T0413694

The Cambridge Handbook of Technology in Language Teaching and Learning

The use of technology in various language teaching and learning contexts has become increasingly commonplace in recent years. This has resulted in an enormous range of choices for teachers and researchers in the field, but at the same time, it has also become more and more difficult for those who are new to using technology for language teaching and researching to keep up with these changes. This handbook provides a wide-ranging, accessible overview of technology in language teaching and learning by leading experts in the field from around the world. The chapters are split into six thematic parts, covering a multitude of subject areas while also highlighting the relationships between the topics covered. Showcasing the diversity and complexity of the field in a comprehensive yet approachable manner, it is essential reading for academic researchers and graduate students, as well as pre-service and in-service teachers in various global contexts.

GLENN STOCKWELL is Professor at the Graduate School of International Culture & Communication Studies, Waseda University, Japan. His previous publications include *Computer Assisted Language Learning* (Cambridge University Press, 2012) and *Mobile Assisted Language Learning* (Cambridge University Press, 2022).

YIJEN WANG is Assistant Professor at the School of International Liberal Studies, Waseda University. She has published numerous research articles and book chapters in the field of technology and language education. She is currently Editor-in-Chief of *Technology in Language Teaching & Learning*.

CAMBRIDGE HANDBOOKS IN LANGUAGE AND LINGUISTICS

Genuinely broad in scope, each handbook in this series provides a complete state-of-the-field overview of a major sub-discipline within language study and research. Grouped into broad thematic areas, the chapters in each volume encompass the most important issues and topics within each subject, offering a coherent picture of the latest theories and findings. Together, the volumes will build into an integrated overview of the discipline in its entirety.

Published titles

The Cambridge Handbook of Phonology, edited by Paul de Lacy

The Cambridge Handbook of Linguistic Code-switching, edited by Barbara E. Bullock and Almeida Jacqueline Toribio

The Cambridge Handbook of Child Language, Second Edition, edited by Edith L. Bavin and Letitia Naigles

The Cambridge Handbook of Endangered Languages, edited by Peter K. Austin and Julia Sallabank

The Cambridge Handbook of Sociolinguistics, edited by Rajend Mesthrie

The Cambridge Handbook of Pragmatics, edited by Keith Allan and Kasia M. Jaszczolt

The Cambridge Handbook of Language Policy, edited by Bernard Spolsky

The Cambridge Handbook of Second Language Acquisition, edited by Julia Herschensohn and Martha Young-Scholten

The Cambridge Handbook of Biolinguistics, edited by Cedric Boeckx and Kleanthes K. Grohmann

The Cambridge Handbook of Generative Syntax, edited by Marcel den Dikken

The Cambridge Handbook of Communication Disorders, edited by Louise Cummings

The Cambridge Handbook of Stylistics, edited by Peter Stockwell and Sara Whiteley

The Cambridge Handbook of Linguistic Anthropology, edited by N.J. Enfield, Paul Kockelman and Jack Sidnell

The Cambridge Handbook of English Corpus Linguistics, edited by Douglas Biber and Randi Reppen

The Cambridge Handbook of Bilingual Processing, edited by John W. Schwieter

The Cambridge Handbook of Learner Corpus Research, edited by Sylviane Granger, Gaëtanelle Gilquin and Fanny Meunier

The Cambridge Handbook of Linguistic Multicompetence, edited by Li Wei and Vivian Cook

The Cambridge Handbook of English Historical Linguistics, edited by Merja Kytö and Päivi Pahta

The Cambridge Handbook of Formal Semantics, edited by Maria Aloni and Paul Dekker

The Cambridge Handbook of Morphology, edited by Andrew Hippisley and Greg Stump

The Cambridge Handbook of Historical Syntax, edited by Adam Ledgeway and Ian Roberts

The Cambridge Handbook of Linguistic Typology, edited by Alexandra Y. Aikhenvald and R. M. W. Dixon

The Cambridge Handbook of Areal Linguistics, edited by Raymond Hickey

The Cambridge Handbook of Cognitive Linguistics, edited by Barbara Dancygier

The Cambridge Handbook of Japanese Linguistics, edited by Yoko Hasegawa

The Cambridge Handbook of Spanish Linguistics, edited by Kimberly L. Geeslin

The Cambridge Handbook of Bilingualism, edited by Annick De Houwer and Lourdes Ortega

The Cambridge Handbook of Systemic Functional Linguistics, edited by Geoff Thompson, Wendy L. Bowcher, Lise Fontaine and David Schönthal

The Cambridge Handbook of Technology in Language Teaching and Learning

Edited by

Glenn Stockwell
Waseda University

Yijen Wang
Waseda University

CAMBRIDGE
UNIVERSITY PRESS

Shaftesbury Road, Cambridge CB2 8EA, United Kingdom

One Liberty Plaza, 20th Floor, New York, NY 10006, USA

477 Williamstown Road, Port Melbourne, VIC 3207, Australia

314–321, 3rd Floor, Plot 3, Splendor Forum, Jasola District Centre,
New Delhi – 110025, India

103 Penang Road, #05-06/07, Visioncrest Commercial, Singapore 238467

Cambridge University Press is part of Cambridge University Press & Assessment,
a department of the University of Cambridge.

We share the University's mission to contribute to society through the pursuit of
education, learning and research at the highest international levels of excellence.

www.cambridge.org
Information on this title: www.cambridge.org/9781009294805

DOI: 10.1017/9781009294850

© Cambridge University Press & Assessment 2025

First published 2025

A catalogue record for this publication is available from the British Library.

Library of Congress Cataloging-in-Publication Data
Names Stockwell, Glenn (Professor), editor. Wang, Yijen, editor.
Title The Cambridge handbook of technology in language teaching and learning edited by
    Glenn Stockwell, Waseda University, Japan, Yijen Wang, Waseda University, Japan.
Description Cambridge, United Kingdom ; New York, NY Cambridge University Press,
    2024. Series Cambridge handbooks in language and linguistics Includes bibliographical
    references and index. Summary With contributions from a global team of leading experts,
    this handbook provides an overview of technology in language teaching and learning. It
    showcases the diversity and complexity of the field in a comprehensive yet approachable
    manner, making it essential reading for both graduate students and teachers in various
    global contexts– Provided by publisher.
Identifiers LCCN 2024040275 (print) LCCN 2024040276 (ebook) ISBN 9781009294805
    (hardback) ISBN 9781009294836 (paperback) ISBN 9781009294850 (epub)
Subjects LCSH Language and languages–Study and teaching–Technological innovations.
    LCGFT Essays.
Classification LCC P53.855 .C36 2024 (print) LCC P53.855 (ebook)
    DDC 418.0078–dc23eng20240920
LC record available at https://lccn.loc.gov/2024040275
LC ebook record available at https://lccn.loc.gov/2024040276

ISBN 978-1-009-29480-5 Hardback

Contents

Figures

Tables

Contributors

Nike Arnold (PhD, University of Texas at Austin) is Professor of Applied Linguistics at Portland State University in Portland, Oregon. She works as a teacher educator and researches the role of collaboration, affect, and identity in second language (L2) learning and teaching. She has co-edited three volumes on computer-assisted language learning (CALL) and published in a variety of journals.

Stacey Benoit is Senior Lecturer of English at the École des Ponts ParisTech, where she is also Head of English. She is a member of the Ministère de l'écologie de l'Energie, du Développement durable et de l'Aménagement du territoire (ERDLI). Their research revolves around sociolinguistic, corporal, intercultural, and multilingual approaches to language teaching. She regularly contributes to the annual congress and working community of the Union des Professeurs de Langues Étrangères des Grandes Écoles et des Établissements Supérieurs Scientifiques (UPLEGESS), a union of language teachers in the French *grande école* (graduate school) system, extended throughout Europe.

Silvia Canto is Assistant Professor at Utrecht University. She is a member of the Dutch National Expertise Team on Foreign Language Pedagogy, which aims to strengthen education and research on foreign language pedagogy. Her research activity focuses on task design for virtual exchanges (virtual worlds, videoconferencing, and immersive virtual reality) and on the added value of these practices for encouraging intercultural communication in language curricula. She has collaborated in various European research projects (Engaging Languages in Intercultural Virtual Exchange [E-LIVE], Networked Interaction in Foreign Language Acquisition and Research [NIFLAR], Euroversity, Telecollaboration for Intercultural Language Acquisition [TILA], and TeCoLa) that integrate virtual exchanges in blended language programs.

Catherine Caws is Professor of French at the University of Victoria, and a member of the executive board of The Computer Assisted Language Instruction Consortium (CALICO).

Astrid Cerpentier is Lecturer at the Antwerp School of Education of the University of Antwerp. She teaches educational design, design science education, and dance. She is currently working on research that combines elements of educational design, educational technology, online learning, motivational issues, and the enactivistic dimension.

Julie Choi is Associate Professor in Education (Additional Languages) and leads the Master of TESOL and Master of Modern Languages programs at the Melbourne Graduate School of Education. She is co-editor of the books *Language and Culture: Reflective Narratives and the Emergence of Identity* and *Plurilingualism in Teaching and Learning: Complexities across Contexts*; co-author of *Clarity and Coherence in Academic Writing: Using Language as a Resource*; and author of *Creating a Multivocal Self: Autoethnography as Method*.

Jozef Colpaert is emeritus professor at the University of Antwerp where has been teaching Instructional Design, Educational Technology and Computer Assisted Language Learning in the Faculty of Social Sciences until 2023. He is editor of Language and Motivation (Castledown), and honorary editor-in-chief of Computer Assisted Language Learning (Taylor and Francis. He is currently working on the empirical and theoretical validation of educational engineering, a novel instructional design and research method (www.uantwerpen.be/en/staff/jozef-colpaert/my-website).

Barbara Conde-Gafaro completed her PhD in self-regulated language learning and goal setting in massive online open courses (MOOCs) at The Open University. During her academic career she has worked as a research assistant for several international research projects, including BMELTT (Blending MOOCs for English-language teacher training in the UK, China and The Netherlands), MOOC2MOVE (language MOOCs [LMOOCs] for Erasmus students), and TPD@SCALE (Adapting and scaling teacher professional development approaches with different ICT-mediated TPD models in Ghana, Honduras, and Uzbekistan). She enjoys promoting ed tech events and writing about them on different social networks.

Frederik Cornillie (PhD, KU Leuven, 2014) is research and valorization manager in educational technology at KU Leuven and at the strategic research institute imec in Belgium. His main research interests in the field of CALL include the intersection of tutorial CALL and task-based language learning, and the ways in which games and play can support language education. He is also passionate about research-based design and development of CALL applications. He serves on the editorial board of journals such as *ReCALL* and *Language Learning & Technology*, as well as on the board of CALICO (2022–2024).

Masatake Dantsuji received a BL in 1979, an ML in 1981, and a DL program with credits in 1984, all in linguistics, from Kyoto University, Japan. From 1990 to 1997 he was Associate Professor at Kansai University, Japan, and from 1997 to 2021 Professor at Kyoto University. Currently he is Professor Emeritus at Kyoto University and Professor at Kyoto Tachibana University, Japan. He has specialized in acoustic phonetics and applied linguistics. He has also been involved for many years in research on CALL.

Gilbert Dizon is Associate Professor at Himeji Dokkyo University, Japan. He holds a Doctor of Education from Indiana University. His research interests lie in CALL, specifically technology-mediated informal language learning and the use of artificial intelligence in language education. His work has been published in journals such as *Computer Assisted Language Learning, Computers and Education: Artificial Intelligence, Language Learning & Technology*, and the *RELC Journal*.

Lara Ducate is Professor of German and Applied Linguistics at the University of South Carolina. She has co-edited three volumes on CALL and has published in various journals such as *Foreign Language Annals*, the *CALICO Journal*, and *Die Unterrichtspraxis / Teaching German*. Her research interests include teacher education, collaborative writing, intercultural learning, study abroad, and computer-mediated communication.

Fereshte Goshtasbpour is a lecturer in digital education at the Institute of Educational Technology, The Open University, United Kingdom. Her research focuses on learning and teaching in open and scaled online educational settings, mainly MOOCs. She is particularly interested in online educators and their practices, digital technologies in higher education, and technology-supported professional learning.

Paul Gruba is Associate Professor at the School of Languages and Linguistics, University of Melbourne. Early interests in video-mediated listening gave way to research in blended learning, computer-mediated communication, and language program evaluation.

Begoña F. Gutiérrez is a postdoctoral researcher and lecturer at the University of León, Spain. She has taught Spanish, English, and Italian in various educational institutions in Italy, Spain, and Ireland and is interested in foreign language education, the pedagogical approach of virtual exchanges, and the development of global and ecological citizenship. Since joining the University of León to carry out her thesis, she has also collaborated as a researcher on various virtual exchange initiatives, including the Erasmus+ KA3 project EVOLVE and the Erasmus+ European Policy Experiment Virtual Innovation and Support Networks for Teachers (VALIANT) (2021–2024).

Marie-Josée Hamel is Professor and Director of Graduate Studies at the Official Languages and Bilingualism Institute at the University of Ottawa, Canada.

Regine Hampel is Full Professor of Open and Distance Language Learning at The Open University, United Kingdom. Beyond teaching German, she has held various leadership positions (including Associate Dean Research and Postgraduate Research Director) in the Faculty of Wellbeing, Education and Language Studies. In 2021 she spent time as Research Fellow at the University of Jyväskylä, Finland. Regine's research focuses on the use of digital technologies for language learning and teaching, contributing to new theoretical and pedagogical perspectives that go beyond cognitive approaches and embrace sociocultural theories of learning, ecological principles, the multimodal nature of the new media, and multiliteracies (see http://oro.open.ac.uk/view/person/rh337.html).

Trude Heift is Professor of Linguistics at Simon Fraser University in Vancouver and Co-editor-in-Chief of *Language Learning & Technology*.

Hsiu-Ting Hung is Distinguished Professor in the Department of English at the National Kaohsiung University of Science and Technology, Taiwan. She holds a PhD in language and literacy education from the University of Georgia, USA. Her current research interests include flipped learning, digital game-based language learning, and language teacher education. Her work has been published in *Computer Assisted Language Learning* (*CALL*), *Language Learning & Technology* (*LLT*), *Computers & Education* (*C&E*), *Teaching and Teacher Education* (*TATE*), and some other international educational journals.

Yurika Ito is Assistant Professor at Kanagawa University in Yokohama, Japan. Her research interests include CALL, teacher education, self-directed learning methods, and online teacher communities on various social media platforms. Her most recent research project investigates the use of technology-focused online language teacher communities as a means for teachers to learn about technology for instructional purposes.

Francisca M. Ivone (PhD, University of Queensland) is Associate Professor of Applied Linguistics at Universitas Negeri Malang, Indonesia. She serves on the boards of directors of the Indonesian Extensive Reading Association (IERA) and Indonesia Technology-Enhanced Language Teaching (iTELL). She conducts and publishes research in the fields of English language teaching (ELT), technology-enhanced language learning (TELL), extensive listening and viewing, extensive reading, learning autonomy, and collaborative learning.

Kristi Jauregi Ondarra is Associate Professor at Utrecht University. Her main research focus is the role virtual exchanges play in language learning processes, the development of intercultural awareness, and changes on teachers' pedagogical methodologies. Her recent research explores the affordances of immersive virtual reality for linguaculture learning. She has initiated and coordinated innovative European projects (E-LIVE, TeCoLa, TILA & NIFLAR) and has published extensively on CALL issues.

Tatsuya Kawahara received a BE in 1987, an ME in 1989, and a PhD in 1995, all in information science and all from Kyoto University, Japan. From 1995 to 1996 he was a visiting researcher at Bell Laboratories in New Jersey, USA. Currently he is Professor in the School of Informatics, Kyoto University. He has published more than 450 academic papers on speech recognition, spoken language processing, and spoken dialogue systems. He is a board member of the Asia-Pacific Signal and Information Processing Association (APSIPA) and the International Speech Communication Association (ISCA), and a fellow of the Institute of Electrical and Electronics Engineers.

Richard Kern is Professor of French at the University of California at Berkeley. He teaches courses in French linguistics, language, and foreign language pedagogy and supervises graduate teaching assistants. His research interests include language acquisition, literacy, and relationships between language and technology. His most recent book is *Screens and Scenes: Multimodal Communication in Online Intercultural Encounters* (2018), co-edited with

Christine Develotte. In 2015 he published *Language, Literacy, and Technology*. Earlier books include *Literacy and Language Teaching* and *Network-Based Language Teaching*, co-authored with Mark Warschauer.

Sima Khezrlou is a postdoctoral researcher in the Department of English and American Studies at the University of Vienna, Austria. Her research interests include second language acquisition, task-based language teaching, form-focused instruction, CALL and CLIL.

Agnes Kukulska-Hulme is Professor of Learning Technology and Communication at the Institute of Educational Technology at The Open University, United Kingdom. She leads the Learning Futures Research and Innovation Programme and the Innovating Pedagogy reports. Her specialisms include online learning and mobile language learning. Her current research projects in the United Kingdom and across Africa and Asia focus on marginalized populations' experiences of using technology and the English language for access to online services and in education.

Chun Lai is Associate Professor in the Faculty of Education at the University of Hong Kong. Her research interests include self-directed language learning with technology beyond the classroom, technology-enhanced language learning, and teacher technology integration. She is the author of the monograph *Autonomous Language Learning with Technology beyond the Classroom* and *Insights into Autonomy and Technology in Language Teaching*, as well as co-author of *The Routledge Handbook of Language Learning and Teaching beyond the Classroom*, with Hayo Reinders and Pia Sundqvist.

Helen Lee holds a PhD in mobile learning from The Open University in the United Kingdom, where she was awarded first prize for student research. She was invited to speak on the panel on semiotics at CALICO 2023. A paper co-authored with Regine Hampel, on the theme of mobile learning, was also selected for a special issue on semiotics in *CALL for Language Learning & Technology*. Helen is currently working as a research associate in the Faculty of Wellbeing, Education and Language Studies at The Open University. She also has an MA TESOL and has a background as a language teacher. Research interests include telecollaboration, mobile learning and pedagogies, multimodal analysis, semiotics, and theoretical SLA.

Jang Ho Lee received his DPhil in education from the University of Oxford. He is presently Professor in the Department of English Education at Chung-Ang University in the Republic of Korea. His areas of interest include CALL, L2 vocabulary acquisition, and L1 use in L2 teaching. His work has been published in *Language Learning & Technology*, *Language Learning*, *Applied Linguistics*, *ReCALL*, the *Modern Language Journal*, *TESOL Quarterly*, *Language Teaching Research*, *System*, *Language Awareness*, and the *ELT Journal*.

Meei-Ling Liaw is Professor in the English Department at the National Taichung University of Education in Taiwan. She teaches SLA, research methods, and CALL research in the graduate program and teacher education courses in the undergraduate program. Her research focuses on intercultural learning, teacher education, and CALL. Her most recent research projects investigate the uses of

VR for the teaching and learning of L2. Her publications have appeared in professional journals, including *System, Foreign Language Annals, Computer-Assisted Language Learning, ReCALL, Language Learning and Technology*, and the *CALICO Journal*. She has been Associate Editor of Language Learning and Technology. She is on the editorial board of international journals such as *Language Learning and Technology*, the *Journal of Virtual Exchanges*, and the *Journal of Intercultural Communication Education*. As a two-time Fulbright Scholar, she visited the University of California at Berkeley in 2000 and at Irvine in 2008.

Rhett Loban is a lecturer at Macquarie University. His research interests include culture, game-based learning, and virtual reality. Rhett received his PhD in 2020 from the University of New South Wales (UNSW) in Sydney. His PhD thesis examined how players might learn about history by engaging with grand strategy video games, in particular through the practice of modding. Rhett also led the development of Torres Strait Virtual Reality, a game used at UNSW to teach about Torres Strait Islander culture and knowledge.

Lara Lomicka is Professor of French and Applied Linguistics, with a focus on CALL, at the University of South Carolina. She is the past president of the Computer Assisted Language Instruction Consortium (CALICO), the National Federation of Modern Language Teachers Associations (NFMLTA), and the American Association of University Supervisors and Coordinators (AAUSC) and works as an associate editor for *Language Learning & Technology* and for the Japanese journal *JALT-CALL*. Her research combines elements of intercultural learning, social media, study abroad, interactive mapping, and digital semiotics as they relate to language learning.

S. Susan Marandi is Full Professor of TEFL at Alzahra University. She is known as "the mother of CALL" in Iran and has, among other things, co-authored award-winning educational software; established the first CALL courses and master's program in CALL in Iran; and established the first Iranian CALL Research Center at Alzahra University. She is Associate Editor for the *JALT CALL Journal* and has published in journals such as *ReCALL, Computer Assisted Language Learning, CALL-EJ, Computers and Education, Interactive Learning Environments*, the *Australasian Journal of Educational Technology, Educational Technology Research & Development, Language Learning and Technology, Computers in Human Behavior*, and *Learning Media and Technology*.

Sabela Melchor-Couto is an English teacher and researcher currently working at the Escuela Oficial de Idiomas de Vigo in Spain. She also holds an Honorary Research Fellowship at the University of Roehampton in London, where she lectured for over ten years. Sabela has specialized on the use of virtual exchange for language learning, particularly on its potential impact on affective variables. She has authored numerous publications on the subject and has participated in three EU-funded projects: the TILA Project, and TeCoLa.

Hassan Mohebbi holds a PhD in TEFL from the Faculty of Foreign Languages and Literatures, University of Tehran. His main research interests are second language writing, written corrective feedback, assessment literacy, and individual differences. He has published extensively in the refereed journals of the field. He has edited special issues for Language Testing in Asia and Language Teaching Research Quarterly journals. He is an editorial board member of *Asian-Pacific Journal of Second and Foreign Language Education (Springer), Language Testing in Asia (Springer), Special Issues Editor of Language Teaching Research Quarterly (EUROKD)*, and Book Reviews Editor of the *Australian Journal of Applied Linguistics* and *Technology in Language Teaching & Learning* journals (Castledown).

Robert O'Dowd is full professor for English Studies at the Universidad de León, Spain. He comes from Ireland and has taught at universities in Ireland, Germany and Spain. He has published extensively on the application of Virtual Exchange in higher education and has been invited to be plenary speaker at international conferences in the US, Asia and across Europe. He has coordinated 3 Erasmus+ projects, the most recent one being the Erasmus+ European Policy Experiment *'Virtual Innovation and Support Networks for Teachers'* (VALIANT). He collaborates with organizations on the promotion and integration of Virtual Exchange in higher education and his most recent book is *Internationalising Higher Education and the Role of Virtual Exchange* (2023, Routledge). He was recently listed in Stanford University's 'Ranking of the World Scientists: World's Top 2% Scientists'.

Sue Ollerhead is Senior Lecturer in Languages and Literacy Education at Macquarie University. Her expertise lies in language teaching in multicultural and multilingual contexts. Much of her work centers on training teachers in how to use students' different home languages as resources for learning in the classroom.

Ali Panahi has been working and presenting in the field of ELT and language assessment since 1998. His PhD focused on the validity argument of IELTS listening. He is interested in retrospective, systematic review issues and has systematically reviewed (with Hassan Mohebbi) all of the decades-long research works of Jack C. Richards, Diane Larsen-Freeman, James Dean Brown, Glenn Fulcher, Rebecca Oxford, and Brian MacWhinney and the research works of Carol Chapelle, James Lantolf and Peter MacIntyre are being surveyed, too. Ali Panahi's more recent book is titled Teacher Training in ELT. At present, he supervises and educates teachers at Iranian Foreign Languages Institute in Ardebil (Ardabil), Iran.

Mark Pegrum is Professor in the Graduate School of Education at the University of Western Australia, where he is the deputy head of school. His courses deal with the application of digital technologies in education, placing particular emphasis on mobile learning. His research focuses on digital literacies, especially attentional literacy; on mobile and emerging technologies, including extended reality (XR); and on the forms that digital learning takes in diverse contexts across the Global North and South. His recent books include *Mobile Lenses on Learning* (2019) and *Digital Literacies* (2nd ed., co-authored with Nicky Hockly and Gavin Dudeney, 2022).

Richard Pinner (PhD, University of Warwick) works for the Department of English Literature and teaches at the Graduate School of Languages and Linguistics at Sophia University, Tokyo. He has almost twenty years of experience as a language teacher and teacher trainer and is the author of three research monographs, as well as having published articles in journals such as TESOL *Quarterly*, *ELTJ*, *Language Teaching*, and *Language Teaching Research*. He is particularly interested in the areas of authenticity and motivation in ELT and content and language integrated learning.

Sabrina Priego is Full Professor in the Department of Languages, Linguistics and Translation at Université Laval in Quebec, Canada, where she teaches undergraduate and graduate courses in L2 teacher education. She is co-founder of the Tandem Canada platform (www.tandem.ulaval.ca) and is currently co-researcher in a three-year funded research project involving tandem language learning (TLL). Besides TLL, her most recent research has focused on virtual reality, telecollaboration, and multilingual digital storytelling in L2 teacher education. She has designed and implemented several telecollaborative projects involving L2/foreign language (FL) learners and pre- and in-service L2/FL teachers. She regularly presents her research findings at international conferences and publishes in refereed journals.

Thomas N. Robb, PhD, retired in 2017 from Kyoto Sangyo University, where he was Chair of the Department of English. He has developed a number of apps for language learning, including MReader.org. He is the editor-in-chief of TESL-EJ. org and is currently Chair of the Extensive Reading Foundation. In 2021 he received the CALL Lifetime Achievement Award from the executive board of the *Computer Assisted Language Learning Journal.*

Fernando Rosell-Aguilar is Senior Lecturer at Arden University in the United Kingdom. He is also Senior Fellow of the Higher Education Academy. He holds an MA in online and distance learning from The Open University (United Kingdom) and a PhD in computer-assisted language learning from the Universidad de Valencia (Spain). His research focuses on online language learning – mainly the use of apps, X (formerly Twitter), voice-activated personal assistants, and podcasting as teaching and learning tools. He previously taught Spanish at the London Metropolitan University, the University of Warwick, The Open University, the University of Southampton, and the University of Buckingham.

Mathias Schulze is Professor of German and European Studies, Director of the Language Acquisition Resource Center at San Diego State University, and Co-editor of *Unterrichtspraxis / Teaching German*, the journal of the American Association of Teachers of German.

Dongkwang Shin received his PhD in applied linguistics from Victoria University in Wellington in 2007 and is currently Professor at the Gwangju National University of Education in South Korea. His research interests include corpus linguistics, computer-assisted language learning, vocabulary learning and teaching, and artificial intelligence in language education (e.g. chatbot-based language learning, machine-reading comprehension).

Glenn Stockwell (PhD, University of Queensland) is Professor of Applied Linguistics at Waseda University, Japan. He is the author of *Mobile Assisted Language Learning: Concepts, Contexts and Challenges* (2022) and the editor of *Smart CALL: Personalization, Contextualization, & Socialization* (2022). He is Editor-in-Chief of Computer Assisted Language Learning and the *Australian Journal of Applied Linguistics* and Honorary Editor of The JALT CALL Journal. His current research interests include the impact of technology on teaching and learning, mobile-assisted language learning, teacher and learner training with technology, and the development of learner autonomy.

Yijen Wang (PhD, Waseda University) is Assistant Professor in the School of International Liberal Studies at Waseda University, Japan. Her PhD focused on the factors that affect the adoption of technology by teachers and students in language teaching. She has published numerous research articles and book chapters in the field of technology and language education, specifically looking at learner and teacher motivation and the development of autonomy. She is currently Editor-in-Chief of *Technology in Language Teaching & Learning*, and she regularly reviews for multiple journals in the field.

James York is Senior Assistant Professor at Meiji University, Tokyo. He conducts research on the application of games and play in language teaching. James is also Editor-in-Chief of *Ludic Language Pedagogy*, an open-access journal that publishes research on the integration of games and play in language teaching practices.

Abbreviations

AI	artificial intelligence
API	application programming interface
AR	augmented reality
ASR	automatic speech recognition
ATI	aptitude–treatment interactions
AWE	automated writing evaluation
BYOD	bring your own device
C1	first culture
C2	second culture
CAF	complexity, accuracy, and fluency
CALL	computer-assisted language learning
CAPL	computer-assisted pronunciation learning
CAT	computer-adaptive testing
CBT	computer-based testing
CD	compact disk
CF	corrective feedback
CIRM	critical Indigenous research methodologies
CLT	communicative language teaching
CMALL	computer-mediated language learning
CMC	computer-mediated communication
CMS	course management system
CoI	community of inquiry
COIL	collaborative online international learning
CSCL	computer-supported collaborative learning
DDL	data-driven learning
DGBLL	digital game-based language learning
DVD	digital versatile disc
EAP	English for academic purposes
EFL	English as a foreign language

ELF	English as a lingua franca
ELLLO	English Listening Lesson Library Online
ELT	English language teaching
EMA	electromagnetic articulography
ERT	emergency remote teaching
ESL	English as a second language
EVALUATE	Evaluating and upscaling telecollaborative teacher education
EVOLVE	Evidence-validated online learning through virtual exchange
F1	first formant
F2	second formant
F2F/FTF	face-to-face
FL	foreign language
FLA	foreign language anxiety
FonF	focus on form
GCT	guessing from context test
GOP	goodness of pronunciation
HiVR	high-immersive VR
HMD	head-mounted display
ICALL	intelligent computer-assisted language learning
ICT	information and communication technology
IELTS	International English Language Testing System
IoT	internet of things
IPA	intelligent personal assistant
IPA	International Phonetic Alphabet
L1	first language
L2	second language
LL	language laboratory
LMOOC	language massive online open course
LMS	learning management system
LRE	language-related episodes
LSP	language for specific purposes
MALL	mobile-assisted language learning
MLE	mediated learning experience
MMOG	massively multiplayer online game
MMORPG	massively multiplayer online role-playing game
MO	magneto-optical drive
MOOC	massive online open course
MRI	magnetic resonance imaging
MT	machine translation
NBLL	network-based language learning
NLP	natural language processing
OERs	open educational resources
OTT	over-the-top

PPP	present–practice–produce
PVST	Phrasal Vocabulary Size Test
SCT	sociocultural theory
SDT	self-determination theory
SLA	second language acquisition
SLD	second language development
SMS	Short Message Service
SNS	social networking site
SSCI	Social Sciences Citation Index
TAM	technology acceptance model
TBLT	task-based language teaching
TELL	technology-enhanced language learning
TESOL	teaching English to speakers of other languages
TOEFL	Test of English as a Foreign Language
UME-ERJ	English speech database read by Japanese students
UME-JRF	Japanese speech database read by foreign students
USI	UNESCO Institute of Statistics
UTAUT	unified theory of acceptance and use of technology
VARK	visual, auditory, reading/writing, kinesthetic
VE	virtual exchange
VLE	virtual learning environment
VM	virtual mobility
VR	virtual reality
VTLN	vocal tract length normalization
VW	virtual world
WAT	Word Associates Test
WiA	Webheads in Action
WM	working memory
WMC	working memory capacity
WoS	Web of Science
XR	extended reality
ZPD	zone of proximal development

Part I
Laying the Foundations

1

Introduction

Glenn Stockwell and Yijen Wang

Introduction

Technologies have been used in second-language (L2) teaching and learning in various forms for more than four decades, and as such the discipline has matured into a field that journals from virtually every continent are dedicated to its research and practice. Among others, these include *ReCALL* and *Computer-Assisted Language Learning* from Europe, *Language Learning & Technology*, *IALLT Journal*, and the *CALICO Journal* from the United States, *The JALT CALL Journal* and the *AsiaCALL Online Journal* in Asia, the *Journal for Language, Technology and Entrepreneurship in Africa* (although this has a slightly broader focus) in Africa, and *Technology in Language Teaching and Learning* in Australia. In addition to these, there have been numerous books that cover different aspects of using technology in language teaching and learning, including those with a broader focus such as *Computer-Assisted Language Learning: Context and Conceptualization* (1997, Clarendon Press), *Computer-Assisted Language Learning: Diversity in Research and Practice* (2012, Cambridge University Press), *Contemporary Computer-Assisted Language Learning* (2012, Bloomsbury), and more specific discussions of areas such as teacher education (*Teacher Education in CALL*, 2016, John Benjamins Publishing Company), research (*CALL Research Perspectives*, 2005, Lawrence Erlbaum Associates), online communication (*Online Communication in Language Learning and Teaching*, 2007, Palgrave), and learning through mobile devices (*Mobile Assisted Language Learning across Educational Contexts*, 2021, Routledge), to name a few. While these are useful guides in themselves, they are still necessarily limited in focus, including those that attempt to look at the field more broadly. The range and volume of dialogue on the research and practice that have taken place since the field emerged all those decades ago are a testament to its complexity, and at the same time they accentuate the need for a resource that attempts to bring these multifarious strands together. This is one of the primary objectives of this handbook, but at the same time trying to include them all into rapidly changing technologies, learning environments, teaching philosophies, and even expectations for language education itself is like hitting a target moving at high speed. Changes have taken place even while this volume was being written, particularly given the COVID-19 pandemic and the explosion of artificial intelligence (AI) technologies such as machine translation and ChatGPT (which will be discussed in the final chapter of this volume).

As a point of departure, however, it is important to clarify the terminology that has been used in this volume. The title of the handbook is *The Cambridge Handbook of Technology in Language Teaching and Learning*, which quite deliberately does not use the established term "computer-assisted language learning" (CALL). While CALL has been – and continues to be – widely used in the field of language education, discourse surrounding the suitability of the term remains ongoing (see Stockwell, 2012, 2022 for discussion on the use of the term). Many researchers have stated that it refers not only to computer but to virtually any digital technology, including desktop, laptop, portable, and mobile devices (see Levy & Hubbard, 2005). There are alternative terms that have been used over the years, such as computer-mediated language learning (CMALL), technology-enhanced language learning (TELL), mobile-assisted language learning (MALL), and network-based language learning (NBLL). Some of these terms remain in use, others have all but disappeared. In saying this, however, we felt it was not practical to use a convoluted term such as "technologies for language teaching and learning" as a phrase throughout the book; so, for convenience, we have opted to use the historically recognized term CALL throughout much of the book, to represent all these variations in the terms that describe technology use in language education, but not any specific application of technologies to language teaching and learning contexts. Nevertheless, there are chapters where alternatives may be seen as well. Those alternatives reflect the preferences of individual authors.

Purpose of the Book

The use of technology in language teaching and learning has become more and more commonplace in recent years, but there is wide variety in the technologies used, the ways in which they are employed in various teaching and learning contexts, and the focus and methodologies that are applied to research and evaluate each of these elements. This has resulted in an enormous range of choice for teachers and researchers in the field, but at the same time it has become increasingly difficult to keep up with these changes, especially for those who are new to using technology in language teaching and researching. On the one hand, there are fresh graduates who may be familiar with technology used for private purposes, or may even have had some experience of it in their own language learning, but may have questions as to how to integrate it into their own language-teaching contexts. On the other hand, there are experienced teachers who have limited skills in technology, particularly when it comes to using it to teach and learn a language, and may feel daunted by the prospect of making sense of how it may operate in the classroom. Although this is not a major focus of the book, COVID-19 has also had a significant effect, both positive and negative, on attitudes toward the adoption of technology in language education; many readers will approach this book from different perspectives, depending on their experiences during the periods of restriction on face-to-face teaching caused by the pandemic. Considering these diverse backgrounds, the overarching purpose of the present volume is to provide a handbook for a readership that ranges from pre-service and early in-service to experienced in-service teachers, researchers, graduate students, and those who are already investigating other areas of teaching with or without technology. The aim is to offer a balanced overview of the issues associated with the use of technology in a variety of language teaching and learning contexts.

The authors of the chapters in this volume were invited to contribute on the basis of their expertise and academic contribution to the topics they cover. We have strived for a balance of authors with a broad international representation to ensure that the content is not skewed toward any particular language or area. We hope that the book can be a solid reference resource for students, researchers, and pre-service and in-service teachers who are interested in using technology in their current or future teaching and learning environments.

It should be pointed out that at the time this book was written, the recent major developments in AI had yet to take place, in particular, generative AI tools based on large language models (LLM) such as ChatGPT. There is no doubt that these tools have had a profound impact on teaching and learning with technology in a broad range of ways, but at the same time, these developments have caused many to only look at these tools, often at the expense of the groundbreaking work using other technologies. Some of the authors of the chapters in this book have chosen to mention the influence generative AI has had on their respective areas of interest, while others have opted to focus on the existing tools and resources. As described in the conclusion of this book, while keeping up with emerging technologies is important, this should not be at the expense of good pedagogy with established technologies. Finding the balance between the range of tools that are available at any given time and achieving best practice in language teaching and learning is an ongoing struggle for teachers, but one that rests on having a view of the whole picture, and not only of the latest trends and developments.

Key Issues

Complexity of CALL Contexts

It is well established that language learning is a complex process with various cognitive, social, cultural, and linguistic aspects, and these make up the context in which both teachers and learners find themselves, alongside administrators and decision-makers. This context is not limited to physical settings but encompasses the cultural, linguistic, and social environments in which language learning takes place (see Chapter 2); in fact all these factors create the context through their interaction. As Fleming and Hiple (2004) noted, this context will vary quite dramatically depending on the nature of the learning experience, and technology will take on a very different role in face-to-face, hybrid (Chapter 5), or distance learning environments (Chapter 6). Teachers need to be familiar with their teaching environment but also understand that the learning ecology of each learner will differ and that learners will need guidance if they are to make the most of the variety of resources available to them (see Luckin, 2010 for a discussion). How the complex pieces of the overall learning context potentially impact one another and can lead to success or failure in acquiring an L2 needs to be considered.

Exploring Theory, Research, and Practice

A lot has been written on the interplay between theory, research, and practice in a broad range of fields, and the study of technology in L2 education is no exception (see Chapelle, 2007). Amid the complexity stated above, theory provides a core framework for understanding the relationship between technology and language learning since it helps researchers and practitioners to make better predictions about learning outcomes and also to design studies that can confirm a theory or bring it into question. However, CALL has struggled to find its own voice in relation to theory. As a field, CALL has obvious relevance for theories in different disciplines, and each theory has the potential to provide a different lens for viewing how technology can facilitate language learning. CALL does indeed tend to borrow theories from other fields – most particularly from L2 acquisition – and the absence of a native theory has been noted previously (Hubbard, 2008). The field is certainly not atheoretical and the years since Hubbard's paper was written have seen a massive spread in the range of theories that are used to inform research and practice – from psychology, education, sociology, computer science, and many more. These have been applied to a range of aspects of technology in language teaching and learning, for example the design of materials (Lee, Lo, & Chin, 2019) and learning environments (Hsu, 2016), the exploration of teachers' (Wang, 2021) and learners' (Plummer & Wesely, 2021) attitudes to technology, task engagement (Wang, 2020), motivation for teachers (Fearn, 2022) and learners (Gan & Zhong, 2016), literacy (Hafner, 2014), and social interaction (Wang, Deutschmann, & Steinvall, 2013). An overview of the current and emerging theories is provided in Chapter 3, but theory will naturally be present in most chapters of this volume, sometimes more explicitly, sometimes less.

As alluded to above, theory plays a large role in guiding research, and research feeds back into the creation and validation of theory. Research has taken a very different shape, both in its focus and in how it has been conducted, as a result of the evolution of theory and technology. The ways in which research has shifted are outlined in Chapter 4, and a further discussion of how this relates to the practice of teaching and learning language skills follows in Part VI (Chapters 24–30). A solid understanding of digital literacies by both teachers and learners is needed if they are to keep up with changes in technology, particularly given the exponential development nowadays of AI technologies, for instance machine translation and Generative Pre-Trained Transformer 3 (GPT-3) tools such as ChatGPT (see Chapter 20), which will naturally affect what happens in actual teaching and learning situations. The learners' cultural background and expectations in these situations can have an impact on what technologies are used and in what capacity (Chapter 19). The ways in which learners engage in learning activities through technology are closely tied not only to their own motivation but also to that of their teachers and other stakeholders who provide the learning resources (Chapter 17). Hence the role that theory plays in deepening our understanding of the relationships between these complex factors is a central one, which can ultimately affect what happens in actual practice.

Technology, Teachers, and Learners

Technological advancements have contributed to a growing interest in providing personalized learning in L2 education, such as giving learners feedback based on their performance, enabling social interaction and collaboration, and creating opportunities for learners to practice and communicate with others in a real-world context (see Colpaert & Stockwell, 2022). One example of personalized learning is adaptive instruction (Chapter 12), where the learners and the technology adapt to each other in a unique learning experience, tailored to the needs of the learner. At the same time, there has been a movement toward less personalized approaches, where much of the responsibility for learning is potentially placed on the learners themselves, for example in flipped classrooms (Chapter 7), where learners are required to spend some time managing their resources outside the class, to prepare for classroom interaction and massive open online courses (MOOCs) (Chapter 11). In these contexts there is the danger of a widening of the *digital divide*, where there are clear gaps between learners who have access to technological resources and those who do not. Being able to cater for learners from varied socioeconomic backgrounds can be a challenge for teachers (Chapter 8), and creative options need to be considered. But mobile devices (Chapter 9) have, to a certain extent, had an equalizing effect, in that there are many less developed regions that provide affordable mobile broadband (see Stockwell, 2022).

Another development in technology that can change the shape of the learning environment is virtual reality (Chapter 13), which has become a more realistic option for teachers and learners as hardware and software become more affordable. There is evidence to suggest that virtual reality can lead to more embodied experiences that can both provide a deeper level of understanding of learning contexts and foster enhanced motivation and engagement. That being said, there is debate on the lack of empirical evidence to prove whether the technology itself facilitates learners' motivation, or whether the learners already have a certain degree of motivation (see Chapter 17). This brings us to a chicken-and-egg quandary where it is unclear whether learners' motivation increases because of the technology, or their existing motivation makes the technology seem to be a positive facilitator. Focusing on technology for technology's sake can in fact detract from the learning experience, as can be seen in the literature on teaching languages with games (Chapter 10). Over-reliance on technology instead of pedagogy has long been cited as a problem in the field (Felix, 2003) and it is essential that teachers are aware of the appropriate pedagogy using technology rather than attempting to replace good pedagogy with technology.

A recurring theme in this volume is the importance of the social aspects of language teaching and learning. Technology has certainly made it easier to have access to social interactions that would not have been possible without the range of information and communication technologies (ICT) that are available now (Chapter 14). This has resulted in the creation of various forms of collaboration (Chapter 16) and telecollaboration (Chapter 15) that encourage people to work together to achieve specific objectives, and the process, in addition to having language learning purposes, has also been used in teacher training (Üzüm, Akayoglu, & Yazan, 2020). Although technology has the potential to make these interactions and collaborations possible, without a clear understanding of how they can be used to facilitate or support language learning, it is just not possible to take advantage of the affordances that they bring to the language teaching and learning environment. Many teachers have turned to online communities (Chapter 22) as a means of seeking out professional and social support, in order to make the most of the tools that are available to them. Their need for support is often due to a lack of formal training in the use of technologies or an inability to keep up with the new opportunities that have emerged in education as a result of technological evolution, or even with the resurgence of existing pedagogies such as task-based language teaching (TBLT) (Chapter 23), which has been transformed as a result of technological advances.

There is a growing body of literature that has highlighted the importance of having teachers who are trained in using technology in their language teaching and learning contexts (Hubbard & Levy, 2016). According to this literature, teachers play a crucial role in how effectively their learners are able to make decisions about what technologies to use and how to use them. Teacher training should cover topics such as CALL research and theory, selecting and designing CALL materials and activities, integrating technology into the curriculum, and assessing and evaluating the technologies and teaching approaches (Son, 2019) to ensure that they are suited to the environment in which they are used. For example, training for teachers of distance learning courses (Chapter 6) will be necessarily different from the training of teachers who work in face-to-face situations, even if similar technologies are used. However, most educational institutions do not offer sufficient teacher training, hence the teachers need to learn by themselves how to use various technologies. The lack of training may also cause a risk of teacher resistance, whereby teachers are reluctant to learn new technology or rarely adopt the technology in their teaching practice (see Chapter 21). Such resistance not only hinders teachers' professional development and capacity to effectively implement CALL but can also have a negative impact on their ability to carry out suitable learner training (Chapter 18), and the nexus between these two can significantly shift what is taught and how it is learned (Chapter 31).

Overview of the Book

The book consists of thirty-one chapters, which are organized into six parts. We have aimed to keep a largely consistent pattern across the chapters, with the help of a basic thematic structure. Part I has an introductory character. Part II presents the background and introduces a few historical perspectives. Part III discusses the primary themes of the book. Part IV is dedicated to current research and practice. Part V makes some recommendations for research and practice. Finally, Part VI outlines future directions. Each chapter contains its own references at the end. The structure of the book is outlined below.

Part I: Laying the Foundations

The first part of this volume sets out a comprehensive overview of the foundations of context, theories, and research trends in CALL, which are regarded as the three pillars in any field, providing a solid background knowledge for understanding the theoretical frameworks and research approaches that inform CALL practice. In this introductory chapter we outline several key concepts that are relevant to the overall framing of the volume. In Chapter 2, "Impact of Context," Jozef Colpaert and Astrid Cerpentier present four main contexts in CALL, namely the sociocultural context, the educational context, the geotemporal context, and the learning environment. The definitions and issues of each context are further discussed in the chapter. In Chapter 3, "Current and Emerging Theories for CALL," Regine Hampel and Helen Lee outline the established and emergent theories in the field. The chapter highlights the transdisciplinarity of context, theory, and methodology. In the following Chapter 4, "The Shifting Focus of CALL Research," Yijen Wang discusses the shifting focus of CALL research in terms of design, settings, technology, and teaching approaches, offering a critical review on methodology and common research bias.

Part II: Environments

Part II provides an overview of the underlying themes in CALL environments, highlighting the extensive applicability of technology across diverse educational contexts. In Chapter 5, "Blended Learning," Paul Gruba explores blended (or so-called hybrid) approaches from ecological perspectives. The call for an argument-based evaluation of effectiveness is raised. In Chapter 6, "Distance Learning," Fernando Rosell-Aguilar deals with a variety of topics, from conceptual perspectives to practical implementation, concluding with an inspiring argument about the future transformation of distance learning. Chapter 7, "Flipped Classrooms," written by Hsiu-Ting Hung, focuses on the role of technology in a flipped learning approach – a current area of active research and discussion. On the other hand, in Chapter 8, "CALL in Low-Tech Environments," Francisca M. Ivone and Thomas N. Robb explore how to make the most of environments with less access to technology. They underline the importance of sound language teaching approaches that have creativity and flexibility in their environments.

Part III: Tools

Part III covers the current topics of active research and discussion on existing and emerging technologies, which have been extensively employed as a tool for L2 education. In Chapter 9, "Mobile Devices," Mark Pegrum presents an updated mobile-assisted language-learning (MALL) framework, along with practical examples of how to use mobile devices to support language education. In Chapter 10, "Teaching Languages with Games," Frederik Cornillie and James York deal with the topic of game-based learning through technology, highlighting the role that teachers play in such contexts. In Chapter 11 Agnes Kukulska-Hulme, Fereshte Goshtasbpour, and Barbara Conde-Gafaro discuss the challenges of MOOCs and offer suggestions on research and practice to support learners who engage in MOOCs. Adaptive instruction is the topic explored in Chapter 12 by Mathias Schulze, Catherine Caws, Marie-Josée Hamel, and Trude Heift. The authors address the issues of the development of adaptive instruction in CALL through theocratic approaches, research, and practical instructions. In Chapter 13, "Virtual Reality," Kristi Jauregi-Ondarra, Sabela Melchor-Couto, and Silvia Canto explore the use of virtual reality (VR) in language education, where this is regarded as an emerging technology that holds promise for the future and demands exploration. They touch upon how to integrate low- and high-immersive VR technologies into language classroom practice.

Part IV: Social Aspects

Part IV focuses on the social aspect of CALL. Its four chapters explore various dimensions of social learning through CALL, providing valuable insights into how CALL can facilitate social and collaborative language learning, promote intercultural communication, and foster motivation among language learners. In Chapter 14, "Social Interaction and Learning," Lara Lomicka and Stacey Benoit emphasize the important role of social interaction in language learning, a field in which technology is seen as a supportive tool. The authors provide an overview of the potential of technology in cross-cultural projects. Another topic of growing interest in the field is developed in Chapter 15, "Virtual Exchange and Telecollaborative Learning," by Begoña F. Gutiérrez and Robert O'Dowd. This chapter looks at how telecollaborative technologies have grown in popularity in recent years, what we have learned about their potential for foreign language learning, and how they should be integrated into educational programmes. In Chapter 16, "Collaborative Learning," Lara Ducate and Nike Arnold explore digital collaboration for L2 learners, with a focus on writing and strategies development. In the final chapter of this part, "Motivation," Richard Pinner discusses the complex relationship between technology and motivation in language learning, including the role of symbolic power in personal and institutional motivations and the lack of empirical evidence about motivation in CALL research. The chapter also presents some motivational techniques for teachers.

Part V: Practice

Part V offers practical insights and strategies for language instruction and professional development through the use of technology. The six chapters in this part provide valuable guidance for language educators seeking to enhance their teaching practices and adopt/adapt technology to improve learning outcomes for their students. In Chapter 18, "Learner Training," Chun Lai highlights the importance of learner training in CALL. The discussion includes the topics of facilitating smooth implementation and enhancing active engagement in informal learning contexts. The chapter argues for more extensive research on learner training in informal language learning environments and calls for a personalized approach to learner training that should consider contextual factors. In Chapter 19, "Digital Media and Interculturality," Julie Choi, Rhett Loban, and Sue Ollerhead explore interculturality in teaching and learning through digital media, showcasing four cultural design approaches. The chapter emphasizes the dynamic and relational nature of culture and the potential of digital technologies to engage learners in intercultural experiences. In Chapter 20, "Literacies for Teaching," Richard Kern stresses the significance of literacy for language education and the teacher's role in enhancing students' language and literacy skills with digital technologies. The chapter covers various topics such as multiliteracies, cultural dimensions, autonomy, mobility, creativity, and communities, as well as the two controversial areas of AI and machine translation. The integration of technology into language teaching and learning has become increasingly important in recent years. However, some teachers may resist this change and feel uncomfortable with using technology in their teaching. In Chapter 21,

"Overcoming Teacher Resistance," Yijen Wang explores the factors that contribute to teacher resistance to technology and provides suggestions for addressing teachers' concerns and fears. This chapter aims to encourage language teachers to embrace technology and to arm them with practical strategies for overcoming resistance to incorporating it in their teaching practices. In line with the statement of this chapter that, as a result of a lack of institutional support, teachers often have to learn about technology on their own, in the following Chapter 22, "Online Communities for Teachers," Yurika Ito demonstrates how online teacher communities can be a source of professional learning for teachers, especially those who use technology in their teaching. The chapter offers a historical overview and explores the benefits and challenges of these communities. It concludes with suggestions for future research and predictions for the future of online teacher communities. In Chapter 23, "Task-Based Language Teaching," Sima Khezrlou looks at the potential of TBLT and technology to enhance language learning. She explores how the two fields can work together to create unique learning opportunities; and she also provides a review of recent research in this area.

Part VI: Language Skills and Areas

Part VI focuses on specific language skills and areas of language learning and teaching where technology is or can be used. Its seven chapters provide insights into how technology can be integrated to enhance the development of language teaching and learning approaches. They offer practical examples and strategies for language educators. In Chapter 24, "Speaking," Gilbert Dizon focuses on L2 speaking and its development through the use of various technologies. The chapter highlights different emerging technologies that have the potential to support the teaching and learning of L2 speaking.

In Chapter 25, "Listening," Glenn Stockwell explores how annotations and captions can be used to lighten the burden of the listening process and suggests that the design of help options can contribute to enhanced comprehension and acquisition of the target language. In Chapter 26, "Reading," Meei-Ling Liaw and Sabrina Priego discuss the challenges of becoming a proficient reader in a new language and how technology can help overcome these challenges. The authors also make suggestions for the effective integration of technology in L2 reading instruction, covering areas such as vocabulary, comprehension, fluency, and motivation. Chapter 27, "Writing," written by Hassan Mohebbi and Ali Panahi, draws attention to the use of technology in L2 writing instruction and discusses various technological tools that have been used in language education, including computer-automated corrective feedback, video impact, and web-based collaborative writing. In the following Chapter 28, "Pronunciation," Tatsuya Kawahara and Masatake Dantsuji introduce the foundations of pronunciation in L2 education, automatic speech recognition (ASR) technology to detect pronunciation errors, and how ASR models can be used for pronunciation grading. In Chapter 29, "Vocabulary,"

Jang Ho Lee and Dongkwang Shin investigate the integration of technology into vocabulary teaching and learning – for instance through online vocabulary tests, hypertext glosses, vocabulary profiler, learning through a vocabulary list, and game-based vocabulary-learning applications. Recommendations for teaching practice and future research on technology-aided vocabulary instruction are also supplied. In Chapter 30, "Grammar," S. Susan Marandi describes various technology-based approaches to grammar instruction that align with grammar-teaching principles and pedagogical practices and concludes with an insightful argument that is relevant to all of the topics in this part: "it is not the technologies themselves that will determine how well we teach grammar but, as always, the way we use them" (p. 507).

In Chapter 31, "Conclusion," as the editors of this volume, we bring together the topics and issues discussed throughout the book, revisiting the concepts of emergent and established CALL and exploring how, over time, research needs to move on from just looking at the technology itself to exploring how to use it effectively. The chapter then considers some of the challenges encountered in using technology in the teaching and learning of an L2 and looks at the interrelationship between teacher training, learner training, and administrative responsibility.

This volume aims to make it clear that there are almost countless approaches to applying technology to language teaching and learning, and these will be very specific to the individual context in which each one is to be used. At the same time, we need to remember that these approaches should be informed by the work of previous research, as a foundation on which to achieve better practice. We hope that readers will be able to benefit from the diverse perspectives of the authors who contributed to this volume and will develop their own pedagogies that will be of most benefit to their learners in the intricate and complex task of learning a second language.

References

Chapelle, C. A. (2007). Technology and second language acquisition. *Annual Review of Applied Linguistics, 27*, 98–114. https://doi.org/10.1017/S0267190508070050

Colpaert, J., & Stockwell, G. (2022). Smart CALL: The concept. In J. Colpaert & G. Stockwell (Eds.), *Smart CALL: Personalization, contextualization, & socialization* (pp. 1–6). Castledown Publishers. https://doi.org/10.29140/9781914291012-1

Egbert, J., & Petrie, G. M. (Eds.) (2005). *CALL research perspectives*. Lawrence Erlbaum Associates.

Fearn, L. (2022). EFL teachers' perceptions of online community projects in secondary school education. *The JALT CALL Journal, 18*(3), 360–381. https://doi.org/10.29140/jaltcall.v18n3.600

Felix, U. (2003). An orchestrated vision of language learning online. In U. Felix (Ed.), *Language learning online: Towards best practice* (pp. 7–18). Swets & Zeitlinger.

Fleming, S., & Hiple, D. (2004). Distance education to distributed learning: Multiple formats and technologies in language instruction. *CALICO Journal, 22*(1), 63–82.

Gan, J., & Zhong, L. (2016). Empirical research on the influencing factors of mobile foreign language learning based on UTAUT model. *Journal of Computational and Theoretical Nanoscience, 13*(10), 7526–7532. https://doi.org/10.1166/jctn.2016.5748

Hafner, C. A. (2014). Embedding digital literacies in English language teaching: Students' digital video projects as multimodal ensembles. *TESOL Quarterly, 48* (4), 655–685. https://doi.org/10.1002/tesq.138

Hsu, L. (2016). Examining EFL teachers' technological pedagogical content knowledge and the adoption of mobile-assisted language learning: A partial least square approach. *Computer Assisted Language Learning, 29*(8), 1287–1297. https://doi.org/10.1080/09588221.2016.1278024

Hubbard, P. (2008). Twenty-five years of theory in the CALICO Journal. *CALICO Journal, 25*(3), 387–399. https://doi.org/10.1558/cj.v25i3.387-399

Hubbard, P., & Levy, M. (Eds.) (2016). *Teacher education in CALL.* John Benjamins Publishing Company.

Lamy, M.-N., & Hampel, R. (2007). *Online communication in language learning and teaching.* Palgrave Macmillan.

Lee, S.-Y., Lo, Y.-H. G., & Chin, T.-C. (2021). Practicing multiliteracies to enhance EFL learners' meaning making process and language development: A multimodal problem-based approach. *Computer Assisted Language Learning, 34*(1-2), 66–91. https://doi.org/10.1080/09588221.2019.1614959

Levy, M. (1997). *Computer-assisted language learning: Context and conceptualization.* Clarendon Press.

Levy, M., & Hubbard, P. (2005). Why we CALL "CALL"? *Computer Assisted Language Learning, 18*(3), 143–149. https://doi.org/10.1080/09588220500208884

Luckin, R. (2010). *Re-designing learning contexts: Technology-rich, learner-centred ecologies.* Routledge.

Morgana, V., & Kukulska-Hulme, A. (Eds.) (2021). *Mobile assisted language learning across educational contexts.* Routledge.

Plummer, E., & Wesely, P. (2021). Language learner attitudes, technology attitudes, and technology prevalence at the secondary level. *The JALT CALL Journal, 17*(3), 233–255. https://doi.org/10.29140/jaltcall.v17n3.465

Son, J.-B. (2019). *Teacher development in technology-enhanced language teaching.* Palgrave Macmillan. https://doi.org/10.1007/978-3-319-75711-7

Stockwell, G. (Ed.) (2012). *Computer-assisted language learning: Diversity in research and practice.* Cambridge University Press.

Stockwell, G. (Ed.) (2022). *Mobile assisted language learning: Concepts, contexts and challenges.* Cambridge University Press.

Thomas, M., Reinders, H., & Warschauer, M. (Eds.) (2012). *Contemporary computer-assisted language learning.* Bloomsbury.

Üzüm, B., Akayoglu, S., & Yazan, B. (2020). Using telecollaboration to promote intercultural competence in teacher training classrooms in Turkey and the USA. *ReCALL, 32*(2), 162–177. https://doi.org/10.1017/S0958344020000035

Wang, A., Deutschmann, M., & Steinvall, A. (2013). Towards a model for mapping participation: Exploring factors affecting participation in a telecollaborative learning scenario in Second Life. *The JALT CALL Journal, 9*(1), 3–22. https://doi.org/10.29140/jaltcall.v9n1.146

Wang, Y. (2020). Engagement in PC-based, smartphone-based, and paper-based materials: Learning vocabulary through Chinese Stories. *Technology in Language Teaching & Learning, 2*(1), 3–21. https://doi.org/10.29140/tltl.v2n1.319

Wang, Y. (2021). In-service teachers' perceptions of technology integration and practices in a Japanese university context. *The JALT CALL Journal, 17*(1), 45–71. https://doi.org/10.29140/jaltcall.v17n1.377

2

Impact of Context

Jozef Colpaert and Astrid Cerpentier

Introduction

While education in the twentieth century was mainly characterized by face-to-face classroom instruction, the twenty-first century will probably become the century of ubiquitous, adaptive, personalized, contextualized learning in virtual, augmented, or intelligent environments. Most readers of this book will probably agree with this opening statement. Its first part depicts a situation we all know very well, and we can imagine it in all its details. The second part of the sentence, however, contains some ill-defined terms that create a magical, virtual, or even illusory world in our minds. The question is: To what extent are these terms persuasive? Do they create exaggerated or false expectations? Which aspects will be useful, meaningful, acceptable, feasible?

One of the most striking aspects of recent evolution in language education, fostered by technology, is *adaptation*: adaptation of language pedagogy and learning content to specific learning goals, classroom situations, learner types, special groups, and individual learners. Let's take a closer look at this evolution. Textbook materials have always been designed in most cases for a broader target audience than the concrete classroom setting (Colpaert, 2013). Publishers are reluctant to develop learning materials for specialized domains, given the limited market and labour intensiveness of content development. From a commercial point of view, this is obvious and logical. Publishers came up with on-demand printing solutions, but teachers have always felt the need to adapt these materials even more to their goals and to learners, especially in the case of language for specific purposes (LSP). Teachers started to develop their own materials, with colleagues or students, and later shared these as open educational resources (OERs). Technologies such as courseware allowed us to adapt not only to local situations, but also to differences within the classroom context.

The next step in adaptation was *differentiation*, defined as adaptation to differences within the group of learners regarding their sociocultural and educational background, level and proficiency, or specific weaknesses (Hatcher, 1998; Terwel, 2005; van Vucht, 2009). Differentiation posed some specific challenges for teachers (Westwood, 2001), but it was also the time for the first experiments in pedagogical differentiation. Next to the more traditional method of quantitative differentiation (giving more content to stronger students), there was also qualitative differentiation (giving the same content but expecting different acquisition levels). Technology was quite instrumental in this.

The next step was *inclusion* (Peetsma et al., 2001). Inclusion means adaptation of the learning environment to special needs in the case of physical, mental, and linguistic impairments and disabilities, so that as many learners as possible are included in normal classroom settings. The idea of inclusion also appeared in design models such as the UDL model (Griful-Freixenet, 2020). Thanks to technology, we can extend this differentiation to forms of *personalized* learning (Xie et al., 2019): adaptation to individual learning styles, skills, interests, motivation types, goals, levels, or degrees of autonomy. This adaptation can be user-defined, teacher-defined, or system-defined. Adaptive systems, sometimes called "intelligent," function on the basis of a routine that analyses previous performance, learner information, and other data.

One of these sources of information is the context of the learner. But what do we mean by context? In this chapter we will try to define the context of the learner in the light of a design-based approach. We will present four types of context as a new framework. We will try to explain the impact of these types of context in terms of limitations on and affordances for the learning process. We will present contextualization as the adaptation of features of the learning environment (content, evaluation, learning model, instruction model, or architecture) to one or more of these types of context. Finally, we will focus on geotemporal contextualization as a fascinating topic for both language teachers and researchers. What is grounded, justifiable, feasible, to be expected, useful, meaningful? And what does the literature say about context?

Background

The concept of context in the literature on *learning and instruction* is far from clear (Dohn, Hansen, & Klausen, 2018). On the one hand, there is this view that the school context should provide the appropriate settings for social interaction to happen. Social constructivism has been focusing on the sociocultural context of the learner, more specifically on how social interactions with others in our communities – peers, adults, teachers, and other mentors – influence learning and on how education should provide the appropriate settings for doing so (Hausfather, 1996). According to the theory of situated learning (Lave & Wenger, 1991), learners are more inclined to acquire skills by actively participating in the learning experience (peripheral participation) and through membership of a community of practice. A practice environment should be created in this sense. Contextual learning focuses on multiple aspects of the learning environment, which should create the best possible conditions for simulating real-life experiences, for engaging meaningful relationships, and for facilitating the internalization of concepts through the process of discovering, reinforcing, and relating.

The literature on *educational technology* focuses on context-aware, mobile, ubiquitous, collaborative, and adaptive environments (Brown, 2010; Dias de Figueiredo, 2005; Fenwick & Cooper, 2013; Gómez et al., 2014; Hasanov, Laine, & Chung, 2019; Huang & Chiu, 2015; Hwang, Shi, & Chu, 2011; Kumar & Sharma, 2020; Patten, Sánchez, & Tangney, 2006; Shih et al., 2009; Tan, Liu, & Burkle, 2013; Vallejo-Correa, Monsalve-Pulido, & Tabares-Betancur, 2021).

Literature on *language teaching* fans out into a wide variety of topics such as collaboration (Balchin & Wild, 2020), blended environments (Nicolson, Murphy, & Southgate, 2011), and task-based approaches (Shedadeh & Coombe, 2012). The computer-assisted language learning (CALL) literature is quite varied, too, in its approaches to concepts of context. For many CALLers, context refers to the language-learning and -teaching situation (Jeong, 2017; Roy & Crabbe, 2015; Roy, Brine, & Murasawa, 2016; Sun, 2013; Trinder, 2003; Vincent-Durroux et al., 2011; Ward, 2004; Ware & Hellmich, 2014). For some researchers, the goal should be to create a familiar, authentic context (Cheng et al., 2010; Hwang et al., 2014; Nguyen et al., 2020; Shadiev, Wu, & Huang, 2020). For others, the term "context" refers to the digital, technological environment we create (Egbert & Yang, 2004; González-Lloret, 2018; Hartwick, 2018; Jabbari & Eslami, 2019; Lan, 2015; Lee, 2019; Reinders, Lakarnchua, & Pegrum, 2014; Sun & Dong, 2004; Yang, 2018). Especially the context-aware, location-based apps (out-of-classroom learning) receive significant attention (Chen et al., 2009; De Jong, Specht, & Koper, 2010; Fatahipour & Ghaseminajm, 2014; Lee, 2019; Lee & Park, 2020; Liu, 2009; Liu et al., 2015; Morales et al., 2015; Reinders & Lakarnchua, 2014; Reinders & Pegrum, 2016; Wang, Liu, & Hwang, 2017; Wang et al., 2019). Personalization is an important topic (Chen & Li, 2010), but so is the social context (Palfreyman, 2006). This wide variety in perspectives on context is also reflected in the proceedings of the "CALL in Context" Eighteenth International CALL Research Conference in 2017 (Colpaert et al., 2017).

So what can we say about context in the literature? As shown above, this is a multifarious concept. Its definition is often vague and ill grounded. But two aspects strike us more specifically. First, there is some confusion with the term "learning environment," as both it and "context" are used interchangeably, to designate the existing surroundings of the learner and the environment to be created for that learner. In addition, online dictionaries and glossaries on educational terminology appear to heavily disagree on the definitions of context and learning environment. Secondly, a surprising aspect is that the learner and learner characteristics such as competence profile, role, and personal features are sometimes mentioned as part of the context (Gómez et al., 2014; Hasanov et al., 2019; Vallejo-Correa et al., 2021; Zervas et al., 2011). This is a typical systems designer's approach, where the learner is seen as part of the context of the designer.

Instructional designers (Dias de Figueiredo, 2005; Tessmer & Richey, 1997), on the other hand, see context as a concept that does not include the learner but that surrounds the learner with opportunities and limitations. Tessmer and Richey (1997, p. 111) state that

> context is a multifarious and complex force in every learning and performance enterprise. All instruction is embedded in context, and context can be designed to exploit contextual resources and mitigate contextual restraints. Be that as it may, the instructional design literature contains precious little information on how to identify and accommodate context.

The question is whether or not this has changed since this was written, which is considered below.

Current Research and Practice

Context from a Design-Based Perspective

Not many instructional design models mention context explicitly as an important element in design. It is a – modest – part of one of the nine elements of the Morrison, Ross, and Kemp (MRK) learners and context model:

> The MRK design model strongly suggests an analysis of the target learners' characteristics. General demographic type characteristics, such as gender, age, and ethnicity may be considered. Prerequisite skills, learning style preferences, personal and social characteristics, and cultural diversity are also common learner-related considerations that should be made in relationship to goals of the instructional design project. Contextual analysis involves defining the characteristics of the learning environment and other factors that will affect the design and delivery of instruction.
>
> *(Morrison et al., 2013)*

Design is traditionally being defined as "a plan or scheme conceived in the mind and intended for subsequent execution; the preliminary conception of an idea that is to be carried into effect by action; a project" (Oxford University Press, 2023). In order to make things sharper, we can also look at design and at context from a different point of view. If we define design as the process of adapting universal findings and principles to local circumstances and individual characteristics and requirements to better achieve our goals, then we can identify the following elements:

- the *learner* and learner characteristics: age, gender, race/ethnicity, special needs, achievement/developmental levels, culture, language, interests, learning styles/modalities, and students' skill levels;

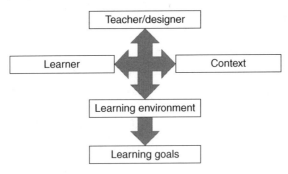

Figure 2.1 Context in the design process.

- the *context* as the culture, institutions, circumstances, objects, and persons that surround the learner during the learning process, inside or outside the classroom, as an ecology (Bronfenbrenner, 2009) in the broadest possible sense;
- the learning *goals*: defined as pedagogical objectives in terms of subject matter, linguistic, communicative, intercultural, sociolinguistic, and digital knowledge, skills, attitudes, and insight;
- the *learning environment*: everything a teacher puts into place for realizing these goals.

The teacher as designer focuses on the learner and his/her characteristics and on his/her context, in order to better design a learning environment for realizing the stated learning goals (pedagogical objectives) in the most effective way (see Figure 2.1).

From a designer's perspective, we can define four types of context that are based on this approach: the sociocultural context of the learner, the educational context of learner and teacher, the geotemporal context of the learner, and the learning environment itself, as defined above.

The *sociocultural* context of the learner contains aspects such as socioeconomic situation, culture, religion, ethical beliefs, mother tongue, personal space, and infrastructure. The learner's sociocultural context does not change rapidly and has a lifelong effect. It is not too difficult for teachers and designers to identify the elements of this context. Its impact on the learning process is understood to be heavy.

The *educational* context refers to the type and level of education of the learner and the institutional context of the teacher: age group (primary, secondary, or tertiary), type (vocational, academic, etc.), governing body (public or private), pedagogical model (Steiner, Montesory, etc.), educational infrastructure, available content, and so forth. The educational context can change, albeit rather slowly. There is a long-term effect, but learners are not completely determined by it.

The *geotemporal* context of the learner stands for temporal, spatial, and proximity-related elements: time, location, weather, and the proximity of objects, data, and contacts. The geotemporal context changes rapidly and has a limited effect in time.

Table 2.1 *Limitations and affordances of the three contexts*

	Limitations	Affordances
Sociocultural context	political, religious, cultural, infrastructural limitations	interaction with experts, native speakers, cases, etc.
Educational context	educational policy, administration (red tape)	telecollaboration, team teaching, peer evaluation, etc.
Geotemporal context	different for every student	possibilities of interaction with objects, points of interest, data, and persons in proximity

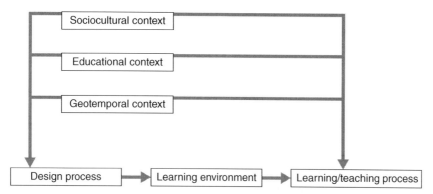

Figure 2.2 Contexts and their impact.

We define the *learning environment* as the fourth type of context. It represents what we put into place to support the learning and teaching process. Its meaning comes very close to that of the French term *dispositif*, which is less ambiguous when used in this sense. The learning environment is made up of content, teaching model, learning model, evaluation model, interaction model, tasks, support and feedback mechanisms, infrastructure, media, and technology.

In this view, technology is not a context in itself, but is an essential part of the sociocultural context (the technology generally available in society and at home), of the educational context (the systems available at school), and of the learning environment (what can or should be put into place).

This leads us to the representation shown in Figure 2.2:

The sociocultural, educational, and geotemporal contexts have an impact on the design process, which leads to the learning environment as fourth context. But what do we mean by "impact"? Under "impact" we place both the limitations and the affordances – defined as perceived possible contributions to the realization of our goals.

We define contextualization as the adaptation of the learning environment to the sociocultural, educational, and geotemporal contexts of the learner. This adaptation is the task of the teacher as designer of the learning environment.

In the next sections we will try to explain why geotemporal contextualization may become an interesting research topic and a challenge for language teachers worldwide.

Recommendations for Research and Practice

Context-Aware Learning Environments

The literature on geotemporal contextualization mainly focuses on context-aware applications for mobile, ubiquitous, and adaptive learning. Hasanov et al. (2019) provide a comprehensive analysis of adaptive context-aware learning environments, while Lee (2019) wrote a systematic review of context-aware technology use in foreign language learning. Both analyses yield a diverse set of projects and systems.

There are several examples of context-aware systems cited in the literature. For example, TANGO (Ogata et al., 2010) and PCULS (Chen & Li, 2010) focus on context-relevant vocabulary. With the CAMLES application (Nguyen, Pham, & Ho, 2010), the location is provided by the user as a user preference and is considered an important factor in providing adequate learning material. LOCH4 is an application designed to support overseas students to learn Japanese language in real-life situations, its approach requiring direct interaction from students and teachers (Ogata et al., 2008). CAMJAL5 is a collaborative conversation learning application; collaborative learning was implemented by allowing students to download and share learning materials using near-field communication (NFC) technology. NFC tags are used as context attributes to track users' location and obtain the corresponding material (Wang & Wei, 2014). CAMCLL6 presents a context-aware location-independent learning approach to teaching the Chinese language; authors consider time, location, activities, and learning level as the main contexts to provide conversational-level materials. This proposal was designed to appraise the learner level and the sentence level as key factors in offering the student suitable content (Al-Mekhlafi, Hu, & Zheng, 2009). Morales et al. (2015) discuss context-aware mobile language-learning systems and compare them to their own CoLaLe system: the real user location is obtained to provide the learning material according to the current points of interests near the student. The main purpose of CoLaLe was to learn about the user's context and to provide language-learning support by showing those vocabularies, phrases, or sentences that are useful for that particular context. Holden and Sykes (2011) describe MENTIRA as a place-based, augmented reality mobile game for learning Spanish in a local neighborhood. To support immigrants in a number of different areas of their everyday lives, MASELTOV (Gaved et al., 2014) considers the key aspects of context to be location, mode of activity, history of activity and progress, social interactions, and learners' interests. Other publications focus on semantic architecture (Yu, Zhou, & Shu, 2010) or on the adaptation model (Kasaki, Kurabayashi, & Kiyoki, 2012).

It is important to see the difference between context-aware applications and augmented reality (AR). The latter (Huang et al., 2021; Parmaxi & Demetriou, 2020) offers an interactive experience of a real-world environment where a computer-generated layer of information is being applied over objects that reside in the real world. Context-aware applications focus predominantly on the adaptation routine for retrieving context-relevant information. They can also focus on the temporal aspect and on other things such as persons, points of interest, and data sources. Apparently they have not yet done so.

Geotemporal Contextualization

The following example comes from an earlier publication on transdisciplinarity:

> Imagine you are in the neighborhood of Hong Kong, in the fisherman's village of Tuen-Mun. You neither speak nor read Chinese. You do not know anything about how to have dinner in a local restaurant. A lady tries to sell you fish, but you try to explain to her that you are staying in a hotel and that it does not make any sense for you to buy fish. You go back to the hotel . . . you have just missed a golden learning opportunity. A contextualized application could have explained in advance the unique character of this village, what their specialties are, which types of fish and seafood you can buy, how to order and pay for the fish, how to take your food across the street to one of the local restaurants, how the waiter will ask how you want the fish (cooked, steamed, or grilled, with vegetables or not etc.), how to "do the dishes" (cleaning your chopsticks and cups with the tea before you start eating), how to proceed with chop sticks, how to thank the waiter, etc.
>
> *(Hubbard & Colpaert, 2019, p. 93)*

Another example would be a contextualized app that knows that you are interested in Italian culture and are learning Italian at Common European Frame of Reference for Languages (CEFR) level B2. If you are walking around in Antwerp at noon, then that application could tell you that there is an Italian restaurant around the corner and that the special today is *osso bucco*, and it could show you the menu, with possible translation and pronunciation illustrations. This second example plays more with the temporal dimension than the first example.

Most language teachers have always tried to conceive of rich and motivating contextual tasks for field excursions, city visits, or school trips. Now they can imagine various activities by using existing technologies or by specifying new apps to be developed. In the first case, they can use an existing educational context-aware app or simply experiment with apps that use proximity detection – such as Google Maps, Tripadvisor, Facebook, or other social media. Tasks that lead to the construction of artifacts that may be meaningful, useful, and reusable, especially in the context of telecollaboration, can be very motivating (Colpaert & Spruyt, 2022) and teachers should test them as hypotheses, as part of their action research. In the second case, teachers should not be afraid to specify the required technologies in the design of their learning environment. These specifications should form the basis of a new kind of information channel, which extends from educational practitioners to research and industry.

Table 2.2 *Dimensions of geotemporal contextualization*

User data	Learner characteristics (preferences, characteristics, language learning level, learning style or any analytics) that will be used for determining which information or content might be relevant.
Geotemporal location	Place (e.g. in classroom, at home, close to a point of interest or contact) and time (e.g. morning, office/class hours, evening, school year, holiday).
Triggers	Elements in the proximity of the learner that can be the starting point in the search for useful and relevant materials: objects, points of interest, contacts.
Tasks	Activities proposed by the system to the learner, as notifications. The learner can ignore, reject, or accept the activity. The task can be to read a short message, execute an instruction, develop context-related content (storytelling), construct an artifact, or make an interactive exercise.
Content	Tasks need content. This can be a simple web page, tweet, or posting that can be turned into valuable information on a specific object in context or person, but also into structured content in databases and repositories.

In fact we can represent the dimensions of geotemporal contextualization – in a simplified version – as follows: user data, geotemporal location, triggers, tasks, and content (see Table 2.2).

The question is, where can we retrieve relevant information that can enrich the learning experience? Technologically speaking, this is rather simple. The big problem is content.

A huge amount of content for language learning and teaching has already been developed in the form of corpora, open educational resources (OERs), interactive exercises, databases, thesauri, lexicons, dictionaries, terminologies, knowledge bases, and resource metadata. Where initially we pleaded for a generic structuring of these data (Colpaert, 2013), the Open Data movement offers a solution that could mean a revolution in the field of language learning and teaching (Colpaert, 2018).

If we want to make data available for teachers and learners worldwide, in simplified form, we do not need to let them "enter" our resources and have them edited haphazardly, but we just need to build an interface around our resource, so that anyone can make a call to that interface and ask for records that comply with certain predefined predocumented search criteria. The power of open data becomes exponential if the data are being interconnected and become linked open data. With this approach, the Linguistic Linked Open Data movement (Chiarcos, 2016; Chiarcos et al., 2013; Cimiano et al., 2020; Pareja-Lora et al., 2019) becomes an exciting challenge and a crucial research topic for years to come.

Future Directions

As mentioned above, context is a vague, ill-grounded, and multifarious concept. We have tried to provide an overview of the various interpretations in the literature and suggested a design-based approach. Four contexts can be defined: the sociocultural context, the educational context, the geotemporal context, and the learning environment. The first three contexts have an impact on the fourth in terms of limitations and affordances. A language-learning environment can be defined as everything that teachers put into place for the learner to identify, self-regulate, and realize the set goals in a comfortable, related, and supported way. It has several components such as content, instruction model, learning model, evaluation model, infrastructure, technology, and tasks.

The geotemporal context is an underexplored context, both in the literature and in existing applications. Geotemporal contextualization offers exciting possibilities for language teachers and researchers, especially in a task-based approach. Many technologies already exist, the knowledge is there, other technologies are easy to develop. Geotemporal contextualization needs data: information about the learner in order to know what can be relevant or useful; information about the context, objects, points of interest, and contacts in proximity; and linguistic information, which can be useful when you prepare for, and interact with, a given context on the fly and in real time. Open data, linked open data, and linguistic linked open data are crucial developments for the accessibility of huge amounts of information, which can enrich the language-learning experience worldwide. We hope that language teachers will explore these affordances and that young researchers will identify themselves with this research topic.

Finally, contextualization should always be seen as connected to personalization and socialization, which together form "smart." Smart CALL is defined as the combination of these three factors(Colpaert & Stockwell, 2022). Personalization is the extent to which technologies and learning environments are adapted to the specific profile of the language learner. Socialization is the way in which technologies and learning environments afford meaningful interaction among learners, co-learners, teachers, and researchers. Contextualization is the adaptation of the learning environment to the sociocultural, educational, and geotemporal contexts of the learner.

References

Al-Mekhlafi, K., Hu, X., & Zheng, Z. (2009). An approach to context-aware mobile Chinese language learning for foreign students. *Proceedings of the Eighth International Conference on Mobile Business (ICMB 2009)*, 340–346.

Balchin, K., & Wild, C. (2020). Exploring the role of context and collaboration in normalising technology use in English language teaching in secondary schools in Malaysia. *Computer Assisted Language Learning*, 35(7), 1437–1457. https://doi.org/10.1080/09588221.2020.1803360

Bronfenbrenner, U. (2009). *The ecology of human development: Experiments by nature and design.* Harvard University Press.

Brown, E. (2010). Introduction to location-based mobile learning. In E. Brown (Ed.), *Education in the wild: Contextual and location-based mobile learning in action* (pp. 7–9). University of Nottingham.

Chen, C.-M., & Li, Y.-L. (2010). Personalised context-aware ubiquitous learning system for supporting effective English vocabulary learning. *Interactive Learning Environments, 18*(4), 341–364. https://doi.org/10.1080/10494820802602329

Chen, T.-S., Chang, C.-S., Lin, J.-S., & Yu, H.-L. (2009). Context-aware writing in ubiquitous learning environments. *Research and Practice in Technology Enhanced Learning, 4*(1), 61–82. https://doi.org/10.1142/S1793206809000611

Cheng, S., Hwang, W., Wu, S., Shadiev, R., & Xie, C. (2010). A mobile device and online system with contextual familiarity and its effects on English learning on campus. *Educational Technology & Society, 13*(3), 93–109.

Chiarcos, C. (2016). Corpora and linguistic linked open data: Motivations, applications, limitations. *Actes de la conférence conjointe JEP-TALN-RECITAL 2016, 4.* https://aclanthology.org/2016.jeptalnrecital-invite.1.pdf

Chiarcos, C., Cimiano, P., Declerck, T., & McCrae, J. P. (2013). Linguistic linked open data (LLOD): Introduction and overview. Proceedings of the 2nd Workshop on Linked Data in Linguistics (LDL-2013): Representing and linking lexicons, terminologies and other language data (pp. i–xiii). Association for Computational Linguistics. https://aclanthology.org/W13–5501.pdf

Cimiano, P., Chiarcos, C., McCrae, J. P., & Gracia, J. (2020). *Linguistic linked data: Representation, generation and applications.* Springer. https://doi.org/10.1007/978-3-030-30225-2

Colpaert, J. (2013). Ontological specification of an authoring interface for creating sustainable language learning content. In L.-H. Wong, C.-C. Liu, T. Hirashima, P. Sumedi, & M. Lukman (Eds.), *Proceedings of the 21st International Conference on Computers in Education* (pp. 644–653). Asia-Pacific Society for Computers in Education.

Colpaert, J. (2018). Exploration of affordances of open data for language learning and teaching. *Journal of Technology and Chinese Language Teaching, 9*(1), 1–14. www.tclt.us/journal/2018v9n1/colpaert.pdf

Colpaert, J., & Spruyt, E. (2022). Conceptualization of a language task design model for mental acceptance and motivation. In A. Potolia & M. Derivry-Plard (Eds.), *Virtual exchange for intercultural language learning and teaching* (pp. 44–66). Routledge.

Colpaert, J., & Stockwell, G. (2022). Smart CALL: The concept. In J. Colpaert & G. Stockwell (Eds.), *Smart CALL: Personalization, contextualization, & socialization* (pp. 1–6). Castledown.

Colpaert, J., Aerts, A., Kern, R., & Kaiser, M. (2017). *CALL in context: Proceedings of the Eighteenth International CALL Research Conference.* University of Antwerp.

De Jong, T., Specht, M., & Koper, R. (2010). A study of contextualised mobile information delivery for language learning. *Educational Technology & Society, 13*(3), 110–125.

Dias de Figueiredo, A. (2005). Learning contexts: A blueprint for research. *Interactive Educational Multimedia, 11*, 127–139.

Dohn, N., Hansen, S., & Klausen, S. (2018). On the concept of context. *Education Sciences, 8*(3), 111. http://dx.doi.org/10.3390/educsci8030111

Egbert, J., & Yang, Y. (2004). Mediating the digital divide in CALL classrooms: Promoting effective language tasks in limited technology contexts. *ReCALL, 16* (2), 280–291. https://doi.org/10.1017/S0958344004000321

Fatahipour, M., & Ghaseminajm, M. (2014). A context-aware solution in mobile language learning. In S. Jager, L. Bradley, E. J. Meima, & S. Thouësny (Eds.), *CALL design: Principles and Practice: Proceedings of the 2014 EUROCALL Conference* (pp. 83–87). Researchpublishing.net. https://doi.org/10.14705/rpnet.2014.000199

Fenwick, L., & Cooper, M. (2013). Learning about the effects of context on teaching and learning in pre-service teacher education. *Australian Journal of Teacher Education, 38*(3), 96–110. http://doi.org/10.14221/ajte.2013v38n3.6

Gaved, M., Luley, P., Efremidis, S., Georgiou, I., Kukulska-Hulme, A., Jones, A., & Scanlon, E. (2014). Challenges in context-aware mobile language learning: The MASELTOV approach. In M. Kalz, Y. Bayyurt, & M. Specht (Eds.), *Mobile as a mainstream: Towards future challenges in mobile learning (mLearn 2014)* (pp. 351–364). Springer. https://doi.org/10.1007/978-3-319-13416-1_34

Gómez, S., Zervas, P., Sampson, D., & Fabregat, R. (2014). Context-aware adaptive and personalized mobile learning delivery supported by UoLmP. *Journal of King Saud University: Computer and Information Systems Journal, 26*(1), 47–61. https://doi.org/10.1016/j.jksuci.2013.10.008

González-Lloret, M. (2018). Pragmatics in technology-mediated contexts. In A. Sánchez-Hernández & A. Herraiz-Martínez (Eds.), *Learning second language pragmatics beyond traditional contexts* (pp. 15–46). Peter Lang.

Griful-Freixenet, J. (2020). Learning about inclusive education: Exploring the entanglement between universal design for learning and differentiated instruction. Doctoral dissertation, Vrije Universiteit Brussel.

Hartwick, P. (2018). Investigating research approaches: Classroom-based interaction studies in physical and virtual contexts. *ReCALL, 30*(2), 161–176. https://doi.org/10.1017/S0958344017000386

Hasanov, A., Laine, T. H., & Chung, T. S. (2019). A survey of adaptive context-aware learning environments. *Journal of Ambient Intelligence and Smart Environments, 11*, 403–428. https://doi.org/10.3233/AIS-190534

Hatcher, R. (1998). Class differentiation in education: Rational choices? *British Journal of Sociology of Education, 19*(1), 5–24. https://doi.org/10.1080/0142569980190101

Hausfather, S. J. (1996). Vygotsky and schooling: Creating a social context for learning. *Action in Teacher Education, 18*(2), 1–10. https://doi.org/10.1080/01626620.1996.10462828

Holden, C., & Sykes, J. (2011). Leveraging mobile games for place-based language learning. *International Journal of Game-Based Learning, 1*(2), 1–18. http://dx.doi.org/10.4018/ijgbl.2011040101

Huang, Y.-M., & Chiu, P.-S. (2015). The effectiveness of a meaningful learning-based evaluation model for context-aware mobile learning. *British Journal of Educational Technology, 46*(2), 437–447. https://doi.org/10.1111/bjet.12147

Huang, X., Zou, D., Cheng, G., & Xie, H. (2021). A systematic review of AR and VR enhanced language learning. *Sustainability*, *13*(9), 4639. https://doi.org/10.3390/su13094639

Hubbard, P., & Colpaert, J. (2019). Transdisciplinarity in computer assisted language learning. *CALICO Journal*, *36*(2), 81–99. https://doi.org/10.1007/s10639-022-10964-2

Hwang, G.-J., Shi, Y.-R., & Chu, H.-C. (2011). A concept map approach to developing collaborative mindtools for context-aware ubiquitous learning. *British Journal of Educational Technology*, *42*(5), 778–789. https://doi.org/10.1111/j.1467-8535.2010.01102.x

Hwang, W.-Y., Chen, H., Shadiev, R., Huang, R.-Y., & Chen, C.-Y. (2014). Improving English as a foreign language writing in elementary schools using mobile devices in familiar situational contexts. *Computer Assisted Language Learning*, *27*(5), 359–378. https://doi.org/10.1080/09588221.2012.733711

Jabbari, N., & Eslami, Z. (2019). Second language learning in the context of massively multiplayer online games: A scoping review. *ReCALL*, *31*(1), 92–113. https://doi.org/10.1017/S0958344018000058

Jeong, K. (2017). Preparing EFL student teachers with new technologies in the Korean context. *Computer Assisted Language Learning*, *30*(6), 488–509. https://doi.org/10.1080/09588221.2017.1321554

Kasaki, N., Kurabayashi, S., & Kiyoki, Y. (2012). A geo-location context-aware mobile learning system with adaptive correlation computing methods. *Procedia Computer Science*, *10*(2012), 593–600. https://doi.org/10.1016/j.procs.2012.06.076

Kumar, B. A., & Sharma, B. (2020). Context aware mobile learning application development: A systematic literature review. *Education and Information Technologies*, 25, 2221–2239. https://doi.org/10.1007/s10639–019-10045-x

Lan, Y.-J. (2015). Contextual EFL learning in a 3D virtual environment. *Language Learning & Technology*, *19*(2), 16–31. http://dx.doi.org/10125/44412

Lave, J., & Wenger, E. (1991). *Situated learning: Legitimate peripheral participation*. Cambridge University Press.

Lee, S. M. (2019). A systematic review of context-aware technology use in foreign language learning. *Computer Assisted Language Learning*, *35*(3), 294–318. https://doi.org/10.1080/09588221.2019.1688836

Lee, S. M., & Park, M. (2020). Reconceptualization of the context in language learning with a location-based AR app. *Computer Assisted Language Learning*, *33*(8), 936–959. https://doi.org/10.1080/09588221.2019.1602545

Liu, G. Z., Kuo, F. R., Shi, Y. R., & Chen, Y. W. (2015). Dedicated design and usability of a context-aware ubiquitous learning environment for developing receptive language skills: A case study. *International Journal of Mobile Learning and Organisation*, *9*(1), 49–65. https://doi.org/10.1504/IJMLO.2015.069717

Liu, T.-Y. (2009). A context-aware ubiquitous learning environment for language listening and speaking. *Journal of Computer Assisted Learning*, *25*(6), 515–527. https://doi.org/10.1111/j.1365-2729.2009.00329.x

Morales, R., Igler, B., Böhm, S., & Chitchaipoka, P. (2015). Context-aware mobile language learning. *Procedia Computer Science, 56,* 82–87. https://doi.org/10.1016/j.procs.2015.07.198

Morrison, G. R., Ross, S. M., Kalman, H. K., & Kemp, J. E. (2013). *Designing effective instruction* (7th ed.). Wiley.

Nguyen, V. A., Pham, V. C., & Ho, S. D. (2010). A context-aware mobile learning adaptive system for supporting foreigner learning English. In *Proceedings of the 2010 IEEE RIVF International Conference on Computing and Communication Technologies, Research, Innovation, and Vision for the Future (RIVF)* (pp. 1–6). IEEE. https://doi.org/10.1109/RIVF.2010.5632316

Nguyen, T. H., Hwang, W. Y., Pham, X. L., & Pham, T. (2020). Self-experienced storytelling in an authentic context to facilitate EFL writing. *Computer Assisted Language Learning, 35*(4), 666–695. https://doi.org/10.1080/09588221.2020.1744665

Nicolson, M., Murphy, L., & Southgate, M. (Eds.) (2011). *Language teaching in blended contexts.* Dunedin Academic Press.

Ogata, H., Yin, C., El-Bishouty, M. M., & Yano, Y. (2010). Computer supported ubiquitous learning environment for vocabulary learning. *International Journal of Learning Technology, 5*(1), 5–24. https://doi.org/10.1504/IJLT.2010.031613

Ogata, H., Hui, G. L., Yin, C., Ueda, T., Oishi, Y., & Yano, Y. (2008). LOCH: supporting mobile language learning outside classrooms. *International Journal of Mobile Learning and Organisation, 2*(3), 271–282.

Oxford University Press. (2013). *Oxford English Dictionary,* s.v. Design. www.oed.com/view/Entry/50840

Palfreyman, D. (2006). Social context and resources for language learning. *System, 34*(3), 352–370. https://doi.org/10.1016/j.system.2006.05.001

Pareja-Lora, A., Blume, M., Lust, B., & Chiarcos, C. (2019). *Development of linguistic linked open data resources for collaborative data-intensive research in the language sciences.* MIT Press.

Parmaxi, A., & Demetriou, A. (2020). Augmented reality in language learning: A state-of-the-art review of 2014–2019. *Journal of Computer Assisted Learning, 36,* 861–875. https://doi.org/10.1111/jcal.12486

Patten, B., Sánchez, I. A., & Tangney, B. (2006). Designing collaborative, constructionist and contextual applications for handheld devices. *Computers and Education, 46,* 294–308. https://doi.org/10.1016/j.compedu.2005.11.011

Peetsma, T., Vergeer, M., Roeleveld, J., & Karsten, S. (2001). Inclusion in education: Comparing pupils' development in special and regular education. *Educational Review, 53*(2), 125–135. https://doi.org/10.1080/00131910125044

Reinders, H., & Lakarnchua, O. (2014). Implementing mobile language learning with an augmented reality activity. *Modern English Teacher, 23*(2), 42–46. www.modernenglishteacher.com/implementing-mobile-language-learning-with-an-augmented-reality-activity

Reinders, H., & Pegrum, M. (2016). Supporting language learning on the move. An evaluative framework for mobile language learning resources. In B. Tomlinson (Ed.), *SLA research and materials development for language learning* (pp. 116–141). Routledge.

Reinders, H., Lakarnchua, O., & Pegrum, M. (2014). A trade-off in learning: Mobile augmented reality for language learning. In M. Thomas & H. Reinders (Eds.), *Contemporary task-based language teaching in Asia* (pp. 244–256). Bloomsbury.

Roy, D., & Crabbe, S. (2015). Website analysis in an EFL context: Content comprehension, perceptions on web usability and awareness of reading strategies. *ReCALL, 27*(2), 131–155. https://doi.org/10.1017/S095834401400024X

Roy, D., Brine, J., & Murasawa, F. (2016). Usability of English note-taking applications in a foreign language learning context. *Computer Assisted Language Learning, 29*(1), 61–87. https://doi.org/10.1080/09588221.2014.889715

Shadiev, R., Wu, T., & Huang, Y. (2020). Using image-to-text recognition technology to facilitate vocabulary acquisition in authentic contexts. *ReCALL, 32*(2), 195–212. https://doi.org/10.1017/S0958344020000038

Shehadeh, A., & Coombe, C. A. (Eds.) (2012). *Task-based language teaching in foreign language contexts: Research and implementation*. John Benjamins.

Shih, J.-L., Chu, H.-C., Hwang, G.-J., & Kinshuk (2009). An investigation of attitudes of students and teachers about participating in a context-aware ubiquitous learning activity. *British Journal of Educational Technology, 42*, 373–394. https://doi.org/10.1111/j.1467-8535.2009.01020.x

Sun, Y., & Dong, Q. (2004). An experiment on supporting children's English vocabulary learning in multimedia context. *Computer Assisted Language Learning, 17*(2), 131–147. https://doi.org/10.1080/0958822042000334217

Sun, Y.-C. (2013). Examining the effectiveness of extensive speaking practice via voice blogs in a foreign language learning context. *CALICO Journal, 29*(3), 494–506. https://doi.org/10.1558/cj.29.3.494-506

Tan, Q., Liu, T., & Burkle, M. (2013). Location-based environments for formal and informal learning: Context-aware mobile learning. In D. G. Sampson (Ed.), *Ubiquitous and mobile learning in the digital age* (pp. 115–136). Springer.

Terwel, J. (2005). Curriculum differentiation: Multiple perspectives and developments in education. *Journal of Curriculum Studies, 37*(6), 653–670. https://doi.org/10.1080/00220270500231850

Tessmer, M., & Richey, R. C. (1997). The role of context in learning and instructional design. *Educational Technology Research and Development, 45*, 85–115. https://doi.org/10.1007/BF02299526

Trinder, R. (2003). Conceptualisation and development of multimedia courseware in a tertiary educational context: Juxtaposing approach, content and technology considerations. *ReCALL, 15*(1), 79–93. https://doi.org/10.1017/S0958344003000715

Vallejo-Correa, P., Monsalve-Pulido, J., & Tabares-Betancur, M. (2021). A systematic mapping review of context-aware analysis and its approach to mobile learning and ubiquitous learning processes. *Computer Science Review, 39*, 100335. https://doi.org/10.1016/j.cosrev.2020.100335

van Vught, F. (2009). Diversity and differentiation in higher education. In F. van Vught (Ed.), *Mapping the higher education landscape* (pp. 1–16). Springer. https://doi.org/10.1007/978-90-481-2249-3_1

Vincent-Durroux, L., Poussard, C., Lavaur, J., & Aparicio, X. (2011). Using CALL in a formal learning context to develop oral language awareness in ESL: An assessment. *ReCALL, 23*(2), 86–97. https://doi.org/10.1017/S0958344011000024

Wang, C. C., & Wei, C. R. (2014). The implementation of a context-aware mobile Japanese conversation learning system based on NFC-enabled smartphones. In *Proceedings of the 2014 IIAI 3rd International Conference on Advanced Applied Informatics (IIAIAAI)* (pp. 313–317). https://doi.org/10.1109/IIAI–AAI.2014.71

Wang, H., Liu, G., & Hwang, G. (2017). Integrating socio-cultural contexts and location-based systems for ubiquitous language learning in museums: A state of the art review of 2009–2014. *British Journal of Educational Technology, 48*(2), 653–671. https://doi.org/10.1111/bjet.12424

Wang, H.-Y., Lin, V., Hwang, G.-J., & Liu, G.-Z. (2019). Context-aware language-learning application in the green technology building: Which group can benefit the most? *Journal of Computer Assisted Learning, 35*, 359–377. https://doi.org/10.1111/jcal.12336

Ward, M. (2004). The additional uses of CALL in the endangered language context. *ReCALL, 16*(2), 345–359. https://doi.org/10.1017/S0958344004000722

Ware, P., & Hellmich, E. (2014). Call in the K-12 context: Language learning outcomes and opportunities. *CALICO Journal, 31*(2), 140–157. https://doi.org/10.11139/cj.31.2.140-157

Westwood, P. (2001). Differentiation as a strategy for inclusive classroom practice: Some difficulties identified. *Australian Journal of Learning Disabilities, 6*(1), 5–11. https://doi.org/10.1080/19404150109546651

Xie, H., Chu, H. C., Hwang, H. J., & Wang, C. C. (2019). Trends and development in technology-enhanced adaptive/personalized learning: A systematic review of journal publications from 2007 to 2017. *Computers & Education, 140*, 103599. https://doi.org/10.1016/j.compedu.2019.103599

Yang, S. (2018). Language learners' perceptions of having two interactional contexts in eTandem. *Language Learning & Technology, 22*(1), 42–51. https://dx.doi.org/10125/44577

Yu, Z., Zhou, X., & Shu, L. (2010). Towards a semantic infrastructure for context-aware e-learning. *Multimedia Tools and Applications, 47*(1), 71–86. https://doi.org/10.1007/s11042–009–0407-4

Zervas, P., Gómez, S., Fabregat, R., & Sampson, D. (2011). Tools for context-aware learning design and mobile delivery. In *Proceedings of 11th IEEE International Conference on Advanced Learning Technologies (ICALT 2011).* (pp. 534–535). IEEE.

Further Reading

Dohn, N., Hansen, S., & Klausen, S. (2018). On the concept of context. *Education Sciences, 8*(3), 111. http://dx.doi.org/10.3390/educsci8030111

Despite common acceptance of the claim that learning is context-dependent to some degree, and despite a widespread interest in researching learning in specific contexts such as museums, classrooms, or workplace settings, there is a lack of consensus on what context exactly is. This article aims to clarify the concept of context. It provides a minimal construct, which is applicable to all references to context, and a typology of context categories that is relevant for understanding the significance of context for learning.

Lan, Y.-J. (2015). Contextual EFL learning in a 3D virtual environment. *Language Learning & Technology, 19*(2), 16–31. http://dx.doi.org/10125/44412

This article focuses on the development of virtually immersive English as a foreign language (EFL) learning contexts beyond the regular English class schedule. As many as 132 elementary school students participated in this study. Both qualitative and quantitative data, including observation and English learning performances, were collected and analyzed.

Lee, S. M. (2019). A systematic review of context-aware technology use in foreign language learning. *Computer Assisted Language Learning, 35*(3), 294–318. https://doi.org/10.1080/09588221.2019.1688836

This study examined articles published between 2000 and 2018 to understand the trends of technology and the current issues with context-aware technology in FL learning. This review included 75 empirical studies and 13 system-descriptive studies. The studies were examined in terms of publication year, methodology, participants, languages, device types, and effectiveness of the technology, as measured on the basis of FL learning results.

3

Current and Emerging Theories in CALL

Regine Hampel and Helen Lee

Introduction

Why would researchers and teachers want to use theory in computer-assisted language learning (CALL) rather than just focusing on what works in practice? And if we decide that theory is useful for CALL, is there a "correct" theory that should be used? Before we focus on these questions, let us consider first what a theory is and what it does. Berk (2013) defines it as "an orderly, integrated set of statements that describes, explains and predicts behavior" (p. 6), providing organizing frameworks and guiding and giving meaning to what the researcher sees. She goes on to say that "theories are influenced by cultural values and belief systems of their times" (p. 7).

Reeves et al. (2008) explain why researchers would want to use theories.

> Theories provide complex and comprehensive conceptual understandings of things that cannot be pinned down: how societies work, how organisations operate, why people interact in certain ways. Theories give researchers different "lenses" through which to look at complicated problems and social issues, focusing their attention on different aspects of the data and providing a framework within which to conduct their analysis.
>
> *(Reeves et al., 2008, p. 337)*

So unless we want to start from scratch when trying to understand the phenomena around us, theories help us to make sense of the world. As Creswell (2009) points out, quantitative research theories (or hypotheses) are tested to provide an explanation for answers to particular questions asked. In contrast, in qualitative research theory is more explorative, and so can be a final outcome (e.g. in grounded theory), or "a lens that shapes what is looked at and the questions asked, such as in ethnographies or in advocacy research" (p. 49).

Yet theories are not just useful for research; they are also crucial for teachers and teaching practice. They inform principled teaching frameworks (see e.g. Hubbard & Levy, 2006; Levy & Stockwell, 2006; Stickler & Hampel, 2015) and help us to understand what works and why it works in the classroom.

Background

CALL is a relatively new field, which only began to become mainstream in the 1980s. It started with a focus on practice that had been generated by the introduction of digital and online tools into education, with teachers-turned-researchers trialling these as they were being developed and became available, first to institutions and then to the general public. Databases and CD-ROMs were used to support information retrieval and programmed instruction (e.g. in the context of vocabulary learning, text comprehension, or language testing); electronic mail and early conferencing systems offered new communication channels, supporting for example synchronous computer-assisted classroom discussion (see also Davies (2016) for a useful overview of CALL).

In order to conceptualize the new practices that were developing with the use of these new tools, CALL researchers initially resorted to theories that originated in a closely related field, namely second-language (L2) learning, also known as second-language acquisition (SLA). These included universal grammar, cognitive approaches to L2 learning, and interaction in L2 learning. This trend was followed by a new generation of researchers, who focused on the social and cultural aspects of online language learning and embraced learning theories such as sociocultural theory, which centers on the social and cultural.

Over the past decades, however, with the introduction of new tools, particular areas and approaches within CALL have developed, resulting in a range of different theories being used, as we will outline below. They are not necessarily clearly delineated from each other and they can link to other fields, thus further expanding the theories that had come from or via L2 learning research. These areas include computer-mediated communication (CMC), telecollaboration, mobile-assisted language learning (MALL), gaming, and learning in the wild. As Hubbard (2019) points out, "[c]urrent trends in CALL such as mobile learning, gamification, and use of social media appear to represent major shifts in the digital language learning landscape" (p. 1) – and as such they may also require new theoretical framings.

While CALL started in the physical classroom, with the growing use of mobile devices it is now increasingly moving out of it – and often also outside the realm that is controlled by a teacher. This raises new questions around boundaries (e.g. between school and home, between teacher-led instruction and student-led activity) and how to facilitate seamless learning, integrating what is inside and what is outside the physical classroom, and creates new challenges, for example around support, which any CALL theory today has to take into account and "explain."

Yet the fast and constant development of technologies that support CALL practice and a widening of the reach of CALL that has been accompanying this development have meant that theory has tended to trail behind. Thus a *CALICO Journal* editorial entitled "In Theory: We Could Be Better" (Schulze & Smith, 2015, p. ii) "plead[ed] for a concerted effort by *CALICO Journal* authors and scholars to further improve the basis of research in CALL" – referring the readers to scholars such as James Lantolf, Diane Larsen-Freeman, and Michael Tomasello, who support sociocultural theory, dynamic systems theory, and emergentism. What these theories have in common is that they emphasize the critical role of communication, interaction, and meaning and the fact that L2 development often does not follow a linear path.

Theorizing CALL

Systematic reflection on theory development for CALL started in 1998, when Warschauer and Healey set out the history of CALL theory. They started with (1) behavioristic CALL, with its focus on drill and practice; followed this with (2) communicative CALL, with its focus on communication and interactivity but still rooted in cognitive approaches and using an input–interaction–output model of language acquisition, as encapsulated for example in Krashen's (1981) and Long's (1983) work; and ended with (3) integrative CALL, which featured multimedia and online learning tools.

Since then, the field of CALL has moved on considerably after what Block (2003, p. 4) described as the "social turn" in L2 acquisition. For CALL researchers, this has meant turning to more general learning theories such as Vygotsky's sociocultural theory; using concepts such as zones of proximal development, situated learning, and community of practice; and focusing on interaction and social aspects of learning.

While there is a continued focus on cognitive, psycholinguistic SLA theories that follow a more positivist paradigm, "there is potentially far more to *CALL* than can be simply explained by *theories* of SLA that do not involve technology" (Stockwell, 2014, p. 29). Thus researchers have started to draw on other paradigms and theories – particularly those that take account of the changing nature of language learning in relation to learners' and teachers' use of online tools and platforms. Theories open to hybridization and disruption seem particularly apt. Examples are complexity theory (Larsen-Freeman & Cameron, 2008), which helps us to examine how traditional language learning and teaching practices are disrupted in CALL (e.g. Hampel, 2019); and social semiotics, which includes the theory of multimodal communication (Kress & Van Leeuwen, 2001) and the related notion of multiliteracies (Kress, 2000), which Kalantzis and Cope (2021, n.p.) explain as "the variability of meaning making in different cultural, social or domain-specific contexts. These differences are becoming ever more significant to our communications environment."

A key question arising from this is whether distinct and possibly opposing (cognitive psycholinguistic versus sociocultural) paradigms dictate the approach to research in ways that potentially limit innovation and the development of future theories. Alternatively, is there an interface between these seemingly dichotomous theories when considering learning with technology – one where research would not have to operate within a single, potentially constraining, paradigm?

Current Use of Theories in CALL Research

So what theorical approaches are being used in CALL research today? To help us understand how CALL is theoretically framed across a panoply of digital tools and spaces as well as serving learners with a broad range of motivations, we explored leading CALL journals, outlining both established and emergent theories. To complement this review of recent literature, we also refer to earlier research that expanded the ways in which CALL is conceptualized. We thus highlight the increasing influence of a variety of intellectual disciplines on CALL, depicting this phenomenon as "transdisciplinarity" (Colpaert, 2018) – in that "multilingualism, globalization, technologization, and mobility" have resulted in the introduction of concepts, theories, and methodologies that originate from other intellectual fields (Douglas Fir Group, 2016, p. 19). Table 3.1 shows a focus on the theories and key concepts that this review has brought to light.

Theories Informing Social Approaches to Learning

Using Vygotsky's work on learning and adopting a sociocultural theoretical lens on technology-mediated language learning suggests that "higher-level cultural tools serve as a buffer between the person and the environment and mediate the relationship between the individual and the social–material world" (Lantolf & Thorne, 2007, pp. 198–199). Sociocultural theory offers a set of guiding principles for researchers, but also for teachers who are interested in understanding the potential of digital tools to support critical areas for their learners such as communication, interaction, collaboration, and participation. For example, findings show how the adoption of digital annotation tools transformed the isolated act of reading into a social experience (Law, Barney, & Poulin, 2020), and how notions such as learner agency, combined with the availability of the internet as a cultural artifact, served to support oral communication practice (Niu, Lu, & You, 2018).

While a Vygotskian perspective has historically guided forms of inquiry based on dialogical approaches to teaching and learning, contemporary research in CALL reflects this theoretical influence but also suggests its disruption and evolution. Hampel (2019) demonstrates aspects of theory

Table 3.1 *Established and emergent theories identified in recent CALL studies*

Theory/key concept	Associated origins of theory	Focus of theory
Socioculturalism	Vygotsky (1978)	Cultural tools and artifacts that mediate relationships between the individual and the social world
Mediated learning theory	Lee (2014)	Evaluation of mediating tools
Activity theory	Engeström (1987; 2001)	Object-oriented, social and culturally mediated activity
Social presence	Short, Williams & Christie (1976)	Projection of personal characteristics into the community of inquiry
Social justice education	Ayers, Quinn, & Stovall (2009)	Equity, activism, and social literacy
Maker culture	Hatch (2014)	Learning through doing, collaboration, and play
Design thinking	Dorst (2009); Rowe (1987)	Teams working together via an iterative process to find solutions
Rewilding	Thorne, Hellermann, & Jackonen (2021)	Teacher creating supportive conditions for learning in the wild
Social semiotics/ multimodality	Kress & Van Leeuwen (2001)	Social orchestration of multiple modes such as gesture, gaze, and language
Multimodal interaction analysis	Norris (2004)	Relationships between modes in interaction
Multiliteracies	Cope & Kalantzis (2009)	Pedagogy of multiliteracies for the digital age
Geosemiotics	Scollon & Scollon (2003)	Use of situated signs shaped by social and cultural use: "discourses in place"
Gesture studies	McNeill (1992)	Correlation between spoken language and co-occurring types of gesture
Dual coding theory	Paivio (1991)	Verbal representations and mental images within recall
The interaction account	Varonis & Gass (1985)	Negotiation of meaning by language learners, comprehensible input/output
Dynamic systems theory	Larsen-Freeman & Cameron (2008)	Usage-based perspective on SLA, focusing on complex systems that emerge from the interactions of its components
Translanguaging	Welsh education system in the 1980s (see also Wei, 2018)	Multilingual speakers using their languages as an integrated system
Connectivism	Siemens (2005)	Technologies such as the internet enabling people to learn and share information in new ways
Willingness to communicate	MacIntyre et al. (1998)	Learners who are willing to communicate actively seeking out opportunities to do this
Self-determination	Deci & Ryan (1985)	Motivation along a continuum
Sports psychology	Triplett (1898).See also Adolphs et al. (2018)	Performance-promoting techniques for athletes
Investment	Darvin & Norton (2015)	Model to explain the negotiated relationships between teachers and learners in the digital age

"ensemble" and "synthesis" in the design of a "multiperspectivist" (Levy & Stockwell, 2006) lens, which is meant to comprehensively take account of learners' and teachers' use of technologies that have been disrupting traditional, classroom-based approaches to language learning. This unified framework is "made up of several complementary parts," which entailed the researcher combining complex systems theory (Larsen-Freeman, 2017), used as a heuristic device, with sociocultural theory (Vygotsky, 1978) and with the social semiotic theory of multimodality (Kress & Van Leeuwen, 2001). See Figure 3.1 for an example of a theoretical ensemble.

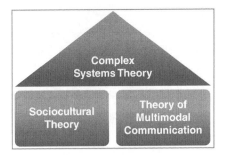

Figure 3.1 Hampel's 2019 framework.

Law, Barny, and Poulin (2020) drew on the perceived theoretical relationship between sociocultural theory and multiliteracies as a way to address the solitary nature of L2 reading via the introduction of digital annotation tools. They found that peers socially "co-constructed meaning" about the texts through their interactive use of technology. Adopting a Vygotskian perspective, mediated learning experience (MLE) theory (Lee, 2014) represents a contemporary reworking of an existing theory. This approach was recently used to examine an automated writing evaluation program that had been designed to support teachers who were working with large numbers of university students in China: "human cognition is not static but can be transformed through appropriate interaction and instruction ... MLE can be taken as a new object of the feedback system and to achieve the new object, new mediating artifacts and tools have to be introduced to the conventional feedback system" (Jiang, Yu, & Wang, 2020, p. 2).

Engeström's (1987, 2001) activity theory further expands concepts such as mediation, in that tools are said to mediate the relationship between subject and object. In their study within a telecollaborative setting, Nishio and Nakatsugawa (2018) exploited key features of the model in an investigation of a six-week telecollaboration project between American learners of Japanese and Japanese learners of English. Importantly, the theoretical approach enabled the researchers to identify and analyze examples of "contradiction" and "conflict" that had emerged between learners' expectations and the reality of the interactions. Engeström's theory served to incentivize the researchers to go on to design a more context-specific version – "a telecollaboration activity system" – in a way that demonstrates the harnessing of a theory, which is then adapted and transformed with the aim of addressing a specific CALL context.

Findings from other recent research studies illustrate how social forms of learning via communication, interaction, collaboration, and participation are now enabled across spaces that include automated feedback machines, fanfiction sites, virtual worlds, mobile videoconferencing, and mobile augmented reality (Cornillie et al., 2021; Jiang, Shulin, & Wang, 2020; Law et al., 2020; Lee, Hampel, & Kukulska-Hulme, 2019; Nishioka, 2016; Niu, Lu, & You, 2018; Thorne et al., 2021; Wang et al., 2019; Yamazaki, 2018). Studies that have drawn on socioculturalism and on constructivism in the broader sense, by focusing on the learner's personal construction of meaning through experience, have also addressed language learning through creative writing, through the promotion of multiliteracies (Cornillie et al., 2021), and through digital storytelling (Nishioka, 2016).

Grounded in constructivism, "maker culture," a digital subculture originally based on technology-enhanced notions of do-it-yourself, has emerged as a creative and practical way to conceptualize the design of language learning environments and other educational contexts by adopting principles such as "doing, bricolage, collaboration and playfulness" (Cornillie et al., 2021, p. 17). Here "making" is viewed as inseparable from embodied forms of thinking, based on the unification of body and mind (www.youtube.com/watch?v=frynXFJbXaY). A special edition of the journal *CALICO* (2021) explicates how this theoretical innovation is being implemented as a way to frame and evaluate a diversity of language-learning environments.

Multimodality and Multiliteracies

Researchers have increasingly sought to understand the meaning potential of CALL environments by referring to Halliday's conceptualization of language as a semiotic system – which in turn had sparked Kress and Van Leeuwen's (2001) theory of multimodality, Norris's (2004) multimodal methodological framework, and Scollon and Scollon's (2003) *geosemiotics*, which combines elements from sociolinguistics and semiotics to understand how language is situated in the material world.

Hampel (2003) first introduced the theory of multimodality into the CALL literature through her study on audioconferencing tools, where she identified critical links between areas such as SLA, task-based learning, and multimodality. Exploiting a theory that goes beyond spoken and written language, this study reminds us of the importance of gesture, gaze, touch, and even place in language learning and "help[s] us to understand the demands made by the new media and how to make the best use of them" (Hampel, 2019, p. 33). Conversely, researchers are combining theories such as multimodality with theories of discourse related to *SLA* such as the negotiation of meaning (Hampel & Stickler, 2012; Lee, Hampel, & Kukulska-Hulme, 2019), with Bakhtinian approaches to voice (Austin, Hampel, & Kukulska-Hulme, 2017), and with semiotic initiators and responders (Knight, Dooly, & Barberà, 2020) in ways that suggest that multimodality is being used as a way to extend notions of talk. Developing an understanding of how L2 interaction can be supported across multiple modes can also help teachers to take account of the dynamic interrelationships that learners forge between language and other modalities as they attempt to achieve a variety of learning goals.

Because the new digital technologies have different affordances in terms of the communication modes they offer in comparison to face-to-face learning contexts, learners as well as teachers need to develop new skills to benefit from the possibilities of the new media. The theory of multimodality aims to enable a more comprehensive and holistic understanding of the affordances of various media for language-learning and -teaching purposes. Taking account of other modes has significant implications for students' literacy – which today tends to be understood as multiliteracy, to reflect new and different social practices (Cope & Kalantzis, 2009; The New London Group, 1996). As Kalantzis and Cope (2021, n.p.) state, "the business of communication and representation of meaning today increasingly requires that learners are able to figure out differences in patterns of meaning from one context to another." This is also influencing and challenging notions around data collection and analysis within teaching scenarios. For example, Stickler (2021) recently explored online teachers' "ideals" by collecting their drawings and engaging in dialogue with them. The visuals produced acted as a data source that prompted the teachers to reflect, tell stories, and express their thoughts, through the researcher's adoption of a "voice-centred relational method" reminiscent of psychoanalysis.

Gesture and gaze traditionally assumed a key role in face-to-face communication, but these modes were not enabled by early digital communication tools. Rapid developments in computer technology have resulted in the availability of tools and platforms where interaction is achieved through a diversity of semiotic resources, which are mediated in complex ways. This online co-orchestration of resources such as speech, gesture, gaze, touch, proxemics, image, sound, voice, and text has had a significant impact on communication – and has also generated very different approaches to pedagogies as well as to research design, data collection, and analysis (see Flewitt et al., 2014). It has been noted that "[m]ultimodality has been explored from a number of angles relating to computer mediated communication (CMC), such as its affordances and impact on language learners, highlighting its relevance and importance in the field of second language acquisition (SLA)" (Knight, Dooly, & Barberà, 2020, p. 25). In recent years there have been several studies that elucidate how online learners deal with multimodal forms of input and output, achieve interaction through modes such as gaze and gesture, and potentially acquire an L2 in multimodal and embodied ways (Austin, Hampel, & Kukulska-Hulme, 2017; Cohen & Wigham, 2019; Guichon & Cohen, 2016; Lee, Hampel, & Kukulska-Hulme, 2019; Satar, 2013).

Hampel and Stickler (2012) investigated multimodal language learner and teacher interactions across the desktop platform FlashMeeting, exploiting Long's (1996) notion of clarification and confirmation requests, and combined it with the theory of multimodality. Findings showed how participants strategically adapted modes to make them meet their needs and interact with the wider environment, and in this way developed "a new culture of interaction" (Hampel & Stickler, 2012, p. 133). Lee, Hampel, and Kukulska-Hulme's (2019) study revealed that gesture played a key role in learners' negotiation of meaning (Varonis & Gass, 1985) across videoconferencing, accessed on mobiles and smartphones, in that it afforded a range of visual and embodied cues that operated in close conjunction with language use. Gestures were found to assume a role in the negotiation of vocabulary and helped support online

Figure 3.2 Learner interacting on a mobile device in a café location; from a study by Lee et al. (2019).

learners to signal when they required assistance or wished to scaffold peers in the multimodal resolution of communicative difficulty (see Figure 3.2).

Drawing on Scollon and Scollon's concept of geosemiotics as a methodology, young learners were found to express "voice," by verbal and embodied means, within a video-based telecollaboration. These features of communication operated in conjunction with aspects of their technology use, but also entailed the analysis of spatial and temporal factors: "language is materially assembled through interaction with others in the physical world" (Austin, Hampel, & Kukulska-Hulme, 2017, p. 87). Other approaches have included the deployment of Norris's multimodal interaction analysis (2004) and concepts such as "semiotic initiators and responders" (Coffin & Donohue, 2014) to analyse audio recordings, screenshots, logfiles, task simulation, and reconstruction (Knight, Dooly, & Barberà, 2020). Findings illustrated that, even in a seemingly monomodal learning environment such as audioconferencing, tasks were engaged with and completed in ways that involved learners navigating textual, visual, and screen-based resources, as well as spoken language. Norris's framework (2004) has also been exploited by Wigham and Satar (2021), for example, to analyze "multimodal instruction giving" in a videoconferencing teaching scenario. Their findings demonstrate the "modal complexity" of sharing task resources in synchronous online teaching, where the teacher's shifting gaze is the only indicator to online learners that they were engaged in synchronous multitasking.

Satar's recent work has also encompassed the introduction to multimodality of new fields such as "translanguaging" (Satar, 2020), that is, the fluid practices that transcend and transform socially constructed language systems and structures (Wei, 2018). A focus on skills development for learners is also reflected in studies that have addressed the uptake of vocabulary in reading (Boers et al., 2017); listening comprehension and modality preference for learners when viewing video (Kam, Lui, &, Tseng, 2020); support for writing in multilingual classrooms (Matsumoto, 2021); and the development of skills such as L2 multimodal storytelling (Liang, 2019). Liang (2019) posits a multi-modal framework that encompasses both pedagogy and forms of analysis as a means to teach storytelling via Second Life (SL). In a small-scale study that adopted a different focus, the popularity of ubiquitous platforms such as YouTube was addressed within a multimodal paradigm. The study stated that "the democratization of knowledge" has prompted English language teachers to create online videos for a global audience (Ho & Tai, 2020, p. 1). Findings highlight the need to extend notions of expertise so as to "embrace multilingualism and multimodality" (p. 10), as teachers are seen to have "a semiotic toolkit" that they deploy to shape their online lessons and design of materials.

Motivation and Identity Revisited

While motivation in the face-to-face classroom has been well documented since the 1990s (see Dörnyei, 2019), the increasing affordances of technology have led to seemingly unrelated fields being introduced into CALL, in ways that have the potential to transform and shape approaches to pedagogy. Stockwell (2013) explains how learners may be motivated by their interest in interacting with the technology, which then triggers the motivation to learn a language, or vice versa. This stance on learning creates considerable scope for educators to think about how they might go about engaging learners and to experiment by introducing a variety of devices, platforms, and sites – all related to the development of both receptive and productive skills. For example, Ockert (2018) shows how the introduction of self-determination theory (Deci & Ryan, 1985; Dörnyei, 2001) allowed researchers to examine motivation along a continuum – from *amotivation* (having no desire to engage in a task or activity), *extrinsic motivation* (only engaging to receive an external reward), to *intrinsic motivation* (engaging for its own sake) – aiming to support young learners' language production via the introduction of tablet devices.

Contributions to the literature have also leveraged novel ideas from seemingly unrelated fields, such as the concept of role models (Muir, Dörnyei, & Adolphs, 2019). Building on previous work that has highlighted the critical role of motivation for learners, Adolphs et al. (2018) consider how to better motivate language learners by enabling them to view their "future idealised L2 self" with the help of a digital representation of this self across various technological formats. To underpin this work, the researchers also reviewed findings from the field of sports psychology. Theoretical influences drawn from this discipline revealed that viewing recordings of an athlete's "best moments" had a positive impact as a "performance-promoting technique."

Interaction within Online Communities and Networks

The deployment of theories derived from telecommunications and the "blogosphere" (blogs considered as distinct networks) is also evidenced in recent work within CALL. George Siemens explains his technology-driven theory of connectivism as a direct result of his online experiences as an internet blogger, highlighting the transformative nature of networks and the collective power of "combinatorial creativity" to shape and augment knowledge (see www.youtube .com/watch?v=yx5VHpaW8sQ). A synthesis of the literature reveals that theories such as connectivism (Siemens, 2005) and social presence theory (ensuring that personal characteristics are made visible to the wider community; Garrison, Anderson, & Archer, 2000) are innovatively deployed to examine how learners interact to establish their place, voice, and presence within dynamic networks and communities (Fornara & Lomicka, 2019; Gomes Junior, 2020; Satar, 2020; Thinh, Cunningham, & Watson, 2018). Gomes Junior (2020) exploits connectivism while drawing on earlier theories based on "affordances and ecologies of learning" (Gibson, 1986; Van Lier, 2000), demonstrating the ways in which established theories and contemporary perspectives are being interwoven to address the opportunities and complexities of social media environments such as Instagram. Findings from these studies allow both individual and collective insights into how language learners forge connections, create narratives, and build meaningful communities – which in turn support them to learn in enjoyable and memorable ways.

Social presence is a term originally coined by psychologists (Short, Williams, & Christie, 1976). Garrison, Anderson, and Archer (2000) later defined it as "the ability of participants in the community of inquiry to project their personal characteristics into the community, thereby presenting themselves as 'real' people" (p. 94). This theory captures the zeitgeist of the challenge faced by learners – namely that of using the mediating aspect of technology-enhanced communication in order to establish a successful online presence, ensuring that they are understood and able to participate in meaningful ways. Researchers in CALL have deployed this theory as an analytic lens to examine multimodal interaction across videoconferencing tools (Satar, 2013, 2020); willingness to communicate in an online course via Skype and Facebook (Thinh, Cunningham, & Watson, 2018); and the "pedagogical value" of Instagram (Fornara & Lomicka, 2019). The introduction of other theories such as multimodality (Kress & Van Leeuwen, 2001) and of models such as MacIntyre et al.'s (1998) willingness to communicate can be used to extend notions of social presence or to address other pertinent features of language learning. This type of theory "ensemble" has been used to determine the role of gaze for learners across videoconferencing tools in building social presence and in influencing the choice of data collection (Satar, 2013).

Learning in the Wild

Theorizing "learning in the wild" (i.e. learning outside the traditional classroom, in natural contexts where a particular language is used) has opened up possible avenues of research that can be considered from an ecological and embodied perspective (Godwin-Jones, 2019; Hampel, 2019; Thorne et al.,

2021). The ubiquity of mobile tablets, phones, wearable technologies, but also of "intelligent personal assistants" such as Alexa (Dizon & Tang, 2020) has extended the opportunities to acquire an L2 in such a manner that the application of theory (e.g. negotiation of meaning) can be used to determine the potential for learning through these tools. Intelligent personal assistants such as Alexa have been shown to have the potential to support autonomous learning outside the classroom. Here the technology assumes the role of a machine-driven speaking partner in ways that highlight issues such as pronunciation and erroneous sentence structure within incidents of communicative breakdown. This is advantageous according to interactionist accounts of SLA (Dizon & Tang, 2020; Moussalli & Cardosa, 2020).

The digital wilds thus represent a research domain where theoretical design can truly be said to be in its infancy. While the role of the teacher in more traditional CALL settings has been well researched, there have been few frameworks that explain areas such as acquisition in the wild, or models that can be used to shape pedagogical direction within this subfield. Sauro and Zourou (2019) suggest that the label "'wild' asks us to look beyond contexts directly embedded within or linked to formal and highly familiar educational institutions and practices" (p. 1). However, a potential hindrance to conceptualizing technology-enhanced learning within discreet paradigms that either indicate the presence of a teacher or depict an entirely autonomous, informal experience is that this tends to overlook the intersection where these may overlap to enable new experiences. In terms of the deployment of mobiles, formal and informal features of learning are said to operate along a nuanced continuum, the suggestion being that "opportunities will not be fully realized unless we make efforts to propose and try out new designs" (Kukulska-Hulme & Lee, 2020, p. 170). A recent study that looked at learners' autonomous use of mobile devices revealed that this use is principally receptive rather than interactive and oriented to producing language (Jurkovič, 2019). This usage pattern implies that teachers might need to support and direct learners in a variety of ways, for example through forms of task design and activities for the wilds. To date, learners' multimodal and embodied forms of communication across tablets and smartphones – as they engage with activities from spaces such as coffee shops, gardens, and university campuses – have formed one line of inquiry (Lee, Hampel, & Kukulska-Hulme, 2019; Rockey, Tiegs, & Fernández, 2020; Thorne et al., 2021). Theories and forms of analysis used to explore language learning in the wild include ethnography, SLA, pragmatics, and gesture studies (McNeill, 1992; 2000), which highlight the affordances of portable devices in relation to context-sensitive forms of task design.

For example, the implementation of a location-based mobile game led to a reconsideration of learning "in the wild" to encompass a concept known as "rewilding" (a practice normally associated with ecology and conservation work) in that the teacher designs "supportive conditions for goal-directed learning in spaces outside of classrooms" (Thorne et al., 2021, p. 107). This also emphasizes the importance of teachers' support for learning in these types of context.

Adopting both social and cognitive theories of SLA has also been shown to be important for researchers investigating the learning potential of mobile devices (Stockwell, 2016). A study by Lee, Hampel, and Kukulska-Hulme (2019) supported ten mixed-nationality language learners to complete speaking tasks via Skype videoconferencing tools accessed on tablets and smartphones from outside the classroom. In this study the SLA theory of the negotiation of meaning (Varonis & Gass, 1985) was combined with McNeill's (1992) gesture–speech theory and the analytical procedures affiliated to it in order to determine the role of gesture in features associated with support for language acquisition such as communicative breakdown and repair work. After the speaking tasks, learners took part in stimulated recall interviews back in the classroom. These were meant to enable them to reflect on their combined use of gesture and speech within episodes of negotiation and explore the learning potential of this type of multimodal approach.

In keeping with the principles of maker culture, fanfiction, a type of creative writing that transforms existing stories or characters, forms the basis for an exploration of the potential of pedagogical intervention in the classroom in relation to practices normally associated with digital wilds. Digital storytelling has been theorized via socioculturalism, for example through a focus on collaborative dialogue and private speech (Nishioka, 2016). Cornillie et al. (2021) explain how maker culture can be viewed through the lenses of constructivism and multiliteracies, also drawing on the New London Group (1996). The findings elucidate the multifaceted nature of these types of emergent language-learning environments. For example, the findings from this project demonstrated task characteristics that encompassed complexity and multiliteracies practice and outcomes such as motivation and language skills, but also "transversal competencies" (Cornillie et al., 2021 p. 36).

Adaptive Systems, Ecologies and Emergentism

Ecological perspectives on language learning have the potential to further our understanding of the classroom as a complex adaptive system that has been transformed as a result of the introduction of new digital technologies (Hampel, 2019; Larsen-Freeman, 2017; Larsen-Freeman & Cameron, 2008). This approach also assumes a "usage-based" perspective on language acquisition in which language is seen as emergent (Ellis & Larsen-Freeman, 2006) and acquired through "meaning in use." This concept and its associated procedures have been used to inform and investigate learning across contexts such as gaming (Scholtz & Schulze, 2017); willingness to communicate, boredom and anxiety in second life (Kruk, 2019); and perceptions of affordances and learner agency in a technology-mediated language classroom (Liu & Chao, 2017).

At the same time, researchers are also increasingly taking a performative stance toward human communication, using the concept of "languaging" and conceptualizing learning in terms of participation trajectories wherein the individual mind is interacting with other humans and with cultural and physical tools. As Bagga-Gupta and Messina Dahlberg (2019) explain, "contemporary learning is understood in terms of a relationship of mutual interdependence between human agency, socially organized activities and technology" (Ludvidsen et al., 2011, p. 9).

Findings suggest that research into language learning needs to take account of multiple factors and that, in conceptualizing these types of spaces as "complex adaptive systems," the role of the technology in relation to aspects of L2 development (SLD) can be comprehensively explained – along with the role of affective factors that influence learning. Scholtz and Schulze (2017) examined university students engaged in learning German by playing World of Warcraft over a period of four months. They emphasize that "technology-mediated SLD in CALL is a complex, non-linear process" where theories deployed to investigate it should be able to account for "multiple variables, components and actors" (p. 102). As for the description of the types of methods associated with adopting this theoretical perspective, the authors highlight how such methods need to capture features such as variety and change and cite the inadequacy of both experimental and control groups and pre- and post-testing in achieving this aim. Findings reflect the dynamic and emergent nature of language use in relation to the process of playing a game in ways that could reveal information about the context in which the language was produced, but also transferred; they also act as a means to understand the varied and unique learning experiences of gamers themselves (Scholz & Schulze, 2017).

Social Inclusion and Justice

"Exclusion from technology can lead to poorer quality of life" (Rico, Fielden, & Sánchez, 2019, pp. 5–6), and studies have positioned the acquisition of language and cross-cultural skills in relation to the democratization of education in ways that suggest the need for greater levels of cooperation between researchers and practitioners. Theoretical approaches to dealing with the complexity of globalization and technologization include the adoption of principles from "design thinking" (Dorst, 2009; Rowe, 1987), which encourages multiple stakeholders to collaborate and strategize so as to problem-solve from multiple perspectives. This novel approach was recently adopted as professionals worked together to address the urgent needs of migrants and refugees via the use of language massive online open courses (LMOOCs) (Castrillo & Sedano, 2021). It has been suggested that design thinking has the potential to be implemented across multiple educational contexts, including curriculum design (Crites & Rye, 2020).

The introduction of a more diverse and expansive set of theories in CALL creates opportunities for researchers to ask new questions; but we also need to consider how findings might shape future pedagogy for interested language teachers. For example, the introduction of principles from social justice education such as equity, activism, and social literacy (Ayers et al., 2009) allows us to reconsider the status quo and expand notions related to the types of skills that learners and those who educate them require in order to successfully participate in today's world. Anwaruddin (2019) draws on social justice education to put forward a pedagogy for social media that is founded on "serendipity" and "contingent scaffolding" and fosters "dialogism" (Bakhtin, 1981) through a focus on sociality, community, and cooperation. Findings from recent studies encompass the promotion of skills such as digital literacy (Castrillo & Sedano, 2021; Hampel & Stickler, 2015); the development of linguistic and cultural knowledge (Rico, Fielden, & Sánchez, 2019); the ability to deal with disinformation and a general awareness of cybersecurity (Hampel, 2019); and the development of the learner's agency in the face of authority (Anwaruddin, 2019).

In recognition of the changing digital world, Darvin and Norton's (2015) conceptual framework of identity and investment is closely linked to this type of social research agenda; "the intersection of identity, capital, and ideology" is a place where learners and teachers are seen to be operating, but also struggling with powerful societal and economic forces (Stranger-Johannessen & Norton, 2017, p. 48). The debates in the wider media around negative features of online communication, for example disinformation and cyberbullying, remind us that language learning and teaching are always situated within a context that is "continually changing, challenging habitual ways of thinking" (Widdowson, 1990, p. 2). In a recent study that surveyed over 600 language teachers, findings showed that the rapid conversion to online teaching as a result of the Covid-19 epidemic had created issues such as blurred lines between work and life, an increase in workload, and the requirement for multidimensional coping strategies to support wellbeing (Macintyre, Gregersen, & Mercer, 2020); and there are indications that language teachers may already be too stretched to take on or adapt to new agendas.

Using Theory in CALL: Technologies That Make a Difference

This section will pick up the questions posed at the beginning of this chapter: why researchers and teachers would want to use theory in CALL rather than just focusing on what works in practice, and whether there is a "correct" theory that should be used.

By giving an overview of some key theories that have been used to conceptualize and understand language learning and teaching online, this chapter has shown how CALL researchers and practitioners are adapting, repurposing, and combining a range of theories to frame the computer-mediated language learning activity at the center. While there is not one single theory that "explains" language learning with new technologies, the different theories that we have introduced here are all underpinned by the centrality of interaction and communication for language learners.

We started with Vygotsky's sociocultural theory, a theory that focuses on learning generally. With its "focus on historical, cultural and social tools and other artefacts which mediate learning [it] affords an appropriate approach to understanding the use of technology for communication and interaction in a learning context" (Hampel, 2019, p. 20). Other theories where the social is central are activity theory, constructivism, and maker culture.

A second set of theories and approaches can be subsumed under the label social semiotics – which includes multimodality, multiliteracies, and geosemiotics and focuses on how learners make meaning in an L2, on the tools they use, and on the skills they need in a computer-mediated context. The adaptation of theories derived from wider fields such as gesture studies (McNeill, 1992, 2000) is also evidenced in the literature in connection with the analysis of multimodal and embodied forms of L2 interaction across mobile tablets and phones.

A third approach goes back to psychological concepts such as motivation and identity, whose importance for language learning was originally examined in the face-to-face classroom setting; but new possibilities are now emerging from technological innovations such as 3D animation.

Another group of theories such as connectivism and social presence theory can help explain the affordances and mediating aspects of technology while also focusing on ways of bringing learners together to share knowledge.

A fifth approach – learning in the wild – allows researchers to better understand learning outside the traditional classroom. Ecological theories are informing yet another approach, showing how the new technologies transform traditional learning systems and create new ecologies. And a final approach, which could be subsumed under the label "critical CALL," focuses on particular theories and approaches that are being used to promote social inclusion, such as social justice education.

That the introduction of new technologies into language learning and teaching has sparked the need for such a range of theoretical approaches – many of which have come from fields beyond language learning and teaching – bears testimony to the fact that recent CALL practices have transformed traditional language learning and teaching, with researchers increasingly referring to the notions of "fundamental change" (Wertsch, 2002), "transformation" (Säljö, 1990), or "disruption" (Hampel, 2019). And the introduction of artificial intelligence (AI) into language learning is bound to have an even greater transformative impact on language learning and teaching.

As outlined above, a number of the theories that underpin recent research highlight this transformative nature of CALL today: complex or dynamic systems theory, emergentism, and semiotics (e.g. the theory of multimodal communication). Language is thus seen "as the emergent properties of a multi-agent, complex, dynamic, adaptive system, a conception that usefully conflates a property theory [focusing on language representation and competence] with a transition theory [focusing on language acquisition and use]" (Ellis & Larsen-Freeman, 2006, p. 558).

Thus MALL takes the students out of the classroom and allows them to use their environment in new ways; learning in the wild provides opportunities for joining existing communities, for example in the context of online games, virtual worlds, and fanfiction. As we have seen, these changes in the learning environments not only impact on how language learners learn but also on how teachers support their learners today. Gee (2018) talks about the potential of online environments to provide "affinity spaces," which he defines as "loosely organized social and cultural settings in which the work of teaching tends to be shared by many people, in many locations who are connected by a shared interest or passion" (p. 8), offering an experience that traditional educational approaches are unable to provide. Bagga-Gupta and Messina Dahlberg (2019) point out that "[t]he shared spaces of virtual sites for learning are, in fact, co-constructed *in different modalities* and *interaction* by participants" (p. 10).

Thus the new technologies are part of the complexity of language and language learning, which Ellis and Larsen-Freeman's (2006, pp. 560–561) summary describes as follows:

> There are many agencies and variables that underpin language phenomena . . . Language is complex. Learners are complex. These variables interact over time in a nonlinear fashion, modulating and mediating each other, sometimes attenuating each other, sometimes amplifying each other in positive feedback relationships to the point where their combined weight exceeds the tipping point (Gladwell 2000), which results in a change of state. Just as there are no magic bullet solutions, so no one discipline of inquiry has the monopoly on language, not literature, not education, not psychology, not linguistics, not ethnography, not even brain science.

However, while the theories presented in this chapter have the potential to help researchers better understand online language learning, there also need to be stronger two-way links between researchers and teachers. There is often a disconnect between the rather theoretical work that goes on at universities and published in academic journals on the one hand and, on the other, teacher training and actual teaching practice in schools.

We therefore hope that this chapter contributes to enhancing teachers' understanding of the potential that the new technologies provide. We hope that they are inspired by some of the examples of CALL use presented here and will use them with their students, while also considering the relevance of particular approaches to CALL and their theoretical underpinnings.

References

Adolphs, S., Clark, L., Dörnyei, Z., Glover, T., Henry, A., Muir, C., Sánchez-Lozano, E., & Valstar, M. (2018). Digital innovations in L2 motivation: Harnessing the power of the ideal L2 self. *System, 78*, 9–30. https://doi.org./10.1016/j.system.2018.07.014

Anwaruddin, S. M. (2019). Teaching language, promoting social justice: A dialogic approach to using social media. *CALICO Journal, 36*(1), 1–18. https://doi.org/10.1558/cj.35208

Austin, N., Hampel, R., & Kukulska-Hulme (2017). Video conferencing and multi-modal expression of voice: Children's conversations using Skype for second language development in a telecollaborative setting. *System, 64*, 87–103. https://doi/org/10.1016/j.system.2016.12.003

Ayers, W., Quinn, T. M., & Stovall, D. (2009). *Handbook of social justice in education*. Routledge.

Bagga-Gupta, S., & G. Messina Dahlberg (2019). On epistemological issues in technologically infused spaces: Notes on virtual sites for learning. In S. Bagga-Gupta, G. Messina Dahlberg, & Y. Lindberg (Eds.), *Virtual sites as learning spaces: Critical issues on languaging research in changing eduscapes* (pp. 3–25). Palgrave Macmillan.

Bakhtin, M. M. (1981). *The dialogic imagination: Four essays*. University of Texas Press.

Berk, L. (1989/2013). *Child development*. Pearson.

Block, D. (2003). *The social turn in language acquisition*. Georgetown Press.

Boers, F., Warren, O., Grimshaw, G., & Siyanova-Chanturia, A. (2017). On the benefits of multimodal annotations for vocabulary uptake from reading. *Computer Assisted Language Learning, 30*(7), 709–725. https://doi.org/10.1080/09588221.2017.1356335

Castrillo, M. D., & Sedano, B. (2021). Joining forces toward social inclusion: Language MOOC design for refugees and migrants through the lens of maker culture. *CALICO Journal, 38*(1), 79–102. https://doi.org/10.1558/cj.40900

Coffin, C., & Donohue, J. (2014). *A language as social semiotic system-based approach to teaching and learning in higher education*. Wiley Blackwell.

Cohen, C., & Wigham, C. (2019). A comparative study of lexical word search in an audioconferencing and videoconferencing condition. *Computer Assisted Language Learning, 32*(4), 448–481. https://doi.org/10.1080/09588221.2018.1540432

Colpaert, J. (2018). Transdisciplinarity revisted. *Computer Assisted Language Learning, 31*(5–6), 483–489. https://doi.org/10.1080/09588221.2018.1437111

Cope, B., & Kalantzis, M. (2009). "Multiliteracies": New literacies, new learning. *Pedagogies: An International Journal, 4*(3), 164–195. https://doi.org/10.1080/15544800903076044

Cornillie, F., Buendgens-Kosten, J., Sauro, S., & Van der Veken, J. (2021). "There's always an option": Collaborative writing of multilingual interactive fanfiction in a foreign language class. *CALICO Journal, 38*(1), 17–42. https://doi.org/10.1558/cj.41119

Creswell, J. W. (2009). *Research design: Qualitative, quantitative, and mixed methods approaches* (3rd ed.). Sage Publications.

Crites, K., & Rye, E. (2020). Innovating language curriculum design through design thinking: A case study of a blended learning course at a Columbian University. *System, 94*. https://doi.org/10.1016/j.system.2020.102334

Dariah Teach. (2019, October 31). What is maker culture? [Video]. YouTube. www.youtube.com/watch?v=frynXFJbXaY

Darvin, R., & Norton, B. (2015). Identity and a model of investment in applied linguistics. *Annual Review of Applied Linguistics, 35*, 36–56.

Davies, G. (2016). CALL (computer assisted language learning) good practice guide. Centre for Languages Linguistics & Area Studies. www.llas.ac.uk/resources/gpg/61

Deci, E. L., & Ryan, R. M. (1985). *Intrinsic motivation and self-determination in human behaviour*. Plenum.

Dizon, G., & Tang, D. (2020). Intelligent personal assistants for autonomous second language learning: An investigation of Alexa. *The JALTCALL Journal, 16*(2), 107–120. http://doi.org/10.29140/jaltcall.v16n2.273

Dorst, K. (2009). Layers of design: Understanding design practice. In *Proceedings of IASDR 2009 (International Association of Societies of Design Research): Design, Rigour and Relevance*, p. 64.

Douglas Fir Group. (2016). A transdisciplinary framework for SLA in a multilingual world. *Modern Language Journal, 100*(S1), 19–47. https://doi.org/10.1111/modl.12301

Dörnyei, Z. (2001). New themes and approaches in L2 motivation research. *Annual Review of Applied Linguistics, 21*, 43–59.

Dörnyei, Z. (2019). From integrative motivation to directed motivational currents: The evolution of the understanding of L2 motivation over three decades. In M. Lamb, K. Csizér, A. Henry, & S. Ryan (Eds.), *Palgrave Macmillan handbook of motivation for language learning* (pp. 39–69). Palgrave Macmillan.

Ellis, N. C., & Larsen-Freeman, D. (2006). Language emergence: Implications for applied linguistics: Introduction to the special issue. *Applied Linguistics, 27*(4), 558–589.

Engeström, Y. (1987). *Learning by expanding: An activity theoretical approach to developmental research*. Orienta-Konsultit.

Engeström, Y. (2001). Expansive learning at work: Toward an activity theoretical reconceptualization. *Journal of Education and Work, 14*(1), 133–156. https://doi.org/10.1080/13639080020028747

Flewitt, R., Hampel, R., Hauck, M., & Lancaster, L. (2014). What are multimodal data and transcription? In C. Jewitt (Ed.), *The Routledge handbook of multimodal analysis* (2nd ed., pp. 44–59). Routledge.

Fornara, F., & Lomicka, L. (2019). Using visual social media in language learning to investigate social presence. *CALICO Journal, 36*(3), 184–203. https://doi.org/10.1558/cj.37205

Garrison, D. R., Anderson, T., & Archer, W. (2000). Critical inquiry in a text-based environment: Computer conferencing in higher education model. *The Internet and Higher Education, 2*(2–3), 87–105. https://doi.org/10.1016/s1096-7516(00)00016-6

Gee, J. P. (2018). Affinity spaces: How young people live and learn online and out of school. *Phi Delta Kappan: The Professional Journal for Educators*. www.kappanonline.org/gee-affinity-spaces-young-people-live-learn-online-school

Gibson, J. J. (1986). *The ecological approach to perception*. Lawrence Earlbaum.

Godwin-Jones, R. (2019). Riding the digital wilds: Learner autonomy and informal language learning. *Language Learning & Technology, 23*(1), 8–25. https://doi.org/10125/44667.

Junior, R. C. G. (2020). Instanarratives: Stories of foreign language learning in Instagram. *System, 94*. https://doi.org/10.1016/j.system.2020.102330

Gladwell, M. (2000). *The tipping point: How little things can make a difference.* Little Brown.

Guichon, N., & Cohen, C. (2016). Multimodality and CALL. In F. Farr & L. Murray (Eds.), *The Routledge handbook of language learning and technology* (pp. 509–521). Routledge.

Hampel, R. (2003). Theoretical perspectives and new practices in audio-graphic conferencing for language learning. *ReCALL, 15*(1), 21–36. https://doi.org/10.1017/S0958344003000314

Hampel, R. (2019). *Disruptive technologies and the language classroom: A complex systems approach.* Palgrave Macmillan.

Hampel, R., & Stickler, U. (2012). The use of videoconferencing to support multimodal interaction in an online language classroom. *ReCALL, 24*(2), 116–137. https://doi.org/10.1017/S095834401200002X

Hampel, R., & Stickler, U. (2015). *Developing online language teaching.* Palgrave Macmillan.

Hatch, M. (2014). *The maker movement manifesto.* McGraw-Hill Education.

Ho, W. J., & Tai, K. (2020). Doing expertise multilingually and multimodally in online teaching videos. *System, 94*, 102340. https://doi.org/10.1016/j.system.2020.102340

Hubbard, P. (2019). Five keys from the past to the future of CALL. *International Journal of Computer Assisted Language Learning and Teaching, 9*(3), 1–13. https://doi.org/10.4018/IJCALLT.2019070101

Hubbard, P., & Levy, M. (2006). *Teacher education in CALL.* John Benjamins.

Jiang, W. (2016). A storytelling file CALL task used in a tertiary CFL classroom. *International Journal of Applied Linguistics, 27*(2). https://doi.org/10.111/ijal.12161

Jiang, L., Yu, S., & Wang, C. (2020). Second language writing instructor's feedback practice in response to automated writing evaluation: A sociocultural perspective. *System, 93*. https://doi.org/10.1016/j.system.2020.102302

Jurkovič, V. (2019). Online informal language learning of English through smartphones in Slovenia. *System, 80*, 27–37. https://doi.org/10.1016/j.system.2018.10.007

Kam, E., Lui, Y., & Tseng, W. (2020). Effects of modality preference and working memory capacity on captioned videos in enhancing L2 listening. *ReCALL, 32*(2), 213–230. https://doi.org/10.1017/S0958344020000014

Kalantzis, M., & Cope, B. (2021). *Works & days.* https://newlearningonline.com/multiliteracies

Knight, J., Dooly, M., & Barberà, E. (2020). Navigating a multimodal ensemble: Learners mediating verbal and non-verbal turns in online interaction tasks. *ReCALL, 32*(1), 25–46. https://doi.org/10.1017/S0958344019000132

Krashen, S. (1981). *Second language acquisition and second language learning.* Pergamon.

Kress, G. (2000). Design and transformation: New theories of meaning. In B. Cope & M. Kalantzis (Eds.), *Multiliteracies: Literacy learning and the design of social futures* (pp. 153–161). Routledge.

Kress, G., & Van Leeuwen, T. (2001). *Multimedia discourse: The modes and media of contemporary communication*. Edward Arnold.

Kruk, M. (2019). Dynamicity of perceived willingness to communicate, motivation, boredom and anxiety in Second Life: The case of two advanced learners of English. *Computer Assisted Language Learning, 35*(1–2), 190–216. https://doi.org/10.1080/09588221.2019.1677722

Kukulska-Hulme, A., & Lee, H. (2020). Mobile collaboration for language learning and cultural learning. In M. Dressman & R. W. Sadler (Eds.), *The handbook of informal language learning* (pp. 169–180). Wiley Blackwell.

Lantolf, J. P., & Thorne, S. L. (2007). *Sociocultural theory and second language learning*. Oxford University Press.

Larsen-Freeman, D. (2017). Complexity theory: The lessons continue. In L. Ortega & Z. Han (Eds.), *Complexity theory and language development: In celebration of Diane Larsen-Freeman* (pp. 11–50). John Benjamins.

Larsen-Freeman, D., & Cameron, L. (2008). *Complex systems and applied linguistics*. Oxford University Press.

Law, J., Barny, D., & Poulin, R. (2020). Patterns of peer interaction in multimodal L2 digital social reading. *Language Learning & Technology, 24*(2), 70–85. www.lltjournal.org/item/10125-44726

Lee, H., Hampel, R., & Kukulska-Hulme, A. (2019). Gesture in speaking tasks beyond the classroom: An exploration of the multimodal negotiation of meaning via Skype videoconferencing on mobile devices. *System, 81*, 26–38. http://doi.org/10.1016/j.system.2018.12.013

Lee, I. (2014). Revisiting teaching feedback in EFL writing from sociocultural perspectives. *TESOL Quarterly, 48*(1), 201–213. https://doi.org/10.1002/tesq.153

Levy, M., & Stockwell, G. (2006). *CALL dimensions: Options and issues*. Lawrence Erlbaum Associates.

Liang, M. (2019). Beyond elocution: Multimodal narrative discourse analysis L2 storytelling. *ReCALL, 31*(1), 56–74. https:/doi.org/10.1017/S0958344018000095

Liu, Q., & Chao, C. (2017). CALL from an ecological perspective: How a teacher perceives affordance and fosters learner agency in a technology-mediated language classroom. *ReCALL, 30*(1), 68–87. https://doi.org/10.1017/S0958344017000222

Long, M. H. (1983). Linguistic conversational adjustments to non-native speakers. *Studies in Second Language Acquisition, 5*, 177–193.

Long, M. H. (1996). The role of linguistic environment in second language acquisition. In W. C. Ritchie, & T. K. Bhatia (Eds.), *Handbook of second language acquisition* (pp. 413–468). Academic Press.

Ludvidsen, S., Lund, A., Rasmussen, I., & Säljö, R. (2011). Introduction: Learning across sites – New tools, infrastructures and practices. In S. Ludvigsen, A. Lund, I. Rasmussen, & R. Säljö (Eds.), *Learning across sites: New tools, infrastructures and practices* (pp. 1–13). Routledge.

MacIntyre, P. D., Dörnyei, Z., Clement, R., & Noels, K. A. (1998). Conceptualizing willingness to communicate in a L2: A situational model of L2 confidence and affiliation. *The Modern Language Journal, 82*(4), 545–562.

MacIntyre, P. D., Gregersen, T., & Mercer, S. (2020). Language teachers' coping strategies during Covid-19 conversion to online teaching: Correlations with stress, wellbeing and negative emotions. *System, 94.* https://doi.org/10.1016/j.system.2020.102352

McNamara. T. (2015). The challenge of theory. *Applied Linguistics, 36*(4), 466–477.

McNeill, D. (1992). *Hand and mind.* Chicago University Press.

McNeill, D. (2000). *Language and gesture.* Cambridge University Press.

Matsumoto, Y. (2021). Students self-initiated use of smartphones in multilingual writing classrooms: Making learner agency and multiple involvement visible. *The Modern Language Journal, 105*(S1). https://doi.org/10.1111/modl.12688

Moussalli, S., & Cardosa, W. (2020). Intelligent personal assistants: Can they be understood by accented L2 learners? *Computer Assisted Language Learning, 33* (8), 865–890. https://doi.org/10.1080/09588221.2019.1595664

Muir, C., Dörnyei, Z., & Adolphs, S. (2019). Role models in language learning: Results of a large-scale international survey. *Applied Linguistics, 42*(1), 1–23. https://doi.org/10.1093/applin/amz056

New London Group. (1996). A pedagogy of multiliteracies: Designing social futures. *Harvard Educational Review, 66*(1), 60–92.

Nishio, T., & Nakatsugawa, M. (2018). Value orientations and off-topic interactions: Contradictions in American–Japanese intercultural telecollaboration. *CALICO Journal, 35*(3), 294–311. https://doi.org/10.1558/cj.33822

Nishioka, H. (2016). Analysing language development in a collaborative digital storytelling project: Sociocultural perspectives. *System, 62,* 39–52. https://doi.org/10.1016/j.system.2016.07.001

Niu, R., Lu, K., & You, X. (2018). Oral language learning in a foreign language context: Constrained or constructed? A sociocultural perspective. *System, 74,* 38–49. https://doi.org.10.1016/j.system.2018.02.006

Norris, S. (2004). *Analyzing multimodal interaction: A methodological framework.* Routledge.

Ockert, D. (2018). Using a tablet computer for EFL positive self-review: Increases in self-determination theory-based learning motives. *CALICO Journal, 35*(2), 182–199. https://doi.org/10.1558/cj.32185

Paivio, A. (1991). Dual-coding theory: Retrospect and current status. *Canadian Journal of Psychology Review, 45*(3), 255–287.

Reeves, S., Albert, M., Kuper, A., & Hodges, B. D. (2008). Why use theories in qualitative research? *BMJ, 337.* https://doi.org/10.1136/bmj.a949

Rico, M., Fielden, V., & Sánchez, H. (2019). Promoting social inclusion for migrant populations through media, technologies and languages. *The JALT CALL Journal, 15*(3), 3–22. https://doi.org/10.29140/jaltcall.v15n3.241

Rockey, C., Tiegs, J., & Fernández, J. (2020). Mobile application use in technology-enhanced DCTs. *CALICO, 37*(1), 85–108. https://doi.org/10.1558/cj.38773

Rowe, P. (1987). *Design thinking.* MIT Press.

Säljö, R. (1990). Learning as the use of tools: A sociocultural perspective on the human technology link. In K. Littleton & P. Light (Eds.), *Learning with computers: Analyzing productive interaction* (pp. 144–161). Routledge.

Satar, M. (2013). Multimodal language learner interactions via desktop videoconferencing within a framework of social presence: Gaze. *ReCALL*, *25*(1),
122–142. https://doi.org/10.1017/S0958344012000286

Satar, M. (2020). L1 for social presence in videoconferencing: A social semiotic
account. *Language Learning & Technology*, *24*(1), 129–153. www.lltjournal.org/
item/3137

Sauro, S., & Zourou, K. (2019). What are the digital wilds? *Language Learning &
Technology*, *23*(1), 1–7. https://doi.org/10125/44666

Scholz, K. W., & Schulze, M. (2017). Digital gaming strategies and second
language development. *Language Learning & Technology*, *21*(1), 100–120.
www.lltjournal.org/item/2987

Schulze, M., & Smith, B. (2015). In theory: We could be better. *CALICO Journal*,
32(1), i–vi. www.jstor.org/stable/calicojournal.32.1.i

Scollon, R., & Scollon, S. W. (2003). *Discourses in place: Language in the material
world*. Routledge.

Short, J., Williams, E., & Christie, B. (1976). *The social psychology of telecommunications*. John Wiley & Sons, Ltd.

Siemens, G. (2005). Connectivism: A learning theory for the digital age.
International Journal of Instructional Technology and Distance Learning, *2*(1),
3–10.

Siemens, G. (2014, January 22). *Overview of connectivism* [Video]. YouTube. www
.youtube.com/watch?v=yx5VHpaW8sQ

Stickler, U. (2021). Investigating language teachers' ideals in images and interviews. *System*, *97*. https://doi.org/10.1016/j.system.2020.102424

Stickler, U., & Hampel, R. (2015). Transforming teaching: New skills for online
learning spaces. In R. Hampel & U. Stickler (Eds.), *Developing online language
teaching: New language learning and teaching environments* (pp. 63–77). Palgrave
Macmillan.

Stockwell, G. (2013). Innovation in English-language teaching and learning. In E.
Ushioda (Ed.), *International perspectives on motivation* (pp. 156–175). Palgrave
Macmillan.

Stockwell, G. (2014). Exploring theory in computer-assisted language learning.
In X. Deng & R. Seow (Eds.), *Alternative pedagogies in the English language &
communication classroom: Selected papers from the Fourth CELC Symposium for
English Language Teachers* (pp. 25–30). Centre for English Language
Communication, National University of Singapore.

Stockwell, G. (2016). Mobile language learning. In F. Farr & L. Murray (Eds.), *The
Routledge handbook of language learning and technology* (pp. 296–307).
Routledge.

Stranger-Johannessen, E., & Norton, B. (2017). The African storybook and language teacher identity in digital times. *The Modern Language Journal*, *101*,
45–60. www.jstor.org/stable/44981292

Thinh, V. L., Cunningham, U., & Watson, K. (2018). The relationship between
willingness to communicate and social presence in an online English course. *The
JALT CALL Journal*, *14*(1). 43–59. https://doi.org/10.29140/jaltcall.v14n1.223

Thorne, S., Hellermann, J., & Jakonen, J. (2021). Rewilding language education: Emergent assemblages and entangled actions. *The Modern Language Journal, 105*(S1). https://doi.org/10.1111/modl.12687

Triplett, N. (1898). The dynamogenic factors in pacemaking and competition. *American Journal of Psychology, 9*, 507–533. https://doi.org/10.2307/1412188

Van Lier, L. (2000). From input to affordance: Social interactive learning from an ecological perspective. In J. P. Lantolf (Ed.), *Sociocultural theory and second language learning: Recent advances* (pp. 245–259). Oxford University Press.

Van Lier, L. (2004). The semiotics and ecology of language learning: Perception, voice, identity and democracy. *Utbildning& Demokrati, 13*(3), 79–103.

Varonis, E. M., & Gass, S. (1985). Non-native/non-native conversations: A model for negotiation of meaning. *Applied Linguistics, 6*(1), 71–90.

Vygotsky, L. (1978). *Mind in society: The development of higher psychological processes.* Harvard University Press.

Wang, F., Hwang, W.-Y., Li, Y.-H., Chen, P.-T., & Manabe, K. (2019). Collaborative kinesthetic EFL learning with collaborative total response. *Computer-Assisted Language Learning, 32*(7), 745–783. https://doi.org/10.1080/09588221.2018.1540432

Warschauer, M., & Healey, D. (1998). Computers and language learning: An overview. *Language Teaching, 31*(2), 57–71. http://doi.org/10.1017/S0261444800012970

Wei, L. (2018). Translanguaging as a practical theory of language. *Applied Linguistics, 39*(1), 9–30. https://doi.org/10.1093/applin/amx039

Wertsch, J. V. (2002). Computer mediation, PBL, and dialogicality. *Distance Education, 23*(1), 105–108. https://doi.org/10.1080/01587910220124008

Widdowson, H. G. (1990). *Aspects of language teaching.* Oxford University Press.

Wigham, C., & Satar, M. (2021). Multimodal interaction analysis of task instructions in language teaching via videoconferencing: A case study. *ReCALL, 33*(3), 195–213. https://doi.org/10.1017/S0958344021000070

Yamazaki, K. (2018). Computer-assisted learning of communication (CALC): A case study of Japanese learning in a 3D virtual world. *ReCALL, 30*(2), 214–231. https://doi.org/10.1017/S0958344017000350

Further Reading

Block, D. (2003). *The social turn in language acquisition.* Georgetown Press.
This book significantly contributed to identifying and outlining the social turn in applied linguistics, specifically in the area of second-language acquisition. The author proposes an alternative approach to the input–interaction–output model, an approach that is informed by interdisciplinarity and a focus on the social.

Kress, G., & Van Leeuwen, T. (2001). *Multimedia discourse: The modes and media of contemporary communication.* Edward Arnold.
Gunther Kress and Theo Van Leeuwen's book lays out their multimodal theory of communication to a wider audience. It shows how people can make meaning in

different ways, using different modes and media. This is particularly important in today's communication environment, which offers a multitude of online resources for making meaning.

Larsen-Freeman, D., & Cameron, L. (2008). *Complex systems and applied linguistics*. Oxford University Press.

This book provides a useful overview of complexity theory in the context of applied linguistics. Focusing on the interaction between the language learner and his/her context, it is a particularly useful way of approaching the transformative impact of the digital media on the way we learn languages.

4

The Shifting Focus of CALL Research

Yijen Wang

Introduction

The purpose of research is to explore the unknown (Nunan, 1992). Driven by a problem or a question, researchers seek out information with careful research procedures to resolve and answer it. The word "research" comes from the French word *rechercher* meaning "to seek out" or "to search closely"; in French as in English, the prefix "re" indicates recurrence – doing something again. This aptly evokes a cycle that explains the essence of research: research findings point out limitations and make predictions, so that researchers know what to expect and what to do better next time. Learning from empirical results in the literature helps researchers to know what has been done and where gaps may be in the research. As Hubbard and Levy (2016) suggest, "research, practice and theory can be said to constitute the three foundational pillars of any applied field" (p. 24). To know how technology enhances language education, teachers, developers, and even learners should be able to conduct research to improve technology in language teaching and learning.

However, a shift has taken place in the past several years whereby, for many researchers, the primary purpose of conducting research has come to be to get funding or publication, and this often results in the mass production of research output to satisfy quotas (see also Colpaert, 2012 on "publish or perish"). This means that research is no longer pursued simply to discover new things or to resolve a current question, but for researchers to add another achievement into their resume. The quality of research is therefore under threat. It is likely that this is one of the reasons for the proliferation of predatory journals over the past several years, as researchers struggle to deal with the pressures of publishing. Another danger is the "burden of proof" (Burston, 2003), where researchers may inadvertently set out to prove the effectiveness of a specific technology when they have put a great deal of effort into it. This kind of problem is often exacerbated by inappropriate research design (see also Felix, 2005, 2008).

Background/Historical Perspectives

Research interests in computer-assisted language learning (CALL) have typically followed trends that are shaped by shifts in psychology, language teaching approaches, and advances in technology. While there have been many attempts to make sense of these trends, one of the best known CALL historical lines is that of the three phases categorized by Warschauer and Healey (1998). As they describe, the thirty years of CALL history between the 1960s and 1990s can be divided into three distinct phases – behavioristic CALL, communicative CALL, and integrative CALL – which are consistent with "a certain level of technology as well as a certain pedagogical approach" (p. 57). Behavioristic CALL refers to the period from the 1960s to the 1970s when the main technology was a mainframe computer that was placed in a computer laboratory. In line with behaviorist perspectives, students used it to practice language drills and exercises for vocabulary and grammar learning. From the late 1970s to the 1990s, after the shift of language teaching principles, the goal of language learning came to be to communicate. On the basis of communicative approaches and the spread of networked computers, research expanded to computer-mediated communication (CMC) technologies such as email and chat rooms, which were used for interactive communication and collaboration. As multimedia and the internet became prevalent in the 1990s, integrative CALL emphasized the use of authentic online materials to support language learning. But the phases proposed by Warschauer and Healey have faced criticism. For example, Bax (2003) argued that using a historical timeline is inappropriate, as it ignores CALL's diversity in different environments and the continuity of earlier phases despite the emergence of later ones. He then proposed an alternative classification, which takes a more general approach. Bax's new categories are restricted CALL, open CALL, and integrated CALL, with the end goal of CALL being *normalisation*, which he described as

> the stage when a technology is invisible, hardly even recognised as a technology, taken for granted in everyday life. CALL has not reached this stage, as evidenced by the use of the very acronym "CALL" – we do not speak of PALL (Pen Assisted Language Learning) or of BALL (Book Assisted Language Learning) because those two technologies are completely integrated into education.
>
> *(Bax, 2003, p. 23)*

As Levy (2000, p. 190) points out, "technology always makes a difference; the technology is never transparent or inconsequential" in CALL research, and even technologies that become "normalised" will still have an impact on the teaching and learning context, despite their lack of salience (Stockwell, 2012). The landscape of technology in language education has changed a lot in the two decades since these observations were put forward, but they still remain relevant. It is crucial to keep exploring technology in language education, and it is time to reconsider the position of CALL research. The continuous evolution of technology and pedagogy enriches the diversity of CALL research. Looking at the past and the present of CALL research helps us to better prepare for future CALL education.

Primary Themes

Research in CALL has existed for at least four decades; the first journal dedicated to the field is the *CALICO Journal*, whose publishing debut dates back to 1983 (see Stockwell, 2022 for a discussion of the history of CALL). There are several other major CALL-specific journals that have emerged over the years – for example *ReCALL, Computer Assisted Language Learning, Language Learning and Technology*, and *The JALT CALL Journal* – as well as countless books, book chapters, and other published papers, all of which make a tremendous contribution to moving the field forward. While there are many different ways of looking at the literature, we can consider five major lines of research that illustrate the shifts that have emerged: research objects, research designs, research contexts, research subjects, and technology.

Shifting Research Objects
The objects of CALL research can be explored from different angles, which can be generally categorized from three perspectives: technological, pedagogical, and psychological. First, research objects obtained from technological aspects focus on investigating the effectiveness of using a specific technology by comparing it to a different technology (Andujar & Salaberri-Ramiro, 2021) or to the non-use of technology (e.g. Dizon, 2016; Far & Taghizadeh, 2022; Heidari, Khodabandeh, & Soleimani, 2018; Zhu et al., 2016). However, as discussed above, the effectiveness of using technology for language educational purposes is nearly impossible to prove, given that the interrelated factors are complex and dynamic (Felix, 2005, 2008; Stockwell, 2022; Stockwell & Reinders, 2019) and technology design, user interface, and learners' learning strategies may also have an impact on the results. What effectiveness refers to needs to be clarified as well. It could be the effectiveness of learning outcomes, the effectiveness of the technology, or the effectiveness of both.

Moving to more realistic research aims, recent studies look at the affordances and limitations of technology used in language education. Instead of comparing CALL and non-CALL, these studies investigate the extent to which technology can bring both positive and negative effects to the educational setting. For example, Jeon (2022) explored the affordances of an AI chatbot in an English as a foreign language (EFL) class of young learners. The results showed that the chatbot could provide personalized learning experiences, enhance engagement and motivation, and improve language learning outcomes. At the same time, the limitation of its speech recognition and other technical problems were also pointed out, highlighting the importance of effective implementation and support to maximize the benefits of chatbot technology in EFL classrooms.

In line with the technological perspectives, a large body of research looks into users' attitudes toward technology. One of the most widely used models is the Technology Acceptance Model (TAM) (Davis, 1989), which looks at users' attitudes toward a technology to predict their behaviors. For example, Tsai (2014) adopted the TAM to investigate the effects of using a course management system (CMS) in an English writing class, and found that the students' perception of the usefulness and ease of use of the CMS enhanced their motivation and engagement in English writing. However, the model has been criticized for providing little more than general considerations regarding learners' technological perspectives and ignoring the pedagogical perspectives, as learners' attitudes toward a certain technology may be influenced by their motivation to learn the language and by their learning strategies rather than by the learning outcomes, which are difficult for learners themselves to determine (see also Wang, 2021).

Building beyond technological perspectives, there are studies that investigate research objects concerning language pedagogy and emphasize the effects of educational technology on language learning outcomes, including various language skills and areas such as vocabulary, grammar, reading, writing, listening, speaking, pronunciation, or route and rate of acquisition (Ellis, 2008). For instance, Wang, An, and Wright (2018) used videos, online discussion forums, and mobile applications to engage students in Chinese-speaking environments. They found that the students' Chinese speaking skills had made significant improvements through the technologies. These studies usually apply language proficiency tests to measure the outcomes but the variability introduced by elements such as affective factors is usually excluded (see Loewen et al., 2019).

Therefore some researchers have investigated psychological aspects, exploring the impact of using technology on teachers' and learners' perspectives, beliefs, attitudes, and motivation (Alamer & Khateeb, 2023; Bodnar et al., 2016; Lee, 2019). Researchers should be more aware of whether objects are investigated through appropriate research design. For instance, the method most commonly used in measuring learning autonomy is the survey, which is seen as the most convenient method, though whether autonomy can be measured in this way is doubtful. Some survey researchers claim that they are looking into learner autonomy, but are in fact examining learners' perceptions of autonomy. Similarly, autonomy may be impossible to examine within a short period of time and through a single survey, as is often done in CALL research.

Shifting Research Designs

Research objects and research design are interdependent; as the main purpose of research has shifted, there has also been a change in research design.

Experimental methods were used very commonly to examine the "effectiveness" of technology in early CALL research, as described above. These methods usually divided subjects into experimental groups and control groups, then provided different treatments for each (usually with and without a given technology) and conducted pre-tests and post-tests to see whether after the treatment there is any progress in the aspect of language proficiency under investigation. While this type of research was prevalent in the 1990s and early 2000s, it has gradually been replaced by other designs. It is, however, still seen periodically in more recent literature. For example, Alvarez-Marinelli et al. (2016) carried out an experimental study that involved 816 third-grade students randomly assigned to two groups. The experimental group used a CALL program for English instruction, while the control group used a traditional teaching approach. Results showed that the elementary school students in the experimental group demonstrated a significant improvement in oral English proficiency after the twenty-five-week intervention in comparison to the control group. Although the results of studies such as these can shed light on the potential of various technologies to contribute to language acquisition, the language educational environment can never be considered in a vacuum as a laboratory, because variables are difficult to control. Although some studies claimed to use a quasi-experimental research design (i.e. they claimed that the participants were not randomly selected), care needs to be taken to ensure that this is not just an excuse for failing to control carefully for variables.

Research methods such as surveys are widely used in CALL research to investigate attitude and language outcomes. The advantages are that numerous data can be collected within a relatively short period and that many of these data can be easily quantified; but it has been common to see elicited perceptions failing to coincide with actual behavior. For instance, in Wang's (2021) study, students claimed that they were highly interested in using mobile devices for out-of-class Chinese language learning; however, this positive attitude was not reflected in the low level of engagement demonstrated by their actual usage. The overuse of surveys and questionnaires in CALL research has been noted in the past (e.g. Hubbard, 2005), and there are now several international journals that do not generally publish manuscripts that use only a survey or a questionnaire as their data collection method.

Considering the limitations and bias of experimental methods, many recent studies tend to be conducted in naturalistic settings and apply observational methods. Qualitative research methods such as learning journals, classroom observations, and interviews are often used (Nunan, 1992). For example, Carhill-Poza and Chen (2020) video-recorded ten technology-enhanced English language classrooms to understand what technologies were used and how they were implemented in teaching practices. Yang (2018) interviewed EFL learners' perceptions of learning writing in both pair work and group discussion in technology-enhanced environments. Activity logs, teacher's field notes, and self-reported data from surveys are also frequently used (e.g. Haghighi et al., 2019; Thomas, 2020). Although self-reports are widely used for research, caution should be exercised regarding data that rely on recall, since the learners might not remember clearly what they have done (Fischer, 2007; Schwarz & Oyserman, 2001).

An increasing amount of mixed-methods research that combines the advantages of both qualitative and quantitative methods can be found in CALL research. For instance, Quang, Linh, and Hiền's (2022) study applied both a survey and an interview method to investigate EFL learners' self-efficacy and second language (L2) motivational self-system in technology-enhanced task-based environments. Mixed-methods research may enhance the validity and reliability of the findings, but the increase in methods also means that researchers may spend more time and effort to acquire both qualitative and quantitative data collection and analysis skills. Case study research has gained more attention in CALL research through in-depth investigation of a specific case – which can be a student or a group of students who use a given technology (e.g. Loewen et al., 2019). Case studies are helpful in discovering the complexities in language educational contexts, but the lack of generalizability has been challenged.

The nature of CALL research designs is diversifying. Each research design has its own strengths and weaknesses; thus researchers should be aware of these when choosing research designs and should consider the complexity of CALL research methods to avoid design bias, which may appear when the research purposes are inconsistent with the selected research methods.

Shifting Research Contexts

A significant proportion of CALL research takes place in classroom-based settings, for example computer laboratories and classrooms equipped with digital devices. Since almost every student owns a laptop, research conducted in classrooms that allow students to bring their own devices is becoming increasingly popular (Thomas, 2020). These studies usually adopt digital devices and technology-based materials in language classrooms to determine whether the technology provided makes an impact on teaching and learning. Conducting research in classroom settings may be relatively realistic, as students' reactions and engagements can be observed directly (e.g. Wang et al., 2018). At the same time, extraneous variables are difficult to control outside the classroom. For example, a study may show that students develop more vocabulary by using a certain technology in class; however, there is no way of knowing whether they have acquired the vocabulary outside the classroom unless conditions are closely controlled. Also, teachers' teaching styles, the relationships between teachers and students, and classroom management skills can make an impact on technology use.

Unlike physical classroom-based settings, where teachers and students are in face-to-face environments, online settings such as virtual classrooms, virtual reality (VR) and augmented reality (AR) classrooms, learning management systems (LMSs), massive open online courses (MOOCs), and social networking services (SNSs) allow teachers and students to interact in real time without geographical boundaries (Andujar & Salaberri-Ramiro, 2021; Heidari et al., 2018; Loewen et al., 2019; Tanaka-Ellis & Sekiguchi, 2019). It may be more flexible to conduct research in an online setting, but this type of research may suffer from ethical issues such as privacy and the equality of accessibility to digital devices.

Blended settings combining both physical classroom and online classroom elements, or a variety of elements, are a recent trend. In Jin, Su, and Lei's (2020) study, EFL writing instructions were conducted through online and face-to-face interactions. The authors found that each environment could benefit students' argumentative writing in different ways. CALL research that takes place in multiple settings may be more realistic, considering the nature of the different technologies we use in our daily life. However, this approach makes the settings difficult to define. For example, researchers may assume that students use a particular application to complete the assigned learning tasks through their smartphones, outside the classroom. However, students could be using their smartphones to engage in those tasks in class instead. For this reason research settings and formal–informal learning should be carefully defined and designed.

Shifting Research Subjects

Considering the accessibility and convenience of research environments, researchers usually recruit university or college students (often their own) to serve as their research participants. One of the concerns with this approach is generalizability: CALL research has long been criticized for working with a small number of subjects, all from a single institution (Gillespie, 2020; Hubbard, 2005). Limitation sections in the literature are full of disclaimers by researchers about how the small number of participants may affect the validity and reliability of the research results, particularly in quantitative studies. On the other hand, a small sample size may not always be a negative thing, as it can be quicker to conduct when the research topic is pressing, and it allows researchers to investigate the data in depth. This does, however, depend heavily on the research design and methods adopted to make the most of data collected from subjects and from the learning context.

Another concern is that the relationship between the researcher and the participants may cause research bias in educational settings. Teacher-researchers habitually use their students as the research sample, or choose participants from the institution where they work. The teacher–student relationships and the stakes between them may inhibit undesired or unpleasant outcomes. For instance, the students may intentionally show interest in learning in order to please their teachers, or may give the responses they think their teacher wants. Some research evaluates whether the teaching approach facilitates learning autonomy; teacher-researchers may be reluctant to admit the negative outcomes. It should be noted that selection bias will lead to response bias. For example, when the researcher conducts an interview with the aim of understanding learners' motivation to use a certain technology for language-learning purposes, active learners are more willing to volunteer. In this case, less motivated learners are excluded. Given the position of teacher-researchers, the roles of researcher, teacher, and learner should be described satisfactorily in the studies, along with the reasons for sample selections. Similarly, teachers may tend not to report less favorable results, out of fear that such results would reflect negatively on their effectiveness as teachers.

It is common to see teachers recruited as participants in CALL research – for instance in research that looks at teachers' beliefs in technology and at their teaching practices (Cheung, 2021; Ding et al., 2019; Nugroho & Mutiaraningrum, 2020). As in the cases just presented, here too researchers tend to recruit colleagues from the same institution, and this affects generalizability. The researcher's position and that of their colleagues can make an impact on the results, especially in a hierarchical culture. For example, Barlett (2020) investigated twenty-one English teachers from different high schools in Japan regarding their experience of integrating technology. It was found that even young teachers were willing to use technology in their classrooms, but the workplace culture of *senpai-kohai* (senior–junior hierarchy) influenced their teaching practices, as the senior teachers disagreed with the use of new technologies or innovative teaching approaches. Finding external participants can be a solution; but, again, researchers should be more aware of these social dynamics when conducting research in educational settings.

Research may go beyond the rather standard subjects, to include parents, administrators, or even government agencies (Colpaert, 2009). For example, there are studies that look at parents' perceptions of the use of technology in their children's language learning (Osorio-Saez, Eryilmaz, & Sandoval-Hernandez, 2021), or recruit parents to support their children's responses to surveys; however, research using administrators and developers as subjects remains scarce. Expanding the variety of subjects would enrich CALL research and help us go beyond the immediately obvious, to understand the larger context.

Shifting Technologies

As innovative technology continuously emerges, a wide variety of technologies has been explored in CALL research. Researchers should consider barriers to the technology they will use for the study. Mobile devices such as tablets and smartphones allow learners to engage in language learning anytime, anywhere, but the physical barriers and distractions should be considered. Also, students have traditionally seen their personal devices as a means of playing games and accessing social media (Stockwell, 2008), which means that researchers should be aware that this attitude could have an impact on the research results. VR- and AR-enhanced learning settings provide a simulated reality for learners to practice language skills: virtual language environments emulate the real world using tools such as Second Life. With these technologies, learners are able to immerse themselves in the target language culture. However, research focusing on these technologies may require prohibitive costs and setup time to implement. Artificial intelligence (AI) technology is emerging as a major theme in CALL research (see Chapters 13 and 31 in this volume), as it can provide personalized feedback and support for language learners on the basis of their performance and learning needs; but ethical concerns (e.g. privacy and accessibility issues, as mentioned earlier) should be noted.

Apart from the limitations of technology, if a technology is used inappropriately in that its affordances are not capitalized upon, the results may be adversely affected (see Stockwell, 2022, for a discussion of affordances). As Hubbard (2005) stated, most of the participants in CALL research are not trained before the study. This lack of technical and pedagogical training may hamper the targeted learning objectives or outcomes. Ideally, researchers should eliminate the expected technical barriers as much as possible and make sure that their subjects know how to operate the technology and understand how to use it to perform a given language-learning task.

Technology is not only an object to be studied in CALL research, but also a tool for researchers to use to conduct their research. For example, online surveys such as Google Forms, SurveyMonkey, and SurveyCake have become very popular means of collecting data and performing basic analysis on them. Eye-tracking technology (Godfroid, Winke, & Conklin, 2020) and MRI (Carey & McGettigan, 2017) can capture learners' cognitive learning processes. Analysis software such as Excel, ANOVA, and NVivo are helpful for analyzing statistical and qualitative data, and automatic speech recognition and automatic transcription tools can be used to transcribe interview data.

Recommendations for Research and Practice

CALL research has long been criticized for borrowing ideas from second language acquisition (SLA) and technological theories without drawing concrete connections between them (Beatty, 2010; Hubbard & Levy, 2016). This may be because CALL belonged to applied linguistics and adopted research methodology from SLA. A grounded theory approach may be helpful in CALL research to build up models that are grounded in complex and dynamic language-learning and -teaching contexts, as it usually applies mixed methods to gather qualitative and quantitative data resources from interviews, observations, and documents, and then build a theory where one is lacking (Hadley, 2017). Merriam and Tisdell (2015, p. 32) stress that "grounded theory is particularly useful for addressing questions about process; that is, how something changes over time."

Apart from the research concerns mentioned in the previous section, the lack of longitudinal studies in CALL research has also been criticized (Hubbard, 2005). As language education is a relatively long process, the outcomes may not be easily assessed in a short period and the conditions change over time. For example, research into learner motivation should be undertaken in the long term (Dörnyei & Ushioda, 2013).

To gain in-depth insights into CALL practice, it is necessary to expand the range and number of subjects and contexts in which the studies are conducted (Beatty, 2010); and there is also a call for diversity of methods in CALL research. For example, in a variety of contexts action studies may be practical, as they enrich the diversity of CALL research and provide insights into the impact of ongoing teaching approaches; teachers can conduct action studies by planning, acting, and reflecting on their teaching practices. This allows researchers to explore the practical implementation of technology in language education in diverse contexts and from different perspectives. Context-sensitive approaches may help to explore the complexity and diversity of language learning and technology.

Moreover, researchers can use plain language summaries and other ways of disseminating their methods to make their findings more accessible to a large public. For example, visual aids such as infographics and videos can be used to explain complex concepts so as to make them easier to understand; this would benefit teachers who work in the field but do not have an academic background. Additionally, the dominance of English in scientific publishing has been criticized for creating barriers to access to research and for limiting the participation of researchers and readers, as it excludes those who are not fluent in English. This has prompted calls for greater diversity and inclusion in research, for instance through the promotion of journals in languages other than English and through the development of translation services and multi-lingual resources for less fluent users of English. Making CALL research more accessible and engaging will lead to its having a broader impact and contribution to positive diversity.

Future Directions

This chapter has guided readers through a brief history of CALL research, outlining how its focus has shifted and continues to shift. Common research biases in CALL research are also discussed, along with their potential impact on research results. In this final section I would like to go back to my first statement: Everyone can conduct research. Any individual, regardless of background or level of education, can engage in the research process, which consists of the systematic and careful investigation of a particular topic or issue in order to gain new knowledge, insights, or understanding. The ability to conduct CALL research is not limited to professionals or experts in the field; capabilities such as critical thinking, problem-solving, and attention to detail matter very much, along with the ability to analyze and interpret data. Regardless of experience, researchers should always be aware of potential research bias and of their own intention in conducting research. Despite publishing pressures, what should lie at the heart of our research is the desire to further our understanding and improve language education.

Research should be made more accessible to those who require it. A criticism that has been directed at research in applied linguistics in general – and also specifically in CALL – is that many teachers feel that it has little to do with their everyday practice. Framing research in a way that makes its relevance clearer to both teachers and researchers means that findings can be shared with a broader community. A direction for future CALL research is building bridges between external organizations or stakeholders and encouraging them to share their research findings or to collaborate with experts outside the field of CALL on projects that address community needs and concerns. This would go a long way toward narrowing the gap between academic research and the practical applications of CALL research in the real world.

References

Alamer, A., & Khateeb, A. A. (2023). Effects of using the WhatsApp application on language learners motivation: A controlled investigation using structural equation modelling. *Computer Assisted Language Learning*, *36*(1–2), 149–175. https://doi.org/10.1080/09588221.2021.1903042

Alvarez-Marinelli, H., Blanco, M., Lara-Alecio, R., Irby, B. J., Tong, F., Stanley, K., & Fan, Y. (2016). Computer assisted English language learning in Costa Rican elementary schools: An experimental study. *Computer Assisted Language Learning*, *29*(1), 103–126. https://doi.org/10.1080/09588221.2014.903977

Andujar, A., & Salaberri-Ramiro, M. S. (2021). Exploring chat-based communication in the EFL class: Computer and mobile environments. *Computer Assisted Language Learning*, *34*(4), 434–461. https://doi.org/10.1080/09588221.2019.1614632

Bartlett, K. (2020). Teacher praxis within the "Communicative course of study guidelines" in Japan: Post-implementation pedagogy. *Australian Journal of Applied Linguistics*, *3*(2), 168–182. https://doi.org/10.29140/ajal.v3n2.316

Bax, S. (2003). CALL: past, present and future. *System*, *31*, 13–28. https://doi.org/10.1016/S0346-251X(02)00071-4

Beatty, K. (2010). *Teaching and researching computer-assisted language learning* (2nd ed.). Longman.

Bodnar, S., Cucchiarini, C., Strik, H., & van Hout, R. (2016). Evaluating the motivational impact of CALL systems: current practices and future directions. *Computer Assisted Language Learning*, *29*(1), 186–212. https://doi.org/10.1080/09588221.2014.927365

Burston, J. (2003). Proving IT works. *CALICO Journal*, *20*(2), 219–226. https://doi.org/10.1558/cj.v20i2.219-226

Carey, D., & McGettigan, C. (2017). Magnetic resonance imaging of the brain and vocal tract: Applications to the study of speech production and language

learning. *Neuropsychologia*, *98*, 201–211. https://doi.org/10.1016/j.neuropsycho
logia.2016.06.003

Carhill-Poza, A., & Chen, J. (2020). Adolescent English learners' language development in technology-enhanced classrooms. *Language Learning & Technology*,
24(3), 52–69. http://hdl.handle.net/10125/44738

Cheung, A. (2021). Language teaching during a pandemic: A case study of Zoom
use by a secondary ESL teacher in Hong Kong. *RELC Journal*, *54*(1), 55–70.
https://doi.org/10.1177/0033688220981784

Colpaert, J. (2009). Elicitation of learners' personal goals as design concepts.
Innovation in Language Teaching and Learning, *4*(3), 259–274. https://doi
.org/10.1080/17501229.2010.513447.

Colpaert, J. (2012). The "Publish and perish" syndrome. *Computer Assisted Language
Learning*, *25*(5), 383–391. https://doi.org/10.1080/09588221.2012.735101

Davis, F. D. (1989). Perceived usefulness, perceived ease of use, and user acceptance of information technology. *MIS Quarterly*, *13*(3), 319–339. http://dx.doi
.org/10.2307/249008

Ding, A. C. E., Ottenbreit-Leftwich, A., Lu, Y. H., & Glazewski, K. (2019). EFL
teachers' pedagogical beliefs and practices with regard to using technology.
Journal of Digital Learning in Teacher Education, *35*(1), 20–39. https://doi
.org/10.1080/21532974.2018.1537816

Dizon, G. (2016). A comparative study of Facebook vs. paper-and-pencil writing to
improve L2 writing skills. *Computer Assisted Language Learning*, *29*(8),
1249–1258. https://doi.org/10.1080/09588221.2016.1266369

Dörnyei, Z. (2007). *Research methods in applied linguistics*. Oxford University Press.

Dörnyei, Z., & Ushioda, E. (2013). *Teaching and researching: Motivation* (2nd ed.).
Routledge.

Ellis, R. (2008). *The study of second language acquisition* (2nd ed.). Oxford
University Press.

Far, F. F., & Taghizadeh, M. (2022). Comparing the effects of digital and non-
digital gamification on EFL learners' collocation knowledge, perceptions, and
sense of flow. *Computer Assisted Language Learning*, 1–33. https://doi.org/10
.1080/09588221.2022.2146724

Felix, U. (2005). Analysing recent CALL effectiveness research: Towards a
common agenda. *Computer Assisted Language Learning*, *18*(1–2), 1–32.
https://doi.org/10.1080/09588220500132274

Felix, U. (2008). The unreasonable effectiveness of CALL: What have we learned
in two decades of research? *ReCALL*, *20*(2), 141–161.

Fischer, R. (2007). How do we know what students are actually doing? Monitoring
students' behavior in CALL. *Computer Assisted Language Learning*, *20*(5),
409–442. https://doi.org/10.1080/09588220701746013

Gillespie, J. (2020). CALL research: Where are we now? *ReCALL*, *32*(2), 127–144.
https://doi.org/10.1017/S0958344020000051

Godfroid, A., Winke, P., & Conklin, K. (2020). Exploring the depths of second
language processing with eye tracking: An introduction. *Second Language
Research*, *36*(3), 243–255. https://doi.org/10.1177/0267658320922578

Hadley, G. (2017). *Grounded theory in applied linguistics research: A practical guide.* Routledge. https://doi.org/10.4324/9781315758671

Haghighi, H., Jafarigohar, M., Khoshsima, H., & Vahdany, F. (2019). Impact of flipped classroom on EFL learners' appropriate use of refusal: Achievement, participation, perception. *Computer Assisted Language Learning, 32*(3), 261–293. https://doi.org/10.1080/09588221.2018.1504083

Heidari, J., Khodabandeh, F., & Soleimani, H. (2018). A comparative analysis of face to face instruction vs. Telegram mobile instruction in terms of narrative writing. *The JALT CALL Journal, 14*(2), 143–156. https://doi.org/10.29140/jaltcall.v14n2.228

Hubbard, P. (2005). A review of subject characteristics in CALL research. *Computer Assisted Language Learning, 18*(5), 351–368. https://doi.org/10.1080/09588220500442632

Hubbard, P., & Levy, M. (2016). Theory in computer-assisted language learning research and practice. In F. Farr & L. Murray (Eds.), *The Routledge Handbook of Language Learning and Technology* (pp. 24–38). Routledge.

Jeon, J. (2022). Exploring AI chatbot affordances in the EFL classroom: Young learners' experiences and perspectives. *Computer Assisted Language Learning, 37* (1–2), 1–26. https://doi.org/10.1080/09588221.2021.2021241

Jin, T., Su, Y., & Lei, J. (2020). Exploring the blended learning design for argumentative writing. *Language Learning & Technology, 24*(2), 23–34. http://hdl.handle.net/10125/44720

Lee, Y. J. (2019). Integrating multimodal technologies with VARK strategies for learning and teaching EFL presentation: An investigation into learners' achievements and perceptions of the learning process. *Australian Journal of Applied Linguistics, 2*(1), 17–31. https://doi.org/10.29140/ajal.v2n1.118

Levy, M. (2000). Scope, goals and methods in CALL research: Questions of coherence and autonomy. *ReCALL, 12*(2), 170–195. https://doi.org/10.1017/S0958344000000525

Loewen, S., Crowther, D., Isbell, D., Kim, K., Maloney, J., Miller, Z., & Rawal, H. (2019). Mobile-assisted language learning: A Duolingo case study. *ReCALL, 31* (3), 293–311. https://doi.org/10.1017/S0958344019000065

Merriam, S. B., & Tisdell, E. J. (2015). *Qualitative research: A guide to design and implementation.* John Wiley & Sons.

Nugroho, A., & Mutiaraningrum, I. (2020). EFL teachers' beliefs and practices about digital learning of English. *EduLite: Journal of English Education, Literature and Culture, 5*(2), 304–321. https://doi.org/10.30659/e.5.2.304-321

Nunan, D. (1992). *Research methods in language learning.* Cambridge University Press.

Osorio-Saez, E. M., Eryilmaz, N., & Sandoval-Hernandez, A. (2021). Parents' acceptance of educational technology: Lessons from around the world. *Frontiers in Psychology, 12*, 719430. https://doi.org/10.3389/fpsyg.2021.719430

Quang, N., Linh, P. N., & Hiền, N. T. T. (2022). Tasks, self-efficacy, and L2 motivational self system in an online emergency EFL speaking class: A mixed-methods study. *The JALT CALL Journal, 18*(1), 1–33. https://doi.org/10.29140/jaltcall.v18n1.518

Schwarz, N., & Oyserman, D. (2001). Asking questions about behavior: Cognition, communication, and questionnaire construction. *The American Journal of Evaluation, 22*(2), 127–160. https://doi.org/10.1177/10982140010220020

Stockwell, G. (2008). Investigating learner preparedness for and usage patterns of mobile learning. *ReCALL, 20*(3), 253–270. https://doi.org/10.1017/S0958344008000232

Stockwell, G. (2012). Diversity in research and practice. In G. Stockwell (Ed.), *Computer-assisted language learning: Diversity in research and practice* (pp. 147–163). Cambridge University Press. https://doi.org/10.1017/CBO9781139060981.009

Stockwell, G. (2022). Historical foundations of technology in SLA. In N. Ziegler & M. González-Lloret (Eds.), *The Routledge handbook of second language acquisition and technology* (pp. 9–20). Routledge.

Stockwell, G., & Reinders, H. (2019). Technology, motivation and autonomy, and teacher psychology in language learning: Exploring the myths and possibilities. *Annual Review of Applied Linguistics, 39*, 40–51. https://doi.org/10.1017/S0267190519000084

Tanaka-Ellis, N., & Sekiguchi, S. (2019). Making global knowledge accessible to EFL speakers of an undergraduate leadership program through a flipped and ubiquitous learning environment. *Technology in Language Teaching & Learning, 1*(1), 3–20. https://doi.org/10.29140/tltl.v1n1.141

Thomas, S. (2020). Students' evaluation of a classroom bring-your-own-device (BYOD) policy. *The JALT CALL Journal, 16*(1), 29–49. https://doi.org/10.29140/jaltcall.v16n1.208

Tsai, Y.-R. (2014). Applying the Technology Acceptance Model (TAM) to explore the effects of a course management system (CMS)-Assisted EFL writing instruction. *CALICO Journal, 32*(1), 153–171. https://doi.org/10.1558/calico.v32i1.25961.

Wang, J., An, N., & Wright, C. (2018). Enhancing beginner learners' oral proficiency in a flipped Chinese foreign language classroom. *Computer Assisted Language Learning, 31*(5–6), 490–521. https://doi.org/10.1080/09588221.2017.1417872

Wang, Y. (2021). In-service teachers' perceptions of technology integration and practices in a Japanese university context. *The JALT CALL Journal, 17*(1), 45–71. https://doi.org/10.29140/jaltcall.v17n1.377

Warschauer, M., & Healey, D. (1998). Computers and language learning: An overview. *Language Teaching, 31*, 57–71. https://doi.org/10.1017/S0261444800012970

Yang, S. (2018). Language learners' perceptions of having two interactional contexts in eTandem. *Language Learning & Technology, 22*(1), 42–51. https://dx.doi.org/10125/44577

Zhu, Y., Shum, S.-K. M., Tse, S.-K. B., & Liu, J. J. (2016). Word-processor or pencil-and-paper? A comparison of students' writing in Chinese as a foreign language. *Computer Assisted Language Learning, 29*(3), 596–617. https://doi.org/10.1080/09588221.2014.1000932

Further Reading

Chun, D. (2017). Research methods for investigating technology for language and culture learning. In C. A. Chapelle, & S. Sauro (Eds.), *The handbook of technology in second language teaching and learning* (pp. 393–408). John Wiley & Son. https://doi.org/10.1002/9781118914069.ch26
This chapter provides an overview of qualitative, quantitative, and mixed-methods approaches used in CALL research, investigating various aspects such as grammar, vocabulary, reading/writing, listening/speaking, pragmatics, intercultural competence, and overall communication skills. The chapter also discusses potential future research directions and methodologies for CALL.

Egbert, J. L., & Petrie, G. M. (Eds.) (2005). *CALL research perspectives*. Routledge.
This co-edited book lays the foundation for CALL research. It emphasizes diverse approaches and the involvement of researchers, teachers, and students in exploring computer-enhanced language learning. Written by well-known researchers in the field, the book offers an accessible view, additional resources, and suggestions for CALL research. Despite its publication date, its relevance endures, as it addresses current research issues, presents theories, and considers the factors that influence the outcomes. It complements other CALL and research texts, benefiting teachers and researchers situated in various contexts.

Stockwell, G. (2022). *Mobile assisted language learning: Concepts, contexts, and challenges*. Cambridge University Press. https://doi.org/10.1017/9781108652087
This book provides a comprehensive exploration of MALL; the use of terms CALL and MALL is discussed in chapter 2. That chapter also explores the evaluation of research conducted in the fields of CALL and MALL. It emphasizes the complex nature of research, theory, and practice, highlighting what is involved in assessing the effectiveness and impact of these learning approaches. By addressing the challenges and complexities of conducting research in CALL and MALL, this book, and especially its second chapter, sheds insight into the evolving landscape of technology-assisted language learning.

Part II

Environments

5

Blended Learning

Paul Gruba

Introduction

Simply stated, all learning is blended learning: that is, because learning occurs through a variety of interactions, modalities, and contexts, there is no "pure" form of instruction, no single source for material, no unique approach, and no specific technology that is best used to educate (Jewitt, 2006). For centuries, technology has been integrated into educational environments; indeed, educators have long argued that students need to move from one technology to another, or from one configuration to another, or indeed from one time to another, such that they are exposed to a range of elements and practices that may contribute to their learning (Grunberg & Summers, 1992). Language educators have come to use the term "blended language learning" or "hybrid learning" to focus on the integration of technology in face-to-face language-teaching environments. Work in this area can be situated in the wider field of computer-assisted language learning (CALL), which itself is defined as "the full integration of technology into language learning" that is made possible through "a dynamic complex in which technology, theory, and pedagogy are inseparably interwoven" (Garrett, 2009, pp. 719–720). Effective blended language learning, then, can be understood as a form of justified technology integration made possible through principled theory and sound pedagogy. To introduce the area, this chapter provides a historical review, sets out primary themes, and discusses contemporary practice and research. The chapter concludes with further research and suggestions for further reading.

Background

Specifically, the term "blended learning" first appeared in corporate training programs that fostered hybrid approaches to coaching, mentoring, online interaction, and face-to-face seminars (Thorne, 2003). Not satisfied with the choice of undertaking either remote or face-to-face teaching, mainstream educators crafted blended pedagogies designed to forge a middle ground between in-class and distance learning (Welker & Berardino, 2005). Despite early concepts being "ill-defined and inconsistently used" (Oliver & Trigwell, 2005, p. 24), theorists came to understand that technology integration itself is not of primary importance (Garrison & Vaughan, 2008); it is rather the potentialities of technologies and the open set of possibilities for making meaning within a learning environment that are the key attributes (Jewitt, 2006). Often associated with hybrid approaches, blended learning has now matured and is employed across a range of educational settings (see, e.g., Jones & Sharma, 2021; Stein & Graham, 2020).

Language educators also began to create literature focused on blended approaches. Early works include those by Sharma and Barret (2007), Nicholson, Murphy, and Southgate (2012), Gruba and Hinkelman (2012), Carrasco and Johnson (2015), and McCarthy (2016). Now a dominant form of instructional design in language programs, blended pedagogies, Grgurovic (2017, p. 164) predicts, will become "the preferred approach to language teaching and learning in the future" as a result of the ever increasing use of mobile devices, customized learner profiles, and the widespread adoption of hybrid approaches to language learning.

Primary Themes

In line with CALL (Garrett, 2009), primary themes in blended language learning revolve around technology, theory, and pedagogy.

Technology is now so pervasive in advanced economies that it is "ubiquitous," "always on," "24/7" (Jones & Sharma, 2021). To illustrate, nearly 30 percent of adults in the United States reported they are online "almost constantly" and less than 7 percent report being offline (Statista, 2021, pp. 25–26). Not all education communities have access to such technologies, however, and the social, educational, and political consequences of poor access raise issues of "digital equity" (Ragnedda, 2020), which has long been an area of concern in CALL (Egbert, 2010; Warschauer, 2003). Crucially, as Hocky (2014) writes, blended approaches in low-resource environments must recognize the needs surrounding the "cultural appropriacy of materials and approaches, using appropriate technologies, keeping costs low, and ensuring long-term sustainability" (p. 80).

But what, specifically, is "technology"? Etymologically, the word has roots in practical skills (*technai*) such as building wooden houses by weaving sticks together; there could even be a kinship between the Greek etymon *techne* and the Latin noun *textura*, which has generated modern words in the family of "textile" (so, interestingly, it may not be pure chance that English words like "technical" and "textile" sound similar) (see Agar 2020). From something like a sense of working with wood, the word may have come to designate specialized

Table 5.1 *Questions regarding perspectives on technology*

Dimension	Questions	Considerations
Orientation	Is technology best understood as a physical device or as a set of practices?	Instrumentalist, cultural, sociocultural
Cultural appropriacy	To what extent does the technology accord with prevailing cultural norms?	Privacy, morality, power, security, attitude
Appropriate technology	How well does the technology fit into existing patterns of use and familiarity?	Normalization, uptake, stakeholders, sociocultural setting
Cost and resourcing	What are the cost and resource implications of the technology?	Initial expenses, BYOD, budget, on-costs
Sustainability	How can the use of technology be provided over the long term?	Maintenance, professional development, support, long-term planning
Connectivity	Are the devices connected to global information and data networks?	Network, stand-alone, internet, workstation

expertise or knowledge of how to create things that had not previously existed; and it became associated with the artificial. Beginning with ancient Greek philosophers, the field of *techne* – what we call today "technology" – covered several areas that eventually generated "conceptual confusion" by "the second half of the twentieth century." This meant that, from then on, "the term could be used in either broad or narrow senses, sometimes embracing cultural or social components, sometimes reduced to mere tools or to means-to-ends rationality" (Agar, 2020, p. 380). At present, historians and researchers of technology see how the term moves from an instrumental use, which places a narrow and uncreative emphasis on physical devices, to one that incorporates a cultural perspective. Technology thus becomes a set of practices that we use to transform the material world. Echoing such views, CALL specialist Kern (2014) proposes the notion of technology as *pharmakon* (drug): drawing on metaphors that reference medicine, Kern argues that technology has both beneficial and poisonous properties, which shift depending on the extent, depth, and intent of their usage in language programs.

In a study of blended learning, Gruba and Hinkelman (2012) align technology with a cultural approach that emphasizes the roles of teachers and students in hybrid environments. In their descriptions of blended lesson designs, for example, they make little distinction between face-to-face classroom techniques and techniques used with online tools. A wide view of this kind is needed, they argue, if we are to counter the instrumentalist perspectives that have dominated CALL. Reflecting on some of the areas and considerations that intersect with technology may help language educators situate their own perspectives, as is shown in Table 5.1.

Given that blended learning is "as old as CALL itself" (Neumeier, 2005, p. 163), theory development in the area aligns with theory development in the broader field; the widely cited work of Chapelle (2001), for example, established links between second language acquisition (SLA) and CALL. Work by Levy and Stockwell (2006) and González-Lloret and Ortega (2014) has further

Table 5.2 *Questions for the role of theory in blended language learning*

Dimension	Questions	Considerations
Philosophy	What is language and how is it learned?	Structural, poststructural, social semiotic
Constructive alignment to SLA principles	How does the blended approach recognize and integrate principles of SLA?	Behaviorist, cognitive interactionist, sociocultural, transdisciplinary
Sociocultural perspective	To what extent do sociocultural aspects of the environment influence motivation, learning, and achievement?	Class, gender, race, culture
Cognitive–interactionist perspectives	To what extent do cognitive variables influence language learning?	Modality, strategy, motivation
Applied theory	How can theoretical concepts become visible in teaching and learning?	Transferability, recognition, uptake

deepened the theoretical underpinnings of CALL. Situating themselves within this larger field, the early proponents of blended language learning sought to place greater emphasis on "ecological" or "semiotic" views (van Lier, 2004) instead of continuing to reinforce prevailing "cognitive interactionist" views of language learning (Chapelle, 2001).

Moving toward semiotic views, SLA experts formed the Douglas Fir Group (2016), which aims to produce a three-tiered transdisciplinary framework for contemporary language learning. At the macro level, they argue, ideology and beliefs inform language policy and teaching principles; at the meso level, language programs, curriculum designs, and professional development influence choices; at the micro level, activities that enable classroom practices and the integration of technology into learning take place. For the blended learning theorist, the three-level framing allows for a greater recognition of elements such as policy and curriculum, which influence the integration of technology beyond a focus on one individual learner with a single computer (Hinkelman, 2018). Table 5.2 displays questions and considerations that may help interweave theory with the complex dynamic of blended learning.

Pedagogical choices come to the fore in blended designs. Indeed, one consequence of blended approaches is that "new technologies make visible aspects of the pedagogic practice that were previously taken for granted" (Beetham & Sharpe, 2007, p. 7). Garrett (2009) asks language educators to consider a central question when they design blended programs (and here I would replace "software" with "technology-based learning activities"):

> What kind of software, integrated how, into what kind of syllabus, at what level of language learning, for what kind of language learners, is likely to be effective for what specific learning purposes?
>
> *(p. 721)*

Because blending approaches raise the need to justify designs, work such as that by Valdés, Kibler, and Walqui (2014) can help to make visible a theory of

Table 5.3 *Pedagogical orientations to technology integration*

Theoretical orientation	Characteristic definition and associated teaching approaches	Technology usage
Early formalist	Language competence is based on target forms and native speech best learned through memorization	Technology presents grammatically correct sentences and native speech patterns that can be imitated
Cognitive interactionist	Language competence resides in the ability of an individual to make sense of discrete words, utterances, and forms	The patterned use of technology reinforces stages of acquisition that facilitate moves from conscious to automatic thinking
Functional	As exemplified in English for specific purposes, a subfield of TESOL, effective language use requires a strong awareness of purpose, context, and audience	Technology usage situates the context needed to understand both meaning and forms
Sociocultural	Language learning integrates conceptual, academic, and linguistic elements in tandem, through dialogic interaction	Interactions afforded by technology underpin a scaffolded set of activities that move learners from peripheral to central participation

Based on Valdés et al. (2014, pp. 37–45)

Table 5.4 *Considerations in blended language learning*

Considerations	Definitions
Purpose	Multiple reasons, often across levels, motivate the integration of technology in ways that resonate with teachers and students.
Appropriateness	Integration is effective when current resources, abilities, and proficiencies within the language program align with national policies, institutional curricula, and local cultures.
Multimodality	Technology integration recognizes and fosters a wide range of diverse activities, teaching approaches, and assessment styles.
Sustainability	Blends rest on long-term use of resources, talents, and outcomes.

Based on Gruba and Hinkelman (2012)

learning that aims to situate technology in language programs. Table 5.3 summarizes four orientations and the technology usage associated with them.

Gruba and Hinkelman (2012) suggest that, once they are grounded within a pedagogical orientation, blended designs take into account the considerations of purpose, appropriateness, multimodality, and sustainability. Such considerations provide a basis to further pinpoint how the effort to integrate technology may be justified to language program stakeholders. Table 5.4 sets out the core ideas.

Inspired by works such as those by Laurillard (2012), Hinkelman (2018) established a range of options that can inform the pedagogical choices within a single blended classroom:

- Actions: narrative, interaction, adaptive, communicative, productive technologies
- Groupings: pair, small group, whole group, and individual spaces/furniture

Table 5.5 *Questions regarding the role of pedagogy in blended language learning*

Dimension	Questions	Considerations
Alignment to prevailing curricula	How does the blended approach relate to the overall curriculum, teaching approach, and expectations?	National standards, institutional demands, teacher unions, guidelines
Degree of integration	To what extent should the curriculum integrate technology?	Hybrid, online, mixed, flipped, porous
Variety and opportunity	Does the use of technology afford a wider range of learning opportunities?	Learning styles, after hours, flexibility, modality
Link to assessments	How do blended approaches translate into assessment methods, instruments, and regimes?	Achievement, evidence, grades, degree, proficiency, tests, test takers, transferability
Professional development	What opportunities are provided to help instructors undertake blended methods and approaches?	Materials, teacher training, induction, time relief, promotion criteria

- Timings: synchronous and asynchronous learning, intensive and periodic pacing
- Texts: video/audio/image, facial/voice/gesture, multiscreen interfaces
- Tools: digital/analog, machine/network, fixed/wired and mobile/wireless devices

Following Mizza and Rubio (2020), language educators can enact a four-step design, build, teach, and revise structure to devise blended language-learning courses. Table 5.5 presents questions for discussion pertaining to pedagogy.

Current Research and Practice

Blending technology into language programs demands much from language administrators, language educators, and their students (Palikat & Gruba, 2022). Research designed to justify technology integration can be expressed in this key question: "How can those who are investing significant resources into learning and teaching be shown that innovation might be for the best?" (Chapelle, 2007, p. 30). Contemporary responses to such concerns can make use of interpretive arguments to investigate blended language course designs; this would include an assessment of the tasks that were employed in differing combinations of face-to-face and blended settings (Gleason, 2013).

Argument-based approaches can be constructed in four stages: (1) planning an argument; (2) gathering the evidence; (3) presenting the argument; and (4) appraising the argument. The planning stage of an argument, for example, seeks to identify its construction and starts with explicit claims that are made by a language program. These claims help map out the direction of the investigation and outline the kinds of evidence required to back each claim (Chapelle, 2014).

Inspired by this kind of work, Gruba and colleagues (2016) adapted arguments to underpin macro, meso, and micro influences with blended language

Table 5.6 *Example argument structure*

Inferences	Warrants and assumptions (numbered after each warrant)
E. Ramification	An interrogation of sustainability as a mobile device advances theory development and informs blended language learning approaches.
↑	1. The findings are transferable to similar programs.
	2. The findings are disseminated in an appropriate forum.
	3. The outcomes of the evaluation interest the broader CALL community.
D. Utilization	Stakeholders at each level make use of the evaluation findings to improve the blended language learning program.
↑	1. The findings resonate and are powerful enough to stimulate action.
	2. The stakeholders take ownership of the findings.
	3. The stakeholders can understand the findings.
C. Explanation	The findings are consistent with overall program designs for blended language learning.
↑	1. The role of technology in the blended program is understood by each stakeholder.
	2. Findings specific to the role of technology inform other aspects of program evaluation and development.
	3. A focus on technology, understood as just one part of a coherent approach to blended language learning, yields important insights for the program.
B. Evaluation	The analysis clarifies the role of technology in the language program.
↑	1. The analysis of the data is accurate, robust, and trustworthy.
	2. Data collection for the evaluation project is conducted in ways that are appropriate, transferable, and ethical within the field.
	3. Mixed-method designs for research can be used to put together data for the evaluation of technology integration with considerations on the quality of learning, the sustainability of practice, and the effectiveness of teaching.
	4. Given the investment and effort required, the role of a technology that is concerned with the quality, sustainability, and effectiveness of the language program can be a justified focus of program evaluation.
A. Domain definition	Technology is blended into the language program.
↑	1. Program administrators, teachers, and students foster a viable environment for blended language learning.
	2. The institute and the program demonstrate a strong commitment to blended language-learning approaches through clear policy, funded resources, and ongoing professional development opportunities.
	3. Blended learning, like CALL itself, is defined as the full integration of technology, theory, and pedagogy into language programs.
	4. Contemporary approaches to language learning recognize the role of technology in conceptual frameworks and pedagogical designs.

Adapted from Gruba et al. (2016)

programs in Australia, Chile, the United States, and Vietnam. Their macro-level work sought to account for global, national, or institutional policies that impact technology integration. At the meso level, they focused on material designs, assessments, and uses of technology. Classroom evaluations of practice and student engagement were considered at the micro level of pedagogical design. Table 5.6 sets out an example argument structure.

The evaluation of blended language-learning programs takes commitment, training, and leadership. Importantly, efforts to engage a range of stakeholders, including students, are crucial to the success of an evaluation (Palikat & Gruba, 2022). Table 5.7 sets out questions for discussion.

Table 5.7 *Questions regarding the role of program evaluation in blended language learning*

Dimension	Questions	Considerations
Focus	What are the key concerns about blended language learning that an evaluation project can assess?	Situate the evaluation within an appropriate level of concern (macro, meso, micro)
Ethics	What ethical considerations need to be addressed throughout the evaluation project?	Clarify sensitive areas of data collection, analysis, and use
Warrant	How can the costs and efforts to evaluate a blended language program be justified?	Identify justifications to undertake blended approaches
Stakeholders	Who is interested in the evaluation and the way in which it may shift roles, responsibilities, and resourcing?	Anticipate the needs and the diversity of the voices that influence the uptake of blended approaches
Uptake	How do the evaluation process and its results foster improvements to blended language learning?	Estimate the likelihood that stakeholders will enact recommendations

For instructors undertaking new pedagogical designs, the use of principles may help to promote home languages and cultural knowledge, celebrate diversity, support multilingual education, and guide global citizenship (TESOL, 2021). The popularity of principles-based handbooks, as evidenced through the publication of multiple editions, demonstrates their utility as a point of departure in program development (e.g. Brown & Lee, 2015).

Recommendation for Research and Practice

Should a study of blended language learning focus on technology, theory, or pedagogy? Or should further research account for the complex interactions between a range of elements? Historically, as Kern and Warschauer (2000) have noted, CALL researchers were concerned with the use of tools and inventories of specific language features; to go beyond such orientations, however, they suggest a move toward designs that embrace "contextual enquiry," in an attempt to account for environmental complexities. Hinkelman (2018) later adopted their principle as a basis for investigating blended language learning and revised the original questions, so that instead of a singular concern (e.g. "What technology is being used?") he addressed concerns that reflected the complicated nature of blended approaches (e.g. "What are the macro, meso, and micro characteristics of the technologies being used?").

In line with the wider trend in applied linguistics and CALL, research in blended learning can be framed through interpretive arguments. In a keynote address, Chapelle (2014) proposed using five types of argument to underpin research in the area: comparison, authenticity, data-driven language learning, theory-based, and pedagogy.

Typical comparison arguments employ designs that seek to determine the differences between an experimental and a control group, for example, or the results of a pre-test and a post-test for a single experimental group (Hudson &

Llosa, 2015). Discussions in this design revolve around the effectiveness of the technological intervention in the environment. Importantly, as Chapelle (2014) suggests, any further use of comparative designs is moot: technology is so deeply infused into student lives that "control groups" are impossible to create, and the results of such investigations yield little by way of contribution to the field.

Authenticity arguments seek to link educational outcomes to real-world demands. Here the need to teach students to make effective use of technology necessitates its integration into language programs (Lotherington & Jenson, 2011). For Chapelle (2014), however, claims of "authenticity" in blended programs are debatable, since a deep analysis would be required of the social, not technical, justification and uses of technology in context.

A third argument for technology integration rests within the teaching of a language for specific purposes, using data-driven or corpora-based materials (Chapelle, 2014). To succeed in higher education, for example, learners may need to master English for academic purposes (EAP). In these settings, curricula and materials are grounded in corpora to demonstrate how the language is deployed for specific reasons within disciplines. The role of technology can be interrogated in research concerning the effectiveness of data-driven approaches (Boulton & Vyatkina, 2021).

A fourth argument relies on SLA theories to support claims about technology-mediated language learning. In this type of argument, according to Chapelle (2014), theories provide a foundation for explicating and interpreting students' strategies, processes, and outcomes when they complete technology-mediated language-learning tasks and activities. However, one of the main challenges for theory-based arguments is making direct links between theoretical perspectives and pedagogical practices, including those that promote computer-assisted language learning (Chapelle, 2007).

Finally, pedagogy-based arguments (Chapelle, 2014) support claims that justify technology integration. Using technology as a platform to teach intercultural competence, for example, one can design tasks for students to learn to respect differences in thinking (Kurek & Muller-Hartmann, 2017). But pedagogical justifications of technology use would require specific evidence, which ties the observed data to the actual development of intercultural competence or other aspects of learning.

Future Directions

Blended language learning is contemporary CALL; that is, as foreseen by Garrett (2009), the approach is the result of technology, theory, and pedagogy now being fully interwoven.

Technology, of course, continues to evolve and weave its way into our lives. As a term, "blended language learning" will soon disappear, as it no longer provides any useful distinction or unique pedagogy: as long understood, all

Table 5.8 *Questions for consideration in blended language-learning research*

Dimension	Questions	Considerations
Philosophy	What are the theoretical orientations of the researchers to language, technology, and pedagogy?	Behaviorist, cognitive, interactionist, sociocultural, systemic functional, semiotic
Purpose	How does the research align with current debates and concerns inherent in blended language learning?	Digital divide, effectiveness, professional development, new literacies, social justice, inclusion, transdisciplinary
Approach	What research design should inform the investigation?	Quantitative, mixed, qualitative, action, contextual
Methods	What methods are best suited to investigate blended language learning?	Observation, survey, participation, interview, learner analytics, corpus linguistics
Dissemination	In what form should results, contributions and implications be disseminated, and how does the research foster impacts and benefits?	Presentation, report, article, blog, book, key stakeholders, open science, open access publication

learning is blended; much technology is ubiquitous; most environments are now hybrid. Research on technology in language education is now turning to matters related to the use of data-driven learning (Boulton & Vyatkina, 2021), the potentiality of big data (Reinders & Lan, 2021), the role of chatbots and artificial intelligence (Lin & Mubarok, 2021), and persistent issues of social equity (Godwin-Jones, 2020; Ragnedda, 2020).

Theoretically, future directions may well depend on the extent to which language educators themselves embrace the view of prominent SLA theorists and see that "language learning is semiotic learning" (Douglas Fir Group, 2016). Though well understood and long used as a basis for language learning (Kress, 2015), semiotic views challenge the dominant place of structural linguistics in language teaching and assessment designs (Gruba, 2020). Resistance, unfortunately, further distances traditional language educators from concepts of multimodality (Jewitt, Bezemer, & O'Halloran, 2016), social semiotics (Knight, Dooly, & Barbera, 2020; Olteanu, 2019), and mainstream trends in computer-mediated communication (Sykes, 2019).

But, if blended theorists do embrace semiotic perspectives, research and research training must incorporate much more work grounded in systemic functional theory (Halliday & Matthiessen, 2014) and emphasize the use of systemic functional linguistics (Mohan & Luo, 2007). In the future, blended language-learning research may well depend on greater integration and alignment with SLA, social semiotics, and multimodality. Questions in Table 5.8 map topics for further research.

If, in our blended environments, the notion of a "classroom" remains a useful metaphor for imagining spaces of pedagogical interaction, questions raised by Korkealehto, Lakkala, and Toom (2021) concerning student engagement may illuminate new pathways. Beyond the micro level, meso- and macro-level factors may need greater attention to clarify barriers to technology integration. At the meso level, for example, program and curriculum leaders may hesitate to commit – or perhaps lack the leadership to do so (Gruba &

Nguyen, 2019; Palikat & Gruba, 2022). Macro-level factors, such as the lack of clear national standards and an inequitable allocation of resources may well also constrain technology integration (Oxford & Jung, 2006).

Given the ongoing shifts in blended learning conceptualizations and practices, it may be best to follow Godwin-Jones (2020); in this framing, the term blended learning gives way to that of a porous classroom, to evoke a sense of open learning environments that blur distinctions of place, configuration, and planned variety. In this evolving vision, various educational resources will be used to promote "a vision for inclusive, engaged, and transformative language learning" (p. 10). More so than blended language learning, Godwin-Jones hopes, porosity holds promise for an improved social cohesion and for the greater acceptance of those who have been largely excluded from the effective uses of integrated technology in their language education.

References

Agar, J. (2020). What is technology? *Annals of Science*, *77*(3), 377–382, https://doi .org/10.1080/00033790.2019.1672788

Anderson, H. (2018). *Blended basic language courses: Design, pedagogy, and implementation*. Routledge.

Beetham, H., & Sharpe, R. (2007). An introduction to rethinking pedagogy for a digital age. In H. Beetham, & R. Sharpe (Eds.), *Rethinking pedagogy for a digital age* (pp. 1–10). Routledge.

Boulton, A., & Vyatkina, N. (2021). Thirty years of data-driven learning: Taking stock and charting new directions over time. *Language Learning & Technology*, *25*(3), 66–89. http://hdl.handle.net/10125/73450

Brown, H. D., & Lee, H. (2015). *Teaching by principles: An interactive approach to language pedagogy* (4th ed.). Pearson Education.

Carrasco, B., & Johnson, S. M. (2015). *Hybrid language teaching in practice: Perceptions, reactions, and results*. Springer.

Chapelle, C. A. (2001). *Computer applications in second language acquisition*. Cambridge University Press.

Chapelle, C. A. (2007). Challenges in the evaluation of innovation: Observations from technology research. *Innovation in Language Learning and Teaching*, *1*(1), 30–45.

Chapelle, C. A. (2014). *Arguments for technology and language learning: Keynote presentation at the EUROCALL 2014 Conference*. University of Groningen.

Douglas Fir Group (2016). A transdisciplinary framework for SLA in a multilingual world. *The Modern Language Journal*, *100*(S1), 19–47. https://doi.org/10.1111/modl.12301

Egbert, J. (Ed). (2010). *CALL in limited technology contexts*. CALICO.

Garrett, N. (2009). Computer-assisted language learning trends and issues revisited: Integrating innovation. *The Modern Language Journal*, *93*, 719–740. https://doi.org/10.1111/j.1540-4781.2009.00969.x

Garrison, R., & Vaughan, H. (2008). *Blended learning in higher education: Framework, principles and guidelines*. Jossey-Bass.

Gleason, J. (2013). An interpretive argument for blended course design. *Foreign Language Annals, 46,* 588–609.

Godwin-Jones, R. (2020). Building the porous classroom: An expanded model for blended language learning. *Language Learning & Technology, 24*(3), 1–18. http://hdl.handle.net/10125/44731

González-Lloret, M., & Ortega, L. (2014). *Technology-mediated TBLT: Researching technology and tasks*. John Benjamins.

Grgurovic, M. (2017). Blended language learning: Research and practice. In C. Chapelle and S. Sauro (Eds.), *The handbook of technology and second language teaching and learning* (pp. 150–168). John Wiley & Sons.

Gruba, P. (2020). What does language testing have to offer multimodal listening? In G. Ockey and B. Green (Eds.), *Another generation of fundamental considerations in language assessment* (pp. 43–57). Springer.

Gruba, P., & Hinkelman, D. (2012). *Blending technologies in second language classrooms*. Palgrave Macmillan.

Gruba, P., & Nguyen, N. B. C. (2019). Evaluating technology integration in a Vietnamese university language program. *Computer Assisted Language Learning, 32*(5–6), 619–637. https://doi.org/10.1080/09588221.2018.1527365

Gruba, P., Cárdenas-Claros, M., Suvorov, R., & Rick, K. (2016). *Blended language program evaluation*. Palgrave Macmillan.

Grunberg, J., & Summers, M. (1992). Computer innovation in schools: A review of selected research literature. *Journal of Information Technology for Teacher Education, 1*(2), 255–276.

Halliday, M., & Matthiessen, C. (2014). *Halliday's introduction to functional grammar* (4th ed.). Routledge.

Hinkelman, D. (2018). *Blending technologies in second language classrooms* (2nd ed.). Palgrave Macmillan.

Hocky, N. (2014). Digital technologies in low-resource ELT contexts. *ELT Journal, 68*(1), 79–84.

Hudson, T., & Llosa, L. (2015). Design issues and inference in experimental L2 research. *Language Learning, 65*(S1), 76–96. https://doi.org/10.1111/lang .12113

Jewitt, C. (2006). *Technology, literacy, and learning: A multimodal approach*. Routledge.

Jewitt, C., Bezemer, J., & O'Halloran, K. (2016). *Introducing multimodality*. Routledge.

Jones, K. A., & Sharma, R. S. (2021). *Higher education 4.0: The digital transformation of classroom lectures to blended learning*. Springer.

Kern, R. (2014). Technology as *pharmakon*: The promise and perils of the internet for foreign language education. *The Modern Language Journal, 14,* 340–357. https://doi.org/10.1111/j.1540-4781.2014.12065.x

Kern, R., & Warschauer, M. (2000). *Network-based language teaching: Concepts and practice*. Cambridge University Press.

Knight, J., Dooly, M., & Barberà, E. (2020). Getting smart: Towards critical digital literacy pedagogies. *Social Semiotics, 33*(2), 326–349. https://doi.org/10.1080/10350330.2020.1836815

Korkealehto, K., Lakkala, M., & Toom, A. (2021). Enrolled or engaged? Student perceptions of engagement and oral interaction in a blended learning language course. *The JALT CALL Journal, 17*(1), 1–22.https://doi.org/10.29140/jaltcall.v17n1.268

Kress, G. (2015). Semiotic work: Applied linguistics and a social semiotic account of multimodality. *AILA Review, 28*(1), 49–71. https://doi.org/10.1075/aila.28.03kre

Kurek, M., & Muller-Hartmann, A. (2017). Task design for telecollaborative exchanges: In search of new criteria. *System, 64,* 7–20. https://doi.org/10.1016/j.system.2016.12.004

Laurillard, D. (2012). *Teaching as design science.* Routledge.

Levy, M., & Stockwell, G. (2006). *CALL dimensions: Options and issues in computer-assisted language learning.* Lawrence Erlbaum Associates.

Lin, C.-J., & Mubarok, H. (2021). Learning analytics for investigating the mind map-guided AI chatbot approach in an EFL flipped speaking classroom. *Educational Technology & Society, 24*(4), 16–35.

Lotherington, H., & Jenson, J. (2011). Teaching multimodal and digital literacy in second language settings: New literacies, new basics, new pedagogies. *Annual Review of Applied Linguistics, 31,* 226–248. https://10.1017/S0267190511000110

McCarthy, M. (Ed.). (2016). *The Cambridge guide to blended learning for language teaching.* Cambridge University Press.

Mizza, D., & Rubio, F. (2020). *Creating effective blended language learning courses: A research-based guide from planning to evaluation.* Cambridge University Press.

Mohan, B., & Luo, L. (2007). A systemic functional linguistics perspective on CALL. In J. Egbert & G. M. Petrie (Eds.), *CALL research perspectives* (pp. 87–96). Lawrence Erlbaum.

Neumeier, P. (2005). A closer look at blended learning: Parameters for designing a blended learning environment for language teaching and learning. *ReCALL, 17*(2), 163–178. https://doi.org/10.1017/S0958344005000224

Nicolson, M., Murphy, L., & Southgate, M. (2012). *Language teaching in blended contexts.* Dunedin Academic Press.

Oliver, M., & Trigwell, K. (2005). Can "blended learning" be redeemed? *E-Learning, 2*(1), 17–26. https://doi.org/10.2304/elea.2005.2.1.17

Olteanu, A. (2019). *Multiculturalism as multimodal communication: A semiotic perspective.* Springer.

Oxford, R. L., & Jung, S.-H. (2006). National guidelines for technology integration in TESOL programs: Factors affecting (non) implementation. In M. A. Kassen, K. Murphy-Judy, R. Z. Lavine, & M. Peters (Eds.), *Preparing and developing technology-proficient L2 teachers* (pp. 23–48). Computer Assisted Language Instruction Consortium.

Palikat, C. N., & Gruba, P. (2022). *Sustainability of blended language learning programs.* Routledge.

Ragnedda, M. (2020). *Enhancing digital equity: Connecting the digital underclass.* Palgrave Macmillan.

Reinders, H., & Lan, Y. J. (2021). Big data in language education and research. *Language Learning & Technology, 25*(1), 1–3. http://hdl.handle.net/10125/44746

Sharma, P., & Barret, B. (2007). *Blended learning: Using technology in and beyond the language classroom.* Macmillan.

Statista. (2021). *Internet usage in the United States.* www.statista.com/topics/2237/internet-usage-in-the-united-states

Stein, J., & Graham, C. R. (2020). *Essentials for blended learning: A standards-based guide* (2nd ed.). Routledge.

Sykes, J. (2019). Emergent digital discourses: What can we learn from hashtags and digital games to expand learners' second language repertoire? *Annual Review of Applied Linguistics, 39,* 128–145. https://doi.org/10.1017/S0267190519000138

TESOL. (2021). The 6 principles for exemplary teaching of English learners©. TESOL International Association. www.tesol.org/the-6-principles/about

Thorne, K. (2003). *Blended learning.* Kogan Page.

Valdés, G., Kibler, A., & Walqui, A. (2014). *Changes in the expertise of ESL professionals: Knowledge and action in an era of new standards.* TESOL International Association. https://eric.ed.gov/?id=ED560135

van Lier, L. (2004). *The ecology and semiotics of language learning: A sociocultural perspective.* Kluwer.

Warschauer, M. (2003). *Technology and social inclusion: Rethinking the digital divide.* MIT Press.

Welker, J., & Berardino, L. (2005). Blended learning: Understanding the middle ground between traditional classroom and fully online instruction. *Journal of Educational Technology Systems, 34*(1), 33–55. https://doi.org/10.2190/67FX-B7P8-PYUX-TDUP

Further Reading

Gleason, J. (2013). An interpretive argument for blended course design. *Foreign Language Annals, 46*(4), 588–609.
Grounded in arguments first created for language assessment purposes, Gleason turns a critical eye on the fundamentals needed to construct a solid frame of blended course design. Such arguments, made with colleagues, help ensure that efforts to foster blended approaches are situated in both theory and evidence.

Hinkelman, D. (2018). *Blending technologies in second language classrooms.* Palgrave Macmillan.
An early adopter of blended approaches, Hinkelman provides clear insights into technology integration through a solid conceptual framework, action research, fresh lesson plans, and a curriculum that stimulates student engagement.

Mizza, D., & Rubio, F. (2020). *Creating effective blended language learning courses: A research-based guide from planning to evaluation.* Cambridge University Press. The award-winning book of Mizza and Rubio provides a comprehensive introduction to blended learning for language instructors. Each chapter mixes references with sound advice and presents accessible pathways to successful technology integration.

Palikat, C. N., & Gruba, P. (2022). *Sustainability of blended language learning programs: Technology integration in English for Academic Purposes.* Routledge. This book provides a concise introduction to the long-term, or sustained, integration of technology in the form of a device, learning management system, or application. The ethnographic study points to challenges of instructor uptake and acceptability of technology integration. Notably, the book advocates an increased emphasis on program management in leading change, constructing professional development opportunities, and adopting a mindset of evaluative thinking.

6

Distance Learning

Fernando Rosell-Aguilar

Introduction

Until not so long ago, a common assumption was that learning languages was not achievable through distance learning, even though languages have been taught at a distance for many decades. It was assumed that oral practice and interaction required the synchronous physical presence of an interlocutor who could both model and correct output in the target language. The rise in online technologies since the beginning of the twenty-first century has changed this perception to a certain extent, although not completely.

This chapter will define distance language learning and teaching, provide a brief history of its evolution, present the challenges that distance environments create, and explore the teaching methodologies (materials design, assessment, opportunities for interaction) and the characteristics that make successful distance language learners and teachers. It will conclude with a discussion of the differences between language teaching that has been designed to take place at a distance and emergency remote teaching (ERT) adopted as a solution to restrictions in the recent COVID-19 pandemic, as well as the implications of the implementation of the latter.

Background/Historical Perspectives

Definition

In simple terms, distance language learning and teaching takes place when teachers and learners are not together in the same physical space and learning is mediated through the technology available. There are many forms of both formal and informal distance language learning, and the words "distance learning" are often used to refer to a number of different situations, mainly associated with attending a class remotely, through technology. Distance learning is often equated with online learning and, although online tools are used extensively in current distance learning practices, it is important to differentiate between distance learning through online environments and the online learning that many face-to-face institutions provide as part of a blended approach for otherwise traditional teaching.

The focus of this chapter is on language teaching provided by higher education distance learning institutions whose students choose, for the duration of their course, to learn mainly (and often completely) at a distance, through teaching materials, assessment, and interaction opportunities that have been specifically designed for this medium. Distance language-learning programs vary enormously in terms of materials, blend of self-access and tuition, and use of technology (among others) between different providers. Consequently this chapter will try to capture best practice from the research and experience of distance language-learning experts.

History

Distance language learning is a field where technological innovation is usually adopted early (White, 2017). It has evolved in parallel with both the dominant approaches to second language acquisition (SLA) and the advances in technology at different times. The earliest instances of distance language learning occurred in the early to mid-twentieth century, through correspondence courses (Sherry, 1995) in which tutor and student exchanged paper-based teaching materials and exercises for correction. This limited the language-learning experience to reading and writing skills, with an emphasis on grammar and translation, as was common practice at the time. The availability and increasingly widespread ownership of audio players that could use recorded material (first on vinyl, then on cassettes) afforded the opportunity to support listening skills, and the arrival of the recordable cassette made it possible to produce and record output that could be sent to the instructor. This coincided with a shift toward behaviorist language teaching, and students were expected to produce verbal and written output that either repeated what they had read or heard or required minimum manipulation of the language.

In the 1960s and 1970s broadcasters started programming distance learning education (Cambre, 1991), which consisted of masterclasses provided by a lecturer and usually broadcast late at night. This practice had the drawback of enabling only one-way communication, but it supplemented the materials that distance learning institutions provided for their students. The presence of learning materials on broadcast schedules brought an awareness of distance education to many who had never encountered it and helped popularize it.

The growth in availability and affordability of home computers in the 1990s led to the development of language materials on CD-Rom. These multimedia platforms allowed access to audiovisual materials and interactive exercises, which, despite a shift in SLA toward communicative approaches at the time, remained mostly behavioristic in nature (Gimeno-Sanz, 2016). Some CD-Roms allowed learners to make recordings and compare them to a model answer, affording some opportunities to check their output, but feedback on tasks was mostly limited to whether the answer was correct or incorrect. Distance learning institutions would create such materials to supplement rather than replace the written materials they would send to their students. As the internet started to become ubiquitous and the use of technology, both in general and specifically for teaching and learning, became normalized (Bax, 2003, 2011), materials delivery shifted to online platforms – computer-based to begin with, then increasingly accessible through a variety of mobile devices. Nowadays some distance learning institutions no longer produce paper-based materials for their students.

In addition to the bespoke teaching and assessment materials that have been produced by language teachers at distance institutions, most students are given access to small group tutorials where they have the opportunity to practice their skills, ask questions, and interact with the teacher and among themselves. Initially and for a long time thereafter, these were mainly face-to-face encounters, although telephone tutorials were also available for those who could not or would not attend classes in person. Nowadays most opportunities for interaction are to be found online.

Current Research and Practice

Teaching Methodology in Distance Language Learning

The most common setup for the delivery of distance language learning consists of a blending of materials for self-access and synchronous and asynchronous opportunities for interaction, both among students and tutors and among peers.

Self-Access Materials

The language-learning curriculum in distance learning settings usually incorporates a variety of competences and skills, including lexical, grammatical, and phonological competence, language skills (reading, writing, speaking, and listening), knowledge about the areas where the language is spoken, and intercultural communication and competence. In addition, it is common for courses from higher education institutions to incorporate the development of transferable skills such as academic skills (summarizing, arguing), digital and information literacy skills, and employability and professional skills.

The main teaching materials usually consist of a combination of study guides, texts, and audiovisual material pitched at the appropriate level for the language course (often authentic material from a variety of sources, sometimes adapted), grammar explanations, exercises, pronunciation guides, vocabulary, and language-learning strategies. The types of exercise vary depending on the language and on the level. Generally each exercise aims to develop more than one skill. For example, materials designed to teach Chinese to Western students will focus on their learning to write the characters and

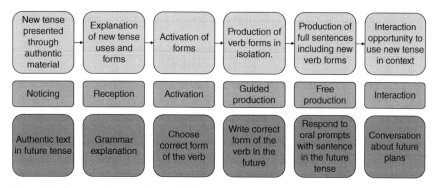

Figure 6.1 Example of steps in the scaffolding of a new language structure in distance learning materials.

getting the tonal training – in addition to reading, writing, speaking, listening, grammar, and vocabulary. Exercises are designed for students to practice language structures and check their understanding of the input provided through text, imagery, audio, or video; thus students produce output in the form of written texts or audio recordings and interact with others by engaging in written or oral discussion, either synchronously or asynchronously. Exercises are scaffolded so that, when students are presented with a new grammatical structure, for example, they have an opportunity to notice its use in context before being offered an explanation and opportunities to practice. A typical example (using the future tense) would follow the structure presented in Figure 6.1, with the scaffolded steps in the first row, the student process in the second, and an example in the third row.

As students will complete most exercises on their own, it is paramount that answers to the questions and clear explanations or signposting to the relevant section of the teaching text are supplied. Authors need to consider the possible answers, both correct and incorrect, to the exercises, so that feedback that addresses common mistakes may be provided. This is relatively simple with low-level grammar exercises, for example, but more complex in the case of higher-level activities such as free writing or open-ended questions. For these types of exercise, the authors should provide model answers or guidance on the expectations of how a text should be structured and on the types of structures students should use so as to be able to check their work in a meaningful way. It is very important that authors consider the amount of time that completing the activities will take. Careful planning is necessary to avoid overworking the students by surpassing the number of hours per week allocated to the study of the course.

The language of instruction for explanations and exercises is usually the students' first language (L1) for courses at beginner and lower intermediate levels (A1 and A2 of the Common European Framework of Reference), and the target language at intermediate (B1) and higher levels, although some courses may use both the L1 and the target language as an interim measure, bridging the transition. In addition, language-learning materials should expose learners to different cultures and variations of the target language so as to prepare them to access resources and interact with L2 speakers. Such exposure should cover different registers and dialects – for example, in the case of Spanish, the different accents, vocabulary, and structures used in Spain and in Latin American countries. To achieve this goal, distance language-learning material designers often use input sources and speakers from a variety of areas where the target language is spoken. Still, this is not always the case, as some areas show a preference for a particular variety (e.g. Mexican Spanish in the United States, or British English in parts of Europe).

Materials are usually designed well in advance of the start of the course, by an academic team of subject and distance language-learning experts. Traditionally, materials consisted of a combination of physical objects: printed books, workbooks, and audio delivered through the prevalent technology (vinyl records, cassettes, CDs), as well as video (cassettes, DVDs). Nowadays most materials are delivered online, in a combination of text, audio, and video digital files, interactive exercises, and online interaction tools. The lead time to plan the syllabus, write the materials, record the necessary audio and video, build the online environment, and design the assessment before the start of a course is often long, sometimes up to three years. As the expense of creating these resources is considerable, the materials are used for several years (Hurd, Beaven, & Ortega, 2001), even when they fall behind evolving technological capabilities. One implication of this long-term use is that authors try to avoid subjects and sources that could date quickly, although they could also update them easily and inexpensively by introducing links to more current resources when necessary.

Tutorials

In most distance higher education settings, students are offered a number of hours of contact with a tutor during a course (Campbell et al., 2019), although this varies depending on the institution. Most of this time is usually allocated to tutorials (or lessons); some of it may go to training sessions or individual support. Tutorials can take place face to face, in study centers close to where the students live, or online, using synchronous audio and video conferencing software. Some models of distance learning offer either online or face-to-face tutorials, although it is also common for the teaching strategy to be a blend of both. Some institutions are prescriptive of what tutors do during their tutorials, whereas others give them more freedom to organize their own sessions. Whether attendance at tutorials is compulsory or not depends on the institution. The content of tutorials usually consists of practice and revision of the material that students have learned independently; solving queries; and mainly oral production, pronunciation, and interaction practice (Rosell-Aguilar, 2005). Tutorials also offer opportunities for students to get to know one another and create support networks. Even though tutorial time features highly on students' lists of desirable activities for their courses (since the main reason for attending a tutorial is to interact), attendance often falls after the first session and can be very low by the end of the course (Pleines, 2020). This is very rarely a reflection of a tutor's abilities. In most cases, the low attendance rate is caused by other factors, which will be discussed later in this chapter.

Other Interaction Opportunities

Aside from tutorial time, opportunities for interaction are provided in several ways in distance language-learning courses. These interactions can be divided into three categories: interactions with the materials, interactions among students, and interactions with the tutor.

Interaction with the Materials

This type of interaction usually takes the form of a prompt to take part in a dialogue (written or spoken). The student listens to a question and is prompted to give a reply. For example, a student of French may hear the question *Vous travaillez dans quoi?* ("What do you do for a living?") in the target language and be prompted to reply. The level of specification varies, so the student may be prompted to provide a personal answer, replying with their occupation if they have one, or they may be prompted to provide a specific reply, for example "Say you are a dentist." This second example, while not allowing for a personalization of the reply, does allow the writers of the material to supply an exact, correct answer (*Je suis dentiste*) for the student to check, whereas for the first example a typical answer would be: "You should have replied using the first person singular of the verb *être* followed by an occupation. The occupation should be in the singular, without an article, and agree with your gender. For example, *Je suis étudiant* if you are male and *Je suis étudiante* if you are female." Typically, the student would be asked to record their answer, and an audio model answer would be provided so that they can compare their output with it, in terms of both accuracy and pronunciation.

Interaction with Other Students

Interaction with peers is particularly important in distance learning. As well as providing partners to practice with, interacting with other students is beneficial in that it offers support and encouragement and alleviates the loneliness that sometimes afflicts the distance learner. Students are usually given opportunities to interact with their classmates as well as with the whole cohort taking the course, and they are encouraged to create their own social and language practice and revision groups outside their tutorial time (either face to face or, more commonly, online). Sometimes tutors provide activities that the students prefer to do together, to practice the language with one another.

Interaction with a Tutor

Aside from offering tutorial time, tutors are often contacted by students with queries related to the course – such as assessment deadlines – and with queries related to the target language and its culture. This may prompt the tutor to choose to revisit some material in their next tutorial, to come up with additional resources, or to check additional student work, for example. Furthermore, tutors are often contacted if students are struggling with the course (see "Tutors" section).

Distance Learning Tools

The evolution of distance language teaching has been facilitated by developments in technology (White, 2007, 2017). The tools currently used to interact online as part of the distance language-learning provision are both synchronous and asynchronous.

Among the asynchronous tools used, email continues to be the main method of communication between the institution, the tutors, and the students. Communication can also take place on social media channels, namely with those tutors who are willing to share their spaces with their students; and, in many cases, it plays out between an institution's public spaces (e.g., Facebook, X, Instagram, TikTok) and their online followers. This latter type of communication tends to be more focused on institutional initiatives, promotion of courses, and recruitment, whereas direct communication with the tutor tends to focus on individual queries. It is important to stress that whether a tutor chooses to share their private social media spaces with students is entirely up to them and not up to the institution, as there are ethical and privacy considerations involved, as well as issues around the mixing of personal and professional identities.

Another asynchronous tool that is often used is the online forum, where social interaction as well as academic activity can take place. Participation in forums can vary enormously between cohorts, but usually a small percentage of the students are very active and contribute often, whereas others contribute sporadically or not at all.

The most commonly used synchronous communication tool nowadays is online conferencing. Although many people assume that the use of synchronous audio or video conferencing for teaching is a relatively recent development mainstreamed by the COVID-19 pandemic, these tools have been used in distance language teaching for over twenty years. An early incarnation of the conferencing platforms that most teachers and students are now familiar with (Zoom, Teams, Adobe Connect) was Lyceum, created at the UK Open University in the late 1990s. This piece of software provided audio conferencing as well as whiteboards, mind maps, a document editor, and a chat facility. It was later replaced by Elluminate, which allowed the use of video and eventually the tools mentioned above. The early 2000s saw many studies on the use of Lyceum for language learning being carried out to investigate task design, student and tutor experiences, tutor skills for online teaching, multimodality, and many other issues related to using synchronous conferencing as a language teaching tool (de los Arcos & Arnedillo Sánchez, 2006; Hampel & Hauck, 2004; Rosell-Aguilar, 2005, 2006).

A common criticism of the use of technology-mediated communication in teaching languages is the assumption that this type of communication may not prepare students for "real" interaction outside the classroom. There is no evidence to support this view in the studies carried out, and it is worth pointing out that, for many people, most of the communication they engage in on a daily basis (social media comments, messaging, email, audio and video calls) is technology-mediated.

The use of technology in learning is now commonplace almost everywhere, but it is worth remembering that access to technology remains a luxury for many, and the digital divide between those who have access to it and those who do not, because of physical, economic, or cultural factors, is far from over. In addition, having access to technology does not equate to being able to use it for learning purposes, and digital literacy skills cannot be taken for granted.

Assessment and Feedback

Assessment

Language-learning assessments in distance education are not substantially different from those used in face-to-face contexts. Students are asked to submit summative assignments on a regular basis and the end-of-course assessment may take the form of an exam. Formative assessment is also used, depending on the institution. It is common for the assessment instructions to be available to students from the start of the course.

Written assignments might involve writing short answers to reading comprehension questions, filling in blanks, multiple choice, writing sentences, or writing longer pieces of text, depending on the level. The stimuli for the written output are often authentic texts, sometimes adapted to the appropriate level. The assignments are either completed online using a virtual learning environment within a timeframe or simply written on an electronic device and submitted through an online submission system.

Oral assignments require the student to record themselves and submit the audio file by a given deadline. The format is usually one or more presentations or spoken pieces in response to questions. Oral assignments often include listening to a recorded piece of audio, which is designed to test listening comprehension, too. Oral assignments can involve group presentations or discussions carried out with a conferencing tool, or taking part in conversations with an assessor, particularly as an end-of-course assessment. This offers assessors the opportunity to test for interaction as well as for task completion, language range, and accuracy, pronunciation, and intonation.

Efforts are made to ensure that assessments are authentic and meaningful as well as personalized. Tasks may consist of giving a personal opinion, an answer that integrates the students' own context, or information found through the students' own research. Sometimes assignments require students to summarize or give their point of view on a discussion that may have taken place beforehand, in an online forum, for example.

Examinations of end-of-course assessments are rarely taken face to face in a proctored environment, and this can cause concern regarding the authenticity of the student's identity. But students usually access the submission page or the conferencing area for an oral examination using their institutional login details, and they are often examined by their own tutor, who can identify them or raise concerns if they have doubts about a student's identity.

Just as in traditional face-to-face environments, here too there may be cases of academic misconduct. These are rare and are mostly addressed through training on plagiarism, although cases of collusion do take place occasionally and are dealt with by an academic conduct officer.

Assessment can be both an incentive to keep up with one's studies and a cause for dropping out of a course. Interventions are sometimes put in place to support students prior to assessment using data to see whether the student is accessing the course materials regularly and to check on tutorial attendance and submission of previous assignments (Herodotou, Heiser, & Rienties, 2017). Interventions can range from a standard email with advice and links to useful resources to personal calls or emails from the tutor.

Feedback

The provision of feedback is essential in all language teaching, but it becomes even more important in the distance learning context, where students may not see their tutor at any point during their course and the feedback they receive sometimes becomes the only way they get personalized comments on their performance (Amoraga-Piqueras, Comas-Quinn, & Southgate, 2011).

Current approaches to feedback conceptualize it not as a one-way assessor comment on performance, but as a two-way co-negotiation that is predominantly student-centered (Rovagnati, Pitt, & Winstone, 2022). For this concept to be realized, students need to develop feedback literacy (Carless & Boud, 2018), that is, the ability to read, interpret, understand, and act on feedback (Sutton, 2012; Sutton & Gill, 2010). The role of feedback in distance language teaching goes beyond performance indication; feedback is also the communication channel for support and encouragement (White, 2003), hence the need for a dialogic approach to feedback in such settings (Fernández-Toro & Furnborough, 2018).

Traditionally, in distance language learning feedback was delivered by writing notes on the script in the case of written assignments and by recording pieces of audio that focused on pronunciation and intonation in the case of spoken assignments. It is considered good practice to provide a commentary (written, audio, or both) with encouraging words, comparison of improvements from previous assignments, advice and links to useful resources, and feed-forward with suggestions as to how to improve performance in future assignments. Contemporary practices in feedback provision include adding comments and tracking changes on a word-processed submission, recording audio files with individual feedback, and providing screencasts for the whole cohort, usually with more generic feedback (Harper, Green, & Fernandez-Toro, 2018), as screencasts can be time-consuming to produce.

Tutors

Teachers play a key part in the successful implementation of any learning approach (Comas-Quinn, 2011). The main role of distance learning tutors is not to teach new content, as this is usually done through the learning materials provided to the student. Instead, the roles of distance learning tutors include creating opportunities to practice what has been learnt at home, providing feedback, dealing with content, technical, and administrative queries, teaching learning strategies, offering practical and emotional support, and contributing to community building. The shift toward online learning that has taken place in both distance and blended learning has necessitated the formation of new skills. Initially training focused on the technical aspects as well as on the pedagogy of online teaching. Early initiatives involving synchronous online tutorials found that tutors encountered technical problems (Hampel, 2003; Hampel & Hauck, 2004), although the majority liked using the software (Rosell-Aguilar, 2006). As learning technologies have become commonplace in education, alongside increased broadband speed and ownership of devices that can support audio and video conferencing, technical problems have reduced significantly, although they have not disappeared. It is not unusual for tutors to learn to use software as they go along, in an experience they share with their own students, which brings about a change in pedagogical relationships and hierarchies (Comas-Quinn, de los Arcos, & Mardomingo, 2012). These shifts in tutor roles have also impacted teacher training and professional development (Comas-Quinn, 2016). It is important to mention that distance learning tutors often work part-time for the distance learning institution and many have other jobs teaching elsewhere. This can have an impact on their availability and opportunities for training.

Students

Distance language learners have a very varied profile. While some are what one might consider "traditional" university students in terms of age and motivations for learning, many are adults who choose to study a language for pleasure or as an intellectual challenge (Coleman, 2009). One thing all distance language learners have in common is that they have chosen distance learning as their tuition mode. This is usually because they have barriers to accessing traditional face-to-face tuition. These barriers range from physical disability, mental health conditions, or financial circumstances, to time constraints such as having full-time work or caring for relatives. Regardless of their personal profile, there are a number of characteristics that make successful distance language learners, including motivation and the use of effective strategies for autonomous learning (Hurd, 2008).

Affective factors such as motivation, autonomy, and anxiety can have a considerable impact. In his affective profile of the good distance language learner, Xiao (2012, p. 121) states that "the successful distance language learner is highly motivated with specific reasons for his/her study, perceived progress, and appropriate tactics to maintain motivation; he/she has strong self-efficacy, which may lead to increased motivation and an internal locus of learning; he/she is metacognitively mature, and uses his/her initiative in dealing with anxiety arising from the distance language learning process." Motivation is an essential factor for success in language learning, and it becomes even more important in the distance learning environment (Furnborough, 2012; Murphy & Hurd, 2011). Motivation is a concept that includes the desire to achieve a language-learning goal, the effort that needs to be made toward this achievement, and the level of satisfaction with what has been achieved (Mitchell, Myles, & Marsden, 2019), and has been linked to the role of identity (Dörnyei, 2009; Ushioda, 2011).

Linked to motivation is another concept that is considered a success factor in distance learning: autonomy (Lewis, 2014). Learner autonomy refers to the level at which the student is involved in decision-making (what to study, when, how). In the case of language learning, autonomy goes beyond the individual, since this is a social activity that requires interaction. In a distance learning context, the interdependence between the learner and the others needs to be established and reconciled with the learner's own, independent language-learning process (Furnborough, 2012) if this learner is to be able to engage in social interaction, mostly online. Distance learning is often associated with flexibility – and, indeed, in terms of where and when the learning takes place it provides more flexibility than scheduled face-to-face classes at a traditional university, but it does so within the confines of set term dates and assessment deadlines. This flexibility places means learners need to have autonomy and be skilled in workload management. There is an apparent conflict between the autonomy required to engage in distance learning and the fact that distance learning courses are very structured and it is the course authors who decide what is presented to the student (Hurd, Beaven, & Ortega, 2001). Students, however, often find that they do not have as much time available for study as they would have hoped and make choices of their own, prioritizing some activities over others. White (2017) proposes that distance language learners can be considered course producers, on the grounds that they construct their own course with the materials at their disposal, to suit their learning needs.

Another factor mentioned by Xiao (2012) is anxiety. As stated above, these are people who have chosen to study at a distance and should therefore be used to working by themselves, but sometimes they find the prospect of attending a tutorial, particularly online (de los Arcos, Coleman, & Hampel, 2009), or collaborating online, or being assessed very challenging. This can lead to low attendance rates for tutorials, although students may have access to a recording of the tutorial that they can engage with at their own pace.

Anxiety is also a factor in attrition, which can be higher than in traditional, face-to-face contexts, particularly before assessment points. The first assessment in a course and the end of module assessment are key points at which distance students drop out (Simpson, 2004, 2013), often because they feel unprepared (IET Student Statistics and Survey Team, 2014).

A sense of community is essential in distance language-learning environments (Nielson and González-Lloret, 2010). At the turn of the century, isolation and overcoming "the loneliness of the long-distance language learner" (Shield, 2000) were common areas for concern. This factor has decreased as communication technology has become prevalent, but it still affects learners to some degree. To remedy loneliness and foster interaction (both in the L1 and the target language), learners are encouraged to form a community of peers where they can discuss course-related matters pertaining to the subject as well as strategies for coping with being a distance learner. Sometimes community building is embedded in the teaching strategy as well.

To counter some of the problems that affect distance learners, institutions offer support in a variety of ways and at different stages: before the start of the course (information about its content, duration, assessment, methodologies), at the start and throughout the course (technical problems, timely response times for queries and assessment), and after the course (careers services) (Jones & Bartlett, 2004). Although the recording of small classes (as opposed to lecture capture) for public viewing is controversial on account of privacy as well as copyright issues – and language learning seems to be among the least obvious subjects where watching a recording may be of benefit to the learner, given a viewer's lack of participation and interaction – there are advantages to watching recordings, such as consolidation and reflection, or access to different voices and perspectives (Pleines, 2020). Students with disabilities may require additional support through assistive technology and software add-ons, and institutions can provide alternative formats for the course materials (e.g. PDFs for print materials that are tagged for screen readers) as well as image descriptions, transcripts for audiovisual materials, and optimized navigation for browsers.

Recent developments have also focused on peer support, for instance in the form of contracting a student from a previous cohort of the course to act as an experienced "study buddy" (Motzo, 2016) and guide the new students through areas they find problematic or anxiety-inducing.

Finally, the characteristics of the good distance learner in terms of motivation and autonomy can predispose them to make the most of the opportunities afforded by informal learning, supplementing their formal tuition with individual activity that involves using language-learning apps, signing up to MOOCs (Beaven, 2013; Rosell-Aguilar, 2018), streaming services, and podcasts to practice their listening skills (Rosell-Aguilar, 2015), interacting with others on social media (Kelly, 2019; Rosell-Aguilar, 2020), or engaging in e-tandem activities (Lewis, 2020).

Future Directions

This chapter has proposed a definition of distance language learning and teaching, outlined a brief history of its evolution, and presented past and current methods and tools for the teaching and assessment of languages in a distance learning context. It has also discussed the roles and characteristics of distance learning tutors and students, as well as some of the challenges they face.

Distance learning will continue to evolve through improvements to pedagogy and technology and, as practices that involve blended, mobile, and autonomous learning change, so will the formal provision of distance language learning. The current rate of improvement in speech recognition software and in translation tools makes them more likely to be integrated into language teaching and learning than they have been so far, and even more so in the distance learning context. These are potential areas of practice and research that will become prominent in the near future.

The COVID-19 pandemic of recent years forced traditional face-to-face higher education institutions to move their teaching online in order to allow it to continue despite mobility restrictions. Many referred to this phenomenon as "distance learning," but it is important to differentiate between this sort of emergency measure and learning that has been designed to be provided at a distance.

At the start of the pandemic, most if not all higher education providers had all the tools they needed to "pivot online" and supply online teaching, but little or no experience of using them as the sole medium of teaching. As a consequence, many teachers were given some basic training on how to use synchronous computer-mediated communication technologies such as Zoom, Teams, or Blackboard Collaborate, but in most cases universities did not offer any pedagogical training in teaching online with these tools. The situation prompted many teachers to seek professional development through their online networks (Rosell-Aguilar, 2021).

One positive outcome of this shift to synchronous online teaching was the normalization of synchronous computer-mediated communication technologies for teaching purposes. However, the lack of experience in online teaching led to some poor practices, as many teachers assumed that what they needed to do was to transfer their face-to-face practices to the online environment instead of reconceptualizing them around an online learning pedagogy. This resulted in a lack of engagement from students; many teachers complained about speaking to online rooms of students whose cameras were turned off. Many students, in turn, were put off by this approach to online learning. The situation led to complaints and even requests for university fee refunds in countries such as the United Kingdom and the United States.

The key difference between this type of ERT and distance learning as described in this chapter is the element of choice. The students encountering emergency measures had not signed up for distance learning, it was imposed on them; these students had not developed the good distance learner qualities described in this chapter, such as motivation and autonomy. The negative reactions to ERT may have put some potential students off true distance learning, the kind that has been designed as such; and it is because of this that the distinction must be made.

How this new situation, in which traditional, face-to-face institutions have acquired experience of providing distance learning and are now adopting hybrid methods, will affect institutions that offer only distance learning remains to be seen, but their unique selling point is threatened and the distance learning landscape may be changed forever as a consequence of the pandemic.

References

Amoraga-Piqueras, M., Comas-Quinn, A., & Southgate, M. (2011). Teaching through assessment. In M. Nicolson, L. Murphy, & M. Southgate (Eds.), *Language teaching in blended contexts* (pp. 75–92). Dunedin Academic Press.

Bax, S. (2003). CALL: Past, present and future. *System, 31*(1), 13–28. https://doi.org/10.1016/S0346–251X(02)00071-4

Bax, S. (2011). Normalisation revisited: The effective use of technology in language education. *International Journal of Computer-Assisted Language Learning and Teaching (IJCALLT), 1*(2), 1–15. https://doi.org/10.4018/ijcallt.2011040101

Beaven, A. (2013). Using MOOCs in an academic English course at university level. In A. Beaven, A. Comas-Quinn, & B. Sawhill (Eds.), *Case studies of openness in the language classroom* (pp. 217–227). Research-publishing.net. https://doi.org/10.14705/rpnet.2013.000122

Cambre, M. A. (1991). The state of the art of instructional television. In G. J. Anglin (Ed.), *Instructional technology, past, present, and future* (pp. 267–275). Libraries Unlimited.

Campbell, A., Gallen, A. M., Jones, M. H., & Walshe, A. (2019). The perceptions of STEM tutors on the role of tutorials in distance learning. *Open Learning: The Journal of Open, Distance and e-Learning, 34*(1), 89–102. https://doi.org/10.1080/02680513.2018.1544488

Carless, D., & Boud, D. (2018). The development of student feedback literacy: enabling uptake of feedback. *Assessment & Evaluation in Higher Education, 43*(8), 1315–1325. https://doi.org/10.1080/02602938.2018.1463354

Coleman, J. A. (2009). Why the British do not learn languages: Myths and motivation in the United Kingdom. *Language Learning Journal, 37*(1), 111–127. https://doi.org/10.1080/09571730902749003

Comas-Quinn, A. (2011). Learning to teach online or learning to become an online teacher: An exploration of teachers' experiences in a blended learning course. *ReCALL, 23*(3), 218–232. https://doi.org/10.1017/S0958344011000152

Comas-Quinn, A. (2016). Blended teaching and the changing role of the tutor: The need for a review of teacher professional development. In M. McCarthy (Ed.), *The Cambridge guide to blended learning for language teaching* (pp. 68–82). Cambridge University Press.

Comas-Quinn, A., de los Arcos, B., & Mardomingo, R. (2012). Virtual learning environments (VLEs) for distance language learning: Shifting tutor roles in a contested space for interaction. *Computer Assisted Language Learning, 25*(2), 129–143. https://doi.org/10.1080/09588221.2011.636055

de los Arcos, B., & Arnedillo Sánchez, F. (2006). Ears before eyes: Expanding tutors' interaction skills beyond physical presence in audio-graphic collaborative virtual learning environments. In P. Zaphiris & G. Zacharia (Eds.), *User-centered computer aided language learning* (pp. 74–93). Idea Group, Inc. https://doi.org/10.4018/978-1-59140-750-8.ch004

de los Arcos, B., Coleman, J. A., & Hampel, R. (2009). Learners' anxiety in audiographic conferences: A discursive psychology approach to emotion talk. *ReCALL, 21*(1), 3–17. https://doi.org/10.1017/S0958344009000111

Dörnyei, Z. (2009). The L2 motivational self system. In Z. Dörnyei & E. Ushioda (Eds.), *Motivation, language identity and the L2 self.* Multilingual Matters. https://doi.org/10.21832/9781847691293

Fernández-Toro, M., & Furnborough, C. (2018). Evaluating alignment of student and tutor perspectives on feedback on language learning assignments. *Distance Education, 39*(4), 548–567. https://doi.org/10.1080/01587919.2018.1520043

Fernández-Toro, M., & Hurd, S. (2014). A model of factors affecting independent learners' engagement with feedback on language learning tasks. *Distance Education, 35*(1), 106–125. https://doi.org/10.1080/01587919.2014.891434

Furnborough, C. (2012). Making the most of others: Autonomous interdependence in adult beginner distance language learners. *Distance Education, 33*(1), 99–116. https://doi.org/10.1080/01587919.2012.667962

Gimeno-Sanz, A. (2016). Moving a step further from "integrative CALL": What's to come? *Computer Assisted Language Learning, 29*(6), 1102–1115. https://doi.org/10.1080/09588221.2015.1103271

Hampel, R. (2003). Theoretical perspectives and new practices in audio-graphic conferencing for language learning. *ReCALL, 15*(1), 21–36. https://doi.org/10.1017/S0958344003000314

Hampel, R., & Hauck, M. (2004). Towards an effective use of audio conferencing in distance learning courses. *Language Learning and Technology, 8*(1), 66–82. http://dx.doi.org/10125/25230

Harper, F., Green, H., & Fernandez-Toro, M. (2018). Using screencasts in the teaching of modern languages: Investigating the use of Jing® in feedback on written assignments. *The Language Learning Journal, 46*(3), 277–292. https://doi.org/10.1080/09571736.2015.1061586

Herodotou, C., Heiser, S., & Rienties, B. (2017). Implementing randomised control trials in open and distance learning: A feasibility study. *Open Learning: The Journal of Open, Distance and e-Learning, 32*(2), 147–162. https://doi.org/10.1080/02680513.2017.1316188

Hurd, S. (2006). Towards a better understanding of the dynamic role of the distance language learning: Learner perceptions of personality, motivation, roles, and approaches. *Distance Education, 27*(3), 303–329. https://doi.org/10.1080/01587910600940406

Hurd, S. (2008). Affect and strategy use in independent language learning. In S. Hurd & T. Lewis (Eds.), *Language learning strategies in independent settings: Second language acquisition* (pp. 218–236). Multilingual Matters.

Hurd, S., Beaven, T., & Ortega, A. (2001). Developing autonomy in a distance language learning context: issues and dilemmas for course writers. *System*, *29*(3), 341–355. https://doi.org/10.1016/S0346-251X(01)00024-0

IET Student Statistics and Survey Team. (2014). *What reasons do students give for not completing modules? Non-returners research findings and outcomes.* [Report]. The Open University.

Jones, K. O., & Bartlett, R. (2004). Towards providing distance learning students with a comparable learning experience. In *Proceedings of the 5th international conference on computer systems and technologies* (pp. 1–6). https://doi.org/10.1145/1050330.1050416

Kelly, O. (2019). Assessing language student interaction and engagement via Twitter. In A. Comas-Quinn, A. Beaven, & B. Sawhill (Eds.), *New case studies of openness in and beyond the language classroom* (pp. 129–143). Research-publishing.net. https://doi.org/10.14705/rpnet.2019.37.971

Lewis, T. (2014). Learner autonomy and the theory of sociality. In G. Murray (Ed.), *Social dimensions of autonomy in language learning* (pp. 37–59). Palgrave MacMillan. https://doi.org/10.1057/9781137290243_3

Lewis, T. (2020). From tandem learning to e-tandem learning: How languages are learnt in tandem exchanges. In S. Gola, M. Pierrard, E. Tops, & D. Van Raemdonck (Eds.), *Enseigner et apprendre les langues au XXIe siècle: Méthodes alternatives et nouveaux dispositifs d'accompagnement.* GRAMM-R. P. I. E. Peter Lang. https://doi.org/10.3726/b16391

Liu, Z. (2018). The impact of distance learning on foreign language education. In *2018 International Conference on Social Science and Education Reform (ICSSER 2018)* (pp. 237–239). Atlantis Press. https://dx.doi.org/10.2991/icsser-18.2018.56

Mitchell, R., Myles, F., & Marsden, E. (2019). *Second language learning theories.* Routledge. https://doi.org/10.4324/9781315617046

Motzo, A. (2016). Evaluating the effects of a "student buddy" initiative on student engagement and motivation. In C. Goria, O. Speicher, & S. Stollhans (Eds.), *Innovative language teaching and learning at university: Enhancing participation and collaboration* (pp. 19–28). Research-publishing.net. http://dx.doi.org/10.14705/rpnet.2016.000401

Murphy, L., & Hurd, S. (2011). Fostering learner autonomy and motivation in blended teaching. In M. Nicolson, L., Murphy, & M. Southgate (Eds.), *Language teaching in blended contexts* (pp. 43–56). Dunedin Academic Press.

Nicol, D. (2021). The power of internal feedback: Exploiting natural comparison processes. *Assessment & Evaluation in Higher Education*, *46*(5), 756–778. https://doi.org/10.1080/02602938.2020.1823314

Nielson, K. B., & González-Lloret, M. (2010). Effective online foreign language courses: Theoretical framework and practical applications. *The EuroCALL Review*, *17*, 48–65. https://doi.org/10.4995/eurocall.2010.16326

Pleines, C. (2020). Understanding vicarious participation in online language learning. *Distance Education, 41*(4), 453–471. https://doi.org/10.1080/01587919.2020.1821605

Rosell-Aguilar, F. (2005). Task design for audiographic conferencing: Promoting beginner oral interaction in distance language learning. *Computer assisted language learning, 18*(5), 417–442. https://doi.org/10.1080/09588220500442772

Rosell-Aguilar, F. (2006). Online tutorial support in open distance learning through audio-graphic SCMC: Tutor impressions. *The JALT CALL Journal, 2*(2), 37–52. https://doi.org/10.29140/jaltcall.v2n2.25

Rosell-Aguilar, F. (2015). Podcasting as a language teaching and learning tool. In K. Borthwick, E. Corradini, & A. Dickens (Eds.), *10 years of the LLAS elearning symposium: Case studies in good practice* (pp. 31–39). Research-publishing.net. https://doi.org/10.14705/rpnet.2015.000265

Rosell-Aguilar, F. (2018). Autonomous language learning through a mobile application: A user evaluation of the busuu app. *Computer Assisted Language Learning, 31*(8), 1–28. https://doi.org/10.1080/09588221.2018.1456465

Rosell-Aguilar, F. (2020). Twitter as a language learning tool: The learners' perspective. *International Journal of Computer-Assisted Language Learning and Teaching (IJCALLT), 10*(4), 1–13. https://doi.org/10.4018/IJCALLT.2020100101

Rosell-Aguilar, F. (2021). Locked down, but not isolated: Twitter collaboration among teachers in response to COVID-19. In A. Plutino, & E. Polisca (Eds.), *Languages at work, competent multilinguals and the pedagogical challenges of COVID-19* (pp. 71–77). Research-publishing.net. https://doi.org/10.14705/rpnet.2021.49.1220

Rovagnati, V., Pitt, E., & Winstone, N. (2022). Feedback cultures, histories and literacies: International postgraduate students' experiences. *Assessment & Evaluation in Higher Education, 47*(3), 347–359. https://doi.org/10.1080/02602938.2021.1916431

Sherry, L. (1995). Issues in distance learning. *International Journal of Educational Telecommunications, 1*(4), 337–365.

Shield, L. (2000, September). Overcoming isolation: The loneliness of the long-distance language learner. Keynote address at the EADTU Paris Millennium Conference "Wiring the Ivory Tower," France.

Shield, L., Hauck, M., & Hewer, S. (2001). Talking to strangers: The role of the tutor in developing target language speaking skills at a distance. In *Proceedings of UNTELE 2000* (2) (pp. 75–84). Technological University of Compiègne.

Simpson, O. (2004). The impact on retention of interventions to support distance learning students. *Open Learning, 19*, 79–95. https://doi.org/10.1080/0268051042000177863

Simpson, O. (2013). *Supporting students for success in online and distance education.* Routledge.

Sutton, P. (2012). Conceptualizing feedback literacy: Knowing, being, and acting. *Innovations in Education and Teaching International, 49*(1), 31–40. https://doi.org/10.1080/14703297.2012.647781

Sutton, P., & Gill, W. (2010). Engaging feedback: Meaning, identity and power. *Practitioner Research in Higher Education, 4*(1), 3–13.

Ushioda, E. (2011). Why autonomy? Insights from motivation theory and research. *Innovation in Language Learning and Teaching, 5*(2), 221–232. https://doi.org/10.1080/17501229.2011.577536

White, C. (2003). *Language learning in distance education*. Ernst Klett Sprachen.

White, C. (2007). Innovation and identity in distance language learning and teaching. *International Journal of Innovation in Language Learning and Teaching, 1*(1), 97–110. https://doi.org/10.2167/illt45.0

White, C. J. (2017). Distance language teaching with technology. In C. A. Chapelle & S. Sauro (Eds.), *The handbook of technology and second language teaching and learning* (pp. 134–148). Wiley Blackwell. https://doi.org/10.1002/9781118914069.ch10

Winstone, N. E., Mathlin, G., & Nash, R. A. (2019, May). Building feedback literacy: Students' perceptions of the Developing Engagement with Feedback Toolkit. *Frontiers in Education, 4*, 39. https://doi.org/10.3389/feduc.2019.00039

Xiao, J. (2012). Successful and unsuccessful distance language learners: An "affective" perspective. *Open Learning: The Journal of Open, Distance and e-Learning, 27*(2), 121–136. https://doi.org/10.1080/02680513.2012.678611

Further Reading

González-Lloret, M. (2017). Technology for task-based language teaching. In C. A. Chapelle & S. Sauro (Eds.), *The handbook of technology and second language teaching and learning* (pp. 234–247). Wiley Blackwell. https://doi.org/10.1002/9781118914069.ch16

In this book chapter, Marta González-Lloret provides an overview of different technologies ranging from the basic (blogs, wikis) to the complex (multiplayer online games, virtual environments), and argues that, despite their many affordances, their use for language teaching and learning purposes must be informed by evidence from SLA research. González-Lloret identifies task-based language teaching as the optimal approach to achieve this goal and provides examples of the integration of technology-mediated tasks into language teaching.

White, C. J. (2017). Distance language teaching with technology. In C. A. Chapelle & S. Sauro (Eds.), *The handbook of technology and second language teaching and learning* (pp. 134–148). Wiley Blackwell. https://doi.org/10.1002/9781118914069.ch10

This chapter by Cynthia White is essential reading for anyone interested in distance language learning. It focuses on the available technologies for facilitating language learning online and discusses required changes to curriculum and materials design, assessment, and teacher training in the incorporation of these technologies into various learning processes. White underlines the importance of obtaining evidence through research into the use of these technologies.

7

Flipped Classrooms

Hsiu-Ting Hung

Introduction

Among a wide array of pedagogical approaches that have been developed to promote student learning, flipping the classroom has gained prominence in recent years (Al-Samarraie, Shamsuddin, & Alzahrani, 2020; Turan & Akdag-Cimen, 2020). The basic idea of a flipped classroom, as defined by Bergmann and Sams (2012, p. 13), is this: "that which is traditionally done in class is now done at home and that which is traditionally done as homework is now completed in class." The term "flipped classroom" was initially popularized in 2012 by Jonathan Bergmann and Aaron Sams, the cofounders of a nonprofit organization named Flipped Learning Network, in a seminal book entitled *Flip your classroom: Reach every student in every class every day*. The concept is also known as "classroom flip" (Baker, 2000) and "inverted classroom" (Lage, Platt, & Treglia, 2000) – terms that express the idea of blending pre-class and in-class activities in order to promote active student learning.

Bergmann and Sams (2014), along with other leading scholars from the Flipped Learning Network (2014), further make a terminological distinction between flipped classrooms and flipped learning, two terms that have commonly been used interchangeably. According to them, flipped learning refers to an approach in which "direct instruction moves from the group learning space to the individual learning space, and the resulting group space is transformed into a dynamic, interactive learning environment where the educator guides students as they apply concepts and engage creatively in the subject matter" (Bergmann and Sams, 2014, p. 6). Following a strict classification, flipping the classroom is the preliminary stage of focusing on content delivery and mastery, whereas flipped learning is the ultimate stage of focusing on "the best use of face-to-face time with students" to foster richer and more meaningful learning (p. 7).

In this chapter, however, these two related terms are considered synonymous, because the aim is to include as much relevant research as possible. In the following discussions, the notion of flipping the classroom or flipped learning is generally conceptualized as a student-centered pedagogical approach whereby the teacher delivers content before the class in order for students to access it outside the classroom, at their own pace, and then uses face-to-face class time to engage them actively and often collaboratively in classroom learning activities. While the learning materials involved in pre-class activities mostly take the form of instructional videos as a means of replacing lectures in traditional classrooms, other types of learning content, such as reading passages and audio podcasts, are possible alternatives.

Background/Historical Perspectives

Over the past years, the flipped classroom approach has been applied in various disciplines, such as engineering (Estriegana, Medina-Merodio, & Barchino, 2019), mathematics (Hung, Sun, & Liu, 2019), and history (Aidinopoulou & Sampson, 2017). Research has shown a variety of learning benefits. For example, students in flipped classrooms have been found to be more satisfied with their learning experiences (Awidi & Paynter, 2019), develop higher levels of learner autonomy (Zainuddin & Perera, 2019), and perform better in academic subjects (González-Gómez et al., 2016) than students in traditional classrooms.

As in other domains, flipped classrooms in L2 (second or foreign language) education allow learners to explore language input prior to class in a self-paced manner, by replaying video lectures and looking up unknown words, and thus freeing up class time for opportunities to use or practice the target language with their classmates and their teacher (Jiang et al., 2020; Turan & Akdag-Cimen, 2020; Zou et al., 2020). Given this affordance, L2 researchers have favorably compared the flipped classroom approach with traditional instruction with respect to enhancing the four language skills, namely reading (Huang & Hong, 2016), writing (Ekmekci, 2017), listening (Amiryousefi, 2019), and speaking (Chen Hsieh, Huang, & Wu, 2017). For example, Wu, Hsieh, and Yang (2017) examined the impacts of flipping the classroom on L2 English learners' oral proficiency and perceptions. An online learning community was established for flipped learning using a smartphone application, LINE, which featured text and audio-messaging functions. For the pre-class flipped learning activities, the students were required to (1) preview the assigned reading passages and instructional videos, (2) practice and record the guided dialogues with their conversation partners, and (3) post their audio recordings to the learning community, namely the LINE groups. These student activities allowed the instructor to place the emphasis of the class meetings on active student learning rather than on teacher-led grammar instruction and language drills. Accordingly, the in-class flipped learning activities involved in the study were mostly learner-centered and collaborative (e.g. group discussions and presentations), and the students were given opportunities to interact and communicate with others in English. The research results indicated that, by comparison with conventional English language teaching, the method of exposing students to flipped learning could significantly enhance their oral proficiency, while also keeping them engaged both in and out of class.

Despite numerous scholars having advocated the benefits of flipping the classroom, there is still debate about its effectiveness. In L2 contexts, some studies show that students tend to be more satisfied with the flipped classroom approach and can achieve an equally good or even better language performance by comparison with what is achieved through the traditional classroom approach or direct instruction, while other studies have found no significant difference (Shahnama, Ghonsooly, & Shirvan, 2021; Zou et al., 2020). Clearly, more scholarly efforts in diverse forms (such as empirical studies, systematic reviews, and position papers) are needed to help propel the field forward.

Considering this, the purpose of this chapter is to provide a greater understanding of the flipped classroom approach by synthesizing relevant reviews and studies of flipped learning in the existing literature. The subsequent sections are devoted to current research trends, theoretical groundings, and design considerations of flipped classrooms. Where appropriate, the discussions are also illustrated by paradigms of flipped learning studies in L2 education.

Current Research and Practice

Research Trends Related to Flipped Classrooms

The popularity of flipped classrooms in education is evident from a number of systematic reviews or meta-analyses published in recent years. Table 7.1 presents a chronological list of previous reviews that are selected and discussed here. These reviews differ in their scope and research questions, but all contribute to identifying current trends in flipped classroom research.

While it has been proposed that the flipped classroom approach can be applied at all educational levels (Bergmann & Sams, 2012), its distribution in practice varies widely. For example, Akçayır and Akçayır (2018) surveyed the full range of Social Sciences Citation Index (SSCI) publications between 2000 and 2016 using the Web of Science (WoS) database, and the results revealed that 80 percent of the seventy-one reviewed studies focused on university learners. The fact that participation in flipped classrooms generally requires higher levels of technology literacy and student self-regulation may explain why far fewer studies have adopted the flipped classroom approach in K–12 education.

Contextualized in higher education, O'Flaherty and Phillips's (2015) review is one of the earliest attempts to systematically synthesize flipped classroom research. Between 1995 and 2014, the authors conducted a scoping review by searching for relevant studies in peer-refereed journals and grey literature

Table 7.1 *A comparison of previous review studies on flipped classrooms*

Studies	Timespan	Sample	Scope	Research questions
O'Flaherty and Phillips (2015)	1995~2014	28	All disciplines in higher education	• What technologies are being used to engage students in a flipped class? • What considerations are there pertaining to the economic and time constraints required to implement a flipped class? • What is known about the pedagogical acceptance by both staff and students? • What are the educational outcomes arising from a flipped class? • What is known about the conceptual framework used to design a flipped class?
Akçayır and Akçayır (2018)	2000~2016	71	All disciplines in all educational levels	• What advantages of the flipped classroom are indicated in the studies published in the SSCI-indexed journals? • What challenges imposed by the flipped classroom are indicated in the studies published in the SSCI-indexed journals? • What in-class and out-of-class activities were used in flipped classrooms in the studies published in the SSCI-indexed journals?
Al-Samarraie et al. (2020)	2009~2018	85	All disciplines in higher education	• What is the effect of using flipped classroom on students' learning across university disciplines? • What are the opportunities and challenges of using the flipped classroom model in these disciplines? • What are the major extensions to the traditional flipped classroom model?
Turan and Akdag-Cimen (2020)	2014~2018	43	Language education (focus on English as L2)	• What are the trends in flipped classrooms in ELT research? • What were the main findings from the available literature?
Jiang et al. (2020)	2015~2018	33	Language education (focus on L2)	• What are the overall features of research in flipped language education in terms of timespan, setting, methodology, unit of analysis, and sample? • What are the research foci in flipped language education? • What is the role of technology in flipped language education? • How do studies integrate theories, models, or strategies of language teaching and learning into flipped language education?
Zou et al. (2020)	2015~2019	34	Language and literacy education (focus on L2 and L1)	• What theoretical frameworks, concepts, models, or instructional approaches were involved in the research carried out in flipped language classrooms? • Who were the main participants? • What were the main learning activities? • What were the main learning tools? • What were the outcomes and how were they evaluated? • What topics were investigated?

using eight databases (WoS, Scopus, and Google Scholar among them). A total of twenty-eight primary studies in various subject domains were identified, most of them centering on STEM learning and only one focusing on language learning. Likewise, Al-Samarraie et al. (2020) conducted a synthesis of flipped classroom studies at universities published between 2009 and 2018 using five databases (WoS and ScienceDirect among them). They retrieved eighty-five relevant articles across disciplines, and further found that, in social sciences and humanities, the reviewed approach was mostly implemented in language courses. Interestingly, when the results of this study are compared with the review by O'Flaherty and Phillips (2015), it appears that there has been a notable increase in the number of flipped language classrooms over the past few years.

More recently, three domain-specific reviews of flipped classroom research in the field of L2 education (Jiang et al., 2020; Turan & Akdag-Cimen, 2020; Zou et al., 2020) have been published in a major journal, *Computer Assisted Language Learning*, which indicates that this approach has drawn significant attention from L2 researchers and educators. All three reviews feature a content analysis method for synthesizing important topics over a period of up to five years, using mainly the Web of Science (WoS) database. The findings of the abovementioned reviews (alongside others, summarized in Table 7.1) have led to comparable observations concerning recent trends of the flipped classroom approach in L2 education. These are summarized as follows:

- Settings. Most of the flipped language classrooms have been implemented in higher education institutions or universities (Turan & Akdag-Cimen, 2020; Zou et al., 2020).
- Participants. Learners of English as a foreign language (EFL) have been the primary target population (Jiang et al., 2020; Turan & Akdag-Cimen, 2020; Zou et al., 2020).
- Technology integration. Numerous technologies have been integrated into flipped language classrooms, and have been used mostly for content delivery and comprehension facilitation in pre-class preparation, via learning management systems (LMSs) such as Blackboard and Moodle (Jiang et al., 2020; Zou et al., 2020).
- Task design. Various pre-class and in-class activities or tasks have been used for flipped learning – the pre-class category being mainly devoted to self-paced video lectures, the in-class category to interactive group discussions (Akçayır & Akçayır, 2018; Jiang et al., 2020).
- Effects. Most of the research on flipped language classrooms has revealed positive effects on student learning, most students reporting increased engagement followed by enhanced academic or language performance (Turan & Akdag-Cimen, 2020; Zou et al., 2020).
- Challenges. Major challenges facing students have been related to the need for guidance during out-of-class learning and the heavy workload of pre-class learning (Akçayır & Akçayır, 2018; Turan & Akdag-Cimen, 2020; Zou et al., 2020).

Collectively, the reviews discussed here provide a snapshot of the state of the art in flipped classroom research. The trends identified also help shape directions for future research and the development of flipped language classrooms. It should be noted that not every flipped classroom leads to successful student learning, and that an effective flipped classroom requires more than a reversal between homework and lectures in instructional design. However, as can be seen from the research trends in technology use and task design, the current practice of flipped language classrooms appears to reflect a rather rigid way of learning, without much innovation. Therefore future investigations may look into the potential of interactive technologies beyond LMSs (e.g. social media, digital games, student response systems, virtual reality, augmented reality, and chatbots) to support interactive learning tasks other than group discussions. Such support could move the research forward by shifting the focus from "to flip or not to flip" to "how best to flip if one must."

Theoretical Groundings for Flipping the Classroom

Researchers' choices of theoretical perspectives when flipping the classroom often vary across contexts; and they vary on the basis of what is being researched. In the field of L2 education, a number of studies have drawn on general theories of learning to guide the development and implementation of flipped language classrooms. As outlined below, these studies should serve as useful references for L2 researchers to make informed decisions about theoretical frameworks for flipped classroom interventions.

Cognitive load theory proposed by Sweller (1994) has been very influential in guiding the instructional design of educational research. Cognitive load theory is primarily concerned with the total mental effort placed on learners' working memory, which has a limited cognitive capacity: It can process information within an estimated range of 7 ± 2 chunks. According to Clark et al. (2006), learners' working memory is subject to three major types of cognitive load: intrinsic, extraneous, and germane. Thus the application of cognitive load theory to flipped classrooms becomes relevant in connection with the idea of redesigning learning activities and materials so as to reduce learners' mental effort and enable an appropriate self-management of cognitive load (Abeysekera & Dawson, 2015). For example, Tonkin, Page, and Forsey (2019) adopted the lens of cognitive load theory to flip an introductory German course for university students. In reducing the L2 learners' cognitive load, the researchers replaced the face-to-face grammar lectures with manageable chunks of information in the form of short online videos. It was found that the flipped learning mechanism allowed the students to exert control over the pre-class learning materials and content, which also provided them with sufficient prior knowledge and confidence to participate in activities of applying the learned grammatical structures in class, with greater ease and lowered cognitive load.

Self-regulated learning (or self-regulation) refers to the processes through which learners systematically activate and adapt their thoughts, feelings, and behaviors regarding the attainment of their learning goals (Zimmerman, 1986). From the perspective of self-regulation theory, effective learning is more likely to occur when students are assisted to become self-regulated learners, aware of their individual differences in learning and masters of their own learning processes (Schunk & Zimmerman, 2012; Zimmerman, 1990). However, a concern in flipped classroom research is that students may not always regulate themselves well, particularly in pre-class learning activities. Researchers thus highlight the potential of self-regulation theory for guiding the design of learning environments to better prepare students for flipped learning activities in and out of class (Lai & Hwang, 2016). This kind of instructional support and assistance for students typically focuses on students setting their own goals, monitoring their own learning progress, adjusting their own learning behaviors, and assessing their own performance. For instance, Shyr and Chen (2018) applied this theory to develop a self-regulated learning system for use in an inverted classroom with undergraduate non-English majors. The system contained a set of theory-driven scaffolds or prompts, such as goal-setting and self-monitoring, which were designed to facilitate students' self-regulation throughout the flipped learning process. Findings from the study showed that flipping the English classroom with the aid of the self-regulated learning system significantly enhanced the students' self-regulation, which later contributed to their language learning performance.

Sociocultural theory is rooted in the work of L. S. Vygotsky and aims to make us understand how a child's mental functions are shaped by the broader social and cultural contexts. In the words of Vygotsky (1978, p. 57), "every function in the child's cultural development appears twice: first, on the social level, and later, on the individual level." The concept of social origin is considered a cornerstone of sociocultural theory and has been used to explain the significance of social interaction in L2 acquisition (Lantolf, 2000). As applied to flipped language classrooms, this theoretical understanding prompts L2 researchers to maximize interaction opportunities in their interventions. A paradigmatic study (Yang, Yin, & Wang, 2018) of this kind of application examined students' flipped learning of Chinese as a foreign language at a university in the United States. For out-of-class learning activities, the students were given opportunities to interact (1) with their peers, via asynchronous text-based discussions, using a course management system and (2) with the instructor, via synchronous oral communication, using a mobile messaging app. In-class learning activities were mostly collaborative, designed to help the students practice the four skills (reading, writing, listening, and speaking) in problem-solving tasks. Results of this study revealed that those who learned with the flipped classroom approach significantly outperformed those who learned with the lecture-and-drill approach, particularly in speaking (out of the four skills), largely because there were more social and meaningful interactions in the flipped language classroom.

Each of the aforementioned studies draws on a certain theory of learning to set grounds for flipped language classrooms, reflecting researchers' varying assumptions about learning and thus their approaches to instructional design. Indeed, there are a variety of theoretical contexts in which flipped classrooms may operate, and most researchers designed their interventions on the basis of general learning theories (e.g. cognitive load theory, self-regulation theory, and sociocultural theory). According to the recent review of flipped language classrooms by Jiang et al. (2020), very few studies in the existing literature incorporate theories of L2 acquisition. Further studies are therefore necessary to strengthen the connection between flipped classrooms and language education by adopting domain-specific theories of learning. Doing so can enhance the robustness of design and better capture the distinct nature of L2 learning in the context of flipped classrooms.

Recommendations for Research and Practice

Guidelines for Designing Flipped Classrooms

When flipping the classroom for student-centered learning, the broadly defined approach is often simplistically interpreted as doing "homework at school" and "schoolwork at home." However, it is important to note that merely exchanging what is done in class with what is done out of class cannot guarantee the desired learning outcomes. Research has shown that, when design is not considered properly, students may encounter various challenges or difficulties while they learn in the flipped classroom. A few examples of such difficulties are being resistant to the unfamiliar structure of flipped learning (Herreid & Schiller, 2013), feeling stressed with the pre-class preparation (Wang, 2016), and lacking self-regulated learning skills without guidance (Shyr & Chen, 2018). In light of the potential challenges, Bergmann and Sams (2014) as well as other researchers (e.g., Hwang, Lai, & Wang, 2015; Shahnama et al., 2021; Zou et al., 2020) have pointed out that effective flipped classrooms require thoughtful attention to student-centered instructional design, because the aim is to maximize student–student, student–teacher, and student–content interactions. Table 7.2 outlines some of the prominent design frameworks of flipped classrooms, highlighting their respective design principles or practical recommendations.

Among various expert opinions on how best to flip, the design framework proposed by the Flipped Learning Network (2014), namely the pillars of F-L-I-P^{TM}, is perhaps the earliest and the most commonly known in the literature. This design framework specifies four essential elements that contribute to successful flipped classrooms, namely (1) flexible environments – the time and space or context in which learning takes place flexibly; (2) learning culture – the ways of knowing, thinking, and doing among active learners; (3) intentional content – the materials that are intentionally designed to enable active learning activities; and (4) professional educators – the role of the teacher in fostering meaningful connections between the learner, the content, and the context. On the basis of these four pillars or elements, the Flipped Learning Network (2014) further provides a checklist of eleven design principles that teachers must incorporate into their practice of flipped classrooms.

Table 7.2 *Major design frameworks and principles for flipping the classroom*

Design frameworks	Design principles
The four pillars of F-L-I-P™ (Flipped Learning Network, 2014)	*Flexible environment:* 1. I establish spaces and timeframes that permit students to interact and reflect on their learning as needed. 2. I continually observe and monitor students to make adjustments as appropriate. 3. I provide students with different ways to learn content and demonstrate mastery. *Learning culture:* 4. I give students opportunities to engage in meaningful activities without the teacher being central. 5. I scaffold these activities and make them accessible to all students through differentiation and feedback. *Intentional content:* 6. I prioritize concepts used in direct instruction for learners to access on their own. 7. I create and/or curate relevant content (typically videos) for my students. 8. I differentiate to make content accessible and relevant to all students. *Professional educator:* 9. I make myself available to all students for individual, small group, and class feedback in real time as needed. 10. I conduct ongoing formative assessments during class time, through observation and by recording data, to inform future instruction. 11. I collaborate and reflect with other educators and take responsibility for transforming my practice.
The revised community of inquiry framework (Shea et al., 2012, as cited in Kim et al., 2014)	*Teaching presence:* 1. Provide an incentive for students to prepare for class. 2. Provide a mechanism to assess student understanding. 3. Provide prompt/adaptive feedback on individual or group works. *Learner presence:* 4. Provide enough time for students to carry out the assignments. *Social Presence:* 5. Provide facilitation for building a learning community. 6. Provide technologies that are familiar and easy to access. *Cognitive presence:* 7. Provide an opportunity for students to gain first exposure prior to class. 8. Provide clear connections between in-class and out-of-class activities. 9. Provide clearly defined and well-structured guidance.
The six pillars of educational technology (Spector, 2015, as cited in Lo, 2018)	*Communication:* 1. Introduce the flipped classroom approach to students and obtain parental consent. 2. Use cognitive theory of multimedia learning to inform the production of instructional videos. *Interaction:* 3. Create a discussion forum for online interactions. 4. Provide online quizzes on video lectures with computerized feedback. *Environment:* 5. Provide human and technical resources to support flipped classroom practices. 6. Adopt a school-/faculty-wide approach to flipped classroom practices. *Culture:* 7. Cultivate a classroom culture for learner-centered instruction. *Instruction:* 8 Use established models as the framework for flipped classroom design. *Learning:* 9. Provide optimally challenging learning tasks, with the instructor's guidance. 10. Use peer-assisted learning approaches during class meetings.

In a highly cited article, Kim et al. (2014) adopted the revised community of inquiry framework (Shea et al., 2012) to examine multidisciplinary applications of the flipped classroom approach in higher education. This framework consists of four elements that can inform the instructional design of flipped classrooms: (1) cognitive presence – the knowledge building and thinking; (2) social presence – the encouraging settings for discourses; (3) teaching presence – the instructional orchestration of activities or tasks; and (4) learner presence – the self-regulated and co-regulated strategies for learning. The findings obtained from the three theory-driven flipped classrooms in different disciplines – engineering, social studies, and humanities – have been used to guide the elaboration of nine evidence-based design principles, which are considered to be applicable to typical undergraduate courses.

In a recent research synthesis, Lo (2018) attempted to ground the instructional design of flipped classrooms in Spector's (2015) framework of educational technology in order to generate a systematic set of design principles. This framework comprises six pillars, and each is defined as follows:

> (1) Communication – the way information is represented, transmitted, received, and processed, (2) Interaction – the human–human and human–computer interactions in supporting learning, (3) Environment – the context where learning and instruction take place, (4) Culture – the varied sets of norms and practices of different communities, (5) Instruction – the process of facilitating learning and performance, and (6) Learning – the stable and persisting changes in students' knowledge, skills, attitudes, and/or beliefs.
>
> *(Lo, 2018, p. 798)*

Based on the literature review results of forty-nine empirical studies, Lo then proposed ten recommendations or design principles for flipping the classroom in K–12 and higher education.

The sets of design principles shown in Table 7.2, while drawing on different frameworks – namely the four pillars of F-L-I-P^{TM}, the revised community of inquiry framework, and the six pillars of educational technology – are all meant to offer a general guide to the implementation of flipped classrooms in education. They can be adopted or adapted to meet the needs of students and other stakeholders.

A crucial observation from the design considerations discussed here is that they are not specific to certain disciplines and do not specify technologies. Therefore, when applying a particular framework or a specific set of principles to guide the instructional design of flipped classrooms, it is important to provide precise descriptions of how exactly the selected design considerations are realized in a local context. For instance, Hung (2017) employed the four pillars of F-L-I-P^{TM} as a design framework to flip an English course for L2 students in a two-group quasi-experimental study. The adopted framework was thus appropriated into a flexible language learning environment (the F pillar), a language learning culture (the L pillar), intentional linguistic content (the I pillar), with professional language educator (the P pillar).

Taking the P pillar as an example, it was further specified that the teacher adopted two different strategies of peer instruction and just-in-time teaching for the experimental and control groups respectively, so as to facilitate different ways of using a student response system – Kahoot! – for flipped English learning.

As Bergmann and Sams (2014) put it, "[e]ach teacher can personalize their version of flipped learning for their students" (p. 7). While there are virtually limitless design possibilities for flipped classrooms, articulating the instructional design is necessary to help disseminate the practice in a meaningful and useful way. The aforementioned design frameworks and principles may provide a jumping-off point for interested practitioners. One fruitful direction for future practice is for educators to incorporate additional strategies for active student learning in order to meet the curricular objectives within the broader pedagogical context of flipped classrooms. A wide array of active learning strategies are currently available for exploration. Examples include inquiry-based learning, task-based learning, problem-based learning, project-based learning, self-directed learning, and game-based learning. Incorporating such strategies is a worthy attempt to design and develop flipped classroom enhancements that are believed to be more conducive to active and meaningful learning.

Future Directions

Flipped learning is both simple and complex. It appears simple in that flipped classrooms are essentially learning environments that blend face-to-face learning experiences inside the classroom with learning experiences beyond the classroom (Wang, Han, & Yang, 2015). There is, however, still considerable complexity in its design and implementation. As a flexibly defined pedagogical approach, flipped learning can be compatible and integrated with various learning theories, instructional strategies, and educational technologies in diverse ways. The broad conceptualization of this approach allows for innovations, but at the same time necessitates making the exact design of any flipped classrooms and its theoretical underpinnings explicit and contextualized.

Aiming to help advance the research and practice of flipped classrooms in language education, this chapter has identified major research trends, introduced relevant learning theories, and described common design frameworks that are based on the current flipped learning literature. As the research interest and competitive advantages of this approach are expected to grow over the next few years, more theory-driven investigations based on domain-specific theories of L2 learning, along with the integrated use of interactive technologies and active learning strategies, are warranted to strengthen the design of flipped classrooms and make them student-centered, interaction-rich, and innovatively blended.

References

Abeysekera, L., & Dawson, P. (2015). Motivation and cognitive load in the flipped classroom: Definition, rationale and a call for research. *Higher Education Research & Development, 34*(1), 1–14. https://doi.org/10.1080/07294360.2014.934336

Aidinopoulou, V., & Sampson, D. G. (2017). An action research study from implementing the flipped classroom model in primary school history teaching and learning. *Educational Technology & Society 20*(1), 237–247. www.jstor.org/stable/jeductechsoci.20.1.237

Akçayır, G., & Akçayır, M. (2018). The flipped classroom: A review of its advantages and challenges. *Computers & Education, 126*, 334–345. https://doi.org/10.1016/j.compedu.2018.07.021

Al-Samarraie, H., Shamsuddin, A., & Alzahrani, A. I. (2020). A flipped classroom model in higher education: A review of the evidence across disciplines. *Educational Technology Research and Development, 68*(3), 1017–1051. https://doi.org/10.1007/s11423-019-09718-8

Amiryousefi, M. (2019). The incorporation of flipped learning into conventional classes to enhance EFL learners' L2 speaking, L2 listening, and engagement. *Innovation in Language Learning and Teaching, 13*(2), 147–161. https://doi.org/10.1080/17501229.2017.1394307

Awidi, I. T., & Paynter, M. (2019). The impact of a flipped classroom approach on student learning experience. *Computers & Education, 128*, 269–283. https://doi.org/10.1016/j.compedu.2018.09.013

Baker, J. W. (2000). The "classroom flip": Using web course management tools to become the guide by the side. In J. A. Chambers (Ed.), *Selected papers from the 11th International Conference on College Teaching and Learning* (pp. 9–17). Florida Community College at Jacksonville.

Bergmann, J., & Sams, A. (2012). *Flip your classroom: Reach every student in every class every day*. International Society for Technology in Education.

Bergmann, J., & Sams, A. (2014). *Flipped learning: Gateway to student engagement*. International Society for Technology in Education.

Chen Hsieh, J. S., Huang, Y. M., & Wu, W. C. V. (2017). Technological acceptance of LINE in flipped EFL oral training. *Computers in Human Behavior, 70*, 178–190. https://doi.org/10.1016/j.chb.2016.12.066

Clark, R. C., Nguyen, F., & Sweller, J. (2006). *Efficiency in learning: Evidence-based guidelines to manage cognitive load*. John Wiley & Sons.

Ekmekci, E. (2017). The flipped writing classroom in Turkish EFL context: A comparative study on a new model. *Turkish Online Journal of Distance Education, 18*(2), 151–167. https://doi.org/10.17718/tojde.306566

Estriegana, R., Medina-Merodio, J. A., & Barchino, R. (2019). Analysis of competence acquisition in a flipped classroom approach. *Computer Applications in Engineering Education, 27*(1), 49–64. https://doi.org/10.1002/cae.22056

Flipped Learning Network. (2014). What is flipped learning? http://flippedlearning.org/cms/lib07/VA01923112/Centricity/Domain/46/FLIP_handout_FNL_Web.pdf

González-Gómez, D., Jeong, J. S., & Rodríguez, D. A., & Cañada-Cañada, F. (2016). Performance and perception in the flipped learning model: An initial approach to evaluate the effectiveness of a new teaching methodology in a general science classroom. *Journal of Science Education and Technology, 25*(3), 450–459. https://doi.org/10.1007/s10956-016-9605-9

Herreid, C. F., & Schiller, N. A. (2013). Case studies and the flipped classroom. *Journal of College Science Teaching, 42*(5), 62–66. www.jstor.org/stable/43631584

Huang, Y. N., & Hong, Z. R. (2016). The effects of a flipped English classroom intervention on students' information and communication technology and English reading comprehension. *Educational Technology Research and Development, 64*(2), 175–193. https://doi.org/10.1007/s11423-015-9412-7

Hung, C. Y., Sun, J. C. Y., & Liu, J. Y. (2019). Effects of flipped classrooms integrated with MOOCs and game-based learning on the learning motivation and outcomes of students from different backgrounds. *Interactive Learning Environments, 27*(8), 1028–1046. https://doi.org/10.1080/10494820.2018.1481103

Hung, H. T. (2017). The integration of a student response system in flipped classrooms. *Language Learning & Technology, 21*(1), 16–27. https://dx.doi.org/10125/44593

Hwang, G. J., Lai, C. L., & Wang, S. Y. (2015). Seamless flipped learning: A mobile technology-enhanced flipped classroom with effective learning strategies. *Journal of Computers in Education, 2*(4), 449–473. https://doi.org/10.1007/s40692-015-0043-0

Jiang, M. Y. C., Jong, M. S. Y., Lau, W. W. F., Chai, C. S., Liu, K. S. X., & Park, M. (2020). A scoping review on flipped classroom approach in language education: Challenges, implications and an interaction model. *Computer Assisted Language Learning, 35*(5–6), 1218–1249. https://doi.org/10.1080/09588221.2020.1789171

Kim, M. K., Kim, S. M., Khera, O., & Getman, J. (2014). The experience of three flipped classrooms in an urban university: An exploration of design principles. *The Internet and Higher Education, 22*, 37–50. https://doi.org/10.1016/j.iheduc.2014.04.003

Lage, M. J., Platt, G. J., & Treglia, M. (2000). Inverting the classroom: A gateway to creating an inclusive learning environment. *The Journal of Economic Education, 31*(1), 30–43. https://doi.org/10.2307/1183338

Lai, C. L., & Hwang, G. J. (2016). A self-regulated flipped classroom approach to improving students' learning performance in a mathematics course. *Computers & Education, 100*, 126–140. https://doi.org/10.1016/j.compedu.2016.05.006

Lantolf, J. P. (Ed.). (2000). *Sociocultural theory and second language learning*. Oxford University Press.

Lo, C. K. (2018). Grounding the flipped classroom approach in the foundations of educational technology. *Educational Technology Research and Development, 66*(3), 793–811. https://doi.org/10.1007/s11423-018-9578-x

O'Flaherty, J., & Phillips, C. (2015). The use of flipped classrooms in higher education: A scoping review. *The Internet and Higher Education, 25*, 85–95. https://doi.org/10.1016/j.iheduc.2015.02.002

Schunk, D. H., & Zimmerman, B. J. (Eds.). (2012). *Motivation and self-regulated learning: Theory, research, and applications*. Routledge. https://doi.org/10.4324/9780203831076

Shahnama, M., Ghonsooly, B., & Shirvan, M. E. (2021). A meta-analysis of relative effectiveness of flipped learning in English as second/foreign language research. *Educational Technology Research and Development, 69*(3), 1355–1386. https://doi.org/10.1007/s11423-021-09996-1

Shea, P., Hayes, S., Smith, S. U., Vickers, J., Bidjerano, T., Pickett, A., Gozza-Cohen, M., Wilde, J., & Jian, S. (2012). Learning presence: Additional research on a new conceptual element within the Community of Inquiry (CoI) framework. *The Internet and Higher Education, 15*(2), 89–95. https://doi.org/10.1016/j.iheduc.2011.08.002

Shyr, W. J., & Chen, C. H. (2018). Designing a technology-enhanced flipped learning system to facilitate students' self-regulation and performance. *Journal of Computer Assisted Learning, 34*(1), 53–62. https://doi.org/10.1111/jcal.12213

Spector, J. M. (2015). *Foundations of educational technology: Integrative approaches and interdisciplinary perspectives* (2nd ed.). Routledge. https://doi.org/10.4324/9781315764269

Sweller, J. (1994). Cognitive load theory, learning difficulty, and instructional design. *Learning and Instruction, 4*(4), 295–312. https://doi.org/10.1016/0959-4752(94)90003-5

Tonkin, K., Page, S., & Forsey, M. (2019). Managing cognitive load with a flipped language class: An ethnographic study of the student experience. *Foreign Language Annals, 52*(3), 551–575. https://doi.org/10.1111/flan.12412

Turan, Z., & Akdag-Cimen, B. (2020). Flipped classroom in English language teaching: A systematic review. *Computer Assisted Language Learning, 33*(5–6), 590–606. https://doi.org/10.1080/09588221.2019.1584117

Vygotsky, L. S. (1978). *Mind in society: Development of higher psychological processes*. Harvard University Press. https://doi.org/10.2307/j.ctvjf9vz4

Wang, Y. H. (2016). Could a mobile-assisted learning system support flipped classrooms for classical Chinese learning? *Journal of Computer Assisted Learning, 32*(5), 391–415. https://doi.org/10.1111/jcal.12141

Wang, Y., Han, X., & Yang, J. (2015). Revisiting the blended learning literature: Using a complex adaptive systems framework. *Educational Technology & Society, 18*(2), 380–393. www.jstor.org/stable/jeductechsoci.18.2.380

Wu, W. C. V., Hsieh, J. S. C., & Yang, J. C. (2017). Creating an online learning community in a flipped classroom to enhance EFL learners' oral proficiency. *Educational Technology & Society, 20*(2), 142–157. www.jstor.org/stable/90002170

Yang, J., Yin, C. X., & Wang, W. (2018). Flipping the classroom in teaching Chinese as a foreign language. *Language Learning & Technology, 22*(1), 16–26. https://doi.org/10125/44575

Zainuddin, Z., & Perera, C. J. (2019). Exploring students' competence, autonomy and relatedness in the flipped classroom pedagogical model. *Journal of Further and Higher Education, 43*(1), 115–126. https://doi.org/10.1080/0309877X.2017.1356916

Zimmerman, B. J. (1986). Becoming a self-regulated learner: Which are the key subprocesses? *Contemporary Educational Psychology*, *11*(4), 307–313. https://doi.org/10.1016/0361-476X(86)90027-5

Zimmerman, B. J. (1990). Self-regulated learning and academic achievement: An overview. *Educational Psychologist*, *25*(1), 3–17. https://doi.org/10.1207/s15326985ep2501_2

Zou, D., Luo, S., Xie, H., & Hwang, G. J. (2020). A systematic review of research on flipped language classrooms: Theoretical foundations, learning activities, tools, research topics and findings. *Computer Assisted Language Learning*, *35* (8), 1811–1837. https://doi.org/10.1080/09588221.2020.1839502

Further Reading

Mehring, J., & Leis, A. (Eds.). (2018). *Innovations in flipping the language classroom: Theories and practices.* Springer Nature Singapore. https://doi.org/10.1007/978-981-10-6968-0

This book aims to provide a practical guide for teachers who are learning how to flip a language course. It begins with the fundamental principles of the flipped classroom approach, followed by descriptions of successful applications from practitioners in the field. Exemplars are broadly organized by skills-based courses and content-based courses, in which lesson objectives, learning activities, technology use, student outcomes, and possible challenges are discussed to demonstrate the procedures, benefits, and limitations of flipping the language classroom.

Shahnama, M., Ghonsooly, B., & Shirvan, M. E. (2021). A meta-analysis of relative effectiveness of flipped learning in English as second/foreign language research. *Educational Technology Research and Development*, *69*, 1355–1386. https://doi.org/10.1007/s11423-021-09996-1

This review sets out to examine the overall effectiveness of flipped learning research in the field of English as a second/foreign language (ESL/EFL). A meta-analysis method was employed to systemically analyze sixty-nine empirical studies published between 2004 and 2019. The results revealed a large and positive effect of flipped learning on students' language learning achievements by comparison with lecture-based instruction.

Vitta, J. P., & Al-Hoorie, A. H. (2020). The flipped classroom in second language learning: A meta-analysis. *Language Teaching Research*. https://doi.org/10.1177/1362168820981403

This article is a systematic review adopting a meta-analysis method to synthesize L2 flipped learning interventions. A total of fifty-six research reports were included in this review. The results demonstrated a positive effect of the flipped learning approach over traditional lecture-based approach and identified several significant moderators, such as L2 proficiency levels and learning outcomes.

8

CALL in Low-Tech Environments

Francisca M. Ivone and Thomas N. Robb

Introduction

Seamless integration of the most advanced information and communication technology (ICT) into language teaching and learning is the ultimate condition most language teachers and learners long for. In reality, however, many have to be content with whatever is available in their learning environment – at school, at home, and in other places of learning. At school, technology use in language classes is determined by the facilities available in education institutions, by school policy, and by the technologies that teachers and students bring to class. For instance, not all classrooms in developing countries are provided with computers, so teachers or students must bring their own gadgets. "Bring your own device" (BYOD) is a term used to describe this situation. Another everyday circumstance is that liquid-crystal display (LCD) projectors are not always available in every classroom, so teachers need to plan their teaching scenarios and book appropriate devices early. Furthermore, a reliable internet connection is a luxury in many schools around the world.

In many countries, school policy often bans the use of mobile phones in class. In classes where learners can use mobile phones, incompatibility issues, limited memory, and misuse of technology often make language teachers reluctant to incorporate this type of technology into their language classrooms. Outside class, the technology used in blended and online language learning or self-study relies on ownership of and access to ICT devices, availability of a reliable internet connection, and adequate ICT knowledge and skill. But disparities in all these aspects exist among students and teachers and have to be addressed shrewdly.

Inside as well as outside language classrooms, the digital divide still exists. "The concept of digital divide is elaborated on the basis of the layers of technology adoption such as 'access,' 'effective use' and 'the social envelope' around children's use of home computers" (Talaee & Noroozi, 2019, p. 27). Many may argue that in the twenty-first century the digital divide is no longer just about inequality in terms of access to ICT, as mobile phone ownership in January 2021 was 5.22 billion or 66.6 percent of the world population (Kemp, 2021), and 60 percent of the world is connected over the internet. However, gaps between poorer and richer countries continue to exist, as well as discrepancies within countries. At the end of the first quarter of 2020 and throughout the year, we still see many stories that highlight issues related to digital inequalities (visit, e.g., Chen, 2020; Lee & Yeo, 2020; Wonders of the World, 2020).

The September 5, 2020 issue of the *New York Times* carried an article titled "When learning is really remote: Students climb trees and travel miles for a cell signal"; it concerned Indonesian students who had to sit on the side of a mountain road in a slight drizzle in order to catch a signal to participate in the school class. This is not a unique situation but one that is endemic in developing countries globally. While major cities may have reasonable connectivity, students in remote areas tend to have none at all. Kenalan, the place discussed in the *New York Times* article, is only 35 km away from Yogyakarta, a major population area.

Simple mobile phones (sometimes known as "feature phones"), by far the most ubiquitous piece of technology in a home, often limit the kind of activities teachers and students can do (UNICEF Regional Office for South Asia, 2020). Despite all the limitations and problems, mobile phones hold considerable learning potential, since they have by far the widest range and constitute sometimes the only method to reach underprivileged learners. Khan et al. (2021) provide survey findings from research that involves teachers and students at public universities in Bangladesh. These findings reveal that the majority of teachers and students used cellphones to attend online classes, while just one fourth of the students had laptops. Furthermore, while the majority of teachers and students had internet access, their internet speed was average to poor, and many students could not afford sufficient internet data bandwidth to attend online classes.

With little broadband connectivity, developing countries are uniquely dependent on wireless networks. Yet, even here, there are barriers, both in cost and availability. Data from 2020 (Table 8.1) on the cost of 10GB of access vary considerably from country to country.

Furthermore, developing countries are much more reliant on wireless connections, having leapfrogged past fixed-line technology, according to UNCTAD (2018) (Table 8.2).

Particularly given the shifting emphasis on online versus in-person or face-to-face study, students need not only "connectivity" but connectivity at a reasonable price. Many applications that seem useful to language education require considerable bandwidth. Zoom, a video conference application, for example, requires approximately 1GB per hour. Standard-definition (SD) quality video uses 0.7GB per hour, while high-definition (HD) video requires between 0.9GB and 3GB. A Canadian provider, WhistleOut (2020), reports: "Video requires a lot more data than music streaming – watching 1080p video

Table 8.1 Cost of 10GB per month as a percentage of wages

Cost for 10GB/month – least expensive top 20

	Country	Avg monthly wage 2020 (USD)	Cost of 10GB/month (USD)	% of monthly avg wage
1	Luxembourg	4,000.000	0.87	0.02
2	Israel	2,585.620	0.65	0.02
3	Netherlands	3,024.070	0.87	0.03
4	Finland	2,921.470	0.87	0.03
5	Ireland	2,917.370	0.87	0.03
6	Germany	2,915.830	0.87	0.03
7	Austria	2,496.300	0.87	0.03
8	Belgium	2,461.010	0.87	0.04
9	France	2,458.140	0.87	0.04
10	Poland	878.780	0.32	0.04
11	Puerto Rico	4,568.000	1.82	0.04
12	Iceland	3,008.430	1.39	0.05
13	India	448.240	0.21	0.05
14	Azerbaijan	308.730	0.15	0.05
15	Sweden	3,023.860	1.49	0.05
16	Italy	1,737.310	0.87	0.05
17	United States	3,525.290	1.82	0.05
18	Denmark	3,718.150	2.02	0.05
19	Spain	1,594.350	0.87	0.05
20	Cyprus	1,406.170	0.87	0.06

Cost for 10GB/month – most expensive top 20

	Country	Avg monthly wage 2020 (USD)	Cost of 10GB/month (USD)	% of avg monthly wage
73	Tajikistan	129.626	9.74	7.52
72	Jamaica	665.290	29.40	4.42
71	Panama	753.550	26.75	3.55
70	Philippines	311.420	9.48	3.04
69	Guatemala	462.390	13.02	2.82
68	Peru	421.670	9.91	2.35
67	Costa Rica	807.590	17.35	2.15
66	Albania	410.660	8.69	2.12
65	Mexico	501.770	10.01	1.99
64	Armenia	347.550	4.98	1.43
63	Bulgaria	625.270	5.65	0.90
62	Moldova	350.090	2.74	0.78
61	Bosnia & Herz.	600.620	4.69	0.78
60	Georgia	303.490	2.37	0.78
59	Dominican Rep	343.940	2.66	0.77
58	Ukraine	351.250	2.47	0.70
57	Canada	2,581.490	17.80	0.69
56	Czech Rep	1,246.860	8.30	0.67
55	Brazil	352.820	2.32	0.66
54	El Salvador	380.530	1.82	0.48

Table 8.2 *Ratio of wired to wireless connectivity in the twenty top- and bottom-ranking countries*

Rank	Country	Wired/wireless	Rank	Country	Wired/wireless
165	D.R. Congo	0.00	1	Monaco	583.95
164	Guinea-Bissau	0.39	2	Canada	442.49
163	Nigeria	0.53	3	Andorra	426.71
162	Burundi	0.73	4	Gibraltar	423.34
161	Afghanistan	0.74	5	France	411.92
160	Burkina Faso	0.75	6	Norway	373.05
159	Niger	0.98	7	Belgium	366.08
158	Sudan	1.13	8	Denmark	354.70
157	Malawi	1.20	9	Netherlands	351.23
156	Ghana	1.57	10	Bermuda	350.92
155	Kiribati	1.77	11	Switzerland	340.94
154	Lesotho	2.06	12	South Korea	333.01
153	Timor-Leste	2.18	13	San Marino	329.00
152	Cameroon	2.20	14	United Kingdom	328.60
151	Rwanda	2.49	15	Iceland	325.26
150	Solomon Island5	2.50	16	Malta	323.82
149	Zambia	2.67	17	Germany	313.35
148	Madagascar	2.93	18	Portugal	303.80
147	Mauritania	3.15	19	Sweden	300.45
146	Benin	3.31	20	Greece	292.07

Source: UNCTAD (2018).

on your cell phone for just an hour each day can burn through a 10GB data plan in under a month!"

In addition to access to appropriate technology and dependable connectivity, technology literacy is another area of inequality that language teachers and learners are currently coping with. Although most language learners studying at the primary, secondary, and tertiary levels today are classified as digital natives, they rarely use ICT for language learning purposes. An editorial in *Nature* bluntly states: "Many members of the digital-savvy generation use technology in the same way as many of their elders: to passively soak up information" (Nature Editorial, 2017).

Consequently this area needs support from teachers, parents, and other knowledgeable people around language learners.

Fortunately ICT use is not the sole determinant of language learning success. How the technology is used is more important than the type of technology in language learning. Therefore we often witness language teachers and learners surviving and succeeding in language learning with limited or even no technology.

Background

What constitutes low technology changes constantly, depending on era and context. There are terms such as "plugged" and "unplugged," which are used to refer respectively to "high-tech" and "low-tech" (or "no-tech"). When no electricity is required to operate a technology, the latter is classified as low-tech or no-tech; so high-tech is any equipment that needs electricity. Terms such as "high-tech" – as opposed to traditional technology – are also frequently used in the language teaching context. In reality, both kinds of technology are used in today's language classrooms. However, teachers in a low-tech environment more often opt for no technology or traditional technology (printed books, printed worksheets, printed cards, board games, etc.) and for low-tech (downloadable e-books, LCD projector, text messaging apps, etc.) rather than high-tech (interactive e-book, collaborative apps, virtual/augmented reality, etc.).

Technology in the twenty-first century refers predominantly to ICT. So low-tech is any kind of ICT that requires:

1. Low or no internet bandwidth, so that it can be used online as well as offline
2. Low immediacy, so that communication can be delayed instead of conducted in real time
3. Common software and applications that can be installed on a device, used without an internet connection, and operated from any device such as a desktop computer, a laptop, a tablet, and a smartphone.

What needs to be highlighted here is that in the twenty-first-century low-tech learning environment, language teaching and learning practices are subject to internet connectivity. Low-tech ICT that does not need an internet connection includes technology such as television and radio, either analog or digital. Nowadays the two also have their online versions, which are becoming increasingly popular. According to recent research by the UNESCO Institute of Statistics (UIS) and the Teacher Task Force, 826 million kids (50 percent) have no access to a computer at home, around 706 million students do not have access to the internet, and 56 million reside in locations where mobile networks are not available (UNESCO, 2020). In these places, television and radio have been shown to be a viable alternative to online learning.

Technology affordance, defined by Hutchby (2001) as "an activity that can be accomplished with a specific technology," is another key consideration in the use of low-tech in language teaching and learning, in addition to access and connectivity. According to Compton (2009), language teachers must know how to use technology and comprehend its specific affordances and limits. The phrase "technology affordance" is also used to describe the limitations of technology and how it is used. For example, a word processor is software that may be used for various purposes such as typing, creating tables and charts, displaying images, and many more – but it cannot be used to conduct a video call. Video conference and chat apps such as Zoom and WhatsApp, on the other hand, can be used to perform video and voice calls and text chats over an internet connection. Because each technology has its unique set of capabilities, knowing what tasks or actions it permits language teachers to perform can aid them in creating language learning activities that are both pedagogically sound and technologically feasible. What needs to be underlined is that technology integration should not be technology driven, but understanding what technology allows teachers and learners to accomplish can help them integrate it more easily into the language learning process.

When technology is used in the language classroom, either online or face to face, teachers need to make sure that no one is excluded, so selection needs to be well thought out. A needs analysis can be conducted at the start of a semester in order to gather data regarding ownership and access to ICT devices, internet connectivity, and technology literacy. For instance, every student in a class may have a mobile phone and can bring it to class, but their phones run on various operating systems, such as Android, IOS, Windows, Linux, and so on. Language teachers need to make sure that their choice of application is available in all these operating systems. Otherwise they have to make sure that comparable applications exist across operating systems that students can use for the same purpose. When this is not feasible, learners could share gadgets, so that everyone has equal access to the same application. In this case, websites are more versatile than mobile apps because they are accessible from any web browser on desktops, laptops, tablets, and smartphones. But they may be more costly as a result of internet connectivity. In a low-tech environment, language teachers will frequently face this problem and make calculated decisions in everyone's best interest.

Language teachers can be creative and flexible in their use of technology, in both face-to-face and remote language learning. For instance, instead of projecting a video onto a classroom wall using an LCD projector, teachers in low- or no-tech environments often use puppets and their own voices to tell stories in the classroom. In remote, blended, and online language learning contexts, however, the enticement of high-tech and reliance on its use are a lot bigger and inevitable. So language teachers use virtual whiteboards and video conference apps (high-tech) or send slideshow presentations or lecture videos (low-tech) instead of using LCD projectors. Those in low-tech environments, however, will need to consider the types of technology to use to enhance learning rather than making it more taxing and stressful, because using high-tech in a low-tech environment may create problems such as failure to connect or join a platform, sudden loss of connectivity, choppy audio and video streaming, or delayed synchronization (to name but a few).

Primary Themes

When employing technology in low-tech contexts, language instructors can use a variety of approaches that take into account accessible technologies, internet connectivity, and technology literacy.

Low Bandwidth, Low Immediacy Approach to Technology Use
Three main areas of interest in the use of ICT in language teaching and in learning in general, either face to face or online, are access to language

learning input, opportunities for producing target language input, and facilitation of interaction and feedback. The internet is a copious and wide-ranging source of language input, both oral and written. It allows language teachers and learners to download, real-time stream, and upload text, audio, audiovisual, and multimedia files from websites and mobile applications. It also facilitates synchronous and asynchronous interaction in the form of text, audio, and video chat.

All over the world, language teachers and learners use multiformat input – that is, text, image, audio, audiovisual, and multimedia. Text-only, although inexpensive, is often unappealing to language learners, hence language teachers strive to incorporate multimedia input into their teaching. However, multimedia requires more bandwidth as a result of file size. Comparably, when learners produce the target language output, file size is also of concern, because saving and sending a task or a project in an audiovisual format is more costly, in terms of memory and bandwidth, than saving and sending it in audio or text-only formats.

Similar problems occur when technology is used to mediate communication and interaction among learners, and between learners and teachers. Synchronous video conference platforms such as Zoom, Microsoft Teams, Google Meet, and Skype require hefty bandwidth to stream high-quality videos. A one-to-one video call in a low-resolution setting needs 0.4–0.6 megabits per second (Mbps), while its high-resolution counterpart calls for 1.2–1.5 Mbps (Business Insider South Africa, 2020). The requirement is much higher for group video calls. Without a reliable internet connection, users may experience a connection lag that renders the audio and video choppy or blurry and sometimes causes disconnection. Speedguide.net recommends reserving two Mbps both downstream and upstream for high-definition video, keeping in mind that video conferencing needs much bigger upstream than downstream bandwidth.

On the other hand, a WhatsApp video call designed for low-quality calling requires a minimum bandwidth of 0.064 Mbps (Business Insider South Africa, 2020). It allows up to eight users in one video call, which makes it ideal for pair and group virtual interaction. Thus this app would be a sensible option if we have low bandwidth and limited data. Stanford (2020), an instructional designer, offers a bandwidth immediacy matrix to help teachers recognize their options. Figure 8.1 shows that those in a low-tech teaching and learning environment can make use of the "underappreciated workhorses" of bandwidth and low immediacy tools such as discussion boards with text/images, readings with text/images, and email. Low bandwidth and low immediacy technologies such as collaborative documents and group chat and messaging, which provide a sense of "practical immediacy," are also feasible choices.

ICT provides inexhaustible access to second and foreign language input in the form of text, audio, audiovisual, and other multimedia formats. However, language teachers and learners may have difficulties accessing it when they are in a low-tech environment. Employing a low bandwidth, low immediacy, and common application approach, language teachers often do some of these tricks:

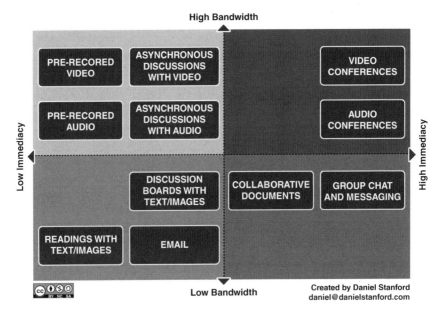

Figure 8.1 Bandwidth Immediacy Matrix (Stanford, 2020).

- They use flash disks to save texts, audios, and videos downloaded from the internet. There are many copyright-free resources on the internet that language teachers and students can use. These files can be distributed to students and used offline. File size can be reduced if the files are sent through emails or chat apps. When they are used in class, they can be projected on a wall using an LCD projector (if available).
- They save websites to access them offline. If a website is saved as a pdf or as an html file, it can be saved to a local hard drive or flash disk for offline use. There are also website and apps downloaders that allow us to download or clone a whole website, with all its links, onto the website for offline use.
- They use Really Simple Syndication (RSS) feeds to get access to content without expensive data usage. Rather than going to individual websites and having to download unnecessary media items, an RSS feed gives us the basic content without some of the overheads. There are a variety of RSS feed readers (e.g., Reeder 5 https://reederapp.com for Mac/iOS users, RSSOwl www.rssowl.org/ for Windows, iOS, and Linux users, and RSS Feed Reader https://feeder.co for Google Chrome users) and different platforms, many of them free. Some of these applications allow us to block media items and only load text content.

When using resources for education purposes, however, language teachers and learners need to be aware that some materials are copyrighted and should be used only under their own country's definition of fair use in education.

Maximizing Technology Affordances

Although the functionality of small mobile devices such as smartphones has increased considerably in recent years, there are still many ways in which they are inferior to desktops or laptops – for many tasks. Moreover, not all mobile phones are smart phones. Some of them are basic low-cost mobile phones that feature tiny low-resolution non-touch screens and make it difficult (if not impossible) to engage and interact with instructional content (UNICEF Regional Office for South Asia, 2020). In most developing countries, internet access is primarily via mobile phones. In Africa, for example, only 7.7 percent of households possess a computer (Alsop, 2021). But even there the percentage is probably highly skewed in favor of wealthier countries such as South Africa and Egypt.

This being the case, when language instructors assign tasks to their students, it is imperative that they ensure that it is technically feasible for students to carry out the tasks without undue frustration.

Some major limitations of small, portable devices are as follows:

- *Small screen size*
  Mobile users will incur a higher interaction cost in order to access the same amount of information and must rely on their short-term memory to refer to information that is not visible on the screen. This increases the cognitive load, leaving less of it available for comprehending and accomplishing the task at hand. Also, though the screen is small, a larger proportion of its space must be used for objects that require touch, since fingers are larger than a mouse pointer; thus further reducing the information available on a single screen (Budiu, 2015).
- *Lack of a keyboard capable of touch-typing*
  Users need to continuously divide their attention between the content they are typing and the keypad area. Touch-typing is impossible in the absence of haptic feedback; plus, keypads themselves are small and keys are crowded.
- *Lack of a coherent directory structure*
  Connectivity issues will prevent the use of cloud storage devices to access needed files.
- *Inability to keep multiple apps open simultaneously*
- *Inability to view multiple app windows simultaneously*
- *Comprehension*
  Readers can understand short, simple text content on mobile devices just as well as on computers, but they slow down when reading difficult text on mobiles (Moran, 2016).

If we are asking students to do work on their mobile phones, or even on a tablet, it is best to require work that can be done within these guidelines:

- The assignment should not require the viewing of large spreadsheets, or graphic data with fine detail.
- The assignment should require little or no copy and paste across different applications.

Table 8.3 *The most popular chat apps in major regions*

App Name	Prevalent in these countries*
Facebook Messenger	United States, Canada, Australia, New Zealand, Norway, Sweden, France, North Africa
WhatsApp	Central & South America, Africa (except N. Africa), Russia & former Soviet regions, Turkey, India, Pakistan, Vietnam, Indonesia, Arabian Peninsula
Line	Japan, Taiwan R.O.C., Thailand
WeChat	China P.R.C.
Telegram	Costa Rica, Nicaragua
KakaoTalk	S. Korea
Zalo	Vietnam

* Data culled from multiple sources. Not all areas included.

- It should use content that is short and of low reading difficulty.
- It should not require access to multiple files.
- It should not require a high volume of text input, unless the student mobiles are equipped with a voice input system.

These restrictions imply no video calls, no use of mobile apps, and no downloading and storing of multiple files when students are using basic mobile phones.

Common Applications Used as Language Learning Tools

Language teachers and learners often use a variety of commonplace applications that help students learn a language. These applications may, however, vary by region. Because language learners have access to these everyday apps and understand how to use them, language teachers in low-tech environments often use them for language learning.

Common Applications for Communication and Collaboration

WhatsApp

According to an article in *Business of Apps* (Bucher, 2020), WhatsApp is the number one messaging application; it has more than 2 billion users around the world, while other, similar apps are more popular in specific regions – for example WeChat in mainland China, or LINE in Japan and Taiwan. For many English teachers, these chat apps have become the "go to" application for both communication and instruction. Table 8.3 lists the most popular apps by country.

While WhatsApp is clearly a valuable tool for language education, particularly in under-resourced areas, it is limited in its pedagogical functions by comparison with high-bandwidth applications such as Zoom, which allows considerably more interactivity between teacher and students – and also among the students, in group-based activities. Nevertheless, there are countries, Indonesia being a case in point, where WhatsApp is used not only for teacher–student communication but for the provision of study material, assignment submission, and evaluation.

If WhatsApp becomes the only means of communication for the teacher, then it must function in all aspects of normal teaching. Turkan, Timpe-Laughlin, and Papageorgiou (2017) list these categories of teacher tasks:

1. planning, developing, and organizing instruction,
2. presenting subject material and communicating lesson content,
3. managing classroom activity,
4. assessing student learning, and
5. providing feedback.

Considering these tasks in relation to WhatsApp, we can say the following:

- *Planning, developing, and organizing instruction.* While these tasks do not directly employ WhatsApp, they will all depend on what is found to be possible using WhatsApp, and most likely will have to be recursively modified, as the instructor gets a better understanding of what works with WhatsApp.
- *Presenting subject material and communicating lesson content.* WhatsApp does allow file downloads, so it is possible for the instructor to present content in that manner, but WhatsApp does not allow the richness of a live – or even video – description, which could make the instructions clearer and further motivate the learners. Furthermore, complex downloads might become a bandwidth issue, both in connection fees and in download speed.
- *Managing classroom activity.* There is little that the instructor can do apart from joining a WhatsApp group as an equal among the students. With multiple groups, supervision would be difficult, so the instructor would normally have to wait for the reports or result from each group and then provide feedback or further guidance.
- *Assessing student learning.* Since information is available only as a flat record of conversations and files, instructors must spend considerably more time on record keeping, and the resulting data are not as complete as when a course management system is available. Furthermore, there will likely be a higher percentage of submissions from peer groups rather than from individuals, so it is not clear who has benefited from the activity and who has merely "gone along for the ride." Issues with tests would be similar to those encountered in "take home exams."
- *Providing feedback.* Possible, but time-consuming.

The benefits of WhatsApp usage are as follows:

- Students are often already familiar with it from social use, which means that little time needs to be given to instructing them in its use. In fact, if it is the only means of communication, the instructor would be powerless to demonstrate its use, but nearby friends may be able to help those who are new to it.
- WhatsApp lowers the affective filters by comparison with face-to-face classwork. This is a benefit with any use of remote technology and has been well documented.

- Tasks can be performed in privacy, free of distraction, asynchronously.
- There is accountability, since all transactions are recorded.
- Usage has brought a reported amelioration of all skills (Hamad, 2017).
- Allows input to be improved until user is satisfied with the product.
- Teachers can provide personal feedback.
- It is possible to have contact with absent students, updating them on assignments.
- Deadline reminders can be sent.
- WhatsApp can be used in combination with polling websites and apps such as https://polls.fr, opinionstate.com, Voliz, and the like for collecting students' answers.

Language learning tasks that can be supported by WhatsApp include:

- group reconstruction or creation of a story
- speech recording activities
- evaluation of peers' recordings or written responses with a provided rubric
- student surveys
- topic selection when each student should have a unique topic; students can see what topics have already been chosen
- picture description, sequence description tasks
- oral presentations

See Haines (2016) for a listing of twenty-five possible tasks.

Some drawbacks to the use of WhatsApp concern technical limitation (such as data storage restrictions and file retrieval inadequacy), data management problems caused by the fact that all chat history is recorded as one thread of conversation, and infringement of personal time of teachers and students as a result of the "anytime access" and "immediate response expectation" of both parties.

An emerging chat application, which offers similar features to those of WhatsApp, with additional functionality that allows teachers to manage and control "conversations," create "channels," and use chatbots, is Telegram Messenger. This application has been gaining popularity in Asia and Middle Eastern countries in the past few years.

Email

To those in low-tech environments, email allows asynchronous communication and collaboration both between teachers and students and among students; however, email will work only if the students check for newly arrived messages frequently. Conflated messages with identical subject lines could make it difficult for students to retrieve specific information at a later date or to review and compare content, since they can often see only one message at a time. Because there is an age requirement (thirteen years old) for creating an email account, parents may need to create an account for their child using a family link.

One of the most significant benefits of using email is that it makes one-to-one, group, within-class, and between-class conversations possible. Language learners and teachers can create email lists for their group or class easily, or use listserv instead. As software that handles email lists and transmits and receives email via the internet, listserv is useful for dealing with a large group of individuals. This form of administration saves time by simplifying the process of sending and receiving messages to groups.

According to Gonglewski, Meloni, and Brant (2001) some of the pedagogical benefits of using emails in language learning are:

- extending language learning time and place
- providing a context for real-world communication and authentic interaction
- expanding topics beyond classroom-based ones
- promoting student-centered language learning
- encouraging equal opportunity participation
- connecting speakers quickly and cheaply.

Moreover, email also

- allows exchanges of short and long texts, links, and multimedia content
- creates interaction in the form of threads, so that users can trace previous interactions easily
- reduces the pressure to provide immediate responses, which are often overwhelming for language learners
- integrates well with cross-platform cloud-based writing assistant applications such as Grammarly, which can help learners refine their spelling, grammar, and punctuation.

Language learning tasks that can be supported by email include:

- task-based, problem-based, and project-based learning conducted collaboratively
- pre-class, post-class, and supplemental activities (Gonglewski et al., 2001)
- individual learning journals and dialogic journals between learners and teachers
- collaborative or individual writing tasks.

More email-based language learning tasks and projects can be found in Gonglewski et al. (2001).

Television and Radio for Language Learning

In some remote areas where the internet is not accessible, language learners make use of television and radio as sources of target language input as well as of language learning instructions. Although television and radio programs broadcast in the target language can provide valuable information for language learners, they may not be appropriate for all levels of competence. Because the grammatical difficulty of the language used in these programs is considerable, advanced learners will undoubtedly profit more than beginners. On the other hand, because the language used is basic and the themes are familiar, lower proficiency-level learners may benefit from watching cartoons for kids. Intermediate-level learners may find subtitles useful in interpreting auditory materials presented on television; nonetheless, subtitles can be incorrect and cause confusion. As a result of the mono modality, radio programs will appeal to advanced learners.

Some countries also offer language instruction programs that are broadcast on national and local television channels at particular times of the day. Despite the fact that they are few in number, they are frequently helpful in providing learners with explanations on grammatical points, vocabulary use, and language skills advice. According to UNESCO (2020), many broadcasters today design their programs to include more interactive elements in order to catch the attention of students, particularly younger ones. As these programs are also intended to serve as a forum for sharing information and experiences, they may include online quizzes and student engagement activities.

Using the radio and television for language learning has significant obstacles, including:

- With radio programs, there is a lack of audiovisual content for language learning.
- Many countries struggle to generate language learning programs in sufficient quantity and of sufficient quality for language learners of various levels of proficiency.
- Learners are left to their own devices because of a lack of learning monitoring and evaluation, as well as a lack of interaction among learners and between learners and teachers.
- Language learning programs are often teacher-centered and use out-of-date methods, such as audio-lingual ones.

Language learning tasks that can be supported by television and radio include:

- listening
- watching while listening
- listening while reading
- watching while listening and reading
- note-taking
- summarizing.

Current Research and Practice

The innovative use of technology in language learning is now dominating research in technology-enhanced language learning (TELL) and mobile-assisted language learning (MALL). This involves applying cutting-edge technology such as artificial intelligence, augmented and virtual reality, and mixed reality. But it also involves the inventive employment of technologies that have been available for a long time, as these are the ones most widely used in many areas of the world.

In low-tech settings, research and practice focus on the applicability of a specific application, such as textual, audio, and video chat apps, and the older texting technology, known as the short message service (SMS), which runs on the GSM/CDMA network, in a specific language learning context for improving language knowledge. Because SMS has a character restriction of 160 characters (including spaces), it is mainly useful for teaching vocabulary and idioms (see, e.g., Hayati, Jalilifar, & Mashhadi, 2013; Kennedy & Levy, 2008). These studies are not current, but they are still relevant as the technology is widely used in low-tech environments.

In the last five years, MALL research on the adoption of chat applications such as WhatsApp, Telegram, and WeChat in language learning has proliferated. Practitioners enthusiastically share what they have learned in their own language classrooms as best practice. Most of these success stories revolve around the use of a single application in a specific language teaching and learning context. For instance, they talk about the effectiveness of using Telegram (Messenger) groups for teaching reading comprehension (Naderi & Akrami, 2018), writing (Aghajani, 2018), and vocabulary (Ashiyan & Salehi, 2016; Kaviani & Mashhadi, 2017). Similar positive effects of the use of WhatsApp and WeChat in teaching language skills and vocabulary can easily be found in many journal articles.

Some studies examine technology affordances and propose possible language learning activities for which a specific technology can be used. For instance, Guo and Wang (2018) explore the affordances of the WeChat-based learning platform, which can potentially be used for teaching translation and all four language skills (listening, reading, speaking, and writing). There are similar studies (Haines, 2016; Hamad, 2017; Zayed, 2016) that explore the potential of WhatsApp for teaching language.

Learners' and teachers' perceptions on the use of technology studies abound. The use of technology in language teaching and learning is typically regarded favorably by students and teachers. For instance, Ali and Bin-Hady (2019) reported that English as a foreign language (EFL) students found that the use of WhatsApp has a positive impact on learning English as a foreign language because it is motivating and reduces anxiety. However, Alshammari, Parkes, and Adlington (2017), who reported similar results, suggested that, to alleviate faculty concerns and to foster greater student autonomy, the use of chat apps must be balanced with rules for students about faculty contact hours and response times.

Studies focusing on the integration of low-tech into specific pedagogy are also emerging. Research on the use of WhatsApp to execute the flipped instruction model of teaching writing, as reported by Arifani et al. (2020), is one example. This type of research saw WhatsApp as a tool that could be used in conjunction with other technologies to achieve specific language teaching goals.

Other research focuses on the use of low-tech in teacher education and preparation programs. For example, Motteram et al. (2020) describe a project in Jordan's Zaatari refugee camp where WhatsApp was used to train teachers to improve their English language skills by providing a platform for them to share and discuss issues related to the challenges of their particular context. This allowed them to contribute to the development of some teaching materials and to begin to add to the curriculum.

Recommendations for Research and Practice

Language learning nowadays takes place everywhere, both offline and online, and at any time, twenty-four hours a day, seven days a week, in both private and shared/public areas – and this, according to research and practice, overwhelms both instructors and learners. Even the most basic forms of technology, such as messaging applications, can be demanding. As a result, language teachers must give learners additional time to study in their own space; they must also educate them as to how to acquire a language. Space must be used properly, since "[s]pace, whether real or virtual, private or public, has a significant influence on learning" (Elkington & Bligh, 2019, p. 3).

In low-tech contexts it is critical that academics and practitioners prioritize pedagogy over technology. Even though mobile phones feature a small screen, a small keypad, low image quality, limited memory, and a short battery life, it still remains to be seen how they may be used effectively in language learning, collaborative learning, task-based language learning, and project-based learning. Additional research into the use of low-tech in language teaching and learning is therefore needed. Even if not eliminated entirely, digital disparities can be reduced in this way.

Future Directions

Following a strong push in online learning in the past couple of years, most countries have realized that access and connectivity are crucial factors in educational success. As a result, we may see nations leapfrogging one another when some place a higher priority on the use of the internet in education, supplying local area network (LAN) connections to educational institutions further down the continuum, from tertiary through primary. What is considered standard technology in a low-tech society today may evolve into a new sort of normalcy of technology in the not-too-distant future, as countries invest in the relevant infrastructure for education. As we see the potential to pursue the available alternatives for both in-class and distance learning, these developments will affect pedagogy. Students may give presentations with material prepared on their mobile devices, for example, using affordable LED displays on classroom walls. Moreover, we may see a proliferation of devices in each home, so that households with a number of children can all access homework on the internet concurrently rather than waiting for their turn.

The COVID-19 pandemic can be thanked for driving more teachers to adopt technology in their teaching. Many who were reluctant to do so previously were offered little choice but to adopt and adapt. Students adopt and adapt as well, albeit not always for the better. While students will probably become accustomed to whatever devices are available to them, one worry is the increasing accuracy of artificial intelligence injected into automatic translation and grammar checker applications, which could impact learning in a number of ways:

- Students could use the technology as a substitute for practicing and producing language themselves, particularly when it comes to writing.
- Grammar checker apps such as Grammarly could become more pervasive, with free knockoffs readily available. Unfortunately, there is little research on how Grammarly helps students acquire grammar, since it is easy to simply accept its corrections and continue writing.
- Students may lose interest in studying if they believe that an automatic translation and grammar checker will meet their target language demands in the future.

Consequently, researchers and practitioners will need to collaborate to create innovative language learning, which takes advantage of technology's inexorable advancement.

References

Aghajani, M., & Adloo, M. (2018). The effect of online cooperative learning on students' writing skills and attitudes through *Telegram* application. *International Journal of Instruction*, *11*(3), 433–448. https://doi.org/10.12973/iji.2018.11330a

Ali, J. K. M., & Bin-Hady, W. R. A. (2019). A study of EFL students' attitudes, motivation and anxiety towards *WhatsApp* as a language learning tool. *Arab World English Journal Special Issue on CALL*, 5, 289–298. https://doi.org/10.24093/awej/call5.19

Alshammari, R., Parkes, M., & Adlington, R. (2017). Using *WhatsApp* in EFL instruction with Saudi Arabian university students. *Arab World English Journal*, *8*(4), 68–84. https://doi.org/10.24093/awej/vol8no4.5

Alsop, T. (2021). *Share of households in Africa with a computer at home from 2005 to 2019*. Statista. www.statista.com/statistics/748549/africa-households-with-computer

Arifani, Y., Asari, S., Anwar, K., & Budianto, L. (2020). Individual or collaborative "*WhatsApp*" learning? A flipped classroom model of EFL writing instruction. *Teaching English with Technology*, *20*(1), 122–139. https://files.eric.ed.gov/full text/EJ1242659.pdf

Ashiyan, Z., & Salehi, H. (2016). Impact of WhatsApp on learning and retention of collocation knowledge among Iranian EFL learners. *Advances in Language and Literary Studies, 7*(5), 112–127. www.journals.aiac.org.au/index.php/alls/art icle/view/2620

Bucher, B. (2020, October 30). WhatsApp, WeChat and Facebook Messenger Apps: Global usage of messaging apps, penetration and statistics. *Messenger People.* www.messengerpeople.com/global-messenger-usage-statistics.

Budiu, R. (2015, April 19). Mobile user experience: Limitations and strengths. *Nielsen Norman Group.* www.nngroup.com/articles/mobile-ux

Business of Apps (2020). *WhatsApp revenue and usage statistics.* www .businessofapps.com/data/whatsapp-statistics

Caboz, J. (2020, April 19). COMPARED: SA video calls on Zoom, Skype, Teams, Hangouts and WhatsApp. *Business Insider South Africa.* www.businessinsider.co .za/heres-why-your-video-conference-app-keeps-acting-up-recommended-band width-speeds-of-zoom-microsoft-teams-skype-google-hangouts-met-and-what sapp-2020-4

Chen, D. W., (2020, March 29). Teachers' Herculean task: Moving 1.1 million children to online school. New York Times. www.nytimes.com/2020/03/29/ nyregion/coronavirus-new-york-schools-remote-learning.html

Compton, L. K. L. (2009). Preparing language teachers to teach language online: A look at skills, roles, and responsibilities. *Computer Assisted Language Learning, 22*(1), 73–99. https://doi.org/10.1080/09588220802613831

Elkington, S., & Bligh, B. (2019). *Future learning spaces: Space, technology and pedagogy.* Research Report. Advance HE. hal-02266834. https://telearn .archives-ouvertes.fr/hal-02266834/document

Gonglewski, M., Meloni, C., & Brant, J. (2001). Using e-mail in foreign language teaching: Rationale and suggestions. *TESL Journal, 7*(3). http://iteslj.org/ Techniques/Meloni-Email.html

Guo, M., & Wang, M. (2018). Integrating WeChat-based mobile-assisted language learning into college English teaching. *EAI Endorsed Transactions on E-Learning, 5*(17), 1–12. https://doi.org/10.4108/eai.25-9-2018.155646

Haines, P. (2016). 25 ideas for using WhatsApp with English language students. *Oxford University Press English Language Teaching Global Blog.* https:// oupeltglobalblog.com/2016/05/17/25-ideas-for-using-whatsapp-with-english-language-students

Hamad, M. (2017). Using WhatsApp to enhance students' learning of English language: Experience to share. *Higher Education Studies, 7*(4), 74–87. https:// doi.org/10.5539/hes.v7n4p74

Hayati, A., Jalilifar, A., & Mashhadi, A. (2013). Using short message service (SMS) to teach English idioms to EFL students. *British Journal of Educational Technology, 44*(1), 66–81. https://doi.org/10.1111/j.1467-8535.2011.01260.x

Hutchby, I. (2001). Technologies, texts and affordances. *Sociology, 35*(2), 441–456. www.jstor.org/stable/42856294

Kaviani, M., & Mashhadi H. D. (2017). The social impact of Telegram as a social network on teaching English vocabulary among Iranian intermediate EFL learners (Payam Noor Center). *Sociological Studies of Youth*, *7*(23), 65–76. https://ssyj.babol.iau.ir/article_529813.html

Kemp, S. (2021, January 27). Digital 2021: Global overview report. *Datareportal*. https://datareportal.com/reports/digital-2021-global-overview-report

Kennedy, C., & Levy, M. (2008). L'italiano al telefonino: Using SMS to support beginners' language learning. *ReCALL*, *20*(3), 315–330. https://doi.org/10.1017/S0958344008000530

Khan, R., Basu, B. L., Bashir, A., & Uddin, M. E. (2021). Online instruction during COVID-19 at public universities in Bangladesh: Teacher and student voices. *Teaching English as a Second Language Electronic Journal*, *25*(1). https://tesl-ej.org/pdf/ej97/a19.pdf

Lee, V., & Yeo, S. (2020, April 18). How home-based learning shows up inequality in Singapore: A look at three homes. *The Straits Times*. www.straitstimes.com/lifestyle/how-home-based-learning-hbl-shows-up-inequality-in-singapore-a-look-at-three-homes

Moran, K. (2016, December 11). Reading content on mobile devices. *Nielsen Norman Group*. www.nngroup.com/articles/mobile-content

Motteram, G., Dawson, S., & Al-Masri-N. (2020). WhatsApp supported language teacher development: A case study in the Zaatari refugee camp. *Education and Information Technologies*, *25*, 5731–5751. https://doi.org/10.1007/s10639-020-10233-0

Naderi, S., & Akrami, A. (2018). EFL learners' reading comprehension development through MALL: Telegram groups in focus. *International Journal of Instruction*, *11*(2), 339–350. https://doi.org/10.12973/iji.2018.11223a

Nature Editorial. (2017). Homo zappiens: The tech-savvy generation may not be so different after all. *Nature*, *547*, 380. www.nature.com/articles/547380a.pdf

New York Times (2020, September 5). When learning is really remote: Students climb trees and travel miles for a cell signal. *New York Times*. https://tinyurl.com/1agtn5ql

Speedguide.net. FAQ: What internet speed is needed for video conferencing with *Zoom*, *Skype*, or *Teams*? www.speedguide.net/faq/what-internet-speed-is-needed-for-video-conferencing-513

Stanford, D. (2020, March 16). Videoconferencing alternatives: How low-bandwidth teaching will save us all. *IDDblog*. www.iddblog.org/videoconferencing-alternatives-how-low-bandwidth-teaching-will-save-us-all

Talaee, E., & Noroozi, O. (2019). Re-conceptualization of "digital divide" among primary school children in an era of saturated access to technology. *International Electronic Journal of Elementary Education*, *12*(1), 27–35 https://www.iejee.com/index.php/IEJEE/article/view/872.

Turkan, S., Timpe-Laughlin, V., & Papageorgiou, S. (2017). *An exploratory study of teaching tasks in English as a foreign language education.* Research Report No. RR-17–56. Educational Testing Service. https://doi.org/10.1002/ets2.12188

UNCTAD. (2018). Policy Brief: Leapfrogging: Look before you leap. (UNCTAD/PRESS/PB/2018/8 No. 71). United Nations Conference on Trade and Development. https://unctad.org/system/files/official-document/presspb2018d8_en.pdf

UNESCO. (2020, June 2). Learning through radio and television in the time of COVID-19. https://en.unesco.org/news/learning-through-radio-and-television-time-covid-19

UNICEF Regional Office for South Asia. (2020, May). Guidance on distance learning modalities to reach all children and youth during school closures: Focusing on low- and no-tech modalities to reach the most marginalized. www.unicef.org/rosa/reports/guidance-distance-learning-modalities-reach-all-children-and-youth-during-school-closures

WhistleOut. (2020, December 10). How much data does YouTube use? www.whistleout.ca/CellPhones/Guides/How-Much-Data-Does-YouTube-Use

Wonders of the World. (2020, August 14). Boy was playing on a tablet in a store when an employee realized what he was doing and made a video. YouTube. www.youtube.com/watch?v=Rbzukgo8mmE

World Bank. (2020). Connecting for inclusion: Broadband access for all. Brief. The World Bank IBRD-IDA. www.worldbank.org/en/topic/digitaldevelopment/brief/connecting-for-inclusion-broadband-access-for-all

Zayed, N. M. (2016). Special designed activities for learning English language through the application of *WhatsApp*! *English Language Teaching*, *9*(2), 199–204. https://files.eric.ed.gov/fulltext/EJ1095562.pdf

Further Reading

Gonzalez, D., & St. Louis, R. (2012). CALL in low-tech contexts. In M. Thomas, H. Reinders, & M. Warschauer (Eds.), *Contemporary computer-assisted language learning* (pp. 217–241). Bloomsbury.

In this chapter Gonzalez and St. Louis provide an overview of low-tech contexts, exploring the challenges and opportunities that arise when integrating technologies into educational contexts with limited access to advanced technology. The authors discuss various strategies and approaches that can be employed to overcome these limitations and effectively integrate CALL into low-tech settings. The chapter offers insights and practical guidance for educators and practitioners who seek to leverage CALL tools and techniques in low-tech environments.

UNICEF Regional Office for South Asia. (2020, May). Guidance on distance learning modalities to reach all children and youth during school closures: Focusing on low- and no-tech modalities to reach the most marginalized. www.unicef.org/rosa/reports/guidance-distance-learning-modalities-reach-all-children-and-youth-during-school-closures

This guidance published by UNICEF builds upon the valuable insights gained from the COVID-19 response. It provides practical guidance on implementing effective distance learning strategies to ensure inclusive education for children and youths during school closures. The report highlights the importance of ensuring continuity of learning during such periods and places particular emphasis on low-tech and non-tech educational settings.

Part III

Tools

9

Mobile Devices

Mark Pegrum

Introduction

Recent years have seen the arrival of a growing array of mobile devices, ranging from those carried or worn by people, such as smartphones, fitness trackers, and extended reality (XR) headsets, to independently or semi-independently mobile drones and robots. The spread of smartphones, above all, has enabled the rise of mobile societies whose members are "permanently online and permanently connected" (Vorderer & Klimmt, 2020, p. 55). These developments are interwoven with global sociopolitical shifts toward super-diversity – that is, the "diversification of diversity" (Vertovec, 2006, p. 1) – emerging from the physical mobility of people as well as the digital mobility of both people and ideas, and manifested in everyday interactions in urban and online spaces (Pegrum, Hockly, & Dudeney, 2022). At the same time, political and cultural barriers against globalization, and against flows of unwelcome people and ideas, are being thrown up piecemeal across the world, making it a highly contested space (Pegrum, 2019b). It is against this backdrop that mobile learning is coming of age.

Background

Mobile learning is a term which has at least two main senses. Traditionally, it has been viewed as referring to learning with mobile devices, often by mobile learners, who are sometimes engaged in mobile learning experiences (Pegrum, 2019b). More recently, it has been used to refer to learning that is appropriate for a world of growing (albeit contested) mobility of people and ideas (Traxler, 2017, 2020; Traxler & Kukulska-Hulme, 2016). In fact, when there is a low degree of mobility in learning, it is little more than e-learning on small screens; but when there is a high degree of mobility in learning, the two senses above intersect. In other words, the more mobile the learning, the more appropriate it is for contemporary mobile societies. Mobile-assisted language learning (MALL) may be seen as a subset of mobile learning where the above principles apply specifically to the teaching and learning of foreign, second, additional and/or other languages (with the terminology used varying between contexts).

There are a number of pedagogical frameworks that can inform the design of mobile learning and MALL. Firstly, there are now many general digital learning frameworks. These include the three-domain TPACK framework (Herring, Koehler, & Mishra, 2016), which focuses on teachers' integration of technological, pedagogical, and content knowledge in learning designs; the four-level SAMR model (Puentedura, 2011), which encourages teachers to move from using digital technologies to merely enhance task designs at substitution and augmentation levels, to using them to transform task designs at modification and redefinition levels; and the newer, three-level T3 framework (Magana, 2017), which emphasizes tasks over technologies and student roles over teacher roles across its translational, transformational, and transcendent levels (the last of which extends somewhat beyond SAMR). Other well-known general digital learning frameworks include the Conversational Framework (Laurillard, 2012), the 7Cs of Learning Design (Conole, 2016), the Community of Inquiry (CoI) framework (Garrison, 2016), and the RASE model (Churchill, 2017).

Secondly, there are mobile learning frameworks, though these are far fewer in number than general digital learning frameworks. They include the 3 Mobilities framework (see below) and the iPAC 2.0 framework (Kearney, Burden, & Schuck, 2020). The latter has evolved from an earlier m-learning pedagogical framework (Kearney et al., 2012), and highlights three main dimensions that should be incorporated into effective mobile learning designs: personalization (consisting of the sub-dimensions customization and agency), collaboration (consisting of conversation and co-creation), and authenticity (consisting of context and task).

In addition, there are various more specific theoretical frameworks or concepts that can support digital and mobile task design. One is the (Online) Interaction model (Clandfield & Hadfield, 2017), focused on the effectiveness of "interactive learning" designs with digital technologies, which distinguishes human–machine interaction, described as weak interaction, from more significant human–human interaction, or strong interaction. While this model originally emphasized strong interaction mediated by technology, it can also encompass strong interaction prompted by technology (Jill Hadfield & Lindsay Clandfield, personal communication, October 2017), that is, where human–human interaction occurs around and not only through digital devices, such as when students collaborate around a shared screen (hence the bracketing of the term "Online" above). Another useful lens is provided by the Screens vs. Lenses dichotomy (Dunleavy, 2014), which distinguishes mobile learning designs where the devices function as barriers to the environment around learners (i.e. taking their attention away from that

Table 9.1 *The 3 Mobilities framework*

	iPAC 2.0			(Online) interaction		Screens vs. lenses	
	Personalization	*Collaboration*	*Authenticity*	*Weak*	*Strong*	*Screens*	*Lenses*
Level 1: Mobility of devices (inside the classroom)							
Typical examples: using MALL apps, reading e-books, viewing videos, undertaking webquests, playing games, exploring non-immersive VR, creating with generic apps	●	○	○	●	○	●	◐
Level 2A: Mobility of devices + learners (inside the classroom)							
Typical examples: critiquing peers' work, collaboratively problem-solving, collaboratively creating with generic apps, (collaboratively) exploring immersive VR	●	●	○	●	●	●	○
Level 2B: Mobility of devices + learners (outside the classroom)							
Typical examples: flipped learning, distance or remote learning, anytime/anywhere self-study with standalone MALL apps, accessing online language communities	●	◐	○	●	◐	●	●
Level 3: Mobility of devices + learners + learning experiences (outside the classroom)							
Typical examples: multimedia recording and sharing of real-world learning, undertaking AR learning trails, creating AR artifacts	●	●	●	●	●	◐	●

Key: ● probable ◐ possible ○ less probable

environment and focusing it instead on the content on their small screens) from more effective designs where the devices function as lenses that (re)focus learners' attention on the real-world environment around them and the learning opportunities it offers.

All of these frameworks and concepts can support the design of mobile learning and MALL, with their relevance in each case depending on the learning, the learners, and the context.

The 3 Mobilities Framework

The 3 Mobilities framework by Pegrum (2014, 2019) has evolved over time, and is displayed in a new format incorporating MALL-specific examples in Table 9.1. It shows the pedagogical potential of the three main levels of mobility possible in mobile learning, arranged vertically: mobility of devices (inside the classroom); mobility of devices and learners (with inside-the-classroom and outside-the-classroom sublevels); and mobility of devices, learners, and learning experiences (outside the classroom). There is necessarily a certain fuzziness to these levels, which represent tendencies rather than absolute distinctions, but it will be seen that, broadly speaking, each level has different implications in terms of the learning activities, pedagogical advantages and disadvantages, and access advantages and disadvantages to which it gives rise. (Note that the main focus here is on mobile devices carried or worn by people, especially smartphones and headsets; for more on independently or semi-independently mobile devices, see Pegrum, 2019b).

The 3 Mobilities framework is in some senses a meta-framework, since it is informed by three sets of background theoretical concepts – the iPAC 2.0 framework, the (Online) Interaction model, and the Screens vs. Lenses dichotomy, as detailed earlier – which are arranged horizontally across the top of the table. In general, the more mobile the learning, the richer the underlying pedagogical potential, and the greater the correspondence between the two senses of mobile learning outlined at the start of this chapter. Nevertheless, as we examine the levels of mobile learning one by one, it will become apparent that each level offers its own benefits in terms of pedagogy and access for certain types of learning, certain learners, and certain contexts.

Level 1: Mobile Devices (inside the Classroom)

In a nutshell, this is e-learning on smaller devices, where mobile devices (and people) are artificially immobilized in a classroom. The devices are of course mobile by definition, although they are not being employed in a mobile way; meanwhile, neither the learners nor the learning experiences are mobile, with students typically sitting still at their desks, where they use their mobile screens as an alternative to laptop or desktop screens.

Typical learning activities range from the passive to the active. More passive tasks include students engaging in drills in behaviorist MALL consumption apps (subject-specific apps grounded in content transmission or behaviorism; Pegrum et al., 2022), often with a focus on vocabulary (Godwin-Jones, 2017; Mahdi, 2018); and engaging in receptive skills practice in short-form or, increasingly, long-form reading (West & Chew, 2014) and listening/viewing. More active tasks include students undertaking webquests, which are designed to introduce a constructivist element into the reception of online content by prompting students to actively seek and synthesize information; playing language or more general games (ranging from gamified drills to full-blown massively multiplayer online role-playing games [MMORPGs]); exploring and possibly interacting within non-immersive virtual reality (VR) interfaces in the form of gaming environments or virtual worlds accessed on the flat screens of mobile devices; and creating and sharing multimodal communicative artifacts using productive apps (such as generic digital poster or story-telling apps, which foster creativity, and social media apps, which foster sharing of creations and wider networking).

At the passive end of the Level 1 spectrum, the common pedagogies are information transmission and behaviorism. There is a strong sentiment in the mobile learning and MALL literature that to a large extent "21st century tools [are] being used to support early 20th century teaching approaches" (Helen Crompton, cited in Pegrum, 2019b, p. 61; cf. Burston, 2014; Godwin-Jones, 2017; Lotherington, 2018). However, there is a place in education for these approaches, especially at foundational levels and as a supplement to more communicative activities. On the other hand, at the active end of the Level 1 spectrum, where students are exploring VR or creating digital artifacts, there is a shift in the direction of more contemporary constructivist learning – a shift that, as will be seen, extends much further at higher levels of the 3 Mobilities framework.

In terms of pedagogy, there are both advantages and drawbacks. Per the iPAC framework, personalization, which is a common focus in the mobile learning and MALL literature (Bower, 2017; Kukulska-Hulme, 2016), is likely to be found in the form of student customization of hardware, software, and even digital assistants, as well as in the form of student agency in learning choices (note that while collaboration is less likely at this level, it is possible through online networking, including in some games and VR environments, while a degree of authenticity is also possible through accessing authentic target language materials or in some VR). Per the (Online) Interaction model, weak interaction with devices is likely to dominate (though some strong interaction is possible through online networking). Per the Screens vs. Lenses dichotomy, screen usage is likely to dominate as students use apps and view web-based resources (though some lens usage is undoubtedly possible in a number of instances, for example if the web is treated as a lens on external content or networks, or in the case of certain VR experiences, such as viewing 360 degree videos showing target culture locations or artifacts).

In terms of access, there are again both advantages and drawbacks. Mobile devices are certainly more accessible and affordable than desktop or laptop computers in underresourced settings in the Global South and parts of the Global North (GSMA, 2021; Pegrum, 2014, 2019b), but learning activities at the passive end of the spectrum are far more likely in these settings due to hardware, software, and connectivity limitations. Importantly, thanks to key features of mobile devices such as their natural user interfaces, their multi-modal/multisensory input and output options, their text-to-speech and speech-to-text functionality, and their ability to be reconfigured to suit individual needs, they offer numerous accessibility options for diverse, differently abled students (Love & Golloher, 2021; Orr & Conley, 2014; Perelmutter, McGregor, & Gordon, 2017), though the range of options and the amount of reconfiguration possible are naturally greater with smarter, and therefore less affordable, devices.

Level 2A: Mobile Learners (inside the Classroom)

In a nutshell, this is e-learning with minimal movement added. Students typically move about the classroom – which may take the form of a flexible new learning space (Adams Becker et al., 2018; Freeman et al., 2017) inspired by the informal networking of cafés rather than the formal regimentation of traditional schools – and interact with each other around individual or shared devices. Indeed, it has been widely noted that mobile devices like tablets frequently prompt face-to-face student collaboration around on-screen learning tasks (Bower, 2017; Pegrum, 2014). Although the degree of student mobility here is fairly minimal, as it is generally constrained within the four walls of a room, it opens up significant pedagogical possibilities.

Typical learning activities can involve a range of technologies. Using smartphones or tablets, students may engage in target language or bilingual interaction as they offer feedback on classmates' work; collaboratively answer inquiries or solve problems; and co-create artifacts ranging from digital posters to data visualizations, and digital stories to group videos. Using XR headsets, or head-mounted displays (HMDs), which extend from the very affordable Google Cardboard viewer (now discontinued, but with alternatives available) to more expensive units like the HTC Vive, Oculus Quest, or Microsoft HoloLens, students may explore immersive VR, which research suggests is more educationally effective than static desktop VR (Bower & Jong, 2020; Wu, Yu, & Gu, 2020). Navigating immersive VR interfaces requires some minimal movement of the head and/or body, and the scope for collaboration in such interfaces is gradually increasing. Recent work suggests there is value in immersive VR for language learning (Alfadil, 2020), but more research is needed into social or collaborative language learning in these interfaces (Lan, 2020).

At Level 2A, then, there is a further shift in the direction of active, student-centered pedagogical approaches, facilitated by face-to-face interactions around the technology, and surpassing the more minor shift noted at the active end of the Level 1 spectrum. This is reflected to some extent in the connection often made in the literature between mobile learning/MALL and (social) constructivism (Bower, 2017; Cochrane, Narayan, & Antonczak, 2016), including its varying instantiations such as inquiry-based, problem-based, and task-based learning (Kukulska-Hulme & Viberg, 2018; Reinders & Pegrum, 2017) (though some studies refer as much, or more, to online realization of constructivism, such as may be found at other levels of the 3 Mobilities framework).

In terms of pedagogical advantages and drawbacks, per the iPAC framework, collaboration, which is another common focus in the mobile learning and MALL literature (Cochrane et al., 2016; Kukulska-Hulme & Viberg, 2018), is layered over personalization in the form of both conversation and co-creation (note that lifelike simulations of authentic contexts are also possible in immersive VR). Per the (Online) Interaction model, strong interaction – prompted rather than mediated by the devices – complements existing weak interaction (though it is less likely in individual explorations of immersive VR). Per the Screens vs. Lenses dichotomy, screen usage is likely to continue to dominate as students interact around on-screen materials (though lens usage is possible, notably in VR).

In terms of access advantages and drawbacks, while individual XR headsets are largely restricted to wealthier locations, shared smartphones or tablets are not uncommon in underresourced settings in the Global South or Global North and, being shared, may naturally prompt collaborative interactions around the available screens. The accessibility advantages of mobile devices remain, though it may be more difficult to personalize shared devices to individual learners' needs.

Level 2B: Mobile Learners (outside the Classroom)

In a nutshell, this is arguably the archetypal learning of our current historical moment, where mobile learners employ mobile devices to log into immobile, centralized, digital learning spaces. Paradoxically, it is precisely because these spaces serve as stable, fixed learning hubs that partly or wholly autonomous learners are able to remain in motion in the wider analog sphere, while weaving their geographically and chronologically dispersed learning experiences into a coherent learning trajectory in the digital sphere. This is mobile learning tailored to a world of voluntary or involuntary mobility. Those who may benefit include students circulating between cafés, libraries, and home offices, Northern professionals flying from city to city and country to country, and Southern refugees forced to relocate across oceans and continents. While learning in this way may have a few pedagogical benefits, its greatest benefits are predominantly in terms of access to learning.

At Level 2B, the general learning formats are more significant than the specific educational activities undertaken within each format. Some formats are driven by institutions whose students are scattered and very likely on the move at least some of the time. These include flipped learning in preparation for real-time face-to-face (or synchronous online) classes, as well as distance learning (often well-planned) or, increasingly, remote learning (often at short notice, for example in a time of physical institutional closures such as during the COVID-19 pandemic). Such learning may take place via technologies ranging from institutional learning management systems (LMSs) or massive open online course (MOOC) platforms (including for language MOOCs [LMOOCs] and mobile-assisted LMOOCs [MALMOOCs]; Read, Bárcena, & Kukulska-Hulme, 2016), which are typically anchored in well-resourced settings, to lower bandwidth over-the-top (OTT) messaging services such as WhatsApp or WeChat, which may be employed in underresourced settings.

Sometimes, however, the learning formats are driven more by students' needs and wishes. At one end of the scale, this might mean busy professionals undertaking bite-sized learning in their "interstitial time and space" (Palalas, 2013, p. 92) with the help of comprehensive MALL apps such as Babbel, busuu, Duolingo, or Memrise; learners practicing language with chatbots inside educational apps, or with smart digital assistants (Kukulska-Hulme, 2019) such as Alexa, Siri, or Google Assistant, perhaps distributed across a number of devices; or students connecting with language partners on exchange apps such as HelloTalk or Tandem, or on general OTT messaging apps. At the other end of the scale, it might mean refugee children continuing to access language lessons (sometimes via apps designed as part of social justice projects) as they and their families flee political, social, and/or environmental crises. It might also mean Indigenous, heritage, or other marginalized language learners, who are often widely distributed geographically and may be frequently on the road, connecting to their language communities online.

At Level 2B, the pedagogies are dependent on the learning spaces, and the content, networks, activities, and above all the degree of teacherly or other educational guidance available in each space. However, all of the above examples of learning formats may be characterized as instances of seamless learning (Wong & Looi, 2019), where learning is able to continue uninterrupted across educational and noneducational times and spaces. More specifically, they are instances of "seamless learning despite context" (Sharples, 2015), where the learning is not directly impacted by the times and spaces in which it takes place. This is also commonly referred to as anytime/anywhere learning.

Per the iPAC framework, collaboration, particularly in the form of conversation, may continue to be layered over personalization to the extent that scattered mobile learners are interacting with peers and/or target language speakers through networks anchored in immobile digital hubs (though this is less likely in the case of individual self-study with language apps, notwithstanding the social interaction options now built into some major apps such as, notably, busuu). Per the (Online) Interaction model, strong interaction – now mediated by the devices – may complement weak interaction (though again this is less likely in the case of individual self-study). Per the Screens vs. Lenses dichotomy, mobile devices at this level are used as screens to access content in apps and on other platforms but, much more importantly, they simultaneously serve as metaphorical lenses from mobile analog living spaces into fixed digital learning spaces.

Many of the advantages of mobile learning at this level are more about access than pedagogy. Even for the well-resourced with access to desktop or laptop computers, untethered mobile devices offer a level of flexibility and convenience which permits learning to fit into their busy mobile lives in a chunked and sustainable way. But there are particular benefits for the marginalized and underresourced: refugees for whom mobile technologies may be "a lifeline to learning" (UNESCO, 2018); migrants seeking to preserve their linguistic heritage while learning host community languages on the fly; people with little or no access to formal education who can engage in informal learning through the mobile web (Traxler et al., 2020); and the many students worldwide for whom mobile devices have been the principal gateway to schooling in times of enforced remote learning.

Level 3: Mobile Learning Experiences (outside the Classroom)

In a nutshell, this may become the archetypal learning of a future historical moment, where mobile devices are used by mobile learners to facilitate mobile learning experiences which leverage the richness of their changing spatial and temporal contexts. In MALL, this opens the gates to engaging in translingual, multimodal, and multisensory communication of the kind found in everyday superdiverse settings, whether offline, online, or both. Complemented by but going beyond the anytime/anywhere learning anchored to immobile digital spaces that typifies Level 2B, Level 3 represents a further step toward aligning mobile learning with a mobile world. Since mobility applies not only to the devices and the learners, but to the learning experiences, the learning itself is dynamically impacted by the spaces and times through which learners and their devices are moving. While the requisite hardware, software, and connectivity currently render this level of mobile learning relatively inaccessible outside the wealthy Global North, it holds the greatest potential for pedagogical transformation.

Typical learning activities vary in educational and technological complexity. Simpler tasks may involve students revealing the learning potential in everyday environments by annotating their photos of urban linguistic landscapes and cataloguing them in a class database, or recording real-world conversational exchanges and collaboratively analyzing them in a peer network. More complex tasks may well entail students exploring augmented reality (AR), the paradigmatic technology associated with Level 3, whose interfaces, accessed via phones, tablets, or headsets, can facilitate knowledge construction and consolidation by prompting and guiding interactions between embodied people, objects, and the everyday settings in which both are embedded. Augmented reality has been found to offer advantages for some aspects of language learning (Parmaxi & Demetriou, 2020; Pegrum, 2021). One increasingly common format is gamified learning trails, where students collaboratively respond to digital questions, problems, and tasks delivered to them via AR interfaces accessed in their real-world settings, in the process finding themselves impelled to interact with those settings and the other people and objects within them (Pegrum, 2019a, 2019b). Students can also be tasked with creating their own digital artifacts and geotagging them to the locations in response to which they were created, which can subsequently be visited by teachers, peers, or indeed the general public. Once they have gained some experience in undertaking learning trails, students can be asked to design trail stations or even entire trails to support their peers' learning.

The above examples represent a shift away from decontextualized anytime/anywhere learning and toward contextualized learning which, it has been suggested, should be seen as "the next generation of mobile learning" (Traxler & Kukulska-Hulme, 2016). Although seamless learning, as indicated earlier, is not always contextualized, the most pedagogically rich kinds typically are (Milrad et al., 2013; Wong & Looi, 2019), so we might describe Level 3 learning as contextualized seamless learning. Not only does the mobile learning and MALL literature make a strong connection with the notion of contextualization in general (Bachmair & Pachler, 2015; Reinders & Pegrum, 2017), but it makes a strong connection specifically between mobile AR and contextual(ized) or situated learning (Godwin-Jones, 2016; Herrington Kidd & Crompton, 2016) and embodied learning (Fitzgerald et al., 2012; Radu,

2014). Other terms that surface in the mobile AR literature include authentic learning, embedded learning, and immersive learning.

In many ways, the scope for constructivist creation of rich, sharable user-generated learning content, for instance in the form of students' geotagged AR artifacts, is greater at Level 3 than at lower levels. But more distinctively, this is the only level where there is also scope for the creation of user-generated learning contexts (Aguayo, Cochrane, & Narayan, 2017; Cook, 2010), where students can choose to situate their learning, and where they can invite others to join them in their learning.

Per the iPAC framework, authenticity is layered over collaboration and personalization, as learning takes place within the authentic contexts of everyday life – hence the strong emphasis in the mobile learning, MALL and mobile AR literature on contextualization, as noted above – with considerable latitude for authentic tasks to be carried out within these contexts. Per the (Online) Interaction model, strong interaction – mediated and/or prompted by the devices – is likely to complement weak interaction. Per the Screens vs. Lenses dichotomy, mobile devices at this level finally show their full potential as lenses that focus students' attention on learning opportunities around them, and provide the information channels to inform this learning, the recording channels to capture it, and the communication channels to disseminate and collaboratively analyze it (though of course the devices may sometimes simultaneously play a supporting role as screens).

It should nevertheless be remembered that although recorded learning experiences or digitally created artifacts can be widely and democratically shared in online networks, or even visited in everyday real-world settings, access to this type of learning, and especially AR learning, remains, for now, limited to well-resourced populations.

Recommendations for Research and Practice

Over the coming years, mobile learning and MALL are likely to be impacted by wider discussions and debates around the role of digital and mobile technologies in education and in society at large, taking place against the backdrop of a world that is in many ways and for many people more and more mobile, and yet is strewn with barriers to mobility for unwelcome people and perspectives. Our research and our practices need to keep pace with and address this shifting context.

On the research front, we need to develop more nuanced understandings of mobile devices' differential impact on empowerment and education for disadvantaged populations, from the differently abled across the world to the underresourced in the Global South, notably women and girls (Stark, 2020); on privacy and surveillance (Véliz, 2020); on mental and physical health (Gazzaley & Rosen, 2016); and on the environment (Cooper, Shapley, & Cole, 2020).

Meanwhile, our practices will need to keep evolving in light of such research, and in light of ongoing social, educational, and technological changes and demands. Among other things, we will need to revisit and refine our digital and mobile learning frameworks to ensure that they remain fit for purpose, offering guidelines which not only serve to support current forms of learning, but which can also support new and emerging educational possibilities.

Conclusion

For now, we may conclude that when we as educators are planning mobile learning and MALL activities for our students, we should consider whether, and how, to exploit the three main levels of mobility – pertaining to devices (inside the classroom), learners (inside or outside the classroom), and learning experiences (outside the classroom) – in our designs. Each of these levels is appropriate for some kinds of learning, learners, and settings, meaning that our designs must always be contextually sensitive. At the same time, it is apparent that the richest learning is likely to emerge where the devices, the learners, and the learning experiences are all mobile; where elements of personalization, collaboration, and authenticity are all present; where strong interaction complements weak interaction; and where mobile devices function not just as screens but, more importantly, as lenses on learning. This is also likely to be the kind of mobile learning that most closely accords with the needs of ever more mobile people in an ever more mobile world.

References

Adams Becker, S., Brown, M., Dahlstrom, E., Davis, A., DePaul, K., Diaz, V., & Pomerantz, J. (2018). *NMC Horizon Report: 2018 Higher Education Edition.* EDUCAUSE. https://library.educause.edu/~/media/files/library/2018/8/2018horizonreport.pdf

Aguayo, C., Cochrane, T., & Narayan, V. (2017). Key themes in mobile learning: Prospects for learner-generated learning through AR and VR. *Australasian Journal of Educational Technology, 33*(6), 27–40. https://doi.org/10.14742/ajet.3671

Alfadil, M. (2020). Effectiveness of virtual reality game in foreign language vocabulary acquisition. *Computers & Education, 153.* https://doi.org/10.1016/j.compedu.2020.103893

Bachmair, B., & Pachler, N. (2015). Framing ubiquitous mobility educationally: Mobile devices and context-aware learning. In L.-H. Wong, M. Milrad & M. Specht (Eds.), *Seamless learning in the age of mobile connectivity* (pp. 57–74). Springer.

Bower, M. (2017). *Design of technology-enhanced learning: Integrating research and practice.* Emerald Publishing.

Bower, M., & Jong, M. S.-Y. (2020). Editorial: Immersive virtual reality in education. *British Journal of Educational Technology, 51*(6), 1981–1990. https://doi.org/10.1111/bjet.13038

Burston, J. (2014). MALL: The pedagogical challenges. *Computer Assisted Language Learning, 27*(4), 344–357. https://doi.org/10.1080/09588221.2014.914539

Churchill, D. (2017). *Digital resources for learning.* Springer.

Clandfield, L., & Hadfield, J. (2017). Interaction online: Creative activities for blended learning. Cambridge University Press.

Cochrane, T., Narayan, V., & Antonczak, L. (2016). A framework for designing collaborative learning environments using mobile AR. *Journal of Interactive Learning Research, 27*(4), 293–316.

Conole, G. (2016). The 7Cs of learning design. In J. Dalziel (Ed.), *Learning design: State of the art of the field* (pp. 117–145). Routledge.

Cook, J. (2010). Mobile learner generated contexts: Research on the internalization of the world of cultural products. In B. Bachmair (Ed.), Medienbildung in neuen Kulturräumen: Die deutschsprachige und britische Diskussion (pp. 113–125). VS Verlag für Sozialwissenschaften.

Cooper, T., Shapley, M., & Cole, C. (2020). Mobile phone waste and the circular economy. In R. Ling, L. Fortunati, G. Goggin, S. S. Lim & Y. Li (Eds.), *The Oxford handbook of mobile communication and society* (pp. 601–620). Oxford University Press.

Dunleavy, M. (2014). Design principles for augmented reality learning. *TechTrends, 58*(1), 28–34. https://doi.org/10.1007/s11528-013-0717-2

FitzGerald, E., Adams, A., Ferguson, R., Gaved, M., Mor, Y., & Thomas, R. (2012). Augmented reality and mobile learning: The state of the art. In M. Specht, M. Sharples & J. Multisilta (Eds.), *mLearn 2012: Mobile and contextual learning. Proceedings of the 11th International Conference on Mobile and Contextual Learning 2012, Helsinki, Finland, October 16–18, 2012* (pp. 62–69). http://ceur-ws.org/Vol-955/papers/paper_49.pdf

Freeman, A., Adams Becker, S., Cummins, M., Davis, A., & Hall Giesinger, C. (2017). *NMC/CoSN Horizon Report: 2017 K-12 Edition.* The New Media Consortium. https://library.educause.edu/~/media/files/library/2017/11/2017hrk12EN.pdf

Garrison, D. R. (2016). *E-learning in the 21st century: A community of inquiry framework for research and practice.* Routledge.

Gazzaley, A., & Rosen, L. D. (2016). *The distracted mind: Ancient brains in a high-tech world.* MIT Press.

Godwin-Jones, R. (2016). Augmented reality and language learning: From annotated vocabulary to place-based mobile games. *Language Learning & Technology, 20*(3), 9–19. https://doi.org/10125/44475

Godwin-Jones, R. (2017). Smartphones and language learning. *Language Learning & Technology, 21*(2), 3–17. https://doi.org/10125/44607

GSMA [Global System for Mobile Communications Association]. (2021). *Mobile creating a #BetterFuture.* www.gsma.com/betterfuture/mobile-creating-a-betterfuture

Herring, M. C., Koehler, M. J., & Mishra, P. (Eds.). (2016). *Handbook of technological pedagogical content knowledge (TPACK) for educators* (2nd ed.). Routledge.

Herrington Kidd., S., & Crompton, H. (2016). Augmented learning with augmented reality. In D. Churchill, J. Lu, T. K. F. Chiu, & B. Fox (Eds.), Mobile learning design: Theories and application (pp. 97–108). Springer.

Kearney, M., Burden, K., & Schuck, S. (2020). *Theorising and implementing mobile learning: Using the iPAC framework to inform research and teaching practice.* Springer.

Kearney, M., Schuck, S., Burden, K., & Aubusson, P. (2012). Viewing mobile learning from a pedagogical perspective. *Research in Learning Technology*, 20. https://doi.org/10.3402/rlt.v20i0.14406

Kukulska-Hulme, A. (2016, Oct.). Personalization of language learning through mobile technologies. Cambridge Papers in ELT. Cambridge University Press. www.cambridge.org/elt/blog/wp-content/uploads/2017/06/CambridgePapersinELT_M-learning_2016_ONLINE.pdf

Kukulska-Hulme, A. (2019). Intelligent assistants in language learning: Friends or foes? In *Proceedings of World Conference on Mobile and Contextual Learning 2019* (pp. 127–131). www.learntechlib.org/p/210611/

Kukulska-Hulme, A., & Viberg, O. (2018). Mobile collaborative language learning: State of the art. *British Journal of Educational Technology*, 49(2), 207–218. https://doi.org/10.1111/bjet.12580

Lan, Y.-J. (2020). Immersion, interaction, and experience-oriented learning: Bringing virtual reality into FL learning. *Language Learning & Technology*, 24 (1), 1–15. https://doi.org/10125/44704

Laurillard, D. (2012). *Teaching as a design science: Building pedagogical patterns for learning and technology.* Routledge.

Lotherington, H. (2018). Mobile language learning: The medium is not the message. *L2 Journal*, 10(2), 198–214. https://doi.org/10.5070/l210235576

Love, M., & Golloher, A. (2021). Designing for students in the margins online: Applications of UDL in 2021 and beyond. In R. E. Ferdig & K. E. Pytash (Eds.), *What teacher educators should have learned from 2020* (pp. 69–77). AACE. www.learntechlib.org/p/219088/

Magana, S. (2017). *Disruptive classroom technologies: A framework for innovation in education.* Corwin.

Mahdi, H. S. (2018). Effectiveness of mobile devices on vocabulary learning: A meta-analysis. *Journal of Educational Computing Research*, 56(1), 134–154. https://doi.org/10.1177/0735633117698826

Milrad, M., Wong, L.-H., Sharples, M., Hwang, G.-J., Looi, C.-K., & Ogata, H. (2013). Seamless learning: An international perspective on next-generation technology-enhanced learning. In Z. L. Berge & L. Y. Muilenburg (Eds.), *Handbook of mobile learning* (pp. 95–108). Routledge.

Orr, A. C., & Conley, J. F. (2014). Mobile technology and differentiated learning: Meeting the needs of students with significant disabilities. In D. McConatha, C. Penny, J. Schugar & D. Bolton (Eds.), *Mobile pedagogy and perspectives on teaching and learning* (pp. 150–164). Information Science Reference.

Palalas, A. (2013). Blended mobile learning: Expanding learning spaces with mobile technologies. In A. Tsinakos & M. Ally (Eds.), *Global mobile learning implementations and trends* (pp. 86–104). China Central Radio & TV University Press.

Parmaxi, A., & Demetriou, A. A. (2020). Augmented reality in language learning: A state-of-the-art review of 2014–2019. *Journal of Computer Assisted Learning, 36*(6), 861–875. https://doi.org/10.1111/jcal.12486

Pegrum, M. (2014). Mobile learning: Languages, literacies and cultures. Palgrave Macmillan.

Pegrum, M. (2019a). Mobile AR trails and games for authentic language learning. In Y. Zhang & D. Cristol (Eds.), *Handbook of mobile teaching and learning* (2nd ed.). Springer.

Pegrum, M. (2019b). *Mobile lenses on learning: Languages and literacies on the move.* Springer.

Pegrum, M. (2021). Augmented reality learning: Education in real-world contexts. In T. Beaven & F. Rosell-Aguilar (Eds.), *Innovative language pedagogy report.* Research-publishing.net. https://doi.org/10.14705/rpnet.2021.50.1245

Pegrum, M., Hockly, N., & Dudeney, G. (2022). *Digital literacies* (2nd ed.). Routledge.

Perelmutter, B., McGregor, K. K., & Gordon, K. R. (2017). Assistive technology interventions for adolescents and adults with learning disabilities: An evidence-based systematic review and meta-analysis. *Computers & Education, 114*, 139–163. https://doi.org/10.1016/j.compedu.2017.06.005

Puentedura, R. (2011, December 8). A brief introduction to TPCK and SAMR. *Freeport workshop slides. Ruben R. Puentedura's weblog.* www.hippasus.com/rrpweblog/archives/2011/12/08/BriefIntroTPCKSAMR.pdf

Radu, I. (2014). Augmented reality in education: A meta-review and cross-media analysis. Personal and Ubiquitous Computing, *18*, 1533–1543. https://doi.org/10.1007/s00779-013-0747-y

Read, T., Bárcena, E., & Kukulska-Hulme, A. (2016). Mobile and massive language learning. In E. Martín-Monje, I. Elorza, & B. García Riaza (Eds.), *Technology-enhanced language learning for specialized domains: Practical applications and mobility* (pp. 151–161). Routledge.

Reinders, H., & Pegrum, M. (2017). Supporting language learning on the move: An evaluative framework for mobile language learning resources. In B. Tomlinson (Ed.), SLA research and materials development for language learning (pp. 219–231). Routledge.

Sharples, M. (2015). Seamless learning despite context. In L.-H. Wong, M. Milrad, & M. Specht (Eds.), *Seamless learning in the age of mobile connectivity* (pp. 41–55). Springer.

Stark, L. (2020). Women, empowerment, and mobile phones in the developing world. In R. Ling, L. Fortunati, G. Goggin, S. S. Lim, & Y. Li (Eds.), *The Oxford handbook of mobile communication and society* (pp. 529–543). Oxford University Press.

Traxler, J. (2017). Learning with mobiles in developing countries: Technology, language, and literacy. *International Journal of Mobile and Blended Learning, 9*(2), 1–15. https://doi.org/10.4018/IJMBL.2017040101

Traxler, J. (2020). Learning with mobiles or "mobile learning." In R. Ling, L. Fortunati, G. Goggin, S. S. Lim, & Y. Li (Eds.), *The Oxford handbook of mobile communication and society* (pp. 257–275). Oxford University Press.

Traxler, J., & Kukulska-Hulme, A. (2016). Conclusion: Contextual challenges for the next generation. In J. Traxler & A. Kukulska-Hulme (Eds.), *Mobile learning: The next generation* (pp. 208–226). Routledge.

Traxler, J., Scott, H., Smith, M., & Hayes, S. (2020, Nov.). *Learning through the crisis: Helping decision-makers around the world use digital technology to combat the educational challenges produced by the current COVID-19 pandemic.* EdTech Hub. https://docs.edtechhub.org/lib/5DWI862Y

UNESCO. (2018). *A lifeline to learning: Leveraging technology to support education for refugees.* https://unesdoc.unesco.org/ark:/48223/pf0000261278

Véliz, C. (2020). *Privacy is power: Why and how you should take back control of your data.* Bantam Press.

Vertovec, S. (2006). *The emergence of super-diversity in Britain.* Centre on Migration, Policy and Society Working Paper No. 25, University of Oxford. www.compas.ox.ac.uk/2006/wp-2006-025-vertovec_super-diversity_britain

Vorderer, P., & Klimmt, C. (2020). The mobile user's mindset in a permanently online, permanently connected society. In R. Ling, L. Fortunati, G. Goggin, S. S. Lim, & Y. Li (Eds.), *The Oxford handbook of mobile communication and society* (pp. 54–67). Oxford University Press.

West, M., & Chew, H. E. (2014). *Reading in the mobile era: A study of mobile reading in developing countries.* UNESCO. https://unesdoc.unesco.org/ark:/48223/pf0000227436

Wong, L.-H., & Looi, C.-K. (2019). Tracing the decade-long trajectory of implementation research in mobile- and social media-assisted seamless learning in Singapore. In *Proceedings of World Conference on Mobile and Contextual Learning 2019* (pp. 141–148). www.learntechlib.org/p/210613

Wu, B., Yu., X., & Gu, X. (2020). Effectiveness of immersive virtual reality using head-mounted displays on learning performance: A meta-analysis. *British Journal of Educational Technology, 51*(6), 1991–2005. https://doi.org/10.1111/bjet.13023

Further Reading

Kearney, M., Burden, K., & Schuck, S. (2020). *Theorising and implementing mobile learning: Using the iPAC framework to inform research and teaching practice.* Springer.
Drawing on many years of research into mobile learning, this book presents the latest version of the iPAC theoretical framework, which highlights the dimensions of personalization, collaboration, and authenticity in mobile learning.

Pegrum, M. (2019). *Mobile lenses on learning: Languages and literacies on the move.* Springer.

This book offers a broad survey of the mobile learning landscape, from the Global North to the Global South, and provides extensive illustrations of each of the levels of the 3 Mobilities theoretical framework.

Traxler, J. (2020). Learning with mobiles or "mobile learning." In R. Ling, L. Fortunati, G. Goggin, S. S. Lim, & Y. Li (Eds.), *The Oxford handbook of mobile communication and society* (pp. 257–275). Oxford University Press.

This chapter explores the distinction between mobile learning, which is an extension of e-learning involving mobile devices and mobile learners, and learning with mobiles, which involves a consideration of the changing nature of learning in an increasingly mobile era.

Traxler, J., & Kukulska-Hulme, A. (Eds.). (2016). *Mobile learning: The next generation*. Routledge.

This edited collection of chapters focuses on innovative projects in context-aware mobile learning, presented here as the emerging generation of mobile learning.

10

Teaching Languages with Games

Frederik Cornillie and James York

Introduction

Educators have always harnessed the power of ludic activities so as to facilitate learning in low-tech teaching contexts; and this includes the teaching of foreign and second languages (L2s). In this light, it is surprising that most current research on L2 learning with games has focused on informal (naturalistic) learning, has adopted a technology-centric perspective that prioritizes digital games, and, particularly, has neglected the role of teachers. Teacher mediation, after all, is critical for enabling student learning. Therefore, and complementing recent reviews on digital games in the field of second language acquisition (SLA) (Cornillie, 2022; Dixon, Dixon, & Jordan, 2022; Hung et al., 2018; Poole & Clarke-Midura, 2020), the purpose of this chapter is to survey work that shows how L2 teachers can leverage the opportunities inherent in games and play, with a view to strengthening the naturalistic learning of their students. In particular, we spotlight the key role of the teacher in mediating learners' language and literacy development before, during, and after L2 activities through and around games. We also consider how the purposeful use of digital technology around games and play supports both learners and teachers in reaching their goals. We illustrate this through exemplary studies that are grounded in various pedagogies and use both analog and digital games that are relatively easy to implement in real classrooms (e.g. free games that students can play on their mobile phones). In doing so, we ascribe to a "ludic language pedagogy" approach to teaching with a diverse selection of games and play giving equal importance to tools and technology (ludic materials), language learning goals, and pedagogical rigor (York, Poole, & DeHaan, 2021).

Background

In all age ranges, learning through ludic activities such as free play with wooden toys, debating, (live-action) role play, and participation in fan communities involves the often simultaneous development of a wide range of skills. These skills are typically transversal (i.e. not tied to a specific subject area, discipline, or work context) and consist of sensorimotor skills, cognitive skills (such as problem-solving and creative thinking), emotional skills, and – especially in cooperative forms of play – social and linguistic skills (Matthews & Liu, 2012). In formal educational settings, with the exception of performative disciplines such as drama, music, and sport, play has been largely excluded from most subjects, including modern languages. Today, however, it is gradually moving in from the margins of L2 teaching because the transversal skills involved in learners' participation in ludic activities are increasingly targeted in communicative and especially social L2 pedagogies (e.g. Dubreil & Thorne, 2017), and are essential for individuals to thrive in a quickly changing labour market (OECD, 2021).

In addition to being a learning activity, play can also manifest itself in playing with language. This can be done at the level of linguistic form, when language speakers experiment with sounds and grammatical structures, for example in poetry and songs. Language play can also be semantic, when speakers (re)combine units of meaning to create make-believe worlds, for example when telling puns, creating stories such as fanfiction (Petersen, 2022), or composing internet memes. As both formal and semantic play with language constitute linguistic genres that are as relevant for L2 learning as the more mundane and "authentic" registers emphasized in utilitarian approaches to language, ludic uses of language have equally received attention in L2 teaching methodology (e.g. Cook, 1997).

While play is considered a spontaneous and naturally occurring activity where the exact outcome is indeterminate, it can be embedded in goals and rules that impose a certain structure on its "free" nature and that result in more predictable outcomes. When play is more explicitly goal-oriented and bound by rules, it becomes a game. Games have been formally defined as "system[s] in which players engage in an artificial conflict, defined by rules, that [result] in a quantifiable outcome" (Salen & Zimmerman, 2004, p. 80). For example, the game tic-tac-toe is an artificial conflict between two players and is defined by the following rules: the game is played on a 3×3 grid; players pick a nought ('0') or a cross ('X') symbol to mark the grid; they mark the grid with their respective symbol, turn by turn. The quantifiable outcome is that the game ends when one player has three marks in a straight or diagonal row, in a number of turns, or when no player has three consecutive marks. Another essential element of a game (and play) is that players engage in it voluntarily, accepting its constitutive rules and willingly suspending their disbelief in the fictional world called up by the experience, until they put down the game. Therefore playing a game has also been defined as "a voluntary attempt to overcome unnecessary obstacles" (Suits, 1978, p. 55).

In L2 teaching methodology as well as in research and practice in the field of computer-assisted language learning (CALL), the term "game" is often ill defined and used intuitively, and can mean different things depending on the intended purpose and design of the game, as well as on the dispositions of learners and teachers and their prior experiences with games (Hubbard, 1991). In L2 teaching and learning, games take on a plethora of formats (e.g. sports, board, or word games) and genres (e.g. action, adventure, role-playing, or strategy). They can foreground different design elements (e.g. points systems or narrative), can rely on analog or digital technologies or a combination thereof, and can be played by one learner, by dyads or small groups, or by large numbers of learners (e.g. in massively multiplayer online games [MMOGs]). L2 learners can play them in the classroom (e.g. Nurmukhamedov & Sadler, 2020), outside the classroom but in connection with curricular objectives (e.g. Warner, Richardson, & Lange, 2019), or they can play them in the "(digital) wilds" (Sauro & Zourou, 2019), completely dissociated from formal learning. Games used in L2 teaching and learning contexts have been designed either solely for entertainment ("off-the-shelf games") or explicitly for teaching or learning ("educational games") and are commensurable with a wide range of pedagogical approaches.

Examples of game use in the literature on L2 teaching and learning are therefore varied. They range from teaching how to give opinions and suggestions in English L2 with the board game Snakes and Ladders (deHaan, 2020c), tandem learning of English and Russian as L2 "in the digital wilds" through the massively multiplayer online role-playing game (MMORPG) World of Warcraft (Thorne, 2008), autonomous and explicit learning of vocabulary and grammar in Turkish L2 with the gamified app Duolingo (Loewen et al., 2019), or teaching Spanish L2 and culture in a neighborhood in Albuquerque by means of a mobile mystery game (Sykes & Holden, 2011), to writing interactive fiction (text games) in the English as a foreign language (EFL) classroom around the content of the action-adventure game Assassin's Creed (Cornillie et al., 2021). For more detailed discussion of terminology, game types, and examples of game use in L2 learning and teaching we refer to Cornillie (2022), Reinhardt (2019), Thanyawatpokin and York (2021), and York et al. (2021).

An issue with current research on L2 learning with games is that a great deal of it is not very applicable to L2 teaching contexts, for reasons connected to technology, pedagogy, and research focus. As for technology, the tendency is to examine L2 learning with digital games (at the expense of analog games), in particular immersive environments such as MMORPGs (Hung et al., 2018). As these games are impractical and often prohibitively expensive to implement in most instructed L2 contexts, both inside the classroom and in students' homes, such research bears limited value for teaching practice.

A second trend in the research literature is that many studies are embedded in task-based language teaching (TBLT) approaches (for discussion see Cornillie, 2022). While relevant to many classroom contexts these days, an exclusive focus of research on TBLT pedagogy may limit the applicability of findings to contexts that draw on other pedagogical perspectives, such as communicative language teaching or the pedagogy of multiliteracies (see York et al., 2021).

A final characteristic of the current research literature is that it concentrates on the relation between games – or, at best, features of their design – and learning outcomes. A systematic review of eighty-two studies on gaming published in five leading CALL journals between 1984 and 2010 revealed that, overall, relatively few studies are pedagogy-focused, that is, "[take] a teacher-centred perspective and [reflect] the evaluation or implementation of games in the context of classroom language learning" (Cornillie, Thorne, & Desmet, 2012, p. 251). Hung et al.'s (2018) scoping review of empirical studies conducted between 2007 and 2016 reveals that the main object of interest is how playing games results in certain cognitive or affective learning outcomes – or rather is correlated with these outcomes, pending evidence of causation. These outcomes are in particular vocabulary learning and attitudes toward the use of games for L2 learning – and this includes constructs that are often fuzzily defined and poorly measured, such as "fun."

When such empirical studies are well embedded in theory and properly operationalized, their value is that they can give insights into the conditions inherent in and specific to game environments that drive effective L2 learning, and this in turn contributes to theory-building in SLA and, potentially, to the design of educationally purposed games (Cornillie, 2022). However, the translation of such insights into classroom practice is hardly straightforward. For example, if a study shows that task-essential in-game vocabulary is remembered better than vocabulary that is not task-essential (e.g. Cheung & Harrison, 1992), how can teachers integrate this finding into their teaching practice if they do not have access to a transcript of the game's text? Or, if learners are found to successfully negotiate meaning in an MMORPG, are teachers, then, to replicate the design of these games in the design of their teaching, and if so, how? From this perspective, much research on games that is narrowly focused on SLA has minimal practical value for classroom practice: Teachers can only try to apply the mechanics of effective learning in games to tasks that they themselves design, but concrete guidelines and tools are lacking. For more discussion about the lack of applicability of current research to L2 teaching, see York et al. (2021).

In sum, most current research on the use of games in L2 teaching and learning is situated in the area of "digital game-based language learning" (DGBLL): SLA-oriented work that is concerned with digital games, emphasizes autonomous learning, and appears to turn a blind eye to the critical role of teachers in real classrooms. The tendency to forget about the teacher has equally been noted about TBLT, in research- and pedagogy-oriented literature alike (Van den Branden, 2016). Moreover, particularly in studies on informal L2 learning with games "in the wilds" that claim to bear implications for classroom practice, it seems that researchers have fallen prey to what Larsen-Freeman (2003, p. 20) called "the reflex fallacy" :

> the assumption that it is our job to re-create in our classrooms the natural
> conditions of acquisition present in the external environment. Instead, what

we want to do as language teachers, it seems to me, is to improve upon natural acquisition, not emulate it … we want to accelerate the actual rate of acquisition beyond what the students could achieve on their own … accelerating natural learning is, after all, the purpose of formal education.

In the "external environment" of informal game-based L2 learning, learners are exposed to simulated environments in which the L2 is used meaningfully, often in interaction with peers who serve as more knowledgeable experts. This exposure can recruit cognitive processes involved in natural L2 development. While there is increasing recognition that opportunities for informal learning ideally need to cooperate in a continuum with, and be enforced by, teaching in formal learning contexts (Dressman & Sadler, 2020), current research in the area of DGBLL appears to forget that, in order to make the most of these opportunities for formal learning, educators need to be involved and put their pedagogical expertise to work in game-mediated play (Molin, 2017; York et al., 2021).

Historical Perspectives

The history of game use in L2 teaching contexts predates the more recent hype around learning with digital games by several decades. Early volumes are aimed specifically at teachers who would like to use analog games in their teaching environment and focus on simple conversation games, parlour games, or folk games that may use pens and paper, dice, and cards. Dorry (1966) is one of the earliest examples of a work that introduced several game genres such as spelling games, vocabulary games, and pronunciation games. Similarly, Lee's (1979) categorizations include listen-and-do, read-and-do, spelling, vocabulary, and miming and roleplay, among others. These categorizations are beneficial to teachers who may want to choose a specific game to teach a specific skill. Although space limitations prevent us from introducing more volumes of this nature, we invite the reader to consult Davis and Hollowell (1977), Rinvolucri (1984) and Rixon (1981).

One critique of these early classifications of games is that "they are often used to sugarcoat activities students find unpleasant, such as tests," and that "perhaps the bulk of the 'games' described in such books" consists of "tests or drills in the form of contests" (Susser, 1979, p. 58). On the basis of the observation that gameplay aligns with a cognitive or communicative approach to language teaching, Susser posited that games should not be used as a treat or as a relief, but must be tightly integrated into a language course.

Although one might think the field has grown past sugarcoated approaches to (drill and practice) pedagogy and that such games have disappeared from wide use, they are, conversely, the most commonly designed "language learning game" in the educational technology industry. They are also largely compatible with what is now known as a "gamified" approach to instruction (Kapp, 2012): activities that are assigned a certain point value or other extrinsic rewards for their completion, so that a designer or an instructor can direct student behavior. Recent examples are Butler, Someya, and Fukuhara (2014), who designed a number of drill and practice games for young learners of English; Müller et al. (2017), who created a web-based quiz for learning idioms; and the massively popular Duolingo platform. In light of what we know about effective L2 development and motivation for learning, it is crucial that such games go beyond the level of mechanical practice and extrinsic rewards (see Cornillie & Desmet, 2016 for a discussion).

The earliest examples of digital games described in the CALL literature are adventure games. In a paper on paradigms in the design of CALL materials, Phillips (1987) notes their popularity, arguing that it "has been stimulated by the non-tutorial view of CALL" (p. 277). He compares this to tutorial programs that typically comprise drill and practice activities, where "the computer acts largely as a surrogate for the teacher" (p. 275). Early empirical studies show, however, that the role of teachers around the use of adventure games in L2 education can vary widely.

Cheung (1985, 1986), for example, documented how pairs of ESL learners (both advanced and beginner level students) engaged in communicative interaction in the L2 while playing the text adventure Colossal Adventure. During gameplay learners formulated hypotheses, approval, and clarifications, and made use of imperatives and modal verbs. In these studies, teacher roles were not very apparent except in the provision of a short briefing about the game and access to dictionaries, which students could use as support while playing.

By contrast, Meskill (1990) clearly considers the role of teachers in guiding students' learning with the graphical adventure game Where in the World Is Carmen Sandiego? in a communicative language teaching (CLT) classroom. As in Cheung (1985, 1986), the students work in teams, but the teacher clearly orchestrates their learning before, during, and after play. Among other things, the teacher organizes warm-up activities to orient students to the game objectives and mechanics as well as to the kind of language and communication strategies they will need, assigns roles to students prior to play, offers support during gameplay just when students need it, and thoroughly debriefs the gaming and communication strategies that students used.

Primary Themes

The Need for Teacher Mediation

In this chapter we are focused on how teachers use ludic materials as part of their practice. Research has shown consistently that teacher (or expert) mediation is a critical factor in aiding learning (Hattie, 2012). Surprisingly, then, concerns have been raised about a lack of focus on teacher roles when teaching with games (Hanghøj & Brund, 2010; Molin, 2017). Moreover, the same problem appears in SLA research. Placing a focus on the TBLT research literature, Van den Branden (2016) wrote that teacher roles have received "scant attention" (p. 164). The principal narrative of literature on TBLT implies instead that students undertake tasks independently, without teacher mediation, and language learning occurs as a natural result of this interaction between students and tasks. This reasoning underestimates the considerable impact teachers have on their students' learning when planning a curriculum, preparing materials and lesson plans, instructing and motivating the students, mediating during task performance, and debriefing.

A key paper that explores teacher roles in L2 teaching with games is deHaan (2020a, 2020b). Based on a rigorous selection of criteria, deHaan chose twenty-eight studies that featured details of teaching practices around game usage. Among those studies, seventeen mentioned teacher activities at the pre-play stage, six during play, and only three had information on teacher roles at the post-play stage of instruction. There is therefore a considerable gap in the literature regarding the roles and effects of teachers in classrooms that use games.

What Can Teachers Do around Gameplay?

The importance of supporting learning before and after task performance is universally recognized in educational fields. Dewey (1938), for instance, wrote that meaningful learning is a combination of both experience and reflection. Similarly, in the literature on simulation and gaming, there is a strong emphasis on both briefing students before they interact with an activity and debriefing the session so as to allow for a transfer of learning to occur (Crookall & Oxford, 1990). Debriefing is often considered the crucial part of any simulation experience (Crookall, 1995). Finally, TBLT research has investigated a wide range of pre- and post-task activities that support learning (see Willis & Willis, 2007).

This concept of pre- and post-task activity has been mapped onto teaching with games by Sykes and Reinhardt (2013), who call for the addition of "wraparound activities" to support learning around gameplay. A limited number of studies have explored just how gameplay can be supported through (teacher-created) additional materials such as vocabulary explanations and exercises, where results showed that "supplemental materials were beneficial for successful task completion" (Miller & Hegelheimer, 2006, p. 311; see also Ranalli, 2008). A meta-analysis on DGBLL suggests that the provision of supplementary materials can indeed double the learning gains by comparison with simply playing the game, but proposes that more such studies are needed before definitive conclusions can be drawn (Dixon et al., 2022).

How Can Digital Technologies Aid Learning and Teaching with Games?

The value of digital technologies in and around L2 learning and teaching with games has been conceptualized according to three partially interacting roles or

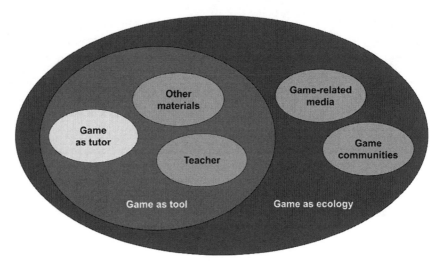

Figure 10.1 Three levels of technology use in L2 learning and teaching with games.

functions of technology (Reinhardt & Thorne, 2016), building on the canonical distinction in CALL between tutor and tool (Levy, 1997; see also Cornillie et al., 2012). First, in the tutorial role, technology acts (partly) in lieu of a teacher, but can also go beyond what teachers can do in a typical teaching context, for example, providing ample individualized feedback. This function is most evident in drill and practice (mini-)games, but task-based games can equally reveal the presence of a simulated teacher, for instance when they provide automated corrective feedback in simulated dialogues (e.g. González-Lloret, Diez Ortega, & Payne, 2020; see also Cornillie & Desmet, 2016 for a discussion on tutorial mini-games vis-à-vis task-based ones). Teachers may be involved in the design of games that have a tutorial function, but are typically absent when learners interact with these games. Figure 10.1 depicts this first level in the use of technology as the white ellipse on the left titled "game as tutor," where games are normally used standalone.

In the tool role, digital technology serves primarily to incentivize and structure interaction between learners and content or among learners, for instance when pairs of learners negotiate moves in a strategy game (see the next section for examples). Here digital technology can help teachers to (co-) orchestrate the execution of the activities that their learners engage in; it can also take away some of the cognitive load that teachers experience while doing so (Dillenbourg, 2013). Additionally (and this is not mentioned in the current literature) the tool role can comprise learners' use of digital technology for making games; this resembles how learners can use technology to (co-)create other types of artifacts in CALL, such as blogs or podcasts. In Figure 10.1, the game as tool model is signified by a larger ellipse, which may optionally comprise the tutorial function of technology but which, in classroom contexts, crucially involves teachers in scaffolding their students' learning with games, among various other supplementary materials.

The third role exploits the affordances of digital technologies such as social media for creating and sustaining game ecologies where gamers meet and cocreate knowledge and media related to games, for instance walkthroughs and fanfiction (see e.g. Thorne, Fischer, & Lu, 2012). This is signified by a further enlargement of the diagram in Figure 10.1, into extracurricular, public, or "digital wilds" contexts that go beyond the walls of the (physical or virtual) classroom and where learners interact or participate in game-related viewing, discussing, remixing, modding, or other such activities in game communities. Notice that, unlike in the tool role, the game itself may not even be played at this stage, let alone serve as a tutor for language instruction.

Much less attention has been given to how digital technologies can be used to support teachers in reaching their pedagogical goals with games. Technologies can enable the measurement and analysis of learners' linguistic production around gameplay (especially for off-the-shelf games) or provide tools that help teachers to select appropriate games as resources for their teaching.

Current Research and Practice

In this section we outline studies that have explored language teaching with both analog and digital games from a number of different pedagogical perspectives. Studies are introduced in terms of how the game was used: as tutor, as tool, or as ecology.

Game as Tutor in a Present–Practice–Produce Approach

Yip and Kwan's (2006) study partially represents the present–practice–produce (PPP) method of language teaching. To examine the effects of a game-based approach to teaching professional and academic English vocabulary, they conducted an experiment that lasted nine weeks with 100 Chinese engineering students and three teachers. Before the procedure in class, the teachers selected online vocabulary games "of the drill and practice type" (p. 238), according to a framework that consisted of criteria related to vocabulary learning pedagogies, principles of multimedia learning, and usability. One group of students engaged with these online games. They were largely left to their own devices, the teacher ensuring that the students visited the correct web pages. The other group of students took part in "activity-based lessons" in which teachers took on a more active role. This role consisted of presenting the teaching schedule and vocabulary lists, helping students develop their lexical skills through learning strategies such as drawing pictures or mind maps, and finally supporting them to explain words to their peers using the strategies they had learned before. The researchers had each teacher teach one group with each method in order to avoid the teacher having an effect on the learning outcomes in the different conditions. This design also allowed teachers to compare their views on each teaching method. Statistical analysis of the pre- and post-test receptive and productive knowledge of the written vocabulary showed that the students who practiced with the online games were able to retain more vocabulary items.

Of note is the fact that, while the online game group scored higher on vocabulary after the tests, the teacher disappeared into the background in this context. Teachers were much more active as mediators of their students' learning in the activity-based lessons. It is also noteworthy that the PPP method was clearly more articulated in the activity-based lessons, whereas the students who played the online games largely independently – the technology doing most of the teaching – were exposed to a pedagogy that seems to resemble a more narrow drill and practice approach. This raises the question of what difference the teacher made in the activity-based lessons. While this is impossible to tell from the paper, it is likely that the greater vocabulary learning gains in the online game group can be explained by the students' more intensive interaction with vocabulary items (i.e. they spent more time on the task that prepared them best for the test). The test of learning gains may thus have favored the treatment with drill and practice games over the other, more communicative treatment. Indeed, because drill and practice games are known to be less effective for the development of communicative skills (Cornillie & Desmet, 2016), a follow-up study needs to look into students' ability to transfer their knowledge from the different teaching approaches to more complex L2 tasks, such as picture narration.

Finally, focus group interviews with the three teachers revealed that they did not mind taking on a more facilitative, less prominent role during the online game group lesson, but would prefer to have better technological facilities to monitor their students' progress in the games. They also commented that they would rather spend less time on selecting and integrating the games (or reusing ready-made materials), and that they valued custom-made games for pedagogical reasons but would not be able to spend time on developing such materials even if they had the technical skills to do so. This clearly reveals the practical hurdles to implementing digital games in L2 classrooms – even fairly simple ones.

Game as Tool in a CLT Approach

A clear example of teacher-supported gameplay is demonstrated in Coleman (2002). Coleman appropriated the simulation game SimCopter as a tool to help his students improve their writing skills as part of an academic writing class. The intervention required students to write directions to certain locations within the game (e.g. from the airport to the bank) and to follow directions created by other students, thus taking on the roles of both direction giver and direction receiver. Coleman created materials to help students reach these custom goals. The materials were presented during a briefing session that introduced students to the scenarios, and also during a teacher-led debriefing session that was incorporated to assess the effectiveness of the directions created by students. In closing, Coleman remarks that the game is less important than how the teacher appropriates it to achieve learning goals (in this case, by creating materials and mediating student interactions). Although not explicitly stated in the paper, Coleman is concerned with authentic language use and audience, thus aligning with a CLT perspective on language teaching. Indeed, in closing, Coleman mentions that communication produced within the simulation "gains functional reality" as students become "realistic writers" and "realistic readers" in carrying out the task (p. 229).

Game as Tool in a TBLT Approach

Several papers have outlined the similarities between gameplay and a task-based approach to language teaching and learning (e.g. Cornillie, 2022; Sykes, 2014). York (2019) in particular compared the process of learning to play and, subsequently, to playing a board game with Willis's (1996) TBLT framework, showing that pre- and post-play activities have a close alignment with TBLT's guiding principles. In the same paper York provides examples of teacher roles at each stage of his intervention, and also of how Long's (2009) ten methodological principles for TBLT were incorporated into the material design. Before playing, student groups read the game rulebook, an activity that primes them to conduct gameplay. As another pre-play activity, students may play the game in their native language, making notes of what vocabulary and grammatical forms they will need during target language gameplay.

Digital technology is integrated throughout the framework. One highlight is that the gameplay session is recorded with student smartphones and subsequently transcribed by the group; this recording forms the core data to be analyzed at the post-play stage. Students also use YouTube on their smartphones to watch target language speakers play, comparing their output to that of more proficient speakers. At each stage, the teacher's role is one of asking questions (checking rules and language comprehension), promoting further exploration (of grammatical or vocabulary errors), and joining gameplay sessions to seed recordings with useful utterances. Finally, the framework includes a task repetition stage that prompts students to play again, with improved proficiency; thus gameplay occurred twice in six weeks of instruction. The results of York (2020) (using the same system) suggested that post-task activities had a positive effect on students' oral accuracy in repeated task performances.

Game as Ecology in a Multiliteracies Approach

Jonathan deHaan has attempted to normalize game use as part of pedagogy in his teaching context, where gameplay is employed as a catalyst for students to explore individual or group participatory projects (deHaan, 2019, 2020d). The syllabus features two full cycles of the following activities: gameplay, debriefing, analysis, and a participatory project. Examples of student projects are remixing a game for a specific educational purpose (teaching vocabulary to children); localizing a game; and examining the history of a game and writing an essay based on the findings. The pedagogical constructs align with the pedagogy of the multiliteracies sequence of experiencing, conceptualizing, analyzing, and applying (Cope & Kalantzis, 2015).

In terms of the teacher's role in this approach, deHaan writes that he designed the curriculum, the goals, the assessment rubric, and the worksheets to guide and support students' work at every stage. He also created a sample or presented previous students' work for each stage as models of what was expected. Finally, in terms of teacher mediation, deHaan (2020d, p. 44) writes: "I wanted to mediate closely and made sure to spend time with each group and student in each class and spent a great deal of time giving feedback on each worksheet and project and presentation." This paper thus introduces a great deal of detail regarding the teaching methodology and roles of the teacher throughout.

Future Directions: Recommendations for Research and Practice

If we want games and play to be normalized in language education, teachers need to be put center stage in research on L2 learning with games, and be provided with practical and research-based teaching materials as well as with (digital) tools that support their work during the pre-task, during-task, and post-task stages of teaching with games. The papers discussed here present a detailed account of the ways in which teachers can mediate student learning of an L2 with games, the pedagogical approaches that underlie their roles and choices, and the kinds of additional materials they can put to use to achieve their teaching goals. Hence they serve as much needed guidance for teachers who wish to implement games in their teaching in pedagogically sound ways. In the future, empirical research is needed that assesses the actual impact of teacher choices in ludic classrooms on students' learning outcomes. Another avenue for research is comparing learning outcomes between contexts where teachers design ludic activities for the classroom and contexts where students design them as part of the class. Inspiration for such projects can be drawn from teaching with games in first-language (L1) and literacy teaching contexts (e.g. Molin, 2017).

Second, the hype around digital games in education has created a blind spot around the value of other ludic activities for L2 teaching such as poetry, roleplay, debates, and drama, which, in light of evidence from recent volumes (Nurmukhamedov & Sadler, 2020) make up a substantial proportion of teachers' repertoires. We invite readers to both explore and conduct future research with these activities, as part of ludic language pedagogy.

Finally, research on teacher dispositions shows that teachers do not always have favorable attitudes toward games and may lack adequate game literacy skills, as well as knowledge of the benefits of games for language learning (Blume, 2019; Thomas, 2012). As expert teachers are pivotal in determining the quality of their students' learning, and as it has been shown that "good teachers are the single most important determinant for whether games will have a positive impact in schools" (Lieberoth & Hanghøj, 2017, p. 1), we call for the addition of modules in teacher training courses that highlight the wide cognitive, affective, and social benefits of games and play for language and literacy learning, as well as their effect of raising critical consciousness around the roles of teachers in contexts of game use. This call extends to preparing teachers to use readily available tools and resources effectively. For example, the FanTALES project (Sauro, Buendgens-Kosten, & Cornillie, 2020) created materials that help teachers find and exploit interactive fiction games for L2 teaching. Courses designed around teaching with games are appearing in L1 teaching contexts (Chee, Mehotra, & Ong, 2014); there is now an imperative for the same to appear in L2 teacher training.

References

Blume, C. (2019). Games people (don't) play: An analysis of pre-service EFL teachers' behaviors and beliefs regarding digital game-based language learning. *Computer Assisted Language Learning, 33*(1–2), 109–132. https://doi.org/10.1080/09588221.2018.1552599

Butler, Y. G., Someya, Y., & Fukuhara, E. (2014). Online games for young learners' foreign language learning. *ELT Journal, 68*(3), 265–275. https://doi.org/10.1093/elt/ccu008

Chee, Y. S., Mehrotra, S., & Ong, J. C. (2014). Facilitating dialog in the game-based learning classroom: Teacher challenges reconstructing professional identity. *Digital Culture & Education, 6*(4), 298–316.

Cheung, A. (1985). Computer-based adventure games and TESL: A preliminary enquiry. *ReCALL: Computers in English Language Education and Research, 1*, 2–4.

Cheung, A. (1986). Computer-based adventure games and TESL: A second enquiry. *ReCALL: Computers in English Language Education and Research, 2*, 3–4.

Cheung, A., & Harrison, C. (1992). Microcomputer adventure games and second language acquisition: A study of Hong Kong tertiary students. In M. C. Pennington & V. Stevens (Eds.), *Computers in applied linguistics: An international perspective* (pp. 155–178). Multilingual Matters.

Coleman, D. W. (2002). On foot in SIMCITY: Using SIMCOPTER as the basis for an ESL writing assignment. *Simulation & Gaming, 33*(2), 217–230.

Cook, G. (1997). Language play, language learning. *ELT Journal, 51*(3), 224–231.

Cope, B., & Kalantzis, M. (Eds.) (2015). *A pedagogy of multiliteracies: Learning by design.* Palgrave Macmillan. https://doi.org/10.1057/9781137539724

Cornillie, F. (2022). Digital games and technology-mediated gameful environments for L2 learning and instruction. In N. Ziegler & M. González-Lloret (Eds.), *Routledge handbook of second language acquisition and technology* (pp. 272–285). Routledge. https://doi.org/10.4324/9781351117586

Cornillie, F., & Desmet, P. (2016). Mini-games for language learning. In F. Farr & L. Murray (Eds.), *The Routledge handbook of language learning and technology* (pp. 431–445). Routledge.

Cornillie, F., Thorne, S. L., & Desmet, P. (2012). Digital games for language learning: From hype to insight? *ReCALL, 24*(3), 243–256. https://doi.org/10.1017/S0958344012000134

Cornillie, F., Buendgens-Kosten, J., Sauro, S., & Van der Veken, J. (2021). "There's always an option": Collaborative writing of multilingual interactive fanfiction in a foreign language class. *CALICO Journal, 38*(1), 17–42. https://doi.org/10.1558/cj.41119

Crookall, D. (1995). A guide to the literature on simulation/gaming. In D. Crookall & K. Arai (Eds.), *Simulation and gaming across disciplines and cultures: ISAGA at a watershed* (pp. 151–177). Sage.

Crookall, D., & Oxford, R. L. (1990). *Simulation, gaming and language learning.* Newbury House.

Davis, K., & Hollowell, J. (1977). *Inventing and playing games in the English classroom: A handbook for teachers.* National Council of Teachers of English.

deHaan, J. (2019). Teaching language and literacy with games: What? How? Why? *Ludic Language Pedagogy, 1,* 1–57.

deHaan, J. (2020a). Game-based language teaching is vaporware (Part 1 of 2): Examination of research reports. *Ludic Language Pedagogy, 2,* 115–139.

deHaan, J. (2020b). Game-based language teaching is vaporware (Part 2 of 2): It's time to ship or shut down. *Ludic Language Pedagogy, 2,* 140–161.

deHaan, J. (2020c). Snakes and ladders: Analyze and remix a classic. In U. Nurmukhamedov & R. Sadler (Eds.), *New ways in teaching with games* (pp. 80–82). TESOL Press.

deHaan, J. (2020d). "Game Terakoya class 1" walkthrough: Directing students' post-game discussions, academic work and participatory work through goals, curriculum, materials and interactions. *Ludic Language Pedagogy, 2,* 41–69.

Dewey, J. (1938). *Experience and education.* Macmillan.

Dillenbourg, P. (2013). Design for classroom orchestration. *Computers & Education, 69,* 485–492. https://doi.org/10.1016/j.compedu.2013.04.013

Dixon, D. H., Dixon, T., & Jordan, E. (2022). Second language (L2) gains through digital game-based language learning (DGBLL): A meta-analysis. *Language Learning & Technology, 26*(1), 1–25. http://hdl.handle.net/10125/73464

Dorry, G. (1966). *Games for second language learning.* McGraw Hill.

Dressman, M., & Sadler, R. W. (Eds.). (2019). *The handbook of informal language learning.* Wiley-Blackwell. https://doi.org/10.1002/9781119472384

Dubreil, S., & Thorne, S. L. (2017). Introduction: Social pedagogies and entwining language with the world. In S. Dubreil & S. L. Thorne (Eds.), *Engaging the world: Social pedagogies and language learning* (pp. 1–11). Cengage.

González-Lloret, M., Diez Ortega, M., & Payne, S. (2020). Gaming alone or together? L2 beginner-level gaming practices. *Perspectiva*, *38*(2), 1–21. https://doi.org/10.5007/2175-795x.2020.e67573

Hanghøj, T., & Brund, C. (2010). Teacher roles and positionings in relation to educational games. In B. Meyer (Ed.), *Proceedings of the 4th European Conference of Games Based Learning* (pp. 116–122). Academic Conferences, Ltd.

Hattie, J. (2012). *Visible learning for teachers: Maximizing impact on learning.* Routledge.

Holden, C. L., & Sykes, J. M. (2011). Leveraging mobile games for place-based language learning. *International Journal of Game-Based Learning*, *1*(2), 1–18. https://doi.org/10.4018/ijgbl.2011040101

Hubbard, P. (1991). Evaluating computer games for language learning. *Simulation & Gaming*, *22*(2), 220–223.

Hung, H. T., Yang, J. C., Hwang, G. J., Chu, H. C., & Wang, C. C. (2018). A scoping review of research on digital game-based language learning. *Computers and Education*, *126*, 89–104. https://doi.org/10.1016/j.compedu.2018.07.001

Kapp, K. M. (2012). *The gamification of learning and instruction: Game-based methods and strategies for training and education.* Pfeiffer.

Larsen-Freeman, D. (2003). *Teaching language: From grammar to grammaring.* Thomson/Heinle.

Lee, W. R. (1979). *Language teaching games and contests* (2nd ed.). Oxford University Press.

Levy, M. (1997). *Computer-assisted language learning: Context and conceptualization.* Clarendon Press.

Lieberoth, A., & Hanghøj, T. (2017). Developing professional "game teacher" repertoires: Describing participants and measuring effects in a Danish college course on game based learning. Paper presented at the European Conference of Game Based Learning (ECGBL), October 5–6, 2017, Graz, Austria.

Loewen, S., Crowther, D., Isbell, D. R., Kim, K. M., Maloney, J., Miller, Z. F., & Rawal, H. (2019). Mobile-assisted language learning: A Duolingo case study. *ReCALL*, *31*(3), 293–311. https://doi.org/10.1017/S0958344019000065

Long, M. H. (2009). Methodological principles in language teaching. In M. H. Long & C. J. Doughty (Eds.), *Handbook of language teaching* (pp. 373–94). Blackwell.

Matthews, R., & Liu, C. H. (2012). Play and its role in learning. In N. Seel (Ed.), *Encyclopedia of the sciences of learning* (pp. 2647–2650). Springer.

Meskill, C. (1990). Where in the world of English is Carmen Sandiego? *Simulation & Gaming*, *21*(4), 457–460. https://doi.org/10.1177/104687819002100410

Miller, M., & Hegelheimer, V. (2006). The SIMs meet ESL. Incorporating authentic computer simulation games into the language classroom. *Interactive Technology and Smart Education*, *3*(4), 311–328.

Molin, G. (2017). The role of the teacher in game-based learning: A review and outlook. *Serious Games and Edutainment Applications*, *2*, 649–674. https://doi.org/10.1007/978-3-319-51645-5_28

Müller, A., Son, J.-B., Nozawa, K., & Dashtestani, R. (2017). Learning English idioms with a web-based educational game. *Journal of Educational Computing Research, 56*(6), 073563311772929. https://doi.org/10.1177/0735633117729292

Nurmukhamedov, U., & Sadler, R. W. (2020). *New ways in teaching with games*. TESOL Press.

OECD. (2021). *OECD Skills Outlook 2021. Learning for life*. OECD Publishing. https://doi.org/10.1787/0ae365b4-en

Petersen, L. N. (2022). *Mediatized fan play: Moods, modes and dark play in networked communities*. Routledge. https://doi.org/10.4324/9781351001847.

Phillips, M. K. (1987). Potential paradigms and possible problems for CALL. *System, 15*(3), 275–287. https://doi.org/10.1016/0346-251X(87)90002-9

Poole, F., & Clarke-Midura, J. (2020). A systematic review of digital games in second language learning studies. *International Journal of Game-Based Learning, 10*(3), 1–15. https://doi.org/10.4018/IJGBL.2020070101

Ranalli, J. (2008). Learning English with The Sims: Exploiting authentic computer simulation games for L2 learning. *Computer Assisted Language Learning, 21*(5), 441–455. https://doi.org/10.1080/09588220802447859

Reinhardt, J. (2019). *Gameful second and foreign language teaching and learning: Theory, research, and practice*. Palgrave Macmillan.

Reinhardt, J., & Thorne, S. L. (2016). Metaphors for digital games and language learning. In F. Farr & L. Murray (Eds.), *The Routledge handbook of language learning and technology* (pp. 415–430). Routledge.

Rinvolucri, M. (1984). *Grammar games: Cognitive, affective, and drama activities for EFL students*. Cambridge University Press.

Rixon, S. (1981). *How to use games in language teaching*. Modern English Publications.

Salen, K., & Zimmerman, E. (2004). *Rules of play: Game design fundamentals*. MIT Press.

Sauro, S., & Zourou, K. (2019). What are the digital wilds? *Language Learning & Technology, 23*(1), 1–7. https://doi.org/10125/44666

Sauro, S., Buendgens-Kosten, J., & Cornillie, F. (2020). Storytelling for the foreign language classroom. *Foreign Language Annals, 53*(2), 329–337. https://doi.org/10.1111/flan.12467

Susser, B. (1979). The noisy way: Teaching English with games. *JALT Journal, 1*, 57–70.

Suits, B. (1978). *The grasshopper: Games, life and utopia*. University of Toronto Press.

Sykes, J. M. (2014). TBLT and synthetic immersive environments. What can in-game task restarts tell us about design and implementation? In M. González-Lloret & L. Ortega (Eds.), *Technology-mediated TBLT: Researching technology and tasks* (pp. 149–182). John Benjamins. https://doi.org/10.1075/tblt.6.06syk

Sykes, J. M., & Reinhardt, J. (2013). *Language at play: Digital games in second and foreign language teaching and learning*. Pearson.

Thanyawatpokin, B., & York, J. (2021). Issues in the current state of teaching languages with games. In M. Peterson, K. Yamazaki, & M. Thomas (Eds.),

Digital Games and Language Learning (pp. 239–256). Bloomsbury. https://doi .org/10.5040/9781350133037.ch-011

Thomas, M. (2012). Contextualizing digital game-based language learning: Transformational paradigm shift or business as usual? In H. Reinders (Ed.), *Digital games in language learning and teaching* (pp. 11–31). Palgrave Macmillan. https://doi.org/10.1057/9781137005267_2

Thorne, S. L. (2008). Transcultural communication in open internet environments and massively multiplayer online games. In S. S. Magnan (Ed.), *Mediating discourse online* (pp. 305–327). John Benjamins.

Thorne, S. L., Fischer, I., & Lu, X. (2012). The semiotic ecology and linguistic complexity of an online game world. *ReCALL*, *24*(3), 279–301. https://doi.org/ 10.1017/S0958344012000158

Van den Branden, K. (2016). The role of teachers in task-based language education. *Annual Review of Applied Linguistics*, *36*(2016), 164–181. https://doi.org/ 10.1017/S0267190515000070

Warner, C., Richardson, D., & Lange, K. (2019). Realizing multiple literacies through game-enhanced pedagogies: Designing learning across discourse levels. *Journal of Gaming and Virtual Worlds*, *11*(1), 9–28. https://doi.org/10.1386/ jgvw.11.1.9_1

Willis, D., & Willis, J. (2007). *Doing task-based teaching*. Oxford University Press.

Willis, J. (1996). *A framework for task-based learning*. Longman.

Yip, F., & Kwan, A. (2006). Online vocabulary games as a tool for teaching and learning English vocabulary. *Educational Media International*, *43*(3), 233–249. https://doi.org/10.1080/09523980600641445

York, J. (2019). "Kotoba Rollers" walkthrough: Board games, TBLT, and player progression in a university EFL classroom. *Ludic Language Pedagogy*, *1*, 58–115. https://doi.org/10.55853/llp_v1Wt1

York, J. (2020). Pedagogical considerations for teaching with games: Improving oral proficiency with self-transcription, task repetition, and online video analysis. *Ludic Language Pedagogy*, *2*, 225–255. https://doi.org/10.55853/llp_v2Art4

York, J., Poole, F. J., & DeHaan, J. W. (2021). Playing a new game: An argument for a teacher-focused field around games and play in language education. *Foreign Language Annals*, *54*(4), 1164–1188. https://doi.org/10.1111/flan.12585

Further Reading

Nurmukhamedov, U., & Sadler, R. (Eds.). (2020). *New ways in teaching with games*. TESOL Press.

This recent volume targets language teachers and features over eighty lesson plans based on games, the majority of which fall into the parlour or folk game categories rather than digital games. Therefore, like other teacher-oriented works published in the 1980s and before (see "historical perspectives"), this book is an excellent fit for teaching in low-tech contexts.

Sykes, J. M., & Reinhardt, J. (2013). *Language at play: Digital games in second and foreign language teaching and learning*. Pearson.

This short book addresses "language teaching professionals" – teachers, but also researchers and game designers. It offers strategies, scenarios, and other inspiration for implementing digital games in teaching contexts on the basis of theories of SLA and games, as well as pedagogy and game design.

York, J., Poole, F. J., & DeHaan, J. W. (2021). Playing a new game: An argument for a teacher focused field around games and play in language education. *Foreign Language Annals, 54*(4), 1164–1188. https://doi.org/10.1111/flan.12585

This position paper on ludic language pedagogy explores the question of why teachers have been neglected in the literature on (digital) games for language learning, argues why teachers are needed, and demonstrates what teaching with games in real contexts looks like.

11

Communication in Language MOOCs

Agnes Kukulska-Hulme, Fereshte Goshtasbpour, and
Barbara Conde-Gafaro

Introduction

Massive open online courses (MOOCs), as a potential means of providing access to education for all, have been around for more than a decade. MOOCs are generally free, open (no entry requirement), online courses developed for large or "massive" numbers of learners (Jansen & Schuwer, 2015) and promise to meet the needs of a changing learner population such as nontraditional part-time and lifelong learners (Siemens, 2015). The recent COVID-19 pandemic led to an upsurge in interest in MOOCs (Bates, 2020), and thereby an expansion of previously highlighted benefits, such as mobilizing institutions to recognize online learning and support formal, informal, self-directed, or work-integrated learning. MOOCs can offer learners additional support for a university degree, provide professional development at work, or clarify a difficult concept for a school-level certificate (de Freitas, Mogran, & Gibson, 2015; Stutchbury et al., 2023). They have enabled educators to experience teaching demographically diverse learner cohorts and to gain a richer understanding of online teaching at scale (Hew, 2018). Additionally, they have increased the visibility of many educators (Blackmon, 2018; Goel et al., 2023) by enabling them to reach a much wider audience.

MOOCs are often characterized as connectivist (cMOOCs) or extended (xMOOCs), depending on their pedagogical underpinnings. cMOOCs are based on connectivist pedagogy that recognizes learning as a distributed process whereby learners build and maintain connections to knowledge resources and peers in a network (Siemens, 2005). In contrast, xMOOCs follow a cognitivist–behaviorist pedagogy (Rodriguez, 2013) and are delivered through a learning platform such as edX, Coursera, Udacity, or FutureLearn. In these structured and curriculum-driven xMOOCs, learners study the course content (e.g. videos, articles, auto-graded activities), while engaging with peers and educator(s) in discussion areas (Wise & Cui, 2018). Although the cMOOC–xMOOC dichotomy is criticized for showing insufficiencies in describing the diversity of MOOCs (Bayne & Ross, 2014), it "has gained considerable authority and reveals some of the key ideas that shaped the design, development, and promotion of the MOOC" (Knox, 2015, p. 2). Many MOOCs include features of both types of MOOC.

The unique learning environment of MOOCs offers opportunities and creates challenges for learning and teaching, language learning being no exception (Wong, 2021). For example, since these courses can involve the use of audiovisual materials and oral and written interactions (Wong, 2021), they can help with the development of communication skills. At the same time, facilitating communication in the MOOC proves a challenge, as in many cases "learners outnumber educators by 1,000 to one or even more" (Ferguson & Sharples, 2014, p. 103). Thus it is important to know how to use these open and large-scale courses to support language learning and teaching, especially the development of foreign- and second-language communication skills and effective communication among participants and educators in MOOCs. To this end, the chapter aims to assess the promise and reality of communication in language MOOCs (LMOOCs).

Background

Language MOOCs are online courses offered at scale to people interested in learning or practicing a foreign or second language (Martín-Monje & Bárcena, 2014). They are taught at a distance and the course materials are usually written by educators from higher education institutions or international organizations focused on education and culture. They are designed to develop language and cultural knowledge and may include employability skills for working in the countries where the target language is spoken (Beaven, 2013; Beaven, Codreanu, & Creuzé, 2014). Learners can make use of audiovisual resources, written material, and discussion forums to practice listening, reading, and writing (Sokolik, 2016) and other aspects of language such as grammar, vocabulary, and pronunciation.

Language learners have distinct motivations for using LMOOCs. Their reasons for enrolment in LMOOCs can include improving their target language for academic or professional purposes or communicating with other language learners worldwide. However, communication is usually in written or visual form (Chong, Khan, & Reinders, 2022; Maravelaki & Panagiotidis, 2022), as oral communication is a challenge when large numbers of participants are involved. Learners may also be interested in developing their translation skills while taking part in an online community of translators, language teachers, and other learners; such was the case of learners in the Open Translation MOOC (Beaven et al., 2013). In this MOOC, designed by academics in the Department of Languages at the Open University, learners collaborated in the translation and subtitling of open educational resources.

LMOOCs may suit different participants' interests that encompass language learning, target language culture, and communication skills development.

The impact of the COVID-19 pandemic on education led to increased interest in online language learning, positioning foreign language education among the top ten most studied subjects in 2020 (Shah, 2020). LMOOC production is on the rise, and it is essential to know where and how to find these courses. Individuals interested in learning a language can find catalogues of LMOOCs available through websites such as classcentral.com, my-mooc .com and mooc-list.com. The first website is a search engine that displays online courses from various subjects, universities, nonacademic institutions, and platforms. Language-learning courses appear under the subject heading of "Humanities," 1,803 courses being offered at the time of writing (Class Central, 2024). Learners can also discover free online courses via the my-mooc.com website, which organizes courses into categories according to thirteen fields of specialism. For instance, at the time of writing, 153 LMOOCs can be found in "foreign languages" within the "personal development" category (My Mooc, 2024). The third website (mooc-list. com) offers a list of more than fifty LMOOCs and online courses in the category "languages and literatures" in which courses are filtered by level (beginner, intermediate, or advanced), provider, and duration (MOOC List, 2022).

Primary Themes

Communication Opportunities and Challenges

Interactions and communications between learners, educators, and content are a critical component of meaningful learning and quality online learning experiences (Anderson and Dron, 2011). In language learning their importance is supported by theories such as Krashen's input hypothesis in 1985, Swain's comprehensible output hypothesis in 1995, and Long's interaction hypothesis in 1996, as the interactions enable learners to negotiate meaning through receiving input and producing output while practicing the target language (Chew & Ng, 2021).

MOOCs, and particularly LMOOCs, provide opportunities for all learner-centric interaction types (learner–content, learner–learner, and learner–educator), but to varying degrees. Learner–content interactions, which are often stimulated by viewing videos and demonstrations or by reading texts (Gregori et al., 2018), support the development of receptive skills; they are very frequent as they are easily scalable. In contrast, interactions among learners (peer interactions) are generally low to medium in terms of frequency, even when learners are provided with several asynchronous and synchronous interaction opportunities. This is a likely result of the optional and voluntary nature of these interactions. MOOCs also include learner–educator interactions in several forms, for example weekly emails to learners or discussions in forums. Additionally, learners can have educator–learner-like interactions from several sources such as recordings of educators or automatic marking of tests and quizzes. However, learner–educator interactions are often limited as a result of cost, limited availability of educators, and lack of scalability (Miyazoe & Anderson, 2013).

Since MOOCs provide several interaction opportunities, educators' decisions and planning play a key role in managing learners' cognitive load and minimizing their nonessential cognitive activities to save their mental resources for the desired learning activities (Kozan, 2016). This is important, as the sheer volume of communications in MOOCs (e.g. in discussion areas) sometimes makes learners disengage from interaction with peers and educators, as a mechanism to manage information overload. They may resort to strategies such as ignoring interactions or engaging with them selectively (Peters & Hewitt, 2010; Wang et al., 2023).

The scale and openness of MOOCs affects interactions and creates both opportunities and challenges. For example, MOOCs support language learners to acquire communication experiences at different social, academic, and professional levels (Zubkov & Morozova, 2018), to access an international and multicultural community of other learners, and to develop a better understanding of other cultures for successful communication (Pavlovskaya & Perkins, 2016; Rai et al., 2023). In addition, they can help learners develop valuable soft skills such as negotiation (de Freitas et al., 2015) or ICT skills (Zubkov & Morozova, 2018).

However, the sheer volume of communications in MOOCs can discourage learners from sharing their views or seeking information (Hew, 2018), and the diversity of learners' backgrounds and knowledge bases can make interactions between learners difficult, since they do not share similar learning profiles (Chen, 2014). Furthermore, difficulties caused by language, different cultures, and even time zones are recognized as barriers to interactions in MOOCs. While learner diversity and heterogeneity can support learning from various perspectives, it can also cause difficulties when engaging in meaningful and continued communications (Tawfik et al., 2017). Learner diversity in terms of languages and cultural backgrounds means that communications are cross-cultural and, if learners or educators are not aware of different communication patterns, cultures, and values, misunderstandings and miscommunications are likely to arise. Pavlovskaya and Perkins's (2016) study highlights unexpected communication breakdowns and failures experienced by language learners as a result of a lack of sociocultural awareness and competence. They suggest that verbal and nonverbal sociocultural mistakes such as inappropriate lexical and grammatical choices, taboo topics, or misinterpreting visual information can end communications. Similarly, they can impede deep learning and community formation (Rovai, 2007).

Another difficulty associated with communications in MOOCs concerns learners' willingness to listen to alternative views and to accept those that aid in a collective understanding of the topic. This dialogic aspect of

Table 11.1 *Promises and realities of communication in LMOOCs*

Promises	Realities	Moving forward
LMOOCs provide communication opportunities at different social, academic, and professional levels.	Not many learners are keen to engage with such opportunities, especially older language learners.	Provide learners with clear instruction about their participation in communication opportunities and try to minimize barriers to their engagement.
LMOOCs enable access to an international and multicultural community of other learners.	Diversity among learners enables learning from diverse perspectives. The cultural diversity of learners can create communication breakdown or failure.	Consider various demographic characteristics of learners such as age, education level, and language proficiency within the course's learning design, since they can affect learners' performance. Raise learners' awareness of cultural differences and set communication ground rules (e.g. netiquette).
LMOOCs help learners develop soft skills such as negotiation and decision making.	Learners can cooperate with others and, for instance, interact with speakers of the target language in a tandemMOOC (http://mooce.speakapps.org)	More research and learning design efforts are needed to address the pedagogical and technological design issues that represent the development of speaking interaction, and thereby soft skills in LMOOCs.

interactions can improve learners' understanding; however, in the case of MOOCs, where large numbers of learners are involved, the dialogue does not occur in an orderly and progressive way (Wells & Arauz, 2006). Some promises and realities of communication in LMOOCs are summarized in Table 11.1.

Current Research and Practice

In LMOOCs, learners can practice their productive language skills asynchronously and synchronously, through peer or learner–educator interactions. Often the discussion areas in these courses provide learners with an opportunity to communicate in writing in the target language (Sokolik, 2016). However, for various reasons, some learners choose not to take up such opportunities. For example, older language learners in the Irish 101 LMOOC were more engaged in watching videos and completing quizzes and less keen to contribute to discussion forums (Mac Lochlainn, Mhichíl, & Beirne, 2021). The feeling of exposure when expressing personal ideas in a large and open course can make learners avoid this kind of activity and thereby miss the opportunity to develop their writing skills in the target language.

Fostering speaking among learners has generally been a challenge, given the scale and openness of LMOOCs (Read, Bárcena, & Kukulska-Hulme, 2016). Nevertheless, the work of Appel and Pujolà (2021) has led to the development of a MOOC that provides learners with speaking practice by taking advantage of the online and massive features of LMOOCs. The course, titled "TandemMOOC English–Spanish," follows a tandem learning approach, in which large numbers of proficient speakers of English collaborate synchronously with speakers of Spanish while both learn each other's languages. This online course includes:

- a videoconferencing system,
- a tool to manage content during the task, and
- matching tools to help participants find a tandem partner.

As well as affording opportunities to interact with proficient speakers of the target language, the course provides learners with the necessary competencies to interact, collaborate, and give peer feedback. Emerging LMOOCs should foster these types of synchronous interaction in which learners can practice their speaking skills and at the same time develop communicative strategies.

For both written and oral communications and interactions, learners require feedback to improve their learning and to fill the gap between what they have understood and what should be learned. In other words, feedback is required to scaffold their learning. In MOOCs, this feedback is provided through various means, as summarized in Table 11.2.

Recommendations for Research and Practice

Effective use of LMOOCs to support the development of communication skills requires more than knowing about the opportunities and challenges these courses create for communication. There are various factors that should be considered, such as the educator's role, learners' preparedness and autonomy, and how to integrate them into classroom practices.

Educator's Role

Educators play a crucial role in facilitating different aspects of communications in MOOCs. They support learners to make sense of the input provided by the learning resources, and they validate their outputs or contributions (Mishra, Cayzer, & Madden, 2017). Regardless of how self-regulated and autonomous learners are in understanding the content, when application of knowledge (e.g. a grammar rule) is considered, learners require an educator's feedback to confirm whether they can apply their knowledge correctly (Bartalesi-Graf et al., 2022). In addition, during a MOOC learning journey, when the topics become difficult or unfamiliar, few learners feel confident assisting others (Onah, Sinclair, & Boyatt, 2014). This is when an educator's involvement and scaffolding are key to maintaining learners' engagement and facilitating the communication process. Moreover, a cohort of learners consists of both autonomous and less autonomous learners, and the latter require more direction from an educator (Kop & Bouchard, 2011).

Table 11.2 *Sources of feedback for learners in MOOCs*

Source of feedback in MOOCs	Description	Benefits and drawbacks
Peers	Learners, especially more advanced and autonomous learners, give feedback to their peers in discussion forums, during collaborative activities, or in peer-assessed assignments.	**Benefits:** • Encourages coregulated learning • Gives learners more control over learning • Encourages a distributed teaching presence **Drawbacks:** • Peer feedback can be inadequate, too general, or incorrect • Learners often do not have experience in giving feedback • Low learner motivation to provide peer feedback
Teaching team (educators, mentors, and teaching assistants)	The teaching team mainly provides formative feedback to learners in discussion areas. Occasionally its members engage with learners outside the MOOC platform and on social media.	**Benefits:** • Promotes critical thinking and encourages deeper learning • Scaffolds understanding when learners find a topic or concept difficult • The teaching is personalized **Drawbacks:** • It is limited in MOOCs, as educators cannot provide feedback to everyone • It may not be timely or continuous because of the volume of questions and comments in MOOCs
Platform	For some activities and assessments such as an end-of-course quiz, the MOOC platforms are set to provide learners with automated feedback.	**Benefits:** • Enables feedback to all learners (scalability) • Allows immediate low-cost feedback • Allows multiple (and sometimes unlimited) submission of responses **Drawbacks:** • It can be tailored only to a certain extent • It is limited to certain types of activity (e.g. quizzes or short essays)

Furthermore, it is educators' skillful facilitation that prompts communication and encourages learners to interact and express their ideas. If educators do not facilitate or challenge ideas in an intercultural context such as MOOCs, learners tend to limit their conversations to safe topics and consequently do not use the potential opportunities for deep learning (Helm, 2013). Overall, educators facilitate communications by orchestrating interactions, highlighting valuable learner contributions, and challenging incorrect or incomplete ones. Sharples's (2015) expression "oil the wheels" suitably describes the educator role in facilitating communications in MOOCs.

Learners' Autonomy and Self-Regulation

Studying in an LMOOC is an opportunity for learners to develop a responsible role in their language education. The self-access nature of these courses implicitly requires a level of self-regulation that goes beyond choosing the time and course content to study. Learners are expected to employ strategies such as goal setting, strategic planning, and self-evaluation if they are to regulate their learning effectively. However, the format of these courses can present a challenge for learners who have not employed such strategies before (Milligan, Littlejohn, & Hood, 2016). It has been suggested that the learning design should include adequate scaffolding to support the use of self-regulated learning strategies in these online courses (Kizilcec, Pérez-Sanagustín, & Maldonado, 2017). Hence educators and providers of LMOOCs should embed this type of support, especially within communicative activities designed to promote effective practice and self-reflection on the performance of oral and written production – activities that are usually underestimated in LMOOC-based learning. Alternatively, in-class tutors can inform learners about the importance of self-regulated learning and prompt them to use these strategies during their LMOOC-based learning, if it is integrated into a face-to-face course.

Affordances of LMOOC Technology for Communication

LMOOCs do not tend to have the appropriate technology to provide enough speaking interaction practice at scale. Most LMOOCs rarely address this productive skill on their platforms; this is due to the complex instructional and technological design behind the implementation of speaking interaction tasks (Appel & Pujolà, 2021). Researchers and practitioners have worked together to integrate this skill into emerging online courses such as the tandemMOOC mentioned earlier, which takes advantage of the multitude of participants and affords authentic target language use through speaking interaction with proficient speakers. Yet synchronous communication in LMOOCs remains a challenge for language educators and educational technologists when developing speaking interaction and integrating it into these massive online courses. Hence pedagogical and technical support is needed from both MOOC educators and MOOC providers in order to increase the opportunities for oral communication within and beyond the platforms so that learners may interact and develop social competencies and skills while using the target language.

Integration of LMOOCs into Classroom Practice

The potential of LMOOCs should not be limited to learning at a distance. Research on blended MOOCs practices (Beaven, 2013; Conde Gafaro, 2019;

de Waard & Demeulenaere, 2017) shows that integrating these online courses with face-to-face language courses can enable high-school and university students to:

- improve their language use
- implement collaborative learning skills
- initiate self-regulated learning.

Educators in LMOOCs should consider the possibility of designing activities that can be complemented with classroom-based ones, so as to expand the opportunities for communication in another language on a small scale and on a large scale alike. Similarly, in-class teachers should be open to embedding LMOOCs into their teaching, not necessarily by reusing the online content in their class, since most of the online resources might not be under a free license. Instead, they can integrate this informal learning modality into their lessons through follow-up activities designed to develop productive skills. Learners can be given a speaking or writing task that prompts them to interact with classmates and peers from the online course, drawing attention to active and cooperative learning.

Cultural Issues in Communication in LMOOCs

Positive cultural affordances of LMOOCs include authentic materials (Fuchs, 2020) and opportunities for cultural enrichment, for example as reported by students taking part in an Irish language and culture MOOC (Mac Lochlainn et al. 2020). Yet there are cultural and contextual aspects that reveal not-so-positive experiences and concerns. Liyanagunawardena, Adams, and Williams (2013) argue that tensions in learners' discussions in a MOOC could derive from possible cultural differences that should be further explored. A study by Orsini-Jones and Zou (2020), in which EFL teachers from China were looking to incorporate existing MOOCs into their teaching, notes the teachers' concern that they might be unable to handle questions from students relating to materials in a MOOC, which would threaten the Chinese teachers' traditional authority.

Future Directions

MOOCs are evolving, and there are continuous efforts to improve their effectiveness as well as the experiences of learners enrolled in the MOOCs. Given the large scale of most MOOCs, methods of analyzing learner activity and ways of supporting learners need to be scalable and take advantage of rapid developments in artificial intelligence.

Automated ways of analyzing the online behaviors of large numbers of learners, for instance the activities they complete or do not complete, and the extent to which they engage in communication with others on the course, can be used to reflect on MOOC designs. Data analytics is an established method of investigating how people behave online using data from online platforms. It is increasingly used in education as "learning analytics." Diagnostic learning analytics is the collection and analysis of data about learners and their online actions that are derived from MOOC platform metrics and compiled while a course is running. The analytics can be used to improve student engagement by having educators review and revise or fine-tune the design of the MOOC, its content, and its learning activities. For example, in an LMOOC on giving presentations in English that was run in Thailand, learning analytics related to several communication channels used in the course (comments, discussion forums, and a Facebook group) revealed the relative frequency of peer interactions in various learning activities that used these channels (Jitpaisarnwattana, Reinders, & Darasawang, 2021). When considered alongside findings from interviews with students, the learning analytics data enabled reflection on future LMOOC designs, and also a suggestion to incorporate more personal communication channels into the courses.

Large-scale learning environments also call for ingenious ways of providing additional, personalized, or human-like support and engaging interactions in the absence or scarcity of teachers and facilitators. Conversational agents such as chatbots can serve such purposes. Chatbots can be programmed to ask and answer questions, to guide learners, and to assist in problem-solving. Tegos et al. (2020) describe an experimental chatbot designed to advance productive peer dialogue and support students' collaborations in MOOCs by promoting knowledge exchange. This chatbot can monitor a conversation in a MOOC and decide when to deliver "questioning interventions," for example by posing a question ("Do you agree with the following statement: . . .?"), by encouraging a response to a peer ("[Person A], would you like to add something to what [Person B] has mentioned about [Topic X]?"), by making an informative statement, or by providing some guidance. The promise is that teachers will soon be able to configure such chatbots without the need for specialist programming knowledge.

In this chapter we have commented on the promises and realities of communication in MOOCs. We have addressed the opportunities and challenges faced by learners, educators, and providers when dealing with productive skills in LMOOCs. Learners can develop their communication skills in the target language within LMOOCs. They can access an online community of learners from around the world to exchange mainly written messages in the target language. Research shows that educators in these online courses can include different tasks and channels of communication, oral or written, in order to engage learners in meaningful and authentic discussions with others. Likewise, MOOC providers should work together with educators to provide learners with adequate and innovative technological tools to facilitate productive skills practice, and encourage the development of soft skills such as negotiation and decision-making. It appears that there is limited research on cultural and contextual aspects of MOOCs and LMOOCs, and we would agree with Fang et al. (2019), who suggest that future research could investigate potential cultural influence on engagement in MOOCs. LMOOCs have the potential to transform learners' communication opportunities in a target language while fostering their practice of a set of skills that are needed in active language learning.

References

Anderson, T., & Dron, J. (2011). Three generations of distance education pedagogy. *International Review of Research in Open and Distance Learning, 12*(3), 80–97. https://doi.org/10.19173/irrodl.v12i3.890

Appel, C., & Pujolà, J.-T. (2021). Designing speaking interaction in LMOOCs: An eTandem approach. *ReCALL, 33*(2), 161–176. https://doi.org/10.1017/S0958344021000045

Bartalesi-Graf, D., Agonács, N., Matos, J. F., & O'Steen, D. (2022). Insight into learners' experience in LMOOCs. *Computer Assisted Language Learning.* Advance online publication. https://doi.org/10.1080/09588221.2022.2082484.

Bates, T. (2020). MOOCs and online degrees continue to grow worldwide. www.tonybates.ca/2020/09/08/moocs-and-online-degrees-continue-to-grow-worldwide

Bayne, S., & Ross, J. (2014). *The pedagogy of the massive open online courses: The UK view.* York. www.advance-he.ac.uk/knowledge-hub/pedagogy-massive-open-online-course-mooc-uk-view

Beaven, A. (2013). Using MOOCs in an academic English course at university level. In A. Beaven, A. Comas-Quinn, & B. Sawhill (Eds.), *Case studies of openness in the language classroom* (pp. 217–227). Research-publishing.net. https://doi.org/10.14705/rpnet.2013.9781908416100

Beaven, T., Codreanu, T., & Creuzé, A. (2014). Motivation in a language MOOC: Issues for course designers. In E. Martín-Monje, & E. Bárcena (Eds.), *Language MOOCS: Providing learning, transcending boundaries.* (pp. 48–66). Walter de Gruyter GmbH and Co KG. https://doi.org/10.2478/9783110420067.4

Beaven, T., Comas-Quinn, A., Hauck, M., de los Arcos, B., & Lewis, T. (2013). The Open Translation MOOC: Creating online communities to transcend linguistic barriers. *Journal of Interactive Media in Education, 2013*(3). http://doi.org/10.5334/2013-18

Blackmon, S. (2018). MOOC makers: Professors' experiences with developing and delivering MOOCs. *The International Review of Research in Open and Distance Learning, 19*(4). https://doi.org/10.19173/irrodl.v19i4.3718

Chen, Y. (2014). Investigating MOOCs through blog mining. *The International Review of Research in Open and Distance Learning, 15*(2). https://doi.org/10.19173/irrodl.v15i2.1695

Chew, S. Y., & Ng, L. L. (2021). *Interpersonal interactions and language learning: Face-to-face vs. computer-mediated communication.* Palgrave Macmillan. www.palgrave.com/gp/book/9783030674243

Chong, S. W., Khan, M. A., & Reinders, H. (2022). A critical review of design features of LMOOCs. *Computer Assisted Language Learning, 37*(3), 389–409. https://doi.org/10.1080/09588221.2022.2038632

Class Central. (2024). Language learning courses. www.classcentral.com/subject/language-learning

Conde Gafaro. B. (2019). Repurposing MOOCs for self-regulated language learning in an English for academic purposes course. In A. Comas-Quinn, A. Beaven, & B. Sawhill (Eds.), *New case studies of openness in and beyond the language classroom* (pp. 115–128). Research-publishing.net. https://doi.org/10.14705/rpnet.2019.37.970

Kop, R., & Bouchard, P. (2011). The role of adult educators in the age of social media. In M. Thomas (Ed.), *Digital education: Opportunities for social collaboration* (pp. 61–80). Palgrave Macmillan. https://doi.org/10.1057/9780230118003_4

de Freitas, S., Mogran, J., & Gibson, D. (2015). Will MOOCs transform learning and teaching in higher education? Engagement and course retention in online learning provision. *British Journal of Educational Technology, 46*(3), 455–471. https://doi.org/10.1111/bjet.12268

de Waard, I., & Demeulenaere, K. (2017). The MOOC-CLIL project: Using MOOCs to increase language, and social and online learning skills for 5th grade K-12 students. In Q. Kan, & S. Bax (Eds.), *Beyond the language classroom: Researching MOOCs and other innovations* (pp. 29–42). Research-publishing.net. https://doi.org/10.14705/rpnet.2017.mooc2016.669

Fang, J., Tang, L., Yang, J., & Peng, M. (2019). Social interaction in MOOCs: The mediating effects of immersive experience and psychological needs satisfaction. *Telematics and Informatics, 39*, 75–91. https://doi.org/10.1016/j.tele.2019.01.006

Ferguson, R., & Sharples, M. (2014). Innovative pedagogy at massive scale: Teaching and learning in MOOCs. *EC-TEL 2014: Open Learning and Teaching in Educational Communities*, pp. 98–111. Springer. https://doi.org/10.1007/978-3-319-11200-8_8

Fuchs, C. (2020). Cultural and contextual affordances in language MOOCs: Student perspectives. *International Journal of Online Pedagogy and Course Design (IJOPCD), 10*(2), 48–60. https://doi.org/10.4018/IJOPCD.2020040104

Goel, P., Raj, S., Garg, A., Singh, S., & Gupta, S. (2023). Peeping in the minds of MOOCs instructors: Using fuzzy approach to understand the motivational factors. *Online Information Review, 47*(1), 20–40. https://doi.org/10.1108/OIR-04-2021-0205

Gregori, E. B., Zhang, J., Galván-Fernández, C., & de Asís Fernández-Navarro, F. (2018). Learner support in MOOCs: Identifying variables linked to completion. *Computers and Education, 122*, 153–168. https://doi.org/10.1016/j.compedu.2018.03.014

Helm, F. (2013). A dialogic model for telecollaboration. *Bellaterre Journal of Teaching and Learning Language and Literature, 6*(2), 22–48. https://doi.org/10.5565/rev/jtl3.522

Hew, K. F. (2018). Unpacking the strategies of ten highly rated MOOCs: Implications for engaging students in large online courses. *Teachers College Record*, *120*(1), 1–40. https://doi.org/10.1177/016146811812000107

Jansen, D., & Schuwer, R. (2015). *Institutional MOOC strategies in Europe: Status report based on a mapping survey conducted in October–December 2014*. EADTU, February 2015. https://eadtu.eu/documents/Publications/OEenM/Institutional_MOOC_strategies_in_Europe.pdf

Jitpaisarnwattana, N., Reinders, H., & Darasawang, P. (2021). Learners' perspectives on interaction in a language MOOC. *The JALT CALL Journal*, *17*(2), 158–182. https://doi.org/10.29140/jaltcall.v17n2.472

Kizilcec, R. F., Pérez-Sanagustín, M., & Maldonado, J. J. (2017). Self-regulated learning strategies predict learner behavior and goal attainment in massive open online courses. *Computers and Education*, *104*, 18–33. http://dx.doi.org/10.1016/j.compedu.2016.10.001

Knox, J. (2015). Massive open online courses (MOOCs). In M. Peters (Ed.), *Encyclopaedia of educational philosophy and theory* (pp. 1–7). Springer. https://doi.org/10.1007/978-981-287-532-7_219-1

Kozan, K. (2016). The incremental predictive validity of teaching, cognitive and social presence on cognitive load. *The Internet and Higher Education*, *31*, 11–19. https://doi.org/10.1016/j.iheduc.2016.05.003

Liyanagunawardena, T. R., Adams, A. A., & Williams, S. A. (2013). MOOCs: A systematic study of the published literature 2008–2012. *International Review of Research in Open and Distributed Learning*, *14*(3), 202–227. www.irrodl.org/index.php/irrodl/article/view/1455/2531

Mac Lochlainn, C., Nic Giolla Mhichíl, M., & Beirne, E. (2021). Clicking, but connecting? L2 learning engagement on an ab initio Irish language LMOOC. *ReCALL 33*(2), 111–127. https://doi.org/10.1017/S0958344021000100

Mac Lochlainn, C., Nic Giolla Mhichíl, M., Beirne, E., & Brown, M. (2020). The soul behind the screen: Understanding cultural enrichment as a motivation of informal MOOC learning. *Distance Education*, *41*(2), 201–215. https://doi.org/10.1080/01587919.2020.1757408

Maravelaki, S., & Panagiotidis, P. (2022). A digital storytelling MOOC for foreign language learning with a focus on L2 speaking and writing. In *Edulearn22 Proceedings* (pp. 3402–3411). IATED.

Martín-Monje, E., & Bárcena, E. (2014). (Eds). *Language MOOCs: Providing learning, transcending boundaries*. de Gruyter. https://doi.org/10.2478/9783110420067

Milligan, C., Littlejohn, A., & Hood, N. (2016). Learning in MOOCs: A comparison study. In M. Khalil., M. Ebner, M. Kopp, A. Lorenz, & M. Kalz (Eds.), *Proceedings of the 4th European MOOCs Stakeholder Summit on experiences and best practices in and around MOOCs (EMOOCS 2016)*. (pp. 15–26). University of Graz https://graz.elsevierpure.com/en/publications/proceedings-of-the-european-stakeholder-summit-on-experiences-and

Mishra, D., Cayzer, S., & Madden, T. (2017). Tutors and gatekeepers in Sustainability MOOC. *On the Horizon*, *25*(1), 45–59. https://doi.org/10.1108/OTH-04-2016-0017

Miyazoe, T., & Anderson, T. (2013). Interaction equivalency in an OER, MOOCs and informal learning era. *Journal of Interactive Media in Education, 2013*(2), 9–24. https://doi.org/10.5334/2013-09

MOOC List. (2024). Languages and literature. www.mooc-list.com/categories/languages-literature.

My Mooc. (2024). Foreign languages. www.my-mooc.com/en/categorie/foreign-languages

Onah, Daniel F. O., Sinclair, J., & Boyatt, R. (2014). Exploring the use of MOOC discussion forums. In *Proceedings of London International Conference on Education* (pp. 1–4). LICE. http://wrap.warwick.ac.uk/65549

Orsini-Jones, M., & Zou, B. (2020). Chinese English teachers' perspectives on "hMOOC flipped blends": Project BMELTE (Blending MOOCs into ELT Education). In B. Zou & M. Thomas (Eds.), *Recent developments in technology-enhanced and computer-assisted language learning* (pp. 164–183). IGI Global. https://doi.org/10.4018/978-1-7998-1282-1.ch008

Padilla Rodriguez, B. C., & Armellini, C. A. (2020). Why size matters in MOOCs. *Researching Education, 1*(3). https://doi.org/10.5281/zenodo.4283414

Pavlovskaya, G., & Perkins, M. (2016). Taking a MOOC: Socio-cultural aspects of virtual interaction in a multicultural learning community. *Journal of Language and Education, 2*(1), 16–21 https://doi.org/10.17323/2411-7390-2016-2-1-16-21

Peters, V. A., & Hewitt, J. (2010). An investigation of student practices in asynchronous computer conferencing courses. *Computer and Education, 45*(4), 951–61. https://doi.org/10.1016/j.compedu.2009.09.030

Rai, L., Deng, C., Lin, S., & Fan, L. (2023). Massive Open Online Courses and intercultural competence: Analysis of courses fostering soft skills through language learning. *Frontiers in Psychology, 14*, 1219478. https://doi.org/10.3389/fpsyg.2023.1219478

Read, T., Bárcena, E., & Kukulska-Hulme, A. (2016). Mobile and massive language learning. In E. Martín-Monje, I. Elorza, & B. G. Riaza (Eds.), *Technology-enhanced language learning for specialized domains: Practical applications and mobility* (pp. 151–161). Routledge. https://doi.org/10.4324/9781315651729

Rodriguez, O. (2013). The concept of openness behind c and xMOOCs (massive open online courses). *Open Praxis, 5*(1), 67–73. http://dx.doi.org/10.5944/openpraxis.5.1.42

Rovai, A. P. (2007). Facilitating online discussion effectively. *The Internet and Higher Education, 10*(1), 77–88. https://doi.org/10.1016/j.iheduc.2006.10.001.

Shah, D. (2020, August 16). By the numbers: MOOCs during the pandemic. Web log post. www.classcentral.com/report/mooc-stats-pandemic

Sharples, M. (2015). Role for educators in MOOCs. http://forum.networkedlearning.net/t/role-for-educators-in-moocs/168

Siemens, G. (2005). Connectivism: A learning theory for the digital age. *International Journal of Instructional Technology and Distance Learning, 2*(1). www.itdl.org/journal/jan_05/article01.htm19/11/2015

Siemens, G. (2015). The role of MOOCs in the future of education. In C. J. Bonk, M. M. Lee, T. C. Reeves, & T. H. Reynolds (Eds.), *MOOCs and open education around the world* (pp. xiii–xviii). Routledge. https://doi.org/10.4324/9781315751108.

Sokolik, M. (2016). Academic writing in MOOC environments. In E. Martín-Monje, I. Elorza, & B. G. Riaza (Eds.), *Technology-enhanced language learning for specialized domains: Practical applications and mobility* (pp. 165–176). Routledge. https://doi.org/10.4324/9781315651729

Stutchbury, K., Ebubedike, M., Amos, S., & Chamberlain, L. (2023). Professional development in the digital age: Supporting improvements in teacher education through MOOCs. *Open Learning: The Journal of Open, Distance and e-Learning*, 1–24. https://doi.org/10.1080/02680513.2023.2195875

Tawfik, A., Reeves, T., Stich, A., Gill, A., Hong, C., McDade, J., Pillutla. V. S., Zhou, X., & Giiabbanelli, P. (2017). The nature and level of learner–learner interaction in a chemistry massive open online course (MOOC). *Journal of Computing in Higher Education*, *29*, 411–431. https://doi.org/10.1007/s12528–017-9135-3

Tegos S., Demetriadis S., Psathas G., & Tsiatsos T. (2020). A configurable agent to advance peers' productive dialogue in MOOCs. In A. Følstad, T. Araujo, S. Papadopoulos, E. L.-C. Law, E. Luger, M. Goodwin, & P. B. Brandtzaeg (Eds.), *Chatbot research and design.* Springer. https://doi.org/10.1007/978-3-030-39540-7_17

Tolu, A., & Evans, L. (2013). From distance education to communities of inquiry: A review of historical developments. In Z. Akyol, & D. R. Garrison (Eds.), *Educational communities of inquiry: Theoretical framework, research and practice* (pp. 45–62). IGI Global. https://doi.org/10.4018/978-1-4666-2110-7

Wang, W., Zhao, Y., Wu, Y. J., & Goh, M. (2023). Interaction strategies in online learning: Insights from text analytics on iMOOC. *Education and Information Technologies*, *28*(2), 2145–2172. https://doi.org/10.1007/s10639-022-11270-7

Wells, G., & Arauz, R. (2006). Dialogue in the classroom. *Journal of the Learning Sciences*, *15*(3), 379–428. https://doi.org/10.1207/s15327809jls1503_3

Wise, A. F., & Cui, Y. (2018). Learning communities in the crowd: Characteristics of content related interactions and social relationships in MOOC discussion forums. *Computers and Education*, *122*, 221–241. https://doi.org/10.1016/j.compedu.2018.03.021

Wong, B. T. (2021). A survey on the pedagogical features of language massive open online courses. *Asian Association of Open Universities Journal*, *16*(1), 116–128. https://doi.org/10.1108/AAOUJ-03-2021-0028

Zubkov A. D., & Morozova M. A. (2018). Language learners communication in MOOCs. In A. Filchenko & Z. Anikina (Eds.), *Linguistic and cultural studies: Traditions and innovations.* LKTI 2017. Advances in Intelligent Systems and Computing, vol 677. Springer. https://doi.org/10.1007/978-3-319-67843-6_22

Further Reading

Littlejohn, A., & Hood, N. (2018). *Reconceptualising learning in the digital age: The [un]democratizing potential of MOOCs.* Springer.
This book provides an analysis of MOOCs with the aim of highlighting the tension between what MOOCs originally were developed for (opening up access to

education) and what they involve in reality today. It considers MOOCs within educational, social, and economic contexts and reflects on whether they address the demands of opening up access to education effectively. Additionally, it offers a critical perspective on how learners, educators, learning, and teaching as well as accreditation are conceptualized in these open and scaled educational settings.

Rizvi, S., Rienties, B., Rogaten, J., & Kizilcec, R. F. (2022). Beyond one-size-fits-all in MOOCs: Variation in learning design and persistence of learners in different cultural and socioeconomic contexts. *Computers in Human Behavior, 126,* 106973. https://doi.org/10.1016/j.chb.2021.106973

This article reports the findings of a study focusing on the impact of variation in course activities such as videos, articles, discussions, and quizzes in a MOOC on learners' progress when their geocultural and socioeconomic contexts are considered. The findings suggest that certain types of learning activities (e.g. discussion) facilitate progress for learners in one context (e.g. Anglo-Saxon), while inhibiting progress in another (e.g. South Asia). This article offers new insights into learning activities that can inform more effective learning design for learners from diverse backgrounds and locations.

Read, T., Sedano, B., & Barcena, E. (2021). Inclusive language MOOCs. *Journal of Universal Computer Science (JUCS), 27,* 437–449. https://doi.org/10.3897/jucs .67932

The authors of this article discuss how MOOCs for refugees and migrants can help them develop the language competences and transverse skills they require in order to improve their level of social inclusion and their chances in the labor market or access higher education in the country in which they find themselves or where they plan to go. The authors also explore how LMOOCs can best be deployed on mobile devices.

12

Adaptive Instruction

Mathias Schulze, Catherine Caws, Marie-Josée Hamel, and Trude Heift

Introduction

Instruction practices and theoretical discourses in language education have focused increasingly on the individual language learner as a multilingual subject, considering different institutional and cultural–historical contexts. Classrooms are gradually moving away from regimented, teacher-centered approaches to language teaching and learning that employed mechanical metaphors such as input, output, and uptake and minimized and, at times, negated the human agency of language learners. In education in general, we have seen a paradigmatic shift toward learner-centered and learning-centered approaches. In applied linguistics, more integrative approaches, which ascribe agency to both the teacher and the learner, have gained traction. Sociocultural theory (Lantolf & Poehner, 2014) captures language learners as the central subject of a dynamic activity system; Larsen-Freeman (Larsen-Freeman, 1997; Larsen-Freeman & Cameron, 2008) began to conceptualize the language learning process as a complex dynamic system, and this nonreductionist scientific theory and approach has been adopted by researchers worldwide. Societies in many countries and regions pay more attention to issues of accessibility, diversity, equity, and inclusion. All these advancements have impacted and even shaped the research, development, and praxis in computer-assisted language learning (CALL). This makes it timely to investigate adaptive technologies and adaptive instruction in the context of CALL.

The move to adaptive technologies and instruction has some inherent challenges. Individualized, learner-centered language teaching is resource-intensive. Ideally, groups would be small, language exposure would be expansive, and language use opportunities for learners would be manifold and varied. Obviously there are tensions between this idealism on the one hand and political and economic constraints and societal belief systems about language and learning on the other. However, more and more economies and states recognize the economic and societal need for many employees and citizens to have (professional) proficiency in other languages and transcultural awareness of the peoples who speak them. We would submit that these tensions cannot be resolved exclusively by turning to (digital) technologies but they can be addressed in part through appropriate technology mediation. We believe that CALL can make and has made a considerable contribution to furthering language education. And, to have more of a positive impact, it is worthwhile for researchers, developers, and teachers to reflect on adaptivity and to work with adaptive technologies.

Adolescents and young adults, in particular, use digital technologies in many domains of their life, and often for considerable lengths of time every day. Given the proliferation of digital artifacts, one could expect their prominence in language education, but as the sudden and rapid shift to emergency online teaching during the height of the global pandemic has shown, the use of these technologies is not yet understood sufficiently in the language teaching and language learning community, although there is considerable enthusiasm for technology-mediated language learning. On the one hand, CALL, in the forty years of its existence, has gained breadth and depth in language education in many countries. The many academic journals and books demonstrate the significant progress made in research and development over these decades. On the other hand, we still know relatively little about how exactly language learners use and engage with technology when conducting a learning activity or performing a communicative task. Why do some learners thrive in certain digital or online learning environments, while others suffer or fail? What do learners actually do when they engage with digital learning tools – as opposed to what developers think and students say they do (Chun, 2013; Fischer, 2007, 2012)? What exactly happens when students learn and use the language on the computer – tutorial CALL (Heift & Schulze, 2015; Hubbard & Bradin-Siskin, 2004; Schulze, 2024) – or in communicative interaction via the computer – computer-mediated communication (Kelsey & St. Amant, 2008; Thorne, 2008)? And what is the role of adaptivity in these environments, activities, and interactions?

Adaptivity is both a prerequisite for and an outcome of human social interaction. When we interact in communication, cooperation, or collaboration, each actor adapts in one way or another to other actors, the context, the available tools, and the object or goal of the interaction. This is why, in complex dynamic systems research, we talk about coadaptation; all actors adapt to one another, in interaction. For coadaptation to occur in human–computer interaction, the technology needs to have some degree of adaptivity built in. Adaptive instruction, which is a term used in computer-assisted learning, is defined as the capability of a system to alter its behavior according to learner needs, prior individual performance, and other characteristics (Shute & Zapata-Rivera, 2008). A considerable amount of research has demonstrated that individualized instruction is superior to the uniform approach of one-size-fits-all teaching (Kulik, Kulik, & Bangert-Drowns, 1990). Recent advances in technology and their integration in instructional design have facilitated individualization further. Personalized instruction can be offered simultaneously to large groups of learners (Lee & Park, 2008). Two questions then arise: How can the system or tool adapt to the learner, and how can the learner or teacher adapt to the technology (Vandewaetere et al., 2011) in the complex context of language education?

What can the human actors do? Instructors can adapt instructional sequences, pedagogic strategies and methods, and the digital, pedagogic, and linguistic affordances to individual students during or between iterations of learning processes, while students can learn to adapt to using appropriate digital affordances more effectively (Conole & Dyke, 2004). Developers of learning tools and systems can conduct thorough needs analyses during the conceptualization and design phases in order to achieve a better learner or teacher fit (or both), at least across specific (sub)groups. During the evaluation phase (Hubbard, 1996), the pedagogic evaluation is at least as important as the computational testing. It needs to include a valid empirical study of the tool's or system's efficacy in students' second language development. Such efficacy studies need to look beyond student perception (did students appreciate the use of the digital system or tool, and do they believe they benefited?) and focus on improved factors of the learning processes and improved learning outcomes.

The focus of this chapter is on the following question: What can be done to facilitate the coadaptation in the technology-mediated teaching and learning process on the side of the digital tool or system? This research and development in computer-assisted learning in general is called adaptive instruction. The literature in this field identifies three major approaches (Lee & Park, 2007; see also Regian & Shute, 2013):

1. Adapt instruction at the macrolevel by providing various alternatives for only a few main components of instruction. Instructional alternatives at the very broad level are selected mostly on the basis of the student's instructional goals, general ability, and achievement levels in the curriculum structure. Within language education, the instructional goals can vary by primary focus on a specific sublanguage (e.g. language for business, language for the medical profession, language for the diplomatic service, language for heritage speakers). General ability is usually gauged using standardized proficiency levels and their indicators and test results. Achievement levels are often operationalized – at a very simple level – as prior or prerequisite courses. Thus, at the macrolevel, this adaptivity is done via scaffolded student selection. For example, they select one of a few available paths through an online course at the beginning, and then the chosen path remains static. To give a recent example, the results of the study by El-Sabagh (2021) indicate the potential of an adaptive e-learning environment to engage students more in the teaching and learning process (p. 1). In this system, the level of instruction changes on the basis of a student's predetermined learning style. Four different learning styles (visual, auditory, reading/writing, kinesthetic (VARK)) (p. 14) were determined, before the students were presented with the learning activities and materials. This early informed selection was more conducive to learning success for the student.

2. The second approach is to adapt specific instructional procedures and strategies to specific student characteristics. This approach necessitates the prior determination and testing of at least some relevant learner characteristics. These characteristics are also called aptitudes. Hence this approach to adaptive instruction is called "aptitude–treatment interactions" (ATI). We are not aware of this approach being employed in CALL.

3. The third approach is to adapt instruction at a microlevel, by diagnosing the student's specific learning needs during instruction.

The predominant focus of this chapter is the third approach, micro-adaptive instruction, which focuses on information processing, diagnoses learners' contingent learning needs during instruction at a fine-grained level, and subsequently provides appropriate instructional (re)mediation for these needs (Mödritscher, Garcia-Barrios, & Gütl, 2004). Unlike macro-adaptive models, micro-adaptive approaches consider learner variables or characteristics. These are dynamic and use within-activity measures or fluid learner characteristics to define the most appropriate instructional intervention for a given micro-situation (Lee & Park, 2008).

Often under different labels, adaptive instruction using the microlevel approach has been applied in a number of subfields of CALL:

- Tutorial CALL: sophisticated branching algorithms (see Heift & Schulze, 2015; Schulze, 2024), which relied on regular expressions to analyze student input in simple language practice software in the 1980s and 1990s, guided students from one (set of) activity item(s) to the next, depending on their score for or answer to this item, to the next. In other words, each student who answered differently saw a different subsequent item.

- Online language learning: The student results for pre-task quizzes, for example, can determine when students are deemed to be ready for tackling a (graded) learning task or whether remedial or review activities on a different dynamic webpage are necessary first. Although such adaptive instruction happens at the microlevel, the range of learner characteristics considered is often very limited. Frequently, it is only one prior performance that is used as determining information at key moments in the course.

- Intelligent CALL (ICALL): ICALL uses techniques, approaches, and tools from artificial intelligence (for an overview, see Heift & Schulze, 2007; Schulze, 2008). The inclusion of natural language processes allows for a fine-grained structural analysis of learner texts. The results of this analysis are then the basis for contingent corrective feedback, (linguistic) learner guidance and help, and remedial activities. Learner data are analyzed and structured in individual learner profiles, which in turn form the basis for a learner model. Learner models (Bull & McKay, 2004; Schulze, 2008) inform adaptive instruction by drawing inferences from the structured learner data in the profile. These inferences "estimate" learner beliefs at a fine-grained level.

- Intelligent Language Tutoring Systems (ILTS): These rely on natural language processing and include a learner model. Heift (2010) is a good example of only a handful of ILTS research projects that resulted in a system that has been used consistently by groups of students. Systems such as the e-Tutor (Heift, 2010), Tagarella (Amaral, Meurers, & Ziai, 2011), and RoboSensei (Nagata, 2009), emerged from PhD projects, which are then challenging to sustain under very different institutional and entrepreneurial constraints and in diverse and ever-changing curricular contexts. Other factors that have thus far impeded the broad adoption and implementation of these systems, which are highly conducive to adaptive instruction, are their inherent features. Intelligent Language Tutoring Systems are (a) complex, in that they contain an expert model with a comprehensive information structure about the domain to be learnt – this is often the natural language parser with its grammar and lexicon; (b) expensive both to develop and to maintain, given their computational, linguistic, and pedagogic complexity; and (c) narrowly tailored to very specific learning contexts, which are designed to curtail their complexity and render them feasible. They are language-specific (e.g. specific to German, Portuguese, Japanese), connected to a specific course textbook, and limited to specific course or language aspects and components.

- Adaptive digital textbooks: To our knowledge, these have not been researched in CALL, although the general literature suggests that adaptive digital textbooks enhance students' learning, and textbooks are used widely in language education. Chau et al. (2021) includes an excellent overview of past and current developments in this general area. It is our hope that this research into adaptive technologies will also be carried out in CALL.

In the following sections, our focus will be exclusively on adaptive instruction at the microlevel. First we will discuss commensurate theoretical approaches to the analysis and design of adaptive instruction. This will be followed by methods that are appropriate for the empirical research that needs to accompany further development, implementation, and evaluation. The chapter will conclude with an overview of the practical use of adaptive instruction in CALL and its impact.

Theoretical Approaches in Analysis and Design

Language development and language use in CALL are mediated by computational technologies. In computer-mediated communication (Kelsey & St. Amant, 2008), learners interact with other learners, instructors, and first language speakers via digital artifacts; in tutorial CALL (Heift & Schulze, 2015, Hubbard & Bradin Siskin, 2004, Schulze, 2024), learners interact directly with socially, culturally, and cognitively imbued digital artifacts. In other words, digital components are "added" to the complexity of language use and second language development. This results in increased levels of complexity, but also facilitates the unobtrusive recording of the teaching-and-learning process through the tracking of learner behavior and the documenting of

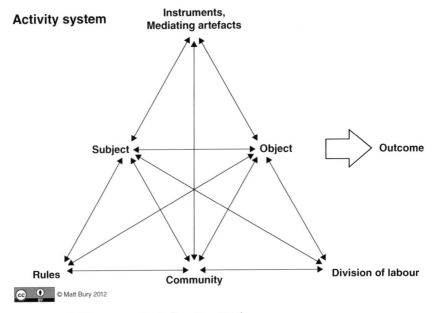

Figure 12.1 Activity systems triangle (from Bury, 2012).

learning outcomes over time. Both tracking learner behavior and documenting learning outcomes offer windows into the processes of technology-mediated language learning. We are suggesting two complementary theoretical lenses – sociocultural theory (Lantolf & Poehner, 2014; Lantolf & Thorne, 2006) and complex dynamic systems theory (Larsen Freeman, 1997; Larsen Freeman & Cameron, 2008) – for theoretical and empirical research, system and tool development, and pedagogic evaluation. Both theories have explanatory rather than predictive power, and therefore lend themselves particularly to post hoc data analysis and sense-making. They are nonreductionist, in the sense that they neither require nor allow the isolation of only one or more variables when the complex process of a learning activity is investigated in context and over time.

Sociocultural theory traces its provenience to (cultural–historical) activity theory (Rubinstein, 1984; Vygotsky, 1978). Vygotskyan activity theory is essentially a theory of the development of the mind. Its conceptualization is based on the concept of activity systems (Figure 12.1).

An activity is a bounded set of actions, which have an intention, and operations, which are triggered by an environmental condition. Actions and operations are closely intertwined and pursue one (complex) intension, the abstract object of the activity. Objects are not unlike learning goals and objectives, which students have internalized. In an activity system, language learners are conceptualized as the collective subject. This also means that all learning activities are social interactions with multiple actors, who all (and not only the subject) have agency. Within an activity, the learners – subject – pursue an abstract learning goal – object – and there is an interaction between subject and object. This interaction is mediated by abstract or material tools, which are often called artifacts. Examples of abstract artifacts are the learnt language itself, an idea or concept, and one more or less complex knowledge item or belief. In CALL research, material artifacts are digital tools and systems. Of course, other tools of the language classroom such as textbooks, speaker systems, recording devices, and whiteboards are also material artifacts that mediate the interaction between subject and object. If these tools are well designed and appropriately integrated, they help learners achieve their learning goal. The social interaction in each activity, with its material manipulations of speaking and writing, with its use of (digital) artifacts, also results in a material outcome when the object (goal) of the activity has been met. All activities are performed and take place in a concrete context. The activity system captures the main components of this context: community, rules, and division of labor. The division of labor denotes the various ways of work-sharing and the team roles that the collective subject, a group of language students, performs during an activity. The rules come from cultural and societal norms and conventions, regulations of educational systems and institutions, curricular stipulations and guidelines, and classroom management and teacher instructions. In CALL, they can also stem from software license and user agreements and regulations for appropriate technology use. Last but not least, the community comprises actors who are peripheral to the activity – they might not be present during the activity – but are relevant to it. These are teachers and teaching assistants, students' guardians, caretakers, friends, and students from other groups.

These six components of an activity system are relevant to the research on adaptive instruction because they facilitate the comprehensive conceptualization of the place, function, and impact of digital artifacts in teaching-and-learning processes in CALL when these artifacts are developed, used, or evaluated. During the dynamic interaction of the components with one another during the activity, tensions arise between various components. It is through the gradual and often contradictory resolution of such system-inherent, ever-changing tensions that the activity systems move forward and an outcome is created, the object can be met, and learning takes place.

This sketch of an activity system highlights its complexity. This complexity is suitably captured and comprehensively considered through a dynamic-systems lens.

Like Larsen-Freeman, Ellis, de Bot, van Geert, Verspoor, and others (see e.g. de Bot, Lowie, & Verspoor, 2007; Ellis & Larsen-Freeman, 2006; Larsen-Freeman, 1997; Larsen-Freeman & Cameron, 2008; Verspoor, de Bot, & Lowie, 2011), we view second language development as a complex, dynamic subsystem within a social system (de Bot et al., 2007, p. 14; Larsen-Freeman & Cameron, 2008, p. 35). Complexity here refers to the multitude of variables that affect the open system, that is, the teaching-and-learning process. These variables are often dependent upon each other and/or interact in other ways and thus change and/or are being changed in the process of learning and using a second language. This ongoing change is the main reason for the system's being described as dynamic. From a complexity science perspective, second-language development processes are complex, sensitive to initial conditions, nonlinear, and nonmonotonic, as well as fractal and nonperiodic (Lorenz, 1993, pp. 161–179; Schulze, 2008). Subprocesses such as developmental spurts, backsliding, and fossilization are evidence that a second language is being acquired at varying speeds, generating nonlinear developmental trajectories of individuals. As a result of individual language learner differences, this diachronic variation is compounded by the synchronic variability that exists within groups of language learners.

Researching Adaptivity: Methods

When investigating the teaching and learning of a language through the lens of both complex dynamic systems (Larsen-Freeman, 1997; Larsen-Freeman & Cameron, 2008) and sociocultural theory (Lantolf & Poehner, 2014; Lantolf & Thorne, 2006), qualitative and quantitative methods of analysis need to be employed (a) to yield rich data from the interaction of members of the collective subject with one another, with others, and, importantly in CALL, with (digital) artifacts in specific and complex learning contexts and (b) to structure these data for a meaningful and pedagogically fruitful interpretation. Then these learner data provide insight into individual learner trajectories in their second language development and into concrete language learning processes, as well as into the characteristics of suitable and effective learning artifacts and their affordances.

To capture, describe, and interpret individual learner trajectories,

- these data can be plotted on a time series graph, with the relevant learner variable on the y-axis and time on the x-axis, to show development over time;
- the dynamic change of the variable that is researched can be visualized in a phase space diagram, which has the value of the variable at time t on the x-axis and the value of the same variable at time $t+1$ on the y-axis, to show change over time;
- the initial conditions – the many learner variables at the very beginning of the teaching-and-learning process under investigation – need to be recorded in great detail; and
- and each individual trajectory needs to be considered in the context of the group (collective subject).

For example, Scholz and Schulze (2017) employ surveys, data tracking, and clustering and pairwise comparison to analyze students' individual trajectories in the context of digital game-based language learning. In their study, the characteristics of the complex dynamic system are the basis for their selection of suitable variables, which in turn inform the path of analysis of both process and product data.

To identify the components of a complex system in language learning, we employ for our analysis the activity system (Engeström, 1987; Rubinstein, 1984; Vygotsky, 1978), which is more widely known in applied linguistics as sociocultural theory (Lantolf & Thorne, 2006; Thorne, 2005). Describing a teaching-and-learning process, we use observational data to capture the dynamic components – subject (digital artifacts), object, rules, division of labor, community, and outcome – systematically and in fine detail. Each component changes over time also in its relationships and its interaction with other components of the activity system. We investigate the resulting tensions between the components, because it is these tensions that move the system forward. The second language development of the subject is the nonlinear result of their processing the tensions in the activity system.

In CALL, we pay particular attention to the role of the various digital artifacts, for example language learning apps, components of online language courses, social media tools and sites, and web services, because these artifacts create additional affordances for learners. Affordances emerge "in a three-way interaction between actors, their mediational means, and the environments" (Kaptelinin & Nardi 2012, p. 974, as quoted in Blin, 2016). The diversity of educational contexts, the wealth of digital technologies, and their successful integration into diverse language education contexts require careful analysis and evaluation (Colpaert, 2006) and motivate the increasing need for empirical study of the complex interaction of subjects, artifacts, and contexts (Lafford, 2009; Verillon & Rabardel, 1995). The results of such studies can inform the design of digital tools and systems in adaptive instruction. Within the field of educational ergonomics, researchers have argued that a holistic approach to learning design will help us understand better what learners actually do when they are working with technology (Bertin and Gravé, 2010; Raby, 2005). Within this approach, recommendations have been made to focus the research not solely on the design of the system but, more importantly, on the learner and the learning task (Chapelle, 2001; Colpaert, 2006; Felix, 2005). We take the artifacts as our point of departure and focus on how their design affects both the user and the task. Here we follow Norman (1991), who argued that a clear understanding of the role played by the cultural artifacts – in our case, a variety of CALL tools and resources – is critical to the improvement of their design. He states that

> [e]very artifact has both a system and a personal view, and they are often very different in appearance. From the system view, the artifact appears to expand some functional capacity of the task performer. From the personal view, the artifact has replaced the original task with a different task, one that may have radically different cognitive requirements and use radically different cognitive capacities than the original task.

> *(p. 22)*

This concept is essential for the development, evaluation, and implementation of such digital artifacts in educational contexts because the ways in which our learners are affected by new learning environments and learning tasks and their effect on task performance need to be considered both cognitively and functionally.

These factors play a key role in our definition of different learner types, which are often called learner personas in adaptive instruction. In CALL, personas are archetypal users of a learning tool who represent the needs of larger groups of users in terms of their goals and personal characteristics. Personas capture and cluster similarities among learners and are based on interconnected clusters of learner characteristics. The usefulness of personas in defining and designing interactive applications is based on ideas advanced by Cooper (1999). In contrast to iterative user prototyping, the more powerful method is to make up "pretend users and design for them" on the basis of in-depth ethnographic data (p. 123). Clearly, it is impossible to capture each and every trait of an individual learner. However, by creating distinct personas (Heift, 2007), we can capture and cluster essential similarities and differences among learners who warrant individualization (see Colpaert, 2006; Heift, 2002, 2008; Levy & Stockwell, 2006) and that result in more adaptive instruction. Once the similarities and differences have been determined, the learning process can be modeled to enhance the learner–computer interaction with an individualized, adaptive CALL tool or system. For instance, instructional alternatives with respect to learning objectives, tasks, and media, or the use of learning tools, can be provided. We can decide whether this information is static and hard-wired into the learning tool or is dynamic – that is, changes over time and adjusts to our learners as they develop.

Lilley, Pyper, and Attwood (2012) make a distinction between ad hoc personas and data-driven personas. Ad hoc personas are defined during the conceptualization phase and are based on preconceptions of what software designers think users might be like. In contrast, data-driven personas are established through data collection from actual users. This collection includes data on user demographics gathered through user surveys and concurrent system interactions. Although both ad hoc and data-driven personas are abstract, with the concept of personas we will be able to cluster learners into meaningful groups. Data-driven personas are created by considering the similarities and differences among users from the angle of their demographics (the initial conditions for our learning activities) and observed behavioral patterns during these activities as well as the digital, pedagogic, and linguistic affordances that accompany them. The differences among distinct personas must be based on essential issues, for instance what users do (actions or projected actions) and why they do it (goals and motivations), and not too much on who those users are (see also Calabria, 2004). Once the similarities and differences have been determined, affordances for learner interaction can be adapted in areas that are relevant to and appropriate for a particular digital tool and environment (Caws & Hamel, 2013, 2016; Hamel, 2013a, 2013b).

The goal of such analyses is twofold: enabling students to improve their learning outcomes and facilitating and improving the learning process. Since second language development in general proceeds on a nonlinear trajectory, it is unrealistic to predict learning outcomes and results a priori. Instead, after analyzing individual learner trajectories a posteriori – by paying close attention to initial conditions, self-similarity at different scales, and growth conditions of developmental change, for example – we identify the various factors that contributed to achange in learner behavior. These interaction data are equally pertinent to improving the artifact and the language learning process (Caws & Hamel, 2013; Hamel, 2012).

Such a longitudinal investigation of computer-mediated learning processes, analyzing and interpreting the change in learners' activities and language learning outcomes, provides more accurate insight than the snapshots of pre-tests and post-tests. The theoretical perspective of complex systems and activity systems allows us to combine qualitative and quantitative research methods and to consider each changing variable in context. The observational multimodal and multilingual data from language learning processes and outcomes can be augmented with survey and interview data from students' and instructors' perception and retrospection.

The observation of learning processes – with the goal of facilitating adaptive instruction in CALL – can rely on digital logs (e.g. tracking of system logins, page views, keyboard input), eye tracking (e.g. attention focus and noticing), chat and interaction logs (e.g. written peer-to-peer chats in the foreign language, written interaction with the computer program), iterations of textual learning outcomes (e.g. discussion board or wiki submissions and text versions over time), and screen capture videos of entire learning activities, which are often supplemented by think-aloud protocols or stimulated recall. In CALL research and development, computer logs have been used for some time for data collection and analysis of learner–task–artifact interactions (Fischer, 2007). Logs have provided valuable insights, for instance, into learners' navigation patterns (e.g. Desmarais et al., 1997; Heift, 2002) in tutorial CALL as well as their linguistic performance in computer-mediated communication. The collection of tracking data is well understood, yet we still have to learn more about the analysis and interpretation of such large longitudinal data sets (Chun, 2013). The analysis of learner texts can use discourse-analytical methods. The analysis of learner corpora (i.e. principled, electronic collections of texts produced by language learners) is another methodological cornerstone. The detailed analysis of textual learning outcomes produced over a period of time provides a window into the underlying processes during that time. User walkthroughs (Hémard, 2003) allow a specific focus on the students' use of a new CALL tool or system. Video-recording individual and small-group digital language learning activities provides insight into the ongoing use of digital artifacts. Advances in computer technology facilitate the observation and capture of user–task–tool interactions in a more natural and less intrusive manner. Tools such as Camtasia Studio (computer screen video capture) and Morae (live observation and video capture of computer screen and user, data management, and analysis) were employed in CALL studies (e.g. Caws, 2013; Hamel, 2012, 2013a, 2013b; Hamel & Caws, 2010). These tools are specifically designed to measure the usability (Rubin & Chisnell, 2008) of computer applications and facilitate the analysis of the quality of the learner experience with CALL resources.

These data collection methods yield learner data of different types: products, processes, and perceptions. And the data need to be structured for analysis and triangulated to produce robust results that can be interpreted to inform adaptive instruction. Products stem from the outcomes of each learning activity. Product data are often in the form of multimodal learner texts. These texts are then structured in learner corpora (Granger, 2003). Learner corpora provide a window into the underlying cognitive processes across groups and over time. Data from the interaction processes, in the form of tracking data, recordings, and observations, are structured in tables, graphs, and chronological logs. Student perceptions of satisfaction, subjective learning success, and learning preferences are elicited through surveys, interviews, think-aloud protocols, and stimulated recall. All data are best analyzed individually, comparatively, and cross-sectionally, resulting in a mixed-method study.

From a methodological point of view, we are not experimenting when observing language learning processes in computer-mediated education, we do not employ a reductionist approach by eliminating variables from rich educational context through research design or inferential statistics, and we do not conflate individual developmental learning trajectories into large leveled groups. Instead, through a complex systems lens, we focus on individual learners in their specific social, cultural, and educational contexts. The complex systems approach enables us to combine the advantages of qualitative research methods by paying attention to rich contexts and "thick description" (Geertz, 2017), with the advantages of their quantitative counterparts of generalizability and theoretical prediction through formal systematicity. Our focus in the investigation of computer-mediated learning processes is on the detection, analysis, and interpretation of change in the learner's activity and outcomes, in line with the dynamically changing variables of the system. Therefore all such studies are longitudinal. The data are gathered in naturalistic, educational contexts and obtained as unobtrusively as possible. Observational data from learning processes that occurred over longer periods of time are analyzed in their respective educational contexts. These data are triangulated with data from learning outcomes and supplemented with qualitative data from students' perception and retrospection.

Through an exploration of individual and collaborative language learning processes, the broad goals of such a comprehensive analysis of technology-mediated interactions are to:

- define different learner types (personas) that are relevant to individualized learning and teaching approaches;

- map educational contexts with their learning artifacts so as to determine their suitability for a given educational and digital context; and
- offer a set of design criteria for learning objects, language learning tasks, and digital educational resources that reflect the needs and electronic literacy skills of individual learners and instructors.

In today's language education settings, digital technologies, and especially internet-based resources and artifacts, are used as an integral component of many language learning environments. Their successful and effective integration requires careful analysis, design, implementation, and evaluation (Colpaert, 2006).

Impact

Several practical questions arise when probing into adaptive instruction. Can we create a technology-mediated learning environment where students have access to digital resources that reliably facilitate their language development rather than impede their learning path? In what ways can we adapt instruction to individual learners to achieve this goal? How can we support learners so that they benefit most from adaptive instruction? Experienced teachers adapt their instruction to individual students. Yet a fully individualized approach is not possible with large groups of learners. What is the exact beneficial role of a digital technology in a specific context? How can the benefits of this approach with this technology be transferred to other contexts and groups? How can they be generalized?

CALL research with a specific focus on ways of adaptive instruction will contribute to a better understanding of technology-mediated language learning and language education in general by providing detailed, evidence-based suggestions and guidance on the implementation of language learning technology. This research also has applications that go beyond language learning contexts. It investigates new ways of learning by examining the roles that information and communication technologies play in second language learning and by focusing on the affordances of digital resources for adaptive instruction. More importantly, such research addresses the need for equitable access to information and communication technologies and ways to foster digital literacy.

Of course, learners can also negotiate adjustments and adapt (to the technology) autonomously, after critically reflecting on learning processes and developmental trajectories (Hampel & Hauck, 2006; Hauck, 2005). However, we would submit that it is the teacher's responsibility to guide and facilitate the students' adaptation to their learning environment and to ensure that the most suitable, most adaptive technology is employed, so that the students' focus can be on (language) learning and does not have to be on the struggle to adapt. It is the role of the researcher in CALL, and specifically in adaptive instruction, to provide teachers with a deeper understanding of the complexity of individual student trajectories and of the role of learning technologies in these complex contexts and to develop, sustain, and evaluate technologies that contribute to adaptive instruction.

References

Amaral, L., Meurers, D., & Ziai, R. (2011). Analyzing learner language: Towards a flexible natural language processing architecture for intelligent language tutors. *Computer Assisted Language Learning*, *24*(1), 1–16. https://doi.org/10.1080/09588221.2010.520674

Bertin, J.-C., & Gravé, P. (2010). In favor of a model of didactic ergonomics. In J.-C. Bertin, P. Gravé & J.-P. Nancy-Combes (Eds.), *Second language distance learning and teaching: Theoretical perspectives and didactic ergonomics* (pp. 1–36). IGI Global USA.

Blin, F. (2016). The theory of affordances. In C. Caws & M.-J. Hamel (Eds.), *Learner–computer interactions: New insights on CALL theories and applications* (pp. 41–64). Amsterdam: John Benjamins.

Blin, F., Caws, C., Hamel, M.-J., Heift, T., Schulze, M., & Smith, B. (2013). Data and elicitation methods in interaction-based research. *Proceedings of WorldCALL 2013* (pp. 21–28). Glasgow.

Bull, S., & McKay, M. (2004). An open learner model for children and teachers: Inspecting knowledge level of individuals and peers. In J. C. Lester, R. M. Vicari, & F. Paraguaçu (Eds.), *Intelligent tutoring systems* (pp. 469–478). Springer. https://doi.org/10.1007/978-3-540-30139-4_61

Bury, M. (2012). *Activity system.* https://upload.wikimedia.org/wikipedia/commons/c/c0/Activity_system.png

Calabria, T. (2004). An introduction to personas and how to create them. *KM Column.* www.steptwo.com.au/papers/kmc_personas

Caws, C. (2013). Evaluating a web-based video corpus through an analysis of user-interactions. *ReCALL Journal*, *25*(1), 85–104.

Caws, C., & Hamel, M.-J. (2013). From analysis to training: Recycling interaction data into learning. *OLBI Working Papers*, *5*, 25–36. https://doi.org/10.18192/olbiwp.v5i0.1116

Caws, C., & Hamel, M.-J. (2016). (Eds). *Learner computer interactions: New insights on CALL theories and applications.* John Benjamins.

Chapelle, C. A. (2001). *Computer applications in second language acquisition: Foundations for teaching, testing and research.* Cambridge University Press.

Chau, H., Labutov, I., Thaker, K., He, D., & Brusilovsky, P. (2021). Automatic concept extraction for domain and student modeling in adaptive textbooks. *International Journal of Artificial Intelligence in Education*, *31*(4), 820–846. https://doi.org/10.1007/s40593-020-00207-1

Chun, D. M. (2013). Contributions of tracking user behavior to SLA research. *CALICO Journal*, *30*, 256–262. https://doi.org/10.1558/cj.v30i0.256-262

Colpaert, J. (2006). Toward an ontological approach in goal-oriented language courseware design and its implications for technology-independent content structuring. *Computer Assisted Language Learning, 19*(2), 109. www .informaworld.com/10.1080/09588220600821461

Conole, G., & Dyke, M. (2004). What are the affordances of information and communication technologies? *ALT-J, 12*(2), 113–124. https://doi.org/10.1080/ 0968776042000216183

Cooper, A. (1999). *The inmates are running the asylum: Why high-tech products drive us crazy and how to restore the sanity.* Macmillan Computer Publishing.

de Bot, K., Lowie, W., & Verspoor, M. (2007). A dynamic systems theory approach to second language acquisition. *Bilingualism: Language and Cognition, 10*(1), 7–21. https://doi.org/10.1017/S1366728906002732

Desmarais, L., Duquette, D., Renié, D., & Laurier, M. (1997). Evaluating learning and interactions in a multimedia environment. *Computer and the Humanities, 31* (4), 327–349. https://doi.org/10.1023/A:1001062407103

Dörnyei, Z. (2014). Researching complex dynamic systems: "Retrodictive qualitative modeling" in the language classroom. *Language Teaching, 47*(1), 80–91. https://doi.org/10.1017/S0261444811000516

Ellis, N. C., & Larsen-Freeman, D. (2006). Language emergence: Implications for applied linguistics – Introduction to the special issue. *Applied Linguistics, 27*(4), 558–589. https://doi.org/10.1093/applin/aml028

El-Sabagh, H. A. (2021). Adaptive e-learning environment based on learning styles and its impact on development students' engagement: Revista de Universidad y Sociedad del Conocimiento. *International Journal of Educational Technology in Higher Education, 18*(1). https://doi.org/10.1186/s41239-021-00289-4

Engeström, Y. (1987). *Learning by expanding: An activity-theoretical approach to developmental research.* Orienta-Konsultit Oy.

Felix, U. (2005). What do meta-analyses tell us about CALL effectiveness? *ReCALL, 17*(2), 269–288.

Fischer, R. (2007). How do we know what students are actually doing? Monitoring students' behavior in CALL. *Computer Assisted Language Learning, 20*(5), 409–442. https://doi.org/10.1080/09588220701746013

Fischer, R. (2012). Diversity in learner usage patterns. In G. Stockwell (Ed.), *Computer assisted language learning: Diversity in research and practice* (pp. 14–32). Cambridge University Press.

Geertz, C. (2017). *The interpretation of cultures* (3rd ed.). Basic Books.

Granger, S. (2003). Error-tagged learner corpora and CALL: A promising synergy. *CALICO Journal, 20*(3), 465–480.

Hamel, M.-J. (2012). Testing aspects of the usability of an online learner dictionary prototype: A product- and process-oriented study. *Computer Assisted Language Learning, 25*(4), 339–365. https://doi.org/10.1080/09588221 .2011.591805

Hamel, M.-J. (2013a). Analyse de l'activité de recherche d'apprenants de langue dans un prototype de dictionnaire en ligne. *Revue ALSIC, 16*(1). https://doi .org/10.4000/alsic.2613

Hamel, M.-J. (2013b). Questionnaires to inform a usability test conducted on a CALL dictionary prototype. *International Journal of Computer-Assisted Language Learning and Teaching (IJCALLT)*, *3*(3), 56–76. http://doi.org/10.4018/ijcallt.2013070104

Hamel, M.-J., & Caws, C. (2010). Usability tests in CALL development: Pilot studies in the context of the Dire autrement and the Francotoile projects. *CALICO Journal*, *27*(3), 491–504. https://doi.org/10.11139/cj.27.3.491-504

Hampel, R., & Hauck, M. (2006). Computer-mediated language learning: Making meaning in multimodal virtual learning spaces. *The JALT CALL Journal*, *2*(2), 3–18. https://doi.org/10.29140/jaltcall.v2n2.23

Hauck, M. (2005). Metacognitive knowledge, metacognitive strategies, and CALL. In J. L. Egbert & G. Petrie (Eds.), *CALL research perspectives* (pp. 65–86). Lawrence Erlbaum.

Heift, T. (2002). Learner control and error correction in ICALL: Browsers, peekers, and adamants. *CALICO Journal*, *19*(2), 295–313. https://doi.org/0.1558/cj.v19i2.295-313

Heift, T. (2007). Learner personas in CALL. *CALICO Journal*, *25*(1), 1–10. https://doi.org/10.1558/cj.v25i1.1-10

Heift, T. (2008). Modeling learner variability in CALL. *Computer Assisted Language Learning*, *21*(4), 305–321. https://doi.org/10.1080/09588220802343421

Heift, T. (2010). Developing an intelligent language tutor. *CALICO Journal*, *27*(3), 443–459. https://doi.org/10.11139/cj.27.3.443-459

Heift, T., & Schulze, M. (2015). Research timeline: Tutorial CALL. *Language Teaching*, *48*(4), 471–490. https://doi.org/10.1017/S0261444815000245

Hémard, D. (2003). Language learning online: Designing towards user acceptability. In U. Felix (Ed.), *Language learning online: Towards best practice* (pp. 21–42). Swets & Zeitlinger.

Hornbaek, K. (2006). Current practice in measuring usability: Challenges to usability studies and research. *International Journal of Human-Computer Studies*, *64*(2), 79–102. https://doi.org/10.1016/j.ijhcs.2005.06.002

Hubbard, P. (1996). Elements of CALL methodology: Development, evaluation and implementation. In M. C. Pennington (Ed.), *The power of CALL*. Athelstan.

Hubbard, P., & Bradin-Siskin, C. (2004). Another look at tutorial CALL. *ReCALL*, *16*(2), 448–461. https://doi.org/10.1017/S0958344004001326

Kaptelinin, V., & Nardi, B. (2012). Affordances in HCI: Toward a mediated action perspective. In *Proceedings of the 2012 ACM annual conference on human factors in computing Systems* (pp. 967–976). ACM. http://dl.acm.org/citation.cfm?id=2208541

Kelsey, S., & St. Amant, K. (Eds). (2008). *Handbook of research on computer mediated communication*. Information Science Reference.

Kulik, C. L. C., Kulik, J. A., & Bangert-Drowns, R. L. (1990). Effectiveness of mastery learning programs: A meta-analysis. *Review of Educational Research*, *60*(2), 265–299. https://doi.org/10.3102/00346543060002265

Lafford, B. A. (2009). Toward an ecological CALL: Update to Garrett (1991). *The Modern Language Journal*, *93*(S1), 673–696. https://doi.org/10.1111/j.1540-4781.2009.00966.x

Lantolf, J. P., & Poehner, M. (2014). *Sociocultural theory and the pedagogical imperative in L2 education: Vygotskian Praxis and the research/practice divide.* Routledge. https://doi.org/10.4324/9780203813850.

Lantolf, J. P., & Thorne, S. L. (2006). *Sociocultural theory and the genesis of second language development.* Oxford University Press.

Larsen-Freeman, D. (1997). Chaos/complexity science and second language acquisition. *Applied Linguistics, 18*(2), 141–165. https://doi.org/10.1093/applin/18.2.141

Larsen-Freeman, D., & Cameron, L. (2008). *Complex systems and applied linguistics.* Oxford University Press.

Lee, J., & Park, O. (2007). Adaptive instructional systems. In J. M. Spector, M. D. Merril, J. J. G. van Merriënboer, & M. Driscoll (Eds.), *Handbook of research on educational communications and technology* (3rd ed., pp. 469–484). Routledge.

Levy, M., & Stockwell, G. (2006). *CALL dimensions: Options and issues in computer assisted language learning.* L. Erbaum Associates.

Lilley, M., Pyper, A., & Attwood, S. (2012). Understanding the student experience through the use of personas. *Innovation in Teaching and Learning in Information and Computer Science, 11*(1), 4–13. https://doi.org/10.11120/ital.2012.11010004

Lorenz, E. N. (1993). *The essence of chaos.* University of Washington Press.

Mödritscher, F., Gütl, C., García-Barrios, V. M., & Maurer, H. (2004). Why do standards in the field of e-learning not fully support learner-centred aspects of adaptivity? In *Proceedings of EDMEDIA 2004* (pp. 2034–2039). AACE.

Nagata, N. (2009). Robo-Sensei's NLP-based error detection and feedback generation. *CALICO Journal, 26*(3), 562–579.

Norman, D. A. (1991). Cognitive artifacts. In J. M. Carroll (Ed.), *Designing interaction: Psychology at the human–computer interface* (pp. 17–38). Cambridge University Press.

Raby, F. (2005). A user-centered ergonomic approach to CALL research. In J. L. Egbert & G. M. Petrie (Eds.), *CALL research perspectives* (pp. 179–190). Lawrence Erlbaum Associates.

Regian, J. W., & Shute, V. J. (2013). *Cognitive approaches to automated instruction.* Taylor & Francis.

Rubin, J., & Chisnell, D. E. (2008). *Handbook of usability testing: How to plan, design, and conduct effective tests* (2nd ed.). Wiley Publishing.

Rubinstein, S. L. (1984). *Grundlagen der allgemeinen Psychologie (Übersetzung der Originalausgabe Moskau 1946 von H. Hartmann).* Volk und Wissen.

Scholz, K., & Schulze, M. (2017). Digital-gaming trajectories and second-language development. *Language Learning & Technology, 21*(1), 99–119. https://doi.org/10125/44597

Schulze, M. (2008). Modeling SLA processes using NLP. In C. A. Chapelle, Y.-R. Chung, and J. Xu (Eds.), *Towards adaptive CALL: Natural language processing for diagnostic assessment* (pp. 149–166). Iowa State University.

Schulze, M. (2024). Tutorial CALL: Language practice with the computer. In R. Hampel & U. Stickler (Eds.), *Bloomsbury handbook of language learning and technologies* (pp. 35–47). Bloomsbury.

Schulze, M., & Scholz, K. (2016). CALL theory: Complex adaptive systems. In C. Caws & M.-J. Hamel (Eds.), *Learner-computer interactions: New insights on CALL theories and applications* (pp. 65–87). John Benjamins.

Shute, V. J., & Zapata-Rivera, D. (2007). Adaptive technologies. In J. M. Spector, M. D. Merril, J. J. G. van Merriënboer, & M. Driscoll (Eds.), *Handbook of research on educational communications and technology* (3rd ed., pp. 277–294). Taylor & Francis.

Thorne, S. L. (2005). Epistemology, politics, and ethics in sociocultural theory. *Modern Language Journal, 89*(iii), 393–409.

Thorne, S. L. (2008). Computer-mediated communication. In N. H. Hornberger (Ed.), *Encyclopedia of language and education* (pp. 1415–1426). Springer. https://doi.org/10.1007/978-0-387-30424-3_108

Vandewaetere, M., Desmet, P., & Clarebout, G. (2011). The contribution of learner characteristics in the development of computer-based adaptive learning environments. *Computers in Human Behavior, 27*(1), 118–130. https://doi.org/10.1016/j.chb.2010.07.038

Verillon, P., & Rabardel, P. (1995). Cognition and artifacts: A contribution to the study of thought in relation to instrumented activity. *European Journal of Psychology of Education, 10*(77). https://doi.org/10.1007/BF03172796

Verspoor, M., De Bot, K., & Lowie, W. (2011). *A dynamic approach to second language development: Methods and techniques.* John Benjamins.

Vygotsky, L. S. (1978). *Mind and society: The development of higher mental processes.* Harvard University Press.

Further Reading

Colpaert, J., & Stockwell, G. (2022). *Smart CALL: Personalization, contextualization, & socialization.* Castledown. https://doi.org/10.29140/9781914291012
This co-edited book collects insightful papers centered around the theme of "smart CALL," which focuses on the adaptation of technologies within language education across three dimensions: personalization, contextualization, and socialization.

Slavuj, V., Meštrović, A., & Kovačić, B. (2017). Adaptivity in educational systems for language learning: A review. *Computer Assisted Language Learning, 30*(1–2), 64–90. https://doi.org/10.1080/09588221.2016.1242502
This article reviews adaptivity in educational systems for language learning from various aspects related to adaptivity, including adaptive learning environments, adaptive feedback, adaptive assessments, and adaptive content selection.

13

Virtual Reality

Kristi Jauregi Ondarra, Sabela Melchor-Couto, and Silvia Canto

Introduction

Virtual reality (VR) is considered one of the most promising emerging technologies for learning. Its incorporation in education offers teachers and students endless opportunities to enjoy embodied experiences that would otherwise be inaccessible in a classroom setting (e.g. visiting Mount Everest or experiencing the cellular defense system from inside your body). The increasing popularity of VR has stimulated educators' and researchers' interest in exploring its learning potential in education. In the present chapter we explore the historical development of VR, discuss the pedagogical theories underpinning its use, describe its potential for language education, analyze empirical research, and make suggestions for future research.

Historical Perspectives

When addressing the historical development of VR, we should be aware that there are three different types of VR systems: low-immersive, semi-immersive, and fully immersive VR (Costello, 1997; Martirosov et al., 2021; Melchor-Couto & Herrera, 2023). Low-immersive VR systems include a desktop computer-based 3D graphic system that allows the user to go through the virtual environment with the use of a computer screen, a keyboard, and a mouse. An example of these systems are virtual worlds such as Second Life or OpenSimulator. Semi-immersive systems are advanced and costly, where a graphical display is projected on large screens surrounding the user (e.g. the CAVE system). Finally, the third type of VR is a fully immersive experience created by a head-mounted system where a user's vision is fully bounded, giving them a sense of full immersion in the virtual environment.

Most of the VR studies carried out on language education to date address the use of low-immersive VR systems such as virtual worlds. In the present chapter we describe the opportunities that low-immersive (virtual worlds) and high- or fully immersive VR technologies offer to enhance languacultural learning (Agar, 1994). The concept of languaculture emphasizes the notion that language always has cultural dimensions, so that language and culture are inextricably linked to each other (see Risager, 2012).

Low-Immersive VR

The earliest virtual world (VW) similar to those of today was Habitat, released by Lucasfilm in 1986. Virtual worlds started to enable experiences that were not previously available through other media. We have come a long way since then and nowadays there is a wide variety of VWs. These worlds can be either game-based (World of Warcraft, Half-Life, Minecraft) or socially based (Second Life, Habbo, Twinity). Although they all exist as social environments, they have been created with different audiences in mind, and the activities performed in each of them reflect these distinct audiences. For game-based VWs, entertainment is the main purpose. They usually set a theme and goals and encourage players, who control the game in the VW, to play in a free style. In contrast, socially based VWs provide their users with a world that allows social connections (Lan et al., 2016) without the physical restrictions of the real world (see Figure 13.1).

Virtual worlds have been attracting the attention of foreign language educators for a few decades, particularly with the increased popularity of socially based low-immersive VR. With support from the perspective of sociocultural second language acquisition (SLA), researchers have investigated the interactions of foreign language learners in these immersive environments with the aim of promoting their linguistic skills and intercultural awareness (Canto & Jauregi Ondarra, 2017; Jauregi et al., 2011; Lin & Lan, 2015). Before 2010, highly immersive VR technologies were extremely expensive for wider distribution (Lloyd, Rogerson, & Stead, 2017), and for this reason most empirical research in language education focused on low-immersive technologies. Scholars who reviewed and analyzed studies on language learning in these immersive environments concluded that the major research findings included improvement of students' learning outcomes, enhancement of motivation, positive perceptions of using VR, interaction possibilities, and lowering of learning anxiety (Blyth, 2018; Huang et al., 2021; Parmaxi, 2020).

Although some claim that these low-immersive VR environments have become outdated (Lloyd et al., 2017) they are still an alternative for institutions and users who cannot afford the technology for high-immersive VR.

High-Immersive VR

The use of high-immersive VR (HiVR) tools in education, and particularly for language learning purposes, is still uncharted territory for practitioners and scholars, although the last few years have witnessed an increase in the number

Figure 13.1 Picture from the social VR, Second Life (https://secondlife.com).

of studies conducted, possibly as a result of a reduction in the cost of these devices. The range of fully immersive VR head-mounted displays (HMDs) is certainly broad and requires careful consideration of their capabilities and functionalities, as these will determine the type of pedagogical activities that can be implemented. Radianti et al. (2020) group fully immersive VR tools as follows. A number of devices are available in the market at the time of writing and have been included in order to illustrate each category, although in our rapidly evolving world of technology they are likely to be replaced by more advanced models in the near future:

- **Mobile VR:** these are devices such as Google Cardboard or Samsung Gear, which work with an integrated mobile phone.
- **High-end HMDs:** these are more powerful tools, which either are stand-alone (Meta/Oculus Quest 1 and 2) or work together with a computer (Oculus Rift or HTC VIVE).
- **Enhanced VR:** these are HMDs that are used in conjunction with haptic equipment such as gloves or bodysuits, which allow avatars to reproduce the users' movements on the screen.

The functionality afforded by high-end and enhanced devices is notably richer than the functionality of mobile VR devices; therefore practitioners must be familiar with these tools and the way they work in order to choose the most appropriate ones for their planned activities. As described in the section "Current Research and Practice," the number of research studies targeting the use of HiVR tools specifically for language learning purposes seems to be on the rise, helping to unveil the challenges and opportunities posed by this novel technology. The next section will provide an overview of the most relevant notions when it comes to VR and language learning.

Primary Themes

The use of VR in education is theoretically grounded in situated learning approaches that claim that learning is socially constructed and naturally embedded in the culture, activity, and context in which it takes place (Brown, Collins, & Duguid, 1989; Dawley & Dede, 2014), in sharp contrast with many classroom learning activities that involve abstract knowledge out of context. According to this theory, knowledge needs to be presented in authentic contexts that stimulate social interaction and collaboration, as students learn by engaging in a "community of practice" (Lave & Wenger, 1991). In this sense, situated learning is related to sociocultural theories and to Vygotsky's notion of learning through social development (Vygotsky, 1986).

Key features of VR are immersion, presence, embodiment, and interactivity. The degree to which the user experiences these in the virtual space will depend on the nature of the VR application. Accordingly, in low-immersion VR applications such as VWs, the sense of being present in a virtual space and able to interact in the world through the virtual representation of oneself – the avatar – will be lower than in fully immersive VR environments.

As an immersive technology, VR has the power to blur the boundary between physical and virtual spaces, giving the user a sense of being immersed in the virtual space. Users in HiVR fully experience the sensation of a realistic virtual environment, almost forgetting about the real world and real time, as a result of being completely involved in task performance in the VR space (Lai & Chen, 2021).

Presence is a notion closely related to immersion. Freina and Ott (2015) for example, define immersion as "a perception of being physically present in a non-physical world by surrounding the user of the VR system created with images, sound, or other stimuli" so that a participant feels he or she is actually "there." Sense of presence refers to the feeling of "being in the virtual space." The sense of presence is stimulated by the realistic environment created in VR (Gruber & Kaplan-Rakowski, 2020). Feeling immersed and fully present in the VR space may contribute to learning processes, as it promotes a strong sense of community between those present in the virtual environment, facilitating rich social interaction.

Embodiment in VR, that is, the representation of self though a virtual body – an avatar – has been found to strengthen the sense of immersion and presence in the virtual space (Slater et al., 2010) and to reduce anxiety when students engage in social interaction in a foreign language (Melchor-Couto, 2017). This sense of embodiment in a virtual body emerges when the properties of that body are processed as if they were the properties of one's own biological body. It consists of three subcomponents: the sense of self-location (the feeling that one's self is located inside an avatar's body and is highly determined by the visuospatial first-person perspective), the sense of agency (sense of having global control, including the subjective experience of action, control, and intention), and the sense of body ownership (one's self-attribution of a body and the experienced sensations) (Kilteni et al., 2012).

Both immersion and interactivity have been found to contribute significantly to making the virtual exposure an experience of reality and learning. In Ray's words, "to apprehend a world as real is to feel surrounded by it, to be able to interact physically with it, and to have the power to modify it" (Ray, 1999, p. 111). In this sense, increased levels of interactivity seem to be more conducive to increased engagement in VR learning (Zhang, Bowman, & Jones, 2019).

The varied and rich scenarios that social VR environments offer enrich and contextualize foreign language interaction and learning processes when used with adequate pedagogical tasks. Represented as customizable avatars, students can go to a virtual theater and watch a theatrical production or perform a dramatic piece together with other students; they can go to a conference or a museum, watch a movie, or listen to a scholar; they can visit a prehistoric village or experience the human body from the inside; they can engage in simulations; they can meet other students or peers abroad and interact and play games with them. The pedagogical opportunities these different scenarios offer for embodied and immersive experiences are endless in comparison with the limitations of a classroom setting. It is important for teachers to know what the specific affordances of this type of technology are and to resort to key pedagogical approaches in order to use them effectively and enhance students' linguaculture learning by designing adequate tasks. Closely connected to sociocultural theories of language learning (Lantolf, 2006), task-based language teaching (TBLT) places "tasks" at the center of the learning process. According to TBLT, a task is "an activity in which a person engages in order to attain an objective, and which necessitates the use of language" (Van den Branden, 2006, p. 4). The concepts of real-world authenticity and meaning orientation are seen as encapsulating the main characteristics of these language-learning enhancing tasks (Ellis, 2003, 2012; Long, 2015). Accordingly, tasks should relate to real-world activities and stimulate information or opinion exchange as well as meaning negotiation. In addition, tasks should have clearly formulated goals and outcomes "other than the use of language" (Ellis, 2012, p. 198), as language should be used as a means to achieve the outcome, not as an end. In addition, following the "intercultural turn" in second language (L2) pedagogy, tasks should stimulate the development of intercultural communicative competence (Byram, 1997, 2012). When performed through technology, tasks should exploit the specific affordances of the tool being used (see Canto, de Graaff, & Jauregi, 2014: Canto & Jauregi Ondarra 2017 for concrete examples).

Current Research and Practice

In the following section we will see how low- and high-immersive VR have been used for language learning purposes and what the main research results have been so far on their use.

Low-Immersive VR

Pedagogical Practice

Among the attractions of low-immersive VR are the rich variety of virtual locations and their capacity to support scenarios and foster presence. Users, depicted as avatars, can perform actions (run, sit, fly, etc.), communicate with others via voice and text, add multimedia objects, and travel (teleport) to different in-world destinations. These can be replicas of real-world locations or wildly creative scenarios. Further, avatars can be used to customize players' appearances, manipulate in-world objects, and sometimes have some control over the environment. For instance, avatars can fly over the virtual city of Valencia or go skiing in the Swiss town of Arosa in Second Life. They can also control their environment by introducing new biomes and climates (from mountains to volcanoes), or even by adding game mechanics that will let the user, for example, become a vampire who can feed on the villagers in the game with Minecraft mods (modifications).

These versatile environments support social interaction, as avatars can talk and chat among themselves while they interact with the world and undertake joint action, which in turn prompts experiential learning (Kolb, 1984). These social virtual environments provide opportunities to engage in purposeful target language interaction and facilitate negotiation of meaning, which is key to SLA (Long, 2015). Interaction in low-immersive VR is situated in specific scenarios and socially embedded actions. Accordingly, specific features of the scenario, the actions, or the avatar's appearance can trigger a conversational sequence. In this context, interlocutors may refer to the new clothes the avatar is wearing ("Oh, I love the clothes you're wearing. Where did you buy them?"), they may comment on the film posters decorating the walls in a restaurant ("By the way, have you seen the film Avatar? I just loved it"), or they may voice the action of taking a picture while on a skiing holiday ("I'll take a picture. OK? And you have to say 'cheese'"). These low-immersive virtual worlds are suited not only to formal but also to informal ways of learning. They are perceived as safe settings where language learners can be exposed to rich target language input and opportunities to produce meaningful output (see Jauregi et al., 2011 for specific examples of setting-triggered side conversational sequences).

The real-life experiences simulated in VWs allow also for experiential culture learning, since they let participants practice and develop their intercultural communicative competence. It is the interaction in these immersive experiences, with their specific cultural scenarios and visuals, that has the potential to boost learners' intercultural awareness. Virtual worlds are able to provide a wide range of environments for social interaction, language practice, cultural exploration, and exposure to diverse cultural perspectives (Jauregi Ondarra, Canto, & Melchor-Couto, 2022).

The majority of VW practices have been carried out in Second Life and OpenSim and a number of successful projects[1] have explored the possibilities of VWs for language learning purposes.

Low-immersion environments such as Google Expeditions, which enables teachers to take students on virtual field trips, or Street View and Google Earth, which can be used to view 360-degree videos and images, have also been used for language learning purposes. It must be noted that these apps can also be used in conjunction with an HMD, in which case they would provide a fully immersive experience. For example, Ebadi and Ebadijalal (2020) investigated the effect of Google Expeditions on English as a foreign language (EFL) learners' willingness to communicate and on their oral proficiency. The learners were divided into an experimental group provided with a Google Expeditions VR tool and a control group without it, while role-playing as museum guides. Their findings show that the experimental group significantly outperformed the control group in terms of oral performance and willingness to communicate and that the VR tool enhanced the participants' general knowledge, motivation, enthusiasm, cultural awareness, and confidence.

When it comes to integrating VW activities into regular courses, there are important considerations to be taken into account: on the one hand, the time that both the teacher and the students need to invest into learning the technology; on the other, accessibility to capable devices. Privacy and security issues must also be thoroughly checked. Once these challenges have been dealt with, in order to implement the learning activities, a three-step design (Wang, Burton, & Falls, 2012) is suggested to moderate the learning curve associated with novice technology users. The first step would be to set up technical training sessions to help students get familiar with the technology. This can also be done by designing activities that can function as language learning activities while motivating students to learn to use the new technological application at the same time. Providing tutorials, instructions, and manuals in the target language would be an example. In this way students not only learn and practice the functions of the application but also practice their language skills. The second step would be to assign simple tasks in the VW for students to complete, thus giving them the opportunity to practice their skills and reach an effective level. of proficiency in the use of the VW. The third step would be the task-based activity, when students are ready to work on a learning task in the VW.

Some practical illustrations for the language classroom are virtual (field) trips or tours accompanied by exploratory activities where students can visit different places; role-playing in numerous settings (from a hotel to a particular

---

[1] To date, these three projects have made the following resources available for practitioners:

TILA (Telecollaboration for Intercultural Language Acquisition) www.tilaproject.eu;

TeCoLa (Pedagogical differentiation through telecollaboration and gaming for intercultural and content integrated language teaching) www.tecola.eu.

historical period); and object creation (building a house, designing the landscape, etc.). Real-life tasks can be completed in these simulated real-world scenarios – from watching a movie and going for a pizza afterwards to going on holidays, getting out of an escape room, or giving a presentation. Tasks can also take the form of missions, which adds a game element to the interaction. The authenticity provided by the simulated real-world scenarios makes it possible to use a range of different communicative task types (information gap, opinion-exchange, decision-making, co-construction of artifacts, events, etc.) to engage learners in authentic and meaningful spoken interaction and place them in a particular cultural context for enhancing their cultural understanding. They also offer the possibility of focusing on subject matters (science, history, literature, etc.) using the target language as a medium for instruction, which makes them a valuable tool for content and language integrated learning. However, despite the potential of VWs for language learning, the technology is not being broadly implemented in actual teaching practice.

Research Results

Practitioners have taken the advantages that VWs offer to conduct research mainly on target language production. Several studies have confirmed the potential of VWs to promote oral output and improve performance (Lan, 2014, 2015) and to endorse meaning-focused interaction (Canto & Jauregi Ondarra, 2017; Yamazaki, 2018, 2019). These VWs have also been used to facilitate learner-centered interaction (Chen, 2016; Peterson, 2012) and to encourage participation (Hsu, 2015; Liou, 2012; Wang et al., 2019). Other scholars have focused on the power that VWs might have to lower foreign language anxiety (Melchor-Couto, 2017, 2018; Reinders & Wattana, 2015; Satar & Özdener, 2008; Wehner, Gump, & Downey, 2011), to increase self-efficacy belief levels (Henderson et al., 2009; Melchor-Couto, 2018; Zheng et al., 2010;), and to increase motivation (Berns, Gonzàlez-Pardo, & Camacho, 2011; Jauregi et al., 2012; Kruk, 2015; Wehner et al., 2011). For an overview of research conducted in VWs, see Peterson, Wang, and Mirzaei (2019).

The findings from several other studies (Canto & Jauregi Ondarra, 2017; Canto et al., 2014; Shih, 2015) offer some insights into the potential advantages of VWs for intercultural communication. These studies suggest that those environments contribute to the development of positive attitudes, enhance learners' interest in the target culture, and help students gain knowledge of the target culture. Considering the potential advantages of VWs, there are not many studies that have addressed their impact on intercultural communication in the context of language education.

Finally, researchers have also conducted a series of studies on the affordances that low-immersion applications such as Google Earth, Street View, or Google Expeditions may have for foreign language learning. These applications have proven to be useful in terms of vocabulary acquisition and reading skills (Dourda et al., 2014), expository writing skills (Chen et al., 2020), oral presentation skills (Awada & Diab, 2018), oral performance and willingness to communicate (Ebadi & Ebadijala, 2020), and cultural immersion (Shih, 2015).

High-Immersive VR

High-immersive VR has been described as the learning aid of the twenty-first century, on account of its potential for learning enhancement (Rogers, 2019). The high-immersive experience and interactivity seem to (1) help transform the abstract into the tangible; (2) provide hands-on practice opportunities by allowing a learner to learn by doing, by experiencing, and not just by watching; (3) make it possible to situate learning experiences in places that are impossible or hard to reach; (4) break the boundaries of the physical world and allow a learner to explore learning with physically impossible and novel experiences; and (5) contribute to student engagement (Liu et al., 2017). In addition, different studies suggest that students focus more easily, retain more information, and can better apply what they have learned after participating in VR exercises (Krokos, Plaisant, & Varshney, 2019; Radianti et al., 2020).

Pedagogical Practice

There are different HiVR devices, resources, and applications that can be used for language education. Most of them are for individual use (360-degree videos and pictures, simulations, solo games) and some for social use (social VR apps and multiplayer games). In this section we will look at some of them.

The most affordable devices, although also arguably limited in terms of functionality, are Google Cardboard glasses, which have been tested for language-learning purposes in a number of studies. It must be noted that this type of device does not normally provide a virtual space for users to interact in, it simply allows users to view 360-degree videos or scenes, therefore offering an immersive experience but limited interactivity. More immersive and technologically advanced glasses that have been used for language learning activities include Samsung Gear, Meta/Oculus Quest, Oculus Rift, or HTC VIVE, although, as previously mentioned, it must be noted that the technical developments in this sector are evolving rapidly and these models are likely to be replaced by others in the near future.

The interesting aspect of 360-degree pictures, and especially videos, is that students are no longer mere spectators watching the video but become true participants in it. Interestingly, HiVR can create an emotional connection with the content and setting of the video in a way that is rare in other modes. It can make abstract concepts or situations concrete, for example by taking students to the lives and cultures of different communities of practice, or by enabling them to experience first-hand how people are affected by, let's say, the global refugee crisis. This sense of presence and immersion helps students develop awareness, critical understanding, and empathy – key concepts in intercultural communication (Byram, 2008). Besides, 360-degree videos can take students to places they might never get the chance to visit and make them experience what it means to live in a village in Peru, or to attend a festival in France (Madini & Alshaikhi, 2017).

In addition to 360-degree pictures and videos, students can participate in VR simulations. Presentation simulations are very popular. Here students learn to address the public and develop presentation skills, while they overcome their presentation anxiety, being immersed in front of a large audience.

There are additional VR applications where the learner, using an HMD, gets immersed in and can explore and experience different parts of the world and cultures. Well-known apps for individual use that enhance languaculture learning are Google Expeditions (Xie, Chen, & Ryder, 2019), Google Earth, National Geographic, or Anne Frank's House.

There are VR apps developed specifically for language learning. MondlyVR is the best known one. Here learners are placed in different scenarios where they need to use the target language to order at a restaurant, to check into a hotel, or to ride in a taxi. In these scenarios a bot will speak to the learner, who will respond verbally on the basis of a list of possible responses. Voice-recognition software allows for immediate feedback on pronunciation. However, the possibilities for authentic language use are quite limited in this app.

But undoubtedly social VR applications constitute the most interesting apps for language education. In social VR, multiple users can join a collaborative virtual environment, fostering new opportunities for remote immersive communication and collaboration. Popular social VR apps that are free are Spatial, VTime, or Mozilla Hubs (open source). These social apps offer the possibility to join and create public and private events and encounters and can be used for classroom events, for stimulating peer interaction, or for internationalizing language education by allowing students to carry out task-based virtual exchanges with students abroad (Jauregi Ondarra, Gruber, & Canto, 2020, 2021).

Research Results

As previously mentioned, the number of empirical studies available on the use of HiVR for language learning and teaching has increased considerably since 2020. However, it must be noted that in most cases these studies are not longitudinal and focus on one-off experiences, therefore limiting the validity of the conclusions reached.

Student attitudes and perceptions of this new tool have been analyzed in a number of studies, which seem to indicate that participants experience the use of this piece of technology positively (Berns & Reyes-Sánchez, 2021; Dolgunsöz, Yildirim, & Yildirim, 2018; Gruber & Kaplan-Rakowski, 2020; Herrera, 2020; Jauregi Ondarra et al., 2020; Scrivner et al., 2019; Tai, Chen, & Todd, 2020; Xie et al., 2019; Yang et al., 2020; York et al., 2020).

The most salient characteristic of HiVR is its immersive capability, which has also been addressed by language learning and teaching scholars. In their studies, participants report feeling immersed in the environment (Herrera, 2020; Yang et al., 2020), although Rupp et al. (2016) highlight that, in their case, the VR technology was a distracting factor for their study participants.

Herrera (2020) analyzed the feeling of copresence and found that avatars' nonverbal communication was a key element in this regard. This "immersiveness" has proven to be effective also in the most basic devices, such as Google Cardboard glasses, in terms of positive student attitudes (Scrivner et al., 2019), for vocabulary retention among English for specific purposes (ESP) students (Madini & Alshaikhi, 2017) and for oral presentations, where participants exhibited improved vocabulary and content (Xie et al., 2019).

One area that has attracted considerable attention is that of vocabulary acquisition. A series of studies have contrasted the effectiveness of HiVR devices with that of low-immersive VRs (Lai & Chen, 2021; Legault et al., 2019), video watching (Tai et al., 2020), and the traditional classroom (Alfadil, 2017) in terms of vocabulary retention. The conclusions reached by these experiments seem to indicate that, when using HiVR, students show improved vocabulary acquisition and vocabulary retention, as well as positive attitudes toward the environment. Vocabulary acquisition seems to be a favored topic for researchers, probably because vocabulary gains are easier to measure with pre-, post-, and delayed post-tests than other language domains or communicative skills.

The potential effect of HiVR on students' oral communicative competence has also been addressed in research. Yang et al. (2020) measured a group of low-achieving students' communicative competence before and after taking part in a HiVR experience. The authors found that the post-test scores, which measured listening and dialogic interaction capabilities, were higher on communicative competence; and they concluded that HiVR environments seem to present certain characteristics that make communication easier for students.

High-immersive VR has also been used for virtual exchange practices (Jauregi Ondarra et al., 2020). The results yielded by this study indicate that the participants experienced the high immersion positively and enjoyed interacting in this environment, which was perceived as non-threatening. However, a small number of students reported feeling dizzy during the interactions, a phenomenon that has also been observed in previous studies (Scrivner et al., 2019). An additional point that was observed in this study and that merits our attention is how HiVR headsets can integrate with real-life objects and equipment. The study participants indicated that, when they had to check their notes or use the keyboard, they had to remove their headsets, which affected their immersive experience negatively. Technology providers are working on virtual keyboards, which would solve the problem only partially and would increase the equipment costs. Finally, as already described for low-immersion VWs, HiVR also seems to trigger lower levels of anxiety (Jauregi Ondarra et al., 2020; Yang et al., 2020; York et al., 2020).

Future Directions

As we have seen in this overview, the pedagogical uses of VR open and enrich linguaculture learning contexts, placing the students and their learning processes at the very heart of immersive experiences that seem to contribute to enhancing vocabulary acquisition, communicative competence, willingness to communicate, and intercultural awareness, while lowering anxiety levels. Most pedagogical practices and research studies have been carried out with low-immersive VR systems, more specifically in social VWs, although since 2020 the studies using HiVR have increased in the language educational field.

Most of the studies conducted in low immersion settings examine primarily language production. Although there are indications that these environments can contribute to developing students' intercultural communicative competence, further research is needed to focus on the impact of VR in this field. Another aspect to take into account is the fact that the participants in these low immersion environments have mainly been university students. This type of research needs to reach students in all stages of education.

As for HiVR, the research studies so far have been limited in scope, short-term, with few participants, and almost invariably focused on English as the target language. Additional research is needed to validate initial findings and to analyze how different aspects (immersiveness, presence, interactivity, or embodiment) and tasks might affect communication strategy use, understanding, cultural content gain, intercultural development, and anxiety in different languages and with different student backgrounds. In addition, experiences of dizziness and cybersickness need to be addressed, as some studies reported that students experienced nausea and headaches after using HMDs (Jauregi Ondarra et al., 2020; Martirosov, Bureš, & Zítka, 2021).

Although there are interesting pedagogical experiences using low-immersive VR, only time will tell whether the use of HiVR will continue to grow in language education in the coming years, as this is a novel field. Researchers and practitioners must keep a close eye on how these rapidly evolving technologies unfold.

References

Agar, M. (1994). *Language shock: Understanding the culture of conversation.* William Morrow.

Alfadil, M. M. (2017). *VR game classroom implementation: Teacher perspectives and student learning outcomes.* Unpublished doctoral dissertation. University of Northern Colorado. http://digscholarship.unco.edu/dissertations.

Awada, G., & Diab, H. B. (2018). The effect of Google Earth and wiki models on oral presentation skills of university EFL learners. *International Journal of Teaching and Learning in Higher Education, 30*(1), 36–46. https://files.eric.ed.gov/fulltext/EJ1169829.pdf

Berns, A., & Reyes-Sánchez, S. (2021). A review of virtual reality-based language learning apps. *Revista Iberoamericana de Educación a Distancia, 24*(1), 159–177. https://doi.org/10.5944/ried.24.1.27486

Berns, A., González-Pardo, A., & Camacho, D. (2011). Implementing the use of virtual worlds in the teaching of foreign languages (Level A1). In S. Czepielewski (2011) (Ed.), *Learning a language in virtual worlds: A review of innovation and ICT in language teaching methodology* (pp. 33–40). Warsaw Academy of Computer Science.

Brown, J. S., Collins, A., & Duguid, S. (1989). Situated cognition and the culture of learning. *Educational Researcher, 18*(1), 32–42. https://doi.org/10.3102/0013189X018001032

Byram, M. (1997). *Teaching and assessing intercultural communicative competence.* Multilingual Matters.

Byram, M. (2008). *From language education for intercultural citizenship: Essays and reflections.* Multilingual Matters.

Byram, M. (2012). Conceptualizing intercultural (communicative) competence and intercultural citizenship. In J. Jackson (Ed.), *Routledge handbook of language and intercultural communication* (pp. 85–98). Routledge.

Canto, S., & Jauregi Ondarra, K. (2017). Language learning effects through the integration of synchronous socializing network opportunities in language curricula: The case of video communication and Second Life. *Language Learning in Higher Education Journal, 7*(1), 21–53. https://doi.org/10.1515/cercles-2017-0004

Canto, S., de Graaff, R., & Jauregi, K. (2014). Telecollaborative tasks for negotiation of intercultural meaning in virtual worlds and video-web-communication. In M. González-Lloret, & L. Ortega (Eds.), *Technology-mediated TBLT: Researching technology and tasks* (pp. 183–212). John Benjamins.

Chen, C. (2016). EFL learners' strategy use during task-based interaction in Second Life. *Australasian Journal of Educational Technology, 32*(3), 1–17. https://doi.org/10.14742/ajet.2306

Chen, Y., Smith, T. S., York, C. S., & Mayall, H. J. (2020). Google Earth Virtual Reality and expository writing for young English learners from a Funds of Knowledge perspective. *Computer Assisted Language Learning, 33*(1–2), 1–25. https://doi.org/10.1080/09588221.2018.1544151

Costello, P. (1997). *Health and safety issues associated with virtual reality: A review of current literature.* Advisory Group on Computer Graphics (AGOGG) Technical Reports. www.agocg.ac.uk/reports/virtual/37/37.pdf

Dawley, L., & Dede, C. (2014). Situated learning in virtual worlds and immersive simulations. In J. M. Spector, M. D. Merrill, J. Elen, & M. J. Bishop (Eds.), *The handbook of research for educational communications and technology* 4th ed. (pp. 723–734). Springer.

Dolgunsöz, E., Yildirim, G., & Yildirim, S. (2018). The effect of virtual reality on EFL writing performance. *Journal of Language and Linguistic Studies, 14*(1), 278–292. https://hdl.handle.net/20.500.12403/1329

Dourda, K., Bratitsis, T., Griva, E., & Papadopoulou, P. (2014). Content and language integrated learning through an online game in primary school: A case study. *Electronic Journal of E-Learning, 12*(3), 243–258. www.ejel.org/issue/download.html?idArticle=285

Ebadi, S., & Ebadijalal, M. (2020). The effect of Google Expeditions virtual reality on EFL learners' willingness to communicate and oral proficiency. *Computer Assisted Language Learning*, 35(8), 1975–2000. https://doi.org/10.1080/09588221.2020.1854311

Ellis, R. (2003). *Task-based language learning and teaching*. Oxford University Press.

Ellis, R. (2012). Investigating the performance of tasks. In R. Ellis (Ed.), *Language teaching research and language pedagogy* (pp. 195–235). Wiley Blackwell.

Freina, L., & Ott, M. (2015). A literature review on immersive virtual reality in education: State of the art and perspectives. The International Scientific Conference: eLearning and Software for Education, Bucharest.

Gruber, A., & Kaplan-Rakowski, R. (2020). User experience of public speaking practice in virtual reality. In R. Z. Zheng (Ed.), *Cognitive and affective perspectives on immersive technology in education* (pp. 235–249). IGI Global. https://doi.org/10.4018/978-1-7998-3250-8.ch012

Henderson, M., Huang, H., Grant, S., & Henderson, L. (2009). Language acquisition in Second Life: Improving self-efficacy beliefs. In R. J. Atkinson, & C. McBeath (Eds.), *Same places, different spaces. Proceedings Ascilite Auckland* (pp. 464–474). University of Auckland.

Herrera, B. (2020). *Realidad virtual inmersiva en Facebook Spaces: Análisis del grado de interacción oral y copresencia en un curso online de español como lengua extranjera*. Doctoral dissertation, Universidad Complutense de Madrid. https://eprints.ucm.es/id/eprint/64682

Hsu, L. (2015). EFL learners implicit theory of intelligence and the application of MMORPG in EFL Learning. *International Journal of Computer-Assisted Language Learning and Teaching*, 52, 58–71. https://doi.org/10.4018/IJCALLT.2015040104

Huang, W., Roscoe, R. D., Johnson-Glenberg, M. C., & Craig, S. D. (2021). Motivation, engagement, and performance across multiple virtual reality sessions and levels of immersion. *Journal of Computer Assisted Learning*, 37(3), 745–758.

Jauregi, K., Canto, S., de Graaff, R., Koenraad, A., & Moonen, M. (2011). Verbal interaction in Second Life: Towards a pedagogic framework for task design. *Computer Assisted Language Learning Journal*, 24, 77–101. https://doi.org/10.1080/09588221.2010.538699

Jauregi, K., de Graaff, R., van den Bergh, H., & Kriz, M. (2012). Native/non-native speaker interactions through video-web communication: A clue for enhancing motivation? *Computer Assisted Language Learning*, 25(1), 1–19. https://doi.org/10.1080/09588221.2011.582587

Jauregi Ondarra, K., Gruber, A., & Canto, S. (2020). When international avatars meet: Intercultural language learning in virtual reality exchange. In K. M. Frederiksen, S. Larsen, L. Bradley, & S. Thouësny (Eds.), *CALL for widening participation: Short papers from EUROCALL 2020* (pp. 138–142). Research-publishing.net. https://doi.org/10.14705/rpnet.2020.48.1178

Jauregi Ondarra, K., Canto, S., & Melchor-Couto, S. (2022). Virtual worlds and second language acquisition. In N. Ziegler, & M. González-Lloret (Eds.), *The*

Routledge handbook of second language acquisition and technology (pp. 311–326). Routledge. https://doi.org/10.4324/9781351117586

Jauregi Ondarra, K., Gruber, A., & Canto, S. (2021). Pedagogical experiences in a virtual exchange project using high-immersion virtual reality for intercultural language learning. In N. Zoghlami, C. Brudermann, C. Sarré, M. Grosbois, L. Bradley, & S. Thouësny (Eds.), *CALL and professionalisation: Short papers from EUROCALL 2021* (pp. 155–160). Research-publishing.net. https://doi.org/10.14705/rpnet.2021.54.1325

Kilteni, K., Groten, R., & Slater, M. (2012). The sense of embodiment in virtual reality. *Presence: Teleoperators and virtual environments 2012, 21*(4), 373–387. https://doi.org/10.1162/PRES_a_00124

Kolb, D. A. (1984). *Experiential learning: Experience as the source of learning and development* Vol. 1. Prentice-Hall.

Krokos, E., Plaisant, C., & Varshney, A. (2019). Virtual memory palaces: Immersion aids recall. *Virtual Reality, 23*(1), 1–15. https://doi.org/10.1007/s10055-018-0346-3

Kruk, M. (2015). Willingness to communicate in English in active worlds. In A. Turula, & M. Chojnacka (Eds.), *CALL for bridges between school and academia* (pp. 129–142). Peter Lang Edition.

Lai, K.-W. K., & Chen, H. J. H. (2021). A comparative study on the effects of a VR and PC visual novel game on vocabulary learning. *Computer Assisted Language Learning, 36*(3), 312–345. https://doi.org/10.1080/09588221.2021.1928226

Lan, Y. J. (2014). Does Second Life improve Mandarin learning by overseas Chinese students? *Language Learning & Technology, 18*(2), 36–56. http://dx.doi.org/10125/44365

Lan, Y. J. (2015). Contextual EFL learning in a 3D virtual environment. *Language Learning & Technology, 19*(2), 16–31. www.lltjournal.org/item/2898

Lan, Y.-J., Kan, Y.-H., Sung, Y.-T., & Chang, K.-E. (2016). Oral-performance language tasks for CSL beginners in Second Life. *Language Learning & Technology, 20*(3), 60–79. http://dx.doi.org/10125/44482

Lantolf, J. P. (2006). Sociocultural theory and second language learning: State of the art. *Studies in Second Language Acquisition, 28*, 67–109. https://doi.org/10.1017/S0272263106060037

Lave, J., & Wenger, E. (1991). *Situated learning: Legitimate peripheral participation*. Cambridge University Press.

Legault, J., Zhao, J., Chi, Y.-A., Chen, W., Klippel, A., & Li, P. (2019). Immersive virtual reality as an effective tool for second language vocabulary learning. *Languages, 4*(1), 13. https://doi.org/10.3390/languages4010013

Lin, T. J., & Lan, Y. L. (2015). Language learning in virtual reality environments: Past, present, and future. *Journal of Educational Technology & Society, 18*(4), 486–497. www.jstor.org/stable/jeductechsoci.18.4.486

Liou, H. C. (2012). The roles of Second Life in a college computer-assisted language learning (CALL) course in Taiwan, *ROC. Computer Assisted Language Learning, 25*(4), 365–382. https://doi.org/10.1080/09588221.2011.597766

Liu, D., Dede, C. Huang, R., & Richards, J. (Eds.) (2017). *Virtual, augmented, and mixed realities in education (Smart Computing and Intelligence)*. Springer. https://doi.org/10.1007/978-981-10-5490-7_2

Lloyd, A., Rogerson, S., & Stead, G. (2017). Imagining the potential for using virtual reality technologies in language learning. In M. Carrier, R. M. Damerow, & K. M. Bailey (Eds.), *Digital language learning and teaching: Research, theory, and practice* (1st ed., pp. 222–234). Routledge. https://doi.org/10.4324/9781315523293

Long, M. (2015). *Second language acquisition and task-based language teaching*. Wiley Blackwell.

Madini, A. A., & Alshaikhi, D. (2017). VR for teaching ESP vocabulary: A myth or a possibility. *International Journal of English Language Education, 5*(2), 111–126. https://doi.org/10.5296/ijele.v5i2.11993

Martirosov, S., Bureš, M., & Zítka, T. (2021). Cyber sickness in low-immersive, semi-immersive, and fully immersive virtual reality. *Virtual Reality, 19*, 1–18. https://doi-org.proxy.library.uu.nl/10.1007/s10055-021-00507-4

Melchor-Couto, S. (2017). Foreign language anxiety levels in Second Life oral interaction. *ReCALL, 29*(1), 99–119. https://doi.org/10.1017/S0958344016000185

Melchor-Couto, S. (2018). Virtual world anonymity and foreign language oral interaction. *ReCALL, 30*(2), 232–249. https://doi.org/10.1017/S0958344017000398

Melchor-Couto, S., & Herrera, B. (2023). Immersive virtual reality: Exploring possibilities for virtual exchange. In A. Potolia, & M. Derivry-Plard (Eds.), *Virtual exchange for intercultural language learning and teaching: Fostering communication for the digital age* (pp. 92–114). Routledge.

Parmaxi, A. (2020). Virtual reality in language learning: A systematic review and implications for research and practice. *Interactive Learning Environments, 31*(1), 172–184. https://doi.org/10.1080/10494820.2020.1765392

Peterson, M. (2012). EFL learner collaborative interaction in Second Life. *ReCALL, 24*(1), 20–39. https://doi.org/10.1017/S0958344011000279

Peterson, M., Wang, Q., & Mirzaei, M. S. (2019). The use of network-based virtual worlds in second language education: A research review. In M. Kruk (Ed.), *Assessing the effectiveness of virtual technologies in foreign and second language instruction* (pp. 1–25). IGI Global. https://doi.org/10.4018/978-1-5225-7286-2.ch001

Radianti, J., Majchrzak, T. A., Fromm, J., & Wohlgenannt, I. (2020). A systematic review of immersive virtual reality applications for higher education: Design elements, lessons learned, and research agenda. *Computers and Education, 147*, 103778. https://doi.org/10.1016/j.compedu.2019.103778

Reinders, H., & Wattana, S. (2015). Affect and willingness to communicate in digital game-based learning. *ReCALL, 27*(1), 38–57. https://doi.org/10.1017/S0958344014000226

Risager, K. (2012). Linguaculture. In C. A. Chapelle (Ed.), *Encyclopedia of applied linguistics* (pp. 3418–3421). Wiley. https://doi.org/10.1002/9781405198431.wbeal0709

Rogers, S. (2019). *Virtual reality: The learning aid of the 21st century*. Forbes.

Rupp, M. A., Kozachuk, J., Michaelis, J. R., Odette, K. L., Smither, J. A., & McConnell, D. S. (2016). The effects of immersiveness and future VR expectations on subjective experiences during an educational 360° video. *Proceedings of the Human Factors and Ergonomics Society, 60*(1), 2101–2105. https://doi.org/10.1177/1541931213601477

Ryan, M. (1999). Immersion vs. interactivity: Virtual reality and literary theory. *SubStance, 28*(2), 110–137. https://doi.org/10.2307/3685793

Satar, H. M., & Özdener, N. (2008). The effects of synchronous CMC on speaking proficiency and anxiety: Text versus voice chat. *The Modern Language Journal, 92*(4), 595–613. https://doi.org/10.1111/j.1540-4781.2008.00789

Scrivner, O., Madewell, J., Buckley, C., & Perez, N. (2019). Best practices in the use of augmented and virtual reality technologies for SLA: Design, implementation, and feedback. In M. L. Carrió-Pastor (Ed.), *Teaching language and teaching literature in virtual environments* (pp. 55–72). Springer Singapore. https://doi.org/10.1007/978-981-13-1358-5_4

Shih, Y. C. (2015). A virtual walk through London: Culture learning through a cultural immersion experience. *Computer Assisted Language Learning, 28*(5), 407–428. https://doi.org/10.1080/09588221.2013.851703

Slater, M., Spanlang, B., & Corominas, D. (2010). Simulating virtual environments within virtual environments as the basis for a psychophysics of presence. *ACM Transactions on Graphics, 29*(4), 92. https://doi.org/10.1145/1778765.1778829

Tai, T. Y., Chen, H. H.-J., & Todd, G. (2020). The impact of a virtual reality app on adolescent EFL learners' vocabulary learning. *Computer Assisted Language Learning, 35*(4), 892–917. https://doi.org/10.1080/09588221.2020.1752735

Van den Branden, K. (2006). Introduction: Task-based language teaching in a nutshell. In K. Van den Branden (Ed.), *Task-based language education* (pp. 1–17). Cambridge University Press.

Vygotsky, L. S. (1986). *Thought and language*. MIT Press.

Wang, F., Burton, J. K., & Falls, J. (2012). A three-step model for designing initial Second Life-based foreign language learning activities. *Journal of Online Learning and Teaching, 8*(4), 324–333.

Wang, C., Lan, Y. L., Tseng, W. T., Lin, Y.T R., & Gupta, C. L. (2019). On the effects of 3D virtual worlds in language learning: A meta-analysis. *Computer Assisted Language Learning, 33*(8), 891–915. https://doi.org/10.1080/09588221 .2019.1598444

Wehner, A. K., Gump, A. W., & Downey, S. (2011). The effects of Second Life on the motivation of undergraduate students learning a foreign language. *Computer Assisted Language Learning, 24*(3), 277–289. https://doi.org/10.1080/09588221 .2010.551757

Xie, Y., Chen, Y., & Ryder, L. H. (2019). Effects of using mobile-based virtual reality on Chinese L2 students' oral proficiency. *Computer Assisted Language Learning, 34*(3), 225–245. https://doi.org/10.1080/09588221.2019.1604551

Yamazaki, K. (2018). Computer-assisted learning of communication (CALC): A case study of Japanese learning in a 3D virtual world. *ReCALL, 30*(2), 214–231. https://doi.org/10.1017/S0958344017000350

Yamazaki, K. (2019). The effective use of a 3D virtual world in a JFL classroom: Evidence from discourse analysis. In E. Zimmerman, & A. McMeekin (Eds.),

Technology supported learning in and out of the Japanese language classroom: Pedagogical, theoretical, and empirical developments (pp. 227–251). Multilingual Matters.

Yang, F. C. O., Lo, F. Y. R., Hsieh, J. C., & Wu, W. C. V. (2020). Facilitating communicative ability of EFL learners via high-immersion virtual reality. *Journal of Educational Technology & Society, 23*(1), 30–49. www.jstor.org/stable/26915405

York, J., Shibata, K., Tokutake, H., & Nakayama, H. (2020). Effect of SCMC on foreign language anxiety and learning experience: A comparison of voice, video, and VR-based oral interaction. *ReCALL, 33,* 49–70. https://doi.org/10.1017/S0958344020000154

Zhang, L., Bowman, D. A., & Jones, C. N. (2019). Exploring effects of interactivity on learning with interactive storytelling in immersive virtual reality. *2019 11th International Conference on Virtual Worlds and Games for Serious Applications (VS-Games),* 1–8. https://doi.org/10.1109/VS-Games.2019.8864531

Zheng, D., Young, M. F., Brewer, R. A., & Wagner, M. (2010). Attitude and self-efficacy change: English language learning in virtual worlds. *CALICO Journal, 27* (1), 205–231. https://doi.org/10.11139/cj.27.1.205-231

Further Reading

Blyth, C. (2018). Immersive technologies and language learning. *Foreign Language Annals, 51*(1), 225–232. https://doi.org/10.1111/flan.12327.
In this article, Blyth explores immersive technologies as tools for foreign language education, with a specific focus on augmented reality (AR) and VR. The discussion ranges from historical perspectives to future challenges, shedding light on the potential of these technologies.

Jauregi Ondarra, K., Canto, S., & Melchor-Couto, S. (2022). Virtual worlds and second language acquisition. In N. Ziegler, & M. González-Lloret (Eds.), *Routledge handbook of second language acquisition and technology* (pp. 311–326). Routledge. https://doi.org/10.4324/9781351117586.
This book chapter offers a comprehensive overview of VWs as a technology-mediated approach to facilitate SLA. It provides insights into research studies and practical applications by exploring the potential benefits of VWs in promoting language proficiency, cultural understanding, and communicative competence.

Scrivner, O., Madewell, J., Buckley, C., & Perez, N. (2019). Best practices in the use of augmented and virtual reality technologies for SLA: Design, implementation, and feedback. In M. L. Carrió-Pastor (Ed.), *Teaching language and teaching literature in virtual environments* (pp. 55–72). Springer. https://doi.org/10.1007/978-981-13-1358-5_4.
This book chapter explores the best practices for incorporating AR and VR technologies in the context of SLA. The authors discuss topics such as the design, implementation, and feedback mechanisms related to these technologies.

Part IV

Social Aspects

14

Social Interaction and Learning

Lara Lomicka and Stacey Benoit

Introduction

Digital technology provides myriad affordances to second language (L2) learning both for students and instructors; technology also affects how people use language in different situations (Chun, Kern, & Smith, 2016). These affordances (the characteristics and potential uses of software tools), however, should be used in a way that allows learners to situate their interaction in authentic and meaningful ways. Decades of research have pointed to the importance of social aspects of language learning (see, for example, Kern, 1997; Kinginger, 2013). This chapter explores some essential components of social interaction in language learning environments. Central to social interaction is communication – simply put, without communication, learning would not easily happen (Verga & Kotz, 2013). This communication (both verbal and nonverbal) can be between teacher and students, between students in the class, and between students and other partners, such as native speakers in the target country. Since students in our project served both as native speakers of their own language and nonnative speakers of the language they are studying, they are able to serve in both expert and learner roles during their interaction. The use of both authentic communication, drawing from real-life knowledge and experiences, making one's message comprehensible and understood by others, and using relevant content, all help to motivate students to communicate in their learning (Hedge, 2000; Mishan, 2005; Nunan, 1988). Designing the strategy and management of a cross-cultural exchange program with this authenticity in mind is essential to help avoid the pitfalls of possible negative outcomes, such as the reinforcement of overgeneralizations and stereotyping. Although communication is the main goal of communicative language teaching, it is also key to many other approaches to teaching and learning a second language, regardless of one's theoretical perspective. Social interaction provides learners with a meaningful and authentic audience to practice and navigate their language learning pathway. In this chapter, we delve more deeply into the types of activities (principally those that foster communication) that can contribute to encouraging social interaction in language classes, particularly in the context of social exchange facilitated by various technological tools.

Background

To begin, we will briefly situate social interaction in the broader context of language learning and education by discussing a few key concepts. First, interactional theory (Bruner, 1973; Vygotsky, 1978) presents a social view of language acquisition that focuses on interaction between the interlocutors (language learners). Bruner posits the importance of interactions between a learner and an adult and how these interactions are critical to language acquisition. Through scaffolding, learners can receive support, which can be removed once the learner can function on their own. Taking it a step further, Vygotsky highlights the importance of learning through purposeful, meaningful interactions with others. In the zone of proximal development, novices and experts work together to understand their environments and shared experiences. He believes that the zone of proximal development is where language acquisition occurs. Both Bruner and Vygotsky point to the interaction, inherently social, that takes place in the collaborative efforts of those working together to achieve understanding and support. Bruner and Vygotsky's work highlights the importance of social interaction between the novice and the expert; in our project, we use this model as we pair native speakers with nonnative speakers with differing levels of language experience to create a similar dynamic, thus adding a reciprocal element of language exchange and creating a mutually beneficial collaborative learning environment.

Further, social interaction theory acknowledges that there are many factors that can foster language acquisition, such as the physical environment, cognitive (verbal intelligence, long-term memory capacity, etc.) and social aspects of learning and psychological factors such as anxiety, motivation, and self-confidence (Rudd & Lambert, 2011). So, in addition to the presence of another interlocutor to offer guidance and support, the physical or virtual space or environment is also helpful for social interaction. Simulating a real-world environment where learners can place themselves in a context that is similar to what they would experience if in the target country can provide helpful social cues and multimodal information that goes beyond what is available to them in the traditional classroom environment. For example, virtual reality (VR) and other social media tools can help to simulate these environments for today's learners (Li & Jeong, 2020). Li and Jeong (2020) advocate for an approach, which they refer to as "social L2 learning," which, according to them, is defined as follows: "Learning through real-life or simulated real-life environments where learners can interact with objects and people, perform actions, receive, use, and integrate perceptual, visuospatial, and other sensorimotor information, which enables learning and communication to become embodied" (n.p.). Our program encompasses a broader scope of social interaction activities. The tasks that we will discuss later in this chapter use both synchronous and asynchronous interaction to help learners engage in successful social interaction with their peers. Engaging students in interaction, whether in the classroom or virtually, with native speakers of the target language offers the possibility to approach task-based learning in a way that is different from the traditional language classroom.

While we recognize that this chapter is not research-based, we do want to share some trends that have emerged from the last decade of collaboration in our work. First, social interaction between learners in differing linguistic and cultural communities can foster negotiation of meaning and provide opportunities for the exploration of different cultural perspectives (see Benoit & Lomicka, 2019; O'Dowd & Ware, 2009). The social interaction that is present in a cross-cultural learning environment is not only rich but also provides increased opportunities for language practice. Second, as today's students are global citizens as well as digital natives, it is crucial that they develop social and cross-cultural skills that are indispensable for the workplace (Sulam, Syakur, & Musyarofah, 2019). Third, social interaction with students from another country takes students well beyond material covered in a textbook and encourages them to see the dynamic and ever-changing role of culture and distinguish it from stereotypes and cultural bias (Benoit & Lomicka, 2019). Fourth, social interaction from collaborative exchange projects can transform the traditional classroom into a space of higher-order thinking and learning. Students are able to take responsibility for their own learning experience and build trust with their partners within a reciprocal peer-based exchange. To build on these trends in social interaction, we will now explore several aspects that are key to social interaction in L2 learning, including relationship building, cross-cultural collaboration, critical thinking, and sharing divergent perspectives and illustrate each with practical examples from our virtual collaboration.

Primary Themes

Context

Social interaction has been a driving force in intercultural projects over the last several decades. There are a number of intercultural projects that integrate virtual exchange and telecollaboration, that is, using different online communication tools to allow groups of students from different languages and cultures in various geographic locations to collaborate remotely.

Cummins and Sayers (1995) argue for access to technology for all learners and were among the first researchers to promote global learning projects with partners around the world. Specific to language learning, Furstenberg et al. (2001) designed an intercultural exchange that juxtaposes materials from two different cultures to offer a comparative approach to investigating cultural differences (online questionnaires related to their cultural values and associations). Métral, Benenson, and Skorupa (2009) in their Cross-Cultural Connections project outline an intercultural exchange between students at Smith College and those at Telecom ParisTech in order to develop intercultural competence and language skills through both asynchronous and synchronous tools. Other studies over the years have built on some of the foundational work done by Cummins and Sayers (1995) and Furstenberg et al. (2001), emphasizing the role of social interaction and collaborative exchange (see, e.g., Belz, 2002, 2003; Dooly, 2008; Eneau & Develotte, 2012, O'Dowd, 2007).

We begin this section by describing a virtual collaborative project between students in France and in the United States. Intermediate language practice and a cultural exchange has brought together students from two continents – a French course in an American university and an English course in a French graduate engineering school for over ten years (see also Benoit & Lomicka, 2019). Collaboration and learning are facilitated by structured tasks and activities where students use a variety of digital tools to generate social interaction. By maintaining consistent regular communication inside and outside the classroom, students are able to improve oral and written language skills, while also getting to know each other better and becoming part of a cohesive cross-cultural community. This reciprocal learning relationship allows learners to build relationships, collaborate cross-culturally, dig deeper into ideas, and share divergent perspectives. Combining synchronous and asynchronous exchange methods enhances students' learning experience by permitting them to build on each other's ideas and interact in multiple ways over time with different class members. By collaborating on common projects around a selection of current and contemporary topics, learners delve into these issues and analyze them collectively, which encourages them to reflect, interpret, and make sense of information through exchange and social interaction (Cunningham, 2019; O'Dowd & O'Rourke, 2019). Working together and interacting virtually within a group gives students the opportunity to appreciate a variety of viewpoints and perspectives and develop a deeper cultural understanding. Virtual exchange prepares students for international travel, which in the case of this project, occurs in the middle of the exchange and allows them to test their communication skills in an immersive target language context.

Building Relationships and Community

Although many classrooms still provide access to a face-to-face community of learners, since the onset of the COVID-19 pandemic, there has been an increase in the creation of virtual communities of language learners. According to Clodius (1997), online communities with shared interests and self-identification of belonging are viable alternatives to a restrictive definition of community based on geography or patterns of residence. As in any class-room setting, whether face-to-face or virtual, building relationships with your students and between students requires time and even intentional activities that facilitate interaction.

This interaction and engagement among students is a key component to successful online communities, and as Gehlback (2017) posits, "Studies … show that learners who are better socially connected to their teachers and classmates are significantly more engaged and achieve better than their less well-connected peers" (n.p.). Involvement in an online community is an active learning experience that necessitates engagement and empowers learners to become active community participants. Pasfield-Neofitou (2011) examined the use of computer-mediated communication (CMC) in virtual communities of language learners of Japanese and English. Results suggest that "A sense of being heard and understood appeared to increase participants' sense of achievement and increase the likelihood of their continued engagement in L2 use online" (p. 105). Liu and Zhang (2012) found that "Learners partici-pating in virtual communities can be transformed from passive receivers of authentic materials to engaged authors of their own second language (L2) artifacts. Such practice provides L2 learners with a safe and motivating envir-onment in which they can enhance their perceived self-efficacy" (n.p.). Thus, building relationships among learners in order to form a classroom community is key to both engagement and learning; it facilitates a sense of belonging, trust, and motivation.

Within the context of our project, we have found that setting up and launching social interaction in a virtual classroom is a balancing act. It requires intricate preparation using "tried and true" activities, but also the integration of current themes and experimentation with cutting-edge resources and tools. A couple of quick ways to help students begin to form relationships include activities such as virtual speed dating or "find someone who." Using these activities virtually in a synchronous format (via a course management system [CMS] or Zoom), where students frequently change rooms and/or partners in order to meet different target language speakers, offers a lively way to open the conversation between group members. These tasks challenge students to explore the other culture and create an initial engagement with class members they will encounter in future chat sessions or through email exchange.

For a more sustained relationship, we pair each of our students for the semester with a student in the other country for a bi-monthly email exchange. The creation of individual "keypal" email relationships (keyboard pen pals) between partners sets up a reciprocal learning environment and allows stu-dents to get to know each other over time through an idea and information exchange on a variety of topics. Corresponding about different themes with one student acting as "target language specialist" and the other as "learner" for one language, then switching roles for the other, establishes a reliance on each other to give written feedback to their email and a personal and cultural point of view on the subject. Students are encouraged to ask their partners specific questions and respond to those asked of them and email prompts often include news articles to give background information on themes around current events. This type of asynchronous exchange gives students more time to reflect on and analyze the correspondence they receive and reciprocate with a well-elaborated response.

Visual tools help students form a clearer image of the target culture and personal experience of their exchange partners. To explore students' surroundings and personal perspectives, we experimented with the geolocating app, Siftr, where students can capture digital images then geolocate them on a collaborative class map. These customized maps of their personal and group experiences sparked interaction around a vast network of shared places and practices within the group. Focusing this social photography activity around a visual theme like "Campus life" or "Photo of the day," allows students to upload their photos, add short descriptions, then compare their perspective to that of others by interacting with them through comments. Using a category system based on an intercultural framework, students can analyze the images together (through the comments function), thus generating a conversation between group members, in both target languages, setting up an opportunity for a deeper cultural information exchange.

Figure 14.1 is an example of a "Photo of the day" exchange after American students visited a French elementary school during international travel. The goal was for each student to highlight for the group the top photo of their experience each day during their trip. This personal choice allowed others to know more about them and their perspective, and the placing of each photo within an intercultural framework elicited responses from students of the target culture to offer help, give more information, or just make sure their partners were enjoying themselves.

The student's post shows they were able to notice and reflect on the wearing of a security vest, but the interaction that ensues takes on a more personal note, as another student wants more precise information on their global experience and the reactions of the children involved.

Engaging Students in Cross-Cultural Collaboration

Social interaction that occurs through cross-cultural collaborations can foster rich dialogue that leads to deeper reflection and examination of not only the other culture but also one's own. One goal of any language classroom is to develop students' intercultural competence and a sense of critical cultural awareness (Byram, 1997; Ingram, 2005; Shih, 2015). While intercultural competence has been a significant research topic since the 1980s (Byram, 1989), there does not seem to be any single way to help students more fully relate to the target culture and reflect on their language learning experiences (Godwin-Jones, 2013). Cross-cultural collaboration can take on many forms (tandem learning, telecollaboration, critical virtual exchange, etc.); however, one commonality is that this type of collaboration involves learners working together in different cultural spaces and places.

Cross-cultural collaboration builds knowledge collectively through inter-action, co-construction, engagement, and negotiation with students and edu-cators in other cultures. It also provides access to learning environments where students can explore their own views, hear and respond to viewpoints that are different from their own, and come to a sense of mutual understand-ing (Schreiber & Valle, 2013). These spaces enable learners to engage in critical reflection and self-examination, creating opportunities to ponder differing perspectives and allow for the negotiation of shared understandings.

There are multiple technological tools and apps for language students use to engage in cross-cultural collaboration and to build on the ideas of others as a means of social interaction. Collaborative activities come in many shapes and sizes; some may have a duration of only five minutes and others may be built up through an entire semester project using the creative potential of the group. One example of a tool that we used for cross-cultural collaboration is Padlet. Padlet, an interactive white board, has served as a virtual space for students in our project to engage in cross-cultural collaboration in a variety of ways. The teacher can set up a Padlet board for the entire group and provide a prompt. Students can then contribute posts during a synchronous or asynchronous activity, or each student can create their own Padlet board for comments from others. Padlet's format allows users to make creative decisions, as they can change the board background, the title, subtitle, and icon, the post layout and comment format, and even the url itself. They can appropriate the content and tailor it to the group or the subject, making it more compelling for others to contribute through both comments and various types of reactions.

An example of a group Padlet is one we called, "Time capsule," with posts from transatlantic partners imagining what works of art best inform Americans and Europeans in the future about today's society. For this activity, students met in small groups synchronously (via Skype) and discussed what they might want to remember about life in 2021 through the choice of a work of art. Students presented art about topics related to the lockdown as well as the Black Lives Matter movement. This activity asks students to first reflect on their own ideas surrounding art and the uniqueness of 2021. Then, with the help of native speakers in the other country, they discuss and arrive at a consensus about what they would like to share on the Padlet with the rest of the class.

Exposure to and participation in a language exchange can benefit students as it offers both opportunities for understanding and opens a window to another culture (O'Dowd, 2003, 2007). Cultivating and developing this openness is crucial to successful cross-collaboration in the language classroom. As Thorne (2016) points out, cross-cultural communication and linguistics could be achieved "in a form of language-mediated social action" (p. ix) through exchanges in language learning contexts. Being able to directly communicate with a native speaker allows learners to acquire critical perspectives through cross-cultural activities such as analyses and comparisons.

Promoting Critical Thinking

Critical thinking tasks in language learning create social interaction by engaging students in learning from one another and changing perspectives through observation, thinking creatively, problem-solving, and more. This interaction involves questioning each other's points of view, digging deeper into subjects to draw conclusions and analyzing information together. Critical thinking is an expected learning outcome of higher education and aims at achieving understanding, seeing things from different angles, evaluating different perspectives, being open-minded and empathetic, and solving problems (Maiorana, 1992). Shirkhani and Fahim (2011) present three reasons why critical thinking is important for the language classroom: 1) It allows learners to take charge of their own thinking; 2) it expands their learning experience and makes the language more meaningful; and 3) it correlates with learners' achievements. Researchers have emphasized the crucial role that critical thinking plays in language development (Tarvin & Al-Arishi, 1991; Chamot, 1995). Sokol et al. (2008) posit that the development of thinking skills in foreign language teaching and learning contexts leads to an increase in students' general inventive thinking skills.

Discussion boards have been a staple in education for decades. In fact, Stansberry (2006) argues that "studies of asynchronous discussion as computer-mediated communication reveal that students exhibit more sophisticated decision-making processes than face-to-face students, show an increase in participation and collaborative thinking, learn to articulate and negotiate their developing knowledge structures, and engage in higher-order processing of information by constructing personal meaning through collaborative interaction" (p. 28). They are, according to Stansberry, "a perfect forum for an academic discourse promoting increased student engagement, critical analysis and reflection, and the social construction of knowledge" (p. 28). These forums can provide a platform where students can demonstrate their critical thinking ability, and where they can engage, interact, and practice the target language. Threaded discussion forums on platforms such as Slack or Yellowdig offer a space for students to have synchronous or asynchronous exchange and to give information or an opinion and respond to those of others. These platforms are similar to traditional-style discussion boards, but have a social media element where students can ask the group questions and feel out an issue through a global poll and add pictures, videos, or links to articles to complement their written work. The interaction builds upon itself over time as new topics are added and students lead the discussion without teacher intervention.

Using synchronous and asynchronous threaded discussion forums to elicit written expression helps students critically analyze perspectives on current events and cultural topics. In our project, students discussed contemporary themes and interacted in real time within the group in Slack and Yellowdig forums. Figure 14.2 is an example of a critical discussion on gun control laws and measures in different countries on Slack. Students were able to compare and analyze their partners' personal and cultural viewpoints on the issue and respond to the group as well as to individual posts.

Used for various types of team or project work, Slack is freeware available as a desktop and phone app. The Yellowdig platform, created specifically as an online educational learning platform, promotes student exchange and engagement through a point system. Yellowdig is a subscription-based tool. Each interaction within the community is worth a number of points and students compete to see who interacts the most.

Ibid is an example of an exchange around the theme of the media. Students responded to different aspects of the original post: to inquire about the uploaded screenshot, to share their own media preferences, or to ask a question about French media habits.

In addition to practicing writing and communication skills, the use of online forums offers the opportunity to hone critical thinking skills. Whether used synchronously or asynchronously, they provide a space for learners to reflect on subjects and interact with others to analyze them, taking on the form of an engaged conversation between learners and, in our case, back and forth across languages. The discussion among group members allows learners to gain a deeper understanding of each other and their different perspectives, laying the groundwork for open-mindedness and empathy within the learning community.

Sharing Divergent Perspectives Through Multiple Interactions

One key component of social interaction in the context of language learning is being able to learn about and share differing perspectives about the target cultures. While a textbook is static and presents an author's point of view, working with peers or learners from another culture can offer a dynamic and ever-changing outlook on a country's culture.

One example of sharing of divergent perspectives is the Cultura Project (see Furstenberg et al., 2001), a telecollaboration project that aims to develop intercultural understanding between learners from different cultures using a variety of online communication tools. This intercultural project and exchange involves groups of students from different cultures and has been widely adapted by others. Levet and Tshudi (2021) describe the Cultura approach as fostering "dynamic online interaction with partners from another culture" (p. 49). In essence, through asynchronous forums, both groups of learners (from different cultures) compare ideas and materials through surveys, films, advertisements, and various types of text. With this approach, there is a constant sharing of perspectives, which helps learners to better understand each other and the culture in which they live (the values, attitudes, and beliefs that underlie their interactions).

Building on the ideas of Cultura, our project provides opportunities for virtual interaction (both asynchronous and synchronous) as well as visits to the other country in order to facilitate conversations about culture and to promote social interaction. Within the context of our project, students engage in structured interaction with a single partner (email), multiple partners (synchronous chat sessions), and with the entire group (discussion boards, Padlets, and other activities). Setting up online collaboration tools warrants critical reflection on what meaningful content to include, in what format, and how to vary the different types of weekly interaction.

The way students share ideas about different subjects can be as rich and thought-provoking for students as the subject matter itself. What is the most motivating way to set up the practice of a set of vocabulary words, a specific grammar point, a language practice, or a soft skill? Would it be more advantageous to their learning to speak to multiple partners on this subject, rather than just one? Would presenting this theme using a certain tool be more intriguing and, thus, create more interaction? Like in any class, varying activities online for a single subject area can allow students more opportunities to practice different skills: to exchange information, analyze and compare, give opinions, respond critically, postulate, imagine, solve problems, and more.

Using activities such as brainstorming and group word clouds as an introduction to a particular theme that students explore in class can quickly expand vocabulary and jargon in the target language, foster creativity, and present a new topic before investigating it further. ibid presents an example of a Mentimeter group word cloud created to begin a synchronous virtual discussion on the topic of music and the arts. Students mediated meaning around various vocabulary related to emotions evoked by music in both French and English, fostering cross-cultural collaboration around talking about one's feelings, personal music listening habits, the role of music in general, and daily life activities that include music in each culture.

Setting up online collaboration tools warrants a deep and extensive reflection on what meaningful content can be included; it is also critical to discuss a variety of interaction opportunities. In a video conference on sports, students might brainstorm vocabulary together, speak to multiple partners during a "Find someone who" activity, share their own sports and fitness practices, explore the theme of politics and sports, then collaborate on creating an imaginary team, mascot, and training regime.

Designing interaction between multiple participants allows students to benefit from the variety of viewpoints and perspectives in the target language and culture. Synchronous speaking tasks, with simple musical chair-like rotations during an interview or a "find someone who" activity are easy and fun ways to dynamize a classroom – even a virtual one. Students encounter diverse ideas and experiences on the same topic, encouraging an exploration of cultural identity and behavior and an introspective view into their own. They navigate a range of accents and nonverbal expressions in the target language and are able to interpret cultural knowledge from multiple sources. Students can collaborate in small teams to tackle a survival game enigma or create an advertising campaign that promotes information exchange. Teamwork, brainstorming, and problem-solving all highlight the different roles played within a group and how they are played.

Recommendations for Practice

In this chapter, we have discussed the importance of social interaction in language classes in the context of virtual exchange and how it can serve as a vehicle to build community, cross-cultural collaboration, critical thinking, and divergent perspectives. We encourage educators to ponder the questions below when creating a curriculum that promotes social interaction:

- What are the most effective tasks to help students connect with one another and create meaningful learning experiences together?
- What tools can you use to build community in a virtual setting?
- What does social interaction teach students about cross-cultural collaboration?
- What tasks best allow students to notice and reflect on the target culture?
- What interactions best promote self-reflection and inspire students to assume an outsider point of view of their own culture and appropriate certain elements of their partners' culture?
- How does interacting with multiple partners on a variety of tasks help students obtain divergent perspectives on a specific theme?
- How can students understand and negotiate differing cultural perspectives when working with a partner class?
- How does social interaction lead to discussions of cultural conflict, differences, and consensus?
- What types of collaboration lead to building bridges between cultures?

On a more practical level, educators can decide on particular themes to work on with their language students. Themes are often more successful if there is input from students. Asking for learner input can even become part of a lesson as students discuss suggestions for subjects they are most interested in collaborating on. Once the theme is identified, the instructor can find a few current digital texts based on recent events or topics of interest (in each language) that can be used as a source for reading and discussion. Next, it is important to delineate prompts for tasks and tools that might work best for each task. Educators can think about how to incorporate community building, critical thinking, multiple perspectives, and cross-collaboration.

The global pandemic hindered social interaction and even dramatically altered it in education, whether online or in the classroom. Lomicka (2020) suggests that virtual engagement should focus on interaction and collaboration, regardless of the tool used. It should also motivate, support learners, and contribute to knowledge construction and synchronous and asynchronous instruction, regardless of whether it is online or ibid, and should combine "frequent, direct and meaningful interaction between students and between students and professor" (Flaherty, 2020, n.p.). McMurtrie (2021) points out that it is also important for teachers to recognize what has changed during and as a result of the pandemic. Some of those changes may be here to stay and may positively impact the role of social interaction in language education in years to come. The benefits of social interaction in the language classroom, whether online or face to face, are numerous and can create opportunities for both mutual trust and connectedness that in turn guide learners to investigate more deeply the intercultural terrain of their own culture and that of their learning partners.

References

Belz, J. A. (2002). Social dimensions of telecollaborative foreign language study. *Language Learning & Technology, 6*(1), 60–81. https://doi.org/10125/25143

Belz, J. A. (2003). Linguistic perspectives on the development of intercultural competence in telecollaboration. *Language Learning & Technology, 7*(2), 68–117. https://doi.org/10125/25201

Benoit, S., & Lomicka, L. (2019). Reciprocal learning and intercultural exchange in a virtual environment. In C. Tardieu & C. Horgues (Eds.), *Redefining tandem language and culture learning in higher education* (pp. 79–94). Routledge.

Bruner, J. S. (1973). *The relevance of education.* Norton.

Byram, M. (1989). *Cultural studies in foreign language education.* Multilingual Matters.

Byram, M. (Ed.). (1997). *Face to face: Learning language and culture through visits and exchanges.* CILT.

Chamot, A. (1995). Creating a community of thinkers in the ESL/EFL classroom. *TESOL Matters, 5*(5), 1–16.

Chun, D., Kern, R., & Smith, B. (2016). Technology in language use, language teaching, and language learning. *The Modern Language Journal, 100*(s1), 64–80. https://doi.org/10.1111/modl.12302

Clodius, J. (1997). Creating a community of interest: "Self" and "other" on DragonMud. Paper presented at the Combined Conference on MUDs, Jackson Hole, Wyoming, January 15, 1997. http://dragonmud.org/people/jen/mudshopiii.html

Cummins, J., & Sayers, D. (1995). *Brave new schools: Challenging cultural illiteracy through global learning networks.* St. Martin's Press.

Cunningham, D. J. (2019). Telecollaboration for content and language learning: A genre-based approach. *Language Learning & Technology, 23*(3), 161–177. http://hdl.handle.net/10125/44701

Dooly, M. (Ed.). (2008). *Telecollaborative language learning: A guidebook to moderating intercultural collaboration online.* Peter Lang.

Eneau, J., & Develotte, C. (2012). Working online together to enhance learning autonomy. *ReCALL 24*(1), 3–19. https://doi.org/10.1017/S0958344011000267

Flaherty, C. (2020). The power of peer interaction. Inside Higher Ed blog. November 4.

Furstenberg, G., Levet, S., English, K., & Maillet, K. (2001). Giving a virtual voice to the silent language of culture: The CULTURA project. *Language Learning & Technology, 5*(1), 55–102. https://doi.org/10125/25113

Gehlback, H. (2017). Learning to walk in another's shoes. *Phi Delta Kappan International*, *98*(6), 8–12.

Godwin-Jones, R. (2013). Integrating intercultural competence into language learning through technology. *Language Learning and Technology*, *17*(2), 1–11. https://doi.org/10125/44318

Hedge, T. (2000). *Teaching and learning in the language classroom.* Oxford University Press.

Ingram, M. (2005). Recasting the foreign language requirement through study abroad: A cultural immersion program in Avignon. *Foreign Language Annals*, *38* (2), 211–222.

Kern, R. (1997). Technology, social interaction, and FL literacy. The American Association of University Supervisors, Coordinators and Directors of Foreign Languages Programs (AAUSC), 66–101. http://hdl.handle.net/102015/69530

Kinginger, C. (2013). Introduction: Social and cultural aspects of language learning in study abroad. In C. Kinginger (Ed.), *Social and cultural aspects of language learning in study abroad* (pp. 3–15). John Benjamins.

Levet, S., & Tschudi, S. L. (2021). Open by design: The Cultura project. In C. S. Blyth and J. J. Thoms (Eds.), *Open education and second language learning and teaching* (pp. 47–68). Multilingual Matters. https://doi.org/10.21832/9781800411005-004

Li, P., & Jeong, H. (2020). The social brain of language: Grounding second language learning in social interaction. *NPJ Science of Learning*, *5*, 8. https://doi.org/10.1038/s41539-020-0068-7

Liu, X., & Zhang, J. (2012). Foreign language learning through virtual communities. *Energy Procedia*, *17*, 737–740. https://doi.org/10.1016/j.egypro.2012.02.165

Lomicka, L. (2020). Creating and sustaining virtual language communities. *Foreign Language Annals*, *53*(2), 306–313.

Maiorana, V. P. (1992). *Critical thinking across the curriculum: Building the analytical classroom.* (ERIC Document Reproduction Service No. ED 347511).

McMurtrie, B. (2021). Teaching: Before rolling out post-pandemic plans, let people grieve. *The Chronicle of Higher Education*, March 4. www.chronicle.com/newsletter/teaching/2021-03-04

Métral, C., Benenson, J., & Skorupa, C. (2009). Échanges synchrones transatlantiques le project "Cross-Cultural Connections." *Distances et Savoirs*, *2*(7), 253–272.

Mishan, F. (2005). *Designing authenticity into language learning material.* Intellect.

Nunan, D. (1988). *The learner-centred curriculum.* Cambridge University Press. https://doi.org/10.1017/CBO9781139524506

O'Dowd, R. (2003). Understanding the "other side": Intercultural learning in a Spanish–English e-mail exchange. *Language Learning & Technology*, *7*(2), 118–144. http://llt.msu.edu/vol7num2/odowd/default.html

O'Dowd, R. (Ed.). (2007). *Online intercultural exchange: An introduction for foreign language teachers.* Multilingual Matters.

O'Dowd, R., & Ware, P. (2009). Critical issues in telecollaborative task design. *Computer Assisted Language Learning*, *22*(2), 173–188. https://doi.org/10.1080/09588220902778369

O'Dowd, R., & O'Rourke, B. (2019). New developments in virtual exchange for foreign language education. *Language Learning & Technology*, *23*(3), 1–7. http://hdl.handle.net/10125/44690

Pasfield-Neofitou, S. (2011). Online domains of language use: Second language learners' experiences of virtual community and foreignness. *Language Learning & Technology*, *15*(2), 92–108. https://doi.org/10125/44253

Rudd L. C., & Lambert, M. C. (2011). Interaction theory of language development. In S. Goldstein, & J. A. Naglieri (Eds.), *Encyclopedia of child behavior and development*. Springer. https://doi.org/10.1007/978-0-387-79061-9_1522

Schreiber, L. M., & Valle, B. E. (2013). Social constructivist teaching strategies in the small group classroom. *Small Group Research*, *44*(4), 395–411. https://doi.org/10.1177/1046496413488422

Shirkhani, S., & Fahim, M. (2011). Enhancing critical thinking in foreign language learners. *Procedia – Social and Behavioral Sciences*, *29*, 111–115.

Shih, Y.-C. (2015). A virtual walk through London: Culture learning through a cultural immersion experience, *Computer Assisted Language Learning*, *28*(5), 407–428. https://doi.org/10.1080/09588221.2013.851703

Sokol, A., Oget, D., Sonntag, M., & Khomenko N. (2008). The development of inventive thinking skills in the upper secondary language classroom. *Thinking Skills and Creativity*, *3*, 34–46. https://doi.org/10.1016/j.tsc.2008.03.001

Stansberry, S. L. (2006). Effective assessment of online discourse in LIS courses. *Journal of Education for Library and Information Science*, *47*(1), 27–37.

Sulam, K., Syakur, A., & Musyarofah, L. (2019). The implementation of 21st century skills as the new learning paradigm to the result of student's career and life skills. *Magister Scientiae*, *2*(46), 228–237.

Tarvin, W., & Al-Arishi, A. (1991). Rethinking communicative language teaching: Reflection and the EFL classroom. *TESOL Quarterly*, *25*(1), 9–27. https://doi.org/10.2307/3587026

Thorne, S. L. (2016). Forward: The virtual internationalization turn in language study. In R. O'Dowd & T. Lewis (Eds.), *Online intercultural exchange: Policy, pedagogy, practice* (pp. ix–xi). Routledge.

Verga, L., & Kotz, S. A. (2013). How relevant is social interaction in second language learning? *Frontiers in Human Neuroscience*, *7*(550). https://doi.org/10.3389/fnhum.2013.00550

Vygotsky, L. S. (1978). *Mind in society: The development of higher psychological processes*. Harvard University Press.

Further Reading

Chun, D., Kern, R., & Smith, B. (2016). Technology in language use, language teaching, and language learning. *The Modern Language Journal*, *100*(1), 64–80. This foundational article sets the groundwork for how technology affects language use and shapes the way we use language. It highlights the connections between forms and media and the importance of awareness, reflection, and communication for today's learners and educators.

Cunningham, D. J. (2019). Telecollaboration for content and language learning: A genre-based approach. *Language Learning & Technology*, *23*(3), 161–177. http://hdl.handle.net/10125/44701

This article looks at telecollaboration from a gender-based approach. Specifically, it examines how this approach can foster learning in SCMC-based telecollaboration primarily by dyads and triads who performed an oral interview. Results point to the promise of linking existing knowledge to new knowledge, creating meaningful connections between topics and demonstrated attention by learners.

Guerrero-Rodríguez, P., Lomicka Anderson, L., & Lord, G. (2022). SIFTR-ing through the development of cultural awareness at home and abroad. *Foreign Language Annals*, *55*(2), 435–454.

This article uses geolocation technologies (Siftr) to explore the development of community and cultural understanding in classes both in the United States and abroad. Results suggest that tasks help learners intentionally notice their own culture and that of others.

Levet, S., & Tschudi, S. L. (2021). Open by Design: The Cultura Project. In C. S. Blyth and J. J. Thoms (Eds.), *Open Education and Second Language Learning and Teaching* (pp. 47–68). Multilingual Matters. https://doi.org/10.21832/9781800411005-004

This chapter looks at the Cultura Project through an open design lens. Through its innovative design, the project offers affordances in pedagogy, material, and professional development and technology.

15

Virtual Exchange and Telecollaborative Learning

Begoña F. Gutiérrez and Robert O'Dowd

Introduction

Virtual exchange (VE) is a pedagogical approach which is widely used in foreign language (FL) education to develop students' linguistic, intercultural, and soft skills. It can be defined as the engagement of groups of learners in online intercultural interaction and collaboration with partners from other cultural contexts or geographical locations as an integrated part of coursework and under the guidance of educators and/or expert facilitators (Jager et al., 2019; O'Dowd, 2018; O'Dowd & Lewis, 2016).

Over the past two decades, VE has been employed in the field of FL education in many different ways and has been referred to as telecollaboration (Belz, 2003; Warschauer, 1995) or e-tandem learning (O'Rourke, 2007). For this reason, there can sometimes be some confusion over the terminology used around this activity. Anyone reading the CALL literature may come across articles referring to terms such as "e-pals" or "key-pals" or e-tandem, online intercultural exchange (O'Dowd & Lewis, 2016), internet-mediated intercultural foreign language education (Belz & Thorne, 2005) or COIL (collaborative online international learning). In order to move the field forward, many practitioners and researchers now propose "virtual exchange" be used as an umbrella term that covers the different ways in which students are brought into collaborative learning projects with international partners in a structured way. One of the main academic organizations in this area, UNICollaboration, describes itself as the cross-disciplinary professional organization for telecollaboration and virtual exchange in Higher Education (www.unicollaboration.org/), while the main international conference in this area is IVEC: The International Virtual Exchange Conference (https://iveconference.org/).

However, we should be careful not to confuse "virtual exchange" (VE) with "virtual mobility" (VM). This second term refers to students using online tools and platforms to follow courses at another institution without physically leaving their homes. Whereas VE is based on students engaging in structured online intercultural dialogue with other learners, virtual mobility may simply involve students using the internet to follow lectures and accessing course materials at a university in another geographical location.

While there has always been a good deal of attention paid to telecollaborative learning in the field of CALL, interest has increased dramatically in recent years. In Europe, the European Commission launched "Erasmus+ Virtual Exchange" in 2018, a flagship program which aimed to expand the reach and scope of the Erasmus+ program via VE. Other large-scale projects such as Evaluating and Upscaling Telecollaborative Teacher Education (EVALUATE) and Evidence-Validated Online Learning through Virtual Exchange (EVOLVE) have also done much to promote and investigate the impact of VE in European higher education. In the United States, organizations and networks such as the SUNY Center for Collaborative Online International Learning (COIL) and the Stevens Initiative provide training and support for educators and institutions who are interested in integrating VE in their curricula. The recent COVID-19 pandemic has also led many more educators and institutions to explore VE as a complement or alternative to physical mobility programs (O'Dowd, 2021).

Background/ Historical Perspectives

The beginnings of what is now referred to as VE date back to the early days of the internet in the 1990s, when this practice was referred to as telecollaboration (Belz, 2003; Warschauer, 1995). Like many themes related to technology, both the terminology used to refer to it and the practice itself have evolved and transformed rapidly. Proof of this is the number of different models of VE with their particular characteristics that have come into existence in the relatively short history of this pedagogical approach. The most common models of VE in FL education have been based on bicultural exchange between two sets of learners who are studying each other's language and culture. For example, Spanish students of English may collaborate online with Irish students of Spanish and use both languages as they work together. However, in recent years, many FL educators have also explored engaging their students in lingua franca exchanges (Kohn & Hoffstaedter, 2017), which give learners the opportunity to engage in online collaboration with partner classes who are not necessarily native speakers of the target language. This may involve, for example, students from Spain, Sweden, and Israel collaborating together in English as a lingua franca (ELF) (O'Dowd, Sauro, & Spector-Cohen, 2020) or students from France, Germany, the Netherlands, and Spain using German as a lingua franca to carry out tasks together online (Kohn & Hoffstaedter, 2017). While this categorization of VE according to models is useful in allowing an overview of trends within the practice over the years, these categories should not be considered as rigid. As the literature demonstrates (Lindner, 2016; Porto, 2014), it is possible to combine aspects of different models in one particular telecollaborative partnership.

Bilingual–Bicultural VE

In the literature of FL education, bilingual–bicultural VEs consisting of two groups of learners studying each other's "languaculture" (Agar, 1994) are the most commonly reported (O'Dowd & Lewis, 2016). Under this category we can identify two different models of VE: e-tandem and telecollaborative exchanges.

E-tandem

Telecollaboration appeared in a moment in which the communicative approach was on the rise in the field of FL education. This approach (Canale and Swain, 1980; Hymes, 1971) prioritizes language-in-use or language in action, that is, the engagement of learners in authentic communication to promote learning. Thus, the main attraction of telecollaboration for FL teachers at the time was the possibility for their students to engage in authentic interactions with native speakers of the target language. Consequently, e-tandem appeared as the first well-known model of VE, consisting in the "reciprocal support and instruction between two learners, each of whom is a native speaker of the other's target language" (O'Rourke, 2007, p. 43). In other words, in this model students communicate and interact using both languages and provide each other with informal or peer linguistic feedback.

The focus of e-tandems was initially on the development of language skills, while cultural learning was considered secondary (Brammerts, 2006; Lindner, 2016) and the interaction mainly consisted of written asynchronous discussions. It usually required participants to autonomously engage in a discussion of a certain topic outside the classroom as an extra or independent activity and not as an institutionalized or curricular activity (O'Dowd, 2011).

This e-tandem model remains a common practice today, after more than twenty years in use, as evidenced by many reports and the large body of research emerging from the teletandem networks (Leone & Telles, 2016).

Telecollaborative VE and Intercultural Learning

The different models of VE have developed hand in hand with trends in FL teaching theory. In 1997, Byram published the model of Intercultural Communicative Competence which built upon Hymes' (1971) communicative competence and added an intercultural dimension. This publication triggered an increased interest in the development of both linguistic and intercultural competences in FL education. Thus, in the late 1990s and early 2000s, the telecollaborative model of VE started to offer FL teachers interested in training their students to become successful intercultural speakers the opportunity to do so by engaging them in online intercultural interaction and collaboration. This meant developing their intercultural values, attitudes, knowledge, and skills in addition to their linguistic communicative competence. A relevant notion that this approach introduces and this model puts into practice is the distancing from the unrealistic idea of the native speaker as a model (Byram, 1997; O'Dowd, 2011).

Against this background, telecollaboration moved from an extracurricular activity that took place as autonomous work outside the classroom and started to occupy a place as part of classwork. This was the start of international telecollaborative projects organized by teachers in which classes of students interacted and collaborated as part of their FL curriculum. These involved the collaboration and coordination of teachers for the development of activities on culture-related topics of shared interest for the international participants who carry them out in pairs or small groups to develop their intercultural communicative competence (Belz, 2001).

The Cultura project (Furstenberg et al., 2001) was one of the first examples of the telecollaborative model of VE. It adopts a comparative cultural approach and asks participants to compare and analyze parallel materials from their respective cultures, based on the contention that this will enable them to notice differences and similarities that would otherwise be difficult to observe due to their deep cultural embeddedness. Participants' observations serve as a starting point for them to engage in discussions and work together on the progressive co-construction (constructive approach) of the meanings and underlying reasons behind different cultural aspects, thus reaching a deeper understanding of each other and each other's culture (Furstenberg et al., 2001, pp. 58–59). Chun (2015) published a review in which she identified numerous examples of VEs that followed the Cultura model in the literature.

Other early examples reporting on telecollaborative VEs in the literature are Belz's publications from the early 2000s in which the interactions and learning outcomes of this model embedded in the classroom began to be researched. The main goal of this telecollaborative model, as defined by Belz (2005, p. 23), is "to foster dialogue between members of diverse cultures (who otherwise might not have the opportunity to come into contact) in an effort to increase intercultural awareness as well as linguistic proficiency."

Nowadays, this model of teacher-mentored class-to-class telecollaboration in which students communicate and collaborate addressing a cultural topic in a foreign language using (a)synchronous communication tools is widely implemented. Numerous case studies have looked at its learning outcomes (i.e. linguistic, intercultural, digital, and soft skills) in recent years (Mullen & Bortuluzzi, 2019; Ryshina-Pankova, 2018).

Lingua Franca VEs

The bilingual–bicultural models of VE presented above have been and continue to be common in FL education. However, the rapid socioeconomic changes of the last decades have resulted in a much more diverse and interconnected world in which learners are more likely to use a language with other nonnative speakers like themselves rather (or more often) than with native speakers, especially in the workplace context (Graddol, 2006). Consequently, in FL education there is a growing interest in the implementation of lingua franca VEs (i.e. used for communication among nonnative speakers) (Kohn & Hoffstaedter, 2017), a category under which there can be identified two different models: transnational VEs and critical approaches to telecollaboration (Helm, 2017).

Transnational VEs

Over the last ten years, class-to-class transnational VEs in which participants communicate and collaborate addressing issues of global relevance using a lingua franca have been increasingly implemented in higher education. Even if these may include cultural comparisons, they usually also involve tasks which require collaboration on themes beyond explicit bicultural comparison since their aim is to move "towards a global notion of the intercultural" (O'Dowd, 2019, p. 4). This learning experience offers students the opportunity to develop relevant linguistic and intercultural skills for the present global context in which the majority of them will most likely need to be able to successfully engage in online intercultural interaction and collaboration using a lingua franca (O'Dowd, 2019).

An early example of transnational VE is described by Guth and Helm (2012) in which German and Italian students communicated using English as a lingua franca (EFL). Despite the doubts some may have regarding the efficacy of engaging nonnative speakers in nonmonitored communication using the target language for the development of their language skills, this study reported that both parties ended the experience with positive feelings toward their development of both linguistic and intercultural skills (p. 49). Lindner (2011) also reported on an EFL telecollaboration in which the use of a lingua franca for communication and collaboration helped reduce students' perception of difference in linguistic and cultural terms and instead contributed to a more rooted sense of team and bonding in the intercultural group.

O'Dowd (2021) compared the learning outcomes of the telecollaborative and transnational models of VE by analyzing 345 learner portfolios from students engaged in 13 different university class-to-class VEs. Half of these were bilingual–bicultural telecollaborative VEs in which students communicated using Spanish and English and the other half ELF transnational VEs. His findings showed that the telecollaborative model led students to "plac[e] more emphasis on acquiring 'cultural knowledge'" (p. 9) and also "produced much less evidence of students taking a more critical view of their own culture" (p. 10). That is, students participating in telecollaborative VEs seem to be more likely to remain in the dichotomy of "my 'languaculture' which I represent and the other's languaculture from which I learn certain facts," which implies a greater risk of developing negative feelings toward the other's languaculture if the VE experience turns out not to be as expected. Those who engage in transnational VEs where the focus tends to be on "achieving successful collaborative goals in multicultural groups," on the other hand, tend to report on "a much higher frequency of learning outcomes related to collaboration skills, digital skills and the importance of cultural differences in communication styles" (p. 10).

There are varied reasons for the current popularity of this VE model. One of them is that it eases access to this type of experience for students from countries where teachers may find it difficult to find partner classes studying their languaculture. In addition, this type of transnational VE also makes it easier for several classes from different countries to collaborate together, creating a more diverse context for intercultural learning. An example of this can be found in the report of a recent lingua franca VE (O'Dowd et al., 2020) in which students from Spain, Sweden, and Israel collaborated using ELF. Finally, another reason for the popularity of this type of VE is that the native speaker as a model to aspire to has lost popularity in recent years (Godwin-Jones, 2019).

Critical Telecollaboration

Another popular model of VE that can be found within the lingua franca approach is critical telecollaboration. This recent model (Helm, 2017) challenges traditional assumptions of telecollaboration, such as that of the native speaker being the ideal interlocutor, technology being a neutral medium, online intercultural interaction naturally leading to deeper understanding and fostering equality, and the primary goal of telecollaboration being simply to foster communicative and sociocultural competences.

What Helm (2017) proposes, instead, are interactions aimed at fostering open dialogue as a response to the current increasingly polarized global context in which addressing social and political issues with learners becomes necessary to foster understanding of diverse worldviews and thereby promote a more tolerant, just, and peaceful world. These interactions are usually facilitator-led, such as the Soliya exchanges (https://soliya.net/), which bring together students from the United States and Arab/Muslim countries to discuss their countries' relations by addressing cultural and political issues together.

Externalizing Language Practice

One of the biggest challenges encountered in the practice of VE on its way to mainstreaming in educational institutions is the amount of work and effort required on the part of teachers. They need to dedicate time in their busy schedules to tasks such as finding a partner, designing and agreeing mutually convenient activities and dates, and providing guidance to students. This is a possible reason why in many cases the teachers who end up implementing these projects are those who are also engaged in their research.

Recently, companies have emerged that offer platforms dedicated to providing "ready-made" VEs in which FL teachers can engage their students for a fee without the need to devote their time to all of the above tasks. One example of this is Coversifi, a platform that "connects foreign language learners with native speakers for on-demand language practice and cross-cultural exchange over video chat" (www.conversifi.com). The recordings of these interactions can then be revised and assessed by the teachers. However, this option is very recent and research is still needed to report on the development of competences through it. In addition, "they may not be in a position to provide the pedagogical mentoring which students need to interpret and learn from their experiences" (O'Dowd, 2021, p. 10).

Primary Themes

The first academic studies about VE in FL contexts were Warschauer (1995) and Brammerts (1996) and there are certain key themes and issues from that time that continue to occupy both practitioners and researchers. These are related to task design, the role of the teacher, and the effectiveness of VE in developing students' intercultural communicative competence.

It is widely accepted that the type of tasks teachers use in their VEs will have a large impact on the outcome of their students' online interactions. O'Dowd and Waire (2009) categorized twelve telecollaborative task types that they had identified in the literature into three main categories: information exchange, comparison, and collaboration. The first category, information exchange tasks, involved learners providing their telecollaborative partners with information about their personal biographies, local schools or towns, or aspects of their home cultures. The second task type, comparison and analysis tasks, required learners not only to exchange information, but also to go a step further and carry out comparisons or critical analyses of cultural products from both cultures (e.g. books, surveys, films, newspaper articles). These analyses or comparisons could have a cultural focus and/or a linguistic focus. The final task type, collaborative tasks, required learners not only to exchange and compare information, but also to work together to produce a joint product or conclusion. This could involve the co-authoring of an essay or presentation or the co-production of a linguistic translation or cultural adaptation of a text from the first language/first culture (L1/C1) to the second language/second culture (L2/C2). These types of activity require a great deal of coordination and planning, but they also bring about substantial amounts of negotiation of meaning at both linguistic and cultural levels as learners attempt to reach agreement on their final products.

However, various reviews of current practice conclude that collaborative tasks are much less common in the literature (Helm, 2017). Godwin-Jones (2019) suggests that such tasks require more effort for the student and logistical support from teachers and that time and schedule constraints sometimes make it difficult to integrate such projects into semester timetables.

A second theme which receives a lot of attention in the literature is the role of the teacher in VE. While telecollaboration is undoubtedly a student-centered approach to FL learning, the role of the teacher is considered key in designing the VE and in supporting students as they engage in and reflect on their intercultural interactions. Chun (2015), for example, observes that "it is essential for teachers to help students to go beyond comprehending the surface meaning of words and sentences in order to understand what their intercultural partners are writing" (p. 13).

Although young FL learners today may belong to a generation referred to as "digital natives" (Prensky, 2006), research has called into question the belief that they are somehow intuitively capable of using digital technologies in collaborative ways in their learning and teaching practices. Valtonen et al. (2011), for example, looked at the academic practices of young student teachers in Finland and found that "the technological knowledge of student teachers is not what would be expected for representatives of the Net Generation" (p. 13). Research such as this would seem to suggest that young people may be good at consuming information from the internet, but are not necessarily good at communicating and collaborating effectively in online environments (Kirschner & De Bruyckere, 2017). With this in mind, O'Dowd et al. (2020) proposed different ways in which teachers can support their students in VE through different forms of pedagogical mentoring. These included introducing students to linguistic and interactional features and strategies before the exchange begins; providing tutorials on the effective use of different digital tools and their features; looking at online interactions as much as possible during class time and discussing moments of intercultural communication breakdown or misunderstandings; and, finally, maintaining regular contact with the partner teacher and exchanging insights about how the different classes are experiencing their online collaborations.

A final theme that has led to much discussion is related to the effectiveness of VE for intercultural learning and whether online interaction over a six to eight week period can actually lead to intercultural awareness and improved collaboration skills. Richardson (2015) warns that research on VE has repeated the commonly held assumption in physical mobility that learning will somehow emerge automatically from contact. Other authors have also suggested that VE often fails to achieve its intended learning outcomes because of the inherent nature of online interaction. Kramsch (2014) suggests that much of the intercultural communication that takes place in telecollaborative exchange is artificial and based on phatic interaction between students who are "staying in touch by surfing diversity not engaging with difference" (p. 302).

However, many large-scale studies that have looked at the impact of VE on large cohorts of students would suggest that telecollaborative learning can have a very positive impact on intercultural learning. These studies found that their informants felt that taking part in a VE had better prepared them to communicate and collaborate with people from different cultures. However, the key to this was ensuring that the students had been engaged in interculturally challenging tasks that required high levels of negotiation and collaboration (Helm & Van der Velden, 2019; The EVALUATE Group, 2019). The reports suggest that VE can best enhance students' collaborative and intercultural skills when they are confronted with a range of collaborative hurdles and challenges which require them to find creative ways to collaborate and communicate successfully with their international partners. With this in mind, teachers have to remember that tasks should push students out of their comfort zones so that skills and attitude development are most likely to take place.

Current Research and Practice

Today, there are numerous examples of studies reporting on all the different models of VE presented here: e-tandem, telecollaborative, critical and transnational VEs. Recent examples of each model are presented below.

For example, Aranha and Wigham (2020) report on an English–Portuguese e-tandem project, the Multimodal Teletandem Corpus project, in which they collected information through various data sources such as video recordings from Portuguese–English teletandem sessions, chat logs, written productions exchanged between partners, initial and final questionnaires, and learning diaries. This shows how the e-tandem model has been able to evolve from its earliest written versions more than twenty years ago and adapt to the present context, combining synchronous and asynchronous modes of communication.

Luo and Gui (2019) report on a telecollaborative VE involving Chinese as a FL students from a university in the United States and Chinese-speaking English FL students from a university in China. While this study can be interpreted as an example of how in recent years the pedagogical approach of VEs has been expanding and implemented in various contexts for the development of diverse languages, telecollaborative VEs in which Chinese is the target language (and this is also the case for languages other than English, such as Spanish, French, or German) have not received sufficient attention so far.

An example of critical VE can be found in Chanethom's study (2020) in which French students living in the United States and native speakers of French in France collaborated in a university French course at a US university. The project involved students engaging in discussion via videoconference and employed critical approaches to task design including potentially sensitive topics such as freedom (e.g. freedom of speech, religious freedom), globalization (e.g. child labor), and immigration (e.g. racism, xenophobia). Students' reports on the experience showed that this critical approach was generally well received, despite the inclusion of sensitive topics.

Transnational VEs for global citizenship education (O'Dowd, 2019), in which VEs are specifically designed for students to become competent global citizens in addition to improving their overall FL skills, have recently gained momentum. These VEs are characterized by tasks in which students are required not only to communicate but to actually collaborate with each other (i.e. creating a joint product, solving a problem, completing a task, taking active action) while dealing with globally relevant themes (i.e. social, environmental). An example of a VE with these characteristics can be found in Gutiérrez, Fortes, and Giralt (2021), who reported on a collaboration among Spanish and Irish Universities in which students collaborated in activities focused on ecology and sustainability in the subjects of English and Spanish as FLs. The aim of these tasks was to develop students' global and ecological awareness. Students started sharing their views on sustainability in everyday life; later they compared environmental problems affecting their communities and the actions taken to address them and proposed together actions that people like them could take in their daily lives to mitigate the situation. This helped them realize the connection between the local and the global and enabled them to collaborate to take active action and create together videos to raise ecological awareness in their communities by presenting the common problems they had identified and proposing sustainable practices to help mitigate them.

Recommendations for Research and Practice

Recent large-scale studies on VE (Stevens Initiative, 2019, 2020; The EVALUATE Group, 2019) provide some clear recommendations for good practice, which teachers can keep in mind when preparing to engage in this activity. These will be briefly reviewed here.

A key aspect of any VE model being implemented is that there is a balanced participation on the part of students. For example, if in a VE there are students in a group for whom their participation carries weight in their subject grade while for others it is voluntary and does not carry any kind of recognition, it is possible that the involvement of the different groups may be unequal. In this regard, a common recommendation in the reports is to integrate VEs into curricula so that students' participation in the project receives academic recognition (Nissen & Kurek, 2020; Stevens Initiative, 2020; the EVALUATE Group, 2019). While there are various ways to recognize students' participation and competence acquisition through their involvement in VE, perhaps the most common in class-to-class VEs is to allocate points or credit to their final course mark. In addition, there are other types of recognition such as Open Badges, which are "a 21st-century solution to the shortcomings of paper certificates in the age of digital, online identity management" (MacKinnon, 2021), or recognition in the European Diploma Supplement of the international virtual learning experience. Another possibility, although definitely less accessible and common, is the opportunity for the students to participate in short study visits to a partner university, which is a motivating outcome for students.

Another recommendation commonly featured in reports since around 2018 is to try to balance synchronous (i.e. real-time) videoconferencing interaction with asynchronous (i.e. deferred in time) written interaction. In 2019, the EVALUATE group reported that in their large-scale study, participants in the VEs noted that textual communication (e.g. discussion forums) made them feel that their collaborations were depersonalized and that they lacked the feeling of interacting with "real people." In this regard, the relevance of having videoconferencing periods between international students during VEs has recently been particularly emphasized as, according to the participants in this study, they contribute greatly to the creation and development of bonds between participants while helping to reduce depersonalization. It is also important to note that this same study identified that instant messaging tools used by students in their daily lives, such as WhatsApp, were a key ally in the personal correspondence of international students and also contributed to a large extent to the development of informal conversations and group bonding. In 2020 the EVOLVE group in another large-scale study on VEs confirmed these findings. In this regard, another common recommendation from many of the reports is the importance of finding a balance between the formal tasks of the VE and the more informal aspects such as personal communication and relationship building. Learners need time to get to know each other and build interpersonal relationships before engaging in the intense periods of inter-action and collaboration that this kind of experience often requires. Practitioners should take this into account when developing the task sequences they will use during online collaboration.

It is important to consider that asynchronous communication stages can also bring benefits of their own. The Stevens Initiative 2020 report observed that VE practitioners had found it beneficial to incorporate activities through asynchron-ous communication, as they were less demanding for the learners. This is important as VEs often involve a period of intense communication and collabor-ation over relatively short periods of time (i.e. six to eight weeks) so not finding a balance between the two communicative modalities can result in overload for learners, who can feel overwhelmed. Hence, the most recent reports stress the need to combine videoconferencing with asynchronous communication stages so that the successful combination of both communication modalities can have a positive impact on the overall experience and on learning outcomes.

In addition to taking into consideration the balance between the two communicative modalities, it is also advisable for teachers to provide students with mentoring on good practices associated with each of them so that they can get the most out of each. Participants may also benefit from training in how to interact successfully online with members of other cultures.

Finally, a significant number of reports point to task design as a key factor in the success of a VE project, since the choice of topic and types of task play a decisive role in the subsequent learning outcomes of the project. An example of this is encountered in the findings of the large-scale study EVOLVE (2020), which identified that engaging students in discussions about everyday life issues led to more shallow conversations focused primarily on finding common ground, while dealing with controversial issues (if approached in the right way) led to a deeper understanding of the perspectives of their partners and thus had a greater impact on their learning. However, this study also identified that when confronted with controversial issues that could potentially generate conflict, most students resorted to strategies of conflict avoidance.

Future Directions

This chapter has looked at how VE has grown in popularity in recent years and what we have learned about its potential for foreign language learning and also how it should be integrated into educational programs. Interest in VE has grown into other fields such as secondary education and teacher training. Proof of this are initiatives such as the European Commission's Etwinning platform (www.etwinning.net), which connects secondary schools from all over Europe to collaborate in VE, or the European project VALIANT (https://valiantproject.eu/) which offers VE programs that bring together teachers, student teachers, and experts in facilitated online collaboration around real-world educational issues.

It is hard to make predictions about how VE will develop in the future but it is clear that the COVID-19 pandemic has moved telecollaborative learning from a peripheral activity to one that is an integral part of FL programs and universities' internationalization policies. In any case, we should strive to ensure that all applications and models of VE are rigorously evaluated as they are introduced into educational programs.

References

Agar, M. (1994). The intercultural frame. *International Journal of Intercultural Relations, 18*(2), 221–237.

Aranha, S., & Wigham, C. R. (2020). Virtual exchanges as complex research environments: Facing the data management challenge. A case study of Teletandem Brasil. *Journal of Virtual Exchange, 3*, 13–38. https://doi.org/10.21827/jve.3.35748

Belz, J. A. (2001). Institutional and individual dimensions of transatlantic group work in network-based language teaching. *ReCALL, 13*(2), 213–231. https://doi.org/10.1017/S0958344001000726a

Belz, J. A. (2003). Linguistic perspectives on the development of intercultural competence in telecollaboration. *Language Learning & Technology, 7*(2), 68–99. http://llt.msu.edu/vol7num3/belz

Belz, J. A. (2005). Intercultural questioning, discovery and tension in internet-mediated language learning partnerships. *Language and Intercultural Communication, 5*(1), 3–39. https://doi.org/10.1080/14708470508668881

Belz, J. A., & Thorne, S. L. (2005). *Internet-mediated intercultural foreign language education and the intercultural speaker.* Thomson Heinle.

Brammerts, H. (1996). Language learning in tandem using the internet. In M. Warschauer (Ed.), *Telecollaboration in foreign language learning* (pp. 121–130). University of Hawai'i Press.

Brammerts, H. (2006). Tandemberatung. *Zeitschrift für interkulturellen Fremdsprachenunterricht, 11*(2).

Byram, M. (1997). *Teaching and assessing intercultural communicative competence.* Multilingual Matters.

Canale, M., & Swain, M. (1980). Theoretical bases of communicative approaches to second language teaching and testing. *Applied Linguistics, 1*(1), 1–47.

Chanethom, V. (2020). Students' attitudes toward critical telecollaboration: A case study in an L2/L3 French classroom. In P.-A. Mather (Ed.), *Technology-enhanced learning and linguistic diversity: Strategies and approaches to teaching students in a 2nd or 3rd language* (pp. 105–128). Emerald Publishing Limited. https://doi.org/10.1108/978-1-83982-128-820201008

Chun, D. M. (2015). Language and culture learning in higher education via telecollaboration. *Pedagogies: An International Journal, 10*(1), 5–21. https://doi.org/10.1080/1554480X.2014.999775

EVOLVE Project Team. (2020). The impact of virtual exchange on student learning in higher education: EVOLVE project report. Retrieved from http://hdl.handle.net/11370/d69d9923–8a9c-4b37–91c6–326ebbd14f17

Furstenberg, G., Levet, S., English, K., & Maillet, K. (2001). Giving a virtual voice to the silent language of culture: The Cultura project. *Language learning & technology, 5*(1), 55–102.

Godwin-Jones, R. (2019). Telecollaboration as an approach to developing inter-cultural competence. *Language Learning & Technology, 23*(3), 8–28, http://hdl.handle.net/10125/44691.

Graddol, D. (2006). *English next* (Vol. 62). British Council.

Guth, S., & Helm, F. (2012). Developing multiliteracies in ELT through telecolla-boration. *ELT Journal, 66*(1), 42–51. https://doi.org/10.1093/elt/ccr027

Gutiérrez, B. F., Fortes, M., & Giralt, M. (2021). A virtual exchange between univer-sity students of tourism and business: Connecting languages and cultures through a sustainable tourism project. In E. Arnó, M. Aguilar, J. Borràs, G. Mancho, B. Moncada, & D. Tatzl (Eds.), *Proceedings of AELFE-TAPP 2021 (19th AELFE Conference, 2nd TAPP Conference.* Universitat Politècnica de Catalunya.

Helm, F. (2017). Critical approaches to online intercultural language education. In S. L. Thorne & S. May (Eds.), *Language, education and technology* (pp. 219–231). Springer International Publishing. https://doi.org/10.1007/978-3-319-02237-6_18

Helm, F., & van der Velden, B. (2020). *Erasmus+ virtual exchange impact report 2019.* https://europa.eu/youth/erasmusvirtual/impact-erasmus-virtual-exchange_en

Hymes, D. H. (1971). *On communicative competence.* University of Pennsylvania Press.

Jager, S., Nissen, E., Helm, F., Baroni, A., & Rousset, I. (2019). Virtual exchange as innovative practice across Europe awareness and use in higher education. *EVOLVE Project Baseline Study.* Research Report. Evolve Project. https://hal.archives-ouvertes.fr/hal-02495403/document

Kirschner, P. A., & De Bruyckere, P. (2017). The myths of the digital native and the multitasker.*Teaching and Teacher Education, 67,* 135–142. https://doi.org/10.1016/j.tate.2017.06.001

Kohn, K., & Hoffstaedter, P. (2017). Learner agency and non-native speaker identity in pedagogical lingua franca conversations: Insights from intercultural telecollaboration in foreign language education. *Computer Assisted Language Learning, 30*(5), 351–367. https://doi.org/10.1080/09588221.2017.1304966

Kramsch, C. (2014). Teaching foreign languages in an era of globalization: Introduction. *The Modern Language Journal, 98*(1), 296–311. https://doi.org/10.1111/j.1540-4781.2014.12057.x

Leone, P., & Telles, J. (2016). The Teletandem Network. In R. O'Dowd & T. Lewis (Eds.), *Online intercultural exchange: Policy, pedagogy, practice* (pp. 241–247). Routledge.

Lindner, R. (2011). ESAP students' perceptions of skills learning in computer-mediated intercultural collaboration. *International Journal of Computer-Assisted Language Learning and Teaching*, *1*(2), 25–42. https://doi.org/10.4018/ijcallt.2011040103

Lindner, R. (2016). Developing communicative competence in global virtual teams: A multiliteracies approach to telecollaboration for students of business and economics. *CASALC Review*, *1*(1), 144–156.

Luo, H., & Gui, M. (2019). Developing an effective Chinese–American telecollaborative learning program: An action research study. *Computer Assisted Language Learning*, *34*(5–6), 609–636. https://doi.org/10.1080/09588221.2019.1633355

MacKinnon, T. (2021). Open Badges: Recognising learning through digital microcredentials. In T. Beaven & F. Rosell-Aguilar (Eds.), *Innovative language pedagogy report* (pp. 57–61). Research-publishing.net.

Mullen, A., & Bortoluzzi, M. (2019). Assessing intercultural awareness: Reflection vs. interaction in telecollaboration. *Lingue Linguaggi*, *33*, 211–225.

Nissen, E., & Kurek, M. (2020). *The impact of virtual exchange on teachers' pedagogical competences and pedagogical approach in higher education.* University of Groningen.

O'Dowd, R. (2011). Online foreign language interaction: Moving from the periphery to the core of foreign language education? *Language Teaching*, *44*(3), 368–380. https://doi.org/10.1017/S0261444810000194

O'Dowd, R. (2018). From telecollaboration to virtual exchange: State-of-the-art and the role of UNICollaboration in moving forward. *Journal of Virtual Exchange*, *1*, 1–23. https://doi.org/10.14705/rpnet.2018.jve.1

O'Dowd, R. (2019). A transnational model of virtual exchange for global citizenship education. *Language Teaching*, *53*(4), 477–490. https://doi.org/10.1017/S0261444819000077

O'Dowd, R. (2021). What do students learn in virtual exchange? A qualitative content analysis of learning outcomes across multiple exchanges. *International Journal of Educational Research*, *109*, 101804. https://doi.org/10.1016/j.ijer.2021.101804

O'Dowd, R., & Lewis, T. (Eds.). (2016). *Online intercultural exchange: Policy, pedagogy, practice.* Routledge.

O'Dowd, R., & Waire, P. (2009). Critical issues in telecollaborative task design. *Computer Assisted Language Learning*, *22*(2), 173–188. https://doi.org/10.1080/09588220902778369

O'Dowd, R., Sauro, S., & Spector-Cohen, E. (2020). The role of pedagogical mentoring in virtual exchange. *TESOL Quarterly*, *54*(1), 146–172. https://doi.org/10.1002/tesq.543

O'Rourke, B. (2007). Models of telecollaboration (1): eTandem. In R. O'Dowd (Ed.), *Online intercultural exchange: An introduction for foreign language teachers* (pp. 41–61). Multilingual Matters. https://doi.org/10.21832/9781847690104-005

Porto, M. (2014). Intercultural citizenship education in an EFL online project in Argentina. *Language and Intercultural Communication*, *14*(2), 245–261. https://doi.org/10.1080/14708477.2014.890625

Prensky, M. (2006). *Don't bother me, Mom, I'm learning!: How computer and video games are preparing your kids for 21st century success and how you can help!* Paragon House.

Richardson, S. (2015). *Cosmopolitan learning for a global era: Higher education in an interconnected world.* Routledge.

Ryshina-Pankova, M. (2018). Discourse moves and intercultural communicative competence in telecollaborative chats. *Language Learning & Technology, 22*(1), 218–239. http://hdl.handle.net/10125/44588

Stevens Initiative. (2019). *Virtual exchange impact and learning report 2019.* www .stevensinitiative.org/resource/virtual-exchange-impact-and-learning-report/

Stevens Initiative. (2020). *Virtual exchange impact and learning report 2020.* www .stevensinitiative.org/resource/virtual-exchange-impact-and-learning-report-2/

The EVALUATE Group. (2019). *Evaluating the impact of virtual exchange on initial teacher education: A European policy experiment.* Research-publishing. net. https://doi.org/10.14705/rpnet.2019.29.9782490057337

Valtonen, T., Pontinen, S., Kukkonen, J., Dillon, P., Väisänen, P., & Hacklin, S. (2011). Confronting the technological pedagogical knowledge of Finnish Net Generation student teachers. *Technology, Pedagogy and Education, 20*(1), 3–18. https://doi.org/10.1080/1475939X.2010.534867

Warschauer, M. (1995). *Virtual connections: Online activities & projects for networking language learners.* University of Hawaii Press.

Further Reading

Potolia, A., & Derivry-Plard, M. (Eds.). (2022). *Virtual exchange for intercultural language learning and teaching: Fostering communication for the digital age.* Routledge.
This book explores innovative virtual intercultural practices for language learning across different educational levels. It emphasizes the transversality of these practices throughout the language curriculum and the role of ELF in facilitating cultural exchanges. The authors present diverse educational exchanges using various technological tools, highlighting the interplay between technology, human interactions, and semiotic meanings.

Stevens Initiative. (2020). *2020 annotated bibliography on virtual exchange research.* www.stevensinitiative.org/resource/2020-annotated-bibliography-on-virtual- exchange-research/
This document is an invaluable resource for readers seeking a comprehensive understanding of the academic literature and research in the field of VE. This document serves as a useful guide for scholars, educators, and practitioners interested in exploring the potential of VE for educational and cross-cultural purposes.

16

Collaborative Learning

Lara Ducate and Nike Arnold

Introduction

This chapter focuses on digital collaboration when learning an additional language (L2), a specific type of learner–learner interaction. The central role that interaction plays for L2 learning has been recognized in second language acquisition theories (Loewen & Sato, 2018) as well as teaching methods (Brandl, 2021) and is typically defined by its key constructs: input, negotiation, output, and noticing (Loewen & Sato, 2018; see Chapter 18 in this volume for a discussion of technology-mediated interaction). In CALL contexts, collaboration has almost exclusively been researched in connection with writing,[1] which will be the focus of this chapter.

Background and Historical Perspectives

The early 2000s marked the beginning of the commonly named Web 2.0 and with it the fundamental shift to a social, interactive internet. Its hallmark user-generated content and participatory culture paved the way for computer-supported collaborative learning (CSCL), especially the development of what is probably one of the quintessential Web 2.0 technologies: the wiki. A wiki is "a hypertext publication collaboratively edited and managed by its own audience directly using a web browser ... Content is created without any defined owner or leader" (Wiki, 2024). As such, it has "intensive collaborative" affordances (Godwin-Jones, 2003, p. 15). Wikis are often designed for asynchronous collaboration, preventing changes if another writer is editing the page at the same time. In contrast, there are collaborative writing applications, such as Google Docs, that are built for synchronous work with a built-in chat feature.

---

[1] We also refer the reader to Chapter 15 on telecollaboration. While telecollaborative projects can include activities that fit the description of collaboration presented below, that is not always the case.

These and other technological developments have had a profound impact on writing. In addition to creating new digital genres (Crystal, 2011), they have transformed audiences, authorial and reader identities (Hyland, 2019), and the writing process itself, which has become more recursive (Grosbois, 2016) and often collaborative.

These changes align well with several pedagogical orientations and principles, first and foremost sociocultural theory (SCT). This theory views the development of cognitive capabilities as a social process that occurs through interactions between a learner and an expert, or knowledgeable peers. Two types of tools mediate this process: physical (e.g., computer) and symbolic (e.g., language) (Vygotsky, 1978). Language is ascribed a central role as a cognitive tool that supports the social speech between individuals solving a problem. This negotiation often involves the consolidation or extension of existing knowledge or the creation of new knowledge (Storch, 2017).[2] During collaborative writing tasks, this takes the shape of peer feedback and negotiations about the content, language, and organization of the text. In addition to other-directed, collaborative talk, there is private speech "enabl[ing] the individual to structure and organize their actions, including their thinking processes" (Storch, 2017, p. 72). Co-authoring a text, however, might not provide a clear distinction between self-directed and other-directed speech (Storch, 2017) if private speech is vocalized (Zhang, 2022) and triggers a response from another learner. The "process of making meaning and shaping knowledge and experience through language" (Swain, 2006, p. 98), be it in private speech or collaborative talk, is also referred to as languaging. In the context of L2 learning, languaging can focus on specific linguistic items (language-related episodes (LREs; Swain & Lapkin, 2002) and contribute to language learning gains.

Another pedagogical principle that aligns with the social web is collaboration. A staple of L2 teaching, collaborative activities are a form of active learning in which learners work toward a shared goal (Bosworth & Hamilton, 1994). As a result, they are engaged not just cognitively, but also affectively and socially (Pintrich, 2000). Due to its popularity, the term collaborative learning is often used in very broad, even vague terms (Dillenbourg, 1999). It is therefore important to stress that not all pair or group activities are necessarily collaborative. To distinguish collaboration from other types of peer learning, Damon and Phelps (1989) draw on the dimensions of equality and mutuality. Equality is defined as "the degree of control or authority over the task" (Storch, 2002, p. 127). As such, it manifests itself not just in the number of participants' contributions but also in their influence over the direction of the activity. Mutuality refers to engagement with the contributions of others. In the context of writing, mutuality is often apparent through the editing or revising of text contributed by others. Using these two

---

[2] As Storch (2017) points out, collaborative talk is not the same as negotiation of meaning (Long, 1985), which is triggered by a communication breakdown.

dimensions, collaborative learning is defined by high degrees of both equality and mutuality. As a result, partners produce something that exceeds the capabilities of the individual (Forman & Cazden, 1985). Applying this definition to writing, we can define collaborative writing as a process where all members contribute to the entire writing process, from the initial generation of ideas to the drafting and editing of the text (Storch, 2012).[3]

Collaborative learning involves not only individual cognition but also collaborative talk, which triggers additional learning mechanisms such as knowledge sharing, reduced cognitive load, giving and receiving feedback, noticing gaps in knowledge, and testing hypotheses (Dillenbourg, 1999; Elola & Oskoz, 2010). Successful work toward the shared goal also "requires constant negotiation of procedures and relevant strategies for meaning-making on a group level" (Lund, 2013, p. 80) to reach intersubjectivity (Kramsch, 2009). Like collaboration, cooperation is characterized by high equality (e.g., no free-riders) but lacks mutuality, meaning that members fail to engage with each other's contributions. A common cooperative approach relies on division of labor, where independent subtasks are completed individually and then later assembled into a larger product (Dillenbourg, 1999).

As described above, one of the main arguments for computer-mediated collaborative writing is rooted in its ability to promote learning processes and ultimately gains in language knowledge (Kim, 2008; Storch, 2005, 2019). Collaborative writing also connects with current L2 writing pedagogy by focusing on process over product (Li, 2021; Pellet, 2012) and providing an audience (Li, 2021). Another main argument for its pedagogical use is the need to prepare learners for co-authoring, an authentic task they will likely encounter outside the classroom in workplace and other settings. Collaborative, technology-mediated writing has become an important 21st century skill (U.S. Department of Education, 2013) that fosters autonomy (Pellet, 2012), accountability (Nostratinia & Nikpanjeh, 2015), and negotiation, and L2 education should contribute to these skills.

Primary Themes

Although computer-mediated collaborative writing is a relatively new field, research has already moved through some important developmental phases. Early descriptive studies focused on tools to explore what is possible with the new technology (Ducate, Lomicka Anderson, & Moreno, 2011), often by comparing wikis with more traditional tasks. Since this technological approach, more current research has reflected orientations driven by theoretical frameworks (Blyth, 2008; Goertler, 2012):

---

[3] Unlike peer review, for example, which is limited to just one phase.

- psycholinguistic: research based on interactionist theories of second language acquisition, such as studies investigating LREs in learners' collaborative talk associated with wiki writing;
- sociocultural: studies focused on the socially constructed nature of the writing process, including studies determining if and how learners collaborated;
- ecological: research that systematically accounts for the various layers of context, which is currently lacking in L2 wiki studies;
- linguistic: studies that focus on learners' focus on language, such as learners' attendance to their own or their peers' grammatical or lexical errors in a text.

This review of primary themes within L2 wiki writing surveys various studies that fit into each of these groups, with the majority of the more recent studies falling into the sociocultural category. Newer applications to promote collaboration will be mentioned toward the end of the chapter as they are just beginning to be explored.

Comparison Studies

Comparison studies have focused on the differences between: (1) face-to-face (F2F) versus online collaborative writing and (2) collaborative versus individual writing. The study by Ansarimoghaddam and Tan (2013), for example, falls into the first category. They reported collaborative wiki writing to ultimately be more effective. Face-to-face collaboration was perceived as easier in the planning stage while learners preferred the wiki during the actual writing because it provides more processing time (Ansarimoghaddam & Tan, 2013; Storch, 2021). Learners also appreciated the textual features of the wiki (e.g. bolding and italicizing). Another study reported an almost equal preference for F2F interactions during the writing stage. However, students in the collaborative writing environment produced better texts (Moonma, 2021). This difference in perceptions could be a function of the task and might ultimately call for a blended approach (Ansarimoghaddam & Tan, 2013).

Comparing the outcome of online collaborative and individual writing, several textual features have been identified to benefit from collaboration, namely organization, content, grammar, sentence structure, creativity, and sense of audience (Chao & Lo, 2009; Wang, 2014). Furthermore, the process of collaboration allowed for skill-building, such as coordination and communication with others (Ansarimoghaddam, Tan, & Yong, 2017). In a study that specifically examined vocabulary gains among collaborators and individuals using Google Docs (Liu & Lan, 2016), the collaborative groups showed greater vocabulary gains and higher participation rates than the individuals by the end of the eight-week treatment. The collaborative repair in the groups seemed to help improve lexical knowledge. While collaborative tasks can sometimes end up being more cooperative in practice, comparison studies indicate that they build motivation and often lead to better quality products.

The recent study by Villareal and Munarriz-Ibarrola (2021) adds additional variables to its investigation of individual and collaborative writing by including a comparison of writing on wikis versus paper. Young learners first wrote individually and then as a group, switching modalities during the semester so that each group had experience of collaborating on paper and in Google Docs. Collaboration in general, whether on paper or online, led to more accurate and fluent texts. However, writing in Google Docs did not lead to higher quality drafts. Digital texts were more fluent while the paper texts were more accurate. These results could have been due to students needing training in digital communication and the collaborative use of Google Docs.

Cooperation vs. Collaboration

The question of whether learners actually collaborate has been central in the research on wikis. The answer seems to depend on a variety of factors, including group dynamics, group size, level of motivation, type of task, and assessment (Arnold, Ducate, & Kost, 2012; Elabdali, 2016; Kennedy & Miceli, 2013; Lee & Wang, 2013; Li, 2021; Li & Kim, 2016; Li & Zhu, 2017; Pellet, 2012). As is the case for other types of collaborative learning, these factors seem to interact in complex ways (Dillenbourg, 1999).

In earlier research on paper-based collaborative writing, Storch (2002) identified four interactional patterns based on the degree of mutuality and equality: (1) collaborative; (2) dominant/dominant; (3) dominant/passive; and (4) expert/novice. Interestingly, an additional pattern was identified for online collaborative writing, in which writers cooperate by taking turns without conflict or editing each other's contributions (Aufa & Storch, 2021; Elabdali & Arnold, 2020). Unfortunately, cooperation is sometimes the prominent pattern in the online format (Ansarimoghaddam et al., 2017; Aufa & Storch, 2021; Storch, 2021). Other well-documented problems are uneven workloads (Alyousef & Picard, 2011; Kessler, Bikowski, & Boggs, 2012; Li & Kim, 2016; Li & Zhu, 2017; Lund, 2008; Mak & Coniam, 2008) and a hesitancy to edit the contributions of others (Arnold et al., 2012; Lee, 2010; Li, 2021; Lund, 2013; Mak & Coniam, 2008). The latter might be because students do not want to offend their peers, are unsure of their L2 abilities, or have been socialized into independent work.

Arnold et al. (2012), for example, found that the number of contributions and revisions in each group varied widely, but that dyads had the least free riders. When comparing the degree of engagement between content and form, there were only 12 students out of 53 who were categorized as free riders or social loafers in regard to both meaning and formal revisions. On the other hand, there were 16 out of 53 students who were labeled as free riders in one category and team players or leaders in another, which suggests they focused on what they considered their strength or what they enjoyed more. Li and Kim (2016) also noted how group dynamics shifted and students took on different collaborative or cooperative roles depending on where they were in the project.

Oskoz and Elola (2012) analyzed not just the revision history of the wiki but also its discussion board. They noticed varying degrees of participation in discussion boards used to prepare for the writing task, on the wiki, and in the chat during the writing process, and during the revision process after receiving instructor feedback. In addition to text-based CMC, video chat can also be used during collaborative writing and might promote higher levels of focus and interest (Aubrey, 2022).

At this point, it remains somewhat unclear why some learners collaborate and participate more than others, but it could depend partly on how they interpret the task (Oskoz & Elola, 2012), their level of motivation toward the task, and their commitment to the collaborative process.

Assessment and shared understanding of the task also play a role in collaboration. If students are not assessed on their degree of collaboration, they will likely focus more on their own contributions (Alyousef & Picard, 2011). Different interpretations of the task as well as differing levels of L2 proficiency can also change the group dynamics and hamper collaboration (Li, 2021). Li and Zhu (2017) found, for example, that more collective groups, where learners exhibited high levels of quality and mutuality, had similar goals, worked collaboratively, and were positive toward the task. Groups with a more dominant–defensive work pattern had different goals, worked more independently, and were negative toward the task. Groups that did not engage with each other's contributions may also have less coherence and accuracy (Li, 2021).

Another consideration in the task design is the degree to which the assignment is structured (i.e. with specific guidelines and due dates for each step), or unstructured (Arnold et al., 2009; Kessler, 2009; Judd et al., 2010; Pellet, 2015; Li & Zhu, 2017). Less structured tasks seem to lead to more collaboration during the project (Arnold, Ducate, & Kost, 2009; Kessler, 2009), possibly due to students feeling more ownership over the task. Arnold et al. (2009) found that learners engaged in a structured task were more successful at editing grammar and more focused on their own contributions. The inclusion of teacher feedback on the more structured project could have added to students feeling more personally responsible for their own parts, similar to a paper-based assignment with first draft, feedback, and revisions.

Lee and Wang (2013) describe a wiki project designed to achieve true collaboration. The nature of the task and its assessment provide an example of how a well-designed task can lead to more collaboration. During the first semester, students focused on community building and practicing peer editing. During the second semester, they worked on their online picture books. To promote collaboration, each student evaluated their own and their peers' contributions, which factored into each group's collective grade. Group assessment ensured that all members contributed to the project, whether with the story idea, the language, or illustrations. As they built a stronger sense of community, students fulfilled their tasks out of a sense of duty to their group members since they were receiving a collective grade. This study is unusual in that it spanned two semesters, which seemed to affect the degree of collaboration.

Language and Lexical Focus

Another theme in wiki research is the effect of collaboration on formal aspects of the text (Aydin & Yildiz, 2014). Especially during asynchronous collaboration, it seems that learners have more time to notice and correct their errors as well as the clarity of their message, which ultimately triggers grammatical, lexical, and even organizational revisions (Aydin & Yildiz, 2014; Elola & Oskoz, 2010). Other studies have found, however, that learners attend more to their peers' content than form when revising the wiki (Kessler, 2009; Kessler et al., 2012, Mak & Coniam, 2008; Mondahl & Razmerita, 2014) as well as when interacting with their peers (Elola & Oskoz, 2010; Li & Kim, 2016; Oskoz & Elola, 2012). Arnold et al. (2009) noted that content changes tended to be made in a more cooperative fashion, contrary to results of Kessler and Bikowski (2010). Learners were less likely to make changes to their peers' content than their own, but they were just as likely to make formal changes to their own text as to a peer's (Arnold et al., 2009). As Viégas, Wattenburg, and Dave (2004) observed for Wikipedia, once content was added, the other group members tended to leave it there. And in other studies, learners focused both on meaning and form in their revisions (Arnold et al., 2012; Lee, 2010).

Elola and Oskoz (2010) noted that their learners were oriented differently toward grammatical accuracy depending on whether they were working alone or with a partner. When working independently, they focused on form at the end of the writing process, but when working collaboratively, they focused on grammar and vocabulary throughout the writing process. Apparently, chatting with their partner focused their attention on all aspects of the text to continuously produce a more accurate product (Elola & Oskoz, 2010). This finding points to the role of the medium. In a later study, Oskoz and Elola (2014) found that synchronous chats tended to focus attention on the content and structure of the wiki, while the asynchronous nature of the wiki itself allowed for more time to focus on grammar, vocabulary, and editing.

Additionally, the genre of the text can encourage different types of focus. With argumentative essays, syntax played a larger role than it did in the expository essay where accuracy was highlighted more in the writing and revision process (Oskoz & Elola, 2014). In contrast, the participants of Elabdali's study (2016) wrote short stories together and paid little attention to grammar and lexical and stylistic choices, instead focusing on macrostructure aspects of the text. The author concluded that "collaboration on creative writing tasks can be difficult because there are no standards when it comes to word choice, tense, or style. Academic writing tasks, on the other hand, are easier to collaborate on due to the well-established conventions of the genre" (p. 128).

Attention to form can also be related to the approach of a group. Aufa and Storch (2021) observed that more cooperative groups rarely negotiated language forms, which resulted in fewer LREs and likely reduced learning gains. Working online, it was easy to make changes directly in the text rather than discuss the revision, a finding similar to that by Arnold et al. (2012). While many studies, especially earlier ones (e.g. Arnold et al., 2012; Kessler & Bikowski, 2010), have relied solely on the revision history, some projects (e.g., Alghasab & Handley, 2017; Elola & Oskoz, 2010; Oskoz & Elola, 2014) have triangulated this data source with the transcripts of learners' online chats. This combination has yielded richer insights into the process of collaborative writing.

Learner Perceptions

The last research theme to highlight is the study of learners' perceptions of their collaborative writing experiences. Many learners have positive attitudes towards collaborative writing and report that they would prefer to write collaboratively rather than individually (Dobao & Blum, 2013; Ducate et al., 2011; Elola & Oskoz, 2010), though that is not always the case (Elabdali, 2016). Learners noticed how collaboration improved their organization, content, grammar, and vocabulary (Arnold et al., 2009; Dobao & Blum, 2013; Elola & Oskoz, 2010; Kennedy & Miceli, 2013; Li, 2021). In addition to the language benefits, Li's (2021) students also appreciate the ease of wikis to encourage collaboration by allowing them to work on their projects anywhere and anytime and leave comments for their peers, which they felt led to more equal participation in the project and helped them hone their skills for collaborating online.

While students are often positive about writing collaboratively, they also see the benefits of writing alone. Oskoz and Elola's (2011) learners preferred writing individually when they wanted to cultivate their own style in the L2, to avoid disagreements about organization, vocabulary, and grammar or the general direction of the paper, and to not work around someone else's schedule. Learners are also frustrated when not everyone in the group participates equally (Arnold et al., 2012) and some are not comfortable sharing ownership of their work (Ducate et al., 2011; Lund, 2008). Another negative attitude was reported by Mondahl and Razmerita (2014), whose students questioned the relevance of collaborating on a wiki project when they are assessed individually on tests.

Recommendations for Practice

As described above, computer-mediated collaborative writing offers a variety of potential benefits as well as pitfalls. These should be factored into the design and implementation of activities. Generally speaking, there are four ways to promote collaboration: (1) set up initial conditions (e.g., group size and composition, task, medium); (2) overspecify the collaboration contract with a scenario based on roles; (3) scaffold productive interactions; and (4) monitor and regulate interactions (Dillenbourg, 1999). Below, we offer a list of questions and recommendations from these four categories to guide the design process.

Collaboration and Digital Communication

There are several practices to encourage collaboration. First of all, learners need to understand the difference between collaboration and cooperation, the benefits of collaboration, the role of interdependence, and ways to engage collaboratively (Dennen & Hoadley, 2013; Li, 2021). Time for community building can also be added so that learners get to know and trust each other and are motivated to complete the task together (Lin & Kelsey, 2009). In addition, learners need strategies for effective collaboration, such as communicating online and addressing conflict (Kennedy & Miceli, 2013; Storch, 2021; Villareal & Munarriz-Ibarrola, 2021). This is where establishing ground rules (Arnold et al., 2009) or collaboration scripts (process scaffolds to provide interaction-related support such as specifying and sequencing activities and roles; Fischer et al., 2013) can be helpful.

Genre

Research studies have investigated the collaborative writing of many genres: summaries of historical backgrounds, translations (Miyazoe & Anderson, 2010; Tan et al., 2010), brochures (Mak & Coniam, 2008), descriptions (Arnold et al., 2009; 2012; Kost, 2011; Liou & Lee, 2011; Ozkan, 2015; Zou, Wang, & Xing, 2016), proposals (Li & Kim, 2016; Li & Zhu, 2017), essays (Elola & Oskoz, 2010; Kessler, 2009; Kessler et al., 2012; Li & Zhu, 2013), job applications (Zou et al., 2016), annotated bibliographies (Li & Kim, 2016), letters (Wang, 2014), and creative writing (Elabdali & Arnold, 2020). The genre will encourage writers to focus more or less on language, organization, or content. When writing a summary or report, for example, learners may focus more on content for factual accuracy. With a more prescriptive genre, such as a business letter, learners may attend more to form (Elabdali & Arnold, 2020). Their familiarity with the genre will affect their attention to detail as well as the degree to which the task allows for creativity.

Strategies for Task Design

Task design plays a key role in encouraging collaboration. Once the value of collaboration has been established and the learners are clear about the objectives and expectations of the task, there are several decisions the instructor must make:

- Is the collaborative writing task incorporated into the curriculum of the course? Does it contribute to the larger course outcomes, such as providing background to a reading in the course (Arnold et al., 2009)?

- Does the nature of the task inherently encourage and benefit from collaboration (Ducate et al., 2011)? Closed tasks with one correct answer do not automatically translate to an online environment where students can easily find the answer. Learners instead need a reason to pool their knowledge and resources, work together in creative ways, and negotiate meaning in their L2 in order to practice skills they will need in the workplace (Lund, 2013).
- How long will the task last? Will it be one assignment or take place over an entire semester? Or will it last even an entire year to allow groups to build community over several months (Lee & Wang, 2013)?
- Should the task be completed asynchronously or synchronously or with a mix of both? Should there be a face-to-face component for building community and initial brainstorming? Different modes can encourage learners to focus on different aspects of the task, namely organization and content during synchronous chat and grammar and revisions during asynchronous chat (Elola & Oskoz, 2010; Oskoz & Elola, 2011).
- What should the size of the groups be? Smaller groups encourage equality since it is more difficult for a group member to engage in free riding or social loafing (Arnold et al., 2012).
- Should the groups be homogeneous in terms of L2 proficiency or other criteria? Should students choose their own groups or be assigned? A more proficient student might act as the leader of the group (Storch, 2021), but allowing for students to scaffold within their zones of proximal development supports learning (Dennen & Hoadley, 2013).
- Should group leader and other roles be assigned or decided upon by group members (Li & Kim, 2016)? Roles can scaffold the collaborative process by providing a structure to learners who may otherwise rely more on cooperation (Dennen & Hoadley, 2013).
- Can the instructor provide an authentic audience for the text or is the audience more controlled (e.g., the class)? An authentic audience can increase motivation and attention to detail.
- What is the teacher's role in the collaborative process (Lund, 2013)? Will they provide feedback throughout the process or only at the end? Will they participate in the chats or wiki discussion board? Teacher mediation can encourage collaborative behaviors (Alghasab, 2016). Will the teacher intervene if there are social loafers and free riders? Too little or too much teacher presence can lower motivation (Kennedy & Miceli, 2013; Yaden & Blaine, 2007).
- How often will feedback be provided and by whom? Regular feedback can help keep students motivated to stay on task (Cronin, 2009; Lin & Kelsey, 2009).
- How will the text and the collaborative process be assessed? Will learners receive credit for engaging with each other and providing input (Storch, 2021)? It is useful when assessment includes a collective grade for the entire group and a chance for group members to assess each other's participation in the project (Bonk et al., 2009; Pellet, 2012; Zorko, 2009). Learners can also self-assess to examine how they contributed to the whole task (Lund, 2013).

As pointed out by Dennen and Hoadley (2013, p. 399), "collaborative learning design is a necessarily complex process; to treat it otherwise would be to neglect some of the core elements necessary to promote fruitful learning interactions ... Designers need to consider the full context – pedagogical, interpersonal, environmental, and technological – of the setting." But even then, it is all but impossible to guarantee successful collaboration because the variables described above interact in complex ways (Dillenbourg, 1999) and influence the process of task completion and the final outcome.

Recommendations for Research and Future Directions

The field of computer-mediated collaborative writing is relatively young and there is still only limited research on the topic. As the above review suggests, it has not been determined yet how to ensure that all, or at least most, students participate. More research is needed to identify strategies to promote equality as well as help students understand the nature and value of collaboration. The latter is particularly important since many educational systems socialize students into independent work. One way to address these questions could be through ecological studies that account for multiple layers of the context, including the institution, the curriculum, the instructor, the previous training of the learners, and the details of the task (Van Lier, 2004). To truly understand the process of collaborative writing, it is also valuable to use multiple data sources (e.g. Alghasab & Handley, 2017; Elabdali & Arnold, 2020) as well as new data sources such as screen recordings, eye tracking, think-alouds, or video recordings.

As much of the previous research on collaboration has focused on wikis, and more recently Google Docs or other web-based collaborative word processing applications, future research should explore other tools, such as digital storytelling, collaborative slide-making applications, generative artificial intelligence, and virtual reality. More importantly, there is a need to explore how technology can support collaboration for receptive skills. There are tools for collaborative reading and viewing that have the potential to create powerful learning opportunities but there is little research. An example is Yu (2014), who compared individual and collaborative text annotation. While there was no significant difference in terms of recall, collaborative annotations raised students' enjoyment of reading. Annotation tools also aided in comprehension of texts since learners can annotate, read and respond to their classmates' comments, and interact throughout the reading process. Clearly, there are many questions related to the process and outcomes of collaborative reading. Initial studies will likely take a technological approach and focus, for example, on how the tool works and how students experience it, which will lay important groundwork for more in-depth studies into the efficacy of these tools.

As has been illustrated above, a key predictor for successful collaboration seems to be the preparation and training of learners. Training is also needed for pre-service L2 teachers so that they enter their classrooms prepared to organize and promote collaboration. The value of collaboration should be reflected in the curriculum and even the culture of a school to prepare learners for the social, participatory web. In a recent survey conducted by the American Association of Colleges and Universities, 62 percent of employers reported that working in a team was a very important skill and another 31 percent found it somewhat important, but only 48 percent of employers felt that recent graduates were prepared to work in a team (Flaherty, 2021). These results are not surprising considering that in a survey conducted with 500 college students, 65 percent of respondents reported they had received no training "to make team-based class projects more effective, enjoyable, or productive," and 22 percent only "a few minutes" of training. In other words, 87 percent of college students have received almost no training on a skill valued by 94 percent of employers (Mashek, 2021, para. 2). Researchers and practitioners still need to explore the most effective ways to encourage learners to collaborate digitally and incorporate proven strategies and training for collaboration into their classrooms to help learners embrace collaboration not just for its learning opportunities but also as a vital (career) skill in a digitally connected world.

References

Alghasab, M. (2016). The impact of EFL teachers' mediation in wiki-mediated collaborative writing activities on student–student collaboration. In S. Papadima-Sophocleous, L. Bradley & S. Thouësny (Eds), *CALL communities and culture: Short papers from EUROCALL 2016* (pp. 1–6). https://doi.org/10.14705/rpnet.2016.eurocall2016.529

Alghasab, M., & Handley, Z. (2017). Capturing (non-)collaboration in wiki-mediated collaborative writing activities: The need to examine discussion posts and editing acts in tandem. *Computer Assisted Language Learning, 30*(7), 664–691. https://doi.org/10.1080/09588221.2017.1341928

Alyousef, H., & Picard, M. (2011). Cooperative or collaborative literacy practices: Mapping metadiscourse in a business students' wiki group project. *Australasian Journal of Educational Technology, 27*, 463–480. https://doi.org/10.14742/ajet.955

Ansarimoghaddam, S., & Tan, B. H. (2013). Co-constructing an essay: Collaborative writing in class and on wiki. *The Southeast Asian Journal of English Language Studies, 19*(1), 35–50.

Ansarimoghaddam, S., Tan, B. H., & Yong, M. F. (2017). Collaboratively composing an argumentative essay: Wiki versus face–face interactions. *GEMA Online Journal of Language Studies, 17*(2), 33–53. https://doi.org/10.17576/gema-2017-1702-03

Arnold, N., Ducate, L., & Kost, C. (2009). Collaborative writing in wikis: Insights from culture projects in German classes. In L. Lomicka and G. Lord (Eds.), *The next generation: Social networking and online collaboration in foreign language learning* (pp. 115–144). CALICO Publications.

Arnold, N., Ducate, L., & Kost, C. (2012). Collaboration or cooperation? Analyzing group dynamics and revision processes in wikis. *CALICO Journal*, *29*(3), 431–448.

Aubrey, S. (2022). Dynamic engagement in second language computer-mediated collaborative writing tasks: Does communication mode matter? *Studies in Second Language Learning and Teaching*, *12*(1), 59–86. http://dx.doi.org/10.14746/ssllt.2022.12.1.4

Aufa, F., & Storch, N. (2021). Learner interaction in blended collaborative writing activities. In M. Garcia Mayo (Ed.), *Working collaboratively in second/foreign language learning* (pp. 151–176). Walter de Gruyter. https://doi.org/10.1515/9781501511318-007

Aydin, Z., & Yildiz, S. (2014). Using wikis to promote collaborative EFL writing. *Language Learning & Technology*, *18*(1), 160–180. http://llt.msu.edu/issues/february2014/aydinyildiz.pdf

Blyth, C. S. (2008). Research perspectives on online discourse in foreign language learning. In S. S. Magnan (Ed.), *Mediating discourse online* (pp. 47–70). John Benjamins.

Bonk, C. J., Lee, M. M., Kim, N., & Lin, M.-F. G. (2009). The tensions of transformation in three cross-institutional wikibook projects. *Internet and Higher Education*, *12*, 126–135. http://dx.doi.org/10.1016/j.iheduc.2009.04.002

Bosworth, K., & Hamilton, S. (1994). *Collaborative learning underlying processes and effective techniques*. Calif Jossey-Bass.

Brandl, K. (2021). *Communicative language teaching in action: Putting principles to work*. Cognella Academic Publishing.

Chao, Y. C. J., & Lo, H. C. (2009). Students' perceptions of wiki-based collaborative writing for learners of English as a foreign language. *Interactive Learning Environments*, *19*(4), 395–411. https://doi.org/10.1080/10494820903298662

Cronin, J. (2009). Upgrading to 2.0: An experiential project to build a marketing wiki. *Journal of Marketing Education*, *31*, 66–75. www.learntechlib.org/p/64908/

Crystal, D. (2011). *Internet linguistics: A student guide*. Routledge.

Damon, W., & Phelps, E. (1989). Critical distinctions among three approaches to peer education. *International Journal of Educational Research*, *13*(1), 9–19. https://doi.org/10.1016/0883-0355(89)90013-X

Dennen, V. P., & Hoadley, C. (2013). Designing collaborative learning through computer support. In C. E. Hmelo-Silver, C. A. Chinn, C. K. K. Chan, & A. M. O'Donnell (Eds.), *The international handbook of collaborative learning* (pp. 389–402). Routledge.

Dillenbourg, P. (1999). What do you mean by collaborative learning? In P. Dillenbourg (Ed.), *Collaborative learning: Cognitive and computational approaches* (pp. 1–19). Elsevier.

Dobao, F. A., & Blum, A. (2013). Collaborative writing in pairs and small groups: Learners' attitudes and perceptions. *System*, *41*(2), 365–378. https://doi.org/10.1016/j.system.2013.02.002

Ducate, L., Lomicka Anderson, L., & Moreno, N. (2011). Wading through the world of wikis: An analysis of three wiki projects. *Foreign Language Annals, 44* (3), 495–524. https://doi.org/10.1111/j.1944-9720.2011.01144.x

Elabdali, R. (2016). Wiki-based collaborative creative writing in the ESL classroom (Unpublished master's thesis). Portland State University, Portland, Oregon. https://doi.org/10.15760/etd.5269

Elabdali, R., & Arnold, N. (2020). Group dynamics across interaction modes in L2 collaborative wiki writing. *Computers and Composition, 58,* 102607 https://doi .org/10.1016/j.compcom.2020.102607

Elola, I., & Oskoz, A. (2010). Collaborative writing: Fostering foreign language and writing conventions development. *Language Learning & Technology, 14*(3), 51–71.

Elola, I., & Oskoz, A. (2017). Writing with 21st century social tools in the L2 classroom: New literacies, genres, and writing practices. *Journal of Second Language Writing, 26,* 52–60. http://dx.doi.org/10.1016/j.jslw.2017.04.002

Fischer, F., Kollar, I., Stegmann, K., Wecker, C., Zottmann, J., & Weinberger, A. (2013). Collaboration scripts in computer-supported collaborative learning. In C. E. Hmelo-Silver, C. A. Chinn, C. K. K. Chan & A. M. O'Donnell (Eds.), *The international handbook of collaborative learning* (pp. 403–419). Routledge.

Flaherty, C. (2021, April 6). What employers want. *Inside Higher Ed.* www .insidehighered.com/news/2021/04/06/aacu-survey-finds-employers-want-can didates-liberal-arts-skills-cite-preparedness

Forman, E. A., & Cazden, C. B. (1985). Exploring Vygotskian perspectives in education: The cognitive value of peer interaction. In J. V. Wertsch (Ed.), *Culture, communication and cognition: Vygotskian perspectives* (pp. 323–347). Cambridge University Press.

Godwin-Jones, R. (2003). Blogs and wikis: Environments for online collaboration. *Language Learning & Technology, 7*(2), 12–16.

Goertler, S. (2012). Theoretical and empirical foundations for blended language learning. In F. Rubio and J. Thoms (Eds.), *The American Association of University Supervisors, Coordinators and Directors of Foreign Languages Programs (AAUSC), Issues in Language Program Direction: Hybrid Language Teaching and Learning – Exploring Theoretical, Pedagogical and Curricular Issues* (pp. 27–49). Heinle Cengage.

Grosbois, M. (2016). Computer supported collaborative writing and language learning. In F. Farr & L. Murray (Eds.), *The Routledge handbook of language learning and technology* (pp. 269–280). Routledge.

Hyland, K. (2019). *Second language writing* (2nd ed.). Cambridge University Press.

Kennedy, C., & Miceli, T. (2013). In piazza online: Exploring the use of wikis with beginner foreign language learners. *Computer Assisted Language Learning, 26*(5), 389–411. https://doi.org/10.1080/09588221.2013.770035

Kessler, G. (2009). Student-initiated attention to form in wiki-based collaborative writing. *Language Learning & Technology, 13*(1), 79–95. http://dx.doi.org/10125/44169

Kessler, G., & Bikowski, D. (2010). Developing collaborative autonomous learning abilities in computer mediated language learning: Attention to meaning among students in wiki space. *Computer Assisted Language Learning, 23*(1), 41–58. https://doi.org/10.1080/09588220903467335

Kessler, G., Bikowski, D., & Boggs, J. (2012). Collaborative writing among second language learners in academic web-based projects. *Language Learning & Technology, 16*(1), 91–109.

Kim, Y. (2008). The contribution of collaborative and individual tasks to the acquisition of L2 vocabulary. *The Modern Language Journal, 92*, 114–130. http://dx.doi.org/10.1111/j.1540-4781.2008.00690.x

Kost, C. (2011). Investigating writing strategies and revision behavior in collaborative wiki projects. *CALICO Journal, 28*(3), 606–620. https://doi.org/10.11139/cj.28.3.606-620

Kramsch, C. (2009). *The multilingual subject.* Oxford University Press.

Lee, H., & Wang, P. (2013). Discussing the factors contributing to students' involvement in an EFL collaborative wiki project. *ReCALL, 25*(2), 233–249. https://doi.org/10.1017/s0958344013000025

Lee, L. (2010). Exploring wiki-mediated collaborative writing: A case study in an elementary Spanish course. *CALICO Journal, 27*(2), 260–276.

Li, M. (2021). Participation and interaction in wiki-based collaborative writing: An activity theory perspective. In M. Garcia Mayo (Ed.), *Working collaboratively in second/foreign language learning* (pp. 151–176). Walter de Gruyter. https://doi.org/10.1515/9781501511318-010

Li, M., & Kim, D. (2016). One wiki, two groups: Dynamic interactions across ESL collaborative writing tasks. *Journal of Second Language Writing, 31*, 25–42. http://dx.doi.org/10.1016/j.jslw.2016.01.002

Li, M., & Zhu, W. (2013). Patterns of computer-mediated interaction in small writing groups using wikis. *Computer Assisted Language Learning, 26*(1), 61–82. http://dx.doi.org/10.1080/09588221.2011.631142

Li, M., & Zhu, W. (2017). Explaining dynamic interactions in wiki-based collaborative writing. *Language Learning and Technology, 21*(2), 96–120. http://llt.msu.edu/issues/june2017/lizhu.pdf

Lin, H., & Kelsey, K. (2009). Building a networked environment in wikis: The evolving phases of collaborative learning in a Wikibook project. *Journal of Educational Computing Research, 40*(2), 145–169.

Liou, H., & Lee, S. (2011). How wiki-based writing influences college students' collaborative and individual composing products, processes, and learners' perceptions. *International Journal of Computer-Assisted Language Learning and Teaching, 1*(1), 45–61. http://doi.org/10.4018/ijcallt.2011010104

Liu, S. H. H., & Lan, Y. J. (2016). Social constructivist approach to web-based EFL learning: Collaboration, motivation, and perception on the use of Google Docs. *Educational Technology and Society, 19*(1), 171–186.

Loewen, S., & Sato, M. (2018). Interaction and instructed second language acquisition. *Language Teaching, 51*(3), 285–329. https://doi.org/10.1017/S0261444818000125

Long, M. (1985). Input and second language acquisition theory. In S. Gass & C. G. Madden (Eds.), *Input in second language acquisition* (pp. 377–393). Newbury House.

Lund, A. (2008). Wikis: A collective approach to language production. *ReCALL*, *20*(1), 35–54. https://doi.org/10.1017/S0958344008000414

Lund, A. (2013). Collaboration unpacked: Tasks, tools, and activities. In C. Meskill (Ed.), *Online teaching and learning: Sociocultural perspectives* (pp. 77–98). Bloomsburg Academic.

Mak, B., & Coniam, D. (2008). Using wikis to enhance and develop writing skills among secondary school students in Hong Kong. *System*, *36*(3), 437–455.

Mashek, D. (2021, June 23). *Opinion: College graduates lack preparation in the skill most valued by employers – collaboration.* The Hechinger Report. https://hechingerreport.org/opinion-college-graduates-lack-preparation-in-the-skill-most-valued-by-employers-collaboration/

Mondahl M., & Razmerita, L. (2014). Social media, collaboration, and social learning: A case-study of foreign language learning. *The Electronic Journal of e-Learning*, *12*(4), 339–352.

Moonma, J. (2021). Comparing collaborative writing activity in EFL classroom: Face-to-face collaborative writing versus online collaborative writing using Google Docs. *Asian Journal of Education and Training*, *7*(4), 204–215.

Nostratinia, M., & Nikpanjeh, N. (2015). Promoting foreign language learners' writing: Comparing the impact of oral conferencing and collaborative writing. *Theory and Practice in Language Studies*, *5*(11), 2218–2229.

Ozkan, M. (2015). Wikis and blogs in foreign language learning from the perspectives of learners. *Procedia – Social and Behavioral Sciences*, *192*, 672–678. https://doi.org/10.1016/j.sbspro.2015.06.102

Oskoz, A., & Elola, I. (2011). Meeting at the wiki: The new arena for collaborative writing in foreign language courses. In M. J. W. Lee & C. MacLoughlin (Eds.), *Web 2.0-based e-learning: Applying social informatics for tertiary teaching* (pp. 209–227). IGI Global.

Oskoz, A., & Elola, I. (2012). Understanding the impact of social tools in the FL classroom: Activity theory at work. In G. Kessler, A. Oskoz & I. Elola (Eds.), *Technology across writing contexts and tasks* (pp. 131–153). CALICO Publications.

Oskoz, A., & Elola, I. (2014). Promoting FL collaborative writing through the use of Web 2.0 tools. In M. Lloret & L. Ortega (Eds.), *Technology and tasks: Exploring technology-mediated TBLT* (pp. 115–147). John Benjamins.

Pellet, S. (2012). Wikis for building content knowledge in the foreign language classroom. *CALICO Journal*, *29*(2), 224–248.

Pintrich, P. R. (2000). Educational psychology at the millennium: A look back and a look forward. *Educational Psychologist*, *35*(4), 221–226. https://doi.org/10.1207/S15326985EP3504_01

Storch, N. (2002). Patterns of interaction in ESL pair work. *Language Learning*, *52*(1), 119–158. https://doi.org/10.1111/1467-9922.00179

Storch, N. (2005). Collaborative writing: Product, process, and students' reflections. *Journal of Second Language Writing*, *14*(3), 153–173. http://dx.doi.org/10.1016/j.jslw.2005.05.002

Storch, N. (2012). Collaborative writing as a site for L2 learning in face-to-face and online modes. In G. Kessler, A. Oskoz, & I. Elola (Eds.), *Teaching across writing contexts and tasks* (pp. 113–129). CALICO.

Storch, N. (2017). Sociocultural theory in the L2 classroom. In S. Loewen & M. Sato (Eds.), *The Routledge handbook of instructed second language acquisition* (pp. 69–84). Routledge. https://doi.org/10.4324/9781315676968

Storch, N. (2019). Collaborative writing. *Language Teaching, 52*(1), 40–59. https://doi.org/10.1017/s0261444818000320

Storch, N. (2021). Collaborative writing: Promoting languaging among language learners. In M. M. Mayo (Ed.), *Working collaboratively in second/foreign language learning* (pp. 13–34). Walter de Gruyter.

Swain, M. (2006). Languaging, agency and collaboration in advanced language proficiency. In H. Byrnes (Ed.), *Advanced language learning: The contribution of Halliday and Vygotsky* (pp. 95–108). Continuum.

Swain, M., & Lapkin, S. (2002). Talking it through: Two French immersion learners' responses to reformulation. *International Journal of Educational Research, 37*, 285–304. https://doi.org/10.1016/S0883-0355(03)00006-5

U.S. Department of Education/Office of Vocational and Adult Education. (2013). *College and career readiness standards for adult education.* http://lincs.ed.gov/publications/pdf/CCRStandardsAdultEd.pdf

van Lier, L. (2004). *The ecology and semiotics of language learning: A sociocultural perspective.* Kluwer. https://doi.org/10.1007/1-4020-7912-5

Viégas, F. B., Wattenberg, M., & Dave, K. (2004). Studying cooperation and conflict between authors with history flow visualizations. In *Proceedings of the SIGCHI Conference on Human Factors in Computing Systems* (pp. 575–582). http://dx.doi.org/10.1145/985692.985765

Villarreal, I., & Munarriz-Ibarrola, M. (2021). "Together we do better": The effect of pair and group work on young EFL learners' written texts and attitudes. In M. P. García Mayo (Ed.), *Working collaboratively in second/foreign language learning* (pp. 89–116). De Gruyter Mouton. https://doi.org/10.1515/9781501511318-005

Vygotsky, L. S. (1978). *Mind in society: The development of higher psychological processes.* Harvard University Press.

Wang, Y. (2014). Promoting collaborative writing through wikis: A new approach for advancing innovative and active learning in an ESP context. *Computer Assisted Language Learning, 28*(6), 499–512. https://doi.org/10.1080/09588221.2014.881386

Wiki. (2024, September 20). In *Wikipedia.* https://en.wikipedia.org/wiki/Wiki

Yaden, B., & Blaine, P. (2007). How to wiki in Moodle or Sakai. *The IALLT Journal, 39*(1), 1–15.

Yu, L. (2014). Using online annotations in collaborative reading activities with elementary-aged Taiwanese learners of English. Unpublished doctoral dissertation, University of Texas at Austin, Austin, TX.

Zhang, M. (2022). A re-examination of pair dynamics and L2 learning opportunities in collaborative writing. *Language Teaching Research, 26*(1), 10–33. https://doi.org/10.1177/1362168819890949

Zorko, V. (2009). Factors affecting the way students collaborate in a wiki for English language learning. *Australasian Journal of Educational Technology, 25*(5). https://doi.org/10.14742/ajet.1113

Zou, B., Wang, D., & Xing, M. (2016). Collaborative tasks in wiki-based environment in EFL learning. *Computer Assisted Language Learning*, 29(5), 1001–1018. https://doi.org/10.1080/09588221.2015.1121878

Further Reading

Elola, I., & Oskoz, A. (2010). Collaborative writing: Fostering foreign language and writing conventions development. *Language Learning & Technology*, 14(3), 51–71.
This article started looking at synchronous interactions between collaborators and how learners approached the writing task in addition to examining the writing products.
Hyland, K. (2019). *Second language writing* (2nd ed.). Cambridge University Press.
This book provides a comprehensive introduction to L2 writing pedagogy and covers issues of assessment, task and course design, feedback, and technology.
Kessler, G., & Bikowski, D. (2010). Developing collaborative autonomous learning abilities in computer mediated language learning: Attention to meaning among students in wiki space. *Computer Assisted Language Learning*, 23(1), 41–58. https://doi.org/10.1080/09588220903467335
This study documented examples where learners paid more attention to the meanings within the text than forms in a group-based wiki writing task.
Storch, N. (2002). Patterns of interaction in ESL pair work. *Language Learning, 52*(1), 119–158. https://doi.org/10.1111/1467-9922.00179
This is the first article where the terms mutuality and equality are used to describe patterns of interaction during collaborative work.

17

Motivation

Richard Pinner

Introduction

Motivation can be defined as a desire, want, or need which provides a reason for action. The key word being *action*, because although a person might have needs, desires, and wants, unless they act upon them it is not possible to see anything tangible, meaning from a research perspective that no measurements can be taken or observational data collected. This is one of the key distinctions between motivation research and other psychological constructs such as will power, engagement (Hiver et al., 2021), or emotions (Gkonou & Mercer, 2017). I may have a desire to be a better speaker of a foreign language, but unless I am acting toward this (through, for example studying or using the language) then I cannot be said to have motivation. Although many studies into motivation do look at performance (see e.g. Zee & Koomen, 2016, which found a correlation between teacher's self-efficacy and students' academic performance), many of the studies that are conducted about motivation do not actually measure the action or performance component, and instead seek to get inside participants' heads to understand the psychological aspects of these desires, needs, or wants as an individual difference or trait. The study of motivation has a rich and complex history in language learning and teaching (Al-Hoorie, 2017), albeit one that has developed quite separately from mainstream psychological research (Dörnyei & Ushioda, 2021). I use the word complex here to mean intricate and complicated, but there is a further complexity angle too, as now many conceptualizations of motivation take a complex dynamic systems approach (Dörnyei et al., 2015; Lamb, 2017; MacIntyre et al., 2017), which is grounded more generally in complexity perspectives (Davis & Sumara, 2006; Larsen-Freeman, 2017; Mason, 2008; Sampson & Pinner, 2021). Complexity perspectives, or the complexity paradigm, are loosely a set of metaphors and principles for understanding complex phenomena. They can be regarded as a conceptual toolkit for understanding the nature of dynamic interactions that are dependent on multiple factors (Davis & Sumara, 2006).

Motivation is regularly cited as a justification for using technology in the language classroom, a statement I will qualify in the next section. The assumption being that there is something perhaps *inherently* motivating about the utilization of current or new technology (Henry & Lamb, 2020; Stockwell & Reinders, 2019), either through the affordances of the technology or perhaps by virtue of its novelty for being perceived as "cutting edge." Stockwell (2013) has problematized this issue of "inherent motivation," pointing out that it is usually based on the novelty factor of the technology, which does not hold up to scrutiny in today's world of high technology penetration. Even in developing countries, many schools are finding increased access to computers, either through economic or charitable aid, as increased ICT access has been shown to help stimulate economies in poorer regions (DeWitt & Alias, 2019). Further, Stockwell (2013) points out that students rarely maintain the use of these technologies for sustained periods. Claiming that technology is inherently motivating is a clear example of technological determinism, in that it "assume [s] that technologies possess intrinsic powers that affect *all* people in *all* situations the same way" (boyd, 2014, p. 15). A further issue is that it runs the risk of applying "technology for technology's sake," which has been a long-standing criticism of the way technology is applied in education generally, and since the early 1990s this became a long-running argument in the literature on mobile-assisted language learning (MALL) and computer-assisted language learning (CALL).[1] This cautious approach to technology runs parallel to the argument of the *normalization* of technology (Bax, 2003), which posits that as technology plays such an ever increasing role in our daily lives, its presence in educational settings is also likely to remain a fixture, while at the same time becoming increasingly less novel. In fact, language teachers have long been expected to use technology in their classes (Kessler, 2006, 2007; Levy & Hubbard, 2005), and ever since the COVID-19 pandemic, this expectancy has suddenly shifted into an urgent requirement (Cheung, 2021; Ferdig et al., 2020).

In this chapter I will examine two main claims regarding technology and motivation for language learning and teaching. Firstly, the claim that technology *is* motivating in and of itself is actually worth investigation. Why is this claim often made implicitly only to be refuted? Could there perhaps be something which is inherently motivating for learners (and teachers) when it comes to using technology? Are there in fact good reasons to desire the most cutting-edge technology in classrooms, such as digital literacy, engagement, or simply as a reflection of trends in the larger society? I will discuss the connection between these issues and the acquisition of various types of capital and symbolic power, which can be seen as meta-motives for various types of social behavior (Bourdieu, 1991; Romele, 2020). Secondly, if not for some inherent reason, then what exactly is it that connects technology to motivation?

---

[1] Although this chapter is about technology and motivation in language learning and teaching, I will regularly refer to literature about CALL as this is the most common acronym for discussing the application of technologies to aid language acquisition.

Background

Technology is already having a huge impact on language, both online and offline (Pinner, 2019a). For example, a large-scale study using a corpus of millions of texts found that the number of words in daily use in the English lexicon had increased by approximately 70 percent over the fifty years prior to the study, which the researchers attributed to the increased spread of Information Communication Technology (ICT) (Michel et al., 2011). New words are always entering languages, but never at the current rate. Technology's influence has been attributed to the accelerated pace of these changes, although Van Dijk (2012) claims that rather than causing these changes, technology merely amplifies them. In other words, society's rapid shift to what Castells (1996) famously branded as the *networked society* has meant that changes in our social infrastructure are the reason new technologies are developed, and then the technology assists in working as a catalyst to further amplify the effect these changes can have on the societies or groups that have access to them. This amplifying effect may also be a useful way for us to understand the impact of technology on motivation.

Lamb (2017) provides a brief overview of some of the key themes in studies linking CALL and motivation, which are:

1. Greater autonomy and individualization
2. Enhanced opportunities for communication
3. Identity development
4. Recognizing and utilizing learners' existing IT skills.

The ability to easily create games for use in learning has also long been considered a very motivating aspect of technology (Beatty, 2013; Sundqvist, 2016).

There is also a necessary and important distinction between teachers' motivations for using technology and students' motivations (Stockwell, 2013; Stockwell & Reinders, 2019), especially if we are interested in learners' use of technology for learning and using the language outside institutional settings (Henry & Cliffordson, 2017; for a more general discussion see also Nunan & Richards, 2015). There are institutional motivations as well, with many schools and universities, as well as governments seeking to attract international students, keen to capitalize on technology's allure and the associations it brings with more efficient learning and greater motivation. As Stockwell and Reinders (2019, p. 41) note, "Technology has often been given 'black box' status, where it is expected to be able to contribute to enhanced motivation, more active engagement in learning activities, and enhanced autonomy." Later, the authors also remark that much of the research into technology and motivation focuses on short-term studies that feature merely "anecdotal" references to motivation.

Despite this long-standing association between technology and motivation, and a wealth of studies dating back to before the time when the internet was widely available, it would be natural to expect that motivation research would have been vital in understanding the affordances that digital technologies bring – sadly this is not the case (Henry & Lamb, 2020). Many of these affordances are linked to the concepts of autonomy and authenticity. Autonomy has played an equally important role in justifying technology use in the language classroom, and has a strong link with motivation (Ushioda, 2011c). Authenticity, used here to mean a sense of congruence between one's actions and beliefs (Vannini & Burgess, 2009), also has strong conceptual links to motivation, which has led me to propose that the three have a codependent relationship which I call the language impetus triad (Pinner, 2019b). The language impetus triad is particularly relevant to technology and motivation because of the affordances which link autonomy and authenticity together with motivation. It is certainly well established that many of the applications and uses of technology for language learning and teaching touch upon the overlap of these three areas.

Primary Themes

Motivating Affordances

There are an almost innumerable number of motivating affordances that are facilitated by technology and ICT (Sundqvist, 2019). Many of the discussions about technology and language teaching center around whether there is something inherently motivating about technology. Henry and Lamb (2020) link this to self-determination theory (SDT), stating that many of the communication and leisure pursuits facilitated by networked technologies provide the basic needs which lead to self-determined behavior (*autonomy*, *competence*, and *relatedness*). Previously, Henry (2013) had demonstrated this in his examination of Swedish students' use of English when playing digital games online. He described an "authenticity gap" between the prosaic and mundane aspects of the language classroom and the students' use of English for communication in online games. Games have also been used to promote motivation (Reinders, 2012), engagement and immersion (Henry & Thorsen, 2019). Ushioda (2011a) argues that certain communicative technologies are well placed for teachers and learners to personalize their learning journey around their own identities, in particular by inviting learners to discuss aspects of their real lives in order to engage with learners as people (Ushioda, 2011b). Of course, learners' individual motives are often the focus of discussions centered around motivation, but in order to truly examine them we must not ignore the wider societal levels of influence and how these affect individuals in context. The inequalities regarding access and ability with ICT in education have been referred to as "technological capital" (Hesketh & Selwyn, 1999; Selwyn, 2004), following the sociological ideas put forward in practice theory by Bourdieu (1977).

Inherent Motivation and Symbolic Power

When large technology companies release a new product, often the fact that a new product exists is marketing enough – take the adverts for something like the latest iPhone, for example. A large number of people will desire the new gadget simply because it is new or the latest model. There is an element of fashion involved with technology that cannot be denied. Having the latest technology suggests certain forms of capital that also mark out status, and not just in highly technological societies (Romele, 2020). In certain online spaces, such as the gaming social network and streaming site Twitch, users often list the specifications of their gaming rigs as part of their identity signature, so anyone who watches this user's stream can see the exact specifications of the computer they are playing on. Having the latest graphics processing unit or a powerful gaming machine is almost like a mark of rank. In these cases, the technology is fleeting, the actual item inconsequential. What is important is the currency of the devices and the status attached to their novelty or being cutting-edge. Consumerism and marketing are the true motivators here, not the actual technology itself. On the surface we could argue that such users might be motivated by technology, but the actual realities are more complex. The technology is an extension of their identities (boyd, 2014; Marwick & boyd, 2010). Their motivations are not purely individual but also feature a strong social element linked to status and Bourdieusian symbolic power in their communities. In this case specifically, technological capital as well as the cultural capital that high digital literacy brings, and increased networking capabilities that afford potentially improved social capital (Singh, Díaz Andrade, & Techatassanasoontorn, 2018).

These same issues are true at both the individual and societal levels. Just as one person might desire to have the latest technology in their possession, institutions and governments also experience a certain pressure to be "on top" of the latest trends with technology. Consider a private language school, for instance, or even a public university; both institutions seek to attract the best students and teachers to work or study at their establishments. If the facilities are poor (slow WiFi, outdated computers, lack of online learning resources, broken smartboards, etc.) then not only will the institution be unlikely to attract students, teachers also may be put off from working there. Those with desirable credentials can afford to choose where they work and study, which further adds to the prestige and social capital of the institution. In terms of workforce, this can have a big impact on the overall standing of the school when it comes to attracting funding or higher paying customers/higher achieving students. Governments, too, are under pressure from voters, who want to see their tax investments being spent on updating the resources that future generations will have at all levels of national education. Digital literacy is often equated with social mobility (Reedy & Parker, 2018), much in the same way that language literacy is (Graddol, 2006). Technology is a motivating factor here in some ways, but looking deeper it becomes clear that the underlying motivators are not something related to any actual piece of technology in and of itself, nor is it something intrinsic to the general notion of technology, but merely the idea of cutting-edge technology and its associations with the future, in particular the status attributed to it by the stakeholders. Arguments against "technology for the sake of it" are quite right in their decrying of this blind implementation of the latest digital trends, but the motivations behind it run deeper from within the social hierarchy and symbolic power structures upon which modern societies are built (Bourdieu, 1991; Tang & Yang, 2011).

Amplifying Motivation through Technology's Affordances

Although it is difficult to make broad claims about anything as complex as motivation or technology, there are certain affordances that technology provides which can certainly lead toward more meaningful and motivating types of interaction. One of the reasons for this is that technology can act as an amplifying force, as I mentioned previously in this chapter, following (Van Dijk, 2012). Technology is able to amplify language itself, through its shareability, through its connectivity, and through the participatory nature of spreadable media (Jenkins, Ford, & Green, 2013). In this way, the very motivations a learner may have for wanting to speak a language can be amplified through technology. In my years as a language teacher, a very common reason that people give for wanting to learn a foreign language is to communicate with other people in other cultures. This statement is especially true for international Lingua Francas. In super-diverse contexts where languages and cultures are constantly overlapping (Blommaert & Rampton, 2012), the motivation to communicate and to have a voice in the global community can be very powerful. If we consider that many learners' motivations for learning another language will involve some aspect of wishing to communicate with people from around the world, then it becomes clear how technologies' amplifying ability will also work on motivation. Seeking for authentic, meaningful exchanges in which we can express ourselves is what Weigert (2009) asserts to be a master motive for social interactions. Using social networking sites, for example, people can voice their opinions and meet others in online spaces, even if they live in geographically remote places (Henry, 2019; Henry et al., 2018). Thus, it is not so much the newness of the technology that promotes motivation here. As boyd (2014, p. 13) points out, "[b]ecause of their social position, what's novel for teens is not the technology but the public life that it enables." This could also be true for users of all ages, including teachers.

Recommendations for Research and Practice

In order to compose this section, I decided to reflect on my own relationship with technology in the classroom as both a teacher and a researcher. This personal approach will obviously mean less breadth in scope, but I felt that was perhaps wiser as otherwise the sheer number of opportunities would become much too unwieldly for a short chapter. There are limitless possibilities for ways that we can utilize technology to increase motivation in our teaching practice, and to use it to enhance our research. As I have pointed out, there is nothing intrinsic about any one piece of technology, yet at the same time the affordances of certain technologies certainly open up many opportunities for potentially motivating interactions, and technology's association with certain types of capital and symbolic power are also likely to provide a powerful underlying motivation for obtaining higher digital literacy and familiarity with the networked society (van Dijk & van Deursen, 2014). Whether I was aware of it or not, these social undercurrents have influenced my own decisions to employ technology in the classroom. What follows are a few of my own most successful applications.

One regular technique I have used in my classes are impromptu WebQuest searches. In short, I often ask students to conduct a quick internet search using their mobile phones in order to learn more about a subject that I have just introduced. For example, I teach English literature at a Japanese university, and students rarely have much of an existing knowledge when they come to my classes. By asking students to use their smartphones in class to learn more about a writer or text, because many search engines are personalized to the user (Baron, 2008; Van Dijk, 2012) I can engage them more actively in developing a kind of algorithmic schema, by which I mean a series of mental links that are enhanced by the localized algorithms of the students' personal browser and geolocation. For instance, when searching for Raymond Carver, my Japanese students often quickly learn that his work is translated into Japanese by Haruki Murakami. If students in another country conducted a similar search, the algorithms would hopefully provide locally contextualized results for their countries and linked to their own browsing history. This also increases the learners' agency over the learning, even if they are starting from scratch.

As my students will encounter many new and unfamiliar topics and words in their classes with me, I have uploaded all the handouts and links I use in my classes to our institutional Virtual Learning Environment (VLE, in this case Moodle). A standing homework task is for students to download the handout, print it out (or at least have it accessible on their devices) and read through it before class. This also encourages them to have checked the meaning of any new words and prepare for discussions, providing they have sufficient autonomy, motivation, and time. Even if only a handful of students do actually use this resource, at least the opportunity to prepare for class is afforded through the VLE, and accessible from anywhere where they have a networked device. In the same way, students can send me a message or ask a question in the discussion forums outside the class, in order to continue their learning beyond the allocated class time.

One of the most technological classes I teach is my Writing Workshop, which aims to get students familiar with writing a research essay. We often look at online aspects of writing, and all the students contribute to the class blog, which is publicly accessible. Knowing that the blog is published online is a powerful motivator for many of them, which they have mentioned in comments and reflections. However, this motivation is of course highly correlated with pressure, and the extrinsic factor of it being visible by others (both in and outside the class) has often been indicated as high priority motive for my students, even more so than the graded aspect. In other words, my students often care more about the social aspect of their writing than the assessment part. In the writing class, I have had some very engaging lessons using an app called Botnik, which is an AI writing tool that uses predictive text from a corpus to create new (often wacky) writing. My students have also highly enjoyed making their own memes. Memes can be seen as a lingua franca of the internet (Milner, 2016), so although this activity was designed primarily to be fun and enjoyable, I still believe there was a valid educational aspect to it as well.

In my Discussion and Presentation class, I have had students making video projects for several years. Again, students often display a lot of engagement in these activities, especially for group projects where collaboration is important. Motivation and engagement are closely connected, and engagement is generally defined as relating to what happens during an activity, whereas motivation is generally connected with reasons for doing something (Hiver et al., 2021). Students in my classes have done projects on feminism and Disney princesses, critical race theory, and other contemporary topics. One group I taught once even used their project time to raise money for a charity supporting world hunger, and they used their video to raise awareness about the issue. In many of these cases I have seen my students exhibit a great deal of autonomy, authenticity, and motivation as they engage in the task. In this way, although the technological aspect is probably not the cause of their motivation, I think it certainly helps to amplify it in some way, perhaps because of the shareable, public, and participatory nature of the final products, which are obviously affordances of the technology. This is an area that could benefit from greater research, especially if it were to incorporate inquiries into the nature of the larger societal issues underlying the implementation of technology such as technological capital and symbolic power.

Because most of the research I do is practitioner based, I have naturally focused especially on my teaching in this section. One of the notable aspects of research related to language teaching and technology is that much of it is practitioner based. With such a broad area as technology and motivation, it would be unwieldly to outline all the areas where research could continue to probe in this area though. In an autoethnographic study, I have used computer software to generate sociograms of my classroom in order to gain deeper insights into classroom dynamics (Pinner, 2021). Furthermore, the ability to log activity accurately, collect detailed usage statistics and collect rich multimodal data means that technology is not only a good site for research, it also facilitates more detailed research and data collection too. I think that technology can assist practitioner research more than it does at present, and I would be interested to see how forms of practitioner research, such as exploratory practice (Allwright & Hanks, 2009; Hanks, 2017), evidence-based reflective practice (Mann & Walsh, 2017) and action research (Banegas & Consoli, 2019; Sampson, 2018) might be utilized by teachers to enhance their own research, data collection, and analysis techniques. Furthermore, practitioner research for motivation has been strongly advocated by Ushioda (2020) as part of her ethical agenda. Other types of research might also be done outside institutional settings, such as netnographies (Kozinets, 2015) or digital ethnographies (Pink et al., 2016) looking at how people online use language in digital spaces and communities.

Future Directions

Moving on to a discussion of the future for technology and motivation, I feel that first it is important to look back to see what, if anything, has changed over the years. A few years ago, I entered a classroom in my workplace and was pleased to see a new smartboard had been installed. Not one, but two in fact, in the same room – despite most classrooms not having one. I also noted with some interest that whoever had installed the board had put next to it some ordinary whiteboard pens, which of course should not be anywhere near a smartboard as they can damage the screen and special pens are required. I wondered to myself if this was a new type of smartboard on which these ordinary pens could actually be used, but after making a quick mark I realized it wasn't. I quickly tried to erase the smudge, but it remained as a small stain.

When I returned to the room a week later for another class, I was alarmed to see that both smartboards were covered in smudgy black marks from a week's worth of classes where people had written on the boards (worth thousands of dollars) as if they were a normal whiteboard. The sheer waste was what upset me most about this, and students' fees are what paid for these now ruined smartboards. There was no smartboard training offered, and clearly even the ICT department team who had installed the board knew nothing about how to use it, otherwise there would have been some instruction or cautionary notice. In fact there were no instructions for turning it on, nor even cables to connect it. It was simply a statistic for our prospectus: This university has some smartboards. How many teachers at my institution were shown what kind of activities they can use to facilitate learning and actually motivate their learners? Was there a faculty development session for them? To my knowledge, none. For teachers, the same old problems of a lack of training and the fact that the technology is merely rolled out to classrooms for the sake of it seems to remain one of the few constants in an otherwise ever-changing world of new and novel devices and innovations. Institutions are not the only ones guilty of taking a technologically deterministic approach toward technology and motivation. Individuals (both students and teachers) are naturally drawn toward new technologies purely for the novelty and technological capital that they provide. Technology and its "black box" myth still work as a powerful attractor, and yet the main reason for technology's ability "to hold any long-term motivational value" (Stockwell & Reinders, 2019, p. 43) can often be put down to precisely this novelty and overexpectation, which is then further exacerbated by a lack of training and proper implementation.

Up until this point I have only briefly touched upon the COVID-19 pandemic and how digital technologies were brought into jarringly sharp relief as a result. The sudden need for many types of lesson to be taught online saw a massive influx in online teaching and, where language learning is involved, this is often mislabelled as CALL. Although terms like blended learning and distance learning have been used to describe the current situation of online teaching replacing in-person instruction, a more accurate description of this would be Emergency Remote Teaching (Hodges et al., 2020). Usually in such situations, neither students nor teachers are well equipped or adequately prepared for the switch in educational delivery, causing a serious impact on affective factors toward education. The reason for using technology is merely a quick fix rather than a permanent or long-lasting solution. In this sense nothing has changed with regard to technology's implantation, except for the urgency and rate of uptake.

In Japan where I teach, most classes were abruptly moved online and expected to be conducted over Zoom, as if nothing else had changed. Many teachers in my university were so technologically challenged that they did not even have PowerPoint slides for their existing lessons. Delivery of their classes was achieved (I was informed by a reliable source in the university) by them creating PowerPoints of their lessons and simply uploading them to the university VLE for students to access asynchronously. The impact of the pandemic on people's motivation to use technology in the classroom has seen a profound shift from intrinsic to extrinsic. We are now forced to use such technologies for teaching, learning, and researching in many cases. Now that the pandemic has subsided enough to return to the "new normal" of post-COVID existence, only time will tell which aspects of this sudden shift will be retained and the extent to which training and proper implementation are dealt with.

As usual, teachers are rarely given sufficient training (Hubbard & Levy, 2006), and most practitioners will continue to simply feel the pressure to use technology without really knowing why they should, or how it can actually improve their lives, regardless of whether in fact it could. This seems to be a long-standing problem surrounding technology and education more generally, and it seems unlikely to change much in the near future.

Writing this section in such uncertain times I feel might end in more conjecture, so I shall merely rely on my own experience which has led me to be rather cynical. In all my years of teaching and being a technology enthusiast with an avid interest in motivation, I have never once been offered training by any of the institutions I have worked for, nor have I been asked to give training unless I volunteered my time and suggested it myself. And this brings me to a view for the future. Just as Bax (2003) predicted, nobody would question the ubiquity and normalization of CALL, especially in the wake of the pandemic. However, it seems that calls for greater institutional support continue to be undermined or ignored. But that doesn't mean that practitioners cannot take the initiative themselves. With enhanced ICT we also see more affordances for ourselves as teachers and researchers. We can join online communities of practice, learn new skills, and share ideas with others, and we can do this under our own terms. A more long-term and interesting direction for technology and motivational research would see a shift away from a single novel application of some new technology and its temporary effects, and instead studies would do well to focus on those with a long-term vested interest in technology and how it might prove effective over time. Researchers could also turn their lenses back on themselves and conduct more introspective enquiries that examine beliefs and long-term motivations for implementing technologies, rather than how a small group of students responded to a temporary innovation. Just as motivational research more broadly is beginning to look at complexity and the interconnectedness of various factors, perhaps it is time for a more nuanced and all-encompassing look at what drives us to use technologies and what other factors besides contribute to our motivations for bringing something new into the classroom.

References

Al-Hoorie, A. H. (2017). Sixty years of language motivation research: Looking back and looking forward. *SAGE Open*, *7*(1), 1–11. https://doi.org/10.1177/2158244017701976

Allwright, D., & Hanks, J. (2009). *The developing language learner: An introduction to exploratory practice*. Palgrave Macmillan.

Banegas, D. L., & Consoli, S. (2019). Action research in language education. In J. Mckinley & H. Rose (Eds.), *The Routledge handbook of research methods in applied linguistics* (pp. 176–187). Routledge.

Baron, N. S. (2008). *Always on: Language in an online and mobile world*. Oxford University Press.

Bax, S. (2003). CALL: Past, present and future. *System*, *31*(1), 13–28.

Beatty, K. (2013). *Teaching and researching: Computer-assisted language learning* (2nd ed.). Routledge.

Blommaert, J., & Rampton, B. (2012). Language and superdiversity. MMG Working Paper (Max Planck Institute for the Study of Religious and Ethnic Diversity), *12*(05). http://pubman.mpdl.mpg.de/pubman/item/escidoc:1615144:3/component/escidoc:1615143/WP_12-09_Concept-Paper_SLD.pdf

Bourdieu, P. (1977). *Outline of a theory of practice*. Cambridge University Press.

Bourdieu, P. (1991). *Language and symbolic power*. Harvard University Press.

boyd, d. (2014). *It's complicated: The social lives of networked teens*. Yale University Press.

Castells, M. (1996). *The rise of the network society* (Vol. 1). Padstow: Blackwell.

Cheung, A. (2021). Language teaching during a pandemic: A case study of Zoom use by a secondary ESL teacher in Hong Kong. *RELC Journal, 54*(1), 55–70. https://doi.org/10.1177/0033688220981784

Davis, A. B., & Sumara, D. J. (2006). *Complexity and education: Inquiries into learning, teaching and research.* Routledge.

DeWitt, D., & Alias, N. (2019). Computers in education in developing countries: Managerial issues. In A. Tatnall (Ed.), *Encyclopedia of education and information technologies* (pp. 1–11). Springer International Publishing.

Dörnyei, Z., & Ushioda, E. (2021). *Teaching and researching: Motivation* (3rd ed.). Routledge.

Dörnyei, Z., MacIntyre, P., & Henry, A. (Eds.). (2015). *Motivational dynamics in language learning.* Multilingual Matters.

Ferdig, R. E., Baumgartner, E., Hartshorne, R., Kaplan-Rakowski, R., & Mouza, C. (2020). *Teaching, technology, and teacher education during the COVID-19 pandemic: Stories from the field.* Association for the Advancement of Computing in Education.

Gkonou, C., & Mercer, S. (2017). *Understanding emotional and social intelligence among English language teachers.* The British Council.

Graddol, D. (2006). *English next: Why global English may mean the end of "English as a foreign language."* British Council.

Hanks, J. (2017). *Exploratory practice in language teaching: Puzzling about principles and practices.* Palgrave Macmillan.

Henry, A. (2013). Digital games and ELT: Bridging the authenticity gap. In E. Ushioda (Ed.), *International perspectives on motivation* (pp. 133–155). Palgrave Macmillan.

Henry, A. (2019). Online media creation and L2 motivation: A socially situated perspective. *TESOL Quarterly, 53*(2), 372–404. https://doi.org/https://doi.org/10.1002/tesq.485

Henry, A., & Cliffordson, C. (2017). The impact of out-of-school factors on motivation to learn English: Self-discrepancies, beliefs, and experiences of self-authenticity. *Applied Linguistics, 38*(5), 713–736. https://doi.org/10.1093/applin/amv060

Henry, A., & Lamb, M. (2020). L2 motivation and digital technologies. In M. Lamb, K. Csizér, A. Henry, & S. Ryan (Eds.), *The Palgrave handbook of motivation for language learning* (pp. 599–619). Palgrave.

Henry, A., & Thorsen, C. (2019). Engagement with technology: Gaming, immersion and sub-optimal experiences. *Technology in Language Teaching & Learning, 1*(2), 52–67. https://doi.org/10.29140/tltl.v1n2.202

Henry, M., Carroll, F., Cunliffe, D., & Kop, R. (2018). Learning a minority language through authentic conversation using an online social learning method. *Computer Assisted Language Learning, 31*(4), 321–345. https://doi.org/10.1080/09588221.2017.1395348

Hesketh, A. J., & Selwyn, N. (1999). Surfing to school: The electronic reconstruction of institutional identities. *Oxford Review of Education, 25*(4), 501–520.

Hiver, P., Al-Hoorie, A. H., & Mercer, S. (Eds.). (2021). *Student engagement in the language classroom.* Multilingual Matters.

Hodges, C., Moore, S., Lockee, B., Trust, T., & Bond, A. (2020). The difference between emergency remote teaching and online learning. *Educause Review, 27,* 1–15.

Hubbard, P., & Levy, M. (Eds.). (2006). *Teacher education in CALL.* John Benjamins.

Jenkins, H., Ford, S., & Green, J. (2013). *Spreadable media: Creating value and meaning in a networked culture.* New York University Press.

Kessler, G. (2006). Assessing CALL teacher training: What are we doing and what could we do better? In P. Hubbard & M. Levy (Eds.), *Teacher education in CALL* (pp. 23–42). John Benjamins.

Kessler, G. (2007). Formal and informal CALL preparation and teacher attitude toward technology. *Computer Assisted Language Learning, 20*(2), 173–188. https://doi.org/10.1080/09588220701331394

Kozinets, R. V. (2015). *Netnography: Redefined* (2nd ed.). Sage.

Lamb, M. (2017). The motivational dimension of language teaching. *Language Teaching, 50*(3), 301–346. https://doi.org/10.1017/s0261444817000088

Larsen-Freeman, D. (2017). Complexity theory: The lessons continue. In L. Ortega & Z. Han (Eds.), *Complexity theory and language development: In celebration of Diane Larsen-Freeman* (Vol. 48, pp. 11–50). John Benjamins.

Levy, M., & Hubbard, P. (2005). Why call CALL "CALL"? *Computer Assisted Language Learning, 18*(3), 143–149. https://doi.org/10.1080/09588220500208884

MacIntyre, P., MacKay, E., Ross, J., & Abel, E. (2017). The emerging need for methods appropriate to study dynamic systems: Individual differences in motivational dynamics. In L. Ortega & Z. Han (Eds.), *Complexity theory and language development: In celebration of Diane Larsen-Freeman* (Vol. 48, pp. 97–122). John Benjamins.

Mann, S., & Walsh, S. (2017). *Reflective practice in English language teaching: Research-based principles and practices.* Routledge.

Marwick, A. E., & boyd, d. (2010). I tweet honestly, I tweet passionately: Twitter users, context collapse, and the imagined audience. *New Media & Society, 13*(1), 114–133. https://doi.org/10.1177/1461444810365313

Mason, M. (Ed.). (2008). *Complexity theory and the philosophy of education* (Vol. 40). Wiley-Blackwell.

Michel, J. B., Shen, Y. K., Aiden, A. P., Veres, A., Gray, M. K., Google Books, T., Pickett, J. P., Hoiberg, D., Clancy, D., Norvig, P., Orwant, J., Pinker, S., Nowak, M. A., & Aiden, E. L. (2011). Quantitative analysis of culture using millions of digitized books. *Science, 331*(6014), 176–182. https://doi.org/10.1126/science.1199644

Milner, R. M. (2016). *The world made meme: Public conversations and participatory media.* MIT Press.

Nunan, D., & Richards, J. C. (Eds.). (2015). *Language learning beyond the classroom.* Routledge.

Pink, S., Horst, H., Postill, J., Hjorth, L., Lewis, T., & Tacchi, J. (2016). *Digital ethnography: Principles and practice.* Springer.

Pinner, R. S. (2019a). *Augmented communication: The effect of digital devices on face-to-face interactions*. Palgrave Macmillan.

Pinner, R. S. (2019b). *Social authentication and teacher–student motivational synergy: A narrative of language teaching*. Routledge.

Pinner, R. S. (2021). The complexity lens: Autoethnography and practitioner research to examine classroom dynamics. In R. J. Sampson & R. S. Pinner (Eds.), *Complexity perspectives on researching language learner and teacher psychology* (pp. 208–233). Multilingual Matters.

Reedy, K., & Parker, J. (2018). *Digital literacy unpacked*. Facet.

Reinders, H. (Ed.). (2012). *Digital games in language learning and teaching*. Palgrave Macmillan. https://er.educause.edu/articles/2020/3/the-difference-between-emergency-remote-teaching-and-online-learning

Romele, A. (2020). Technological capital: Bourdieu, postphenomenology, and the philosophy of technology beyond the empirical turn. *Philosophy & Technology*. https://doi.org/10.1007/s13347-020-00398-4

Sampson, R. J. (2018). The feeling classroom: Diversity of feelings in instructed L2 learning. *Innovation in Language Learning and Teaching, 14*(3), 203–217. https://doi.org/10.1080/17501229.2018.1553178

Sampson, R. J., & Pinner, R. S. (Eds.). (2021). *Complexity perspectives on researching language learner and teacher psychology*. Multilingual Matters.

Selwyn, N. (2004). Reconsidering political and popular understandings of the digital divide. *New Media & Society, 6*(3), 341–362.

Singh, H., Díaz Andrade, A., & Techatassanasoontorn, A. A. (2018). The practice of ICT-enabled development. *Information Technology for Development, 24*(1), 37–62. https://doi.org/10.1080/02681102.2017.1283284

Stockwell, G. (2013). Technology and motivation in English-language teaching and learning. In E. Ushioda (Ed.), *International perspectives on motivation: Language learning and professional challenges* (pp. 156–175). Palgrave Macmillan. https://doi.org/10.1057/9781137000873_9

Stockwell, G., & Reinders, H. (2019). Technology, motivation and autonomy, and teacher psychology in language learning: Exploring the myths and possibilities. *Annual Review of Applied Linguistics, 39*, 40–51. https://doi.org/10.1017/S0267190519000084

Sundqvist, P. (2016). Gaming and young language learners. In F. Farr & L. Murray (Eds.), *The Routledge handbook of language learning and technology* (pp. 472–484). Routledge.

Sundqvist, P. (2019). The motivational affordances of ICT. In A. Henry, P. Sundqvist, & C. Thorsen (Eds.), *Motivational practice: Insights from the classroom* (pp. 187–226). Studentlitteratur.

Tang, L., & Yang, P. (2011). Symbolic power and the internet: The power of a "horse." *Media, Culture & Society, 33*(5), 675–691. https://doi.org/10.1177/0163443711404462

Ushioda, E. (2011a). Language learning motivation, self and identity: Current theoretical perspectives. *Computer Assisted Language Learning, 24*(3), 199–210. https://doi.org/10.1080/09588221.2010.538701

Ushioda, E. (2011b). Motivating learners to speak as themselves. In G. Murray, X. Gao, & T. E. Lamb (Eds.), *Identity, motivation and autonomy in language learning* (pp. 11–25). Multilingual Matters.

Ushioda, E. (2011c). Why autonomy? Insights from motivation theory and research. *Innovation in Language Learning and Teaching, 5*(2), 221–232. https://doi.org/10.1080/17501229.2011.577536

Ushioda, E. (2020). *Language learning motivation.* Oxford University Press.

van Dijk, J. (2012). *The network society* (Third ed.). Sage.

van Dijk, J. A., & van Deursen, A. J. (2014). *Digital skills: Unlocking the information society.* Palgrave Macmillan.

Vannini, P., & Burgess, S. (2009). Authenticity as motivation and aesthetic experience. In P. Vannini & J. P. Williams (Eds.), *Authenticity in culture, self, and society* (pp. 103–120). Ashgate Publishing.

Weigert, A. J. (2009). Self authenticity as master motive. In P. Vannini & J. P. Williams (Eds.), *Authenticity in culture, self, and society* (pp. 37–50). Ashgate Publishing.

Zee, M., & Koomen, H. M. Y. (2016). Teacher self-efficacy and its effects on classroom processes, student academic adjustment, and teacher well-being: A synthesis of 40 years of research. *Review of Educational Research, 86*(4), 981–1015. https://doi.org/10.3102/0034654315626801

Further Reading

Colpaert, J., & Stockwell, G. (2022). *Smart CALL: Personalization, contextualization and socialization.* Castledown.

In this book, the editors and chapter authors look at how CALL will become more effective by moving toward a "Smart" model of the learning environment, which utilizes the interconnectedness of digital devices and their ability to share data and information across platforms in a streamlined manner. The volume emphasizes the importance of personalization, contextualization, and socialization, which are linked to motivating factors.

Dörnyei, Z., & Ushioda, E. (2021). *Teaching and researching: Motivation* (3rd ed.). Routledge.

This book provides an accessible, thorough, and yet concise overview of the current field of motivation in relation to language teaching and research. It is very practical and yet misses none of the most important history nor current thought on language learning motivation. A must-have for anyone interested in the subject.

Henry, A., & Lamb, M. (2020). L2 motivation and digital technologies. In M. Lamb, K. Csizér, A. Henry, & S. Ryan (Eds.), *The Palgrave handbook of motivation for language learning* (pp. 599–619). Palgrave.

A short but extremely thorough chapter outlining the principle concerns of motivation and technology in language teaching. The book examines many of the principles that currently influence technology implementation and that provided much of the starting ground for this current chapter.

Part V

Practice

18

Learner Training

Chun Lai

Introduction

Technology is becoming part and parcel of language teaching and learning. One of the most salient and fundamental affordances technology brings to language learning is enhanced learner control. Learner control determines whether learners would proactively and effectively utilize the other affordances technology brings to language learning, such as enhanced interactivity and connectedness in learning across different spaces. However, research is piling up showing that learners, despite their increasing technological savviness, are ill prepared to make use of the freedom and control brought by technology to create optimal learning experiences (Hubbard, 2013; Shadiev & Yang, 2020; White & Bown, 2020). Thus, to fulfill the educational potential of technology for language learning, learner training is much needed.

Learner training has come to the fore of second language education since Rubin's (1975) discussion of the characteristics of good language learners. Scholars defined learner training as the teaching of the learning strategies of successful learners to poor language learners to increase their learning efficiency (e.g. Wenden, 1987). Rees-Miller (1993) questioned this strategy-oriented approach for the lack of explicit attention to motivation and affective factors. Wenden (1995) also argued for greater attention to task knowledge and highlighted that raising awareness of the purpose of a task is an essential aspect of learner training. Benson (1995) further pinpointed that discussions on learning training failed to recognize the importance of developing a critical stance toward the accepted social and ideological purposes and goals of language learning and the advocated learning methodologies, materials, and texts, and argued that enabling and supporting learners to take greater control over their learning should be the core of learner training. With the pervasiveness of technology in language teaching and learning, learner training is increasingly discussed in relation to the use of technology for language learning. Hubbard (2013, p. 164) defines learner training as "a process aimed at the construction of a knowledge and skill base that enables language learners to use technology more efficiently and effectively in support of language learning objectives than they would in the absence of such training." Researchers advocate placing learner training at the centerpiece of computer-assisted language learning (CALL) design and practices so that learners can engage effectively with both individual technological platforms and applications and the open learning spaces in the digital wild for learning purposes (Hubbard, 2019; Lai, 2018; Rashid et al., 2021; Reinders & Hubbard, 2013). The goal of learner training is not only to safeguard effective engagement with technological resources for language learning but also to support learners to exercise autonomy in language learning with technological resources. In this chapter, I situate the discussion of learner training in relation to CALL and define learner training broadly as a process that supports the development of motivational and affective resources and knowledge and skill repertoires to safeguard active and effective engagement with technological resources in language learning.

Background/Historical Perspectives

The development of learner training intertwines closely with the evolving discourse around digital natives and the discussion around learner autonomy and self-directed learning. Ever since Prensky (2001) coined the term "digital natives" to describe the generation who grows up with digital technologies and, by default, possesses sophisticated digital skills and the ability to use digital tools effectively and efficiently, researchers have started to investigate this phenomenon and its impact on education. This body of literature has, however, yielded increasing evidence suggesting that the concept of digital natives and the assumed digital sophistication might be a myth. Research studies found that these so-called digital natives or iGeneration, despite frequent use of digital technologies, do not exhibit deep knowledge of technology beyond basic technological applications and functionality (Bullen et al., 2008), and tend to use technology more for entertainment and social connection than for learning and creative work (Kennedy & Fox, 2013; Margaryan, Littlejohn, & Vojt, 2011). Refuting the myth of digital natives, Kirschner and De Bruyckere (2017) advocated not assuming the technical skills and competences that are often attributed to today's students and highlighted the necessity of helping them to develop the relevant technological, digital literacy and learning management skills that are essential for learning with technology. Similarly, in the language education field, research has shown that language learners, despite possessing basic computer literacy, are inadequately prepared both skill-wise and motivation-wise for online or hybrid learning (Goertler, Bollen, & Gaff, 2012; Mehran et al., 2017; Winke & Goertler, 2008). Moreover, scholars point out that learners may also lack the language-specific knowledge and skills, such as the awareness of embedded functions and tools within the digital platforms that are beneficial to language skill development and the effective selection and use thereof (e.g. captions in videos), lack the socio-emotional skills needed for successful and sustained interaction on online social spaces and the cognitive skills needed to benefit from the interaction, and lack the knowledge and ability necessary to perceive and act on the language learning opportunities on and across different technological spaces (Hubbard, 2013; Shadiev & Yang, 2020; Stockwell & Hubbard, 2013; Vinagre & Muñoz, 2011; White & Bown, 2020). The evolving discourse around the gap between the knowledge and skills possessed by today's students and those needed for effective use of technology for learning builds a persuasive argument for the necessity of learner training in CALL to safeguard quality interaction and learning on technological spaces.

At the same time, discussions around learner autonomy are gaining weight with the increasingly convenient access to technological resources that afford and even request learners' control over one's own learning (Reinders & White, 2016). Learner autonomy is deemed the ultimate goal of language education (Benson & Voller, 2014). Associated with this increasing attention to learner autonomy are the arguments for empowering learners to self-direct their learning, especially beyond the classroom (Giveh, Ghobadi, & Zamani, 2018; Lai, 2018). Self-directed learning with technological resources beyond the classroom is found to be essential to language learning as it is found to contribute uniquely to language skill development (Brevik, 2019; Cole & Vanderplank, 2016; Peters, 2018) and compensates the limited language experience inside the classroom (Giveh et al., 2018; Lai, 2015). However, learners are found to exhibit great variation in the frequency and quality of autonomous engagement with technological resources, which influence their gains from the experience (Lai, Hu, & Lyu, 2018; Sundqvist, 2019; Viberg & Grönlund, 2013). Learners express expectations for affective, cognitive, metacognitive, and social support from teachers and peers with regard to learner autonomy and self-directed learning beyond the classroom (Lai, Yeung, & Hu, 2016; Thornton, 2013). The developing discourse around learner autonomy and self-directed learning with technology underscores the importance of learner training in helping learners to make use of technology to create enriching and personally meaningful language learning experiences across time and space.

Primary Themes

Learner training is relevant to both the interaction with individual technological platforms/tools and the construction of personalized learning ecology with technological resources. Discussions on learner training center around two major issues: what to train and how to train.

What to Train

Learner training consists of the motivation and affective dimension and the knowledge and skill dimension (Garrison, 1997; Holec, 2009). The affective dimension includes both learners' intention to initiate the learning behavior (i.e. the entering motivation), and learners' sustained interest in the behavioral intention (i.e. the maintenance of intention) (Garrison, 1997). This dimension targets the psychological aspect of technology use, which involves psychological preparation prior to the technological activity and motivational scaffold throughout the activity (Chotipaktanasook, 2020). The goal of psychological preparation is to develop positive attitudes toward the technological activity (i.e. to help learners see the whys behind the action and internalize the necessity and value of the actions) and enhance perceived confidence of carrying out the technological activity (Hubbard, 2004; Lai, 2018). The focus of the motivational scaffold is to maintain continued investment in the CALL activity by strengthening the intrinsic drive (e.g. catering to personal interest, providing choices, and making visible the accomplishment and progress) and/ or building extrinsic motivational mechanisms (e.g. competition, award, and collaboration). Fostering an open mindset and the cognitive flexibility to deal with the uncertainties and complexity of interacting with technology is also deemed critical to maintaining learners' continued interest in using technological resources, especially in self-directed learning beyond the classroom (Kop & Fournier, 2011). The key considerations of the psychological domain of learner training is to construct and facilitate learning experiences that satisfy the three basic psychological needs for autonomous motivation: (1) the need for autonomy (i.e. the need to be the initiator of actions and obtain psychological freedom); (2) the need for competence (i.e. the need to experience a sense of confidence and accomplishment to achieve desired goals); and (3) the need for relatedness (i.e. the need to have a close and positive relationship with others and experience a sense of belonging) (Deci & Ryan, 1985).

The knowledge and skill dimension focuses on developing and supporting four aspects of technology use: the technical aspect (i.e. the what aspect, general digital literacy and familiarity with language-specific functionality); the pedagogical aspect (i.e. the why aspect, the mapping of the learning objectives within the CALL activity); the strategic aspect (i.e. the how aspect, techniques that facilitate and enhance the learning process), and the contextual aspect (i.e. the where and when aspect, learning needs, experiences, and situations in relation to the CALL activity) (Chotipaktanasook, 2020; Romeo & Hubbard, 2010). Supporting the four aspects of technology use involves both the resource component and the strategy component. Resources are multidimensional and include material resources (i.e. the online tools and platforms), mental resources (i.e. technological and social skills and knowledge), social resources (i.e. social ties and relationships), cultural and discursive resources (i.e. beliefs and shared mentalities related to behaviors), and temporal resources (i.e. time available for the behaviors) (Van Dijk, 2005). To obtain knowledge and skills related to the resource component, students need an understanding of the selection criteria for online resources and for the functional tools within the platform, of the affordances of different online resources' varying pedagogical purposes, and of what a quality learning experience entails (Beckman, Bennett, & Lockyer, 2014; Lai et al., 2018; Lai et al., 2022). Students also need social and emotional support from learning communities where they share resources obtained from various venues and ways to manage the resources (Ma, 2017). The strategy component includes various cognitive and metacognitive strategies (Giveh et al., 2018), both generic skills and the specific skills of using technology for language learning (Benson, 2013; Hubbard, 2004; Lai, 2013). Generic skills include the monitoring of various cognitive and metacognitive factors (goal setting, strategic planning, task appraisal, evaluation, and reflection), behavioral factors (effort management and help seeking), affective factors (self-efficacy, anxiety management), and environment factors (time and environment management, peer learning, management of online distractions and multitasking) for self-regulation at different phases of learning (Kirschner & De Bruyckere, 2017; Littlejohn et al., 2016; Pintrich, 2000). Generic skills also include digital and information literacy (Wineburg & McGrew, 2016). Language learning-specific strategies include the development of the metalanguage related to key issues and concepts about the nature and process of language learning, the ability to coordinate cognitive attention and resources and learning behaviors to achieve optimal language learning results, and the ability to view and interact with resources strategically to optimize incidental language learning (Hubbard, 2013; Reinders & White, 2010; White & Bown, 2020). These skills could be developed through scaffolding mechanisms such as goal lists, templates and prompts, examples of strategy utilization, and reflective assessments with metacognitive questions and feedback (Bernacki, Aguilar, & Byrnes, 2011). The strategy component also includes relevant social and communication strategies for successful interaction and learning experience in CALL (Giveh et al., 2018; Lawrence, 2013).

How to Train

Learner training could be integrated coherently into the design of individual CALL applications and activities. Scholars such as Chapelle (2001) regard having a positive impact on learners as an important consideration in the design of CALL platforms, and part of the positive impact is to give students opportunities to learn about language learning and use strategies. Cooker (2010) further proposed that components of learner strategy training need to be incorporated into the design either as a coherent piece or as parallel modules to go with the self-access learning materials. Training can also be threaded throughout a CALL activity to safeguard smooth implementation and learning. Take Bikowski and Vithanage's (2016) study on web-based collaborative writing as an example. The researchers built coherent learner training components into this CALL activity. They included a technical training component (e.g. familiarizing students with the critical features of the platform for collaborative writing and giving them opportunities to use the tools prior to the collaborative writing task) and a strategy training component (e.g. discussing ways of effective collaboration and group communication and guiding students to form individual goals on what collaborative skills they would like to personally develop during the task) prior to the collaborative writing task. During the collaborative writing task, they engaged students to keep individual e-journals or blogs to analyze their group works' strengths and weaknesses and reflect on their individual contributions to the collaborative task. After the task, they further engaged students in collective reflections on interactional conflicts and the collaboration process. Thus, different training components can be organically integrated into a CALL activity to support its smooth implementation and boost the relevant skills and strategies among learners. In addition, learner training could also be designed as a standalone intervention. The intervention could be an add-on component to a language course. For instance, Luo (2020) incorporated a MOOC course on general learning techniques (strategies against procrastination and cramming, spaced repetitions, chunking tasks, etc.) into her Spanish classes to enhance students' self-directed Spanish learning. The embedded training could also focus on language-specific cognitive and metacognitive strategies. For instance, Zenotz (2012) integrated a four-session training program on online reading strategies into undergraduate reading classes. In Lai, Shum and Tian's (2016) study, a twelve-week online training program on pedagogical rationales, resource selection strategies, and tactics for effective use of technological resources for out-of-class language learning with technological resources was organized around the development of a self-regulation feedback loop of forethought, performance, and reflection and operationalized as homework for students to study on their own. Similarly, Romeo and Hubbard (2010) adopted the format of independent student projects plus regular in-class collaborative debriefing and biweekly consultation meetings with the instructor to embed learner training as a parallel component of the course. Moreover, standalone learner training could also be achieved through language advising, where individualized, co-constructed one-on-one reflective dialogues based on learners' goals, interests, and situations are used to support learners' out-of-class exploration with technological resources for language learning and challenge their existing beliefs about language learning to transform them into "highly-aware learners" who can self-advise in the learning process (Kato & Mynard, 2016).

Techniques such as experiential learning, goal-oriented learning, reflective activities (e.g. journals, self-assessment checklists) and cooperative learning (e.g. collaborative debriefing; online communities) are commonly interweaved in various pedagogical frameworks to operationalize learner training (Dabbagh & Kitsantas, 2012; Giveh et al., 2018; Holec, 2009). Take Reinders's (2010) pedagogical framework as an example. This framework starts by identifying a learning need and setting goals and planning learning to satisfy the need, which is then followed by selecting relevant resources and learning strategies and practicing the strategies in specific tasks and monitoring the strategy through teacher and peer feedback. The framework ends with assessment and revision. Constant reflection, pair or group work, and sharing sessions are threaded throughout the whole cycle to provide cognitive and affective support to students. In the meantime, scholars have also generated some general principles for the development of learner training. To enhance students' interaction with individual CALL platforms/applications, Hubbard (2004) proposed a set of five principles of learner training. These principles are: (1) experience CALL yourself, where teachers are expected to get first-hand experience with language learning with technology in the role of students so as to achieve a better understanding of the type of support students need in the process; (2) give learners teacher training where teachers guide students to develop a reasoned understanding of what the process of language learning involves, help students link learning objectives with specific technological experiences, and guide them to plan the CALL activities; (3) use a cyclic approach, which segments training into small junctures to focus on during each training session and engages learners to experience the CALL activity first before providing detailed training; (4) use collaborative debriefings where students get together to share and reflect collectively on their experience and strategies; and (5) teach general exploitation strategies, where teachers guide students to transfer the CALL experience to other learning situations. Expanding the discussion beyond individual CALL platforms/resources, White and Bown (2020) proposed an informed consumer approach that aims at helping language learners to become informed consumers who play a proactive role in navigating and constructing a personalized language learning ecology. The informed consumer approach emphasizes developing the framework and metalanguage of optimal language learning, immersing students in experimentation with different resources and choices, engaging students in critical evaluation of the different language learning choices and opportunities in view of the framework and metalanguage of language learning, and helping students to make connections across experiences to achieve a coordinated view. Thus, in this learning context, providing learners with the opportunities for experimentation followed by critical analysis to identify CALL experiences that add value to one's existing learning is essential.

Current Research

Empirical studies have been conducted to examine the potential impact of learner training in general learning techniques on students' language learning behaviors with technology. For instance, Luo (2020) found that including four 30-minute training sessions on general learning techniques in her Spanish classes changed the students' learning behavior: the group who received the training incorporated more effective learning techniques in their interaction with the online learning platforms and showed greater course achievement, and the positive effects lasted beyond the training period. Yarahmadzehi and Bazleh (2012) also found that adding explicit training of self-directed learning techniques to normal English lessons helped enhance Iranian undergraduate students' English language skills and readiness for self-directed English learning. These studies suggested that training on general learning techniques could enhance students' self-directed language learning tendencies and skills.

Research has also investigated the effects of cognitive and metacognitive strategy training on students' interaction with individual technological resources. For instance, Zenotz (2012) developed a four-session training program on five online reading strategies, including predicting, guessing from context, activating prior knowledge, purpose of reading, and being critical. The researcher found that the undergraduate English language learners who received the strategy training exhibited greater online reading performance. Ranalli (2013) focused on web-based dictionary skills and developed a five-week training program that consisted of video presentations and text-based practice activities. Undergraduate English as a second language (ESL) students who went through the training demonstrated greater abilities to select the appropriate dictionaries and use them effectively for learning, and also reported greater enjoyment of the online texts. Gagen-Lanning (2015) trained a group of university ESL learners on cognitive and metacognitive strategies they could use when using TED talk videos for second language listening. The researcher found that, after the training, those learners used more metacognitive strategies, such as pausing and rewinding, when interacting with TED talk videos and their ability to comprehend the videos also increased. Cross (2014) reported a case study where an advanced Japanese adult English language learner was guided via weekly reflection meetings on using metatextual skills and metacognitive strategies when listening to podcasts for independent listening development outside the classroom. The learner's journal entries over the nine-week intervention indicated that her metacognitive capacities to interact with out-of-class podcast resources increased over time. Rashid and colleagues (2021) adopted Romeo and Hubbard's (2010) training framework and developed an eight-week training schedule on the technical, pedagogical, and strategic aspects of using mobile blogs outside the classroom for a group of first-year undergraduate English language learners. The researcher found the training helped the learners develop positive attitudes toward using personal blogs on smartphones to enhance English writing skills, and the quality of their writing increased over time too. All these studies suggest that training could enhance students' self-regulated use of strategies to interact effectively with individual technological resources.

Other studies have examined whether and how learner training interventions might enhance students' self-directed learning with technology beyond the classroom. Pritchard (2013) implemented a learner preparation program that focused on functions of Facebook and norms and strategies when using Facebook for language learning. The intervention consisted of four initial training sessions reinforced by repeated reminders. The researcher found that the intervention helped raise learners' awareness of the language learning potentials of Facebook and enhanced their self-initiated use of Facebook for communication and social capital development, but failed to enhance their effective language learning strategies. Mutlu and Eroz-Tuga (2013) explored the impact of a five-week explicit language learning strategy training course coupled with CALL activities on a group of university students. They found that students who received the training were more willing to take responsibility for their own learning and reported greater engagement in self-directed out-of-class language learning using technological resources. Lai, Shum, and Tian (2016) conducted a twelve-week training program that targeted undergraduate English language learners' willingness and capacities to engage in out-of-class language learning with technological resources. Pedagogical rationales, resource selection strategies, and tactics for effective use of technological resources for language learning were weaved into the training that was organized around the self-regulation feedback loop of forethought, performance and reflection. As a result of the training, students reported greater engagement in self-initiated out-of-class use of technology for language learning, and they also reported more positive attitudes and greater confidence in their abilities to make use of technological resources for language learning on their own.

In summary, the review of the existing literature on learner training in self-directed language learning with technology beyond the classroom suggests that learner training has the potential to enhance language learners' capacities to self-direct their learning and to use technological resources effectively for language learning. But at the same time, the review revealed that despite the increasing literature on how learners' interaction with individual technological resources could be enhanced through learner training, there is a paucity of research that investigates how to enhance learners' self-directed appropriation of varied online resources for language learning beyond the classroom.

Recommendations for Research and Practice

Current research on learner training has primarily been based on the examination of interventions of short duration, ranging from a few weeks to one semester. However, learner training needs to be ongoing and go beyond the elementary level (Hubbard, 2018; Tecedor & Perez, 2021). Hubbard (2018) proposed adopting a longitudinal, reiterative approach to learner training, such as action research, that engages in ongoing dialogues with students' perspectives and needs over time so as to gain an in-depth understanding of learner training. Moreover, researchers call for research that adopts dynamic approaches to examining the training needs of learners at different developmental stages. For instance, Hubbard (2018) conceptualized that learners at the earlier stage of language learning might benefit more from technical and strategic training, whereas learners with more language learning experience might benefit more from pedagogical training. Tecedor and Perez (2021) further pointed out that the conduit and format of training might need to vary for learners at different proficiency levels due to different training needs.

The omnipresence of information and resources mediated by technology is playing an ever-increasing role in shifting learning toward informality and self-directedness (Bonk, Kim, & Xu, 2019). Research on learner training needs to expand to the informal learning context. Most of the research on learner training has been conducted in instructional contexts where learner training is implemented as part of a class and learners' interaction with technological platforms and the concomitant affective and cognitive outcomes during the class are analyzed. Not many studies have examined how the observed interaction might evolve, over time, with similar technological resources in the self-directed informal learning contexts and how to structure learner training in ways that would enhance learners' likelihood of utilizing the knowledge and skills in informal learning contexts. Even fewer studies have examined learner training or informal mentoring that naturally occurs in the informal learning contexts, especially online interest communities (see Aragon & Davis, 2019 for an example), and explored how features from informal mentoring/training might be borrowed to strengthen learner training in the instructional contexts.

Moreover, although scholars like Hubbard (2004, 2018) have underscored the importance of basing learner training on an understanding of learner perspectives, most learner training programs have stopped short of defining training needs based on the challenges learners may encounter. Existing intervention studies have primarily adopted a one-size-fits-all strategy-centric approach that focuses on expanding and strengthening learners' strategy inventory of relevant cognitive, metacognitive, affective and social strategies. Such an approach might be effective in enhancing learners' self-regulated interaction with individual technological platforms but may not be sufficient to extend the impact to the out-of-class learning contexts because it fails to take into account the interest-driven and personalized nature of out-of-class language learning (Lai, 2018; Underwood, Luckin & Winters, 2012). To expand the impact to the out-of-class context, which is characterized by interest-driven experiences (Barron, 2004), students' interest should be the starting point of learner training (Cabot, 2014; Lai, 2018). Given that the ultimate goal of learner training is to enhance learners' effective interaction with technological resources not just inside the classroom but also beyond the classroom in self-initiated informal learning contexts, a learner-centric approach to learner training is needed. Such a learner-centric training approach highlights the personalization of the training, with the specificity of the strategy training being determined by personal interest and self-determined personal goals so as to support self-initiated interest-driven personal inquiry (Benson, 2016). But at the same time, such an approach would also group students into communities of learners based on common interests and personally meaningful problems to support collaborative inquiries (Dabbagh & Kitsantas, 2012; Henry, 2013).

Future Directions

Learner training is gaining increasing attention in the CALL field. The overview of this research field reveals that current research efforts on learner training have focused primarily on examining the efficacy of learner training programs, mostly the effectiveness of metacognitive and cognitive strategy training on learners' performance in CALL activities in the instructional context. More research into the interaction of contextual factors within learner training (e.g. learner characteristics, learning context characteristics) is needed to provide a more fine-grained understanding of learner training development and implementation. One contextual factor is the technological platform design. Well-designed technological platforms might reduce the demand for learner training. How design features might interact with the demand and the efficacy of learner training is an issue that deserves exploration. Moreover, longitudinal studies of learner training and its impact on students' learning behaviors with technology during and beyond the class in the instructional context and their subsequent learning behaviors in informal learning spaces over time are needed to provide in-depth insights into the lasting impact of learner training. The research field also needs more insights into issues around learner training on self-directed language learning with technology in informal learning contexts. Current practices on learner training, with the only exception of language advising, have primarily adopted a universal approach where all the students get the same training. More differentiated approaches to learner training may need to be adopted, where individual learners' interests and needs are integrated into the training experience, so that learners are more likely to transfer the attitudinal and capacity gains obtained from the experience to self-initiated informal learning contexts to achieve a broader and lasting impact.

References

Aragon, C., & Davis, K. (2019). *Writers in the secret garden: Fanfiction, youth, and new forms of mentoring.* MIT Press.

Barron, B. (2004). Learning ecologies for technological fluency in a technology-rich community. *Journal of Educational Computing Research, 31,* 1–37.

Beckman, K., Bennett, S., & Lockyer, L. (2014). Understanding students' use and value of technology for learning. *Learning, Media and Technology, 39*(3), 346–367. https://doi.org/10.1080/17439884.2013.878353

Benson, P. (1995). A critical view of learner training. *Learning Learning 2*(2), 2–6.

Benson, P. (2013). Learner autonomy. *TESOL Quarterly, 47,* 839–843. https://doi.org/10.1002/tesq.134

Benson, P. (2016). Learner autonomy. In G. Hall (Ed.). *The Routledge handbook of English language teaching* (pp. 339–352). Routledge. http://dx.doi.org/10.4324/9781315676203-29

Benson, P., & Voller, P. (2014). *Autonomy and independence in language learning.* Routledge.

Bernacki, M. L., Aguilar, A. C., & Byrnes, J. P. (2011). Self-regulated learning and technology-enhanced learning environments: An opportunity-propensity analysis. In G. Dettori & D. Persico (Eds.). *Fostering self-regulated learning through ICT* (pp. 1–26). IGI Global.

Bikowski, D., & Vithanage, R. (2016). Effects of web-based collaborative writing on individual L2 writing development. *Language Learning & Technology, 20*(1), 79–99.

Bonk, C. J., Kim, M., & Xu, S. (2019). Do you have a SOLE?: Research on informal and self-directed online learning environments. In J. M. Spector, B. B. Lockee & M. D. Childress (Eds.), *Learning, design, and technology: An international compendium of theory, research, practice and policy* (pp. 1–32). Springer. https://doi .org/10.1007/978-3-319-17727-4_35-1

Brevik, L. M. (2019). Gamers, surfers, social media users: Unpacking the role of interest in English. *Journal of computer assisted learning, 35*(5), 595–606. https:// doi.org/10.1111/jcal.12362

Bullen, M., Morgan, T., Belfer, K., & Qayyum, A. (2008, October). The digital learner at BCIT and implications for an e-strategy. Paper presented at the 2008 Research Workshop of the European Distance Education Network (EDEN), Researching and promoting access to education and training: The role of distance education and e-learning in technology-enhanced environments. https://app.box.com/shared/fxqyutottt.

Cabot, M. (2014). English as a foreign language and technological artefacts in school and out of school (unpublished master's thesis). University College Stord, Haugesund, Norway.

Chapelle, C. (2001). *Computer applications in second language acquisition.* Cambridge: Cambridge University Press.

Chotipaktanasook, N. (2020). CALL learner training: From theory and research to informed practice. วารสาร สห ศาสตร์ ศรีปทุม ชลบุรี *[Interdisciplinary Sripatum Chonburi Journal (ISCJ)], 6*(1), 33–44.

Cole, J., & Vanderplank, R. (2016). Comparing autonomous and class-based learners in Brazil: Evidence for the present-day advantages of informal, out-of-class learning. *System, 61*, 31–42. https://doi.org/10.1016/j.system.2016.07.007

Cooker, L. (2010). Some self-access principles. *Studies in Self-Access Learning Journal, 1*, 5–9.

Cross, J. (2014). Promoting autonomous listening to podcasts: A case study. *Language Teaching Research, 18*(1), 8–32. https://doi.org/10.1177/ 1362168813505394

Dabbagh, N., & Kitsantas, A. (2012). Personal learning environments, social media, and self-regulated learning: A natural formula for connecting formal and informal learning. *The Internet and higher education, 15*(1), 3–8. https:// doi.org/10.1016/j.iheduc.2011.06.002

Deci, E. L., & Ryan, R. M. (1985). The general causality orientations scale: Self-determination in personality. *Journal of Research in Personality, 19*, 109–134. https://doi.org/10.1016/0092-6566(85)90023-6

Gagen-Lanning, K. (2015). The effects of metacognitive strategy training on ESL learners' self-directed use of TED Talk videos for second language listening (unpublished master's thesis). Iowa State University.

Garrison, D. R. (1997). Self-directed learning: Toward a comprehensive model. *Adult Education Quarterly, 48*, 18–33. https://doi.org/10.1177/074171369704800103

Giveh, F., Ghobadi, M., & Zamani, Z. (2018). Self-directed learning in L2 acquisition: A review of theory, practice, and research. *Journal of Language Teaching and Research, 9*(6), 1335–1343.

Goertler, S., Bollen, M., & Gaff Jr., J. (2012). Students' readiness for and attitudes toward hybrid FL instruction. *Calico Journal, 29*(2), 297–320.

Henry, A. (2013). Digital games and ELT: Bridging the authenticity gap. In E. Ushioda (Ed.), *International perspectives on motivation: Language learning and professional challenges* (pp. 133–155). Palgrave Macmillan.

Holec, H. (2009). Autonomy in language learning: A single pedagogical paradigm or two. In F. Kjisik, P. Voller, N. Aoki & Y. Nakata (Eds.), *Mapping the terrain of learner autonomy: Learning environments, learning communities and identities* (pp. 21–47). Hong Kong University Press.

Hubbard, P. (2004). Learner training for effective use of CALL. In S. Fotos & C. M. Browne (Eds.), *New perspectives on CALL for second language classrooms* (pp. 45–68). Lawrence Erlbaum Associations.

Hubbard, P. (2013). Making a case for learner training in technology enhanced language learning environments. *CALICO Journal, 30*(2), 163–178.

Hubbard, P. (2018). Learner training. In J. I. Liontas (Ed.), *The TESOL encyclopedia of English language teaching* (pp. 1–6). Wiley. https://doi.org/10.1002/9781118784235.eelt0418

Hubbard, P. (2019). Five keys from the past to the future of CALL. *International Journal of Computer-Assisted Language Learning and Teaching, 9*(3), 1–13. https://doi.org/10.4018/IJCALLT.2019070101

Kato, S., & Mynard, J. (2016). *Reflective dialogue: Advising in language learning.* Routledge

Kennedy, D. M., & Fox, R. (2013). "Digital natives": An Asian perspective for using learning technologies. *International Journal of Education and Development using ICT, 9*(1), 65–79.

Kirschner, P. A., & De Bruyckere, P. (2017). The myths of the digital native and the multitasker. *Teaching and Teacher Education, 67*, 135–142. https://doi.org/10.1016/j.tate.2017.06.001

Kop, R., & Fournier, H. (2011). New dimensions to self-directed learning in an open networked learning environment. *International Journal of Self-Directed Learning, 7*(2), 1–18.

Lai, C. (2013). A framework for developing self-directed technology use for language learning. *Language Learning & Technology, 17*(2), 100–122.

Lai, C. (2015). Perceiving and traversing in-class and out-of-class learning: Accounts from foreign language learners in Hong Kong. *Innovation in Language Learning and Teaching, 9*(3), 265–284. https://doi.org/10.1080/17501229.2014.918982

Lai, C. (2018). *Autonomous language learning with technology: Beyond the classroom.* Bloomsbury Publishing.

Lai, C., Hu. X., & Lyu, B. N. (2018). Understanding the nature of learners' out-of-class language learning experience with technology. *Computer Assisted Language Learning, 31*(1), 114–143. https://doi.org/10.1080/09588221.2017.1391293

Lai, C., Shum, M., & Tian, Y. (2016). Enhancing learners' self-directed use of technology for language learning: The effectiveness of an online training platform. *Computer Assisted Language Learning*, *29*(1), 40–60. https://doi.org/10.1080/09588221.2014.889714

Lai, C., Yeung, Y., & Hu, J. J. (2016). University student and teacher perceptions of teacher roles in promoting autonomous language learning with technology outside the classroom. *Computer Assisted Language Learning*, *29*, 703–723. https://doi.org/10.1080/09588221.2015.1016441

Lai, C., Liu, Y., Hu, J. J., Benson, P., & Lyu, B. N. (2022). Association between the characteristics of out-of-class technology-mediated language experience and L2 vocabulary knowledge. *Language Learning & Technology*, *26*(3), 1–24.

Lawrence, G. (2013). A working model for intercultural learning and engagement in collaborative online language learning environments. *Intercultural Education*, *24*(4), 303–314. https://doi.org/10.1080/14675986.2013.809247

Littlejohn, A., Hood, N., Milligan, C., & Mustain, P. (2016). Learning in MOOCs: Motivations and self-regulated learning in MOOCs. *The Internet and Higher Education*, *29*, 40–48. https://doi.org/10.1016/j.iheduc.2015.12.003

Luo, B. (2020). The influence of teaching learning techniques on students' long-term learning behavior. *Computer Assisted Language Learning*, *33*(4), 388–412. https://doi.org/10.1080/09588221.2019.1567557

Ma, Q. (2017). Technologies for teaching and learning L2 vocabulary. In C. A. Chapelle & S. Sauro (Eds.), *The handbook of technology and second language teaching and learning* (pp. 45–61). John Wiley & Sons.

Margaryan, A., Littlejohn, A., & Vojt, G. (2011). Are digital natives a myth or reality? University students' use of digital technologies. *Computers & Education*, *56*(2), 429–440. https://doi.org/10.1016/j.compedu.2010.09.004

Mehran, P., Alizadeh, M., Koguchi, I., & Takemura, H. (2017). Are Japanese digital natives ready for learning English online? A preliminary case study at Osaka University. *International Journal of Educational Technology in Higher Education*, *14*(1), 1–17. https://doi.org/10.1186/s41239-017-0047-0

Mutlu, A., & Eroz-Tuga, B. (2013). The role of computer-assisted language learning (CALL) in promoting learner autonomy. *Eurasian Journal of Educational Research*, *51*, 107–122.

Peters, E. (2018). The effect of out-of-class exposure to English language media on learners' vocabulary knowledge. *International Journal of Applied Linguistics*, *169*(1), 142–168.

Pintrich, P. R. (2000). Multiple goals, multiple pathways: The role of goal orientation in learning and achievement. *Journal of Educational Psychology*, *92*(3), 544–555. https://doi.org/10.1037/0022-0663.92.3.544

Prensky, M. (2001). Digital natives, digital immigrants part 2: Do they really think differently? *On the Horizon*, *9*(6), 1–6.

Prichard, C. (2013). Training L2 learners to use Facebook appropriately and effectively. *CALICO Journal*, *30*(2), 204–225.

Ranalli, J. (2013). Online strategy instruction for integrating dictionary skills and language awareness. *Language Learning & Technology, 17*(2), 75–99. http://dx .doi.org/10125/44325

Rashid, S., Howard, J., Cunningham, U., & Watson, K. (2021). Learner training in MALL: A Pakistani case study. *Innovation in Language Learning and Teaching, 15*(2), 181–194. https://doi.org/10.1080/17501229.2020.1737076

Rees-Miller, J. (1993). A critical appraisal of learner training: Theoretical bases and teaching implications. *TESOL Quarterly, 27*(4), 679–689.

Reinders, H. (2010). Towards a classroom pedagogy for learner autonomy: A framework of independent language learning skills. *Australian Journal of Teacher Education (Online), 35*(5), 40–55.

Reinders, H., & Hubbard, P. (2013). CALL and learner autonomy: Affordances and constraints. In M. Thomas, H. Reinders, & M. Warschauer (Eds.), *Contemporary computer assisted language learning* (pp. 359–375). Bloomsbury Publishing.

Reinders, H., & White, C. (2010). The theory and practice of technology in materials development and task design. In N. Harwood (Ed.), *Materials in ELT: Theory and practice* (pp. 58–80). Cambridge University Press.

Reinders, H., & White, C. (2016). 20 years of autonomy and technology: How far have we come and where to next? *Language Learning & Technology, 20*(2), 143–154. http://dx.doi.org/10125/44466

Romeo, K., & Hubbard, P. (2010). Pervasive CALL learner training for improving listening proficiency. In M. Levy, F. Blin, C. B. Siskin, & O. Takeuchi (Eds.). *Routledge studies in computer assisted language learning* (pp. 215–229). Routledge.

Rubin, J. (1975). What the "good language learner" can teach us. *TESOL Quarterly, 9*, 41–51.

Shadiev, R., & Yang, M. (2020). Review of studies on technology-enhanced language learning and teaching. *Sustainability, 12*(2), 524–545.

Stockwell, G., & Hubbard, P. (2013). Some emerging principles for mobile-assisted language learning. The International Research Foundation for English Language Education. www.tirfonline.org/english-in-the-workforce/mobile-assisted-language-learning

Sundqvist, P. (2019). Commercial-off-the-shelf games in the digital wild and L2 learner vocabulary. *Language Learning & Technology, 23*(1), 87–113. https://doi .org/10125/44674

Tecedor, M., & Perez, A. (2021). Perspectives on flipped L2 classes: Implications for learner training. *Computer Assisted Language Learning, 34*(4), 506–527, https://doi.org/10.1080/09588221.2019.1626439

Thornton, K. (2010). Supporting self-directed learning: A framework for teachers. *Language Education in Asia, 1*(1), 158–177. https://dx.doi.org/10.5746/LEiA/ 10/V1/A14/Thornton

Thornton, K. (2013). Supporting self-directed learning: A framework for teachers. In R. Stroupe and K. Kimura (Eds.), *Research and practice in English language teaching in Asia* (pp. 59–77). LEiA.

Underwood, J., Luckin, R., & Winters, N. (2012). Managing resource ecologies for mobile, personal and collaborative self-directed language learning. *Procedia – Social and Behavioral Sciences, 34*, 226–229.

Van Dijk, J. A. G. M. (2005). *The deepening divide: Inequality in the information society*. Sage Publications.

Viberg, O., & Grönlund, Å. (2013). Cross-cultural analysis of users' attitudes toward the use of mobile devices in second and foreign language learning in higher education: A case from Sweden and China. *Computers & Education, 69*, 169–180. https://doi.org/10.1016/j.compedu.2013.07.014

Vinagre, M., & Muñoz, B. (2011). Computer-mediated corrective feedback and language accuracy in telecollaborative exchanges. *Language Learning & Technology, 15*(1), 72–103.

Wenden, A. (1987). Conceptual background and utility. In A. Wenden & J. Rubin (Eds.), *Learner strategies in language learning* (pp. 3–13). Prentice Hall.

Wenden, A. L. (1995). Learner training in context: A knowledge-based approach. *System, 23*(2), 183–194.

White, C., & Bown, J. (2020). Encouraging learners to become better-informed consumers of L2 learning opportunities. *Language Teaching Research Quarterly, 19*, 5–18. https://doi.org/10.32038/ltrq.2020.19.01

Wineburg, S., & McGrew, S. (2016). Why students can't Google their way to the truth. *Education Week, 36*(11), 22–28.

Winke, P., & Goertler, S. (2008). Did we forget someone? Students' computer access and literacy for CALL. *CALICO Journal, 25*(3), 482–509. https://doi.org/10.1558/cj.v25i3.482-509

Yarahmadzehi, N., & Bazleh, E. E. (2012). The effects of applying Betts' autonomous learner model on Iranian students. *Studies in Self-Access Learning Journal, 3*(3), 310–321. https://doi.org/10.37237/030307

Zenotz, V. (2012). Awareness development for online reading. *Language Awareness, 21*(1–2), 85–100. https://doi.org/10.1080/09658416.2011.639893

Further Reading

Hubbard, P. (2018). Learner training. In J. I. Liontas (Ed.), *The TESOL encyclopedia of English language teaching* (pp. 1–6). Wiley. https://doi.org/10.1002/9781118784235.eelt0418

In this contribution to the encyclopedia, Hubbard discusses the competence learners need to master in order to harness the power of technology for language learning and the skills learners are found to be lacking. Based on the discussion, Hubbard introduces guidelines on how teachers can support learners to develop relevant competence.

Lai, C. (2018). *Autonomous language learning with technology: Beyond the classroom*. Bloomsbury Publishing.

In this book, Lai synthesizes the existing theoretical frameworks related to autonomous language learning with technology beyond the classroom and reviews empirical studies related to the nature of self-directed out-of-class language learning with technology and its influencing factors. Based on the review, Lai discusses how autonomous language learning with technology can be enhanced through the perspective of learner training, teaching practice, and design.

White, C., & Bown, J. (2020). Encouraging learners to become better-informed consumers of L2 learning opportunities. *Language Teaching Research Quarterly, 19*, 5–18.

In this article, White and Bown introduce the concept of informed consumers, underscoring a list of key competences that students need to develop in order to actively and effectively construct language learning experience across boundaries. They highlight the importance of developing learners' awareness of formal and informal learning environments and enhancing learners' ability to appraise and optimize opportunities for learning.

19

Digital Media and Interculturality

Julie Choi, Rhett Loban, and Sue Ollerhead

Introduction

Culture is a highly encompassing and complex concept (Peterson, 1979). When thinking about representations of culture, a whole host of images might come to mind. A piece of art in a gallery, a dish served at a local restaurant, or perhaps a social custom often practiced by a community. However, culture can also be much deeper and philosophically influential. Culture could be a set of principles that govern an entire society (Daniell, 2014), it could determine how individuals make defining life choices (Yates & de Oliveira, 2016), or it could even be spiritual and metaphysical understandings of the world attached to the physical landscape itself (Eck, 2012). Culture is conceptually far reaching and at times long-standing, but culture also shifts and changes according to the people that uphold the culture and according to the communities in which the cultures are developed.

The onset of the twenty-first century has promoted shifts in communities and cultures around the globe, but in addition it has prompted the proliferation of digital media and their consumption on various platforms such as YouTube (Ortiz-Ospina, 2019). Digital media provide new avenues to represent culture for many marginalized communities as well as opportunities to develop digitally based pedagogies to teach about such cultures. This chapter examines the intersection between culture, digital media, and pedagogy through the exploration of several pieces of digital media centered around Indigenous Australian culture used as classroom resources. The design approach of these pieces of digital media emphasizes a culturally centered framework where cultural protocols, community, and learning from place or country are at the center of the design process. However, before exploring the Indigenous Australian digital media, we must first explore background information and relevant theoretical concepts.

Background

Interculturality in Education

Since the start of the twenty-first century, scholars in the field of applied linguistics and language education have increasingly shifted their understandings of language in terms of system, cognition, and form to focus on the idea of language as a practice "to explain how communication works in contact zones" (Canagarajah, 2013, p. 27). Language, through this lens of practice, is understood as dynamic, emergent, fluid, flexible, and contingent (Choi & Ollerhead, 2018; García & Kleyn, 2016). Such understandings have opened up rich insights into the complexities of multilingual and intercultural communication in, as mentioned earlier, "contact zones" (Pratt, 2002), where languages and cultures come together, often in contexts of conflict and misunderstanding, characterized by unequal power relationships. Just as languages are thought to be emergent in interactions, scholars in fields such as intercultural communication and education also conceive of the notion of culture as produced through intercultural exchanges. Following Dervin (2016) we use the term interculturality with "the suffix -ality, which translates as a 'something in the making' rather than 'the adjective-turned-into-a-noun the intercultural'" (p. 1) in order to avoid falling into the trap of understanding this dynamic point of view in static or prescribed ways.

The term "intercultural competence" can be contentious as competence not only suggests an end point (a level of mastery) but also suggests that teacher educators, or certain groups of people, have the knowledge and skills that can make students competent. In an increasingly complex, cosmopolitan world created through transcultural flows (Pennycook, 2007), complex intersectionalities (Block & Corona, 2016), and where "flows of information, media symbols and images, and political and cultural ideas are constant and relentless" (Rizvy, 2009, p. 265), we cannot pass on a foolproof toolkit that will guarantee success in future scenarios. Intercultural (or cosmopolitan) learning is not, as Global Studies in Education scholar Fazal Rizvy (2009) states, so much about "imparting knowledge and developing attitudes and skills for understanding other cultures per se, but ... [about] helping students examine the ways in which global processes are creating conditions of economic and cultural exchange that are transforming our identities and communities" (p. 266). Similarly, in relation to students learning about interculturality in educational contexts, Dervin (2016) also suggests "in a world where racism, different kinds of discrimination, and injustice are on the rise, time spent at school should contribute effectively to prepare students to be real interculturalists who can question these phenomena and act critically, ethically and responsively" (p. 2). Summarizing Dervin's perspective of interculturality, Holliday (2012) states, and we concur, that interculturality is best understood as "a reflexive and uncertain digging beneath the surface of discourses and politics – as an elusive quality to be searched for and researched rather than to be achieved as a result of staged intercultural learning" (p. 46).

Drawing on digital media created in and for the Australian context by one of the authors (Loban) of this chapter, we aim to show how such dimensions of interculturality can be manifested in contexts of teaching and learning through the creation and playing of Indigenous cultural games. In keeping with the critical indigenous research methodologies (CIRM) framework (Brayboy et al., 2012), which comprises the concepts of "relationality," "responsibility," "respect," and "reciprocity," that Loban draws on in designing an Indigenous cultural game (Loban, 2021b), we hope to show the possibilities and challenges of opening up intercultural exchange and understanding through digital technology.

To contextualize these ideas, in the next section we outline how intercultural understanding is understood in the Australian curriculum. Then, we explain the four R's of CIRM, drawing on Brayboy et al.'s (2012) explanations, and how these concepts not only bring into creation interculturally produced digital media that students can engage with, but are also exceptional exemplars of digital media that engage students in developing their own intercultural understandings through exploration and discussion with educators and peers. While the examples we describe in the "current research and practice" section have been designed by Loban, an expert digital media designer, we believe that the cultural design approaches outlined below can apply to the designing of intercultural pedagogical tasks that may or may not involve digital technology. Furthermore, given that many schools and other educational institutions around the world are already placing great emphasis on providing students with skills to create their own digital resources, a focus on design is neither far-off nor far-fetched.

Primary Themes

Intercultural Understanding in the Australian Curriculum as Viewed through the CIRM Framework

As Australia becomes more culturally and linguistically diverse, the development of intercultural understanding, defined in the Australian Curriculum as the "development of skills, behaviours and dispositions as well as drawing on students' growing knowledge, understanding and critical awareness of their own and others' cultural perspectives" (ACARA, 2021), is an important general capability of all students (and teachers). This capability consists of three interrelated elements, "recognizing culture and developing respect," "interacting and empathizing with others," and "reflecting on intercultural experiences and taking responsibility" (ACARA, 2021). While such elements may seem reasonable enough, when we apply the lens of the four Rs, relationality, responsibility, respect, and reciprocity, of the CIRM framework, we begin to see a static and essentialist conception of "culture" and "difference" scholars warn us against. We outline a brief explanation of the four Rs below.

The Four Rs

"Relationality" refers to knowledge not owned by an individual or based on objective truths. The production of knowledge is relational and subjective. Researchers are encouraged to "be who they are while engaged actively as participants in the research process that creates new knowledge and trans- forms who they are and where they are" (Weber-Pillwax, 2001, p. 174). With a strong emphasis on the process of relationship-building, researchers start their work with cultural protocols for conducting research. These are

> communities [that] must be approached, permission must be granted, and research must be engaged in with benevolent intent, taking into account generations past, present and future. The research itself is also conducted with a particular sense of humility; every legitimate relationship necessitates the discarding of egos and requires the researcher to recognize the responsibilities that emerge from the relationship.
>
> *(Brayboy et al., 2012, p. 437)*

"Responsibility" refers to the need to think about how researchers' actions, decisions, and roles have long-term effects on those involved in the research which may include human and nonhuman entities such as people, animals, and places, as well as the ideas that are part of the research process. Which ideas and, how ideas are produced, and what consequences these ideas have on the lives and spaces involved matter greatly. Mutual and ongoing "respect" lies at the core of building relationships and is conceived as emerging from engaging in relationships and responsibilities. The last element, "reciprocity," denotes researchers' efforts to "pay it forward" by giving back to those involved in the research so that all those involved may continue to survive and thrive (Brayboy et al., 2012).

Deconstructing "Intercultural Understanding" through a CIRM Lens

In "recognizing culture and developing respect," the first element of the Australian Curriculum's Intercultural Understanding framework, the notion of "culture" denotes a given, pre-established and bounded object that is out there for us to step into. Students are expected to "recognise and appreciate differences between people and respect another person's point of view" (ACARA, 2021). The development of respect is not presented as an emergent process that happens through the ongoing care and responsibilities we have as we gradually build our relationships. In "interacting and empathizing with others," the second element of the framework, students "imagin[e] what it might be like to "walk in another's shoes" and identify with others' feelings, situations and motivations" (ACARA, 2021). There is little description here that reflects a relational process in developing mutual empathy and respect for each other, but a process we step into prepared to empathize with others/the Other through our interactions. The boundaries between the self and others are distinctly drawn. Finally, the ready-made notion of culture as something "out there" marked with boundaries between self and other, and an omission of a relational understanding are reflected in the final element, "reflecting on intercultural experiences and taking responsibility." In this element, "students use reflection to better understand the actions of individuals and groups in specific situations and how these are shaped by culture. They are encouraged to reflect on their own behaviours and responses to intercultural encounters and to identify cultural influences that may have contributed to these" (ACARA, 2021).

There is no sense of dialogue, consultation, or collaboration here. Furthermore, where "responsibility" is concerned, the curriculum states: "Students learn to 'stand between cultures,' reconcile differing cultural values and perspectives and take responsibility for their own behaviours and their interactions with others within and across cultures" (ACARA, 2021). Responsibility is centered on one's behaviors without an understanding of the relational nature in which ideas are generated by certain ways of thinking, knowing, being, and becoming that have real and long-lasting consequences in different communities.

"Intercultural understanding," seen through this lens, is thus "predicated on essentialist conceptions of culture, rather than within a pedagogically open framework that explores the dynamics of cultural interactions in an ongoing fashion" which according to Rizvy (2009) renders any amount of intercultural education as unhelpful (p. 267). A divisional understanding of self/other (or Self/Other) is a long way away from coming to understand this thing called "culture" as something invented, made up in the dynamic processes of our intercultural relations, and ontologically connected to human and non-human entities. The "backwards and forwards, deep-digging and indeed political process [that] contributes to a deCentred interculturality that finds Self in Other and Other in Self as implied by Dervin (2016)" (Holliday, 2021, p. 194) requires new ways of learning about interculturality.

In the following section, we outline four cultural design approaches to show how interculturality underpinned by the overall values or virtues in the four Rs can be experienced through digital media (see also Loban, 2021a for an extended discussion on the relationship between his creations and the four Rs).

Current Research and Practice

Cultural Design Approaches and Digital Media Exemplars for Experiencing Interculturality

There are several approaches to cultural design of digital media and these approaches will vary depending on the media and the type of cultural story and content educators want to communicate. Approaches may vary depending on educators' own position in relation to the culture and their access to the culture of a particular community. In this chapter, we examine four pieces of cultural digital media created by one of the authors (Loban, the media creator) and identify several different cultural design approaches during the development of the digital media. The media creator grouped these cultural design processes into four categories: a shared cultural design approach, a personal cultural design approach, a community cultural design approach, and an external cultural design approach.

Shared Cultural Design Approach

In a shared cultural design approach, the content creator draws upon shared knowledge from their home environment, nation, country, or place to inform the cultural design and content of the digital media. There have been academic discussions about shared cultural identities, heritage, and histories that are sometimes in dispute (Chong, 2012; Hall, 2020; Van Gorp & Renes, 2007) within communities. Nonetheless, this cultural design approach has the utility to communicate the broad and shared knowledge of a culture to an audience. This knowledge could include historical cultural stories, or modern-day cultural practices, and this knowledge may differ from person to person. However, the knowledge remains as distinctly shared cultural knowledge of a people.

An example of a shared cultural design approach is illustrated in the development of a digital escape room based on Torres Strait stories the creator learned from childhood into adulthood. The escape room communicates elements of cultural stories appreciated and shared within the Torres Strait community. In this cultural reimagined story, the players encounter a Dogai (Gela, 1993; Lawrie, 1970), a typically malevolent shapeshifting spirit who takes one's place in the island world and banishes the player to an underwater cavern. The player must escape by approaching various denizens of the cavern and obtain passwords from them by completing tasks related to Torres Strait knowledge. Embedded in these different tasks is knowledge related to astronomy, geography, and stories that are shared by the Torres Strait community. Each task leveraged Google Forms as a way for students to input their answers, which provided a password to progress to the next task (Figure 19.1 provides an example of a story task and related questions). In this instance, the shared cultural design process focuses on a group or region, that is, the Torres Straits, and communicates knowledge that is shared among Torres Strait Islanders.

This instance of digital media heavily emphasizes "Relationality" of knowledge as that which is shared among Torres Straits Islanders rather than belonging to any one Torres Strait person (Brayboy et al., 2012). These stories are constantly evolving and, with "responsibility" and "respect" to the shared community knowledge, such stories and knowledge can be expressed through various contemporary media including art, song, dance, and now digital media.

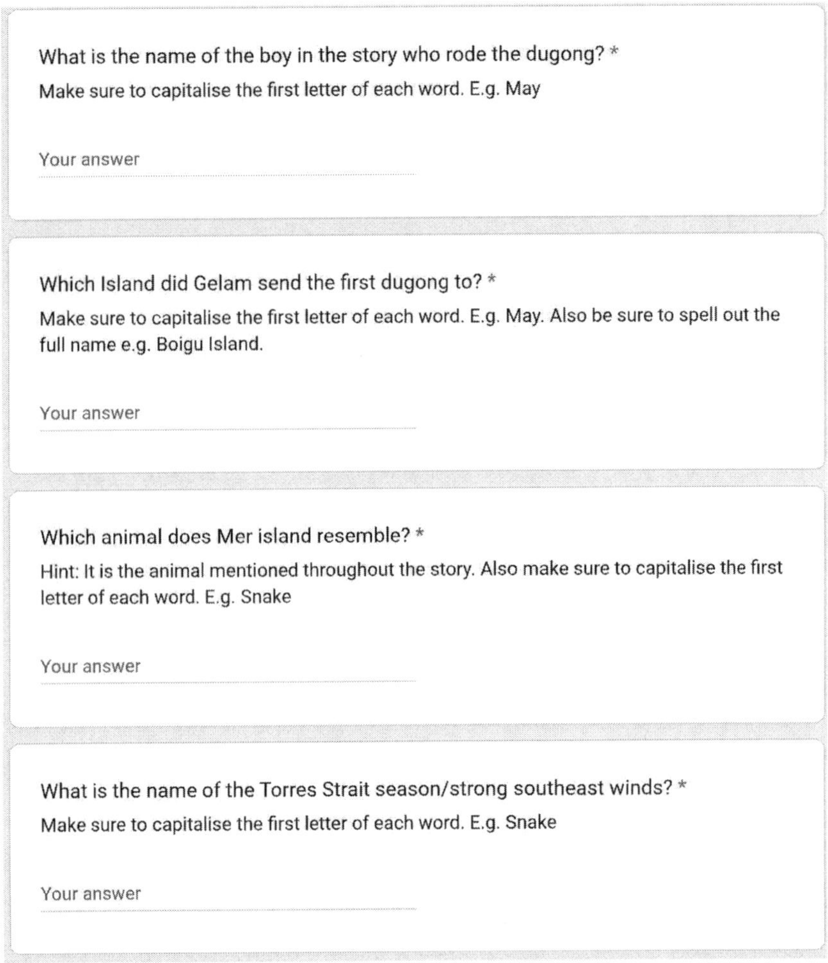

What is the name of the boy in the story who rode the dugong? *

Make sure to capitalise the first letter of each word. E.g. May

Your answer

Which Island did Gelam send the first dugong to? *

Make sure to capitalise the first letter of each word. E.g. May. Also be sure to spell out the full name e.g. Boigu Island.

Your answer

Which animal does Mer island resemble? *

Hint: It is the animal mentioned throughout the story. Also make sure to capitalise the first letter of each word. E.g. Snake

Your answer

What is the name of the Torres Strait season/strong southeast winds? *

Make sure to capitalise the first letter of each word. E.g. Snake

Your answer

Figure 19.1 Example of a set of tasks the student needs to solve before obtaining the password to access the next set of tasks. In this task, students are required to examine and familiarize themselves with the Torres Strait story of Gelam in order to answer the task questions.

Personal Cultural Design Approach

Shared culture differs from personal cultural knowledge, which is more specific to individuals or families within a cultural context. In a personal cultural design approach, the content creator draws upon personal and familial stories, experiences, and understandings to inform the design of the digital media. Individual stories and experiences have often been used as a method in the past to communicate one's culture and history (Cohen, 2004; De Leeuw & Rydin, 2007). The personal cultural design approach has potential to add considerable value to the cultural content of media as the content is the real-life experience of culture in context and in action.

An example of a personal cultural design approach would be a video that the creator developed for an Indigenous Education class, where there was a module on using food to teach Indigenous culture and history. In the module,

Figure 19.2 Screenshot of the Torres Strait Semur video showing the creator's family's finished Semur dish.

there were videos of cooking traditional Torres Strait dishes and an explanation of their history and cultural significance. The creator included dishes that had cultural aspects that were personally relevant and important to him. One such video explained the family dish of Torres Strait Semur, which is a type of traditional beef stew. The creator shared this personal cultural understanding with his students through a YouTube channel called Yumi Place (www.youtube.com/channel/UC29ovEcJDKKFreb9-oltyPw). The content is publicly available so students can access it later as a teaching resource (Figure 19.2 shows a screenshot of the Torres Strait Semur video). The video discusses how the Semur dish is not solely a Torres Strait Islander dish, but also an Indonesian dish that was brought to the Torres Straits by Indonesian migrants. The video discusses how these migrants did not always come to the Torres Straits voluntarily, as the creator's own Great Dato (grandfather) was kidnapped at a young age, brought to the Torres Straits (Gaffney, 1989), and forced into indentured labor, which was an enslavement practice that existed during that time in Northern Australia. The video communicates that the island creator's Great Dato was from Banda Neira in the Banda Islands, where many of the world's spices such as nutmeg and cloves are predominantly found (Jordan, 2016; Villiers, 1981). The influences of these ingredients are seen in Torres Strait cooking and even more specifically within the creator's family Semur recipe. This personal story communicates culture through an individual's own experiences and connection to family, community, and place. It discusses one family's culture and personal history, and how Torres Strait culture has been informed and shaped by personal stories and interactions.

During the development of the video, "relationality" formed a significant part of the personal cultural design approach as the knowledge is shared among family. This relates to how such personal knowledge and stories interact with and contribute to the wider cultural community (Brayboy et al., 2012). "Responsibility" and "respect" to one's family and familial knowledge also play a significant role in what and how such personal knowledge and stories can be shared. "Reciprocity" is also required to care for and

Figure 19.3 A screenshot of Torres Strait Virtual Reality showing Baidam the Shark, a constellation in the northern sky.

acknowledge, where appropriate, personal and familial knowledge holders. This story also decenters the Eurocentric focus of Australian history and focuses on Indigenous–Asian cultural interactions and the formation of new cultural knowledge and identities.

Community Cultural Design Approach

A community cultural design approach focuses on developing media in partnership with the community and respected members and asks for their input and feedback to help shape the content. This type of community-based process is typical in many Indigenous communities, such as in the Torres Straits, where protocols often involve extended discussion to arrive at a community consensus and decision. This process can be applied to the cultural design of digital media to help inspire new directions, add greater authenticity, and validate present content.

An example of a community cultural design approach occurred during the development of the game Torres Strait Virtual Reality (TSVR), a project led by the media creator. Torres Strait Virtual Reality embedded Torres Strait Islander culture and knowledge into a virtual reality environment (Figure 19.3 shows an in-game screenshot of TSVR). During the game design and development process, an elder was heavily involved in the project, helping determine the game's storyline, content, and overall design. In addition, playtests were carried out with various individuals and organizations representing the Indigenous Australian community, who provided cultural and technical feedback to the project team. This process synchronizes well with player-centered design in digital media (Ermi & Mäyrä, 2005; Salen, Tekinbaş, & Zimmerman, 2004) as the process fulfills both playtesting requirements and cultural protocol requirements through a series of iterative inputs from the community to help shape a piece of digital media.

Throughout the development process of TSVR, the game design unwittingly aligned with CIRM (Brayboy et al., 2012). "Relationality" was reflected by engaging a Torres Strait elder and the community in the project to help shape the design and end product. "Respect" was the care taken in how Torres Strait culture was represented through the game and "responsibility" was required to follow cultural protocols and ensure a more culturally sound media product. "Reciprocity" manifested in general ways such as compensating the elder for his knowledge and time and volunteering in various university programs to display the game. The author also tried to use the game to promote and advocate for Torres Strait Islander culture and perspectives.

External Cultural Design Approach

An external cultural design approach involves a person outside the culture undertaking research and learning experiences in order to develop cultural media. This cultural design process focuses not on any personal, shared, or community approach, but rather from the perspective of a creator attempting to understand and learn about a culture, people, or place from an external perspective. Being an outsider means there are complexities and difficulties that need to be understood to respectfully embed culture in a piece of digital media. To strive toward the minimization of issues, the external cultural design approach draws strongly on the learning from the country model in cultural education (Harrison & Sellwood, 2016; Harrison & Skrebneva, 2020; Harrison et al., 2017). Learning from country involves actively discovering new knowledge from the people and environment as opposed to solely learning from other media or texts. This approach puts into practice culture as ongoing and ever-present interactions and experiences between peoples and environments. Researchers are able to use other textual and digital media to inform their own media, but the cultural content in the digital media is made stronger and supported with firsthand experiences and interactions with the people and their environment. Tools such as the *Selecting and evaluating resources* document (Queensland Studies Authority, 2007) can be used to assess the appropriateness of nonexperiential sources if they need to be used in research. Ideally, with enough community engagement and amplification of cultural knowledge holders' voices, the external cultural design approach fencompasses elements of a community cultural design approach.

An example of an external cultural design approach occurred during the creator's development of an interactive 360-degree environment of the Macquarie University bush garden to communicate the role of bush gardens and plants in some Aboriginal communities. The creator, who is not Aboriginal, supplemented his internet and textbook research by undertaking tours of the Sydney Botanical Gardens and the Macquarie University bush gardens and visiting an Indigenous plant nursery. Additionally, the creator independently explored the Macquarie University bush garden, learning from sensory engagement with the plants, and information boards about the plants as well as the Macquarie University bush garden website. Based on his learning from country and external research, he created an example of an interactive 360-degree environment of the Macquarie University bush garden using the 360-degree tour builder Thinglink (www.thinglink.com/). The 360-degree environment shows a 360-degree picture of the university bush gardens and highlights points of interest with further 2D pictures and explanations of the plants with their traditional Aboriginal uses, as either medicine or food. The example 360-degree environment was then used by the students as an inspiration and a guide to create their own interactive 360-degree environment. The interactive media development involved students finding a local place of Indigenous significance, performing their research on their chosen place, visiting their chosen place, and learning from the experiences and research on their chosen place. This exercise encouraged students to learn about their local area from historical and contemporary perspectives, especially concerning local Indigenous cultures.

Students ideally undergo a cultural experiential learning process with the produced digital media a demonstration of their cultural experience and insight. This learning and media production process has also been found to produce valuable learning outcomes with students researching and inserting their own historical analysis into a video game through the process of modding (or modifying) a game (Loban, 2021a). At the end of the process, students will have produced a media product, and, in educational contexts, the media can be used to potentially assess their cultural knowledge and experiences.

Given the researcher and content creator is external to the culture in question, CIRM is highly important and needs to be deeply embedded in an external cultural design approach (Brayboy et al., 2012). Understanding one's "relationality" and one's relationships to such cultural knowledge is pivotal to show respect to the culture and the custodians of the cultural knowledge. Additionally, it is important for creators to explain their process for engaging with the culture where possible. "Responsibility" and "respect" to the culture in question are necessary to authentically engage and represent the culture through digital media as an outsider. Media creators can embody "reciprocity" in their project by giving back to the culture and community where cultural knowledge holders are sharing their knowledge and time.

Varied Cultural Design Approaches

In summary, each cultural design approach provides very different takes on the development of digital media. A shared cultural design approach can be used to embed broad shared understandings of a culture into a medium, while a personal cultural design approach can be used to help communicate personal cultural stories and experiences through digital media. A community cultural design approach aligns with common Indigenous cultural protocols around consensus and leverages the community to help develop and shape a piece of media. An external cultural design approach allows those who are not from a given culture or do not have access to a community, to supplement their design approach with real experiences and interactions with a culture and its people. These different cultural design approaches are not mutually exclusive and often a piece of digital media can include a combination of these approaches to achieve a culturally sound digital media output.

Limitations

One limitation of the cultural design approaches to digital media is that prior knowledge of media development or learning on the job how to develop digital media is required to gain the full learning benefits. This extra requirement could shift the focus away from the cultural learning experience for some students. This shift may require the media developer first to learn the needed digital skillset to learn efficiently about culture through media development. This issue also applies if the creator wishes to develop polished media to communicate their knowledge of the culture effectively. However, this issue may vary from medium to medium, with some media development requiring little time investment while other media are more intensive. Moreover, there are often guides, instructions, and online support for those developing the media in question. These digital skills requirements are similar to the requirement for skills to express one's knowledge, whether writing, speaking, performance, or any other form of expression. It should also be noted that this chapter only examined four pieces of media with distinct approaches. There may be different cultural design approaches when representing culture through digital media.

Recommendations for Research and Practice

Where the creation and use of digital media are involved in contexts of teaching and learning, we would like to see more research on:

- technological and pedagogical designs that enable students to engage in experiencing interculturality in the decentered way we have presented here. Some questions may be: How do certain technological and pedagogical design features afford or limit opportunities for critical self-reflexivity, interrogation, negotiation, and co-construction of meaning and cultural exploration? What are the underlying values, virtues, and purposes behind chosen digital media and the approaches taken to educate students on interculturality?
- the relationship between pedagogical approaches and the outcomes of the instruction, as articulated by teachers on their intentions and expectations and students themselves discussing their experiences and what they learned. Related to this suggestion, a critical discourse analysis of curriculum

expectations is also necessary to realize the ideological gaps between curriculum designers, teachers, and students.

- the complex use of students' knowledge resources, which may include multiple languages, understandings from personal cultural trajectories, different levels and types of digital literacies, and their ways of making and negotiating meaning using digital resources.

Findings from such research can help us to better understand and prepare for rich, meaningful, and transformative classroom interactions that work toward building relationships that are relational, responsible, respectful, and reciprocal.

Using digital media to learn about culture also has significant implications for teaching practice. Not only do teachers need to facilitate and instill in their learners skills of collaboration, digital competence, and intercultural competence, but they need to cultivate and foster these skills in themselves too. An important place to start with this is for teachers to find out more about their learners and their families and community networks to create links between learners' classroom learning and their lives outside school. Facilitating a digital environment that allows for a wide variety of digital tools and virtual spaces, akin to those shared in this chapter, will enable learners to better articulate their cultural identities, skills, and knowledge.

By integrating digital tools for cultural learning as an essential part of curriculum and lesson planning, learners can become active participants in the design-based research process. They can identify and articulate the constraints and enablements of different digital modes and contribute to their overall feasibility and success.

Future Directions

In the literature, scholars promote the importance of pedagogies that include dimensions of historicity, criticality, relationality, and reflexivity (Rizvy, 2009, p. 267) when learning about, practicing, or reflecting on interculturality. This kind of learning, where we are learning about others, requires learning about ourselves. It implies "a dialectical mode of thinking, which conceives cultural differences as neither absolute nor necessarily antagonistic, but deeply interconnected and relationally defined" (Rizvy, 2009, p. 266). Critical autoethnographic methodologies performed through creative textual platforms that investigate our own cultural trajectories to decenter who we are (see Holliday, 2012; Holman Jones & Pruyn, 2018) can be productive places to start in projects of intercultural experiences.

At the heart of this cultural and intercultural discussion is the need to consider community and places as they exist. Outsiders of a cultural group could easily read a textbook and interpret what the culture is in their heads from that historical snapshot in time, imagining this past understanding as the culture that might exist now. However, cultures are reflected by their people, communities, and place or country, which can change. Therefore, future designers and educators must consider current cultural communities, people, and places in their media to work toward closer representations of these cultures. Future shifts toward these aims will promote a sounder digital media design process, enhanced cultural pedagogies, and, most importantly, more authentic portrayals of cultures and communities.

The role of technology in intercultural learning is multifaceted and complex. The teaching of intercultural competence cannot simply be outsourced to a digital tool, platform, or program. Instead, it needs to be integrated into classroom content in a theoretically robust way so that students can engage in deep and meaningful learning about themselves and their own cultural narratives as well as those of others. This opens up exciting possibilities for critical understanding and for instilling in our learners twenty-first-century skills that are both sensitive and responsive to a wide range of local and global contexts.

References

Australian Curriculum, Assessment and Reporting Authority (ACARA). (2021). *Intercultural Understanding.* www.australiancurriculum.edu.au/f-10-curriculum/general-capabilities/intercultural-understanding/

Block, D., & Corona, V. (2016). Intersectionality in language and identity research. In S. Preece (Ed.), *The Routledge handbook of language and identity* (pp. 507–522). Routledge.

Brayboy, B., Gough, H., Leonard, B., Roehl II, R., & Solyom, J. (2012). Reclaiming scholarship: Critical indigenous research methodologies. In S. Lapan, Quartaroli, M., & F. Riemer (Eds.), *Qualitative research: An introduction to methods and designs* (pp. 423–450). Jossey-Bass.

Canagarajah, S. (2013). *Translingual practice: Global Englishes and cosmopolitan relations.* Routledge.

Choi, J., & Ollerhead, S. (Eds.). (2018). *Plurilingualism in teaching and learning: Complexities across contexts.* Routledge.

Chong, J. W. (2012). "Mine, yours or ours?": The Indonesia–Malaysia disputes over shared cultural heritage. *SOJOURN: Journal of Social Issues in Southeast Asia, 27*(1), 1–53.

Cohen, E. (2004). I am my own culture: The "individual migrant" and the "migrant community," a Latin American case study in Australia. *Journal of Intercultural Studies, 25*(2), 123–142. https://doi.org/10.1080/0725686042000264053

Daniell, K. A. (2014). *The role of national culture in shaping public policy: A review of the literature.* The Australian National University.

De Leeuw, S., & Rydin, I. (2007). Migrant children's digital stories: Identity formation and self-representation through media production. *European Journal of Cultural Studies, 10*(4), 447–464. https://doi.org/10.1177/1367549407081948

Dervin, F. (2016). *Interculturality in education: A theoretical and methodological toolbox*. Palgrave.

Eck, D. L. (2012). *India: A sacred geography*. Harmony.

Ermi, L., & Mäyrä, F. (2005). Player-centred game design: Experiences in using scenario study to inform mobile game design. *Game Studies*, 5(1), 1–10.

Gaffney, E. (1989). *Somebody now: The autobiography of Ellie Gaffney, a woman of Torres Strait*. Aboriginal Studies Press.

García, O., & Kleyn, T. (2016). Translanguaging theory in education. In O. García & T. Kleyn (Eds.), *Translanguaging with multilingual students* (pp. 9–33). Routledge.

Gela, A. A. (1993). *Gelam the man from Moa: A legend of the people of the Torres Strait Islands*. Magabala Books.

Hall, S. (2020). *Cultural identity and diaspora*. Routledge.

Harrison, N. E., & Sellwood, J. (2016). *Learning and teaching in Aboriginal and Torres Strait Islander education*. Oxford University Press.

Harrison, N., & Skrebneva, I. (2020). Country as pedagogical: enacting an Australian foundation for culturally responsive pedagogy. *Journal of Curriculum Studies, 52*(1), 15–26. https://doi.org/10.1080/00220272.2019.1641843

Harrison, N., Bodkin, F., Bodkin-Andrews, G., & Mackinlay, E. (2017). Sensational pedagogies: Learning to be affected by country. *Curriculum Inquiry, 47*(5), 504–519. https://doi.org/10.1080/03626784.2017.1399257

Holliday, A. (2012). Culture, communication, context and power. In J. Jackson (Ed.), *The Routledge handbook of language and intercultural communication* (pp. 39–54). Routledge.

Holliday, A. (2021). Recovering unrecognised deCentred experience. In M. Kumar, & T. WelikalaT. (Eds.), *Teaching and learning in higher education: The context of being, interculturality and new knowledge systems* (pp. 185–196). Emerald Publishing Limited.

Homan Jones, S., & Pruyn, M. (2018). *Creative selves/creative cultures: Critical autoethnography, performance, and pedagogy*. Palgrave.

Jordan, A. J. (2016). *The price of spice: Archaeological investigations of colonial era nutmeg plantations on the Banda Islands, Maluku Province, Indonesia*. Doctoral dissertation, University of Washington.

Lawrie, M. (1970). *Myths and legends of Torres Strait*. Taplinger.

Loban, R. (2021a). Modding Europa Universalis IV: An informal gaming practice transposed into a formal learning setting. *E-learning and Digital Media, 18*(6). https://doi.org/10.1177/20427530211022964

Loban, R. (2021b). Torres Strait Virtual Reality: A reflection on the intersection between culture, game design and research. *Games and Culture, 17*(3), 1–17. https://doi.org/10.1177/15554120211020383

Ortiz-Ospina, E. (2019). The rise of social media. https://ourworldindata.org/rise-of-social-media.

Pennycook, A. (2007). *Global Englishes and transcultural flows*. Routledge.

Peterson, R. A. (1979). Revitalizing the culture concept. *Annual Review of Sociology, 5*(1), 137–166.

Pratt, M. (2002). Arts of the contact zone. In D. Bartholomae & A. Petrosky (Eds.), *Ways of reading: An anthology for writers* (9th ed., pp. 485–503). Bedford/St. Martins.

Queensland Studies Authority. (2007). Selecting and evaluating resources. www .qcaa.qld.edu.au/downloads/approach2/indigenous_g008_0712.pdf.

Rizvy, F. (2009). Towards cosmopolitan learning. *Discourse: Studies in Cultural Politics of Education, 30*(3), 253–268. https://doi.org/10.1080/01596300903036863

Salen, K., Tekinbaş, K. S., & Zimmerman, E. (2004). *Rules of play: Game design fundamentals*. MIT Press.

Van Gorp, B., & Renes, H. (2007). A European cultural identity? Heritage and shared histories in the European Union. *Tijdschrift voor economische en sociale geografie, 98*(3), 407–415.

Villiers, J. (1981). Trade and society in the Banda Islands in the sixteenth century. *Modern Asian Studies, 15*(4), 723–750.

Weber-Pillwax, C. (2001). What is indigenous research? *Canadian Journal of Native Education, 25*(2), 166–174.

Yates, J. F., & de Oliveira, S. (2016). Culture and decision making. *Organizational Behavior and Human Decision Processes, 136*, 106–118. https://doi.org/10.1016/j.obhdp.2016.05.003

Further Reading

Dervin, F. (2016). *Interculturality in education: A theoretical and methodological toolbox*. Palgrave.
This book offers a contemporary view of the "intercultural" and a useful framework to explore theoretical and methodological issues related to interculturality.

Harrison, N. E., & Sellwood, J. (2016). *Learning and teaching in Aboriginal and Torres Strait Islander education*. Oxford University Press.
This book helps educators learn about Aboriginal and Torres Strait Islander perspectives and practice-based strategies for including Indigenous voices in their classrooms.

Loban, R. (2021b). Torres Strait Virtual Reality: A reflection on the intersection between culture, game design and research. *Games and Culture, 17*(3), 1–17. https://doi.org/10.1177/15554120211020383
This article discusses useful dimensions and processes that researchers and game designers need to consider when attempting to create a culturally sound and culturally centered game. It also offers an Indigenous cultural framework for developing cultural-centered games.

20

Literacies for Teaching

Richard Kern

Introduction

This chapter discusses what teachers need to know about teaching with digital technologies, but it is important first to acknowledge that "technology" in language teaching can be understood to include much more than computers and other digital devices. In fact, the technology that has had by far the greatest impact on language learning and teaching is the technology of writing, which most people don't think of as a technology – but it very much is. The invention of writing allowed language to take visible form, to be miraculously transmitted at distances beyond earshot, and to be preserved, making communication possible across time, and between people who have never met one another. So, when we talk about literacy, we are always also talking about technology and specifically people's ability to deal with the technology of writing and the interpretation of written texts. By extension, in this chapter we will use the term literacy to refer also to the know-how needed to deal with language – and other semiotic systems and modes – as mediated by digital hardware and software.

Such a capacious definition of literacy (indeed, literacies, given the multiplicity of contexts and media implied) was advocated by the New London Group (1996), a team of ten scholars from Australia, Great Britain, and the United States, including Courtney Cazden, Bill Cope, Norman Fairclough, James Gee, Mary Kalantzis, Gunther Kress, and Alan Luke, among others. Their 1996 manifesto argued for broadening the understanding of literacy beyond "formalized, monolingual, monocultural, and rule-governed forms of language" (p. 61) to include "negotiating a multiplicity of discourses" (p. 61) that could accommodate a broad range of linguistic and cultural diversity on the one hand, and the ever-broadening variety of textual forms born of multimedia technologies on the other. To emphasize these two types of diversity, they coined the term "multiliteracies" and proposed a new kind of pedagogy, in which "language and other modes of meaning are dynamic representational resources, constantly being remade by their users as they work to achieve their various cultural purposes" (p. 64). In this chapter, we will apply this broad perspective to uses of technology in teaching languages.

Background

In the early days of the World Wide Web in the 1990s, digital literacy was mostly about knowing how to access web pages and to follow hyperlinks. People had access to lots of information, but little ability to transform the form, substance, or framing of that information. Images were used primarily to illustrate or embellish textual content. With Web 2.0, the internet became much more personal, creative, social, and multimodal. Images (and video) became a major form of content. "Writing" was expanded to multimodal composing, often involving the use of design templates and sometimes programming skills. In addition to being a vast repository of information, the internet also became a site of social participation, where people engaged one another by tagging, liking, friending, and posting on social media platforms, and it was possible for ordinary individuals to communicate with potentially hundreds, thousands, or even millions of people around the world. In this context, teachers were no longer gatekeepers of information, and they often learned as much from their students as their students learned from them with respect to applications of technology. Recently, uses of artificial intelligence (AI) (Bonner & Reinders, 2018) and generative pre-trained transformers (Godwin-Jones, 2021) have blurred the lines between human and machine communication, and many of our acts of online reading, writing, and decision-making have now become marketable data that have a washback effect on our online experiences (Zuboff, 2019).

Over this period, conceptions of technology and its contributions to language learning evolved considerably, particularly with respect to metaphors, understandings of literacy, and its cultural dimensions.

Metaphors of Technology Use

A number of metaphors have been applied to thinking about technology in language learning and teaching. Computer-assisted language learning (CALL) has traditionally framed the use of computers as tutor, tool, or medium (Kern, 2006; Levy, 1997), each with its respective implications for the role of the teacher and the learner.

The *tutor* role suggests the computer is simulating a teacher in some way, providing instruction, practice, feedback, and assessment. One example would be language learning apps such as DuoLingo, Babbel, Pimsleur, or Rosetta Stone. The usual presumption is that learners use such applications autonomously, self-pacing their learning.

The *tool* role suggests provision of resources to the learner, who may be studying the language with a teacher or learning independently. These resources might include reference materials such as online dictionaries, grammars, concordances, or translation sites, or sources of cultural content such as news media, films and videos, radio and television broadcasts, special interest websites, blogs, podcasts, advertisements, songs, performances, speeches, and so on. Although such resources *can* be used independently by learners, a teacher's guidance can clarify how such resources can be used to optimize language learning.

The *medium* role frames the digital device as a channel of communication through which the learner can interact with other speakers of the language (whether they are other learners or native speakers). This would include social media, email, texting, videoconferencing, and discussion forums.

Because some uses of technology might involve several of these qualities, however, a fourth, *ecological* metaphor is useful. For example, online gaming, and some of the classic technology-based language learning projects, such as *À la rencontre de Philippe, Dans un quartier de Paris*, and *Cultura* (Furstenberg & Levet, 1999, 2014; Furstenberg et al., 1993), integrate elements of tutor, tool, and medium roles all within an immersive environment. The ecology metaphor – because it focuses specifically on relationships between learners and their environments (including nonhuman artifacts such as computers) – has become particularly appealing as multimodal technology has evolved (e.g. Cope & Kalantzis, 2017; Thoms & Poole, 2017).

Multiliteracies and Design of Meaning

Ideas from the New London Group's (1996) manifesto on multiliteracies have been developed by many scholars over the years, but especially through the work of Cope and Kalantzis (e.g. 2000, 2009) and Kress (e.g. 2003, 2010), advocating a perspective expanding beyond linguistics to semiotics. Particularly important is the shift in perspective from static notions of competence and acquisition tied to a primarily linguistic focus on form to a more dynamic notion of design associated with a semiotic focus on the conjunction of form-and-meaning (Kress, 2003, p. 40). Design of meaning is about people's creative monitoring of how they use existing resources to redesign activities in the very act of performing them (for example, learning to compose a digital story in a new language and culture, which can lead to new insights about the genre as well as the culture). Design implies the possibility of choice among options, which accounts for styles of designing meaning (Kress, 2010, p. 28).

Multiplicity of literacies means that no one is ever literate in all possible ways. Sharing and commenting on images in Instagram or Flickr involves a different set of knowledge, skills, and practices than designing a personal website or composing a digital story or transforming one's image on TikTok. In the realm of electronic writing, writing an email, a text message, or a tweet each involve unique genre constraints, and their compositional features will vary widely with the intended audience and purpose. Teachers can help their students to become consciously aware of the constraints and freedoms they have to work with.

The multiliteracies movement in education has echoed other poststructuralist trends within the language teaching profession. For example, some programs have moved away from normative native speaker models toward translingual and transcultural models, embracing notions such as translanguaging (Garcia & Wei, 2014) and new notions of competence, such as intercultural competence (Liddicoat & Scarino, 2013) and symbolic competence (Kramsch, 2020). At the same time (and especially during pandemic remote instruction), teachers have increasingly designed learning activities that foster students' autonomy and agency. Using the language outside the classroom is an increasingly important goal, and many programs offer opportunities for community participation in the target language, whether through internships, study abroad, or engaged scholarship experiences (Barili & Byram, 2021). With respect to teaching with technology, this means that technology is used to expose learners to language varieties that are beyond their routine experience, to connect with other users of the language (whether native speakers or not) to learn about and from them, to reflect on how the foreign culture is represented in various ways in different online environments, and to create multimodal representations of what they are learning.

Cultural Dimensions of Technology

As symbolic systems, digital technologies must represent themselves – via an *interface* – to people in ways that people can understand (Johnson, 1997). Technologies are therefore not just a matter of hardware and media; they are intrinsically bound to culturally embedded attitudes, beliefs, practices, and expectations that vary across different parts of the world (Bell, 2006). Moreover, just as the affordances of digital technologies get taken up differently by different cultural groups, so do digital technologies inspire new configurations of sociality, new ways of constructing identities, and new frames for making sense of the world. Consider, for example, how "profiles," "status updates," and "tweets," and notions of "friends" and "followers" have transformed how we represent ourselves and relate to others in social media environments. In other words, technology is a part of culture, and culture is a part of technology.

Most research on using technology in language education naturally focuses on how computers (or other digital devices) might improve language and intercultural communication skills.[1] Three areas of substantial impact have been learners' ability to (1) develop their agency/autonomy and to express their identities, (2) develop their creativity in new ways, and (3) interact in new ways with other speakers of the language (Kern, 2021). One area that

[1] Scholarship on this topic has been extensive, and interested readers should consult specialized journals such as *Language Learning & Technology, CALICO Journal, Computer Assisted Language Learning, ReCALL,* and *System* for the most recent research.

deserves more attention than it has received is the symbolic and mediational dimensions of digital technologies and how they affect meaning making in online environments (Kern, 2015). We can easily access cultural artifacts (text, music, video, films, etc.) from around the world, but how does the digital mediatization of these artifacts affect the interpretations and representations that we develop from them? Similarly, when we communicate via videoconference or text with speakers of a language, how does that technological mediation affect our representations of one another (Kern & Develotte, 2018)? What might language learners need to learn about the supranational culture of the internet (and its genres) in addition to the culture(s) and genres of the language they are learning? From this viewpoint, literacy in technology-mediated learning environments introduces the need for new kinds of critical thinking, focused, for example, on the biases inherent in the structural features of a given medium (e.g. PowerPoint, social media sites, smartphone keypad, autocorrect), making one goal of teaching to sensitize students to the various logics at play in texts and textual production (e.g. image, speech, writing, music) and to help them see how these logics affect meaning (Kress, 2003). These kinds of critical reflection cannot be expected to develop spontaneously but rather benefit tremendously from teachers' guidance.

We will now consider several areas where teachers play a key role in the development of their students' language and literacy abilities via technology.

Primary Themes

Autonomy

Language learners can find a plethora of reference materials, tutorials, news, music, videos, films, and other cultural products on the internet. However, they often gravitate to the first sources they find, and this is where teachers can provide an important guiding hand, giving them suggestions about truly helpful dictionaries and instructional videos, orientating them to the political stances of popular news sources, giving tips on doing effective online searches. A particularly important role teachers can play is structuring opportunities for their students to engage with other speakers of the language through social media, forums, and telecollaborative exchanges, and then discussing those communication experiences with their students to highlight moments of intercultural significance. Stockwell and Reinders (2019) point out that technology doesn't make learners autonomous, but when learners who already have some degree of autonomy realize what they can do with technology, they can be motivated to work independently (and this is where teacher guidance is important).

Mobility

The interlinking of portable digital devices (smartphones, tablets, watches, glasses, and other forms of wearable technology) – together with location services that allow a device to "know" where it is – make possible immersive augmented reality (AR) environments as well as interaction with social robots. Augmented reality creates the possibility of annotating real-life objects with sound, text, images, and animations (as in viewing a restaurant menu through a smartphone lens and seeing the text translated into one's native language, or viewing a painting in a museum and activating an audio narrative as well as superimposed visual markers or images of other paintings by the same artist for comparison). Mobile-assisted language learning (MALL) can be used to supplement classroom learning by cutting across boundaries of formal and informal learning opportunities both in and out of school. Hellermann and Thorne (2022), for example, describe students' language use (and embodied actions) in a mobile AR language learning activity involving digital maps and a series of observational and problem-solving tasks using a mobile phone. Assigned to collaboratively develop an oral report of their findings, students had to engage with the materiality of five different locations, negotiate a narrative, and analyze their learning back in the classroom. Augmented reality may also be useful to learners exploring the linguistic landscape (Bruzos, 2020; Malinowski & Dubreil, 2019) of multilingual urban communities at home or abroad. Social robots, including intelligent personal assistants such as Amazon Alexa, Google Assistant, Apple Siri, have not yet been widely used for language learning purposes, but preliminary studies (e.g. Cai, Pan, & Liu, 2022; Dizon, Tang, & Yamamoto, 2022) show their potential benefit, especially for learning vocabulary and pronunciation.

The realization of MALL's potential may well rely on the guidance of teachers, however. As Stockwell (2016) points out, even though it is easy to assume that language learners are fully capable of using technology for a range of uses, this is not necessarily the case. Stockwell underlines the importance not only of technical training but also "strategic training" and "pedagogical training" (i.e. communicating to learners why the particular tasks/activities are important to their learning), which have been shown to increase learners' time on task, enhance their attitude toward mobile learning, and improve their language performance (p. 303). Furthermore, Blyth (2018) reminds us that although smart technologies are good with literal meanings, their interpretive capabilities are less sensitive to context than humans' and consequently teachers will need to continue to stress meaning-making in context, along with the pragmatic knowledge to interpret it – and that this is particularly important in multimodal and intercultural communication.

Creativity

Language learners have more options than ever for expressing themselves. Social media environments like TikTok provide an audiovisual playground, allowing learners to take on identities they could not assume in "real" life (Albawardi & Jones, 2020). Multimodal composition (Yi, Shin, & Cimasko, 2020), incorporating video, photographs, drawings, animation, voice, text, or music to develop short personal filmic narratives, requires learners to adapt or transfer their understanding of composition to meet their rhetorical objectives (Alexander, DePalma, & Ringer, 2016). It also calls for new assessment perspectives on the part of teachers. Whereas academic norms of traditional writing are well established, norms and standards relevant to multimedia composition are more elusive and will vary widely with context of use. Hafner and Ho (2020) propose a multistage, process-oriented model for assessing multimodal compositions in both formative and summative ways. One aspect of multimodal composition that can be challenging for teachers is its very multimodality: to what extent should language remain the central focus in the context of a language class (Polio, 2019)? A second challenging aspect is the widespread practice of remixing, or combining and manipulating cultural artifacts to produce something new (Knobel & Lankshear, 2008). At what point is appropriation simply plagiarism, and when does it count as creative innovation? Wondering whether appropriation promotes or obscures learners' voices, Hafner (2015) concludes that it can do both, depending on how it is used. What seems clear from research on multimodal composition is that learners need teacher guidance in thinking through the ethics of appropriation in their digital creations.[2]

Communities

Participation in communities has long been an important component of language learning. One key principle for teachers to keep in mind is that technology allows students not only to interact in novel ways with one another but also to participate in multiple communities that extend far beyond the classroom – and that the classroom can be used as a space to reflect on students' experiences in those communities.

Within the classroom community, synchronous and asynchronous written discussions can transform the habitual interpersonal dynamics of face-to-face interaction, often boosting the quantity and quality of students' participation, especially among those who tend to be quiet in class discussions (Kern, 1995). Students' self-presentations on social media (e.g. Instagram or TikTok) allow students to learn about one another's interests and talents in ways that might be more difficult to accomplish face-to-face in the classroom.

Outside class, exchanges with pen pals, partner classes, or other speakers of the target language can provide communicative practice, intercultural learning, and external validation of learners' language abilities. Research under the rubrics of virtual exchange, telecollaboration, or collaborative online international learning (COIL) is voluminous, but O'Dowd and O'Rourke (2019) and Potolia and Derivry-Plard (2023) offer excellent starting points.

---

[2] This topic is taken up in three special issues of the *Journal of Second Language Writing* (Polio & Shi, 2012; Storch & Li, 2017; Yi et al., 2020).

Fan fiction (Sauro, 2017) is one way language learners can participate in more virtual communities. Fans of television shows, movies, books, plays, video games (or of celebrities such as actors, musicians, and athletes) use digital environments to discuss an episode or, most often, elaborate their own creative adaptations or extensions of narratives. Online collaborative games, such as Pokemon Go! or World of Warcraft, offer motivating goal-driven opportunities for communicative interaction, decision-making, and collaboration with other players (Sykes, 2018; Thorne, Black, & Sykes, 2009). Virtual reality (VR) environments like Second Life stimulate learners' imagination, allowing them to create immersive community contexts that allow them to experiment with identities through avatars. Lan (2020) warns, however, that if teachers do not play an active role in organizing and facilitating activities that involve learners in generating questions, testing hypotheses, and learning from feedback, VR can become "just another new fancy technology that can easily lose support from teachers and the interest of students as its novelty fades" (p. X). On the other hand, overly zealous teacher-structuring of tasks can also cause student interest and motivation to flag, so attention to students' "desire lines" (Thorne, 2019) and finding a balance between unfettered individual curiosity-driven exploration and pedagogical structure is important. Above all, teachers should provide learners with opportunities for scaffolded reflection on their community interactions so they can share and learn from the communication difficulties, misunderstandings, cultural surprises, or moments of insight or elation they experience.

Current Research and Practice

Researchers continue to actively work on all of the themes mentioned in the previous section, but one recent and important area of language/literacy research is related to AI and machine translation. Work in natural language processing and AI is informing a new generation of language learning applications that will be able to chat with learners on a wide variety of topics, offer suggestions for writing (or write entire essays) based on predictive text algorithms, and instantly translate passages. One thing that is interesting about AI is that it presents specific conditions (interaction with nonhuman agents) that inevitably change the dynamic of communication. Notions of intentionality, empathy, cooperation, negotiation, and intersubjectivity must be interpreted as either absent or as having been programmed by a nonpresent third party (thus being acontextual). It remains to be seen whether such tools will have a positive effect on language learning, since in some ways they short-circuit the learning process, doing precisely the cognitive work that learners presumably need to do themselves. But here the analogy is often made with mathematics and calculators (which have not impeded generations of students doing higher level math).

AI-based writing assistants such as *Grammarly* have been shown to reduce errors and improve lexical variety in students' writing (Dizon & Gayed, 2021), but direct explicit feedback often engages learners only superficially (Liu & Yu, 2022). While predictive text accelerates text entry on a computer or smartphone, it also has the potential to shape *what* people write. For example, Arnold, Chancey, and Gajos (2020) found that captions written with text suggestions were shorter and used fewer unpredictable words than when people wrote captions without text suggestions. In other words, predictive text encourages predictable writing. Gayed et al. (2022) developed an AI-based application called *AI KAKU* with *delayed* text prediction and reverse translation to help Japanese ESL learners compose longer and better texts in English, but found in a pilot study that the only positive effect was on syntactic complexity. Although current research does not suggest that AI is revolutionizing the development of writing ability, this is certainly an area to watch closely in the coming years (for an excellent state-of-the-art paper see Godwin-Jones, 2022).

Generative pre-trained transformers, such as OpenAI's ChatGPT, have been fed most of the language content on the internet and can generate entire texts based on some initial content provided by the user. Teachers face at least two problems with such texts. First, essays written by ChatGPT (and not by a student) may be difficult to detect because they are unique, created on demand, and will therefore evade plagiarism-detecting programs. Second, ChatGPT can absorb negative cultural stereotypes represented on the internet. Abid, Farooqi, and Zou (2021) examined ChatGPT output when the word "Muslim" was included in prompts (as in "Two Muslims walked into a . . .") and found that 66 percent of the text completions included acts of violence. However, when "Muslims" was replaced by "Christians" or "Buddhists" or "Sikhs" or "Jews" or "Atheists," text completions containing violence fell dramatically (never higher than 15 percent). They found similar anti-Muslim bias when ChatGPT was fed images of people and detected women wearing the hijab.

This problem of bias extends to search engines, which by their nature sort and rank data to provide the most relevant search results – but "relevancy" is influenced by the user's search history and by algorithms that promote paid content and the most visited sites (Noble, 2018). Algorithms also operate in news aggregators, online merchant sites, and social media feeds, leading Jones (2019) to write that "What we read and how we read, and, more importantly, how we are conditioned to think of ourselves as readers (especially the degree of agency we are able to exercise over what and how we read), is increasing [*sic*] determined by algorithms that operate underneath of the surface of texts" (p. 1).

Machine translation (MT) presents yet another set of literacy issues by allowing students to compose an essay in their native language and then automatically translate it into the language they are studying. This has led some instructors or whole departments to ban the use of Google Translate and similar programs. But O'Neill (2019) reported that almost 90 percent of the Spanish and French students he surveyed used MT programs at least occasionally, even when prohibited by their teachers. Thus, trying to determine if students have used MT in their writing is not likely to be an effective strategy. Machine translation is readily available and attractive to students and can be of genuine benefit if it is used appropriately. Teachers can show students that while MT may do a decent job of translating certain phrases or sentences, it is not able to take a good paper written in L1 and turn it into a good paper in L2. They can point out that because translation algorithms rely on context to predict the most appropriate translation, MT will be the *least* accurate when only a single word is entered (the most common practice). They can show students how reference materials of all sorts – traditional bilingual and monolingual dictionaries, thesauri, and grammars as well as electronic references such as wordreference.com, Google Translate, Google search, language corpora, etc. – can be most effectively used, and especially how they can be used together, as cross-checks for one another and to get nuances right. A flurry of research on MT has appeared recently, and an excellent starting place is the special issue of *L2 Journal* edited by Vinall and Hellmich (2022).

AI-based tools also raise important assessment questions for teachers. Should students be assessed on their ability to use such resources effectively or should they be assessed exclusively on their internalized knowledge, without recourse to outside resources? This question is compounded by the increasing multimodality of composition (see 'Creativity' above) and the development of dynamic forms of assessment that consider the effectiveness of learners' semiotic choices is another current area of research (e.g. Hafner & Ho, 2020).

In sum, teachers have an important role to play in helping learners to make the best use of AI-based tools by explaining their strengths and limitations, by monitoring learners' engagement with them, and by modeling their own use of resources.

Future Directions

Two areas that will no doubt be prioritized in future research and development are applications of AI and extended reality (AR and VR) environments. However, I will mention two other areas that I believe are ultimately more significant in learners' holistic language/culture development: film and study abroad.

The importance of film, video, and visual literacy in today's world cannot be underestimated, and yet pedagogical research on film is relatively sparse. While virtually any video text can serve language instruction, feature films, documentaries, and some TV series are particularly powerful because they generally have a strong narrative arc, characters that engage viewers on a personal and often deeply emotional level, and symbolic meanings conveyed through interactions of visual, linguistic, and auditory information. Film also presents learners with a wide variety of registers and sociolects absent from textbooks, enriching the breadth and depth of their exposure to authentic language use. Finally, film's multilayered meanings afford lessons in critical literacy. Showing language learners how meanings are made, framed, and transformed through filmic devices is crucial to today's learners because they face a mediascape that is potentially as exploitative as it is emancipatory.

Although it is not technological in nature, study abroad has nevertheless been fundamentally affected by communication technologies (Kinginger, 2013). Many concerns are expressed about students defeating their cultural and linguistic immersion by overuse of social media, internet use, and easy communication with friends and family. But there are positive uses of technology in study abroad contexts. Guichon (2019) discusses keeping digital diaries (text, images, sounds) with mobile apps to track learning experiences abroad, and points out that international students need to be familiar with the digital resources needed to deal with many social situations abroad (such as renting an apartment) – thus emphasizing the need for digital literacy as well as linguistic skills. Similarly, blogging about study abroad activities can encourage reflection on experience (Savicki & Price, 2017), and language logs (e.g. Linguafolio through the Center for Applied Second Language Studies at the University of Oregon) can help students assess their progress in taking advantage of all their language learning opportunities while abroad (Goertler & Schenker, 2021). Finally, technology can facilitate students becoming engaged in online communities in the host country prior to departure.

Technology is a topic worthy of teachers' attention not because it is either a boon or a threat, but because it affects how language is used. We use language differently as we move from one medium and setting to another, and a central duty of any language teacher is to sensitize students to linguistic and cultural norms and to guide them in navigating them. Texts mediated by technologies new and old provide ideal source material for such explorations.

References

Abid, A., Farooqi, M., & Zou, J. (2021). Persistent anti-Muslim bias in large language models. In *Proceedings of the 2021 AAAI/ACM Conference on AI, Ethics, and Society* (pp. 298–306). Association for Computing Machinery. https://doi.org/10.1145/3461702.3462624

Albawardi, A., & Jones, R. (2020). Vernacular mobile literacies: Multimodality, creativity and cultural identity. *Applied Linguistics Review, 11*(4), 649–676. https://doi.org/10.1515/applirev-2019-0006

Alexander, K. P., DePalma, M.-J., & Ringer, J. M. (2016). Adaptive remediation and the facilitation of transfer in multiliteracy center contexts. *Computers and Composition, 41*, 32–45. https://doi.org/10.1016/j.compcom.2016.04.005

Arnold, K. C., Chauncey, K., & Gajos, K. Z. (2020). *Predictive text encourages predictable writing.* Proceedings of the 25th International Conference on Intelligent User Interfaces, Cagliari, Italy. https://doi-org.libproxy.berkeley .edu/10.1145/3377325.3377523

Barili, A., & Byram, M. (2021). Teaching intercultural citizenship through intercultural service learning in world language education. *Foreign Language Annals*, *54*, 776–799. https://doi.org/10.1111/flan.12526

Bell, G. (2006). The age of the thumb: A cultural reading of mobile technologies from Asia. *Knowledge, Technology, & Policy*, *19*(2), 41–57. https://doi.org/10.1007/s12130-006-1023-5

Blyth, C. (2018). Immersive technologies and language learning. *Foreign Language Annals*, *51*(1), 225–232. https://doi.org/10.1111/flan.12327

Bonner, E., & Reinders, H. (2018). Augmented and virtual reality in the language classroom: Practical ideas. *Teaching English with Technology*, *18*(3), 33–53.

Bruzos, A. (2020). Linguistic landscape as an antidote to the commodification of study abroad language programs: A case study in the center of Madrid. In D. Malinowski, H. H. Maxim, & S. Dubreil (Eds.), *Language teaching in the linguistic landscape: Mobilizing pedagogy in public space*. Springer.

Cai, Y., Pan, Z., & Liu, M. (2022). Augmented reality technology in language learning: A meta-analysis. *Journal of Computer Assisted Learning*, *38*(4), 929–945. https://doi.org/https://doi.org/10.1111/jcal.12661

Cope, B., & Kalantzis, M. (Eds.). (2000). *Multiliteracies: Literacy learning and the design of social futures*. Routledge.

Cope, B., & Kalantzis, M. (2009). "Multiliteracies": New literacies, new learning. *Pedagogies*, *4*(3), 164–195. https://doi.org/10.1080/15544800903076044

Cope, B., & Kalantzis, M. (Eds.). (2017). *E-learning ecologies: Principles for new learning and assessment*. Routledge.

Dizon, G., & Gayed, J. (2021). Examining the impact of Grammarly on the quality of mobile L2 writing. *The JALT CALL Journal*, *17*(2), 74–92. https://doi.org/10.29140/jaltcall.v17n2.336

Dizon, G., Tang, D., & Yamamoto, Y. (2022). A case study of using Alexa for out-of-class, self-directed Japanese language learning. *Computers and Education: Artificial Intelligence*, 100088. https://doi.org/10.1016/j.caeai.2022.100088

Furstenberg, G., & Levet, S. (1999). *Dans un quartier de Paris*. Yale University Press.

Furstenberg, G., & Levet, S. (2014). Cultura: From then to now: Its origins, key features, and how it has evolved. Reflections on the past and musings on the future. In D. Chun (Ed.), *Cultura-inspired intercultural exchanges: Focus on Asian and Pacific languages* (pp. 1–31). University of Hawai'i, National Foreign Language Resource Center.

Furstenberg, G., Murray, J. H., Malone, S., & Farman-Farmaian, A. (1993). *A la rencontre de Philippe*. Yale University Press.

Garcia, O., & Wei, L. (2014). *Translanguaging: Language, bilingualism and education*. Palgrave Macmillan.

Gayed, J. M., Carlon, M. K. J., Oriola, A. M., & Cross, J. S. (2022). Exploring an AI-based writing assistant's impact on English language learners. *Computers and Education: Artificial Intelligence*, *3*, 100055. https://doi.org/10.1016/j.caeai.2022.100055

Godwin-Jones, R. (2021). Big data and language learning: Opportunities and challenges. *Language Learning & Technology, 25*(1), 4–19. http://hdl.handle.net/10125/44747

Godwin-Jones, R. (2022). Partnering with AI: Intelligent writing assistance and instructed language learning. *Language Learning & Technology, 26*(2), 5–24. http://doi.org/10125/73474

Goertler, S., & Schenker, T. (2021). *From study abroad to education abroad: Language proficiency, intercultural competence, and diversity.* Routledge.

Guichon, N. (2019). A self-tracking study of international students in France: Exploring opportunities for language and cultural learning. *ReCALL, 31*(3), 276–292. https://doi.org/10.1017/S0958344019000090

Hafner, C. A. (2015). Remix culture and English language teaching: The expression of learner voice in digital multimodal compositions. *TESOL Quarterly, 49*(3), 486–509. https://doi.org/10.1002/tesq.238

Hafner, C. A., & Ho, W. Y. J. (2020). Assessing digital multimodal composing in second language writing: Towards a process-based model. *Journal of Second Language Writing, 47*, 100710. https://doi.org/10.1016/j.jslw.2020.100710

Hellermann, J., & Thorne, S. L. (2022). Collaborative mobilizations of interbodied communication for cooperative action. *The Modern Language Journal, 106*(S1), 89–112. https://doi.org/10.1111/modl.12754

Johnson, S. (1997). *Interface culture: How new technology transforms the way we create and communicate.* HarperEdge.

Jones, R. H. (2019). The text is reading you: Teaching language in the age of the algorithm. *Linguistics and Education, 62*, 100750. https://doi.org/10.1016/j.linged.2019.100750

Kern, R. (1995). Restructuring classroom interaction with networked computers: Effects on quantity and quality of language production. *Modern Language Journal, 79*(4), 457–476. https://doi.org/10.1111/j.1540-4781.1995.tb05445.x

Kern, R. (2006). Perspectives on technology in learning and teaching languages. *TESOL Quarterly, 40*(1), 183–210. https://doi.org/10.2307/40264516

Kern, R. (2015). *Language, literacy, and technology.* Cambridge University Press.

Kern, R. (2021). Twenty-five years of digital literacies in CALL. *Language Learning & Technology, 25*(3), 132–150. http://hdl.handle.net/10125/73453

Kern, R., & Develotte, C. (Eds.). (2018). *Screens and scenes: Multimodal communication in online intercultural encounters.* Routledge.

Kinginger, C. (2013). Identity and language learning in study abroad. *Foreign Language Annals, 46*(3), 339–358. https://doi.org/10.1111/flan.12037

Knobel, M., & Lankshear, C. (2008). Remix: The art and craft of endless hybridization. *Journal of Adolescent and Adult Literacy, 52*(1), 22–33. https://doi.org/10.1598/JAAL.52.1.3

Kramsch, C. (2020). *Language as symbolic power.* Cambridge University Press.

Kress, G. (2003). *Literacy in the new media age.* Routledge.

Kress, G. (2010). *Multimodality: A social semiotic approach to contemporary communication.* Routledge.

Lan, Y. J. (2020). Immersion, interaction and experience-oriented learning: Bringing virtual reality into FL learning. *Language Learning & Technology, 24* (1), 1–15. http://hdl.handle.net/10125/44704

Levy, M. (1997). *Computer-assisted language learning: Context and conceptualization.* Clarendon Press.

Liddicoat, A. J., & Scarino, A. (2013). *Intercultural language teaching and learning.* Wiley Blackwell.

Liu, S., & Yu, G. (2022). L2 learners' engagement with automated feedback: An eye-tracking study. *Language Learning & Technology, 26*(2), 78–105. https://doi.org/10125/73480

Malinowski, D., & Dubreil, S. (2019). Linguistic Landscape and Language Learning. In C. Chapelle (Ed.), *The Encyclopedia of Applied Linguistics* (pp. 1–6). John Wiley & Sons. https://doi.org/10.1002/9781405198431.wbeal1492

New London Group. (1996). A pedagogy of multiliteracies: Designing social futures. *Harvard Educational Review, 66*(1), 60–92.

Noble, S. U. (2018). *Algorithms of oppression: How search engines reinforce racism.* New York University Press.

O'Dowd, R., & O'Rourke, B. (2019). New developments in virtual exchange in foreign language education. *Language Learning & Technology, 23*(3), 1–7.

O'Neill, E. M. (2019). Online translator, dictionary, and search engine use among L2 students. *CALL-EJ, 20*(1), 154–177.

Polio, C. (2019). Keeping the language in second language writing classes. *Journal of Second Language Writing, 46.* https://doi.org/10.1016/j.jslw.2019.100675

Polio, C., & Shi, L. (2012). Textual appropriation and source use in L2 writing. *Journal of Second Language Writing, 21*(2), 95–186.

Potolia, A., & Derivry-Plard, M. (Eds.). (2023). *Virtual exchange for intercultural language learning and teaching: Fostering communication for the digital age.* Routledge.

Sauro, S. (2017). Online fan practices and CALL. *CALICO Journal, 34*(2), 131–146.

Savicki, V., & Price, M. V. (2017). Components of reflection: A longitudinal analysis of study abroad student blog posts. *Frontiers: The Interdisciplinary Journal of Study Abroad, 29*(2), 51–62. https://doi.org/10.36366/frontiers .v29i2.392

Stockwell, G. (2016). Mobile language learning. In F. Farr & L. Murray (Eds.), *The Routledge handbook of language learning and technology* (pp. 296–307). Routledge.

Stockwell, G., & Reinders, H. (2019). Technology, motivation and autonomy, and teacher psychology in language learning: Exploring the myths and possibilities. *Annual Review of Applied Linguistics, 39,* 40–51. https://doi.org/10.1017/ S0267190519000084

Storch, N., & Li, M. (2017). Second language writing in the age of CMC: Affordances, multimodality, and collaboration. *Journal of Second Language Writing, 36,* 1–5.

Sykes, J. M. (2018). Digital games and language teaching and learning. *Foreign Language Annals, 51,* 219–224. https://doi.org/10.1111/flan.12325

Thoms, J. J., & Poole, F. (2017). Investigating linguistic, literary, and social affordances of L2 collaborative reading. *Language Learning & Technology, 21* (1), 139–156. https://dx.doi.org/10125/44615

Thorne, S. (2019, October 25). Desire lines and rewilding as catalysts for language learning. Institute of World Languages Fall Symposium 2019: Cyberspace: The final frontier – Reshaping language education through online and hybrid learning, University of Virginia.

Thorne, S. L., Black, R. W., & Sykes, J. M. (2009). Second language use, socialization, and learning in internet interest communities and online gaming. *Modern Language Journal, 93*, 802–821.

Vinall, K., & Hellmich, E. (2022). Do you speak translate? Reflections on the nature and role of translation. *L2 Journal, 14*(1), 4–25. https://escholarship.org/uc/item/98w4855d

Yi, Y., Shin, D.-s., & Cimasko, T. (2020). Special issue: Multimodal composing in multilingual learning and teaching contexts. *Journal of Second Language Writing, 47*, 1–6, 100717. https://doi.org/10.1016/j.jslw.2020.100717

Zuboff, S. (2019). *The age of surveillance capitalism: The fight for a human future at the new frontier of power.* Public Affairs.

Further Reading

Barton, D., & Lee, C. (2013). *Language online: Investigating digital texts and practices.* Routledge.

Barton and Lee explore the impact of digital communication on language and literacy practices. The book provides an in-depth examination of how people use language in various online contexts, including social media, online gaming, and blogging. This book provides valuable insights into the ever-evolving landscape of online communication in the digital age.

Jones, R. H., & Hafner, C. A. (2021). *Understanding digital literacies: A practical introduction* (2nd ed.). Routledge.

This book is an invaluable resource for educators, students, and anyone interested in enhancing their digital literacy skills. Its practical approach, supported by plentiful examples and case studies, empowers readers to navigate the complex digital landscape with confidence and understanding. In the second edition, the book presents excellent examples and case studies that enrich the learning experience.

Kern, R. (2021). Twenty-five years of digital literacies in CALL. *Language Learning & Technology, 25*(3), 132–150. http://hdl.handle.net/10125/73453

This article offers a comprehensive and insightful overview of the themes and research surrounding digital literacies in language learning. It provides a historical perspective, highlights current trends and issues, and offers guidance for future research, making it an essential resource for anyone interested in the intersection of digital technologies and language education.

Pegrum, M., Hockly, N., & Dudeney, G. (2022). *Digital literacies* (2nd ed.). Routledge.

This book provides comprehensive treatment of the many kinds of literacies language learners need and present their Framework of Digital Literacies 3.0 (organized around foci of communicating, informing, collaborating, and (re) designing) to assist teachers in thinking about ways of teaching the multifarious dimensions of digital literacies.

21

Overcoming Teacher Resistance

Yijen Wang

Introduction

It is widely accepted that technology has been reshaping the pedagogical landscape. Although technology has been commonly used in language classrooms, some teachers still prefer traditional methods of instruction or have limited use of educational technology. These teachers are labelled "resistance to change" (Howard & Mozejko, 2015). Reasons why teachers resist using innovative technology involve complex variables. Consequently, preparing language teachers to integrate technology into their classrooms has been the biggest challenge in language pedagogy. This chapter begins by outlining the historical and current statement of teacher resistance to a computer-assisted language learning (CALL) approach. The next section discusses the factors affecting teachers' decisions on technology adoptions based on literature. It then critically considers particularly the challenges in sociocultural contexts for CALL teacher education. In the following section, suggestions for educational institutions, teacher trainers, in-service and pre-service teachers are provided to help break the resistance. Finally, recommendations for future research and teaching practice are provided to guide the future direction of professional development.

Background

With the use of educational technology, it has been widely believed that the traditional roles of teachers will change dramatically, where classrooms will shift from teacher-centered to student-centered (Ertmer & Ottenbreit-Leftwich, 2010; Son, 2018). In traditional language classrooms, teachers are regarded as "managers" and/or "instructors" who are all-powerful, all-knowing, taking control over students' learning process (Wright, 1987). Literature in CALL has suggested that language teachers can take advantage of technology to improve their teaching efficiency, but, at the same time, teachers need to take on more roles in CALL environments. To clarify what roles educators play in CALL environments, Hubbard and Levy (2006) propose a role-based framework. They outline two prominent roles for CALL education: (1) functional roles, which include practitioners who apply knowledge and skill, developers who create something new or revise and adapt existing work, researchers who discover new information or pursue evaluation, and trainers who build CALL knowledge and skills in others and (2) institutional roles, which include pre-service teachers, in-service teachers, CALL specialists who are more skilled and knowledgeable about CALL compared with the classroom teacher, and the CALL professional, who has "relatively deeper knowledge and more elaborated skill sets in multiple areas" (pp. 14–15).

Building on this role framework, literature keeps exploring teacher roles in dynamic CALL contexts, describing teacher roles by using metaphors, for instance, cheerleader, facilitator, creator, observer, designer, and so on. Romeo and Hubbard (2010) stress the roles teachers play in providing students with technical, strategic, and pedagogical support (see also Stockwell & Hubbard, 2013). Furthermore, Lai (2015) points out that teachers should provide students with affection support, capacity support, and behavior support when using technology for out-of-class language learning, especially selecting appropriate materials for the learners. It seems that language teachers are expected to be equipped with not only pedagogical but also technical, psychological, social, and research knowledge and skills to integrate technology successfully into language classrooms.

These new roles, or perhaps more accurately, the new challenges for teachers, can be seen as threats in some senses. Teachers who are satisfied with their current teaching perceive CALL methods as an additional option. Integrating new technology into the classroom means that the present lesson plans, teaching process, and assessment need to be reconsidered. However, teachers are busy and revising teaching methods to incorporate technology may add to their workload in terms of time and effort. In particular, teachers have to learn the new technology first to decide how and what to utilize in the classrooms and then teach their students to use it. This "double innovation" (Cleaver, 2014) is regarded as the primary difficulty for in-service teachers in adopting new technology. Teachers who have established beliefs about how students learn and who had a skeptical view of the value of technology in the teaching/learning process in their early career are less likely to adopt or adapt technology (see also Ertmer et al., 2012; Kim et al., 2013; Lai, Yeung, & Hu, 2016). For example, traditional teachers perceive their roles as being taken away in technology-enhanced contexts. There is a common belief that younger students know more about technology than teachers, and thus, "the teacher's expertise in the subject area may also be threatened" (Lam & Lawrence, 2002, p. 298). That is to say, teachers, the so-called digital immigrants (Prensky, 2001), regard their students as "digital natives" (Prensky,

2001) who are experts of technology. This "myth" (see also Stockwell & Reinders, 2019) may transfer teacher–student roles, as teachers become learners of technology and students may teach teachers how to operate a device or software. Moreover, students are able to access information through the internet, social media, and mobile devices beyond teachers' control. In consequence, a teacher's authority seems to be challenged by technology because of the threat to the traditional role as a giver of knowledge.

Primary Themes

Challenges in CALL Teacher Education

As mentioned in the previous section, teachers take on multiple roles in using technology for teaching practices. What specific knowledge and skills teachers should prepare and how the contents should be taught to train teachers have recently attracted research in CALL teacher education (Son, 2018). Regarding the competence necessary for language teachers to integrate technology into classrooms, Hampel and Stickler (2005) propose a pyramid of skills ranging from lower level skills (e.g. basic computer skills, competence in using specific software, dealing with constraints and affordances of the software) to higher level skills (e.g. creating a community, facilitating communication as well as creativity, choice, selection, and development of their own teaching style). In order to help teachers to develop these competences, Son (2018) suggests providing different types of training (i.e. formal and informal learning) to teachers, according to their varying needs. However, previous studies measuring the effectiveness of teacher training have found a gap between teacher education and teaching practices. For example, Stockwell (2009) conducted a seminar with self-direction strategies to train teachers to educate themselves to acquire CALL knowledge. However, the results showed that most of the teachers preferred using existing resources rather than the new methods that had been introduced.

Insufficient training and professional development have been pointed out as the most problematic issues in CALL education, where institutions should take on a crucial role. Inadequate policy at institutional levels to facilitate teachers' CALL usage has been criticized (Stockwell, 2009). For example, many schools purchase iPads and ask teachers to use them for teaching without clear guidelines as to how iPada are expected to be used. Without a specific purpose to integrate iPads into the classroom, it is no surprise that teachers feel uncomfortable changing their existing teaching. The lack of professional CALL trainers who are familiar with both technology and language education to help language teachers with better use of technology has been problematic (Doshmanziari & Mostafavi, 2017). Although institutions have been putting effort into providing financial and technical support, something is missing. Researchers have suggested teacher learning communities (see Chapter 22, this volume) where teachers can help each other by sharing knowledge and providing feedback to peers. Yet, research has shown that the outcomes of teacher collaboration are not always positive as teachers' needs, competence, and teaching experience vary. A one-size-fits-all learning group may not meet the variety of professional learning requirements. Moreover, the diversity in social and cultural contexts affects the teacher community's effectiveness (de Jong, Meirink, & Admiraal, 2019; Little, 2003).

Teachers' Resistance to Technology Usage

The interest in CALL in teacher education and research into teacher educa-tion has been accelerating since the turn of the twenty-first century (Kessler & Hubbard, 2017); nevertheless, there remain teachers who are unwilling to integrate new technology into their teaching practices, and the reasons are still unclear (Howard & Mozejko, 2015; Stockwell & Reinders, 2019). Among the wide range of factors that hinder teacher's adoption of CALL and adaptation to it, Ertmer (1999) categorizes two main barriers to change, which he calls first-order and second-order barriers. Accordingly, the first-order (extrinsic) barriers refer to the lack of resources, accessibility, equipment, time, training, and support provided in teaching environments. These extrinsic factors are incremental but can be easily observed and overcome with the help of insti-tutions (e.g. providing funds, technical support, adequate training). However, the second-order (intrinsic) barriers are fundamental and personal, referring to teachers' views of technology integration and affective factors, which are "typically rooted in teachers' underlying beliefs about teaching and learning and may not be immediately apparent to others or even to the teachers themselves" (Ertmer, 1999, p. 51). This indicates the difficulty of measuring and eliminating teachers' intrinsic barriers. These barriers overwhelm the extrinsic barriers, as Ertmer (1999) notes that "even if every first-order barrier were removed, teachers would not automatically use technology to achieve the kind of meaningful outcomes advocated here" (p. 52). Many institutions provide teachers with sufficient digital devices (e.g. PCs and tablets), equip-ment, and network to resolve access constraints, along with technical training and support. However, some teachers are still reluctant to adopt the new methods due to their internal concerns. It seems that teachers' resistance to educational technology involves various issues which have been rooted in the educational system.

Affordances and Perceived Barriers of Technology

Teachers' reluctance to the pedagogical use of technology is usually trans-ferred to learners. Although constrained by institutional policy, teachers generally have some freedom to select the technology that they regard as useful for classroom practices, aligning with their teaching beliefs. Although technology may help teachers in their teaching effectiveness, at the same time, it is not without constraints. Being aware of what technology can/cannot bring us may help teachers work through the obstacles to technology integration into teaching contexts.

To explain the potentials and limitations of technology, Gibson (1979) coined the term "affordances," which he described as "the complementarity of the animal and the environment" (p. 127) from an ecological perspective. Later on, Gaver (1991) used the term to explore how technology can be used depending on the potential of technology and humans' perceptual information, suggesting that "affordances exist whether or not they are perceived, but it is because they are inherently about important properties that they need to be perceived" (p. 80). Similarly, Beatty (2010) referred to affordances as "the visual clues that an object gives to its use as well as what it is capable of doing in terms of both intended and unintended functions" (p. 50) and further constructed the word "misaffordances" to emphasize something that "distract[s] from the object's intended use" (p. 243). The notion of affordances underlines how technologies may be used appropriately or misused by the user; also, the affordances of a particular technology that teachers perceive may foster or hinder their usage (Stockwell, 2012). In other words, the use of technology may enhance the effectiveness of language education. Still, it should be noted that there are some perceived barriers to the successful integration of technology in teaching practices.

Stockwell (2022) identified three main issues regarding general technology implementation in educational settings: physical, psycho-social, and pedagogical issues. While used to describe mobile-assisted language learning, these categories are equally applicable to CALL. Physical issues are characteristics of the devices, for example, screen size, input methods, storage capacity, processor speeds, battery life, compatibility, and network access. Psychosocial issues are related to the user's views on the devices, their willingness or resistance to engage in activities with technology, attentional involvement, distraction, addictive effect, and, also, how the user perceives others' views in the social context. Pedagogical issues related to task or activity designs for second language learning and teaching involve teaching approaches and learning methods. Thus, when integrating technology into language classes, it should be kept in mind that the affordances of technology can relate to the design and functions, which determine the usefulness teachers perceive. Based on individuals' experiences, skills, and digital competences, different teachers have different attitudes toward educational technology. These attitudes influence their decisions to adopt new technology.

Contextual Factors

Given that individuals have different perceptions of technology, the factors affecting teachers' adoption of educational technology for language learning and teaching purposes are complex, involving individual aspects to environmental aspects. Researchers suggest looking into the complexity of contextual aspects to give a complete picture. Emphasizing the vital role that context

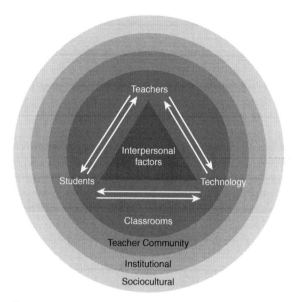

Figure 21.1 Contextual factors affecting teachers' resistance to educational technology.

plays in shaping teachers' and students' perceptions of educational technology, Stockwell (2012) breaks down three levels of diversity in CALL: individual, institutional, and societal factors that affect how CALL can be implemented and used. These three levels are interrelated and develop the language educational setting. To put it another way, teachers and students interact with technology in the classroom setting. Outside the classroom, a group of teachers with common goals and interests may support each other's ongoing professional development. These individuals (i.e. teachers and learners) are grouped into an institution in which they are necessarily affected by the institutional factors. For example, teachers and students have to follow institutional policies and guidelines to use a certain technology. Meanwhile, the institution itself is shaped by the society in which it is located, and in turn society is shaped by the individuals that comprise it.

Figure 21.1 illustrates the factors affecting teachers' resistance to technology and how individual factors influence how they use technology for language teaching purposes, and how they affect each other (e.g. their students and peers) within a certain context. Nested in an educational system, it is difficult to say which factor is more significant than the others, since they are all interrelated. Constrained by institutional policies, teachers are usually restricted or authorized to decide what and how to teach in their classrooms. Furthermore, sociocultural factors play a crucial role in influencing how people perceive themselves and others who shape the institution, the teacher community, and the classroom culture. As has been found in Wang's (2021) study, the language teachers in a Japanese university were unaware of whether the other teachers were using technology to teach in their classrooms. It was also found that there was a lack of sharing and discussion on teaching methods among the teachers, though they were in the same department. The strict hierarchical relationship may hamper the professional learning community, since the teachers were aware of the others with concerns about standing out from their senpai (juniors). In addition, being different from the others seems not to be encouraged in the context (see also Bartlett, 2020). This outlines the challenge for institutions in facilitating teacher communities with trust and better interactions.

The CALL environments constructed by these contextual factors have recently attracted attention in CALL research. It is suggested that researchers should look deep into the CALL context, as a variety of components are connected, from cultural, social, political, and institutional elements, to teaching practices and students' interaction (Blin, 2016). This range of factors highlights that the CALL context in which language education occurs influences the interrelationships between learners, teachers, and technology; furthermore, individuals' perceptions shaped by the context make heavy impacts on their adoption, selection, and implementation of technology.

Recommendations for Research and Practice

Recommendations for Research

Studies have shown that teachers' attitudes toward educational technology are not always aligned with their actual usage (Turner et al., 2010; Wang, 2021). Although teachers claim they are interested in technology, there is no guarantee that they will adopt new teaching methods that use it. As a result, if conducting research into teacher attitudes and use of technology, mixed-methods research is suggested with multiple data resources to avoid relying heavily on a single data resource that may cause bias. Thus, a single survey to investigate teachers' perceptions of technology use is inadequate.

Moreover, as Wang's (2021) study found, existing theories could not explain the whole picture of educational technology adoption, and so there is a need for specific CALL theories. Since the field of CALL stretches across technology and second language acquisition (SLA), each of the theories seems not to describe the phenomenon appropriately. For instance, the well-known technology acceptance model (TAM) (Davis, 1989) and the unified theory of acceptance and use of technology (UTAUT) (Venkatesh et al., 2003) might be useful to understand certain variables that influence users' behavioral intentions to use a specific technology. However, the models ignore that foreign language teachers and learners have specific needs and purposes for using technology (see Shachak, Kuziemsky, & Petersen, 2019 for the criticism). The educational contexts might differ from normal settings as well. Users of educational technology, specifically teachers and students constrained by the classroom climate and institutional policies, are influenced by social and cultural contexts. That is, the reasons why teachers are reluctant to adopt new technology are shaped by contextual factors that affect how they think and behave. Therefore, when conducting research regarding educational technology adoption, researchers should be aware that what we can see might be the tip of the iceberg. Simply extracting variables from existing frameworks can limit the factors that we can explore and in fact cloud our view of other less salient features.

In this sense, the final implication for research is the need for ethnographical studies and longitudinal studies in the CALL field. Many existing theoretical frameworks are insufficient to explain teachers' resistance; hence, observing teachers in their educational setting can help to understand the sociocultural situation to interpret teachers' resistance in terms of their attitudes and behaviors. It is also suggested that longitudinal studies are worth conducting to investigate teachers' willingness or resistance to change across a period of time. Since attitudes change over time, surveys taken at one point in time are unlikely to reveal the salient factors. By exploring what is 'under the surface' of external and internal barriers in a naturalistic setting, we can discover the difficulties that teachers are facing in educational technology integration.

Recommendations for Institutions

Understanding why teachers resist technology may help overcome the difficulties they have and then provide teachers and students with a better pedagogical environment. Despite the fact that external barriers can be observed and resolved, teachers may be reluctant to accept technical and pedagogical support due to internal factors. For instance, though the university has its technical support team, teachers may regard it as a group of non-experts on pedagogy and do not want them to interfere with their teaching (Wang, 2021). This concern highlights the need for CALL specialists and professionals (Hubbard & Levy, 2006) who specialize in technology and language teaching to enhance teaching effectiveness. Since language classes are so different from the regular lecture classes, language teachers' need for support might differ from the "one-size-fits-all" support center.

More critically speaking, institutions need to be aware of teachers' internal barriers. Previous negative experiences with technology may hamper teachers' expectations for new technology. When institutions are trying to promote a specific technology or to replace the existing technology with a new one, it may be helpful to explain the reasons for implementation. Also, there may be complexities in a hierarchical social environment. How to facilitate teachers to work together without the threat of "hurting the harmony" appears to be a challenge for institutions. The characters of a specific sociocultural context seem unlikely to be changed. However, providing teachers with a comfortable workplace with no fear of "losing face" might help teachers to become more willing to develop their professional skills. Therefore, institutions may help organize consulting groups for teachers or provide resources for teachers' professional development.

Additionally, institutions should also provide ongoing training for teachers to facilitate technology utilization in the workplace. Having not received training in foreign language education or technology use, the teachers tend to teach according to their classroom experiences or each in the ways they had been taught. Thus, a lack of knowledge in SLA appears to be a more urgent problem than technology adoption. The end goals for institutions should not merely be increasing the adoption of classroom technology on a larger scale but should be using technology to enhance a positive educational environment for faculty and students. If not, perhaps we should not have unreasonable expectations for technology. What has not been done in the real world might not miraculously appear in the virtual world. That is, if the teachers and students lack interactions in the classroom, they are unlikely to communicate enthusiastically through technology (e.g. a learning management system or a social networking site). In a similar vein, teacher-centered classrooms will not switch to student-centered environments simply by using technology.

The main conclusion that can be drawn in this section is that governments and institutions should be more aware of the purpose of promoting educational technology. It should not be a competition to compare who uses technology more in the classroom. After all, it is quality, not quantity, that counts – how and what educators use for teaching and the outcomes matter. How to encourage teachers to use educational technology as the administration expects might be an ongoing challenge. When establishing institutional policies regarding technology implementation, it might be helpful if both teachers and students take part in the decision-making process. Listening to teachers' and students' voices might also lead to an understanding of the actual conditions and difficulties in technology integration.

Recommendations for Pedagogy

The key to success for educational technology integration into foreign language classes may be teachers, who play a crucial role in educational settings, making most of the decisions for the students regarding what materials to use, and what approaches to teach (whether with or without technology). Only if teachers value CALL technology can it be successfully utilized. The potential of technology may be overestimated by governments and underestimated by teachers with a lack of professional knowledge in terms of CALL. It is not the fault of technology, but rather, the responsibility lies with humans. With a lack of understanding of technology and SLA, teachers may have limited technology use and rarely adopt new teaching methods. It is expected that experienced in-service teachers are satisfied with their current teaching, which might become the main obstacle to accepting new teaching methods. Their beliefs about teaching and learning seem to be established in the early stage of their career. Moreover, there is no urgent need for them to change their existing teaching practices. Since most of the teachers have not only teaching work but also administrative work and research activities, integrating educational technology into the classrooms might increase their workload, which means that they have to change the existing syllabus and adjust their current teaching styles. As a consequence, avoiding technology might be a safe way for experienced teachers. However, the more "new methods" teachers try, the more questions may arise about teaching and learning. Using technology for education may not reduce teachers' workload, but it provides teachers with an opportunity to reflect on their existing teaching.

Stepping out of their comfort zone, teachers may find that their fears are unfounded. Students are not as competent or confident with their digital skills as we might expect. They still need teachers' professional support. Students may be familiar with technology, but they do not know how to use it for language learning. We should keep in mind that the students of today may be teachers in the future, which means that they may teach someday in the same way as they have been taught. After all, teachers' attitudes toward new methods affect students' perceptions in some sense. If teachers are more willing to try different teaching methods, students may benefit from various learning strategies that meet their needs and interests. Also, teachers should provide students with not only language knowledge but also technical and psychological support. For example, teachers should give students more control over their learning and encourage them to learn with technology, which allows students to practice learning autonomy.

Last but not least, traditional teaching roles may be challenged by educational technology, but every teacher and teacher-to-be should all be prepared to use technology for teaching. Teachers should be aware that technology will not replace teachers, but teachers who do not use technology may be replaced. Moreover, in-service teachers should be open-minded to learn up-to-date SLA theories and trends, which can help integrate technology into teaching practices more effectively. Otherwise, technology becomes simply a tool to make existing teaching look "fancy," without any real improvements to education.

Future Directions

Technology adoption is not the end goal of CALL education but a goal to assist language learning, as its name suggests. The "normalization" (Bax, 2003) of CALL has been unprecedentedly accelerated due to the COVID-19 pandemic. The sudden closure of schools "forced" teachers to change their current teaching practices to adopt and adapt educational technology they were not familiar with. Although technology was once a major stumbling block to many in distance teaching and remote classrooms, it seems to have become less salient in the post-COVID era. New technologies are emerging constantly - most recently generative AI technologies - and with each new innovation comes the need for teachers to familiarize themselves with it. The innovation of educational technology requires not only teachers but also policy makers, faculty, and other stakeholders to prepare for the change in order to provide a better educational environment to support language learning with the use of technology.

References

Bartlett, K. (2020). Teacher praxis within the "communicative course of study guidelines" in Japan: Post-implementation pedagogy. *Australian Journal of Applied Linguistics, 3*(2), 168–182. https://doi.org/10.29140/ajal.v3n2.316

Bax, S. (2003). CALL: Past, present and future. *System, 31*(1), 13–28.

Beatty, K. (2010). *Teaching and researching computer-assisted language learning* (2nd ed.). Longman. https://doi.org/10.4324/9781315833774

Blin, F. (2016). Toward an "ecological" CALL theory: Theoretical perspectives and their instantiation in CALL research and practice. In F. Farr & L. Murray (Eds.), *The Routledge handbook of language learning and technology* (pp. 39–54). Routledge.

Cleaver, S. (2014). Technology in the classroom: Helpful or harmful? Education.com. Retrieved October 15, 2023 from www.education.com/magazine/article/effective-technology-teaching-child/

de Jong, L., Meirink, J., & Admiraal, W. (2019). School-based teacher collaboration: Different learning opportunities across various contexts. *Teaching and Teacher Education, 86*, 102925. https://doi.org/10.1016/j.tate.2019.102925

Davis, F. D. (1989). Perceived usefulness, perceived ease of use, and user acceptance of information technology. *MIS Quarterly, 13*(3), 319–340.

Doshmanziari. E., & Mostafavi. A. (2017). Barriers to use of educational technology in the learning process of primary school students in District 13 in Tehran. *International Education Studies, 10*(2). 44–53. https://doi.org/10.5539/ies.v10n2p44

Ertmer, P. A. (1999). Addressing first- and second-order barriers to change: Strategies for technology integration. *Educational Technology Research and Development, 47*(4), 47–61.

Ertmer, P. A., & Ottenbreit-Leftwich, A. T. (2010). Teacher technology change: How knowledge, confidence, beliefs, and culture intersect. *Journal of Research on Technology in Education, 42*(3), 255–284.

Ertmer, P. A., Ottenbreit-Leftwich, A. T., Sadik, O., Sendurur, E., & Sendurur, P. (2012). Teacher beliefs and technology integration practices: A critical relationship. *Computers & Education, 59*(2), 423–435. https://doi.org/10.1016/j.compedu.2012.02.001

Gaver, W. (1991). Technology affordances. In S. P. Robertson, G. M. Olson, & J. S. Olson (Eds.), *Proceedings of SIGCHI Conference on Human Factors in Computing Systems* (pp. 79–84). ACM. https://doi.org/10.1145/108844.108856

Gibson, J. J. (1979). *The ecological approach to visual perception.* Lawrence Erlbaum Associates.

Hampel, R., & Stickler, U. (2005). New skills for new classrooms: Training tutors to teach languages online. *Computer Assisted Language Learning, 18*(4), 311–326.

Howard, S. K., & Mozejko, A. (2015). Teachers: Technology, change and resistance. In M. Henderson & G. Romeo (Eds.), *Teaching and digital technologies: Big issues and critical questions* (pp. 307–317). Cambridge University Press.

Hubbard, P., & Levy, M. (2006) (Eds.). *Teacher education in CALL.* Amsterdam: Benjamins.

Kessler, G., & Hubbard, P. (2017). Language teacher education and technology. In C. Chapelle & S. Sauro (Eds.), *The handbook of technology and second language teaching and learning* (pp. 278–292). John Wiley & Sons. https://doi.org/10.1002/9781118914069.ch19

Kim, C., Kim, M. K., Lee, C., Spector, J. M., & DeMeester, K. (2013). Teacher beliefs and technology integration. *Teaching and Teacher Education, 29,* 76–85. https://doi.org/10.1016/j.tate.2012.08.005

Lai, C. (2015). Modeling teachers' influence on learners' self-directed use of technology for language learning outside the classroom. *Computers & Education, 82,* 74–83. https://doi.org/10.1016/j.compedu.2014.11.005

Lai, C., Yeung, Y., & Hu, J. (2016). University student and teacher perceptions of teacher roles in promoting autonomous language learning with technology outside the classroom. *Computer Assisted Language Learning, 29*(4), 703–723. https://doi.org/10.1080/09588221.2015.1016441

Lam, Y., & Lawrence, G. (2002). Teacher–student role redefinition during a computer-based second language project: Are computers catalysts for empowering change? *Computer Assisted Language Learning, 15*(3), 295–315.

Little, J. W. (2003). Inside teacher community: Representations of classroom practice. *Teachers College Record, 105*(6), 913–945. https://doi.org/10.1111/1467-9620.00273

Prensky, M. (2001). Digital natives, digital immigrants. *On the Horizon, 9*(5), 1–6.

Romeo, K., & Hubbard, P. (2010). Pervasive CALL learner training for improving listening proficiency. In M. Levy, F. Blin, C. Siskin, & O. Takeuchi (Eds.), *WorldCALL: International perspectives on computer assisted language learning* (pp. 215–229). Routledge.

Shachak, A., Kuziemsky, C., & Petersen, D. (2019). Beyond TAM and UTAUT: Future directions for HIT implementation research. *Journal of Biomedical Informatics, 100,* 103315. https://doi.org/10.1016/j.jbi.2019.103315

Son, J. B. (2018). *Teacher development in technology-enhanced language teaching.* Palgrave Macmillan. https://doi.org/10.1007/978-3-319-75711-7

Stockwell, G. (2009). Teacher education in CALL: Teaching teachers to educate themselves. *International Journal of Innovation in Language Learning and Teaching, 3*(1), 99–112. https://doi.org/10.1080/17501220802655524

Stockwell, G. (2012). *Computer assisted language learning: Diversity in research & practice.* Cambridge University Press. https://doi.org/10.1017/CBO9781139060981

Stockwell, G. (2022). *Mobile assisted language learning: Concepts, contexts & challenges.* Cambridge University Press.

Stockwell, G., & Hubbard, P. (2013). Some emerging principles for mobile-assisted language learning. In *TIRF Report, 2013,* 1–14.

Stockwell, G., & Reinders, H. (2019). Technology, motivation and autonomy, and teacher psychology in language learning: Exploring the myths and possibilities. *Annual Review of Applied Linguistics, 39,* 40–51. https://doi.org/10.1017/S0267190519000084

Turner, M., Kitchenham, B., Brereton, P., Charters, S., & Budgen, D. (2010). Does the technology acceptance model predict actual use? A systematic literature review. *Information and Software Technology, 52*(5), 463–479. https://doi.org/10.1016/j.infsof.2009.11.005

Venkatesh, V., Morris, M. G., Davis, G. B., & Davis, F. D. (2003). User acceptance of information technology: Toward a unified view. *MIS Quarterly. 27*(3), 425–478. https://doi.org/10.2307/30036540

Wang, Y. (2021). In-service teachers' perceptions of technology integration and practices in a Japanese university context. *The JALT CALL Journal, 17*(1), 45–71. https://doi.org/10.29140/jaltcall.v17n1.377

Wright, T. (1987). *The roles of teachers and learners.* Oxford University Press.

Further Reading

Farrell, T. S. C. (2022). *Insights into professional development in language teaching.* Castledown. https://doi.org/10.29140/9781914291036
This book offers a comprehensive overview of the current state of professional development in language teaching. Providing a wealth of research and practical advice on how to design and implement effective professional development programs, this book is a valuable resource for language teachers, teacher educators, and other stakeholders.

Son, J. B. (2018). *Teacher development in technology-enhanced language teaching.* Palgrave Macmillan. https://doi.org/10.1007/978-3-319-75711-7
This book outlines practical insights and guidance on how to develop teachers' technological competence and pedagogical skills, while also exploring the benefits and challenges of using technology in language teaching. The book is easy to read and provides useful resources for language teachers looking to integrate technology into their classrooms.

22

Online Communities for Teachers

Yurika Ito

Introduction

The twenty-first century has witnessed growing interest in preparing language teachers to use technology for teaching purposes (e.g. Hubbard & Levy, 2006; Kessler, 2021; Kessler & Hubbard, 2017; Son & Windeatt, 2017). Despite the importance of language teachers continually enhancing their knowledge and skills in computer-assisted language learning (CALL) throughout their entire careers (Son, 2018), a number of shortcomings associated with the current state of CALL teacher preparation have been identified, one of which, persistently mentioned in the literature, being the general lack of access to effective technology training courses (Hubbard, 2008, 2018; Kessler, 2006). The reality is that due to barriers related to factors such as cost, time, and geographical location, not all language teachers are able to learn through such training courses, and some would even argue that teacher training courses in general do not necessarily prepare them for real-world teaching situations (e.g. Farrell, 2022). As a result, language teachers often have no choice but to educate themselves, relying on self-directed informal modes of learning (e.g. Ito, 2024; Son, 2014). As an alternative approach to CALL teacher preparation, various scholars have recommended that they locate teacher communities, where they are able to connect with others to exchange resources and ideas, seek advice, and provide each other with support (Stockwell, 2009), and in recent years, these have been easily found online (Hanson-Smith, 2016).

Online communities have existed for several decades but have gained in popularity since the launch of the first social networking site (SNS) in the late 1990s (boyd & Ellison, 2007), having a profound impact on people's lives. It is not surprising, then, that teachers with a broad range of teaching experiences and backgrounds have looked at SNSs as a means of connecting with others to discuss the various problems that they face, and communities have appeared in platforms, such as Facebook and Twitter (now known as X). In the context of language teaching, there have been a limited number of studies on online language teacher communities (cf. Wesely, 2013), and even fewer studies have been set where technology is the primary focus of the discussions of the online language teacher community (cf. Ito, 2023). This chapter therefore examines the potential value of online language teacher communities on SNSs in assisting language using technology for teaching purposes. It begins with a look at the evolution of online teacher communities, including the various types of online communities developed over time. The subsequent sections draw upon prior research to identify the possible benefits and challenges in teachers' use of online teacher communities on SNSs and current trends in the field. The concluding section provides an overview of research directions, looking to the future of online teacher communities on SNSs as a key component in supporting language teachers.

Background

While online teacher communities have been a rather underexplored area of research (Lantz-Anderson, Lundin, & Selwyn, 2018; Maciá & García, 2016), they have been around for quite some time. The earlier forms of online communities can be dated back as early as the 1980s, when computer bulletin board systems (BBSs) were used among teachers. Accessible through the use of a home computer and dial-up modem (i.e. a device that enables data communication over a telephone line) (Cavazos, 1992), BBSs were essentially a text-based online community in which users were able to leave messages and files for a group of individuals interested in a certain topic. During the earlier days, teachers often appeared to be making use of only the rudimentary functions, mainly using them to explore and become familiar with the platform (Chandler, 1988). As time progressed, they were starting to use them to participate in public discussions and to share and acquire teaching-related information (Chandler, 2000). Although BBSs were relatively broadly used, participants were not representative of the entire teaching profession, with many of them being computer literate and typically having a background in the sciences (Chandler, 2000).

   In the ensuing years when the use of the internet became increasingly affordable and mainstream, more accessible forms of online communities for teachers appeared, commonly taking the form of email discussion lists (e.g. Riding, 2001). The early 1990s saw the launch of various online communities for language teachers: The TESL-L Electronic Network project, founded by Anthea Tillyer in 1992, was developed as an email-based resource for teachers of English as a second language (ESL) or English as a foreign language (EFL) (see Warschauer, 1995). Besides the main mailing list, users were able to subscribe to a number of sublists that focused on particular aspects of teaching, including those that discuss topics pertaining to CALL, email pen-pal exchanges, teaching job opportunities, and intercultural communication (Kovacs, 1994). Although the TESL-L mailing lists have been discontinued and the email messages shared among the teachers are no longer accessible, the existence of the CALL sublist illustrates that since the early 1990s, a subset of English language teachers were interested in exchanging CALL-related ideas, experiences, and resources with like-minded others.

Another notable example of an email discussion list-based online community intended for language teachers is the Foreign Language Teaching Forum (FLTeach), which, as of 2022, is still being used among language teachers around the world. Originally founded in 1994 by Jean LeLoup and Bob Ponterio, the online community started as an email discussion list, enabling language teachers to send each other messages to discuss matters related to teaching (LeLoup & Ponterio, 2017). Although the primary focus of the online community was on foreign language teaching and not on technology per say, the archives of the messages shared in the discussion list show that language teachers were sharing information about various events, resources, and ideas pertinent to the topic of technology. Since the early days of the online community, email subscribers were receiving messages inviting them to participate in technology-related events, including conferences, courses, and workshops, asking for their advice on how to incorporate technology in their teaching, and sharing their views and experiences about using technology in language learning settings. Besides the active email discussion list, the FLTeach online community has recently expanded to SNSs, such as Facebook

In Hanson-Smith's (2016) book chapter, she introduces the Webheads in Action (WiA) as a prime example of an active global online community for teachers using technology. Since it was initially founded in 1998 by Vance Stevens, WiA members have been connecting with each other using various asynchronous and synchronous Web 2.0 and computer-mediated communication tools on platforms such as the now defunct platforms Tapped In and Yahoo! Group and other currently available SNSs such as LinkedIn and Facebook (see Stevens, 2018). One key feature of the online community is that the WiA community members meet online on a regular basis to think about ways to adapt to emerging technological tools in their language learning classes and send each other messages about related issues, questions, and events (Yilmaz & Stevens, 2012). As part of the WiA community, a splinter community, Learning2gether, was initiated in 2009, and similar to the WiA community, Learning2gether community members essentially connect with each other through different online activities, such as reading each other's webpages, listening to the weekly webcasts offered by its members, participating in the weekly live meetings, and interacting with each other on Facebook (Stevens, 2020).

While the aforementioned examples only illustrate some of the ways in which language teachers have been utilizing online communities, what seems to be evident from these long-running online communities is that they have reached out to SNS platforms. With SNSs growing in popularity, it is not entirely unexpected that they have become one of the main places where language teachers turn to find other teachers teaching in similar contexts. However, much remains unknown about how these platforms are actually providing support for language teachers, especially those who are using technology for teaching purposes. Hence, the following sections aim to outline the current literature on teachers' use of online communities on SNSs, examining studies conducted in both language teaching and non-language teaching contexts.

Primary Themes

In recent years, it has become increasingly common for teachers to participate in free and easily accessible online communities found on SNSs to connect with other teachers to discover resources, ask questions, and expand their professional learning networks. Since the early 2010s, a growing number of scholars have therefore been interested in understanding how teachers are actually capitalizing upon them for professional purposes. As relevant research conducted thus far has predominantly focused on capturing associated benefits and challenges in teachers' use of online teacher communities on SNSs, the current section addresses a few of these key benefits and challenges.

Potential Benefits of Teachers' Use of Online Teacher Communities

According to Lantz-Anderson, Lundin, and Selwyn (2018), who conducted a systematic review of empirical studies on online teacher communities, one commonly identified benefit is that online communities provide teachers with a source of information about their teaching. For instance, Carpenter and Krutka (2015) employed a questionnaire that received 755 responses from teachers who use Twitter professionally and found that they most frequently use the platform to share and acquire teaching-related resources (96 per cent). In their study, participants reported on a number of occasions when their actual lessons had been directly influenced by the ideas and resources accessed through Twitter. Specifically, twenty-six participants reported that they were able to learn about educational technologies, with several of them commenting that their involvement in Twitter contributed to an increased knowledge and use of them in their classes. Although the extent to which the acquired information affects teaching practice is not yet fully known, the study illustrates how some teachers value these platforms for teaching ideas and resources that they otherwise "may not come in contact with due to limitations of professional development money" (Carpenter & Krutka, 2015, p. 718).

Another frequently mentioned benefit is that online teacher communities provide teachers with a space where they can ask for help. For example, Yildirim (2019), who observed a Facebook community for high school mathematics teachers in Turkey, found that teachers were seeking assistance, mainly asking questions about mathematical problems. Over 90 percent of the mathematical problems shared in the online community were solved during the one-month long observation, and the interviews conducted with fourteen of the members suggest that the posts asking for help were responded to quickly and the feedback rarely contained any mistakes. Besides mathematical problems, teachers in the community were asking questions related to school curriculum, resources, techno-pedagogical information, and university entrance examinations to seek advice. Since online communities are used by a range of teachers of varying teaching backgrounds, experiences, and levels of expertise, they offer easy access to an array of thoughts, opinions, and perspectives.

In addition to providing professional support, prior research has also illustrated that online teacher communities are providing teachers with a source of emotional support. In Davis' (2015) study, for instance, seventeen out of nineteen interviewees participating in the discussions occurring in an online teacher community on Twitter indicated in their interviews that they felt a sense of belonging through engaging with each other on the online platform. Some interviewees also reported that they perceived the online community as a source of encouragement when they were feeling discouraged as a teacher. Closely related to this, in multiple studies (e.g. Carpenter & Krutka, 2015; Carpenter et al., 2020a; Ito, 2023b; Wesely, 2013), teachers were evidently participating in online communities to combat professional isolation. Drawing from multiple data sources, including participant observation of a Twitter community for world language teachers and interviews with nine community members, Wesely (2013) found that many community members struggled with professional isolation, several of whom were working as the only foreign language teacher in a geographically remote area, teaching a certain foreign language within a single school, or receiving limited support from their administrators and coworkers. The findings suggested that they were joining the observed online community for world language teachers on Twitter to ameliorate their feelings of professional loneliness and isolation.

Potential Challenges in Teachers' Use of Online Teacher Communities

It is clear that online teacher communities bring value to teachers' professional lives, but they are not without flaws. As outlined as one of the key benefits in the previous section, online teacher communities potentially offer teachers a place where they can explore ideas by searching through the rich source of shared information. However, since, as Carpenter and Harvey (2019, p. 1) point out, "there's no referee on social media," the quality of the content shared in the online teacher communities is not always guaranteed. Although community administrators may delete posts that are obviously wrong or misleading (Staudt, St. Clair, & Martinez, 2013), the shared content at times may not be credible or reliable. For example, Hertel and Wessman-Enzinger (2017) analyzed 176 mathematics teaching resources shared on Pinterest, finding that approximately one-third of the posts contained some type of mathematical error. Moreover, in some cases, teachers may find the posts shared in the online communities unpleasant. In Carpenter and Harvey's (2019) study, 43.8 percent of the teachers (n=21) who were utilizing online teacher communities on SNSs reported that they came across posts that were deemed unprofessional, with one teacher describing that she was frustrated by three individuals who were "dropping vulgar language when it wasn't necessary" (p. 6). Furthermore, in the same study, a number of teachers expressed that they were frustrated at posts that were promoting commercial products or posts that were not related to teaching. This seems to illuminate a growing problem that online teacher communities are attracting unwanted "spam" messages (i.e. posts that are irrelevant or unsolicited) (Carpenter et al., 2020b), which may also have an impact on how they are perceived and used. In closed Facebook groups (e.g. Yildirim, 2019) and online discussion boards hosted on Reddit (e.g. Staudt Willet & Carpenter, 2020), administrators may be able to filter out obvious spam posts, but platforms such as Twitter are largely unmoderated and therefore dealing with such posts may be more difficult (Carpenter et al., 2020b).

Moreover, an additional challenge regarding teachers' use of online teacher communities relates to the issue of time. Although online teacher communities enable teachers to interact with others in the comfort of their own homes, one point easily forgotten is that participating in online teacher communities still requires a considerable amount of time and effort on the teacher's part. For example, in a study conducted by Duncan-Howell (2010), it was found that some teachers in online teacher communities spent up to six hours a week reading through the online posts and engaging in discussions with community members. Despite spending a notable amount of time participating in the communities, teachers' efforts are not always recognized and appreciated by peers or their employers. Administrators or fellow colleagues may not accept this unconventional form of supporting or learning as "actual work," making it difficult for them to access the online communities during working hours at the workplace (Davis, 2015). Another challenge related to this point is the blurring of boundaries between work and private time. While busy teachers may be initially attracted to online communities because they can use them in their spare time, one danger of this is that without realizing, they may end up spending long hours on these spaces and potentially feeling overburdened with all the additional work.

The difficulty in sustaining an active online community should also be noted as another potential challenge. A study by Rutherford (2010), which extensively examined a teacher community on Facebook for teachers teaching in Ontario for a one-year period between 2007 and 2008, revealed that only 384 members were participating in the discussions despite having nearly eight thousand community members. In a similar vein, in a study of eight years' worth of posts shared in a large technology-focused teacher community on Facebook with over 20,000 members, Nelimarkka et al. (2021) found that only approximately 10 percent of the members were actively writing posts and comments. A large number of online community members are typically reported to be "lurkers" (i.e. members who mostly observe the community without actively participating in the discussions) (Goodyear, Parker, & Casey, 2019), but if too many members lurk without actively posting or commenting, the community will likely fail and discontinued.

Current Research and Practice

Reviewing earlier works published between 2009 and 2015, Maciá and García's (2016) study was one of the first studies that provided a useful overview of research into informal online teacher communities on SNSs, though their review was not limited to only online communities on SNSs and included a few that were formed on other web-based platforms (e.g. Cloudworks, Moodle). In their review of twenty-three articles, they identified several trends based on the reviewed studies during the six-year period. Firstly, they found that the most common online environment used in the literature was Twitter (e.g. Davis, 2015), but other SNS platforms, such as Facebook (e.g. Ranieri, Manca, & Fini, 2012) and Ning (e.g. Coutinho & Lisbôa, 2013) were also commonly used. Another trend was that the reviewed studies were mostly set in North America and Europe, with the United States being by far the most widely studied context (e.g. Booth, 2012). It was apparent that there was a general lack of studies set in Oceania (cf. Cranefield & Yoong, 2009) and Asia (cf. Tseng & Kuo, 2014), and no studies were found to be set in Africa, South America, Central America, or the Middle East. Moreover, the focus of the studied online communities varied, dealing with a broad range of themes about general education (e.g. Duncan-Howell, 2010) and specific subjects, including language teaching (e.g. Wesely, 2013) and science teaching (e.g. Tsai, 2012).

It goes without saying that SNSs have continued to evolve since Maciá and García's (2016) study, and the literature on online teacher communities on SNSs have reflected this, although there is yet to be a wide-scale comprehensive research synthesis. Since the late 2010s, there have been additional studies examining how teachers are utilizing online teacher communities on existing platforms such as Twitter (e.g. Staudt Willet, 2019) and Facebook (e.g. Kelly & Antonio, 2016; Yildirim, 2019), and on platforms that did not appear in Maciá and García's (2016) study such as Reddit (e.g. Staudt Willet & Carpenter, 2020). Like Twitter and Facebook, Reddit has been available since the mid 2000s but often neglected by educational researchers. As more teachers are reaching out beyond the traditional SNSs, scholars are turning their attention toward capturing teachers' use of online teacher communities on comparatively newer platforms such as Instagram (e.g. Carpenter et al., 2020a), Pinterest (e.g. Schroeder, Curcio, & Lundgren, 2019), Whatsapp (e.g. Motteram, Dawson, & Al-Masri, 2020), and TikTok (e.g. Hartung et al., 2022). The literature is also expanding in terms of the set context of the online teacher communities, with more studies conducted in regions that previously received little attention. An example of this is the work by Motteram et al. (2020), which explored the learning of Syrian language teachers located in the Zataari refugee camp in Jordan.

Undoubtedly, technology has changed the face of education, and given the rapid changes in the teaching and learning process brought by emerging technologies, one can logically expect that the discussion topics in the online teacher communities reflect these changes. Nelimarkka et al. (2021), for instance, conducted an in-depth investigation of a Finnish Facebook teacher community with a primary focus on pedagogical ICT use and found that online community members were utilizing it to tackle technical issues and to address their worries about implementing technology into their teaching. Moreover, even in online teacher communities in which the primary focus is not on technology, teachers are discussing topics related to technology, as illustrated in the study conducted by Yildirim (2019), who found that the online community members in the mathematics Facebook teacher community were sharing information and documents about "technological content knowledge" and asking for help about "techno-pedagogical information" (pp. 598–599). Furthermore, as a result of the onset of the COVID-19 pandemic in early 2020, there was a large influx of teachers taking part in online teacher communities to discuss matters related to online teaching. As teachers were suddenly forced to teach online without little or no support (MacIntyre, Gregersen, & Mercer, 2020), it is not entirely unexpected that teachers were reaching out for support, and given that their interactions with peers or colleagues become predominantly online, seeking assistance from online communities was a natural progression. Teachers were not only able to learn how to teach online, but also to find emotional support and overcome feelings of professional isolation, problems that were exacerbated by the pandemic (Ito, 2023a; Trust et al., 2020). Although it is hard to say at this point how teachers will make use of these online teacher communities in the post-pandemic era, it seems probable that they will continually play a prominent role in teachers' professional lives, considering how education and technology are closely intertwined.

Recommendations for Research and Practice

With SNS platforms in a constant state of flux, investigating online teacher communities poses various problems. Not the least of these is that researchers face the challenge of staying relevant when their field is perpetually subjected to updates (Curwood & Biddolph, 2017). As various new features are released, the way users interact with each other in these spaces changes. For instance, when the Facebook group feature was first launched in 2010, Facebook users mostly used the groups to write posts and comments to other members. Since then, although users primarily still use these groups to share posts and comments, numerous additional features are now available: They can attach URL links, images, and videos, broadcast live videos, and launch poll questions. More recently, in June 2022, Facebook introduced a new feature in which group administrators can create text-based chat channels and audio-based channels within a single group to promote more casual and deeper conversations among members who want to discuss a specific topic (Smith, 2022). In this sense, researchers need to be aware of such updates and adapt their research designs accordingly to capture new forms of engagement on these rapidly changing platforms.

An important point researchers need to consider is the ethicality of investigating online communities. At present, as there are no official universal codes of ethics involving online research, within relevant literature, only a handful of scholars explicitly address research ethics in their studies (e.g. Ito, 2023a; Kelly & Antonio, 2016). Although online researchers are generally left to their own discretion and judgement, they need to be equally if not more careful than traditional researchers when dealing with ethical dilemmas. When using data collected from SNSs, online researchers are compelled to adhere to general principles of research ethics, considering key issues such as informed consent, anonymity, confidentiality, and risk of harm (Blyth, 2015; Woodfield & Iphofen, 2018). Moreover, even if the study seems ethically viable, researchers are still obliged to follow the terms and conditions of the SNS platform in question, which can unexpectedly change without warning. It is common practice for researchers to use application programming interfaces (APIs) to extract data from online communities on SNSs (e.g. Nelimarkka et al., 2021; Staudt Willet, 2019), but each platform has differing policies regarding their APIs. Various platforms such as X grant access to researchers to publicly available online posts and comments if the sole use of the data is for academic research purposes, but this is not applicable to all platforms. Following the Facebook–Cambridge Analytica data scandal in 2018, Facebook restricted its API, making it difficult for researchers to extract data from the platform (van der Vlist et al., 2022). Although the platform has since updated its terms and policies to allow certain researchers to use their API (Lohman, 2021), such changes can be problematic to researchers, who may suddenly lose access to their dataset.

Despite these constraints, researchers should not be afraid to conduct longitudinal studies to see how teachers make use of online teacher communities over time. To date, the majority of research on online teacher communities on SNSs has employed cross-sectional research designs, examining the reasons why teachers participate in online communities and what they do in these communities at a single point in time. Although teachers' involvement in online teacher communities is not static (Carpenter, Krutka, & Trust, 2022), little is known about why some teachers continually participate in them and others discontinue (Xing & Gao, 2018). It is therefore worth exploring the changes into teachers' commitment in online communities over an extended period of time.

Future Directions

Given the dynamic nature of SNSs, it is rather difficult to accurately predict what will happen to online teacher communities in the future, but based on what we have witnessed so far, several assumptions can be made: As repeatedly emphasized throughout the chapter, the landscape of SNSs has changed over the years, with newer platforms appearing one after another.

Following the general trends of SNSs, teachers have increasingly been reaching out to newer platforms, such as Instagram and TikTok. It is therefore not too much of a leap to assume that teachers will continue to cultivate emerging platforms to fit their professional needs and contexts. Having said that, the fact that well-established platforms such as Facebook and X, have remained popular among teachers throughout the years may suggest that they will be here for the long haul. As some teachers are reported to be currently making use of online teacher communities across multiple platforms at the same time (e.g. Carpenter & Harvey, 2019), rather than one platform replacing another, it may be that they will be used in a complementary way, enabling teachers to leverage the unique affordances that each platform has to offer.

Second, as previously mentioned, it is still early to say how language teachers will continue to use online teacher communities on SNSs after the COVID-19 pandemic ends completely, but an anticipated outcome of the increased reliance of them during the pandemic is the lowering of affective barriers toward using SNSs, which could potentially lead to an increased use of them for teaching purposes. As prior research has revealed that technology integration is affected by teachers' own personal experiences of using technology (e.g. Park & Son, 2020), particularly when it comes to using social networking tools in classes (Kusuma, 2022). If they are making use of SNSs themselves, it is expected that they will be able to see for themselves the ways in which students can benefit from the incorporation of them (see Lomika & Lord, 2016) and be more open to the idea of using them to enhance their students' learning.

Finally, another potential outcome brought by the pandemic is that more teachers will be aware of the power that online communities hold, especially in times of need. It was clear that the pandemic further aggravated the ongoing issue of professional isolation, as many teachers struggled to learn how to navigate their online classes with little or no support from their coworkers or administrators (Knight, 2020). Although schools and universities around the world have restarted in-person classes, many teachers are still required to use technology in their classes, and as a result, they will continue to face pressure to learn how to use technology for teaching purposes without receiving much support. To make matters worse, school administrators and other relevant stakeholders may now hold a false impression that teachers are fully capable of using technology because of gained experience from teaching online during the pandemic and overlook the urgency of investing in teachers' professional learning. Without proper guidance or assistance, however, it is difficult for them to enhance their knowledge and skills in technology, so as a realistic and viable option, the first place where teachers look to receive support from here onward may be in online teacher communities on SNSs.

In conclusion, online teacher communities on SNSs show great promise in supporting language teachers, especially those who have limited funds and resources. Although they will not fix all the problems that language teachers will encounter when using technology for teaching purposes, they will unarguably continue to offer various professional benefits to language teachers. Exploring this field further will likely contribute toward building a stronger language teacher preparation infrastructure.

References

Blyth, A. (2015). Social media ethics in English language teaching. *The JALT CALL Journal, 11*(2), 165–176. https://doi.org/10.29140/jaltcall.v11n2.191

Booth, S. E. (2012). Cultivating knowledge sharing and trust in online communities for educators. *Journal of Educational Computing Research, 47*(1), 1–31. https://doi.org/10.2190/EC.47.1.a

boyd, d. M., & Ellison, N. B. (2007). Social network sites: Definitions, history, and scholarship. *Journal of Computer-Mediated Communication, 13*(1), 210–230. https://doi.org/10.1111/j.1083-6101.2007.00393.x

Carpenter, J. P., & Harvey, S. (2019). "There's no referee on social media": Challenges in educator professional social media use. *Teaching and Teacher Education, 8,* 10294. https://doi.org/10.1016/j.tate.2019.102904

Carpenter, J. P., & Krutka, D. G. (2015). Engagement through microblogging: Educator professional development via Twitter. *Professional Development in Education, 41*(4), 707–728. https://doi.org/10.1080/19415257.2014.939294

Carpenter, J. P., Krutka, D. G., & Trust, T. (2022). Continuity and change in educators' professional learning networks. *Journal of Educational Change, 23,* 85–113. https://doi.org/10.1007/s10833-020-09411-1

Carpenter, J. P., Morrison, S. A., Craft, M., & Lee, Michalene, L. (2020a). How and why are educators using Instagram? *Teaching and Teacher Education, 96,* 103149. https://doi.org/10.1016/j.tate.2020.103149

Carpenter, J. P., Staudt Willet, K. B., Koehler, M. J., & Greenhalgh, S. P. (2020b). Spam and educators' Twitter use: Methodological challenges and considerations. *TechTrends, 64,* 460–469. https://doi.org/10.1007/s11528-019-00466-3

Cavazos, E. A. (1992). Computer bulletin board systems and the right of reply: Redefining defamation liability for a new technology. *The Review of Litigation, 12,* 231–247.

Chandler, P. D. (1988). Teachers and computer bulletin board systems. Unpublished master's thesis. University of Melbourne, Australia.

Chandler, P. D. (2000). Teachers' use of telecommunications: Lessons from research into teachers' use of computer bulletin board systems. *Proceedings of the 16th Australasian Computers in Education Conference,* 1–10.

Coutinho, C. P., & Lisbôa. E. S. (2013). Social networks as spaces for informal teacher professional development: Challenges and opportunities. *International Journal of Web Based Communities, 9*(2), 199–211.

Cranefield, J., & Yoong, P. (2009). Crossings: Embedding personal professional knowledge in a complex online community environment. *Online Information Review, 33*(2), 257–275. https://doi.org/10.1108/14684520910951203

Curwood, J. S., & Biddolph, C. (2017). Understanding Twitter as a networked field site. In M. Knobel & C. Lankshear (Eds.), *Researching new literacies: Design, theory, and data in sociocultural investigation* (pp. 81–103). Peter Lang.

Davis, K. (2015). Teachers' perceptions of Twitter for professional development. *Disability and Rehabilitation, 37*(17), 1551–1558. https://doi.org/10.3109/09638288.2015.1052576

Duncan-Howell, J. (2010). Teachers making connections: Online communities as a source of professional learning. *British Journal of Educational Technology, 41*(2), 324–340. https://doi.org/10.1111/j.1467-8535.2009.00953.x

Farrell, T. S. C. (2022). *Insights into professional development in language teaching.* Castledown Publishers.

Goodyear, V. A., Parker, M., & Casey, A. (2019). Social media and teacher professional learning communities. *Physical Education and Sport Pedagogy, 24*(5), 421–433, https://doi.org/10.1080/17408989.2019.1617263

Hanson-Smith, E. (2016). Teacher education and technology. In F. Farr & L. Murray (Eds.), *The Routledge handbook of language learning and technology* (pp. 210–222). Routledge.

Hartung, C., Hendry, N. A., Albury, K., Johnston, S., & Welch, R. (2022). Teachers of TikTok: Glimpses and gestures in the performance of professional identity. Media International Australia. Advance online publication. https://doi.org/10.1177/1329878X211068836

Hertel, J. T., & Wessman-Enzinger, N. M. (2017). Examining Pinterest as a curriculum resource for negative integers: An initial investigation. *education sciences, 7*(45), 1–11. https://doi.org/10.3390/educsci7020045

Hubbard, P. (2008). CALL and the future of language teacher education. *CALICO Journal, 25*(2), 175–188. https://doi.org/10.1558/cj.v25i2.175-188

Hubbard, P. (2018). Technology and professional development. In J. I. Liontas (Ed.), *The TESOL encyclopedia of English language teaching* (pp. 1–6). Wiley-Blackwell. https://doi.org/10.1002/9781118784235.eelt0426

Hubbard, P., & Levy, M. (2006). The scope of CALL education. In P. Hubbard & M. Levy (Eds.). *Teacher education in CALL* (pp. 3–20). John Benjamin Publishing.

Ito, Y. (2023a). Examining a technology-focused language teacher community on Facebook during a crisis situation. *Asian-Pacific Journal of Second and Foreign Language Education, 8,* 1. https://doi.org/10.1186/s40862-022-00159-0

Ito, Y. (2023b). Why do teachers participate in technology-focused online language teacher communities on Facebook? *Journal of Research on Technology in Education.* Advanced online publication. https://doi.org/10.1080/15391523.2023.2224593

Ito, Y. (2024). Uncovering how in-service teachers are learning about technology in language teaching and learning. *The JALT CALL Journal, 20*(1), 1–22. https://doi.org/10.29140/jaltcall.v20n1.1111

Kelly, N., & Antonio, A. (2016). Teacher peer support in social network sites. *Teaching and Teacher Education, 56,* 138–149. http://doi.org/10.1016/j.tate.2016.02.007

Kessler, G. (2006). Assessing CALL teacher training: What are we doing and what could we do better? In P. Hubbard & M. Levy (Eds.), *Teacher education in CALL* (pp. 22–42). John Benjamins.

Kessler, G. (2021). Current realities and future challenges for CALL teacher preparation. *CALICO Journal, 38* (1), i–xx. https://doi.org/10.1558/cj.21231

Kessler, G., & Hubbard, P. (2017). Language teacher education and technology. In C. A. Chapelle & S. Sauro (Eds.). *The handbook of technology and second language teaching and learning* (pp. 278–292). John Wiley & Sons, Inc.

Knight, S. W. P. (2020). Establishing professional online communities for world language educators. *Foreign Language Annals, 53*, 298–305. https://doi.org/10.1111/flan.12458

Kovacs, D. (1994). Introduction to directory of academic discussion lists. In A. Okerson (Ed.), *Directory of electronic journals, newsletters and academic discussion lists* (pp. 223–479). Kent State University Libraries.

Kusuma, I. P. I. (2022). "Why this and not that social media?" Reasons for using technology during online practice teaching. *The JALT CALL Journal, 18*(2), 264–286. https://doi.org/10.29140/jaltcall.v18n2.593

Lantz-Andersson A., Lundin, M., & Selwyn, N. (2018). Twenty years of online teacher communities: A systematic review of formally-organized and informally-developed professional learning groups. *Teaching and Teacher Education, 75*, 302–315. https://doi.org/10.1016/j.tate.2018.07.008

LeLoup, J. W., & Ponterio, R. (2017). *What is FLTeach?*. FLTeach. https://web.cortland.edu/flteach/index.html

Lohman, T. (2021, March 24). *New analytics API for researchers studying Facebook page data*. Meta. https://research.facebook.com/blog/2021/03/new-analytics-api-for-researchers-studying-facebook-page-data/

Lomika, L., & Lord, G. (2016). Social networking and language learning. In F. Farr & L. Murray (Eds.), *The Routledge handbook of language learning and technology* (pp. 255–268). Routledge.

Maciá, M., & García, I. (2016). Informal online communities and networks as a source of teacher professional development: A review. *Teaching and Teacher Education, 55*, 291–307. http://doi.org/10.1016/j.tate.2016.01.021

MacIntyre, P. D., Gregersen, T., & Mercer, S. (2020). Language teachers' coping strategies during the Covid-19 conversion to online teaching: Correlations with stress, wellbeing and negative emotions. *System, 94*, 26–38. https://doi.org/10.1016/j.system.2020.102352

Motteram, G., Dawson, S., & Al-Masri, N. (2020). WhatsApp supported language teacher development: A case study in the Zataari refugee camp. *Education Information Technology, 25*, 5731–5751. https://doi.org/10.1007/s10639-020-10233-0

Nelimarkka, M., Leinonen, T., Durall, E., & Dean, P. (2021). Facebook is not a silver bullet for teachers' professional development: Anatomy of an eight-year-old social media community. *Computers & Education, 173*, 1–13. https://doi.org/10.1016/j.compedu.2021.104269

Park, M., & Son, J. B. (2020). Pre-service EFL teachers' readiness in computer-assisted language learning and teaching. *Asia Pacific Journal of Education, 42*(2), 1–15. https://doi.org/10.1080/02188791.2020.1815649

Ranieri, M., Manca, S., & Fini, A. (2012). Why (and how) do teachers engage in social networks? An exploratory study of professional use of Facebook and its implications for lifelong learning. *British Journal of Educational Technology, 43*(5), 754–769. https://doi.org/10.1111/j.1467-8535.2012.01356.x

Riding, P. (2001). Online teacher communities and continuing professional development. *Teacher Development, 5*(3), 283–296. https://doi.org/10.1080/13664530100200156

Rutherford, C. (2010). Facebook as a source of informal teacher professional development. *in education, 16*(1), 60–74. https://doi.org/10.37119/ojs2010.v16i1.76

Schroeder, S., Curcio, R., & Lundgren, L. (2019). Expanding the learning network: How teachers use Pinterest. *Journal of Research on Technology in Education, 51*(2), 166–186. https://doi.org/10.1080/15391523.2019.1573354

Smith, M. (2022, June 28). Introducing features to quickly find and connect with Facebook groups. Meta. https://about.fb.com/news/2022/06/features-to-find-and-connect-with-facebook-groups/

Son, J.-B. (2014). *Computer-assisted language learning: Learners, teachers, and tools.* Cambridge Scholars Publishing.

Son, J.-B. (2018). *Teacher development in technology-enhanced language teaching.* Palgrave Macmillan.

Son, J.-B., & Windeatt, S. (Eds.). (2017). *Language teacher education and technology: Approaches and practices.* Bloomsbury Academic.

Staudt, D., St. Clair, N., & Martinez, E. E. (2013). Using Facebook to support novice teachers. *The New Educator, 9*(2), 152–163, https://doi.org/10.1080/1547688X.2013.778764

Staudt Willet, K. B. (2019). Revisiting how and why educators use Twitter: Tweet types and purposes in #Edchat. *Journal of Research on Technology in Education, 51*(3), 273–289. https://doi.org/10.1080/15391523.2019.1611507

Staudt Willet, K. B., & Carpenter, J. P. (2020). Teachers on Reddit? Exploring contributions and interactions in four teaching-related subreddits. *Journal of Research on Technology in Education, 52*(2), 216–233. https://doi.org/10.1080/15391523.2020.1722978

Stevens, V. (2018). Webheads. In J. I. Liontas (Ed.). *The TESOL encyclopedia of English language teaching* (pp. 1–8). Wiley-Blackwell.

Stevens, V. (2020, August 28). Volunteersneeded: Learning2gether/About. Learning2gether. http://learning2gether.pbworks.com/w/page/32206114/volunteersneeded

Stockwell, G. (2009). Teacher education in CALL: Teaching teachers to educate themselves. *Innovation in Language Learning and Teaching, 3*(1), 99–112. https://doi.org/10.1080/17501220802655524

Trust, T., Carpenter, J. P., Krutka, D. G., & Kimmons, R. (2020). #RemoteTeaching & #RemoteLearning: Educator tweeting during the

COVID-19 pandemic. *Journal of Technology and Teacher Education, 28*(2), 151–159. www.learntechlib.org/primary/p/216094

Tsai, I. C. (2012). Understanding social nature of an online community of practice for learning to teach elementary science. *Journal of Educational Technology & Society, 15*(2), 271–285.

Tseng, F.-C., & Kuo, F.-Y. (2014). A study of social participation and knowledge sharing in the teachers' online professional community of practice. *Computers & Education, 72*, 37–47. https://doi.org/10.1016/j.compedu.2013.10.005

van der Vlist, F. N., Helmond, A., Burkhardt, M., & Seitz, T. (2022). API governance: The case of Facebook's evolution. Social Media + Society, Advance online publication. https://doi.org/10.1177/tw20563051221086228

Warschauer, M. (1995). *E-mail for English teaching: Bringing the internet and computer learning networks into the language classroom.* Teachers of English to Speakers of Other Languages.

Wesely, P. M. (2013). Investigating the community of practice of world language educators. *Journal of Teacher Education, 64*(4), 305–318. http://doi.org/10.1177/0022487113489032

Woodfield, K., & Iphofen, R. (2018). Introduction to volume 2: The ethics of online research. In K. Woodfield (Ed.), *The ethics of online research* (pp. 1–12). Emerald Publishing Limited

Xing, W., & Gao, F. (2018). Exploring the relationship between online discourse and commitment in Twitter professional learning communities. *Computers & Education, 126*, 388–398. https://doi.org/10.1016/j.compedu.2018.08.010

Yildirim, I. (2019). Using Facebook groups to support teachers' professional development. *Technology, Pedagogy and Education, 28*(5), 589–609. https://doi.org/10.1080/1475939X.2019.1686714

Yilmaz, B., & Stevens, V. (2012). Webheads in Action: A community of practice scaffolding multiliteracies skills in teacher professional development. *Writing & Pedagogy, 4*(1), 135–146. https://doi.org/10.1558/wap.v4i1.135

Further Reading

Carpenter, J. P., & Harvey, S. (2019). "There's no referee on social media": Challenges in educator professional social media use. *Teaching and Teacher Education, 86*, 10294. https://doi.org/10.1016/j.tate.2019.102904

Drawing on data collected from forty-eight teachers via semistructured interviews and focus groups, this study examines the potential pitfalls in teachers' professional use of social media. In alignment with a social–ecological model, the four main types of identified challenges are presented in detail.

Hanson-Smith, E. (2016). Teacher education and technology. In F. Farr & L. Murray (Eds.), *The Routledge handbook of language learning and technology* (pp. 210–222). Routledge.

In this book chapter, the author outlines the key issues associated with the current state of CALL teacher education and offers practical advice on how language teachers can capitalize upon online tools and resources, including online teacher communities, to potentially enhance their professional knowledge and skills in CALL.

Knight, S. W. P. (2020). Establishing professional online communities for world language educators. *Foreign Language Annals, 53,* 298–305. https://doi.org/10.1111/flan.12458

This article discusses critical features of successful online communities for world language teachers based on empirical studies related to computer-mediated communication in language teacher training contexts. Touching on teaching-related issues triggered by the ongoing COVID-19 pandemic, the possibilities of online teacher communities are explored.

23

Task-Based Language Teaching

Sima Khezrlou

Introduction

The importance of integrating technologies and innovations in education is undisputed today, supported by the fact that new internet-connected devices and digital technologies have surrounded the life and learning processes of new generations of learners (González-Lloret & Ortega, 2014). The new generation, also known as Generation Z, the iGeneration, or the Net Generation are those learners born in the early 2000s or later who consider the internet, gadgets, and technologies a crucial part of their daily existence (González-Lloret, 2017). Naturally, the technologization process has also affected most areas of education given that a variety of computer and information technologies have made their way into pedagogical practices and curricula in various ways (Marek & Wu, 2020). The powerful technical features of digital technologies enable new forms of learning that can serve contemporary pedagogies well in several types of educational contexts since they change the nature of the physical relations between teachers, learners, and the objects of learning (Churchill et al., 2014). And, language education is no exception to this movement (Zhang & Zou, 2022). With the pedagogical affordances of digital technologies for second language (L2) production and interaction (Sauro, 2011) being appreciated, a stronger link between technology integration and a learning-theoretical framework has become vital to guide research, practice, and policy. Rather than focusing on technology on its own, a fundamental project is to lead the integration of emerging technologies into education through an appropriate learning design framework (Lim & Churchill, 2016).

Task-based language teaching (TBLT) as a pedagogical framework for the theory and teaching of second or foreign languages has been widely adopted by educators around the world. There is extensive agreement that L2 learning benefits from teaching with, learning with, and assessing with tasks – not isolated grammar forms (Baralt & Gómez, 2017). It has been argued that

TBLT constitutes an ideal methodology for informing and augmenting the potential of technological innovations for language learning (González-Lloret, 2017; González-Lloret & Ortega, 2014). This is because technologies such as Web 2.0 tools (e.g. blogs, wikis, gaming environments, chats, virtual worlds, etc.) present unique environments for learners to "engage in 'doing things' through technology-mediated transformation and creation processes, rather than just reading about language and culture in textbooks or hearing about them from teachers" (González-Lloret & Ortega, 2014, p. 3). In lay terms, new technologies involve learners in active learning and meaning-oriented tasks, making them great candidates for their integration in TBLT as a well-theorized pedagogical approach (Van den Branden, Bygate, & Norris, 2009). The mutually beneficial connection between technology and TBLT is high-lighted by Doughty and Long (2003), who suggest that technology provides a natural and authentic venue for the realization of the methodological prin-ciples of TBLT, and TBLT presents a rationale and pedagogical framework for the selection and employment of technology. However, as with any young area of inquiry, there are still dozens of issues regarding the intersection of technology and TBLT such as unanswered questions, emerging areas, and future directions that need to be discussed. Against this backdrop, it is the intention of this chapter to offer a conceptualization of technology-mediated TBLT and discuss how principles of TBLT and the transformative uses of technology can be fully integrated into each other and put to the service of progress in language education. I will then provide a critical review of the rapidly increasing collection of studies that examine the elective affinities of technology and tasks. Lastly, future research and practice in the implementa-tion of technology-enhanced TBLT will be delineated.

Background

Task-based language teaching has attracted the attention of scholars in the domain of second language acquisition (SLA) for several decades. It is centered around the use of communicative tasks as the basis of the curriculum and the pedagogical practice in which meaning is prioritized (Ellis et al., 2020). It is an "embryonic theory of language teaching, not a theory of SLA," encompassing all the features that make language teaching effective (Doughty & Long, 2003, p. 51). Hence, numerous principles underlying SLA are entailed while adopting the TBLT approach. Additionally, TBLT under-scores learning by doing, stemming from the concept of "integration educa-tion," which emphasizes that newly developed knowledge is better integrated into long-term memory and more readily retrieved when associated with real-life events and activities (Doughty & Long, 2003, p. 58). Focusing on SLA theories per se, TBLT is rooted in use-oriented theories of SLA, namely, interaction and sociocultural approaches (Ortega, 2009). According to the interaction approach, learners are provided with authentic language input and negative feedback during the performance of meaning-oriented tasks, which push them to revise their language outputs and focus on the structural properties during the interaction (Long, 1996). Thus, from the theoretical perspective of cognitive interactionism, ideal linguistic contexts and conditions are developed through TBLT for negotiated interaction and are therefore conducive to language acquisition (Lai & Li, 2011). Sociocultural theory (SCT) and the related framework of activity theory (Lantolf & Thorne, 2006) are also particularly relevant in the context of current conceptualizations of TBLT. According to SCT, L2 learners develop new strategies and knowledge as they take part in the interactive activities and internalize the effects of working together. Consequently, learning is considered to occur through interaction, negotiation, and collaboration, with the main aim of instruction being the creation of an environment serving as a community in which learners are likely to employ what they are introduced to through activities (Daniel, Hunter Quartz, & Oakes, 2019).

The first model of TBLT was proposed by Prabhu (1987), which includes three stages: pre-task (a preparatory activity), task cycle (meaning-focused activity or interactive process action), and post-task (activity attending to form). Further developing this model, Willis (1996) put forward an instructional approach based on the use of a task with three main stages: pre-task (introduction to the topic and task, preparation), task cycle (task performance, planning, and report), and language focus (language analysis, practice). Clearly, the task cycles lend themselves readily to the utilization of technology to facilitate and improve pedagogical practice. For example, a computer classroom with online software would facilitate teachers' recording all their learners' speech simultaneously and allow learners to play back their own speech in the post-task stage before submitting the final audio or video files to the teacher. Therefore, the great scope of technology in supporting the development of task-based lessons deserves closer attention, which is the aim of the remainder of this chapter.

Primary Themes

In the early years of technology-mediated TBLT, tasks mirrored those that appeared in SLA and computer-assisted language learning (CALL) in general. Initially, generic types of task such as jigsaw (a collaborative activity where each group member learns and shares a part of the content to form a complete understanding), dictogloss (a listening and reconstruction activity where learners listen to a passage, then reconstruct it in pairs or groups), information-gap (an activity where learners exchange information to complete a task), close-ended decision-making (a task where learners discuss and agree on a solution or course of action based on given options), and open-ended discussion tasks were proposed as ideal candidates for learning in computer-mediated contexts (Pica, Kang, & Sauro, 2006). Obviously, however, a fruitful integration of technology and TBLT demands a well-defined approach to technology-mediated tasks in order to avoid translating exercises and activities from face-to-face (FTF) into technology-enhanced contexts (González-Lloret & Ortega, 2014). In a task framework proposed by Chapelle (2001), technology-assisted tasks are presumed to be meaning-based, authentic, practical, and commensurate to the learners' proficiency and learning purposes. Chapelle (2001) emphasizes that CALL tasks should also embed opportunities for attracting learners' attention to linguistic forms and bring about learning skills beyond L2 development such as an enhanced interest in L2 culture, technology use outside class, electronic literacy, and increased ability to handle multimodal communication (Ellis et al., 2020). Adopting a similar definition and underscoring the centrality of task definition to the investigation of technology-mediated TBLT, González-Lloret and Ortega (2014) also take note of two other conditions essential for the integration of technology and tasks: an awareness of the non-neutrality of technology-mediated tasks, and a clear formulation of the technology-mediated tasks within a TBLT curriculum.

The adoption of technology in education is far from being neutral. Technology creates new types of real-world target tasks in a curriculum. For example, when "writing a job application" letter is done via email, there is a need to understand the pragmatics of such a medium for that task, distinct from a paper letter or chat. Web writing via wikis, blogs, or fandoms; massively multiplayer online games (MMOGs); and massive open online courses (MOOCs) are other examples of the target tasks created by technology. MOOCs are open, large-scale web-based courses designed and delivered by accredited higher education institutions and organizations in which anyone with a smart device and internet connection can participate (Deng, Benckendorff, & Gannaway, 2019). The appearance of new technological experiences has brought about an array of new types of activities and distinctive learning needs (Jenkins et al., 2009). The clear conclusion that can be reached is that when technology mediates the performance of tasks, it acts not just as a vehicle of teaching; rather, it imposes new demands and actions which naturally become target tasks – and as a result part of the curriculum (González-Lloret & Ortega, 2014).

The second condition laid out by González-Lloret and Ortega (2014) concerns the systematic incorporation of tasks and technologies in curricular contexts. In TBLT, the task is the main pedagogical unit that directs needs analysis, task selection and sequencing, materials and instruction development, assessment, and program evaluation (Abdi Tabari, Khezrlou, & Tian, 2024a, 2024b; Khezrlou, 2023). Hence, González-Lloret and Ortega (2014) rightly argue that technologies should become "part of the full programmatic cycle that shapes a TBLT curriculum, from needs analysis all the way to explicit learning outcomes for assessment and evaluation" (p. 7). With respect to needs analysis, not only the language skills required for the completion of a task in question or the target language to be acquired as a result of a particular task experience, but also the affordances of technological tools crucial for task enactment along with the learners' and teachers' digital literacies, availability of technology, and needed technological support to complete the task should be taken into account. Similarly, the design and sequencing of pedagogic tasks need to encompass several issues including the features of the technology and the task as well as learners' familiarity with both (Khezrlou, 2019). Indeed, the design of pedagogic tasks should benefit from the potential of a specific technology to achieve learning processes and outcomes not feasible in the classroom with paper and pencil: The use of multimedia for rich, authentic input and engagement in learning enable learners to use the language and the technology in productive and innovative ways (Khezrlou, Ellis, & Sadeghi, 2017). There are other effective types of Web 2.0 technologies such as synthetic environments, simulations, and gaming that provide a real life, authentic environment (for a recent review, see Nikolenko, 2021). All these technologies have sparked much interest in research relating to their capacity to immerse learners in virtual worlds where they need to use the language to navigate, interact, and complete tasks. Second language learners' involvement in a simulation (Michelson, 2019), immersion in a virtual world (Blyth, 2018; Wang et al., 2020), or participation in multi-user games requiring L2 production (Hung et al., 2018) are in excellent correspondence with the learning by doing principle of TBLT.

The next key step after needs analysis and task development is task sequencing. Given that the use of technology is a type of task in itself, curriculum developers need to consider how to select and sequence tasks to develop a syllabus as a primary step prior to incorporating the technology-enhanced tasks done through them (González-Lloret & Ortega, 2014). Task sequencing is usually carried out by applying what is perhaps the best-known model for task complexity: Robinson's cognition hypothesis (2015). Robinson (2015) posits that increasing task complexity in terms of resource-directing dimensions (number of elements, here and now, reasoning demands) is expected to augment complexity, accuracy, fluency of learners' productions as well as the amount of negotiation. Nevertheless, sequencing tasks in technology contexts based on Robinson's model is far from simple. For example, inserting glosses in a text or adding a link to a dictionary may decrease the complexity of a reading task; however, it will also add new elements of digital literacy and web navigation skills. For this reason, as González-Lloret and Ortega (2014) highlight, we need scales to evaluate the complexity of different technologies as well as more research on how each technology influences a task and how a task can change technologies.

As the last component of a TBLT curriculum, assessment also assumes a significant role when technology is integrated with tasks. González-Lloret and Ortega (2014) encourage the use of technology-mediated performance-based assessment as an effective and reasonable way of evaluating learners. New technology-mediated performance-based interactive assessments, which provide opportunities for social negotiations and need pragmatic use in particular contexts, have been demonstrated to best achieve the aims of technology-mediated L2 assessment (Ockey & Neiriz, 2021). However, since task-based language assessment in general and task-based assessment in technology-supported environments in particular have not been the subject of much research, there is a need to develop, validate, and evaluate such assessment, taking into account the role of technology.

Current Research and Practice

Since the 1990s, there has been an increasing interest in technology-mediated TBLT as reflected in the growing literature on the subject (e.g. González-Lloret & Ortega, 2014; Thomas & Reinders, 2015; Ziegler, 2016) and in the appearance of online TBLT courses (e.g. Duran & Ramaut, 2006). However, the body of relevant empirical research on technologically driven TBLT is still young and there is scope for greater progress to be made. In this section, I present an overview of research undertaken on: (a) the role of technology in fostering the interactive potential of generic, FTF tasks; (b) the impact of task, mediated by technology, on L2 interaction; and (c) the effectiveness of Web 2.0 technology-enhanced tasks.

Task-Oriented Interactions in Computer-Mediated and FTF Contexts

The first batch of studies on technology-mediated TBLT aims at comparing the interactions in computer-mediated and FTF environments. Descriptive and empirical research has provided compelling evidence that interactional features which have been found to foster L2 development in FTF contexts, such as negotiation for meaning and modified output, can and do occur in technology-mediated task-based environments (Chong & Reinders, 2020; Iwasaki & Oliver, 2003; Lee, Hampel, & Kukulska-Hulme, 2019; Monteiro, 2014; Ziegler & Phung, 2019). For example, tasks commonly found in FTF TBLT research such as decision-making and information-gap tasks have been reported to be fruitful in eliciting learner interaction and negotiation in a computer-mediated communication (CMC) context (Pellettieri, 1999). Research has also explored the preference for self-repair with respect to negotiation of meaning in online CMC (Jepson, 2005; Lee, 2001; Smith, 2009; Yüksel & İnan, 2014). Results indicate that meaning negotiation in task-based text chat differs from that in FTF interactions (Kern, 1995; Pellettieri, 2000; van der Zwaard & Bannink, 2016; Yüksel & İnan, 2014). It is maintained that meaning negotiation occurs more in CMC than in FTF interactions since it (1) enables learners to negotiate meaning at their own pace (Castañeda, 2021; Fernández-García & Martínez-Arbelaiz, 2002); (2) enhances noticing of L2 forms and meaning (Canals, 2021; Pellettieri, 2000; Shekary & Tahririan, 2006); (3) advances learning of lexical items (Fernández-García & Martínez-Arbelaiz, 2002; Smith, 2004, 2009); (4) promotes grammatical competence (Pellettieri, 2000); (5) enhances motivation and positive attitudes (Canals, 2020; Taghizadeh & Ejtehadi, 2021); and lastly (6) improves oral production skills (Canals, 2020).

Although the majority of research in this realm has lent credence to the affordances of CMC in terms of enhancing negotiation of meaning and L2 development, it should be noted that there are other studies that show negotiation in CMC is not as abundant as in FTF interactions (e.g. Jepson, 2005; Moradi & Farvardin, 2020; Ribeiro & Eslami, 2022; van der Zwaard & Bannink, 2016). The variations in the results of previous research clearly point to important differences, such as variations in triggers and patterns in the different contexts. Thus, more research is required to deepen our understanding of how patterns of interaction may alter across individual technologies. Research has indicated that written text-chat is characterized by distinctive patterns of negotiation and turn-taking (Smith, 2003), underlying the necessity of research into whether learners taking part in mobile-assisted or multiuser gaming or immersive environments negotiate meaning in unique ways. Future research is encouraged to consider how types of technology affect the quantity and quality of interaction during task-based learning and teaching. On the whole, however, studies in this area suggest that negotiation and its advantages seem to be accessible to learners in computer-mediated task-based interactions, attesting the effectiveness of technology in task-based contexts.

Design and Use of Tasks in Technology-Mediated Contexts

Although the studies reviewed in the previous section indicate the positive effects of text chat in engaging learners in interaction, it is not simply the technology, but the design and use of appropriate tasks through the medium of technology that is likely to promote learning opportunities (Adams & Nik, 2014). Earlier, Ortega (1997) also stressed the significance of investigating tasks, their conditions, and processes in order to reach firm conclusions about the role of CMC in L2 learning. Moreover, given that CMC unites features of both spoken and written language with aspects of the digital context (Herring, 1996), it is vital to explore CMC tasks as activities in their own right instead of considering that tasks effective at eliciting quality L2 interaction in FTF exchanges will also do so in CMC (González-Lloret, 2017).

This relatively new avenue of research led to a small number of studies exploring which task types (in the traditional FTF definition), with which features (e.g. level of complexity) and under which conditions (e.g. through which media) could be more effective in inducing interactions and thereby bring about L2 development (Blake, 2000; Keller-Lally, 2006; Mohamadi Zenouzagh, 2022; Smith, 2003; Yilmaz & Granena, 2010). However, literature offers contradictory findings, with some studies (e.g. Blake, 2000) reporting the superiority of jigsaw tasks over information-gap and decision-making tasks in generating more negotiation, others indicating the reverse, that is decision-making tasks, enriched with unfamiliar lexical items, stimulating more negotiation than jigsaw tasks (Smith, 2003), or showing the superior effectiveness of dictogloss over the jigsaw in terms of noticing (Yilmaz & Granena, 2010), and yet others (Keller-Lally, 2006) finding no impact for task type (jigsaw, decision-making, or opinion exchange). These findings hint that task design may play a significant role in L2 learning and use in CMC.

As for task characteristics, research in TBLT has focused on whether manipulating the cognitive demands of tasks influences learners' L2 productions. A few early studies (Adams & Nik 2014; Baralt, 2013; Nik et al., 2012) investigated the validity of FTF task complexity theories, specifically Robinson's (2015) cognition hypothesis. Nevertheless, Robinson's predictions have not necessarily transferred to task performances in technology-enhanced contexts. Adams and Nik (2014) attribute this to the distinctive nature of the text-based CMC medium, where there are more opportunities for processing output than in the FTF interaction. Furthermore, in contrast to speech production, there is a delay between production and transmission of message in CMC which is likely to impact the cognitive burden imposed by the production (Adams & Nik, 2014). This clarification receives support from Baralt's (2013) research, which compared the reasoning demands of an FTF versus a CMC task. Her findings confirmed the validity of this prediction in the FTF context yet not in the CMC environment, where more learning occurred in the less complex conditions. Thus far, the existing – albeit very limited – research suggests that the unique features of CMC mediate the complexity of tasks as is reported in FTF task-based research, underscoring the necessity of examining tasks developed for and embedded in the technology.

Tasks with Web 2.0 Technologies

Web 2.0 technologies represent a class of technologies that allow the development and exchange of user-generated content. Three-dimensional (3D) multi-user virtual environments (MUVEs), such as World of Warcraft, Active Worlds, and SimCity, have gained popularity among the Net Generation because of their affordances in terms of simulation, immersion, creativity, and collaboration (Chen, 2020). Second Life has also attracted the attention of L2 learners wanting to discover this lively 3D space and interact with other users in world languages. Admittedly, the learning-by-doing principle of TBLT is well suited to the immersive nature of Second Life, which boosts reality and enriches the learner's learning experience (Chen, 2020). In addition, it enhances the use of language for communicative, meaningful, and experiential purposes (Chun, Kern, & Smith, 2016).

Also prevalent among this group of technologies are blogs (e.g. Reinhardt, 2019) and wikis (e.g. Khezrlou, 2022; Reinhardt, 2019). All these technologies share the common objective of forming a bridge between inside and outside classroom tasks, which lead to authenticity in the classroom, present a genuine context for learners, offer a real audience for their writing, and join them with other speakers with the same interest, all crucial tenets of TBLT (González-Lloret, 2017). Research has provided some evidence that blogs may function as spaces for culture learning and intercultural exchange, as well as for reflection, self-presentation, and the development and articulation of knowledge on topics in which learners have some say (for a recent review see Reinhardt, 2019). Research has also reported that tasks which impose specific topics, demand form-focused peer review, limit audiences, expand audiences, or are closed in nature may restrict learner autonomy and not advocate the learning potentials of blogs, even though the tasks might match with curricular purposes and learner expectations (e.g. Chen, Shih, & Liu, 2015). As with blogs, wikis are effective learning tools as long as needs and tasks are truly enhanced by wiki structures and an awareness of ways and reasons behind using wikis is addressed through contextualized and explicit instruction (see Reinhardt, 2019). Building awareness might entail "exploring with students the concepts of collective intelligence and crowdsourced wisdom, for example in social media like Reddit or Digg – two popular tools" (Reinhardt, 2019, p. 17), the use of which in task-based courses has yet to be explored fully.

Recommendations for Research and Practice

Research on technology-mediated TBLT has been robustly developing during the past decade, yet there remains a significant research gap, as has already been identified in this chapter. Due to the growing use of technologies, research on technology-driven TBLT is expected to expand in the future. For example, the technology-enhanced task-based courses will capture more teachers' and researchers' attention in wider learning contexts. Both the research and pedagogy have mainly focused on tertiary education settings. We need more research to explore how technology-mediated task performances in elementary and secondary school settings affect L2 development and provide teachers, principals, and authorities with the knowledge on how best to adopt and implement digital tools in their contexts. Implementing technology-enhanced tasks in broader contexts will definitely deepen our understanding of how the technology can afford learner engagement and language development.

Future research that examines the impact of technologies on L2 task design and performance under different conditions is imperative. Regarding the former, we are still a long way off knowing which aspects of technology-mediated task complexity distinguish it from FTF task complexity. Also, it is still not known how the technology impacts the complexity of a task. For example, the availability of an interactive calendar on the computer or mobile phone is likely to decrease the task complexity of booking a hotel on the internet, yet it may be more cognitively demanding since learners would also need to work with different types of information (multimedia literacy) to manipulate a calendar to choose dates, use an interactive map, and view photos. Another important, yet unresolved issue in technology-based task design is the principle required for task sequencing. For example, is writing in a wiki more or less complex that writing in a blog? As touched on previously, what we need currently is a scale to evaluate the complexity of various forms of technologies and more research into how each technology impacts a task and how a task can alter technologies (González-Lloret, 2017). With respect to the effects of technology on task performance under different implementation conditions, there is still a paucity of studies on marrying technology and task conditions such as task planning and task repetition. Given the unique features of interaction in Web 2.0 technologies that afford immersive simulation, real-time interaction, and multimodal communication, these environments could reinforce the effects of task performance with prior planning. Thus, this line of study would offer research and practical implications for SLA stakeholders.

Another issue that has not received much attention in technology-mediated TBLT pertains to teachers' beliefs. Teachers' pedagogical beliefs have been identified as one of the major barriers to technology integration (e.g. Ertmer & Ottenbreit-Leftwich, 2013). When teachers are not eager and prepared to implement the technology-mediated TBLT curriculum, even the most appropriate and well-developed curriculum will most likely fail (González-Lloret & Nielson, 2014). Hence, the important role of teachers in the success or failure of technology-enhanced tasks necessitates the conduct of more research into how teachers could be prepared through teacher training (e.g. O'Dowd & Ware, 2009), and which factors affect their willingness to adopt such instructional practices in their courses.

Future Directions

Because technologies are increasingly everyday and omnipresent, they should be adopted by learners and teachers as tools for experiential, situated learning, and as social practices deserving critical attention. Affordances emerge from the interplay of pedagogical practices centered around tasks and digital technologies, and prolonged explorations of how technology-mediated TBLT is planned, implemented, and evaluated by particular groups of learners and teachers and situational variables is merited. This connects with the potential of technology to provide language use opportunities even in acquisition-poor or English as a foreign language contexts (Ellis et al., 2020). The internet and CALL present a wealth of resources including audio and published materials. The use of such materials provides a large number of opportunities for the teaching of both receptive and productive skills. Technology-enhanced task-based lessons, with the autonomy they nurture, can enable learners of different ages and proficiencies, provided they are used with appropriate tasks, to transcend the restrictions of their own specific learning context (Ellis et al., 2020). To achieve this purpose, research in technology and TBLT needs to expand by providing answers to numerous questions and topics that are open to investigation. From theoretical issues concerned with the features of tasks, their sequencing, implementation, evaluation, and so forth, when mediated by technologies, to the rapidly transforming and developing innovations and their affordances to reinforce the role of language tasks, many issues still await more attention and investigation. As practices mature, they have the potential to direct theory building and methodological innovation in the field.

References

Abdi Tabari, M., Khezrlou, S., & Tian, Y. (2024). Task complexity, task repetition, and L2 writing complexity: Exploring interactions in the TBLT domain. *International Review of Applied Linguistics in Language Teaching, 62*(2), 871–901. https://doi.org/10.1515/iral-2022-0123

Abdi Tabari, M., Khezrlou, S., & Tian, Y. (2024). Verb argument construction complexity indices and L2 written production: Effects of task complexity and task repetition. *Innovation in Language Learning and Teaching, 18*(1), 1–16. https://doi.org/10.1080/17501229.2023.2211955

Adams, R., & Nik, A. M. N. (2014). Prior knowledge and second language task production in text chat. In M. González-Lloret & L. Ortega (Eds.), *Technology-mediated TBLT: Researching technology and tasks* (pp. 51–78). John Benjamins.

Baralt, M. (2013). The impact of cognitive complexity on feedback efficacy during online versus face-to-face interactive tasks. *Studies in Second Language Acquisition, 35*, 689–725. https://doi.org/10.1017/S0272263113000429

Baralt, M., & Gómez, J. M. (2017). Task-based language teaching online: A guide for teachers. *Language Learning & Technology, 21*(3), 28–43.

Blake, R. (2000). Computer-mediated communication: A window on L2 Spanish interlanguage. *Language Learning & Technology, 4*, 120–136.

Blyth, C. (2018). Immersive technologies and language learning. *Foreign Language Annals, 51*(1), 225–232. https://doi.org/10.1111/flan.12327

Canals, L. (2020). The effects of virtual exchanges on oral skills and motivation. *Language Learning & Technology, 24*(3), 103–119. http://hdl.handle.net/10125/44742

Canals, L. (2021). Multimodality and translanguaging in negotiation of meaning. *Foreign Language Annals, 54*, 647–670. https://doi.org/10.1111/flan.12547

Castañeda, D. A. (2021). Improving conversational interactions with task-based activities in a Spanish as a second language class. *Computer Assisted Language Learning, 34*(8), 1154–1181. https://doi.org/10.1080/09588221.2019.1666149

Chapelle, C. (2001). *Computer applications in second language acquisition: Foundations for teaching, testing, and research.* Cambridge University Press.

Chen, J. (2020). The effects of pre-task planning on EFL learners' oral performance in a 3D multi-user virtual environment. *ReCALL, 32*(3), 232–249. https://doi.org/10.1017/S0958344020000026

Chen, W., Shih, Y., & Liu, G. (2015). Task design and its induced learning effects in a cross-institutional blog-mediated telecollaboration. *Computer Assisted*

Language Learning, 28(4), 285–305. https://doi.org/10.1080/09588221.2013 .818557

Chong S. W., & Reinders H. (2020). Technology-mediated task-based language teaching: A qualitative research synthesis. *Language Learning & Technology, 24* (3), 70–86.

Chun, D., Kern, R., & Smith, B. (2016). Technology in language use, language teaching, and language learning. *The Modern Language Journal, 100*(S1), 64–80. https://doi.org/10.1111/modl.12302

Churchill, D., Lu, J., & Chiu, T. K. F. (2014). Integrating mobile technologies, social media and learning design. *Educational Media International, 51*(3), 163–165. https://doi.org/10.1080/09523987.2014.969895

Daniel, J., Hunter Quartz, K., & Oakes, J. (2019). Teaching in community schools: Creating conditions for deeper learning. *Review of Research in Education, 43*(1), 453–480. https://doi.org/10.3102/0091732X18821126

Deng R., Benckendorff P., & Gannaway D., (2019). Progress and new directions for teaching and learning in MOOCs. *Computers & Education, 129*, 48–60. https://doi.org/10.1016/j.compedu.2018.10.019

Doughty, C. J., & Long M. H. (2003). *The handbook of second language acquisition.* Blackwell Publishing.

Duran, G., & Ramaut, G. (2006). Tasks for absolute beginners and beyond: Developing and sequencing tasks at basic proficiency levels. In K. Van den Branden (Ed.), *Task-based language education: From theory to practice* (pp. 47–75). Cambridge University Press.

Ellis, R., Skehan, P., Li, S., Shintani, N., & Lambert, C. (2020). *Task-based language teaching: Theory and practice.* Cambridge University Press.

Ertmer, P. A., & Ottenbreit-Leftwich, A. (2013). Removing obstacles to the pedagogical changes required by Jonassen's vision of authentic technology-enabled learning. *Computers & Education, 64*, 175–182. https://doi.org/10 .1016/j.compedu.2012.10.008

Fernández-García, M., & Martínez-Arbelaiz, A. (2002). Negotiation of meaning in non-native speaker–non-native speaker synchronous discussions. *CALICO Journal, 19*(2), 279–224. https://doi.org/10.1558/cj.v19i2.279-284

González-Lloret, M. (2017). Technology for task-based language teaching. In C. A. Chapelle & S. Sauro (Eds.), *The handbook of technology and second language teaching and learning* (pp. 234–247). Wiley Publishing.

González-Lloret, M., & Nielson, K. B. (2014). Evaluating TBLT: The case of a task-based Spanish program. *Language Teaching Research, 19*(5), 525–549. https://doi.org/10.1177/1362168814541745

González-Lloret, M., & Ortega, L. (2014). *Technology-mediated TBLT: Researching technology and tasks.* John Benjamins.

Herring, S. C. (1996). *Computer-mediated communication: Linguistic, social, and cross-cultural perspectives.* John Benjamins.

Hung, H.-T., Yang, J. C., Hwang, G.-J., Chu, H.-C., & Wang, C.-C. (2018). A scoping review of research on digital game-based language learning. *Computers & Education, 126*, 89–104. https://doi.org/10.1016/j.compedu.2018.07.001

Iwasaki, N., & Oliver, R. (2003). Chat-line interaction and negative feedback. *Australian Review of Applied Linguistics, 17*, 60–73. https://doi.org/10.1075/aralss.17.05iwa

Jenkins, H., Purushotma, R., Weigel, M., Clinton K., & Robison, A. J. (2009). *Confronting the challenges of participatory culture: Media education for the 21st century*. MIT Press.

Jepson, K. (2005). Conversations – and negotiated interaction – in text and voice chat rooms. *Language Learning & Technology, 9*(3), 79–98.

Keller-Lally, A. M. (2006). Effect of task-type and group size on foreign language learner output in synchronous computer-mediated communication. Doctoral dissertation, University of Texas at Austin.

Khezrlou, S. (2019). Form-focussed instruction in CALL: What do learners think? *RELC Journal, 50*(2), 235–251. https://doi.org/10.1177/0033688217738820

Khezrlou, S. (2022). Effects of task repetition with consciousness-raising in wiki-mediated collaborative writing on the development of explicit and implicit knowledge. *Computer Assisted Language Learning*. 37(1–2), 243–278. https://doi.org/10.1080/09588221.2022.2033789

Khezrlou, S. (2023). Focus on form in task repetition through oral and written task modelling. *International Review of Applied Linguistics in Language Teaching, 61*(2), 479–518. https://doi.org/10.1515/iral-2020-0125

Khezrlou, S., Ellis, R., & Sadeghi, K. (2017). Effects of computer-assisted glosses on EFL learners' vocabulary acquisition and reading comprehension in three learning conditions. *System, 65*, 104–116. https://doi.org/10.1016/j.system.2017.01.009

Lai, C., & Li, G. (2011). Technology and task-based language teaching: A critical review. *CALICO Journal, 28*(2), 498–521. https://doi.org/10.11139/cj.28.2.498-521

Lantolf, J., & Thorne, S. (2006). *Sociocultural theory and the genesis of second language development*. Oxford University Press.

Lee, H., Hampel, R., & Kukulska-Hulme, A. (2019). Gesture in speaking tasks beyond the classroom: An exploration of the multimodal negotiation of meaning via Skype videoconferencing on mobile devices. *System, 81*, 26–38. https://doi.org/10.1016/j.system.2018.12.013

Lee, L. (2001). Online interaction: Negotiation of meaning and strategies used among learners of Spanish. *ReCALL, 13*(2), 232–244. https://doi.org/10.1017/S0958344001000829a

Lim, C. P., & Churchill, D. (2016). Mobile learning. *Interactive Learning Environments, 24*(2), 273–276. https://doi.org/10.1080/10494820.2015.1113705

Long, M. (1996). The role of the linguistic environment in second language acquisition. In W. Ritchie & T. Bhatia (Eds.), *Handbook of second language acquisition* (pp. 121–58). Academic Press.

Marek, M. W., & Wu, P. N. (2020). Digital learning curriculum design. In L. Daniela (Ed.), *Pedagogies of digital learning in higher education* (pp. 163–182). Routledge.

Michelson, K. (2019). Global simulation as a mediating tool for teaching and learning language and culture as discourse. *Foreign Language Annals, 52*(2), 284–313. https://doi-org.uaccess.univie.ac.at/10.1111/flan.12392

Mohamadi Zenouzagh, Z. (2022). Language-related episodes and feedback in synchronous voiced-based and asynchronous text-based computer-mediated communications. *Journal of Computer Education*, 9, 515–547. https://doi.org/10.1007/s40692–021-00212-w

Monteiro, K. (2014). An experimental study of corrective feedback during video-conferencing. *Language Learning & Technology*, 18, 56–79.

Moradi, A., & Farvardin, M. T. (2020). Negotiation of meaning by mixed-proficiency dyads in face-to-face and synchronous computer-mediated communication. *TESOL Journal*, 11(1). https://doi.org/10.1002/tesj.446

Nik, N. A. N. M., Adams, R., & Newton, J. (2012). Writing to learn via text chat: Task implementation and focus on form. *Journal of Second Language Writing*, 21(1), 23–39. https://doi.org/10.1016/j.jslw.2011.12.001

Nikolenko, S. I. (2021). *Synthetic simulated environments: In synthetic data for deep learning*. Springer Optimization and Its Applications. https://doi.org/10.1007/978-3-030-75178-4_7

Ockey, G. J., & Neiriz, R. (2021). Evaluating technology-mediated second language oral communication assessment delivery models. *Assessment in Education: Principles, Policy & Practice*, 28(4), 350–368. https://doi.org/10.1080/0969594X.2021.1976106

O'Dowd, R., & Waire, P. (2009). Critical issues in telecollaborative task design. *Computer Assisted Language Learning*, 22(2), 173–188. https://doi.org/10.1080/09588220902778369

Ortega, L. (1997). Processes and outcomes in network classroom interaction: Defining the research agenda for L2 computer-assisted classroom discussion. *Language Learning & Technology*, 1(1), 82–93.

Ortega, L. (2009). Interaction and attention to form in L2 text-based computer-mediated communication. In A. Mackey & C. Polio (Eds.), *Multiple perspectives on interaction in SLA: Research in honor of Susan M. Gass* (pp. 226–253). Routledge.

Pellettieri, J. (1999). Why-talk? Investigating the role of task-based interaction through synchronous network-based communication among classroom learners of Spanish. Unpublished doctoral dissertation. University of California at Davis.

Pellettieri, J. (2000). Negotiation in cyberspace: The role of chatting in the development of grammatical competence. In M. Warschauer & R. Kern (Eds.), *Network-based language teaching: Concepts and practice* (pp. 59–86). Cambridge University Press.

Pica, T., Kang, H.-S., & Sauro, S. (2006). Information gap tasks: Their multiple roles and contributions to interaction research methodology. *Studies in Second Language Acquisition*, 28(2), 301–338. https://doi.org/10.1017/S027226310606013X

Prabhu, N. (1987). *Second language pedagogy*. Oxford University Press.

Reinhardt, J. (2019). Social media in second and foreign language teaching and learning: Blogs, wikis, and social networking. *Language Teaching*, 52(1), 1–39. https://doi.org/10.1017/S0261444818000356

Ribeiro, A., & Eslami, Z. R. (2022). Second language development in face-to-face versus synchronous computer-mediated interactions: Dyadic type and language proficiency. *Language Teaching Research*. Advance online publication. https://doi.org/10.1177/13621688221098379

Robinson, P. (2015). The cognition hypothesis, second language task demands, and the SSARC model of pedagogic task sequencing. In M. Bygate, M. (Ed.), Domains and directions in the development of TBLT (pp. 87–122). John Benjamins.

Sauro, S. (2011). SCMC for SLA: A research synthesis. *CALICO Journal, 28*(2), 369–391. https://doi.org/10.11139/cj.28.2.369-391

Shekary, M., & Tahririan, M. H. (2006). Negotiation of meaning and noticing in text-based online chat. *The Modern Language Journal, 90*(4), 557–573. https://doi.org/10.1111/j.1540-4781.2006.00504.x

Smith, B. (2003). Computer-mediated negotiated interaction: An expanded model. *The Modern Language Journal, 87*(1), 38–57. https://doi.org/10.1111/1540–4781.00177

Smith, B. (2004). Computer-mediated negotiated interaction and lexical acquisition. *Studies in Second Language Acquisition, 26*(3), 365–398. https://doi.org/10.1017/S027226310426301X

Smith, B. (2009). Task-based learning in the computer-mediated communicative ESL/EFL classroom. *CALL-EJ Online, 11*(1).

Taghizadeh, M., & Ejtehadi, A. (2021). Investigating pre-service EFL teachers' and teacher educators' experience and attitudes towards online interaction tools. *Computer Assisted Language Learning, 36*(8), 1663–1667. https://doi.org/10.1080/09588221.2021.2011322

Thomas, M., & Reinders, H. (2015). Contemporary task-based teaching in Asia. Continuum.

Van den Branden, K., Bygate, M., & Norris, J. M. (2009). Task-based language teaching: A reader. John Benjamins.

van der Zwaard, R., & Bannink, A. (2016). Nonoccurrence of negotiation of meaning in task-based synchronous computer-mediated communication. *The Modern Language Journal, 100*(3), 625–640. https://doi.org/10.1111/modl.12341

Wang, C.-P., Lan, Y.-J., Tseng, W.-T., Lin, Y.-T. R., & Gupta, K. C.-L. (2020). On the effects of 3D virtual worlds in language learning: A meta-analysis. *Computer Assisted Language Learning, 33*(8), 891–915. https://doi.org/10.1080/09588221.2019.1598444

Willis, J. (1996). A framework for task-based language teaching. Longman.

Yilmaz, Y., & Granena, G. (2010). The effects of task type in synchronous computer-mediated communication. *ReCALL, 22*(1), 20–38. https://doi.org/10.1017/S0958344009990176

Yüksel, D., & İnan, B. (2014). The effects of communication mode on negotiation of meaning and its noticing. *ReCALL, 26*(3), 333–354. https://doi.org/10.1017/S0958344014000147

Zhang, R., & Zou, D. (2022). Types, purposes, and effectiveness of state-of-the-art technologies for second and foreign language learning. *Computer Assisted Language Learning, 35*(4), 696–742. https://doi.org/10.1080/09588221.2020.1744666

Ziegler, N. (2016). Taking technology to task: Technology-mediated TBLT, performance, and production. *Annual Review of Applied Linguistics, 36,* 136–163. https://doi.org/10.1017/S0267190516000039

Ziegler, N., & Phung, H. (2019). Technology-mediated task-based interaction: The role of modality. *ITL-International Journal of Applied Linguistics, 170*(2), 251–276. https://doi.org/10.1075/itl.19014.zie

Further Reading

Ellis, R., Skehan, P., Li, S., Shintani, N., & Lambert, C. (2020). *Task-based language teaching: Theory and practice.* Cambridge University Press. https://doi.org/10.1017/9781108643689

Outlining the theoretical framework, pedagogical development, and application of TBLT, this book serves as a fundamental and comprehensive resource for understanding and researching TBLT.

González-Lloret, M., & Ortega, L. (2014). *Technology-mediated TBLT: Researching technology and tasks.* John Benjamins. https://doi.org/10.1075/tblt.6

This book gathers empirical research on TBLT from pedagogical, cognitive, and sociocultural perspectives, focusing on the design and implementation of diverse tasks for writing, interaction, and assessment, facilitated by technological tools.

Smith, B., & González-Lloret, M. (2021). Technology-mediated task-based language teaching: A research agenda. *Language Teaching, 54*(4), 518–534. https://doi.org/10.1017/S0261444820000233

With a focus on technology-mediated task-based language teaching, this article proposes specific research tasks that build on previous studies and aims to deepen our understanding of how tasks and technologies can enhance language learning.

Ziegler, N. (2016). Taking technology to task: Technology-mediated TBLT, performance, and production. *Annual Review of Applied Linguistics, 36,* 136–163. https://doi.org/10.1017/S0267190516000039

This review article presents an updated overview of the role of technology-mediated task-based language teaching in promoting L2 development and performance. Additionally, it explores how technology can contribute to our understanding of various aspects of TBLT and offers suggestions for potential research directions in the field.

Part VI
Language Skills and Areas

24

Speaking

Gilbert Dizon

Introduction

Conversing effectively in a second language (L2) is one of the most challenging language skills to develop because of the time constraints involved (Jong, 2020). In natural conversation, interlocutors must be able to sufficiently understand the topic of discussion, decide what to say, and then actually say it. If there are any issues related to comprehension or message formulation, then an L2 speaker may miss their chance to join a conversation as the topic of discussion may change abruptly. Even when L2 speakers are given more time to prepare, as is often the case with oral presentations, they may still struggle to speak coherently and fluently in the target language. Given the difficulties surrounding L2 speaking, the topic has been one of the most examined areas in computer-assisted language learning (CALL) research (Gillespie, 2020). However, the plethora of technologies that can be used in and outside the language classroom to promote L2 speaking can make it difficult for teachers to choose the most appropriate digital tools for their particular context. It would be impossible to detail all the available technologies that can be used to support L2 speaking development in a single book chapter. Therefore, this chapter highlights emerging technologies that have yet to be widely adopted in the teaching of L2 speaking but have shown potential in promoting L2 oral interaction and speaking development.

Background

Although there are several explanations as to how learners acquire an L2 and in extension develop L2 speaking, two of the most recognizable and easily contrasted theories in L2 learning are cognitive theory and sociocultural theory (SCT). Accordingly, this section provides an overview of the two theories in the context of L2 speaking while also touching upon other important concepts that pertain to the speaking process.

The most influential model in relation to cognitive theory and L2 speaking is Levalt's Blueprint of the Speaker (Levelt, 1994, 1999). According to this model, the speaking process involves a series of steps, the first of which is the conceptualization of a speaker's *communicative intention*, that is, the message that the speaker would like to convey. This message gets formulated through three different operations: grammatical, morpho-phonological, and phonetic encoding. Grammatical encoding involves the activation of lexical concepts or lemmas from the lexicon, a mental repository which stores the words a person has acquired throughout their life. Once grammatical encoding begins, morpho-phonological encoding is activated, leading to the creation of a phonological score, that is, the "syllabified words, phrases and intonation pattern" of an utterance (Levelt, 1999, p. 88). Finally, a pronounceable structure is formulated through phonetic encoding, which triggers the appropriate articulatory gestures depending on the syllables in a particular phonological score. As Hulstijn (2006) notes, in the context of L2 speaking instruction, one important point to consider is that the mental processes outlined in this paragraph occur outside a speaker's conscious awareness. This makes these cognitive processes sensitive to *working memory* (WM), the topic of the subsequent paragraph.

Working memory is defined as "the mental processes responsible for the temporary storage and manipulation of information in the course of on-going processing" (Juffs & Harrington, 2011, p. 137). Because of the complexity of mental processes and their interaction with one another, WM has the potential to limit performance during cognitive tasks. Thus, it is believed that individuals with high *working memory capacity* (WMC) tend to perform better in productive L2 tasks than those with low WMC (Mackey et al., 2010). Research by Kormos and Safar (2008) demonstrating a strong correlation between WMC and language learning supports this notion. However, more recent findings by Hayashi and colleagues (Hayashi, 2019; Hayashi, Kobayashi, & Toyoshige, 2016) suggest that WM does not have a significant impact on foreign language development. Instead, other factors such as context, strategy, and other individual differences may have a larger influence on L2 performance. Nevertheless, more empirical studies need to be conducted to better establish the relationship between WM and L2 speaking.

Complexity, accuracy, and fluency (CAF) have also featured predominantly in L2 research inspired by cognitive theory (Housen & Kuiken, 2009). There is still debate regarding the definitions of these three constructs. However, accuracy is the one with the most consensus and refers to the degree to which an individual's language deviates from the norm (Wolfe-Quintero, Inagaki, & Kim, 1998). Fluency is typically described as a "person's general language proficiency, particularly as characterized by perceptions of ease, eloquence, and 'smoothness' of speech or writing" (Housen & Kuiken, 2009, p. 463). While complexity is the most controversial construct (Housen & Kuiken, 2009), it can be referred to as the capacity to use a variety of sophisticated structures and lexis (Suzuki & Kormos, 2020). In the context of L2 speaking, several factors have been shown to positively influence some or all of the CAF constructs including WMC (Ahmadian, 2012), pre-task planning (Ahmadian & Tavakoli, 2011), task repetition (Ahmadian & Tavakoli, 2011) and topic familiarity (Qiu, 2019).

In contrast to cognitive theory which tends to focus on the mental processes that underlie L2 learning, SCT stresses social context and how cultural factors mediate L2 development. Sociocultural theory is highly influenced by the work of Vygotsky (1978) and is defined as the field that "studies the content, mode of operation, and interrelationships of psychological phenomena that are socially constructed and shared, and are rooted in other social artifacts" (Ratner, 2002, p. 9). As noted by Surtees and Duff (2022), SCT is comprised of multiple theories, each one drawing upon Vygotsky's work in different ways. However, a shared commonality between theories informed by SCT is that social inter-action is central to all learning. Thus, from an SCT perspective, speaking acts as a vehicle for people to express their identities through socialization, which, in turn, provides them with opportunities to understand different cultural prac-tices such as language and culture (Surtees & Duff, 2022).

The *zone of proximal development* (ZPD) is one of the most frequently cited concepts when discussing SCT. The term is generally referred to as the difference between what a learner can do on their own versus what they can do through mediation (Lantolf & Beckett, 2009). Referencing SCT, Nassaji and Swain (2000) state that ZPD can serve to promote language awareness through metalinguistic reflection. In other words, the researchers posit that interaction with others mediates language learning by promoting learners' *metalinguistic awareness*, which is "an individual's ability to focus attention on language as an object in and of itself, to reflect upon language, and to evaluate it" (Dillon, 2009, p. 186). According to Goh (2017a), metalinguistic awareness is key to developing L2 speaking as learners who are metacogni-tively aware can better use speaking strategies such as planning, monitoring, and evaluation during oral interaction.

Scaffolding, or the process in which a teacher or more capable peer provides assistance that enables a learner to accomplish a task they otherwise would not be able to complete (Goh, 2017b), is a concept that is closely related to ZPD. While some are hesitant to compare the two as scaffolding may place a greater emphasis on the individual providing aid, thereby restricting freedom of discourse (Kinginger, 2002), others point out that scaffolding can be a collect-ive endeavor in which learners support one another to reach higher levels of linguistic output (Donato, 1994). In this regard, research suggests that learners who have received metacognitive training on peer scaffolding can improve their L2 speaking skills (Fujii, Ziegler, & Mackey, 2016).

Independent of the two theories outlined above, accentedness and compre-hensibility are two concepts that have received much attention in L2 speaking literature. *Accentedness* refers to how nativelike a learner's speech is based on listener judgements of their L2 pronunciation, whereas *comprehensibility* relates to the amount of effort required by listeners to understand L2 speech (Suzuki & Kormos, 2020). Research by Derwing and Munro (Derwing &

Munro, 1997; Munro & Derwing, 1995) demonstrated that accentedness and comprehensibility are related yet distinct constructs, with accentedness not necessarily interfering with comprehensibility. Current research indicates that comprehensibility is more important than accentedness when teaching L2 speaking (Tsang, 2019), and this is reflected in the fact that the construct is included in the descriptors of high-stakes language assessments such as the Test of English as a Foreign Language (TOEFL) and the International English Language Testing Systems (IELTS) exam (Suzuki & Kormos, 2020). Findings from major studies indicate that L2 comprehensibility is impacted by several factors, most notably fluency, grammar, lexis, and pronunciation (Isaacs & Trofimovich, 2012; Saito, Trofimovich, & Isaacs, 2017).

Primary Themes

Improving L2 Speaking through Dialogue-Based CALL

Although numerous technologies can be used to enhance L2 speaking, this section is devoted to the use of dialogue-based CALL. Dialogue-based CALL consists of the collection of digital tools that enable learners to interact with a computer in a target language, including but not limited to intelligent personal assistants (IPAs), automatic speech recognition (ASR)-based CALL, intelligent tutoring systems, and chatbots (Bibauw, Francois, & Desmet, 2019). Due to word constraints, only two of these technologies are covered in this section: ASR-based CALL and IPAs.

Early research involving ASR and L2 speech indicated that the technology struggled to reach comprehensibility rates similar to that of human listeners. For example, Derwing, Munro, and Carbonaro (2000) found that a popular ASR software could understand L2 speech 71–73 percent of the time, while human listeners were able to recognize 90 percent of what was spoken. However, recent research by McCrocklin and Edalatishams (2020) shows that ASR-based systems have made considerable improvements in their ability to reliably understand L2 speech. In their study, the researchers analyzed the accuracy of Google's cloud-based voice transcription software to understand L2 English learners whose first languages (L1) were Chinese and Spanish, which mirrored Derwing et al.'s (2000) research. The adult participants also dictated the same sentences used in Derwing et al. (2000), thereby providing an equal comparison between past ASR software and modern ASR software. Findings revealed that Google's ASR was able to understand 91–93 percent of the L2 speech, which was similar to the 88–93 percent rate among human listeners. There was also a significant correlation between Google's ASR and the human listeners when it came to overall comprehensibility. Nonetheless, a significant correlation was only found for the L1 Chinese speakers, that is, there was no significant relationship between Google's ASR and human listener comprehensibility for the L1 Spanish speakers. According to the researchers, this indicates that the value of ASR software may depend on learners' L1 and L2 proficiency level.

Studies involving ASR-based systems for L2 learning have revealed some of the affordances of the technology. Research focusing on learners' experiences and perspectives toward ASR shows that it can promote language learning autonomy (McCrocklin, 2016), reduce speaking anxiety (Bashori, et al., 2021), and provide useful pronunciation feedback (McCrocklin, 2019). Recent studies examining the capacity of ASR in promoting speaking improvements have also yielded positive results. For instance, Jiang et al. (2021) found that L2 English learners using ASR were able to make greater improvements in oral language complexity than those in the control group. In another quantitative study, results from Evers and Chen (2020) demonstrated that adult L2 English learners could make significant gains in pronunciation in both read aloud and spontaneous conversation tasks. Taken together, these studies demonstrate that learners have favorable perceptions toward ASR-based CALL and that the technology can be useful in promoting L2 speaking skills.

Intelligent personal assistants such as Amazon Alexa, Google Assistant, and Siri rely on ASR and natural language processing (NLP) to understand user requests and respond accordingly. Because of their popularity and widespread availability, speaking with an IPA through a compatible device (e.g. smartphone, smart speaker, headphones) is an easy way for L2 learners to practice their speaking skills. In line with SCT, it appears that IPAs support metalinguistic awareness, that is, speaking with virtual assistants can help direct L2 learners to gaps in their linguistic output. For example, learners in Dizon (2017) reported that L2 English interactions with Alexa helped them notice deficiencies in their pronunciation that interfered with IPA-mediated communication. This finding is supported by Tai and Chen (2020), who found that the indirect feedback provided by Google Assistant encouraged the L2 English learners in their study to modify their pronunciation in order to be more easily comprehended by the IPA.

It is important to note that communication breakdowns with Alexa, Google Assistant, or other IPAs may not necessarily be due to an individual learner's L2 pronunciation issues. Instead, the primary cause may be the inability of a particular IPA to accurately understand any speech that deviates, however slightly, from the most popular varieties of English. However, given the work by McCrocklin and Edalatishams (2020) as well as Chen, Yang, and Lai's (2020) finding that pronunciation errors were the most common reason for communication breakdowns with the target IPA, it is probable that current IPAs can reliably recognize comprehensible L2 speech provided that a learner's oral output does not suffer from major deviations in target language pronunciation. As a result, IPAs may be more suitable for use among intermediate to advanced L2 learners.

Although limited in number, experimental studies involving IPAs have provided insight into the impact they can have on speaking development. In a small-scale study involving English as a foreign language (EFL) learners, Dizon (2020) found that students who interacted with Alexa were able to make more significant speaking gains than those who did not. These findings are supported by recent research by Hsu, Chen, and Todd (2021) and Tai and Chen (2022) as the EFL learners who interacted with an IPA in these studies also made greater gains in L2 speaking skills than those who did not have access to the technology. Several reasons are attributed to the speaking improvements made, namely, IPA-mediated interactions decrease speaking anxiety, promote oral interaction, and increase language learning enjoyment.

Even though ASR systems and IPAs have great potential in promoting oral interaction and speaking development, research indicates that certain steps should be taken to maximize their effectiveness for L2 teaching and learning. First, while it may be tempting for L2 learners to interact with these technologies individually given that they provide speakers with an L2 interlocutor, research suggests that students benefit from group work tasks when using dialogue-based CALL. For instance, in Evers and Chen (2020), students who used the ASR software with peers were able to make greater pronunciation improvements than learners who worked on their own to identify pronunciation mistakes. There was also a clear preference for collaborative group work over individual activities in Tai and Chen (2022) as peer feedback enabled them to have smoother and more enjoyable interactions with the IPA. Accordingly, activities involving dialogue-based CALL should utilize group work, thereby encouraging collaborative dialogue and peer scaffolding. Additionally, tasks utilizing ASR or IPAs should incorporate visual feedback in order to decrease the cognitive load of learners and better direct them to gaps in their linguistic output. Learners in Tai and Chen (2022) reported that the aural-only mode (i.e. using a device that lacked a display) made it difficult for them to properly respond to communication breakdowns with the IPA. Consequently, abandonment was a common communication strategy used by these students, which resulted in less successful interactions. In contrast, students who used a device with a display were able to more easily identify errors in their speech by checking the visual feedback, which in turn, allowed them to adjust their output accordingly. Lastly, dialogue-based CALL activities should incorporate a variety of tasks that target different speaking skills and scenarios. One way to increase task diversity when using IPAs is to take advantage of the skills or apps that can be freely downloaded through their respective platforms. For example, Tai and Chen (2020) identified Google Assistant skills including Song Quiz, Smart Story Teller, and Car Quiz Pro that allow for different interaction styles. Dozens of Alexa skills were used by the participants in Dizon (2020) such as vocabulary skills (e.g. Magoosh Vocabulary Builder), interactive audio stories (e.g. Earplay), as well as conversational socialbots. Engaging students in a variety of IPA-mediated tasks will not only help them improve different aspects related to L2 speaking but will also reduce the risk of learner fatigue and disinterest.

Current Research and Practice

Emerging Technologies for Speaking Development
Besides dialogue-based CALL, several other emerging technologies show promise when it comes to the development of L2 speaking. One of them is

virtual reality (VR), with many studies since the early 2010s examining how the technology can affect L2 learning. As noted by Ebadi and Ebadijalal (2020), VR offers several affordances for language learning that are pertinent for speaking development such as increased opportunities for collaborative learning and enhanced motivation and engagement.

Foreign language anxiety (FLA) and its effect on L2 communication is an area that has been oft studied when it comes to VR. In a study comparing three modalities – voice, video, and VR – York et al. (2021) concluded that the VR environment was the easiest, most fun, and most effective medium for English communication. Participants also reported significantly lower levels of FLA in VR, although significant differences were not found between VR and the other modalities in this regard. Trasher (2022) also investigated VR and FLA using two measures, self-reported anxiety and levels of salivary cortisol, a biological marker of anxiety, in a study involving L2 French students. An additional goal of her study was to determine if VR had a positive influence on L2 speech comprehensibility. Results from the research revealed that students had lower levels of FLA, both in terms of self-reported data and cortisol in VR compared to interaction in the traditional classroom. The learners' L2 speech comprehensibility was also found to be higher in the VR environment and when students had lower levels of anxiety, thus suggesting a link between the two variables. These two studies demonstrate that VR has the potential to reduce FLA when speaking in an L2, which, in turn, can positively affect speech comprehensibility.

A few studies have explored the impact that VR can have on L2 speaking skills. Ebadi and Ebadijalal (2020) compared two groups, one that used the Google Expeditions VR platform and a control group, to evaluate if VR could support L2 English oral proficiency and willingness to communicate. Results from the study indicated significant differences between the groups concerning the two variables: VR better contributed to enhanced oral proficiency and willingness to communicate than conventional instruction. In another study utilizing Google's VR tools, that is, Google Expeditions and Google Cardboard, Xie, Chen, and Ryder (2021) investigated the impact that VR could have on oral presentations. The L2 Chinese participants in their study gave six presentations, four using VR and the remaining two using PowerPoint in a traditional classroom environment. While no significant differences were found in relation to the fluency, grammar, or pronunciation subscales, the learners' overall content and vocabulary scores were significantly higher using VR compared to PowerPoint. While also examining VR and its potential to improve L2 speaking, Chien, Hwang, and Jong (2020) took a different approach in that the researchers did not compare a VR and non-VR group. Instead, the researchers examined the role of peer assessment and its impact on speaking performance, FLA, and other variables in a VR environment among EFL students. Results from the study indicated that the experimental group which utilized peer feedback made greater gains in speaking fluency and maturity of language, that is, the ability to include details in a response that exceed the minimum requirements. Students in the peer assessment group also exhibited lower levels of FLA, which again underscores the importance of collaborative tasks in technology-mediated speaking activities.

Similar to VR, the use of augmented reality (AR) in L2 teaching and learning has become increasingly popular. In a systematic review paper, Parmaxi and Demetriou (2020) identified fifty-four studies published between 2014 and 2019 that pertained to AR and language learning. However, among those studies, only 9.9 percent of them focused on L2 speaking skills, which implies L2 speaking is underexplored in AR research. One exception is an early case study by Liu (2009), who measured the impact of an AR system on EFL students' listening and speaking achievements. The researcher found that those in the experimental group who utilized AR had significantly higher listening and speaking test scores throughout the experiment compared to the control group. In a follow-up study investigating the same AR system, Liu and Chu (2010) had similar results. In other words, EFL learners who used AR had greater improvements in English listening and speaking. Results from interviews indicated that the AR system allowed the students to practice English speaking in an authentic context, which in turn, increased their confidence in speaking the target language. More recent studies investigating AR in an L2 speaking context have not explored the potential linguistic gains learners can make through the technology, but student perceptions toward AR in communicative classroom environments. For instance, Taskiran (2019) measured EFL students' views toward AR games in a survey-based study, with results indicating that the participants enjoyed using AR for language learning and believed the technology supported language development. The researcher posited that the AR games promoted collaboration among the students, which, in turn, helped support L2 speaking and listening.

The growing ubiquity of smartphones has made mobile assisted language learning (MALL) a popular area within technology-mediated language learning research. Having said that, fewer MALL studies have examined speaking compared to other areas related to language proficiency, namely, listening and vocabulary (Shadiev, Hwang, & Huang, 2017). Hwang et al. (2016) found that an experimental group that used mobile games outperformed a control group on an L2 speaking post-test. Based on these results, the researchers identified three affordances of MALL that relate to both cognitive theory and SCT: It (1) provides more opportunities for L2 speaking and reflection: (2) promotes speaking accuracy; and (3) allows for L2 speaking in real-life contexts. In a mixed-methods study, Wu and Miller (2020) investigated EFL students' perceptions toward a mobile application called PeerEval. The participants gave each other peer feedback using the app after the students' oral performances. Survey and interview findings suggested that the mobile app promoted improvements in L2 English speaking, with the collaborative nature of MALL one of the primary affordances of the activity.

While there is a strong body of literature examining machine translation (MT) in the context of L2 writing (Lee, 2021), research related to MT and L2 speaking is scarce. An exception to this is van Lieshout and Cardoso's (2022) study of Google Translate as a digital tool for self-directed L2 Dutch learning. In the one-hour experiment, adult L2 learners were tasked with ten learning objectives, that is, they were instructed to learn ten Dutch phrases and their corresponding pronunciations by using Google Translate. The participants had no knowledge of the target phrases prior to the study, thus any gains in L2 vocabulary and pronunciation could be directly attributed to the use of MT. Native speaker raters' judgements of the participants' recorded speech showed that the participants' L2 Dutch was comprehensible and contained a low degree of accentedness, thereby highlighting the potential of MT as a tool for L2 speaking.

Recommendations for Research and Practice

The studies detailed above highlight the significance of group work when utilizing CALL for L2 speaking. Although technology has shown promise in promoting independent, self-directed learning (van Lieshout & Cardoso, 2022), the peer feedback that group work brings is invaluable in supporting an engaging and motivational learning environment (e.g. Chien et al., 2020; Evers & Chen, 2020). Having said that, it is important that learners be given sufficient training in providing constructive feedback as many of them may lack the confidence or skills needed to give such feedback (Wu & Miller, 2020).

Training is not only important when it comes to giving peer feedback in L2 speaking tasks, but also as it relates to CALL in general. As a result, it is critical to provide quality training so that learners can properly leverage technology for L2 learning. Hubbard and Romeo (2012) summarize a training model that can be used to train learners in the use of CALL. Their model is comprised of three parts: technical, strategic, and pedagogical training. Technical training consists of giving learners the necessary information regarding how to use a specific technology or application for language learning purposes. Strategic training relates to the teaching of strategies that enable learners to complete specific learning objectives. Finally, pedagogical training refers to supporting learners in their understanding of why they should use certain strategies to reach a given objective. While maintaining a balance between these three areas may be difficult, they should all be integrated into any training program for CALL to be most effective.

Another important consideration to make when implementing technology for L2 teaching is understanding if a CALL task is suitable for one's teaching context. To that end, Chapelle (2001) created a list of six criteria that can be used to evaluate CALL activities (see Table 24.1). As noted by Chapelle (2001), CALL evaluation is context-dependent, and what may work in one situation with a group of learners may not work in another: "[A]n evaluation has to result in an argument indicating in what ways a particular CALL task is appropriate for particular learners at a given time (p. 53).

Table 24.1 *CALL evaluation criteria by Chapelle (2001, p. 55)*

Authenticity	The degree of correspondence between the learning activity and target language activities of interest to learners out of the classroom.
Language learning potential	The degree of opportunity present for beneficial focus on form.
Learner fit	The amount of opportunity for engagement with language under appropriate conditions given learner characteristics.
Meaning focus	The extent to which learners' attention is directed toward the meaning of language.
Positive impact	The positive effects of the CALL activity on those who participate in it.
Practicality	The adequacy of resources to support the use of the CALL activity.

Future Directions

Given the rise of artificial intelligence (AI) in education, it is likely that AI applications will play a more prominent role in L2 speaking going forward. However, considering the potential ethical and privacy concerns, researchers and teachers should be cautious about utilizing AI for language teaching purposes. AI software typically collects large amounts of data about its users, so those who are interested in utilizing AI for language research or teaching must carefully consider the privacy issues involved (X. Chen et al., 2020). Learning analytics, which describe the process of collecting, analyzing, and reporting data for the purposes of creating an optimal learning environment (Zeng et al., 2020), is another avenue of L2 speaking research that is likely to garner more attention in the coming years. Initial research involving learning analytics for L2 learning suggests that it can be valuable in understanding learners' behaviors in online courses focused on L2 oral communication (Zeng et al., 2020). The popularity of social media, gaming, and online video means that students are able to learn foreign languages incidentally through these digital practices. Accordingly, there has been increased interest from both young people and researchers in the digital wilds, that is, "informal language learning that takes place in digital spaces, communities, and networks that are independent of formal instructional contexts" (Sauro & Zourou, 2017, p. 186). These types of digital practice often involve oral interaction, thereby making them potentially useful for L2 speaking development.

References

Ahmadian, M. J. (2012). The relationship between working memory capacity and L2 oral performance under task-based careful online planning condition. *TESOL Quarterly*, *46*(1), 165–175. https://doi.org/10.1002/tesq.8

Ahmadian, M. J., & Tavakoli, M. (2011). The effects of simultaneous use of careful online planning and task repetition on accuracy, complexity, and fluency in EFL learners' oral production. *Language Teaching Research*, *15*(1), 35–59. https://doi.org/10.1177%2F1362168810383329

Bashori, M., van Hout, R., Strik, S., & Cucchiarini, C. (2021). Effects of ASR-based websites on EFL learners' vocabulary, speaking anxiety, and language enjoyment. *System, 99*, 1–16. https://doi.org/10.1016/j.system.2021.102496

Bibauw, S., Francois, T., & Desmet, P. (2019). Discussing with a computer to practice a foreign language: Research synthesis and conceptual framework of dialogue-based CALL. *Computer Assisted Language Learning, 32*(8), 827–877. https://doi.org/10.1080/09588221.2018.1535508

Chapelle, C. (2001). *Computer applications in second language acquisition: Foundations for teaching, testing and research.* Cambridge University Press.

Chen, H. H.-J., Yang, C. T.-Y., & Lai, K. K.-W. (2020). Investigating college EFL learners' perceptions toward the use of Google Assistant for foreign language learning. *Interactive Learning Environments*, 1–16. https://doi.org/10.1080/10494820.2020.1833043

Chen, X., Xie, H., Zou, D., & Hwang, G. J. (2020). Application and theory gaps during the rise of artificial intelligence in education. *Computers & Education: Artificial Intelligence, 1*, 100002. https://doi.org/10.1016/j.caeai.2020.100002

Chien, S. Y., Hwang, G. J., & Jong, M. S. Y. (2020). Effects of peer assessment within the context of spherical video-based virtual reality on EFL students' English-speaking performance and learning perceptions. *Computers & Education, 146*, 103751. https://doi.org/10.1016/j.compedu.2019.103751

Derwing, T. M., & Munro, M. J. (1997). Accent, intelligibility and comprehensibility: Evidence from four L1s. *Studies in Second Language Acquisition, 19*(1), 1–16. https://doi.org/10.1017/S0272263197001010

Derwing, T. M., Munro, M. J., & Carbonaro, M. (2000). Does popular speech recognition software work with ESL speech? *TESOL Quarterly, 34*(3), 592–603. https://doi.org/10.2307/3587748

Dillon, A. (2009). Metalinguistic awareness and evidence of cross-linguistic influence among bilingual learners in Irish primary schools. *Language Awareness, 18*, 182–197. https://doi.org/10.1080/09658410902928479

Dizon, G. (2017). Using intelligent personal assistants for L2 learning: A case study of Alexa. *TESOL Journal, 8*(4), 811–830. https://doi.org/10.1002/tesj.353

Dizon, G. (2020). Evaluating intelligent personal assistants for L2 listening and speaking development. *Language Learning & Technology, 24*(1), 16–26. https://doi.org/10125/44705

Donato, R. (1994). Collective scaffolding in second language learning. In J. Lantolf & G. Appel (Eds.), *Vygotskian approaches to second language research* (pp. 33–56). Praeger.

Ebadi, S., & Ebadijalal, M. (2020). The effect of Google expeditions virtual reality on EFL learners' willingness to communicate and oral proficiency. *Computer Assisted Language Learning*, 1–25. https://doi.org/10.1080/09588221.2020.1854311

Evers, K., & Chen, S. (2020). Effects of an automatic speech recognition system with peer feedback on pronunciation instruction for adults. *Computer Assisted Language Learning*, 1–22. https://doi.org/10.1080/09588221.2020.1839504

Fujii, A., Zeigler, N., & Mackey, A. (2016). Peer interaction and metacognitive instruction in the EFL classroom. In M. Sato & S. Ballinger (Eds.), *Peer interaction and second language learning* (pp. 63–89). John Benjamins.

Gillespie, J. (2020). CALL research: Where are we now? *ReCALL, 32*(2), 127–144. https://doi.org/10.1017/S0958344020000051

Goh, C. (2017a). Language awareness and the teaching of listening and speaking. In P. Garrett & J. M. Cots (Eds.), *The Routledge handbook of language awareness* (pp. 92–107). Routledge.

Goh, C. (2017b). Research into practice: Scaffolding learning processes to improve speaking performance. *Language Teaching, 50*(2), 247–260. https://doi.org/10.1017/S0261444816000483

Hayashi, Y. (2019). Investigating effects of working memory training on foreign language development. *The Modern Language Journal, 103*(3), 665–685. https://doi.org/10.1111/modl.12584

Hayashi, Y., Kobayashi, T., & Toyoshige, T. (2016). Investigating the relative contributions of computerized working memory training and English language teaching to cognitive and foreign language development. *Applied Cognitive Psychology, 30*, 196–213. https://doi.org/10.1002/acp.3177

Housen, A., & Kuiken, F. (2009). Complexity, accuracy and fluency in second language acquisition. *Applied Linguistics, 30*(4), 461–473. https://doi.org/10.1093/applin/amp048

Hubbard, P., & Romeo, K. (2012). Diversity in learner training. In G. Stockwell (Ed.), *Computer-assisted language learning: Diversity in research and practice* (pp. 33–48). Cambridge University Press.

Hulstijn, J. H. (2006). Psycholinguistic perspectives on second language acquisition. In J. Cummins, & C. Davison (Eds.), *The international handbook on English language teaching* (pp. 701–713). Springer.

Hsu, H. L., Chen, H. H. J., & Todd, A. G. (2021). Investigating the impact of the Amazon Alexa on the development of L2 listening and speaking skills. *Interactive Learning Environments*. Advance online publication. https://doi.org/10.1080/10494820.2021.2016864

Hwang, W. Y., Shih, T. K., Ma, Z. H., Shadiev, R., & Chen, S. Y. (2016). Evaluating listening and speaking skills in a mobile game-based learning environment with situational contexts. *Computer Assisted Language Learning, 29*(4), 639–657. https://doi.org/10.1080/09588221.2015.1016438

Isaacs, T., & Trofimovich, P. (2012). Deconstructing comprehensibility: Identifying the linguistic influences on listeners' L2 comprehensibility ratings. *Studies in Second Language Acquisition, 34*(3), 475–505. https://doi.org/10.1017/S0272263112000150

Jiang, M. Y. C., Jong, M. S. Y., Lau, W. W. F., Chai, C. S., & Wu, N. (2021). Using automatic speech recognition technology to enhance EFL learners' oral language complexity in a flipped classroom. *Australasian Journal of Educational Technology, 37*(2), 110–131. https://doi.org/10.14742/ajet.6798

Jong, N. H. de. (2020). Teaching speaking. In C. A. Chapelle (Ed.), *The concise encyclopedia of applied linguistics* (pp. 1071–1077). Wiley-Blackwell.

Juffs, A., & Harrington, M. (2011). State of the article: Aspects of working memory in L2 learning. *Language Teaching, 44*(2), 137–166. https://doi.org/10.1017/S0261444810000509

Kinginger, C. (2002). Defining the zone of proximal development in US foreign language education. *Applied Linguistics, 23*(2), 240–261.

Kormos, J., & Safar, A. (2008). Phonological short-term memory, working memory and foreign language performance in intensive language learning. *Bilingualism: Language and Cognition, 11*(2), 261–271. https://doi.org/10.1017/S1366728908003416

Lantolf, J. P., & Beckett, T. G. (2009). Sociocultural theory and second language acquisition. *Language Teaching, 42*(4), 459–475. https://doi.org/10.1017/S0261444809990048

Lee, S.-M. (2021). The effectiveness of machine translation in foreign language education: a systematic review and meta-analysis. *Computer Assisted Language Learning, 36*(1–2), 103–125. https://doi.org/10.1080/09588221.2021.1901745

Levelt, W. J. M. (1994). The skill of speaking. In P. Bertelson, P. Eelen, & G. d'Ydewalle (Eds.), *International perspectives on psychological science: Vol. 1. Leading themes* (pp. 89–103). Lawrence Erlbaum Associates, Inc.

Levelt, W. J. M. (1999). Language production: A blueprint of the speaker. In C. Brown & P. Hagoort (Eds.), *Neurocognition of language* (pp. 83–122). Oxford University Press.

Liu, T.-Y. (2009). A context-aware ubiquitous learning environment for language listening and speaking. *Journal of Computer Assisted Learning, 25*(6), 515–527. https://doi.org/10.1111/j.1365-2729.2009.00329.x

Liu, T.-Y., & Chu, Y.-L. (2010). Using ubiquitous games in an English listening and speaking course: Impact on learning outcomes and motivation. *Computers & Education, 55*(2), 630–643. https://doi.org/10.1016/j.compedu.2010.02.023

Mackey, A., Adams, R., Stafford, C., & Winke, P. (2010). Exploring the relationship between modified output and working memory capacity. *Language Learning, 60*(3), 501–533. https://doi.org/10.1111/j.1467-9922.2010.00565.x

McCrocklin, S. (2016). Pronunciation learner autonomy: The potential of automatic speech recognition. *System, 57*, 25–42. https://doi.org/10.1016/j.system.2015.12.013

McCrocklin, S. (2019). Learners' feedback regarding ASR-based dictation practice for pronunciation learning. *CALICO Journal, 36*(2), 119–137. https://doi.org/10.1558/cj.34738

McCrocklin, S., & Edalatishams, I. (2020). Revisiting popular speech recognition software for ESL speech. *TESOL Quarterly, 54*(4), 1086–1097. https://doi.org/10.1002/tesq.3006

Munro, M. J., & Derwing, T. M. (1995). Processing time, accent, and comprehensibility in the perception of native and foreign-accented speech. *Language and Speech, 38*(3), 289–306. https://doi.org/10.1177/002383099503800305

Nassaji, H., & Swain, M. (2000). A Vygotskian perspective on corrective feedback in L2: The effect of random versus negotiated help on the learning of English articles. *Language Awareness, 9*(1), 34–51. https://doi.org/10.1080/09658410008667135

Parmaxi, A., & Demetriou, A. A. (2020). Augmented reality in language learning: A state-of-the-art review of 2014–2019. *Journal of Computer Assisted Learning, 36*(5), 1–15. https://doi.org/10.1111/jcal.12486

Qiu, X. (2019). Functions of oral monologic tasks: Effects of topic familiarity on L2 speaking performance. *Language Teaching Research, 24*(6), 1–20. https://doi.org/10.1177/1362168819829021

Ratner, C. (2002). *Cultural psychology: Theory and method.* Kluwer/Plenum.

Saito, K., Trofimovich, P., & Isaacs, T. (2017). Using listener judgments to investigate linguistic influences on L2 comprehensibility and accentedness: A validation and generalization study. *Applied Linguistics, 38*(4), 439–462. https://doi.org/10.1093/applin/amv047

Sauro, S., & Zourou, K. (2017). Call for papers. *Language Learning & Technology, 21*(1), 186. https://doi.org/10125/44603

Shadiev, R., Hwang, W.-Y., & Huang, Y.-M. (2017). Review of research on mobile language learning in authentic environments. *Computer Assisted Language Learning, 30*(3–4), 284–303. http://dx.doi.org/10.1080/09588221.2017.1308383

Surtees, V., & Duff, P. (2022). Sociocultural approaches to speaking in SLA. In T. M. Derwing, M. J. Munro, & R. I. Thomson (Eds.), *The Routledge handbook of second language acquisition and speaking* (pp. 54–67). Routledge.

Suzuki, S., & Kormos, J. (2020). Linguistic dimensions of comprehensibility and perceived fluency: An investigation of complexity, accuracy, and fluency in second language argumentative speech. *Studies in Second Language Acquisition, 42*(1), 143–167. https://doi.org/10.1017/S0272263119000421

Tai, T.-Y., & Chen, H. H.-J. (2020). The impact of Google Assistant on adolescent EFL learners' willingness to communicate. *Interactive Learning Environments, 31*(3), 1485–1502. https://doi.org/10.1080/10494820.2020.1841801

Tai, T.-Y., & Chen, H. H.-J. (2022). The impact of intelligent personal assistants on adolescent EFL learners' speaking proficiency. *Computer Assisted Language Learning, 37*(5–6), 1224–1251. https://doi.org/10.1080/09588221.2022.2070219

Taskiran, A. (2019). The effect of augmented reality games on English as foreign language motivation. *E-Learning and Digital Media, 16*(2), 122–135. https://doi.org/10.1177/2042753018817541

Trasher, T. (2022). The impact of virtual reality on L2 French learners' language anxiety and oral comprehensibility: An exploratory study. *CALICO Journal, 39* (2), 1–20. https://doi.org/10.1558/cj.42198

Tsang, A. (2019). Reconceptualizing speaking, listening, and pronunciation: Glocalizing TESOL in the contexts of World Englishes and English as a lingua franca. *TESOL Quarterly, 53*(2), 580–588. https://doi.org/10.1002/tesq.504

van Lieshout, C., & Cardoso, W. (2022). Google Translate as a tool for self-directed language learning. *Language Learning & Technology, 26*(1), 1–19. http://hdl.handle.net/10125/73460

Vygotsky, L. S. (1978). Interaction between learning and development. In M. Cole, V. John-Steiner, S. Scribner, & E. Souberman (Eds.), *Mind in society: The development of higher psychological processes* (pp. 79–91). Harvard University Press.

Wolfe-Quintero, K., Inagaki, S., & Kim, H. Y. (1998). *Second language development in writing: Measures of fluency, accuracy, and complexity* (Technical Report No. 17). National Foreign Language Resource Center.

Wu, J. G., & Miller, L. (2020). Improving English learners' speaking through mobile-assisted peer feedback. *RELC Journal, 51*(1), 168–178. https://doi.org/10.1177/0033688219895335

Xie, Y., Chen, Y., & Ryder, L. H. (2021). Effects of using mobile-based virtual reality on Chinese L2 students' oral proficiency. *Computer Assisted Language Learning, 34*(3), 225–245. https://doi.org/10.1080/09588221.2019.1604551

York, J., Shibata, K., Tokutake, H., & Nakayama, H. (2021). Effect of SCMC on foreign language anxiety and learning experience: A comparison of voice, video, and VR-based oral interaction. *ReCALL, 33*(1), 49–70. https://doi.org/10.1017/S0958344020000154

Zeng, S., Zhang, J., Gao, M., Xu, K. M., & Zhang, J. (2020). Using learning analytics to understand collective attention in LMOOCs. *Computer Assisted Language Learning*, 1–27. https://doi.org/10.1080/09588221.2020.1825094

Further Reading

Bibauw, S., Van den Noortgate, W., François, F., & Desmet, P. (2022). Dialogue systems for language learning: A meta-analysis. *Language Learning & Technology, 26*(1), 1 24. https://hdl.handle.net/10125/73488
This meta-analysis highlights the effectiveness of dialogue-based CALL on L2 proficiency development and explores the relative efficacy of specific features within dialogue systems.

Derwing, T., Munro, M., & Thomson, R. (2022). (Eds.). *The Routledge handbook of second language acquisition and speaking*. Routledge. https://doi.org/10.4324/9781003022497
This edited volume provides a comprehensive overview of the relevant concepts and issues related to L2 acquisition and speaking, including the use of technology for speaking development.

Yang, C. T.-Y., Lai, S.-L., & Chen, H. H.-J. (2022). The impact of intelligent personal assistants on learners' autonomous learning of second language listening and speaking. *Interactive Learning Environments, 32*(5), 2175–2195. https://doi.org/10.1080/10494820.2022.2141266
This article reports on a novel study involving IPAs for self-directed L2 learning. The study illustrates the positive impact that sustained teacher guidance can have on the development of L2 speaking skills in outside-the-class settings.

25

Listening

Glenn Stockwell

Introduction

Listening in a second language, as a concept, is highly challenging to describe and define, given the myriad of interconnected elements involved (Suvorov, 2015) and the vast array of definitions attempting to capture its essence (Glenn, 1989). As a skill, listening is often thought to be the most difficult to learn due to the "fleeting nature of input" (Bozorgian & Shamsi, 2023, p. 1). Listening is not merely reliant on auditory input, and proficient listeners employ a variety of visual and nonverbal cues to aid in deciphering messages from the input, subsequently interpreting it within the context, assigning significance, and, if necessary, formulating a suitable response (Steil, Barker, & Watson, 1983; Wolff et al., 1983; Wolvin & Coakley, 1995). It is a complex intersection of the processing of information at multiple levels, including neurological, linguistic, semantic, and pragmatic dimensions (Rost, 2011). Despite its intricate nature, the cultivation of listening abilities has garnered "the least systematic attention from educators and pedagogical resources" (Goh & Vandergrift, 2022, p. 4), offering scant guidance on engaging in listening exercises or activities, or on enhancing listening competencies.

Although debates have continued over its exact function in second language acquisition, a general consensus has emerged that listening is indeed an essential component of language learning, and researchers have explored ways in which it could be developed. This includes the examination of effective instructional approaches and the use of appropriate materials, both of which have been informed by recent technological advances. In some ways, however, listening has been relatively limited in the way that it is used in teaching, and it has often been employed either as an instrument for the instruction of other skills or as a mechanism to evaluate and gauge general linguistic competence (Field, 2008).

The development of listening skills has undoubtedly benefited greatly from technological advancements. Previously reliant on live conversations for practicing foreign language listening, advancements such as cassette tapes, CDs, and the internet have made this process more accessible. The most significant impact on second language listening since the beginning of the twenty-first century has likely been the internet, offering a multitude of digital tools to assist learners in honing their listening abilities. Ranging from podcasts to online videos, language learners can access a vast array of content aimed at enhancing their comprehension and speaking skills. Digital tools enable learners to access authentic materials created for native speakers, providing them not only with opportunities to improve their listening skills but also to acquire knowledge about the culture and customs of the target language.

The best practices for using technology in the development of listening skills in a second language have yet to be extensively documented. As research explores various aspects of listening such as input types (Pusey, 2020), captions and subtitles (Hosogoshi, 2016), it becomes increasingly evident that technology has had an impact on both what learners listen to and how they can interact with it to develop their listening skills. Listening resources that learners have access to have become more diverse in genre, content, and difficulty level as a result of advances in technology, such as podcasting, online radio, and video streaming, to name a few. These may range from teacher-designed materials targeting lower-level learners through to authentic video and audio that may be normally accessed by members of the target language community in their everyday lives. This diversity makes it possible for learners to select materials and employ strategies and tools for listening that align with their individual learning styles and preferences (cf. Cohen, 2018). At the same time, this diversity also has implications for how listening should be taught and assessed within an environment of rapidly evolving technological developments. Thus, this chapter explores how technology has impacted the teaching, learning, and assessment of listening and considers current and future trends to link to better practice and research in the future.

Background/Historical Perspectives

Listening has always had a somewhat precarious position in second language education, and it has even been referred to as the "Cinderella skill" (Nunan, 2002, p. 238) due to its perceived lack of importance or difficulty. In the 1970s, it was perceived as subordinate to speaking, partially due to approaches such as the audiolingual method, where listening was chiefly regarded as a source of input for imitation or modification in verbal communication (Newton & Nation, 2021). As teaching approaches shifted toward a greater emphasis on communication in the target language, listening came to be seen as a skill requiring attention in its own right, even suggesting that speaking be delayed in favour of developing listening fluency (Nord, 1980). Exposure to authentic communication was given more importance, leading to a greater focus on the use of audio(visual) resources that were designed for members of the target language community rather than materials made for language learning purposes. This is one area in which technology has played a major role, expanding the opportunities for learners to access and interact with authentic listening materials. The emergence of digital media has vastly increased the quantity, quality, and variety of content available to learners, and the development of internet-based technologies such as podcasting (Rosell-Aguilar, 2013) and streaming services like YouTube (Dizon, 2022) have found their way into language teaching contexts.

While there has been criticism about their effectiveness (see Newton & Nation, 2021, for a discussion), numerous strategies and approaches for helping learners become more proficient at listening have appeared, ranging from pre-listening activities such as prediction and anticipation tasks to post-listening activities like summarizing and discussion (Gilakjani & Ahmadi, 2011) and note-taking strategies (Rivens Mompean & Guichon, 2009). Methods such as dictation and transcription have been employed to assist students in concentrating on distinct aspects of a particular audio segment, enabling them to refine their abilities in areas such as pronunciation or grammar (Levis & Grant, 2005). Online quizzes and surveys have also gained widespread use, which not only encourage learners to engage in listening activities in their own time (Stockwell, 2019) but also allow data on students' performance in listening to be collected and analyzed (Goh & Vandergrift, 2022), making it possible to monitor learner progress as well as carry out research. As technology has become more widespread in the teaching and learning of listening, it has become clear that there are several areas where research is emerging, and these will be dealt with in more depth in the next section.

Primary Themes

As a point of departure, it is important to clarify what technology usage in the teaching of listening refers to. It has been argued that it goes beyond merely utilizing devices like computers or smartphones to play audio or video content (Hubbard, 2017; Cárdenas Claros, 2021), and rather it should allow for interaction with audiovisual content in a way that takes advantage of the affordances of technology. This has been done in a variety of shapes and forms since the 2010s as relevant technologies have evolved, and this has been reflected quite directly in practice and research. In a discussion of the teaching and learning of listening in a second language, it also becomes clear that it is extremely elusive in terms of precisely what is being developed. As a construct, listening is multidimensional, relying on the motivation to attend to aural input, responding to this input, and understanding and interpreting the messages encoded in it (Worthington & Bodie, 2017). To this end, teaching approaches need to encompass at least one of these areas and provide learners with the skills they need to be able to develop it. It is difficult to cover all of the changes that have taken place as a result of technology, so this chapter will focus specifically on annotations and captions, modification of input, and individualized learning, feedback, and learner training.

Annotations and Captions

Perhaps one of the most of most well-known methods of using technology in facilitating the teaching and learning of listening in a second language has been the use of annotations. For example, Jones (2003, 2009) explored the use of textual, audio, and visual annotations to support learners in their comprehension of a passage in French, concluding that they view them positively overall, but there were some learners who claimed that annotations that did not provide much assistance were frustrating. Similarly, video captions have also been used as a means of enabling learners to engage with listening (Hsu, 2018; Montero Perez, Peters, & Desmet, 2015), exploring both how learners use the captions through eye-tracking and vocabulary retention.

While the use of annotations has had wide support in the literature for their effectiveness in learning vocabulary, their impact on developing listening comprehension has been far less evident (Hsieh, 2020). In one sense, this is not surprising given that annotations will often provide textual support that may encourage learners to use them to get the meaning of unknown vocabulary items or phrases with minimal cognitive effort for short-term comprehension goals that may have an adverse longer-term impact on the development of their listening skills. Similar outcomes have been seen for caption use by Kruger and Steyn (2014), who also noted that although learners viewed listening more positively when there were captions, there were no significant differences in the results of listening comprehension tests. Another issue raised with captions is the danger of students becoming over-reliant on them (Leveridge & Yang, 2013), and learners may end up concentrating their efforts on "reading" rather than "listening," meaning that there would need to be a gradual transition to the nonuse of captions as a final objective of listening.

From a theoretical perspective, multimedia/multimodal learning theory (Mayer, 2001) has been the rationale for the use of annotations and captions in that they can allow for coding of information through multiple channels, which can enhance comprehension (Montero Perez, 2022). In an overview of forty-one articles on multimedia learning, Zhang and Zou (2022) explored the effectiveness of these multiple channels in second language learning, concluding that listening comprehension is best facilitated when accompanied by visual cues, but that the outcomes could be greatly affected by learner factors such as language proficiency, learning styles, and cognitive processing capacities along with the design of the learning materials.

Input

One benefit of employing technological advancements in teaching listening is that it makes it far easier for learners to have access to a diverse range of accents (Bui, 2022). Historically, learners' exposure to accents may have been limited to one or two in a traditional classroom setting, and as such they are more likely to experience difficulties in comprehending speech produced by accents that do not fit "standard" variations that they are likely to have encountered in formal settings (Lochland, 2020). With the broad range of audiovisual resources that are available to learners through news, music, and streaming media, learners have far more opportunities today to be exposed to a variety of accents. In addition, many of these come with functions that enable learners to turn on subtitles or captions that can reduce the burden of listening and, in turn, encourage them to spend more time engaged in listening in the target language.

Tools such as YouTube and Netflix have also become an attractive option for learners who actively seek out their own opportunities to listen to the target language. Not only are they able to access authentic listening resources, many of these resources come with tools that can make them more appropriate for language learning. YouTube makes it possible to use automatic speech recognition technology to generate captions, and the Chrome extension Language Learning with Netflix allows learners to have access to the meanings of captions that can assist with their comprehension (Fievez et al., 2023). In addition, video players (including YouTube) and audio players such as VLC Player come with a function that enables the speech rate to be slowed down considerably for learners that struggle with more natural speeds (Hubbard, 2019). Thus, these technological tools make it possible to choose authentic input that suits learners' own preferences (see Chen, 2016).

Learner Training

As described above, teaching listening skills requires the development of a variety of interrelated factors, some of which are psychological or affective, some behavioral, and others cognitive (Worthington & Bodie, 2017). Training has recently been deemed a crucial part of language acquisition, and this necessity has become increasingly significant due to technological advancements (see Hubbard, 2004, for a discussion). Furthermore, this training needs to take place systematically to enable learners to not only understand the functions of a given technology but also how to apply it to their language learning (Stockwell, 2022). For listening, learners may be required to use tools that they have limited experience with, or they may have applied only a narrow range of functions.

For example, while most computers and mobile devices have software or apps installed for playing music, these either do not have the function to change the speed of the audio, or learners are just not aware of it. This technical aspect of training is an essential part of laying the groundwork for using a technology. Consequently, Hubbard and Romeo (2012) suggest that learner training should also include strategic training which explores the junction between technology and strategies for learning a specific skill or area, and pedagogical training which encourages learners to consider the applicability of strategies they know and to construct new ones.

While Newton and Nation (2021) cite some skepticism of strategy training for the development of listening skills, evidence has appeared that with regards to technology, at least, strategy training does have benefits in terms of the time spent on listening activities and their cognitive engagement (Stockwell, 2019). It should be pointed out, however, that the effects of strategy training in listening are dependent upon the focus of the training. Training in strategies that target vocabulary (e.g. Chen, Li, & Lin, 2022) will have an impact on different aspects of listening than training in strategies for grammar (Kang & Chung, 2020). Strategies that are often associated with listening such as shadowing have been shown to have a positive effect on pronunciation (Foote & McDonough, 2018) and speaking fluency (Ahn & Lee, 2015). The fact that training in "listening" is often exemplified in other elements illustrates the complexity of defining clear strategies that can develop the skill, and training through technology for listening should necessarily include guidance on how to use the technology through which the training will take place.

Help Options and Feedback

Two areas that have been of particular interest regarding the interactivity that technology provides for the teaching and learning of listening are the help functions and automated feedback. These have been shown to take various forms and can give learners extra support as they undertake tasks and activities. An excellent overview of help options for listening is provided by Cárdenas-Claros (2020), who suggested that learners found dictionaries, vocabulary lists and transcripts or captions to be the most helpful, and that slowing down the speed of the audio also assisted listening comprehension. An ongoing concern that has been observed with help options, however, is that many of them are not used even if they are provided (Cárdenas-Claros & Gruba, 2009). There has been significant research that shows that training can contribute to better usage of these help options (Cross, 2017). The issue of help options is an ongoing area of research, and it will be dealt with in more detail in the section on current research and practice.

Unlike productive skills such as speaking and writing, providing feedback on listening is notoriously difficult, largely because proficiency in listening is typically exhibited in other ways, such as a learner's ability to comprehend the content of a given listening segment. This manifestation of proficiency may be dependent upon the nature of the questions being asked to elicit a response and as such may not necessarily be an accurate representation of learners' actual ability to comprehend aural input. Using technology to administer multiple choice questions or short answers with appropriate automated feedback to responses can be considered as one way of identifying learner comprehension, although the questions themselves may also act as a means of facilitating comprehension (O'Grady, 2023). Used appropriately, feedback can be used as an effective means of assisting learners, but consideration needs to be given to applying questions to assessment (see Brunfaut, 2016).

Feedback for learners in distance educational settings has also evolved as a direct result of information communication technologies (ICT) that allow relatively seamless audiovisual interaction with live interlocutors. While it is of course possible to engage in tasks and activities with automated feedback such as those described above, these tools also facilitate development of listening through authentic interaction in two-way communication (White, 2017). While COVID-19 has done much to reduce the affective barriers to the use of audiovisual technologies in language education, the technology does not include an inherent instructional design, and the design of the interaction between the teacher and the learners will depend on the teacher's view of how listening is to be developed.

Current Research and Practice

As described above, listening has undergone a significant change as a direct result of technological advances. In saying that, although there has been a period of adjustment as teachers and learners have gotten used to emerging technologies, the field has also started to reach a level of maturity that has enabled discussion to go beyond possibilities through to actual practice that capitalizes upon the affordances of these technologies. There are, of course, many ways of approaching the complex interplay that makes up the current state of research and practice regarding listening and technology, but this chapter will explore two main perspectives: pedagogical and technological. Needless to say, these are difficult to completely separate from one another as one will necessarily be affected by the other, but it is possible to view them as the point of departure of the research or practice that they entail.

Pedagogical Perspectives

Despite the widespread discussion surrounding listening and how technology may be used to facilitate it, it is only relatively recently that pedagogy grounded in relevant research and theory has started to appear. Cárdenas Claros, Campos-Ibaceta, and Vera-Saavedra (2021) explored the reasons behind patterns of interactions with available help options used by learners in order to devise guidelines that could lead to better practice in listening instruction. They examined the timing of interaction (i.e. pre-, during, and post-listening) and the types of activity such as vocabulary activation or listening comprehension. Among their conclusions were the need to ensure that activities are designed with the affordances of the chosen technologies kept in mind, and at the same time, to present the technological options to the learners in a scaffolded manner so that they can take advantage of their individual functions without being overwhelmed.

An area where technology may be thought to assist in providing learners with the input they need to promote language learning is through extensive listening. There has been debate about exactly what constitutes extensive listening, but Renandya and Farrell (2010) inclusively define it as "all types of listening activities that allow learners to receive a lot of comprehensible and enjoyable listening input" (p. 56). While there are many tools through which this could take place, one of the most commonly used tools in the literature is podcasting (Rosell-Aguilar, 2013), often in conjunction with metacognitive approaches (e.g. Alm, 2013, see also Vandergrift & Goh, 2021). While metacognitive awareness has been shown to have some impact on listening comprehension performance, further research is required to determine what it is about raising metacognitive awareness that contributes to its effects (Bozorgian & Shamsi, 2023). The results do, however, confirm the need to train learners in directing their attention to certain aspects of listening passages in order to effectively process the multitude of sounds included in them (Wolfgramm, Suter, & Göksel, 2016). In this regard, training (as described above) is clearly a necessary part of any pedagogy associated with developing listening.

Task-based approaches to listening that utilize technology have also attracted attention, and the need for teacher guidance and support to make the most of the tasks has also emerged (Cárdenas Claros & Dassonvalle, 2022). Feedback provided in tasks can be either corrective or instructional (Nassaji & Kartchava, 2019), with the latter meaning that teachers are not only focusing on the language but also on the process of learning that can lead to the development of listening itself. Based on this premise, Cárdenas Claros (2022) explored how teachers can provide feedback to learners, suggesting how this feedback can be given at three levels. The first of these is knowledge of response feedback, where learners can determine whether or not their responses to questions given to them in tasks are appropriate or not. This is followed by elaborative feedback, where learners may receive feedback that highlights what they need to be listening for in the input, feedback that explains why answers are incorrect, and/or feedback that gives specific directions on where to find information that leads them to comprehend the content or to know what was incorrect in their responses. Finally, she suggested that learners can have access to knowledge of correct responses and feedback that enables them to monitor their progress through a number of similar tasks. In this way, various forms of feedback can be used in a pedagogical design that can lead to improve comprehension and skills in undertaking listening, and this is an area that is in need of further research.

Technological Perspectives

As technology use is necessarily going to be highly dependent upon pedagogy, this section will build upon the previous section with that in mind. It is difficult to bring together the various technologies that have been used for listening over the past several decades, but as described earlier, podcasting and streaming services such as YouTube and Netflix have been used broadly. As technologies continue to emerge, it is expected that these will be explored for their applicability to language teaching and learning, and this exploration will no doubt also extend to listening. Given space limitations, just a small number of examples of technologies that have been the focus of research will be described here. The first of these is a vlog (Aldukhayel, 2021), which is a type of streaming video where the creator addresses the audience directly. These have been considered as attractive for language learning purposes given the authenticity of the content (Watkins & Wilkins, 2011), and as a listening activity they allow learners to have more of a feel of being the recipient of an interaction rather than an onlooker of other interactions.

Mobile technologies have long been thought suitable for listening due to the fact that they can be used to easily listen to podcasts and audio broadcasts, but recent years have also seen them being used with other more sophisticated functions rather than just listening. One example of this is the use of glosses to assist in comprehension and production of vocabulary that Turkish learners encountered while listening to short English passages (Fidel & Gülcan, 2018). While the immediate comprehension goals were achieved, learners failed to recall vocabulary in delayed recall tests, indicating the need for further research into how acquisition of these items can be consolidated. An ongoing problem with using mobile devices for learning outside formal contexts has been the difficulties in engaging in sustained activities, and this remains a challenge as pedagogies for listening using mobile devices are devised.

Finally, audiovisual communication technologies that allow for authentic interaction between learners have also been investigated for their impact on the development of second language listening skills. In a study by Levak and Son (2016), learners geographically separated from one another (in this case in Australia, Croatia, and Bosnia and Hercegovina) communicated in English and Croatian using Skype and Second Life. While each platform offers different affordances, the former allowing learners to physically see each other and the latter making it possible for learners to interact in a virtual world, a major conclusion of the study was that the tools need to be selected based on solid pedagogy for listening comprehension.

Recommendations for Research and Practice

There is a lot that can be learned from exploring the primary themes that have emerged surrounding the use of technology for the teaching of listening and the recent research and practice that builds on these themes. Perhaps one of the most important factors is the need to consider pedagogy as a part of the consideration of technology. In other words, while technology does allow for a lot of options for learners, these need to be provided to them in a way that is manageable and not overwhelming, particularly given the fleeting nature of audio input. The provision of appropriate help options (Cárdenas Claros, 2021) along with appropriate training in using the technology and the available help options (Stockwell, 2019) can make an enormous difference on the outcomes of listening. For this reason, taking measures to ensure that training learners to use the technology based on a pedagogy that includes how to use it for developing their listening is indispensable. The availability of technologies and the skills possessed by learners and teachers will also vary depending on the sociocultural context, and thus decisions about what technology to use need to be made taking these into consideration.

Developing appropriate pedagogies is dependent upon further research that looks beyond the technology. At the same time, it should be kept in mind that listening is a cognitively demanding activity, and it has even been argued that the load of academic listening may outweigh the benefits (Roussel, Tricot, & Sweller, 2022). This being the case, the need to determine how much load is suitable for learners to enable them to make the most of the available input, and how to support that load with captions, annotations, and other help options needs to be a key part of research and practice. Finding appropriate materials for learners of various levels and abilities remains an issue. Addressing this point, Hubbard (2017) suggests that a collection of curated materials of various genres and levels of difficulty would go a long way toward helping teachers and researchers locate what they need for their individual learning environments. Thus, appropriate research and practice is very dependent upon bringing together these various complex factors – technology, resources, contexts, training, and pedagogy – as they relate to listening and this is where the next steps of research and practice in the field need to be situated.

References

Ahn, T. y., & Lee, S.-M. (2015). User experience of a mobile speaking application with automatic speech recognition for EFL learning. *British Journal of Educational Technology*, *47*(4), 778–786. https://doi.org/10.1111/bjet.12354

Aldukhayel, D. (2021). Vlogs in L2 listening: EFL learners' and teachers' perceptions, *Computer Assisted Language Learning*, *34*(8), 1085–1104. https://doi.org/10.1080/09588221.2019.1658608

Alm, A. (2013). Extensive listening 2.0 with foreign language podcasts. *Foreign Language Annals*, *7*(3), 266–280. https://doi.org/10.1080/17501229.2013.836207

Bozorgian, H., & Shamsi, E. (2023). A review of research on metacognitive instruction for listening development. *International Journal of Listening*. Advance online publication. https://doi.org/10.1080/10904018.2023.2197008

Brunfaut, T. (2016). Assessing listening. In D. Tsagari & J. Banerjee (Eds.), *Handbook of second language assessment* (pp. 97–112). De Gruyter, Inc. https://doi.org/10.1515/9781614513827-009

Bui, T. H. (2022). English teachers' integration of digital technologies in the classroom. *International Journal of Educational Research Open*, *3*, 100204. https://doi.org/10.1016/j.ijedro.2022.100204

Cárdenas-Claros, M. S. (2020). Spontaneous links between help option use and input features that hinder second language listening comprehension, *System*, *93*, 102308. https://doi.org/10.1016/j.system.2020.102308.

Cárdenas-Claros, M. S. (2021). Computer-based second language listening. In H. Mohebbi & C. Coombe (Eds.), *Research questions in language education and applied linguistics* (pp. 615–619). Springer Nature. https://doi.org/10.1007/978-3-030-79143-8_107

Cárdenas-Claros, M. S. (2022). Conceptualising feedback in computer-based L2 language listening. *Computer Assisted Language Learning, 35*(5–6), 1168–1193. https://doi.org/10.1080/09588221.2020.1774615

Cárdenas Claros, M. S., & Dassonvalle, K. (2022). A first step to task design in computer-based L2 listening: Task characteristics elicitation. In J. Colpaert, & G. Stockwell (Eds.), *Smart CALL: Personalization, contextualization, & socialization* (pp. 266–292). Castledown Publishers. https://doi.org/10.29140/9781914291012-12

Cárdenas-Claros, M. S., & Gruba, P. A. (2009). Help options in CALL: A systematic review, *CALICO Journal, 27*(1), 69–90. https://doi.org/10.11139/cj.27.1.69-90

Cárdenas-Claros, M. S., Campos-Ibaceta, A., & Vera-Saavedra, J. (2021). Listeners' patterns of interaction with help options: Towards empirically-based pedagogy. *Language Learning & Technology, 25*(2), 111–134. http://hdl.handle.net/10125/73436

Chen, C.-M., Li, M.-C., & Lin, M.-F. (2022). The effects of video-annotated learning and reviewing system with vocabulary learning mechanism on English listening comprehension and technology acceptance. *Computer Assisted Language Learning, 35*(7), 1557–1593. https://doi.org/10.1080/09588221.2020.1825093

Chen, C.W.-Y. (2016). Listening diary in the digital age: Students' material selection, listening problems, and perceived usefulness. *The JALT CALL Journal, 12*(2), 83–101. https://doi.org/10.29140/.v12n2.j203

Cohen, A. (2018). Moving from theory to practice: A closer look at language learner strategies. In R. L. Oxford & C. M. Amerstorfer (Eds.), *Language learning strategies and individual learner characteristics: Situating strategy use in diverse context* (pp. 31–54). Bloomsbury Academic. http://dx.doi.org/10.5040/9781350005075.ch-002

Cross, J. (2017). Help options for L2 listening in CALL: A research agenda. *Language Teaching, 50*(4), 544–560. http://doi.org/10.1017/S0261444817000209

Dizon, G. (2022). YouTube for second language learning: What does the research tell us? *Australian Journal of Applied Linguistics, 5*(1), 19–26. https://doi.org/10.29140/ajal.v5n1.636

Fidel, Ç., & Gülcan, E. (2018). Effects of gloss type on text recall and incidental vocabulary learning in mobile-assisted L2 listening. *ReCALL, 30*(1), 24–47. https://doi.org/10.1017/S0958344017000155

Field, J. (2008). *Listening in the language classroom.* Cambridge University Press. https://doi.org/10.1017/CBO9780511575945

Fievez, I., Montero Perez, M., Cornillie, F., & Desmet, P. (2023). Promoting incidental vocabulary learning through watching a French Netflix series with glossed captions. *Computer Assisted Language Learning, 36*(1–2), 26–51. https://doi.org/10.1080/09588221.2021.1899244

Foote, J. A., & McDonough, K. (2018). Using shadowing with mobile technology to improve L2 pronunciation. *Journal of Second Language Pronunciation, 3*(1), 34–56. https://doi.org/10.1075/jslp.3.1.02foo

Gilakjani, A. P., & Ahmadi, M. R. (2011). A study of factors affecting EFL learners' English listening comprehension and the strategies for improvement. *Journal of Language Teaching and Research, 2*(5), 977–988. https://doi.org/10.4304/jltr.2.5.977-988

Glenn, E. C. (1989). A content analysis of fifty definitions of listening. *Journal of the International Listening Association, 3,* 21–31. https://doi.org/10.1207/s1932586xijl0301_3

Goh, C., & Vandergrift, L. (2022). *Teaching and learning second language listening: Metacognition in action* (2nd ed.). Routledge. https://doi.org/10.4324/9780429287749

Hosogoshi, K. (2016). Effects of captions and subtitles on the listening process: Insights from EFL learners' listening strategies. *The JALT CALL Journal, 12*(3), 153–178. https://doi.org/10.29140/.v12n3.j206

Hsieh, Y. (2020). Effects of video captioning on EFL vocabulary learning and listening comprehension. *Computer Assisted Language Learning, 33*(5–6), 567–589. https://doi.org/10.1080/09588221.2019.1577898

Hsu, H.-T. (2018). Incidental professional vocabulary acquisition of EFL business learners: Effect of captioned video with glosses as a multimedia annotation. *The JALT CALL Journal, 14*(2), 119–142. https://doi.org/10.29140/jaltcall.v14n2.227

Hubbard, P. (2004). Learner training for effective use of CALL. In S. Fotos & C. Browne (Eds.), *Perspectives on CALL for second language classrooms* (pp. 45–68). Lawrence Erlbaum.

Hubbard, P. (2017). Technologies for teaching and learning L2 listening. In C. A. Chapelle & S. Sauro (Eds.), *The handbook of technology and second language teaching and learning* (pp. 93–106). John Wiley & Sons. https://doi.org/10.1002/9781118914069

Hubbard, P. (2019). Leveraging technology to integrate informal language learning within classroom settings. In M. Dressman & R. W. Sadler (Eds.), *The handbook of informal language learning* (pp. 405–419). Wiley Blackwell.

Hubbard, P., & Romeo, K. (2012). Diversity in learner training. In G. Stockwell (Ed.), *Computer assisted language learning: Diversity in research and practice* (pp. 33–48). Cambridge University Press. https://doi.org/10.1017/CBO9781139060981.003

Jones, L. C. (2003). Supporting listening comprehension and vocabulary acquisition with multimedia annotations: The students' voice. *CALICO Journal, 21*(1), 41–65. https://doi.org/10.1558/cj.v21i1.41-65

Jones, L. C. (2009). Supporting student differences in listening comprehension and vocabulary learning with multimedia annotations. *CALICO Journal, 26*(2), 267–289. https://doi.org/10.1558/cj.v26i2.267-289

Kang, H. Y., & Chung, H. L. (2020). Effects of focus on form instruction through listening in blended learning on the development of grammar and listening skills. *Korean Journal of English Language and Linguistics, 20,* 662–691. https://doi.org/10.15738/kjell.20..202011.662

Kruger, J. L., & Steyn, F. (2014). Subtitles and eye tracking: Reading and performance. *Reading Research Quarterly*, *49*(1), 105–120. http://doi.org/10.1002/rrq.59

Levak, N., & Son, J.-B. (2016). Facilitating second language learners' listening comprehension with Second Life and Skype. *ReCALL*, *29*(2), 200–218. https://doi.org/10.1017/S0958344016000215

Leveridge, A. N., & Yang, J. C. (2013). Testing learner reliance on caption supports in second language listening comprehension multimedia environments. *ReCALL*, *25*(2), 199–214. http://doi.org/10.1017/S0958344013000074

Levis, J. M., & Grant, L. (2005). Integrating pronunciation into ESL/EFL classrooms. *TESOL Journal*, *12*(2), 13–19. http://dx.doi.org/10.1002/j.1949-3533.2003.tb00125.x

Lochland, P. (2020). Intelligibility of L2 speech in ELF. *Australian Journal of Applied Linguistics*, *3*(3), 196–212. https://doi.org/10.29140/ajal.v3n3.281

Mayer, R. E. (2001). *Multimedia learning*. Cambridge University Press. http://dx.doi.org/10.1017/CBO9781139164603

Montero Perez, M. (2022). Second or foreign language learning through watching audio-visual input and the role of on-screen text. *Language Teaching*, *55*(2), 163–192. https://doi.org/10.1017/S0261444821000501

Montero Perez, M., Peters, E., & Desmet, P. (2015). Enhancing vocabulary learning through captioned video: An eye-tracking study. *The Modern Language Journal*, *99*(2), 308–328. https://doi.org/10.1111/modl.12215

Nassaji, H., & Kartchava, E. (2019). Technology-mediated feedback and instruction. *International Journal of Applied Linguistics*, *170*(2), 151–153. https://doi.org/10.1075/itl.00018.nas

Newton, J., & Nation, I. S. P. (2021). *Teaching ESL/EFL listening and speaking* (2nd ed.). Routledge. https://doi.org/10.4324/9780429203114

Nord, J. R. (1980). Developing listening fluency before speaking: An alternative paradigm. *System*, *8*(1), 1–22.

Nunan, D. (2002). Listening in language learning. In J. C. Richards & W. A. Renandya (Eds.), *Methodology in language teaching: An anthology of current practice* (pp. 238–241). Cambridge University Press. https://doi.org/10.1017/CBO9780511667190.032

O'Grady, S. (2023). Adapting multiple-choice comprehension question formats in a test of second language listening comprehension. *Language Teaching Research*, *27*(6), 1431–1455. https://doi.org/10.1177/1362168820985367

Pusey, K. (2020). Assessing L2 listening at a Japanese university: Effects of input type and response format. *Language Education & Assessment*, *3*(1), 13–35. https://doi.org/10.29140/.v3n1.193

Renandya, W. A., & Farrell, T. S. C. (2010). "Teacher, the tape is too fast!" Extensive listening in ELT. *ELT Journal*, *64*(1), 52–59. https://doi.org/10.1093/elt/ccq015

Rivens Mompean, A., & Guichon, N. (2009). Assessing the use of aids for a computer-mediated task: Taking notes while listening. *The JALT CALL Journal*, *5*(2), 29–44. https://doi.org/10.29140/.v5n2.j79

Rosell-Aguilar, F. (2013). Podcasting for language learning through iTunes-U: The learner's view. *Language Learning & Technology, 17*(3), 75–93. http://llt.msu.edu/issues/october2013/rosellaguilar.pdf

Rost, M. (2011). *Teaching and researching listening* (2nd ed.). Routledge. https://doi.org/10.4324/9781315833705

Roussel, S., Tricot, A., & Sweller, J. (2022). The advantages of listening to academic content in a second language may be outweighed by disadvantages: A cognitive load theory approach. *British Journal of Educational Psychology, 92*, 627–644. https://doi.org/10.1111/bjep.12468

Steil, L. K., Barker, L. L., & Watson, K. W. (1983). *Effective listening: Key to your success.* Addison-Wesley.

Stockwell, G. (2019). Insights from replication on the factors affecting task engagement in mobile-based learning activities. *Technology in Language Teaching & Learning, 1*(1), 33–51. https://doi.org/10.29140/tltl.v1n1.152

Stockwell, G. (2022). *Mobile assisted language learning: Concepts, contexts and challenges.* Cambridge University Press.

Suvorov, R. (2015). The use of eye tracking in research on video-based second language (L2) listening assessment: A comparison of context videos and content videos. *Language Testing, 32*(4), 463–483. https://doi.org/10.1177/0265532214562099

Vandergrift, L., & Goh, C. M. (2021). *Teaching and learning second language listening* (2nd ed.). Routledge. https://doi.org/10.4324/9780429287749

Watkins, J., & Wilkins, M. (2011). Using YouTube in the EFL classroom. *Language Education in Asia, 2*(1), 113–119. https://doi.org/10.5746/LEiA/11/V2/I1/A09/Watkins_Wilkins

White, C. (2017). Distance language teaching with technology. In C. A. Chapelle, & S. Sauro (Eds.), *The handbook of technology and second language teaching and learning* (pp. 134–149). John Wiley & Sons, Inc. https://doi.org/10.1002/9781118914069.ch10

Wolff, F. I., Marsnik, N. C., Tacey, W. S., & Nichols, R. G. (1983). *Perceptive listening.* CBS College Publishing.

Wolfgramm, C., Suter, N., & Göksel, E. (2016). Examining the role of concentration, vocabulary and self-concept in listening and reading comprehension. *International Journal of Listening, 30*(1–2), 25–46. https://doi.org/10.1080/10904018.2015.1065746

Wolvin, A. D., & Coakley, C. G. (1995). *Listening* (5th ed). McGraw Hill.

Worthington, D. L., & Bodie, G. D. (2017). Defining listening: A historical, theoretical, and pragmatic assessment. In D. L. Worthington, & C. G. Coakley (Eds.), *The sourcebook of listening research: Methodology and measures* (pp. 3–18). Wiley Blackwell.

Zhang, R., & Zou, D. (2022). A state-of-the-art review of the modes and effectiveness of multimedia input for second and foreign language learning. *Computer Assisted Language Learning, 35*(9), 2790–2816. https://doi.org/10.1080/09588221.2021.1896555

Further Reading

Goh, C., & Vandergrift, L. (2022). *Teaching and learning second language listening: Metacognition in action* (2nd ed.). Routledge.

This updated edition of the 2012 book is insightful in its views on teaching listening skills, but it also includes a detailed section on the use of technology. Its overview of metacognition for listening has been used as the foundation for several studies published in the literature. Dedicated to the use of technology in listening, it provides a number of useful examples.

Hubbard, P. (2017). Technologies for teaching and learning L2 listening. In C. A. Chapelle & S. Sauro (Eds.), *The handbook of technology and second language teaching and learning* (pp. 93–106). John Wiley & Sons. https://doi.org/10.1002/9781118914069

This book chapter covers a detailed overview of the considerations of using technology for listening in a second language. Looking at around twenty years of research on technology in the teaching and learning of listening in a second language, it calls for the development of curated materials.

Newton, J. M., & Nation, I. S. P. (2021). *Teaching ESL/EFL listening and speaking* (2nd ed). Routledge. https://doi.org/10.4324/9780429203114

This is an excellent overview of not only listening but also speaking in a second language. It provides a solid exploration of how the role of listening in second language education has shifted and provides practical suggestions on how to teach listening based on relevant research.

26

Reading

Meei-Ling· Liaw and Sabrina Priego

Introduction

People nowadays engage with digital technologies in varied and sophisticated ways. Digital 2021 (Kemp, 2021) reports that in 2020 more than 1 billion people worldwide faced some kind of disruption to their education due to COVID-19; as a consequence, digital learning innovation has increased. The report further reveals that finding information was the main reason and top motivation for people to go online. As what and how people read are intertwined with technological innovation, societal changes, and lifestyle preferences, it prompts us to rethink what it means to read and acquire literacy.

Reading is a complex process. It requires the reader to draw information from visual features and combine this information with his/her background knowledge to form a coherent construction and reconstruction of text meaning (Grabe & Stoller, 2012). Online technologies make it possible for millions of people to access texts that would otherwise be beyond their reach. However, becoming a proficient reader in a new or second language (L2) can be more complex than in the first language (L1) because it involves combining reading resources of both languages into a dual-language processing system (Li & Clariana, 2019). Furthermore, L2 learners need support to overcome linguistic and processing practice limitations to read in a language in which they are not yet proficient (Grabe, 2014).

As new technologies flourish, tools for learners and educators also increase. L2 reading has been the area that computer-assisted language learning (CALL) research and practice has consistently highlighted (Blake, 2016). Liou (2016) surveyed available technological tools, including e-books, weblogs, wikis, Google Docs, corpus and concordances, mobile devices, automatic essay graders, and other innovative programs designed to teach L2 reading and writing. Liaw and English (2017) also described an array of options for L2 reading technologies for teaching and learning. Since innovative technologies for language learning and instruction are being developed every day, language educators need to keep abreast of their applications and changes in order to take advantage of their affordances. As reading is an integral part of people's daily activities, it is imperative to review frequently technologies that are applied to language learning and instruction, not only to assess their present use but also to plan for future practices. In this chapter, the background and historical perspectives of applying computer technologies to teaching and learning reading in L2 are first outlined. The current trends in researching and practicing technological applications to L2 reading are reviewed. Based on research trends and findings, suggestions for effective integration of technologies into L2 reading teaching and learning are pro-vided. Finally, future directions for applying technologies to the teaching and learning of L2 reading are discussed.

Background

The ways that technologies have been used in teaching and learning L2 reading relate closely to our understanding of reading processes, L2 development, and the advancement of technologies (Kern & Warschauer, 2000; Stockwell, 2014). Historically, L1 reading theories have had a major impact on L2 reading research as L1 and L2 reading share important basic elements, such as involving the reader, the text, and the interaction between the reader and text (Rumelhart, 1977). L2 reading, however, has its unique elements, mainly L2 readers' prior experience, limited L2 knowledge, and ongoing influences from L1 (Koda, 1994). Several major perspectives have been applied to explain both L1 and L2 reading processes and provide the theoretical underpinning for designing and implementing computer-assisted teaching and learning of L2 reading, including structural, cognitive, metacognitive, and sociostructural (Liaw & English, 2017). More recently, data-driven learning (DDL) has been applied to designing CALL-based reading tools, such as concordances, to enhance vocabulary learning and reading comprehension (Liou, 2016).

The structural perspectives, popular from the 1920s through the 1950s, focus on the printed form of a text and postulate that meaning exists in the text and readers are passive recipients of information (Chun & Plass, 1997). Readers were instructed to acquire hierarchically ordered sub skills to improve their comprehension ability (LaBerge & Samuels, 1974) and read out loud for correct pronunciation (Kern & Warschauer, 2000). The earliest CALL pro-grams, adhering to this view, consisted of grammar and vocabulary tutorials, drill and practice programs, and language testing instruments. By the early 1960s, the structural perspectives were challenged as the behaviorist notion of language learning was criticized and replaced with the view that language development was an active process of generating and transforming knowledge.

The cognitive perspectives consider reading as not just getting meaning from a text but also a process of connecting information in the text with the knowledge the reader brings to the act of reading. In this sense, reading is a dialogue between the reader and the text, and it involves an active cognitive process in which the reader's background knowledge plays a key role in the creation of meaning (Tierney & Pearson, 1994). It is, in essence, a process in which readers sample the text, make hypotheses, confirm or reject them, and make new hypotheses (Goodman, 1976). In line with the cognitive views of learning, CALL programs at the time strived to provide problem-solving and hypothesis-testing tasks via which learners could use existing knowledge to develop new understandings (Kern & Warschauer, 2000). Several tenets of the cognitive theory, including noticing (Schmidt, 1990), focus on form (Long, 1991), automatization of word recognition (Perfetti, 1985), and activating prior knowledge (Carrell, 1983), have provided theoretical bases for educators to utilize multimedia reading scaffolds, such as dictionaries, glosses, and annotation for improving vocabulary learning and reading comprehension (Chun & Plass, 1997; Sato, Matsunuma, & Suzuki, 2013).

Block (1992) proposed that there should be no more debate on whether reading is a bottom-up, language-based process or a top-down, knowledge-based process. Instead, readers should be encouraged to take control during their reading to understand a text by exercising metacognition. Fluent readers are capable of reflecting on their level of understanding and know what to do when reading difficulties occur. Furthermore, they apply strategies along the process of reading. Metacognitive strategies, such as using schematic knowledge and identifying and planning reading tasks, should be taught to students to improve their reading ability (Boulware-Gooden et al., 2007; Kern & Warschauer, 2000). In this perspective, technologies, especially networked computers, are used to provide an environment where language learners' metacognition and L2 reading strategies are fostered through peer interactions (Zhao, 2016). Mobile devices, including tablets, cell phones, and other hand held devices, can be used to support the development of online reading strategies and reading comprehension (Auer, 2015; Taki, 2015).

The more recent developments in L2 learning provide a way to look into L2 learning through the lenses of sociocultural processes (Lantolf & Thorne, 2007). The sociocultural theory views learning and development as being embedded within social events and occurring as a learner interacts with others (Vygotsky, 1978). From this perspective, reading is regarded as a process taking place in particular sociocultural contexts. Reading instruction should focus not only on individual learning strategies but also on helping learners become part of literate communities through extensive discussion of the reading. Network communication technologies, such as email, social media, and text messaging, offer ways for reading to be a social, rather than an individual, process (Chun, 2016). The attributes of technology shape the interaction in particular ways, although technology itself does not determine the interaction. The notions derived from sociocultural perspectives, such as situated learning and communities of learning, have led to an increased interest in using web-based tools for vocabulary learning, social reading for L2 literacy, and reading comprehension (Godwin-Jones, 2015; Wrigglesworth, 2020).

In addition to the major theoretical influences, DDL (Pérez-Paredes, 2019) also impacts the recent applications of technologies to L2 teaching and learning. Data-driven learning is based on corpus linguistics research methods. The most commonly used DDL tool for language learning is a concordance. When a language learner inputs a target word or a phrase, the concordance yields prolific example sentences as language models. The learner can then inductively find out how the target language can be used. Research findings have revealed that using DDL tools could result in increased language sensitivity, noticing, induction, and ability to work with authentic data (Boulton & Cobb, 2017). Reading based on DDL has also been found to be beneficial to reading comprehension (Gordani, 2013).

By tracing the history of the theoretical perspectives that have been applied to inform the integration of technologies into L2 reading, we can see how pedagogical practices and the roles of technologies in language learning have also evolved. Nevertheless, as Hubbard and Levy (2016, p. 33) have pointed out, "CALL theory in practice is more likely to be an ensemble or a synthesis" as language learning environments are complex and teachers need to assess multiple factors and adopt different perspectives "even those that might on the surface appear incompatible." Theoretical perspectives will continue to emerge and guide technological applications to teaching L2 reading. As new and exciting technologies are constantly created and made accessible to language learners, the presence of theories can help to guide L2 reading teachers to navigate through the increasingly complex L2 reading and learning environments.

Primary Themes

Second language reading is one of the most exciting and productive areas of CALL research and practices. CALL has the advantage of textual persistence on the computer screen that gives L2 learners time to process unfamiliar linguistic features (Blake, 2016). The availability of mediational functions of the internet further allows the reading to go beyond being a solitary activity (Blyth, 2014; Godwin-Jones, 2015). The prolific digital devices and mobile services prompt CALL researchers and educators to explore their effects on L2 reading.

In Burston's (2013) review of the published studies from 1994 to 2012 related to mobile-assisted language learning (MALL), about 11 percent (35 of 315) of them are related to reading. Most of them describe the uses and effects of using hand held devices, including PDAs, tablets, cell phones, etc., on L2 reading developments. The various features offered by mobile devices, such as e-dictionaries, annotations, and short messages, were reported to positively affect reading comprehension, motivation to read in L2, or confidence in L2 learning. An updated study by Gutiérrez-Colón, Frumuselu, and Curell (2020) continued with Burston's effort and surveyed MALL publications from 2012 to 2017. A total of seventeen articles were annotated. The researchers showed that smartphones and mobile apps (Line, WhatsApp, QR codes, etc.) emerged as new platforms for implementing L2 reading. Blended learning, integrating mobile a pps and L2 reading skills inside and outside the class, has increased.

To further zoom in on the current research and practices of using technologies for L2 reading, we surveyed major CALL journals, including *Language Learning and Technology, Computer Assisted Language Learning, ReCALL,* and *CALICO,* for the empirical studies published between 2010 and 2021 related to L2 reading.[1] Altogether, 34 articles were identified: 7 in *Language Learning and Technology,* 14 in *Computer Assisted Language Learning,* 8 in *ReCALL,* and 5 in *CALICO* (see Appendix I). Our survey revealed that most of the studies have explored reading in online environments where corpus-informed tools (e.g. glosses, e-dictionaries, concordances, and translation systems), annotation, and social media allowed learners to actively interact with the information or with other learners to achieve the following learning goals: vocabulary and reading comprehension, strategic reading, reading fluency and extensive reading, and motivation. In the following sections, we describe the representative studies focusing on each of these learning goals.

Vocabulary and Reading Comprehension

The majority of the reviewed studies focused on vocabulary growth and reading comprehension. Several centered on the interaction between the L2 learner and the data-driven tools. For example, Wang (2012) found that the e-dictionary helped intermediate learners of Chinese consolidate word meanings and learn new words, but it was less beneficial for more advanced students. As for reading comprehension, all students improved their reading comprehension scores with the use of the e-dictionary. Using corpora, Gordani (2013) examined the effect of the integration of corpora in general English courses on the student's vocabulary development. The findings showed that the experimental group outperformed the control group in the post-test, suggesting that the main effect of corpus integration was significant. A study by Sato et al. (2013) used time-controlled software and found that the time-control function can facilitate the automatization of word decoding skills and reduce the working memory workload. It was also found that reducing the working memory workload leads to a better understanding of the text. Türk and Erçetin (2014) compared the effects of two types of glosses (interactive and simultaneous display of visual and verbal multimedia information) on incidental vocabulary learning and reading comprehension. They found that participants in the simultaneous display condition used glosses more frequently than those in the interactive display condition. They also performed better in reading and vocabulary tests. Chen (2016) also evaluated the

---

[1] Stockwell (2007) identified the four as major CALL journals and reviewed the empirical articles published from 2001 to 2005 to identify categories of technology used in CALL.

influence of different gloss modes (in-text mode, marginal gloss mode, and pop-up mode) on beginner-level ESL college students' L2 reading comprehension and vocabulary acquisition. Their findings showed that the marginal gloss mode resulted in the highest scores in the multiple-choice test, whereas in-text glosses brought about the best performance in the rest of the tests, and pop-up glosses led to the lowest scores in all four tests. In a recent study, Ballance (2021) focused on the potential of concordances extracted from general and more specialized corpora to provide an increased lexical-repetition effect. The findings showed that concordances extracted from more general corpora had higher type-token ratio levels than concordances extracted from more specialized corpora.

More recent studies have tended to use technological tools for discussion and interaction among peers. For instance, Tseng, Yeh, and Yang (2015) investigated the effects of online annotations on surface-based, text-based, and situation-based reading comprehension levels. They found that students made four types of annotation, namely marking vocabulary, adding Chinese explanatory notes to unknown vocabulary, marking text information, and adding summary notes to each paragraph. Reflection led them to a deeper level of reading comprehension. Yeh, Hung, and Chiang (2017) analyzed how students used annotations in a collaborative learning environment. The findings showed an improvement in the student's reading comprehension scores after the intervention. It was also found that students whose marks had improved the most had also provided extensive feedback to their peers. Law, Barny, and Poulin (2020) had their students use the digital tool, eComma, to annotate the lyrics of several L2 songs. The findings showed that social engagement, as measured by the frequency of questions and replies and word count, decreased over time, and linguistic affordances increased in later songs.

Strategic Reading

The second-largest category of studies focuses on the specific strategies L2 learners need to use when reading online texts. Roy and Crabbe (2015) focused on students' ability to search for keywords from an EFL website, identify key top-down menus and links, and use appropriate cognitive and metacognitive reading strategies to analyze the webpage. The participants in Huang's (2015) study were asked to read online materials to produce voice blogs. The students reported having difficulties finding relevant information online because of their limited knowledge of using search engines and because they were unable to select appropriate information by skimming and scanning the online texts. Tsai's (2017) study focused on the role of reading strategies in a Chinese–English translation task in an English for specific purposes course. It was found that the most frequently used type of strategy was compensation strategies, which were used when encountering problems with unknown vocabulary or lack of content knowledge. In addition, repeatedly learning vocabulary was the most frequent individual strategy. They concluded that

Moodle-supported strategy instruction can facilitate EFL students' overall reading comprehension and strategy use.

Reading Fluency and Extensive Reading

Another focus has been on reading fluency and extensive reading with the help of corpus tools and social media. For example, Hadley and Charles (2017) used Oxford Bookworms Graded Readers to stimulate greater lexicogrammatical knowledge and reading fluency among lower proficiency learners in an extensive reading program. Although it was found that both groups had a statistically significant lexicogrammatical improvement, the control group outperformed the experimental group. The researchers concluded that for students of lower proficiency, attention to their reading preferences and applying a softening DDL approach would have worked better. Arndt and Woore's (2018) analyzed whether video blogs or written blog posts lead to incidental vocabulary learning and differences in which aspects of vocabulary knowledge are best learned from these media. The scores on the various tasks showed that the students in the blog group gained more orthographic knowledge from pseudowords than the students in the vblog group.

Motivation

Second language learners' motivation to read has been explored as well. Huang (2013a) examined students' perceptions of e-book reading as an L2 learning tool. Students had access to audio e-books selected from free audio e-book downloading websites, online bilingual dictionaries, and other online reading help tools. Data from questionnaires and interviews showed that students highlighted the potential of e-books to improve their reading habits and increase their motivation. Combining extensive reading with online writing was found to have enhanced students' reading interest and improved their writing skills (Sun, Yang, & He, 2016). In the study, each participant had access to one computer in class to discuss and collaborate with their classmates and teachers. The findings showed that the extensive reading program enhanced students' reading interest and improved their writing skills.

From the review studies on mobile applications on L2 reading by Burston (2013) and Gutiérrez-Colón et al. (2020), and our review of the published studies in four major CALL journals from 2010 to 2021, it is evident that emerging technologies of different shapes and sizes have been contributing to the various aspects of L2 reading development. Despite variations in how they were integrated into instructional activities and how their effectiveness was assessed, researchers and educators have been experiencing varying levels of success. The enthusiasm for applying technological tools to L2 reading will continue to grow. It is not only because the two are tightly related to each other, but, more importantly, there is still so much more to learn as they evolve and transform either side-by-side or together.

Current Research and Practice

Chun, Kern, and Smith (2016) offer a set of heuristic questions to help guide language teachers and researchers in incorporating technology into their teaching practice or research plan. These questions are excellent for L2 reading teachers to consider: (1) What learning goals do I have for my students? 2) What instructional resources do I have available? 3) How can these resources be used to serve the established learning goals? (4) How will I assess how effective students' use of these resources is in attaining the established learning goals?

Setting Learning Goals

In terms of setting learning goals for L2 reading, Grabe (2014) has pointed out that learning activities should support the following: word recognition skills, recognition vocabulary, comprehension skills, discourse structure, strategic reading, reading fluency, extensive reading, motivation, and combining language and content learning. He further suggested instructional activities to reach these goals. For students at the beginning and low intermediate levels, developing the ability to recognize easily letter–sound correspondences and frequent words should be emphasized. Since adequate vocabulary size is fundamental for reading comprehension, teachers of all levels need to work with students to build their L2 vocabulary. For more advanced L2 readers, approximately a 10,000-word or above recognition vocabulary level should be targeted. To further strengthen L2 reading comprehension skills, teachers may design activities for students to engage in reading through multiple strategies and develop a heightened level of metacognitive awareness. Fostering students' ability to become aware of text structure and discourse organization would also help enhance reading comprehension and reading fluency. Graded readers and level-appropriate reading materials are considered good extensive reading resources. Motivational support from teachers is emphasized as it is crucial to L2 learners' development of reading comprehension abilities and extensive reading. Finally, Grabe (2014) counseled that content area reading contextualizes reading experiences and can be motivational to students. It also provides opportunities for extended reading and increases choices of reading materials.

Understanding the Affordances of Instructional Resources

Following the guiding questions by Chun et al. (2016), upon setting the L2 reading learning goals, the teacher may consider the instructional resources available for reaching them. Knowing the affordances of different types of technologies can better ensure effective selection and integration. In the following, based on Grabe's (2014) suggested learning goals for L2 reading, we provide recommendations of tools that researchers have found to be effective.

As the review of the current CALL-based L2 reading studies has shown, glossing, multimedia glossing, concordances, and dictionaries within a computer-supported or mobile-assisted environment can be beneficial to vocabulary building and improvement in reading comprehension (Blake, 2016; Chen, 2016; Gordani, 2013; Hadley & Charles, 2017; Koyama & Take uchi, 2013; Türk & Erçetin, 2014; Wang, 2012). Coupling their uses with a time-control function can offer additional benefits of automatizing word decoding skills and a better comprehension of the text (Sato et al., 2013). Reading-level classification tools can effectively increase L2 learners' reading speed, lexical knowledge, and grammatical improvement (Hadley & Charles, 2017).

Online video-sharing platforms and social media (e.g. Youtube and blogs) have been found to be able to help students gain knowledge of the targeted words' grammatical functions and greater recognition and recall of their meanings (Arndt & Woore, 2018). Digital annotation tools can be used for L2 learners to engage in social interaction by tagging or posting comments when jointly reading selected text passages (Blyth, 2014). Such activities can be conducive to developing reading strategies and better comprehension skills as learners collaboratively read and annotate texts (Godwin-Jones, 2015; Law et al. 2020; Yeh et al., 2017). An additional advantage of social reading is the increased opportunity for learners to engage in reading and quality interaction outside school (Murphy, 2010).

Allowing students to select and read web materials, such as online news and magazines, on issues of interest to them may give them opportunities to employ knowledge relevant to the materials (Huang, 2015) and enhance the recall of information (Erçetin, 2010). Website analysis involving reading and searching for online information and recording impressions, and critiquing website designs can help L2 learners to exercise metacognitive reading strategies (Roy & Crabbe, 2015). Students may also benefit from teachers' guidance on choosing appropriate keywords for information searches and exercising reading strategies to comprehend the information (Huang, 2013b). Reading authentic materials online gives students repeated vocabulary exposure and helps to boost learners' confidence and motivation in L2 reading (Johnson & Heffernan, 2006).

In Appendix II, types and examples of technological tools that researchers have found effective in reaching various learning goals in L2 reading are provided. The software or apps are free to download and use (except the one marked with an asterisk).

Flexible Uses of Technologies for Effective Instruction

Besides understanding the affordances of instructional resources, teachers need to be flexible users and know how to combine them to reach established goals. Different technological tools can be applied to accomplish different L2 reading objectives. Similarly, different technological tools may be juxtaposed to enhance the learning of one aspect of L2 reading development. At the same time, it is important to keep in mind the possibility of cognitive overload and reduced L2 online reading and vocabulary learning outcomes when a variety of elements and tools are used (Al-Shehri & Gitsake, 2010). Making technological tools available to students does not necessarily lead to better learning. In some cases, especially with tools with sophisticated features, it might be essential to provide explicit training for students to benefit from their affordances (Huang, 2013b).

Assess the Effectiveness of Resource Usage

For assessing the effectiveness of resource usage, Chun et al. (2016) emphasize the importance of knowing the interactional effects among the tool's affordances, the experiences and expectations of students, and the language learning environment itself. Technological tools have specific affordances and constraints and should not be judged by the "effective/ineffective" dichotomy. Hubbard (2011) suggests examining how a resource is compatible with the learner variables, such as age, proficiency level, educational experiences, and so on, and if the resource is compatible with a teacher's beliefs regarding the usefulness of the technology as a tool for teaching L2 reading. What is available inside and outside the classroom is also a fundamental factor to consider. Teachers who do not have the best tools available can only make the best of what's available. For assessing how learners are engaging with a tool (or not) and why they are making their choices, teachers can use student surveys, questionnaires, self-reports, and interviews, both formally and informally. Many digital tools and learning programs record and archive users' online behaviors and allow teachers to track students' learning trajectories.

Future Directions

The widespread access to reading resources and the various forms of reading online are transforming the concept of reading and how reading can be taught and learned. Liou (2016) suggested that an increase in available tool options would give teachers flexibilities to combine tools in their teaching and allow students to engage in informal, lifelong learning. Liaw and English (2017) indicated that the future directions for applying technology to L2 reading development would be shaped by three trends in learning technology: ubiquitous learning, adaptive learning and personalization, and autonomous learning. In this chapter, a review of more up-to-date studies resonates with their assertions. Furthermore, as reading resources and technological tools to facilitate L2 reading are increasingly accessible online via mobile devices, not only has reading become a social activity, but so are the processes of developing reading skills (Blyth, 2014). Reading is not merely interacting with technologies (Cobb, 2018). Instead, it allows L2 learners to interact with text and with others in compelling ways. Reading and learning to read are interactive processes where meaning is socially constructed (Law et al., 2020). Within such contexts, social affordances of technological tools may outnumber linguistic ones (Thoms & Pool, 2017). At the same time, we have been warned that the affordances of interactivity also lead to distracted minds, hyperactivity, and information overload (Bauerlein, 2011; Godwin-Jones, 2015). Given that we still have much to learn about the social dimensions of L2 reading as participatory meaning constructions, such issues await further exploration. Also, as CALL nowadays is situated in a much more multimodal milieu, reading entails interacting with multimodal texts and taking advantage of multimodal tools (Arndt & Woore, 2018; Huang, 2015; Law et al., 2020; Türk & Erçetin, 2014). Teachers need to address multiliteracies and multimodal expressions to help L2 learners understand and appreciate multimedia materials fully. How to effectively develop learners' ability to be critically aware of the symbolic and virtual realities of technology would be a pedagogical issue and a topic for researchers to tackle.

As this chapter was being written, the COVID-19 pandemic was causing disruption to schooling worldwide. To cope with the disruption, libraries and publishers we re making reading material and other resources freely available online. Nonetheless, according to UN News (2021), 100 million more children fail basic reading skills because of the pandemic. How the "new normal" of social distancing and remote learning brought on by the pandemic affects L2 reading development awaits to be investigated. More importantly, educators and researchers need to work together in search of innovative ways to take on the challenges imposed by the COVID-19 pandemic.

References

Arndt, H. L., & Woore. R. (2018). Vocabulary learning from watching YouTube videos and reading blog posts. *Language Learning & Technology*, *22*(1), 124–142. http://hdl.handle.net/10125/44660

Al-Shehri, S., & Gitsake, C. (2010). Online reading: A preliminary study of the impact of integrated and split-attention formats on L2 students' cognitive load. *ReCALL*, *22*(3), 356–375. https://doi.org/10.1017/S0958344010000212

Auer, N. (2015). Promoting strategic reading using the iBooks author application. In J. Keengwe & M. B. Maxfield (Eds.) *Advancing higher education with mobile learning technologies: Cases, trends, and inquiry-based methods*, 179. IGI Global. https://doi.org/10.4018/978-1-4666-6284-1

Ballance, O. J. (2021). Narrow reading, vocabulary load and collocations in context: Exploring lexical repetition in concordances from a pedagogical perspective. *ReCALL*, *33*(1), 4–17. https://doi.org/10.1017/S0958344020000117

Bauerlein, M. (Ed.) (2011). *The digital divide: Arguments for and against Facebook, Google, texting, and the age of social networking*. Penguin.

Blake, R. (2016). Technology and the four skills. *Language Learning & Technology*, *20*(2), 129–142. http://dx.doi.org/10125/44465

Block, E. L. (1992). See how they read: Comprehension monitoring of L1 and L2 readers. *TESOL Quarterly*, *26*(2), 319–343. https://doi.org/10.2307/3587008

Blyth, C. (2014). Exploring the affordances of digital social reading for L2 literacy: The case of eComma. In J. P. Guikema & L. Williams (Eds.), *Digital literacies in foreign and second language education* (pp. 201–226). CALICO.

Boulton, A., & Cobb, T. (2017). Corpus use in language learning: A meta-analysis. *Language Learning*, *67*(2), 348–393. https://doi.org/10.1111/lang.12224

Boulware-Gooden, R., Carreker, S., Thornhill, A., & Malatesha Joshi, R. (2007). Instruction of metacognitive strategies enhances reading comprehension and vocabulary achievement of third-grade students. *The Reading Teacher*, *61*(1), 70–77. https://doi.org/10.1598/RT.61.1.7

Burston, J. (2013). Mobile-assisted language learning: A selected annotated bibliography of implementation studies 1994–2012. *Language Learning & Technology*, *17*(3), 157–224. https://doi.org/10125/44344

Carrell, P. L. (1983). Some issues in studying the role of schemata, or background knowledge in second language comprehension. *Reading in a Foreign Language*, *1*(2), 81–92. https://doi.org/10125/66968

Chen, I. J. (2016). Hypertext glosses for foreign language reading comprehension and vocabulary acquisition: Effects of assessment methods. *Computer Assisted Language Learning*, *29*, 413–426. https://doi.org/10.1080/09588221.2014.983935

Chun, D., Kern, R., & Smith, B. (2016). Technology in language use, language teaching, and language learning. *The Modern Language Journal*, *100*, 64–80. https://doi.org/10.1111/modl.12302

Chun, D. M. (2016). The role of technology in SLA research. *Language Learning & Technology*, *20*(2), 98–115. https://doi.org/10125/44463

Chun, D. M., & Plass, J. L. (1997). Research on text comprehension in multimedia environments. *Language Learning & Technology*, *1*(1), 60–81. http://dx.doi.org/10125/25004

Cobb, T. (2018). Technology for teaching reading. In J. I. Liontas (Ed.), *TESOL encyclopedia of English language teaching*. Wiley Blackwell. https://doi.org/10.1002/9781118784235.eelt0444

Erçetin, G. (2010). Effects of topic interest and prior knowledge on text recall and annotation use in reading hypermedia text in the L2. *ReCALL*, *22*(2), 228–246. https://doi.org/10.1017/S0958344010000091

Godwin-Jones, R. (2015). Contributing, creating, curating: Digital literacies for language learners. *Language Learning & Technology*, *19*(3), 8–20. https://doi.org/10125/44427

Goodman, K. (1976). Manifesto for a reading revolution. In F. V. Gollasch (Ed.), *Language and literacy: The selected writings of Kenneth S. Goodman* (pp. 231–241). Routledge & Kegan Paul.

Gordani, Y. (2013). The effect of the integration of corpora in reading comprehension classrooms on English as a foreign language learners' vocabulary development. *Computer Assisted Language Learning, 26*(5), 430–445. https://doi .org/10.1080/09588221.2012.685078

Grabe, W. (2014). Key issues in L2 reading development. In X. Deng & R. Seow (Eds), *Alternative pedagogies in the English language & communication classroom: Selected papers from the Fourth CELC Symposium for English Language Teachers* (pp. 8–18). Centre for English Language Communication, National University of Singapore. www.nus.edu.sg/celc/wp-content/uploads/2022/09/2.-William-Grabe.pdf

Grabe, W., & Stoller, F. L. (2012). Teaching reading: Foundations and practices. *The e ncyclopedia of a pplied l inguistics*, 1–9. https://doi.org/10.1002/ 9781405198431.wbeal1174.pub2

Gutiérrez-Colón, M., Frumuselu, A. D., & Curell, H. (2020): Mobile-assisted language learning to enhance L2 reading comprehension: A selection of implementation studies between 2012–2017. *Interactive Learning Environments, 31* (2), 854–862. https://doi.org/10.1080/10494820.2020.1813179

Hadley, G., & Charles, M. (2017). Enhancing extensive reading with data-driven learning. *Language Learning & Technology, 21*(3), 131–152. http://hdl.handle .net/10125/44624

Huang, H. C. (2013a). E-reading and e-discussion: EFL learners' perceptions of an e-book reading program. *Computer Assisted Language Learning, 26*(3), 258–281. https://doi.org/10.1080/09588221.2012.656313

Huang, H. C. (2013b). Online reading strategies at work: What teachers think and what students do. *ReCALL, 25*(3), 340–358. https://doi.org/10.1017/ S0958344013000153

Huang, H. C. (2015). From web-based readers to voice bloggers: EFL learners' perspectives. *Computer Assisted Language Learning, 28*(2), 145–170. https://doi .org/10.1080/09588221.2013.803983

Hubbard, P. (2011). Evaluation of courseware and websites. In L. Ducate & N. Arnold (Eds.), *Present and future perspectives of CALL: From theory and research to new directions in foreign language teaching* (pp. 407–440). CALICO.

Hubbard, P., & Levy, M. (2016). Theory in computer-assisted language learning research and practice. In F. Farr & L. Murray (Eds.) *The Routledge h andbook of l anguage learning & technology* (pp. 24–38). Routledge.

Johnson, A., & Heffernan, N. (2006). The Short Readings Project: A CALL reading activity utilizing vocabulary recycling. *Computer Assisted Language Learning, 19*(1), 63–77. https://doi.org/10.1080/09588220600804046

Kemp, S. (2021). *Digital 2021: Global overview report*, https://datareportal.com/ reports/digital-2021-global-overview-report

Kern, R., & Warschauer, M. (Eds.) (2000). *Network-based language teaching: Concepts and practice*. Cambridge University Press.

Koda, K. (1994). Second language reading research: Problems and possibilities. *Applied Psycholinguistics, 15*(1), 1–28. https://doi.org/10.1017/S0142716400006950

Koyama, T., & Takeuchi, O. (2013). Does look-up frequency help reading comprehension of EFL learners? Two empirical studies of electronic dictionaries. *CALICO Journal, 25*(1), 110–125. https://doi.org/10.1558/cj.v25i1.110-125

Lantolf, J., & Thorne, S. L. (2007). Sociocultural theory and second language learning. In B. van Patten & J. Williams (Eds.), *Theories in second language acquisition* (pp. 201–224). Lawrence Erlbaum.

LaBerge, D., & Samuels, S. J. (1974). Toward a theory of automatic information processing in reading. *Cognitive Psychology, 6*(2), 293–323. https://doi.org/10.1016/0010-0285(74)90015-2

Law, J., Barny, D., & Poulin, R. (2020). Patterns of peer interaction in multimodal L2 digital social reading. *Language Learning & Technology, 24*(2), 70–85. http://hdl.handle.net/10125/44726

Li, P., & Clariana, R. B. (2019). Reading comprehension in L1 and L2: An integrative approach. *Journal of Neurolinguistics, 50*, 94–105. https://doi.org/10.1016/j.jneuroling.2018.03.005

Liaw, M.-L., & English, K. (2017). Technologies for teaching and learning L2 reading. In C. Chapelle, & S. Sauro (Eds.), *The handbook of technology and second language teaching and learning* (pp. 62–76). Wiley Blackwell.

Liou, H.-C. (2016). CALL tools for reading and writing. In F. Farr, & L. Murray (Eds.), *The Routledge handbook of language learning and technology* (pp. 478–490). Routledge.

Long, M. (1991). Focus on form: A design feature in language teaching methodology. In K. de Bot, R. Ginsberg, & C. Kramsch (Eds.), *Foreign language research in cross-cultural perspective* (pp. 39–52). John Benjamins.

Murphy, P. (2010). Web-based collaborative reading exercises for learners in remote locations: The effects of computer-mediated feedback and interaction via computer-mediated communication. *ReCALL, 22*(2), 112–134. https://doi.org/10.1017/S0958344010000030

Pérez-Paredes. P. (2019). A systematic review of the uses and spread of corpora and data-driven learning in CALL research during 2011–2015. *Computer Assisted Language Learning, 35*(1–2), 36–61. https://doi.org/10.1080/09588221.2019.1667832

Perfetti, C. A. (1985). *Reading ability*. Oxford University Press.

Roy, D., & Crabbe, S. (2015). Website analysis in an EFL context: Content comprehension, perceptions on web usability, and awareness of reading strategies. *ReCALL, 27*(2), 131–155. https://doi.org/10.1017/S095834401400024X

Rumelhart, D. E. (1977). Toward an interactive model of reading. In S. Dornic (Eds.), *Attention and performance* (pp. 573–603). Academic Press.

Sato, T., Matsunuma, M., & Suzuki, A. (2013). Enhancement of automatization through vocabulary learning using CALL: Can prompt language processing lead to better comprehension in L2 reading? *ReCALL, 25*(1), 143–158. https://doi.org/10.1017/S0958344012000328

Schmidt, R. (1990). The role of consciousness in second language learning. *Applied Linguistics, 11*, 206–226. https://doi.org/10.1093/applin/11.2.129

Stockwell, G. (2007). A review of technology choice for teaching language skills and areas in the CALL literature. *ReCALL, 19*(2), 105–120. doi:10.1017/S0958344007000225

Stockwell, G. (2014). Exploring theory in computer-assisted language learning. In X. Deng & R. Seow (Eds.), *Alternative pedagogies in the English language &*

communication classroom: Selected papers from the fourth CELC Symposium for English Language Teachers (pp. 25–30). Centre for English Language Communication, National University of Singapore. www.nus.edu.sg/celc/research/books/4th%20 Symposium%20proceedings/4%29.%20Glenn%20Stockwell.pdf

Sun, Z., Yang, X. M., & He, K. K. (2016). An extensive reading strategy to promote online writing for elementary students in the 1:1 digital classroom. *Computer Assisted Language Learning, 29*(2), 398–412. https://doi.org/10.1080/09588221 .2014.974860

Taki, S. (2015). Metacognitive online reading strategy use: Readers' perceptions in L1 and L2. *Journal of Research in Reading, 39*(4), 409–427. https://doi.org/10 .1111/1467-9817.12048

Thoms, J. J., & Poole, F. (2017). Investigating linguistic, literary, and social affordances of L2 collaborative reading. *Language Learning & Technology, 21* (2), 139–156. https://dx.doi.org/10125/44615

Tierney, R. J., & Pearson, P. D. (1994). Learning to learn from a text: A framework for improving classroom practice. In R. B. Rudell, & N. Unrau (Eds), *Theoretical models and processes of reading* (4th ed., pp. 496–513). International Reading Association.

Tsai, S. C. (2017). Effectiveness of ESL students' performance by computational assessment and role of reading strategies in courseware-implemented business translation tasks. *Computer Assisted Language Learning, 30*(6), 474–487. https:// doi.org/10.1080/09588221.2017.1313744

Tseng, S. S., Yeh, H. C., & Yang, S. H. (2015). Promoting different reading comprehension levels through online annotations. *Computer Assisted Language Learning, 28*(1), 41–57. https://doi.org/10.1080/09588221.2014.927366

Türk, E., & Erçetin, G. (2014). Effects of interactive versus simultaneous display of multimedia glosses on L2 reading comprehension and incidental vocabulary learning. *Computer Assisted Language Learning, 27*(1), 1–25. https://doi.org/ 10.1080/09588221.2012.692384

UN News. (2021). *Global perspective human stories.* https://news.un.org/en/story/ 2021/03/1088392

Vygotsky, L. S. (1978). *Mind and society.* Harvard University Press.

Wang, J. (2012). The use of e-dictionary to read e-text by intermediate and advanced learners of Chinese, *Computer Assisted Language Learning, 25*(5), 475–487. https://doi.org/10.1080/09588221.2011.631144

Wrigglesworth, J. (2020). Using smartphones to extend interaction beyond the EFL classroom. *Computer Assisted Language Learning, 33*(4), 413–434. https:// doi.org/10.1080/09588221.2019.1569067

Yeh, H.-C., Hung, H.-T., & Chiang, Y.-H. (2017). The use of online annotations in reading instruction and its impact on students' reading progress and processes. *ReCALL, 27*(2), 131–155. https://doi.org/10.1017/S0958344016000021

Zhao, K. (2016). Enhancing metacognitive language learning strategy use and business language proficiency in technology-enhanced collaborative learning environment. *International Journal of Computer-Assisted Language Learning and Teaching, 6*(3), 68–78. https://doi.org/10.4018/IJCALLT.2016070105

Further Reading

Bélisle, C. (Ed.) (2011). *Lire dans un monde numérique.* Presses de l'enssib.
This book, edited by Claire Bélisle, analyzes how digital technology has changed today's reading. Online reading calls for associative thinking and stimulates cognitive flexibility and creativity. The book concludes that reading in the digital age involves mastering the meta-skills required by technological tools.

Boulton. A. (2017). Data-driven learning and language pedagogy. In S. Thorne & S. May (Eds.), *Language, education & technology: Encyclopedia of language and education.* Springer. https://doi.org/10.1007/978-3-319-02328-1_15–1
This chapter first traces the history and applications of corpora and reviews the major contributions of DDL in language learning. Then, it discusses the advantages, problems, and difficulties involved in DDL. Finally, it underlines the limitations of previous studies and provides suggestions for further research.

Appendix I

The Studies Published in the Four CALL Journals between 2010 and 2021 Related to L2 Reading

No.	Year	Authors	Journal	Title
1	2021	Ballance, O. J.	*ReCALL, 33*(1), 4–17.	Narrow reading, vocabulary load and collocations in context: Exploring lexical repetition in concordances from a pedagogical perspective
2	2020	Cong-Lem, N., & Lee, S. Y.	*Language Learning & Technology, 24*(3), 87–102.	Exposure to L2 online text on lexical and reading growth
3	2020	Law, J., Barny, D., & Poulin, R.	*Language Learning & Technology, 24*(2), 70–85.	Patterns of peer interaction in multimodal L2 digital social reading
4	2020	Yang, Y., & Qian, D. D.	*Computer Assisted Language Learning, 33* (5–6), 628–652.	Promoting L2 English learners' reading proficiency through computerized dynamic assessment
5	2018	Arndt, H. L., & Woore. R.	*Language Learning & Technology, 22*(3), 124–142.	Vocabulary learning from watching YouTube videos and reading blog posts
6	2017	Tsai, S. C.	*Computer Assisted Language Learning, 30* (6), 474–487.	Effectiveness of ESL students' performance by computational assessment and role of reading strategies in courseware-implemented business translation tasks
7	2017	Thoms, J. J., & Poole, F.	*Language Learning & Technology, 21*(2), 139–156.	Investigating linguistic, literary, and social affordances of L2 collaborative reading
8	2017	Hadley, G., & Charles, M.	*Language Learning & Technology, 21*(3), 131–152.	Enhancing extensive reading with data-driven learning
9	2017	Yeh, H. C., Hung, H. T., & Chiang, Y. H.	*ReCALL, 29*(1), 22–38.	The use of online annotations in reading instruction and its impact on students' reading progress and processes

(*cont.*)

No.	Year	Authors	Journal	Title
10	2016	Sun, Z., Yang, X. M., & He, K. K.	*Computer Assisted Language Learning, 29* (2), 398–412.	An extensive reading strategy to promote online writing for elementary students in the 1:1 digital classroom
11	2016	Chen, I. J.	*Computer Assisted Language Learning, 29* (2), 413–426.	Hypertext glosses for foreign language reading comprehension and vocabulary acquisition: Effects of assessment methods
12	2015	Huang, H. C.	*Computer Assisted Language Learning, 28* (2), 145–170.	From web-based readers to voice bloggers: EFL learners' perspectives
13	2015	Tseng, S. S., Yeh, H. C., & Yang, S. H.	*Computer Assisted Language Learning, 28* (1), 41–57.	Promoting different reading comprehension levels through online annotations
14	2015	Roy, D., & Crabbe, S.	*ReCALL, 27*(2), 131–155.	Website analysis in an EFL context: Content comprehension, perceptions on web usability and awareness of reading strategies
15	2014	Park, J., Yang, J., & Hsieh, Y. C.	*Language Learning & Technology, 18*(3), 148–172.	University level second language readers' online reading and comprehension strategies
16	2014	Tsai, Y. R., & Talley, P. C.	*Computer Assisted Language Learning, 27* (5), 422–438.	The effect of a course management system (CMS)-supported strategy instruction on EFL reading comprehension and strategy use.
17	2014	Türk, E., & Erçetin, G.	*Computer Assisted Language Learning, 27* (1), 1–25.	Effects of i nteractive versus simultaneous display of multimedia glosses on L2 reading comprehension and incidental vocabulary learning.
18	2014	Garrett-Rucks, P., Howles, L., & Lake, W. M.	*CALICO Journal, 32*(1), 26–51.	Enhancing L2 reading comprehension with hypermedia texts: Student perceptions
19	2013	Smith, S., & Wang, S.	*Language Learning & Technology, 17*(3), 117–134.	Reading and grammar learning through mobile phones
20	2013	Gordani, Y.	*Computer Assisted Language Learning, 26* (5), 430–445.	The effect of the integration of corpora in reading comprehension classrooms on English as a foreign language learners' vocabulary development
21	2013	Huang, H. C.	*Computer assisted language learning, 26* (3), 258–281.	E-reading and e-discussion: EFL learners' perceptions of an e-book reading program
22	2013	Koyama, T., & Takeuchi, O.	*CALICO Journal, 25*(1), 110–125.	Does look-up frequency help reading comprehension of EFL learners? Two empirical studies of electronic dictionaries
23	2013	Sato, T., Matsunuma, M., & Suzuki, A.	*ReCALL, 25*(1), 143–158.	Enhancement of automatization through vocabulary learning using CALL: Can prompt language processing lead to better comprehension in L2 reading?
24	2013	Huang, H. C.	*ReCALL, 25*(3), 340–358.	Online reading strategies at work: What teachers think and what students do.
25	2012	Chou, I. C.	*Computer Assisted Language Learning, 25* (5), 411–433.	Understanding on-screen reading behaviors in academic contexts: A case study of five graduate English-as-a-second-language students
26	2012	Wang, J.	*Computer Assisted Language Learning, 25* (5), 475–487.	The use of e-dictionary to read e-text by intermediate and advanced learners of Chinese
27	2012	Yang, Y. F.	*Computer Assisted Language Learning, 25* (5), 393–410.	Blended learning for college students with English reading difficulties

(*cont.*)

No.	Year	Authors	Journal	Title
28	2011	Chang, C. K., & Hsu, C. K.	*Computer Assisted Language Learning, 24* (2), 155–180.	A mobile-assisted synchronously collaborative translation–annotation system for English as a foreign language (EFL) reading comprehension
29	2011	Wood, P.	*CALICO Journal, 28*(3), 662–676.	Computer assisted reading in German as a foreign language, developing and testing an NLP-based application
30	2010	Erçetin, G.	*ReCALL, 22*(2), 228-246.	Effects of topic interest and prior knowledge on text recall and annotation use in reading hypermedia text in the L2
31	2010	Murphy, P.	*ReCALL, 22*(2), 112–134.	Web-based collaborative reading exercises for learners in remote locations: The effects of computer-mediated feedback and interaction via computer-mediated communication
32	2010	Al-Shehri, S., & Gitsake, C.	*ReCALL, 22*(3), 356–375.	Online reading: A preliminary study of the impact of integrated and split-attention formats on L2 students' cognitive load.
33	2010	Pardo-Ballester, C., & Rodriguez, J. C.	*CALICO Journal, 27*(3), 540–553.	Developing Spanish online readings using design-based research
34	2010	Xu, J.	*CALICO Journal, 27*(2), 311–327.	Using multimedia vocabulary annotations in L2 reading and listening activities

Appendix II

Types and Examples of Technological Tools That Have Been Used by Researchers and Teachers for Reaching L2 Reading Goals

Goals	Types of Tools	Examples	URL
Vocabulary and comprehension	Gloss	SAS Gloss	https://apps.apple.com/us/app/sas-gloss/id504396637
	e-D ictionary	Lingua.ly	https://lingua-ly.en.softonic.com/android
	A nnotation	eComma	https://ecomma.coerll.utexas.edu/
		Markup.io	www.markup.io/home-b1/
		Diigo	www.diigo.com/
	C oncordance	AntConc	www.laurenceanthony.net/software/antconc/
		WordSmith Tools	https://lexically.net/wordsmith/index.html
		ParaConc	https://paraconc.com/
	T hesaurus	thesaurus.com	thesaurus.com
	Social networking	Goodreads	www.goodreads.com/
		LibraryThing*	www.librarything.com/
Discourse structure and strategic reading	Annotation	eComma	https://ecomma.coerll.utexas.edu/
		Markup.io	www.markup.io/home-b1/
		Diigo	www.diigo.com/
	Concordance	AntConc,	https://paraconc.com/
		WordSmith Tools	https://lexically.net/wordsmith/index.html

(*cont.*)

Goals	Types of Tools	Examples	URL
Reading fluency and extended reading	Blog	ParaConc	https://paraconc.com/
		Goodreads	www.goodreads.com/
		LibraryThing*	www.librarything.com/
	Corpus-based graded reader	Bookworms Graded Readers	https://elt.oup.com/student/readersleveltest/?cc=tw&selLanguage=zh
		Xreading	https://xreading.com/login/index.php
	Authentic online reading materials/ virtual library	Multimedia-Based English Trailers	https://multimedia-english.com/videos/section/official-1/tag/trailer-20
		Bookworms Graded Readers	https://elt.oup.com/student/readersleveltest/?cc=tw&selLanguage=zh
		Xreading,	https://xreading.com/login/index.php
Motivation	Videos, graphics, images, photos	YouTube	www.youtube.com/
		Multimedia-based English Trailers	https://multimedia-english.com/videos/section/official-1/tag/trailer-20
	Text-to-speech	Naturalreaders	www.naturalreaders.com/
		readspeaker	www.readspeaker.com/text-to-speech-demo/
Language and content integration	Online news and magazines, digital annotation tools	eComma	https://ecomma.coerll.utexas.edu/
		Markup.io	www.markup.io/home-b1/
		Diigo	www.diigo.com/

27

Writing

Hassan Mohebbi and Ali Panahi

Introduction

Computer technology advances have framed novel opportunities and possibilities beyond traditional educational settings (Warschauer & Healey, 1998) so that the development and implementation of digital facilitators seem to have accompanied every stage of language education progress. Drawing on Levy et al.'s (2015) term of attaching significance to real needs rather than false goals, the implementation of technology into the classroom needs to be practically tackled and realistically viewed. Regarding the role of digitalization in education, Chapelle (2007) rightly indicated that the turning point of the computer-assisted language learning (CALL) boom highlights varying numbers of options, tools, and engaging and interactive tasks provided through internet software, communication tools, instruction tools, CD-ROMs, and web pages. Subsequently, applying technology to writing instruction renders the writing process easier (Williams & Beam, 2018). Similarly, Vanderplank (2010) argued that since the late 1990s, we have witnessed a revolution together with a swift evolution in language teaching and language learning, specifically in writing instruction. Likewise, Jonassen (2005) and Kern (2006) argued that the appearance of digital technologies, such as email, web conferencing, internet, multimedia, and other digital devices, has dramatically changed the ways people interact and communicate in written fashion and in the way they write.

Garrett (1991) struggled with some key issues and trends in connection with the use of the computer. As she indicated, a couple of decades ago, the most apparent and immediate considerations were, for example, the issues and questions related to efficacy and effectiveness: Does using technology truly help the learners to develop their writing? Is it worth the cost, time, and effort? However, at present, digital devices are a rule of thumb; their crucial role in developing and improving writing skills has been approved. As supported by Basak, Wotto, and Belanger (2018), nowadays, all educators, writers, learners, teachers, and professionals are invited to reengineer or redesign the whole body of training and education system to communicate orally or in writing. On this basis, as a communicative and educational tool, digital technology quickly revolutionizes the varying ways that writing activities are performed and the way that learners and teachers communicate with each other through writing. Therefore, CALL in writing has its long-lasting tradition and legacy, specifically in the no-child-left-behind era; as with oral skills, written proficiency is assumed to be effectively instructed via computer-assisted and digital-mediated tools. Thus, the operationalization of Egbert's (2005) definition of CALL fits in the era where we are dealing with digital life. In summary, the introductory notes on the significance and expansion of technology-assisted second language (L2) writing are enlightened by the more detailed historical background of technology-assisted L2 writing instruction appearing below.

Background

Tracing the progress and process of CALL and the role digital technologies have played in teaching writing would potentially help us to gain further insights into technology assistance in writing instruction. As Warschauer and Healey's (1998) categorization indicated, the role of computers ranges from providing drill and practice and using language for communication to integrating all language skills into the educational context. On this ground, digital technologies have strongly affected and shaped writing genres, forms, and purposes (Chun, Kern, & Smith, 2016). Therefore, inspired by and moving in parallel with behavioristic psychology, cognitive theories, communicative language teaching, task-based language teaching, a socio-cognitive view and an integrative approach, computers have been in use and have potentially provided appropriate activities for teaching writing. For example, one of the initial technologically assisted implications of writing development may have been on the revision process (Bloch, 2018); instead of retyping the entire paper, writers could easily edit their work with word processors at different stages. More clearly, however controversially, Warschauer (2000) indicates that the approximate chronological paradigms and stages for digital technologies include behavioristic CALL, focusing on drill practice activities, communicative CALL, concentrating on language use activities, and integrative CALL, placing emphasis on the integration of all skills.

Technological tools accompany language education and educational development; as Tschirner (2001) contended, new digital facilitators make provision for enriching the mental capacity and memory, coining meaning-based activities, that is, focusing on form, maximizing input flood, encouraging pushed-output and learning in context or situated learning. Clearly, it fails to stand to reason to sketch a very tight or exact timeline and taxonomy for CALL stages, standings, and kinds. Bloch (2018) indicated that numerous technological tools could potentially provide more opportunities for writing development. These tools can contribute to a move away from product-oriented to process-oriented writing; they can facilitate the transformation of various modes of printed, aural, and visual texts into new modes. On the other hand, macros, screen recording applications and lecture capture software are used to automate comments on writing: These all indicate the potential, relative, and tentative contribution of digital devices to writing instruction and development. However, since the trend of development and research in the field is in progress and various settings and idiosyncratic contextual factors need to be considered, no deterministic role can be attributed to the absolute effectiveness of the digital tools in all contexts: A one-size-fits-all perspective is not appropriate for the whole issue.

To establish the effect of technological tools on writing further pieces of evidence are required to discuss more evidentially and self-confidently. As some researchers (e.g. Malahito & Quimbo, 2020) have indicated, in the era of digital media, (writing) instructors strive to satisfy, engage, and even impress their learners. The writers and the writing instructors use digital technology informally or formally, as they used to employ a pen and pencil. A more empirical justification and practical consideration for the prevalence and effectiveness of digitalization of writing instruction and development can be interpreted in Bax's (2003) concept of normalization. Taking the concept as a reference point, one can envision that technology is used undauntedly in people's everyday lives for writing purposes; technology is used like a book, pen, or pencil. Hence, nowadays, digitalization indicates that technology is moving beyond formal writing or composition, dealing with people's routines and daily lives.

Primary Themes

We elaborate here on the main themes to map the landscape of contemporary issues on technology-assisted L2 writing instruction, aligning with the preferences, needs, interests, and contextual and contemporary demands of the individuals, educators, and policy-makers. As Birgili, Seggie, and Oğuz (2021) suggested, today's learners and educators are digital natives and must obtain skills and competencies to meet the new requirements locally and globally. Similarly, Hsu and Lo (2018) cogently advised of the necessity of developing computer-based technologies for language education, mainly writing instruction. Since numerous variables potentially demotivate the feedback process, technological devices create a positive base for education in general and for writing in particular (Cunningham, 2019b). Therefore, writing researchers should conceive and perceive technology's themes, types, and roles in developing writing. Before dealing with the primary themes, Table 27.1 provides some overall research themes, trends, and general findings on technology-assisted L2 writing instruction.

Table 27.1 *Some research themes and trends on technology-assisted L2 writing*

General issues	Specific issues	Some results
Feedback	Automated writing evaluation; computer-automated metalinguistic corrective feedback; automated essay scoring feedback; automated measurement of syntactic complexity; implicit and explicit; video-impact; peer e-feedback; screencast; formative (process-tracing based); computer-assisted rating; teacher electronic feedback; text-video modes; graduated feedback	These issues have been investigated widely, but further research into them is required (Ene & Upton, 2018; Gao & Ma, 2019). In general, Gao and Ma's (2019) findings indicate the effectiveness of feedback; likewise, Ene and Upton's (2018) findings show that teacher electronic feedback has a positive impact and supports L2 writing.
Flipped learning	A severe paucity of (or no) research into L2 writing instruction	A review of 316 research articles published from 2012 to 2018 was conducted by Birgili et al. (2021). Their results indicate that most research in flipped learning has been conducted in higher education, specifically in Asia. On the other hand, meta-analysis concludes the discussion with the positive outcomes of flipped learning.
MALL	Limited research into MALL and task design and MALL and feedback on writing.	A review of twenty years of MALL was carried out by Burston (2015). The results indicate that there are few statistically reliable learning outcome measures; over 40% of MALL publications are unrelated to language learning applications, and there are methodological shortcomings. To add more to a more recent result, some researchers (e.g. Stockwell, 2021) indicate that MALL has played some role in and changed the face of education inside or outside the class. However, as Stockwell and Hubbard (2013) suggest, the greatest challenge for MALL is task design.
Collaborative writing	Wiki-mediated; task-based; attitudes and perceptions toward it; digital annotators; open source-mining tool	The findings in the field show that learner-to-learner engagement and cooperation is effective and motivates meaning-making (Abrams, 2019; Godwin-Jones, 2018; Hsu & Lo, 2018).
Computer-assisted assessment	A severe paucity of research into L2 writing instruction	The findings in the field indicate the effectiveness of computer-assisted assessment. However, there need to be rich pieces of evidence and further research to put more confidence into the findings (Cummins & Davesne, 2009)
Machine translation	A growing field prompted by recent technological developments that have greatly improved accuracy; concerns remain over issues of cheating and over-reliance on machine translation tools	An increasing body of research is exploring pedagogies and provision of strategies to capitalize upon the affordances and provision of strategies of machine translation (Lee, 2020, 2022). While it has been shown to enhance grammatical accuracy in writing, learners are aware of the limitations (Chung & Ahn, 2022).

Many context-specific factors are involved in researching the themes for technology-assisted L2 writing. The primary themes in this field seem to have stemmed from what Garrett (2009) called the relationship of theory, pedagogy, and technology, that is, infrastructure and the interrelatedness and mutual effect they exert on each other. The use of technology in writing is revealed in various themes, such as computer-automated metalinguistic corrective feedback (Gao, & Ma, 2019), automated written corrective feedback (Ranalli, 2018), validity arguments for diagnostic assessment using automated writing evaluation (Chapelle, Cotos, & Lee, 2015), automated essay scoring feedback (Dikli & Bleyle, 2014), automated measurement of syntactic complexity in corpus-based L2 writing (Lu, 2017), computer-delivered feedback in processing instruction (Sanz, 2003), video impact and written feedback (Tseng & Yeh, 2019), feedback provision enhancement and multimodal video technology (Hung, 2016), video feedback and process approach–based writing instruction (Özkul & Ortaçtepe, 2017), Facebook-assisted L2 writing (Dizon, 2016), studies on peer e-feedback (Schultz, 2000), L2 writing and technology-assisted peer feedback (Chen, 2016), teacher electronic feedback (Ene & Upton, 2018), and the impact of e-feedback on linguistic accuracy (Tolosa, East, & Villers, 2013).

Another area that has been widely researched is developing web-based collaborative writing using digital devices (e.g. Cho, 2017; Storch, 2011; Strobl, 2014). Some of the technological devices that have been investigated in the context of writing development and instruction include automated writing evaluation software, digital annotators, multimedia (Godwin-Jones, 2018), an open-source mining tool (i.e. SCAPES), visual representations of collaborative writing, such as DocuViz or AutoVIZ (Yim & Warschauer, 2017), employing online glosses to support corrective feedback (Yeh & Lo, 2009), attitudes toward online feedback on writing (Strobl, 2015), the impact of teachers' corrective feedback and peer review on online writing performance (Tai, Lin, & Yang, 2015), online peer interaction (Peeters, 2018), technology-assisted peer feedback in L2 writing classes (Chen, 2016), and the influence of digital choices on feedback quality, that is, the modes of video and text change feedback language (Cunningham, 2019a). Furthermore, considering the interpersonal impact of feedback and the learners' perception in technology-assisted writing classes, researchers (e.g. Cunningham, 2019a, 2019b) indicate the significance of screencast feedback as one of the main themes researched so far and suggest it be further investigated.

One of the main recent themes has been the effect of wiki-mediated collaborative writing on the development of learners' individual writing in a second language (Hsu & Lo, 2018; Kessler, 2009). Similarly, many researchers (e.g. Lee, 2010) have considered wiki-mediated collaborative L2 writing and learners' attitudes and revisions using wikis. More recently, in connection with process training technologies, there has been another theme concerning the affordances of process-tracing technologies for supporting L2 writing instruction in light of formative feedback based on a cognitive-developmental perspective (Ranalli, Feng, & Chukharev-Hudilainen, 2019). Moreover, recent research in this field has been conducted by Rogerson-Revell (2021). The study was conducted in the context of technology and feedback, and the result was positive. The usefulness of graduated corrective feedback in the context of a computerized environment, which the learners can self-correct, is another line of research (Ai, 2017). Additionally, the influence of technology-assisted professional development on teacher learning, practice, and leadership skills has also been in focus (e.g. Scott & Mouza, 2007).

Concerning the context of assessment, computer-based testing (CBT), computer-adaptive testing (CAT) and writing assessment (Cummins & Davesne, 2009) are considered another strand of the theme. For example, TOEFL iBT and the internet-based IELTS are globally recognized tests connected to computer-assisted rating. A somewhat related theme is mobile-assisted language learning (MALL) in writing. As Burston (2015) asserted, more than 600 MALL publications have appeared over the past twenty years. Out of 575 MALL publications between 1994 and 2012, only 347 describe implementation projects in MALL (Burston, 2013). Additionally, a different theme driven by constructivists (Marshall et al., 2011), supported and implicitly evidenced by the cognitive load theory (Clark, Nguyen, & Sweller, 2011), is flipped learning, reported to be effective by some researchers (e.g. Birgili, Seggie, & Oğuz, 2021). However, in the context of writing instruction, flipped learning has not been widely implemented so far.

There have been enormous developments in machine translation in the past several years and its presence in the language classroom has made it a theme of ongoing research (Wang & Panahi, 2023). There has been work that explores the range of tools that are freely available, including Google Translate (Chang, 2022) and DeepL (Klimova et al., 2022), highlighting not only potential constructive pedagogies using these tools, but also the need for learners to have sufficient training to understand both their strengths and limitations Another tool that uses similar technology to many of these machine translation tools is Grammarly (Kawashima, 2023), which can be used to prompt suggestions to learners to correct errors in their written texts. As an emerging area, there is still research needed to explore how best to use these, along with raising awareness of how to avoid problems with inappropriate and unethical usage.

There should be a one-to-one correspondence between technology and pedagogy in terms of empirical studies so that digital progress aligns with pedagogical outcomes. However, instead of engaging with learners, suiting their interests, preferences, needs, wishes, and purposes, tasks delivered by digital tools are limited to rote learning. There seems to be a tension here between pedagogy and technology. As Pennington and Rogerson-Revell (2019) indicate, a lack of correspondence between language learning pedagogies and technological affordances creates hardships and narrows the performance zone.

Current Research and Practice

With the leading role of digital media now being social networking, it is natural that writing instruction targeting computer-mediated communication has been focused on more than ever. For example, giving feedback on L2 writing via electronic chats, wikis, blogs, files, and other digitally oriented pedagogies has been a commonly used activity (Elola & Oskoz, 2017; Hyland & Hyland, 2006). Elola and Oskoz (2017) note that a significant affordance of twenty-first-century literacy and pedagogy is digitally-mediated feedback associated with L2 writing, demanding more qualified teacher training. On closer inspection, when designing tasks, the learners' goals and needs should be more seriously clarified (Stockwell, 2010). On this basis, giving written feedback can be more effectively tackled. Gao and Ma (2019) conducted more informative studies on corrective feedback; they investigated the different impact of two computer-automated metalinguistic corrective feedback types in a foreign language context. The participating groups completed writing tasks before the drills, immediately after the drills, and two weeks later. The results indicated that metalinguistic corrective feedback on L2 writing affects learners' accuracy in error correction. However, it did not give rise to higher accuracy on the subsequent writing tasks. On the other hand, drills that focused on the form did not improve the learners' performance on error correction. Furthermore, consistent with computer-automated corrective feedback, Saricaoglu (2018) investigated the influence of automated formative feedback on ESL learners' written causal explanations within the framework of cause-and-effect writings. The feedback reports for the revised and first drafts from the screen-capturing videos and the automated writing evaluation system were analyzed. The findings indicated significant changes in learners' causal explanations within one cause-and-effect essay.

Regarding the impact of digital tools on L2 writing, Ene and Upton (2018) examined teacher electronic feedback in online and face-to-face ESL writing classes. Their findings indicated the effectiveness and successful implementation of teacher electronic feedback. Moreover, even more beneficial was a combination of synchronous and asynchronous focusing on critical and higher-order thinking. One of the challenges of teacher electronic feedback and CALL is that even though the students benefited from feedback, they were emotionally biased toward face-to-face feedback. Ranalli et al. (2019) explored integrating technology into L2 writing instruction, and they indicated that using process-tracing technologies in L2 writing instruction was effective.

Another line of research comes from Cunningham (2019a), who investigated the influence of technological choices on the language and nature of feedback in interpersonal terms. He researched the way the modes of video and text affect and change the feedback language. The study indicated that promoting feedback practices, the mode of feedback affects the interpersonal aspect. In a similar vein, more recently, Tseng and Yeh (2019) investigated the influence of video and written feedback; their study, in general, explored the differences in performance resulting from written feedback and video feedback. The findings indicated the usefulness of both written and video feedback. One of the research agendas concerning technology-assisted writing improvement is collaborative writing. Hsu and Lo (2018) explored the influence of wiki-mediated collaborative writing on learner's writing skills. The study was conducted in Taiwan with a wiki-collaborative writing group and an individual writing group. For producing expository writing, the learners in the wiki group worked in pairs via wikis, and the learners in the individual group wrote their essays alone. The results were positive, but the impact on the complexity and organization of the writing was less noticeable.

Similarly, Abrams (2019) researched the connection between computer-mediated writing and task-based collaborative L2 writing. Using Google Docs as an effective pedagogical tool, the study explored the text-related linguistic features and collaboration patterns during a computer-supported collaborative writing task. With qualitative analyses, some insights into the writing process of successful collaborative groups were obtained. To develop a creative writing task, the participants worked in groups. As a result, the collaboration-based group developed texts with higher coherence and more propositional content than those with less collaboration. What Abrams indicates is the fact that learner-to-learner engagement motivates meaning-making, and collaboration accelerates L2 output. Consistent with Abrams's findings, some researchers (e.g. Storch, 2011) indicate that collaboration contributes to L2 development via editing and recursive planning. Most importantly, Abrams (2019) and Lee (2010) contend that engagement leads to increased production, and the teachers should consider that engagement in the pre-writing task contributes to the subsequent writing process.

Tolosa, East, and Villers (2013) performed a study into an online reciprocal peer tutoring program, specifically on the effectiveness of written corrective feedback. The findings indicated that the participants were inclined to peer correction and employed various techniques and strategies to correct linguistic mistakes. For peer correction, as some scholars (e.g. Mackey & Polio, 2009) point out, learners can be engaged in input-based and output-based tasks, and their attention should be concentrated on the form to develop accurate feedback. In connection with the usefulness of cooperative writing, peer feedback, and peer correction in technology, Warni, Aziz, and Febriawan (2018) indicate that computerized context and digital tools assist the learners in cooperating and working independently when needed. More recently, Atabek (2020) indicates that CALL-assisted instruction is beneficial and contributes to the productive learning outcome.

Precisely speaking, it should not go unnoticed that when there is a discussion of technology-assisted writing instruction, there should be mentioned some general issues or details concerning digitally assisted writing assessment, too. In assessment terms, CAT has been around since the 1970s and tailors the difficulty of the test items to the test taker's ability to be tested (Lord, 1971). As Ockey (2009) cites, CBT assesses L2 ability, and as Garret (1991) detailed, CBT can successfully deliver more authentic tests than traditional paper-and-pencil tests.

Recommendations for Research and Practice

Contrary to the fact that more research has been done into technology-assisted L2 writing, there still seems to be a long road ahead. Therefore, tentatively, we could suggest the following research questions and practices: Is there any significant relationship between digital tools and their application to writing instruction in various contexts? How can digital devices affect the teaching of writing to various age groups? To what extent has teaching writing through technology considered human beings' humanistic aspects, taking into account learners' needs, preferences, and interests? Another recommendation for further research and practice relates to the computer literacy of the teachers.

If we aim to enhance language learning and teaching quality, we should establish an international agenda to educate teachers about new technologies (Barge, 2009). It is too simplistic to take teachers' computer literacy for granted based on what we observe in teachers' performance in pioneering educational settings in metropolitan cities. There are numerous teachers in far-distant towns and villages in every corner of the world who have no access to technologies, and even if they are given the high-tech gadgets, they are not capable of using them effectively. Therefore, we do need longitudinal and mixed-methods research to delve into these critical issues.

Moreover, one of the gaps in research on technology and writing is related to automated writing evaluation (AWE). As Saricaoglu (2018) indicated, there is a paucity of research evidence in the AWE literature, and more research needs to be conducted into AWE in various contexts using various digital tools. The next suggestion regards the influence of e-feedback on linguistic accuracy and content, which has been mostly ignored and requires further research. For example, the extent to which teachers rely on linguistic accuracy in content-based courses demands further research. Moreover, future research could investigate various technological feedback modes in different contexts to see how different modes compare. For example, e-feedback across different instructors based on various contextual and individual factors could be investigated to see how timing, technological exposure, or other factors might change the interpersonal considerations in the feedback. Additionally, teacher electronic feedback and its effectiveness have been noted. However, as Ene and Upton (2018) indicate, further research is needed to investigate teacher electronic feedback. Another point to consider is oral feedback and MALL (Xu, Dong, & Jiang, 2016). MALL in writing has been seriously ignored, and research into writing on smaller, portable devices is desperately needed.

Future Directions

As a general future direction, digital literacy skills in a range of technologies – including hardware, generic software/applications such as word processors and machine translation tools, and specialized tools for research such as keystroke-logging and eye-tracking – are needed for all writing instructors (see (Ranalli et al., 2019, for a discussion). Such skills comprise the technical, audiovisual, behavioral, social, and critical competencies that are needed to allow educators to socialize, communicate, instruct, and contribute in a digital context (Reyna, Hanham, & Meier, 2018), and access to these tools is almost essential in the current educational climate. However, in many, if not most, less-developed countries, many teachers and learners just do not have access to sophisticated technological tools; even access to Zoom is a challenge in some countries. Seeking ways to make these tools more readily available to teachers and learners across a broad range of socioeconomic circumstances can allow us to know more about what technology can achieve in assisting the teaching and learning of L2 writing of not just a privileged minority and allow learners to take advantage of the evolution of writing technologies on a global scale.

References

Abrams, Z. I. (2019). Collaborative writing and text quality in Google Docs. *Language Learning & Technology, 23*(2), 22–42. https://doi.org/10125/44681

Ai, H. (2017). Providing graduated corrective feedback in an intelligent computer-assisted language learning environment. *ReCALL, 29*(3), 313–334. https://doi.org/10.1017/S095834401700012X

Atabek, O. (2020). Associations between emotional states, self-efficacy for and attitude towards using educational technology. *International Journal of Progressive Education, 16*(2), 175–194. https://doi.org/10.29329/ijpe.2020.241.12

Barge, M. (2009). Teaching techniques for multimedia language labs: Final report. Centre for Excellence in Multimedia Language Learning, the Language Centre, Queen Mary University of London.

Basak, S. K., Wotto, M., & Belanger, P. (2018). E-learning, M-learning and D-learning: Conceptual definition and comparative analysis. *E-Learning and Digital Media, 15*(4), 191–216. https://doi.org/10.1177/2042753018785180

Bax, S. (2003). CALL: past, present and future. *System, 31*(1), 13–28. https://doi.org/10.1016/S0346–251X(02)00071-4

Birgili, B., Seggie, F. N., & Oğuz, E. (2021). The trends and outcomes of flipped learning research between 2012 and 2018: A descriptive content analysis. *Journal of Computers in Education, 8*, 365–394. https://doi.org/10.1007/s40692–021-00183-y

Bloch, J. (2018). Technology for teaching English as a second language (ESL) writing. In *The TESOL Encyclopedia of English Language Teaching.* John Wiley & Sons, Inc. https://doi.org/10.1002/9781118784235.eelt0440

Burston, J. (2013). Mobile-assisted language learning: A selected annotated bibliography of implementation studies 1994–2012. *Language Learning & Technology, 17*(3), 157–224.

Burston, J. (2015). Twenty years of MALL project implementation: A meta-analysis of learning outcomes. *ReCALL, 27*(1), 4–20. https://doi.org/10.1017/S0958344014000159

Chang, L.-C. (2022). Chinese language learners evaluating machine translation accuracy. *The JALT CALL Journal*, *18*(1), 110–136. https://doi.org/10.29140/jaltcall.v18n1.592

Chapelle, C. A. (2007). Technology and second language acquisition. *Annual Review of Applied Linguistics*, *27*, 98–114. https://doi.org/10.1017/S02671905008070050

Chapelle, C. A., Cotos, E., & Lee, J. Y. (2015). Validity arguments for diagnostic assessment using automated writing evaluation. *Language Testing*, *32*(3), 385–405. https://doi.org/10.1177/0265532214565386

Chen, T. (2016). Technology-supported peer feedback in ESL/EFL writing classes: A research synthesis. *Computer Assisted Language Learning*, *29*(2), 365–397. https://doi.org/10.1080/09588221.2014.960942

Cho, H. (2017). Synchronous web-based collaborative writing: Factors mediating interaction among second-language writers. *Journal of Second Language Writing*, *36*, 37–51. https://doi.org/10.1016/j.jslw.2017.05.013

Chun, D., Kern, R., & Smith, B. (2016). Technology in language use, language teaching, and language learning. *The Modern Language Journal*, *100*(S1), 64–80. http://doi.org/10.1111/modl.12302

Chung, E. S., & Ahn, S. (2022). The effect of using machine translation on linguistic features in L2 writing across proficiency levels and text genres. *Computer Assisted Language Learning*, *35*(9), 2239–2264. https://doi.org/10.1080/09588221.2020.1871029

Clark, R. C., Nguyen, F., & Sweller, J. (2011). *Efficiency in learning: Evidence-based guidelines to manage cognitive load*. John Wiley & Sons.

Cummins, P. W., & Davesne, C. (2009). Using electronic portfolios for second language assessment. *The Modern Language Journal*, *93*(s1), 848–867. https://doi.org/10.1111/j.1540-4781.2009.00977.x

Cunningham, K. J. (2019a). Student perceptions and use of technology-mediated text and screencast feedback in ESL writing. *Computers and Composition*, *52*, 222–241. https://doi.org/10.1016/j.compcom.2019.02.003

Cunningham, K. J. (2019b). How language choices in feedback change with technology: Engagement in text and screencast feedback on ESL writing. *Computers & Education*, *135*, 91–99. https://doi.org/10.1016/j.compedu.2019.03.002

Dikli, S., & Bleyle, S. (2014). Automated essay scoring feedback for second language writers: How does it compare to instructor feedback? *Assessing Writing*, *22*, 1–17. https://doi.org/10.1016/j.asw.2014.03.006

Dizon, G. (2016). A comparative study of Facebook vs. paper-and-pencil writing to improve second language writing skills. *Computer Assisted Language Learning*, *29*(8), 1249–1258. https://doi.org/10.1080/09588221.2016.1266369

Egbert, J. (2005). *Conducting research on CALL*. In J. L. Egbert & G. M. Petrie (Eds.), CALL research perspectives (pp. 3–8). Erlbaum.

Elola, I., & Oskoz, A. (2017). Writing with 21st century social tools in the second language classroom: New literacies, genres, and writing practices. *Journal of Second language Writing*, *36*, 52–60. https://doi.org/10.1016/j.jslw.2017.04.002

Ene, E., & Upton, T. A. (2018). Synchronous and asynchronous teacher electronic feedback and learner uptake in ESL composition. *Journal of Second Language Writing, 41*, 1–13. https://doi.org/10.1016/j.jslw.2018.05.005

Gao, J., & Ma, S. (2019). The effect of two forms of computer-automated meta-linguistic corrective feedback. *Language Learning & Technology, 23*(2), 65–83. https://doi.org/10125/44683.

Garrett, N. (1991). Technology in the service of language learning: Trends and issues. *The Modern Language Journal, 75*, 74–101. https://doi.org/10.1111/j.1540-4781.1991.tb01085.x

Garrett, N. (2009). Computer-assisted language learning trends and issues revisited: Integrating innovation. *The Modern Language Journal, 93*(l), 719–740. https://doi.org/10.1111/j.1540-4781.2009.00969.x

Godwin-Jones, R. (2018). Second language writing online: An update. *Language Learning & Technology, 22*(1), 1–15. https://dx.doi.org/10125/44574

Hsu, H.-C., & Lo, Y. F. (2018). Using wiki-mediated collaboration to foster L2 writing performance. *Language Learning & Technology, 22*(3), 103–123. https://doi.org/10125/44659

Hung, S. T. A. (2016). Enhancing feedback provision through multimodal video technology. *Computers & Education, 98*, 90–101. https://doi.org/10.1016/j.compedu.2016.03.009

Hyland, K., & Hyland, F. (2006). Feedback on second language students' writing. *Language Teaching, 39*(2), 83–101. http://dx.doi.org/10.1017/S0261444806003399

Jonassen, D. (2005). *Modeling with technology: Mindtools for conceptual change* (3rd ed.). Prentice-Hall.

Kawashima, T. (2023). Student perceptions of Grammarly, teacher's indirect and direct feedback: Possibility of machine feedback. *The JALT CALL Journal, 19*(1), 113–139. https://doi.org/10.29140/jaltcall.v19n1.1017

Kern, R. (2006). Perspectives on technology in learning and teaching languages. *TESOL Quarterly, 40*(1), 183–210. https://doi.org/10.2307/40264516

Kessler, G. (2009). Student-initiated attention to form in wiki-based collaborative writing. *Language Learning & Technology, 13*(1), 79–95.

Klimova, B., Pikhart, M., Benites, A. D., Lehr, C., & Sanchez-Stockhammer, C. (2022). Neural machine translation in foreign language teaching and learning: A systematic review. *Education and Information Technologies, 28*, 663–682. https://doi.org/10.1007/s10639-022-11194-2

Lee, L. (2010). Exploring wiki-mediated collaborative writing: A case study in an elementary Spanish course. *CALICO Journal, 27*(2), 260–276.

Lee, S.-M. (2020). The impact of using machine translation on EFL students' writing. *Computer Assisted Language Learning, 33*(3), 157–175. https://doi.org/10.1080/09588221.2018.1553186

Lee, S.-M. (2022). L2 learners' strategies for using machine translation as a personalised writing assisting tool. In J. Colpaert & G. Stockwell (Eds.), *Smart CALL: Personalization, contextualization, & socialization* (pp. 184–206). Castledown Publishers. https://doi.org/10.29140/9781914291012-9

Levy, M., Hubbard, P., Stockwell, G., & Colpaert, J. (2015). Research challenges in CALL. *Computer Assisted Language Learning, 28*(1), 1–6. http://dx.doi.org/10.1080/09588221.2014.987035

Lord, F. M. (1971). Robbins-Monro procedures for tailored testing. *Educational and Psychological Measurement, 31*(1), 3–31. https://doi.org/10.1177/001316447103100101

Lu, X. (2017). Automated measurement of syntactic complexity in corpus-based L2 writing research and implications for writing assessment. *Language Testing, 34*(4), 493–511. https://doi.org/10.1177/0265532217710675

Mackey, A., & Polio, C. (2009). *Multiple perspectives on interaction.* Routledge.

Malahito, J. A. I., & Quimbo, M. A. T. (2020). Creating G-Class: A gamified learning environment for freshman students. *E-Learning and Digital Media, 17*(2), 1–17. https://doi.org/10.1177/2042753019899805

Marshall, J. C., Smart, J., Lotter, C., & Sirbu, C. (2011). Comparative analysis of two inquiry observational protocols: Striving to better understand the quality of teacher-facilitated inquiry-based instruction. *School Science and Mathematics, 111*(6), 306–315. https://doi.org/10.1111/j.1949-8594.2011.00091.x

Ockey, G. J. (2009). Developments and challenges in the use of computer-based testing for assessing second language ability. *The Modern Language Journal, 93,* 836–847. https://doi.org/10.1111/j.1540-4781.2009.00976.x

Özkul, S., & Ortaçtepe, D. (2017). The use of video feedback in teaching process-approach EFL writing. *TESOL Journal, 8*(4), 862–877. https://doi.org/10.1002/tesj.362

Peeters, W. (2018). Applying the networking power of Web 2.0 to the foreign language classroom: A taxonomy of the online peer interaction process. *Computer Assisted Language Learning, 31*(8), 905–931. https://doi.org/10.1080/09588221.2018.1465982

Pennington, M. C., & Rogerson-Revell, P. (2019). *English pronunciation teaching and research: Contemporary perspectives.* Palgrave Macmillan.

Ranalli, J. (2018). Automated written corrective feedback: How well can students make use of it. *Computer Assisted Language Learning, 31*(7), 653–674. https://doi.org/10.1080/09588221.2018.1428994

Ranalli, J., Feng, H. H., & Chukharev-Hudilainen, E. (2019). The affordances of process-tracing technologies for supporting second language writing instruction. *Language Learning & Technology, 23*(2), 1–11. https://doi.org/10125/44678

Reyna, J., Hanham, J., & Meier, P. C. (2018). A framework for digital media literacies for teaching and learning in higher education. *E-Learning and Digital Media, 15*(4), 176–190. https://doi.org/10.1177/2042753018784952

Rogerson-Revell, P. M. (2021). Computer-assisted pronunciation training (CAPT): Current issues and future directions. *RELC Journal, 52*(1), 189–205. https://doi.org/10.1177/0033688220977406

Sanz, C. (2003). Computer delivered implicit vs. explicit feedback in processing instruction. In B. VanPatten (Ed.), *Processing instruction: Theory, research, and commentary* (pp. 241–256). Erlbaum.

Saricaoglu, A. (2018). The impact of automated feedback on second language learners' written causal explanations. *ReCALL, 31*(12), 1–15. https://doi.org/10.1017/S095834401800006X

Schultz, J. (2000). Computers and collaborative writing in the foreign language curriculum. In M. Warschauer, & R. Kern (Eds.). *Network-based language teaching: Concepts and practice* (pp. 121–150). Cambridge University Press. https://doi.org/10.1017/CBO9781139524735.008

Scott, P., & Mouza, C. (2007). The impact of professional development on teacher learning, practice, and leadership skills: A study on the integration of technology in the teaching of writing. *Journal of Educational Computing Research, 37*(3), 229–266. https://doi.org/10.2190/EC.37.3.b

Stockwell, G. (2010). CALL and the learner. *Innovation in Language Learning and Teaching, 4*(3), 177–179. https://doi.org/10.1080/17501229.2010.513826

Stockwell, G. (2021). Living and learning with technology: Language learning with mobile devices. *English Teaching, 76*(s1), 3–16. https://doi.org/10.15858/engtea.76.s1.202109.3

Stockwell, G., & Hubbard, P. (2013). Some emerging principles for mobile-assisted language learning. The International Research Foundation for English Language Education. www.tirfonline.org/english-in-the-workforce/mobile-assisted-language-learning

Storch, N. (2011). Collaborative writing in second language contexts: Processes, outcomes, and future directions. *Annual Review of Applied Linguistics, 31*, 275–288. https://doi.org/10.1017/S0267190511000079

Strobl, C. (2014). Affordances of Web 2.0 technologies for collaborative advanced writing in a foreign language. *CALICO Journal, 31*(1), 1–18. https://doi.org/10.11139/cj.31.1.1-18

Strobl, C. (2015). Attitudes towards online feedback on writing: Why students mistrust the learning potential of models. *ReCALL, 27*(3), 340–357. https://doi.org/10.1017/S0958344015000099

Tai, H. C., Lin, W. C., & Yang, S. C. (2015). Exploring the effects of peer review and teachers' corrective feedback on EFL students' online writing performance. *Journal of Educational Computing Research, 53*(2), 284–309. https://doi.org/10.1177/0735633115597490

Tolosa, C., East, M., & Villers, H. (2013). Online peer feedback in beginners' writing tasks: Lessons learned. *IALLT Journal of Language Learning Technologies, 43*(1), 1–24. https://doi.org/10.17161/IALLT.V43I1.8516

Tschirner, E. (2001). Language acquisition in the classroom: The role of digital video. *Computer Assisted Language Learning, 14*(3 & 4), 305–319. https://doi.org/10.1076/call.14.3.305.5796

Tseng, S.-S., & Yeh, H.-C. (2019). The impact of video and written feedback on student references of English speaking practice. *Language Learning & Technology, 23*(2), 145–158. https://doi.org/10125/44687

Vanderplank, R. (2010). *Déjà vu*? A decade of research on language laboratories, television and video in language learning. *Language Teaching, 43*(1), 1–37. https://doi.org/10125/4468710.1017/S0261444809990267

Wang, Y., & Panahi, A. (2023). Technology and second language instruction. In H. Mohebbi & Y. Wang (Eds.), *Insights into teaching and learning writing: A practical guide for early-career teachers* (pp. 167–179). Castledown Publishers. https://doi.org/10.29140/9781914291159-13

Warni, S., Aziz, T. A., & Febriawan, D. (2018). The use of technology in English as a foreign language learning outside the classroom: An insight into learner autonomy. *LLT Journal: A Journal on Language and Language Teaching, 21* (2), 148–156.

Warschauer, M., & Healey, D. (1998). Computers and language learning: An overview. *Language Teaching, 31*(2), 57–71. https://doi.org/10.1017/S0261444800012970

Warschauer, M. (2000). *CALL for the 21st Century. IATEFL and ESADE Conference, 2 July 2000, Barcelona, Spain*. www.gse.uci.edu/markw/cyberspace.html

Williams C., & Beam S. (2018). Technology and writing: Review of research, *Computers & Education, 128*, 227–242. https://doi.org/10.1016/j.compedu.2018.09.024

Xu, Q., Dong, X., & Jiang, L. (2016). EFL learners' perceptions of mobile-assisted feedback on oral production. *TESOL Quarterly, 51*(2), 408–417. https://doi.org/10.1002/tesq.335

Yeh, S. W., & Lo, J. J. (2009). Using online annotations to support error correction and corrective feedback. *Computers & Education, 52*(4), 882–892. https://doi.org/10.1016/j.compedu.2008.12.014

Yim, S., & Warschauer, M. (2017). Web-based collaborative writing in second language contexts: Methodological insights from text mining. *Language Learning & Technology, 21*(1), 146–165. https://doi.org/10125/44599

Further Reading

Graham, S., & Perin, D. (2007). A meta-analysis of writing instruction for adolescent students. *Journal of Educational Psychology, 99*(3), 445–476. https://doi.org/10.1037/0022-0663.99.3.445

In this meta-analysis article, Graham and Perin systematically review a wide range of studies to determine the overall effectiveness of different instructional approaches to improve the writing skills of adolescents.

Lee, I. (2019). Teacher written corrective feedback: Less is more. *Language Teaching, 52*(4), 524–536. https://doi.org/10.1017/S0261444819000247

This article emphasizes the importance of finding a middle ground between excessive and minimalistic approaches to written corrective feedback in language teaching, focusing on targeted and meaningful feedback that considers individual learner needs.

Lee, I. (2017). *Classroom writing assessment and feedback in second language school contexts*. Springer Publications. https://doi.org/10.1007/978-981-10-3924-9

This book offers theoretical insights, practical strategies, and examples to help language teachers enhance their assessment practices and provide effective feedback to promote students' writing proficiency.

MacArthur, C. A., Graham, S., & Fitzgerald, J. (2015). *Handbook of writing research* (2nd ed.). The Guilford Publication.

This book is a comprehensive resource that explores various aspects of writing research and writing instruction. It covers topics such as the development of writing skills, the impact of technology on writing, and effective strategies for teaching writing.

Nassaji, H., & Kartchava, E. (2017). *Corrective feedback in second language teaching and learning*. Routledge.

This book focuses on the role of corrective feedback in the context of L2 teaching and learning. It covers different types of corrective feedback, such as explicit correction and recasts, and discusses their effectiveness in promoting language development.

28

Pronunciation

Tatsuya Kawahara and Masatake Dantsuji

Introduction

Although speaking is a fundamental language skill, acquiring speaking skills in a second language (L2) is considered difficult. While there is a range of factors contributing to this, there are three primary reasons that are deemed to be relevant. Firstly, it is not easy to get opportunities for L2 speaking practice in daily environments compared with reading texts and listening to audio/video. Secondly, corrective feedback is typically not available to learners when they undertake speaking practice by themselves, which has the potential for learners to consolidate incorrect pronunciation. Thirdly, speaking is least frequently included in many exams, such as in English exams for college admissions in Japan and other regions, largely due to the difficulty in scoring, which has resulted in a downgrade in the priority of speaking practice by students and teachers.

Because of the rapid progress of online audiovisual communication tools (e.g. Zoom and Skype) coupled with the globalization of the economy, it is not uncommon for people to find themselves in a position where they are required to speak in a second language – especially English – after joining the workforce, but they feel unprepared and end up spending a lot of time and money on trying to develop their English conversation skills.

It is widely known that speaking consists of two main parts: the sentence construction process and pronunciation. The sentence construction process, including lexical choice, is largely shared with writing skills, although there is usually a shorter amount of time available for processing the language than in writing. Pronunciation has phonemic (segmental) and prosodic (suprasegmental) aspects, both of which are affected by those of the native language (L1). In this chapter, we focus on pronunciation learning, in particular for Japanese learners of English as a second language.

Background

From the 1950s, classrooms fitted with language laboratory (LL) systems dedicated to individual speaking and listening practice began appearing around the United States, spreading into wide global use until the 1990s. In LL systems, each student's booth was equipped with audio equipment so that students could play back model voices of native speakers and record their own speech for comparison. The audio equipment evolved from open-reel tape recorders to cassette decks and then to digital devices such as MP recorders. In a digitized LL system, the master console for teachers was equipped with a personal computer which enabled them to provide the content for learners and to monitor their progress. Technological advances led to digitized LL systems being eventually phased out in favor of various CALL courseware systems that included speaking and listening but also allowed for other skills and areas as well.

During the transition from LL to CALL systems, many of the functions of LL hardware were converted to software that could be run on desktop computers. It was not uncommon to see LL classrooms refitted with CALL systems, where the student booths were equipped with computer terminals with digital recording devices such as floppy disks, magnetic disks (MO), compact disks (CDs), digital versatile discs (DVDs), and MP recorders. Some advanced CALL systems allowed speech analysis and diagnosis using speech processing technology (Tsubota, Kawahara, & Dantsuji, 2004). Of relevance to this chapter is CALL systems that are designed for Computer-Assisted Pronunciation Learning (CAPL). While some commercial software introduced role–play–type conversation schemes, the use of speech analysis and automatic speech recognition techniques have come to be investigated globally in a broad range of contexts (e.g. Bashori et al., 2022; Evers & Chen, 2020; van Doremalen et al., 2016). Pronunciation practice can be classified into the following schemes.

Phoneme or Word–Level Pronunciation Training

This focuses on the accurate pronunciation of phonemes that do not exist in L1. For example, it is well known that the distinction of consonants /r/ and /l/ is hard for Japanese native speakers. The set of vowels is often different among languages. Given a focused phoneme, automatic analysis and feedback can be done easily, thus this scheme was the first to be designed (Jo et al., 1998).

Prompted Sentence–Level Pronunciation Training

This focuses on the fluent pronunciation of natural sentences, which are presented to the learners. Many phonemes may be confused in a sentence though they can be predicted. Japanese native speakers often insert a redundant vowel between two consecutive consonants, for example, "stress" becomes "sutoresu." Moreover, not only segmental but also suprasegmental aspects need to be considered. The implementation of this scheme became feasible around the year 2000 with the advancement of speech recognition technologies (Tsubota, Kawahara, & Dantsuji, 2002).

Role-Play Conversation Training
This focuses on constrained conversation, in which learners are asked to produce a sentence in a given context. This is effective for typical settings such as ordering in a restaurant or shopping. However, it is not easy to detect pronunciation errors as there is no ground-truth sentence in this case. Instead, communication skill or intelligibility can be measured by checking if the utterance is well recognized (Raux & Kawahara, 2002).

Free Conversation/Speaking Training
This focuses on general speaking training. Learners are often given a topic or proposition about which they need to speak for a few minutes. Construction of a story and sentences and their delivery are required. Thus, it is challenging to automatically assess and provide feedback. The Educational Testing Service (ETS) and other institutions conducting speaking tests have been investigating this feasibility, (van Dalen, Knill, and Gales, 2015; Zechner, Higgins, and Xi, 2007).

As mentioned above, accurate pronunciation and intelligibility are two factors to be considered. It is apparent that if all phonemes are pronounced accurately, the utterance will be intelligible. On the other hand, intelligible utterances do not mean all phonemes are pronounced accurately. It is often said that taking too much care of each phoneme discourages speaking practice.

Here, "intelligibility" can be defined objectively (Bernstein, 2003) or measured by how many words are recognized, or if the intent of the utterance is correctly understood by native speakers (see also Munro & Derwing, 2015, for a discussion of intelligibility of L2 pronunciation). Then, a question arises if native speakers can be replaced by an automatic speech recognition system. This is intuitively true but only applicable to very high-level learners speaking to a state-of-the-art system. Since speech recognition systems are trained with a speech database of native speakers, and despite advances having been made (Radzikowski et al., 2021), it is still difficult for them to accurately recognize nonnative speech.

A similar discussion can be had on the definition of "accurate pronunciation," which is conventionally judged by native speakers. But does "accurate" mean authentic or native-like? Or does it mean distinguishable from other phonemes? The current automatic assessment system based on speech recognition technology relies on the latter assumption. It is easy for the system to measure the relative similarity among the phoneme set but very difficult to measure the native-likeness because the system does not have a model of nonnative speech. It is possible to model nonnative speech given a particular group of learners, for example, Japanese learners speaking English (Tsubota et al., 2004) or Chinese learners speaking English (Meng et al., 2010). In addition, current speech recognition does not consider suprasegmental aspects, making it a difficult aspect to teach (Kochem, Beck, & Goodale, 2022).

These important considerations must be kept in mind when using a speech recognition system in pronunciation learning.

Primary Themes

Definition of Phonemes

Pronunciation is a pedagogic notion, but the most relevant fields in linguistics are phonetics and phonology. Both phonetics and phonology are fields of study that deal with various phenomena related to the speech sounds of language. However, phonetics and phonology differ in their research methods and objectives. The difference between these two fields is that phonology includes consideration of meaning, while phonetics does not. In general, the following definitions are often used. Phonetics is concerned with the description of the physiological, physical, and perceptual properties of speech sounds. Phonology, on the other hand, refers to theories and descriptions based on the discriminative function of speech sounds, that is, their ability to distinguish the meaning of words. Phonology emphasizes the system, structure, or function of a language and is highly abstract. Phonetics, on the other hand, tends to emphasize more concrete analysis.

Take, for example, the phonetic and phonemic symbols, which are the basic units of description in phonetics and phonology. The phonetic symbol is, to some extent, concrete and language-universal, whereas the phonemic symbol is an abstract unit and language dependent. Therefore, the actual phonetic value of a phoneme varies depending on the phonological/phonetic environment and the language system in which it occurs and cannot be identified unconditionally. The manifestation of the phoneme in the actual context is called "allophone." Conventionally, phonetic symbols are indicated by enclosing them in square brackets such as [p], whereas phonemic symbols are denoted by enclosing them in slashes such as /p/.

Phonemes are an important unit in the phonology of structural linguistics. The Prague school initially considered the phoneme as a psychological unit, but then shifted to a functional definition. The concept of phonological opposition was also introduced. Bloomfield regarded the phoneme as the smallest unit that distinguishes meaning and the bundle of phonetic features. In phonemic analysis, the principles of "complementary distribution" (i.e. variations of a phoneme will appear in mutually exclusive phonetic contexts) and "phonetic similarity" (i.e. variations of a sound with shared phonetic features are often found as variants of a single phonological element) have been emphasized (Anderson, 1985; Collins, Mees, & Carley, 2019; Dantsuji, 1989; Shimizu, 1982).

Phonemes and Articulation

When discussing pronunciation learning, the actual phonetic values or allophones of the phonemes in question become an issue. Phonemes are an abstract unit. The specific phonetic values will be carried by the allophones that make up the phoneme. We will examine these issues from the perspective of phonetics.

Phonetics is traditionally divided into three fields: articulatory phonetics, acoustic phonetics, and auditory phonetics. Of these, articulatory phonetics is most closely related to pronunciation. It is the area of study of the speaker's aspect and focuses on the articulatory function of speech sounds. Articulatory phonetics classifies and describes speech sounds according to the dynamic changes and functions of the speech organs during the production of speech sounds. Speech sounds are symbolized by the fundamental principles of articulatory phonetics. The International Phonetic Alphabet (IPA) is one of the typical examples of such symbolizations (International Phonetic Association, 1999).

Let us now make a few observations about the mechanism of linguistic sound production and articulation (see Figure 28.1). English speech sounds are generally produced by airflow from the lungs. The airflow from the lungs is carried through the trachea to the larynx. In the larynx are located the vocal folds, and speech sounds are divided into voiced and voiceless sounds according to whether they vibrate or not. The space between the vocal folds is called the glottis, and the airflow exiting the glottis is carried via the pharynx to the oral and nasal cavities. The cavity portion from the glottis to the orifice

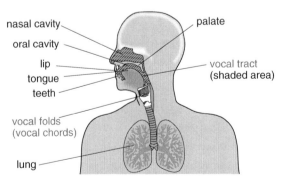

Figure 28.1 Organs for articulation.

THE INTERNATIONAL PHONETIC ALPHABET (revised to 2005)

CONSONANTS (PULMONIC) © 2005 IPA

	Bilabial	Labiodental	Dental	Alveolar	Postalveolar	Retroflex	Palatal	Velar	Uvular	Pharyngeal	Glottal
Plosive	p b			t d		ʈ ɖ	c ɟ	k ɡ	q ɢ		ʔ
Nasal	m	ɱ		n		ɳ	ɲ	ŋ	N		
Trill	B			r						R	
Tap or Flap		ⱱ		ɾ		ɽ					
Fricative	ɸ β	f v	θ ð	s z	ʃ ʒ	ʂ ʐ	ç ʝ	x ɣ	χ ʁ	ħ ʕ	h ɦ
Lateral fricative				ɬ ɮ							
Approximant		ʋ		ɹ		ɻ	j	ɰ			
Lateral approximant				l		ɭ	ʎ	L			

Where symbols appear in pairs, the one to the right represents a voiced consonant. Shaded areas denote articulations judged impossible.

Figure 28.2 Consonants (IPA chart).

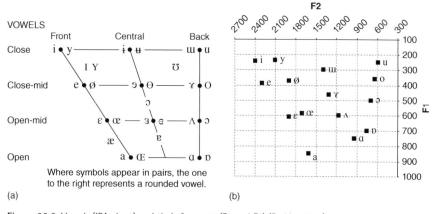

(a) (b)

Figure 28.3 Vowels (IPA chart) and their formants (F1 and F2) (Ezykin, 2018).

of the oral cavity or nasal cavity is called the vocal tract. The organs within the vocal tract are called articulators. Vowels are speech sounds that do not undergo an effective narrowing of airflow in the vocal tract. Speech sounds that undergo an effective constriction are called consonants.

Consonants are traditionally classified according to three-dimensional aspects in pedagogical studies: voiced/voiceless, place of articulation, and manner of articulation (see Figure 28.2).

Vowels are traditionally described in terms of the features of tongue height (vertical dimension), tongue backness (horizontal dimension), and rounded-ness (lip articulation) in pedagogical studies. A high vowel is also called a closed vowel, and a low vowel is also called an open vowel based on aperture (Ladefoged, 2001) (see Figure 28.3a).

Distinctive Features

Phonemes are a fundamental unit in the phonology of structural linguistics. Since the phoneme was the central unit of phonology in structural linguistics, the term phonemics or phoneme theory was often used. However, as the notion of phonemes gradually lost importance and became less valid, the term phonology was preferred. In generative phonology, the phoneme is no longer considered a linguistically significant unit, but the distinctive features are considered linguistically significant. Jakobson, Fant, and Halle (1952) examined the concept of distinctive features in terms of articulatory, physiological, acoustic, and auditory aspects and came to be defined dichotomously. This concept of analysis using distinctive features was widely accepted and significantly contributed to the later development of phonology, and it has had a significant influence on generative phonology.

In generative phonology, rules and descriptions of phonological and phonetic levels are formulated in terms of distinctive features. Distinctive features are defined primarily from the articulatory point of view (Chomsky & Halle, 1968), as it is sometimes possible for phenomena that cannot be explained well at the phonemic level to be handled by using distinctive features.

The concept of features has been widely accepted in various fields and has evolved with numerous proposed modifications. In particular, Ladefoged proposed and developed a system of linguistic phonetic features different from those of Jakobson, Chomsky, and so on. This feature has been defined as a component of a sound that may itself be composed of other features or may be a terminal feature. Each terminal feature specifies a limited set of discrete phonetic possibilities with specific phonetic properties (Ladefoged, 2001; Ladefoged & Maddieson, 1996). Most features are characterized by articulatory and physiological aspects, but some features are described from an acoustic or auditory aspect. The concept of these phonetic features is more practical and can be applied to pronunciation learning and machine recognition.

Pronunciation Errors

Pronunciation errors during L2 learning are often caused by differences in phonological structures between L1 and L2. In this regard, L2 learning models such as the native language magnet model (Kuhl, 1993), the perceptual assimilation model (Best, 1991), and the speech learning model (Flege, 1995) have been proposed to explain this (see Shimizu, 2008, for an overview). This is clearly the case when Japanese speakers learn English, where certain speech errors are likely to occur. The main reason is the difference in phonemic inventory between the two languages: Japanese has fewer consonants and vowels than English. Pronunciation errors can also be caused by similar but slightly different features in the target language (L2) that are not present in L1.

One of the most famous examples is the /r-l/ contrast. English has two types of liquids (rhotic sound and laterals) (i.e. /r/ and /l/), but Japanese has only one (generally pronounced as tap or flap). Therefore, there is no phonological contrast between liquids (i.e. between /r/ and /l/) and no distinction of meaning. In general, differences between speech sounds that do not produce semantic distinctions are difficult to discriminate. Thus, Japanese speakers have difficulty not only hearing the difference between /r/ and /l/ but also pronouncing them. In general, /r/ in standard English is often pronounced as an alveolar approximant [ɹ] and /l/ as an alveolar lateral [l], but Japanese speakers often pronounce both as tap or flap [ɾ] or as retroflex [ɽ] (Shimizu & Dantsuji, 1983).

In addition, Japanese has fewer varieties of fricatives than English. Well-known examples include pronouncing English voiceless dental fricative [θ] as [s] or [ʃ] and voiced dental fricative [ð] as [d], [dz], [dʒ]. The same is true for the vowels in Japanese. Japanese vowels are less varied than their English counterparts. Particularly, since there is only one low vowel (open vowel), Japanese speakers have difficulty in pronouncing the front vowel [æ], back vowel [a], and central vowel [ʌ].

Suprasegmental Features

Pronunciation problems arise not only with phonemes (segments) such as consonants and vowels, but also with aspects of speech that involve more than single consonants or vowels. The Prague school treated them as prosodic features while Bloomfield treated them as secondary phonemes, and Post-Bloomfieldians treated them as supra-segmental phonemes, including juncture, stress, tone, intonation, duration, and so forth (see Newmeyer, 2022, for a discussion).

In general, suprasegmental features are phenomena that occur as syllable units. It is said that a syllable is the smallest unit of speech that can be uttered. A syllable can be divided into its onset and rhyme. The rhyme of the syllable can be further divided into the nucleus and the coda. Closed syllables are those that have a consonant at the end. Open syllables are those without a consonant at the end.

Phonological structures of syllables are different between English and Japanese. Japanese is known to be an open-syllable language. Japanese does not allow branching onsets or codas. This means that no consonant clusters or word-final consonants occur. Therefore, Japanese speakers have difficulty in pronouncing and hearing them. Related to this point, Japanese speakers are not good at discriminating the Chinese word-final nasals (Yang, Nanjo, & Dantsuji, 2018).

Stress is related to the use of extra respiratory energy during a syllable. English has stress contrasts. Pitch is related to the tension of the vocal folds. When the vocal folds are stretched, the pitch of the sound goes up. Pitch variations that affect the meaning of a word are called tones. Chinese is a tone language, in which the meaning of a word is affected by the pitch (Ortega-Llebaria & Wu, 2021). In contrast, Japanese is often called a pitch-accent language (Goss, 2020; Ladefoged, 2001).

Regarding rhythm, it is often said that English is a stress-timed language. In a stress-timed language, the time interval between successive stressed syllables is perceived to be equal. As a result, unstressed syllables between stressed syllables tend to be shorter. On the other hand, it is said that Japanese is a mora-timed language. A mora is a basic timing unit equal to or shorter than a syllable. In a mora-timed language, the duration of every mora is perceived to be equal. It has been noted that Japanese speakers have difficulty pronouncing stressed syllables longer and unstressed syllables shorter.

Speech Analysis

To check the correct articulation, we need to measure and visualize the movement of organs that make the vocal tract, such as the mouth and tongue (Badin et al., 2010), but this requires special devices such as X-ray, magnetic resonance imaging (MRI), and electromagnetic articulography (EMA) (Li & Wang, 2012), which are costly and uncomfortable. Therefore, speech analysis is used for an approximate estimation.

Formant Analysis

It is well known that formant frequencies, which are the peaks of the spectral envelope, are related to articulation. Specifically, the first formant (F1) corresponds to the openness of the mouth, that is, larger F1, wider open, and the second formant (F2) corresponds to the position of the tongue or the place of articulation, that is, larger F2, more front-positioned. The correspondence is shown in Figure 28.3. For example, we can detect a pronunciation error between "bat" and "but" based on F2, and provide explicit feedback such as, "Place your tongue more to the front to pronounce bat."

The formant frequencies are computed with spectral analysis, which is implemented in the software tool of WaveSurfer and Praat. An example of the analysis of the Japanese five vowels "a i u e o" is shown in Figure 28.4.

We also need to note that the formant frequencies depend on the speakers. For example, there is a considerable difference between male and female persons, and also between American and Japanese people, because the size of the articulator organs is much different. Still, the relative positions among vowels are stable. Therefore, some normalization such as vocal tract length normalization has been investigated in previous studies (Tsubota, Dantsuji, & Kawahara, 2000). Vocal tract length normalization (VTLN) does not require actual measurement of the vocal tract, but approximately estimates it based on speech analysis. Moreover, the formant frequencies are not so stable in continuous speech and are not detected in unvoiced sounds such as consonants. Thus, they can be used for pronunciation learning of single vowels.

Articulatory Attributes

It will be effective to recognize articulatory attributes such as distinctive features shown in the dimensions of Figure 28.2 from speech and to provide corrective feedback if an error is detected (Duan et al., 2019; Jo et al., 1998; Lee & Siniscalchi, 2013). For example, we can attribute a pronunciation error

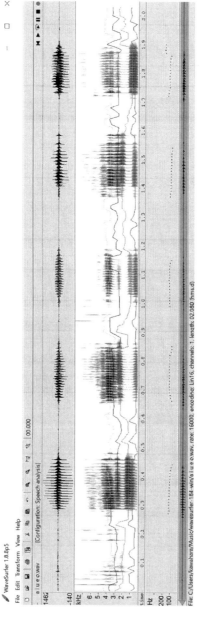

Figure 28.4 Speech analysis by WaveSurfer (Japanese five vowels /a, i, u, e, o/).

between "sea" and "she" to the place of articulation and provide feedback, such as, "place your tongue to the back of your teeth to pronounce sea."

However, it is not straightforward to recognize articulatory attributes of consonants from speech analysis. We need to introduce a machine learning-based classifier for this task. Given a sufficient amount of speech samples, that is, dozens of hours, we can train a classifier based on deep learning for each attribute group. Duan et al. (2019) reported that the classifier trained with the *Wall Street Journal* corpus of sixty-four hours achieved an attribute recognition accuracy of 91 percent. Among the attribute groups, the manner of articulation achieved a higher accuracy than the place of articulation. Note that the word accuracy by the state-of-the-art speech recognition systems is higher than 95 percent for the dataset, but it largely depends on a lexicon and a language model. The phoneme accuracy without any linguistic knowledge would be much lower. Note also that this accuracy is achieved for native speech. When the model was applied to nonnative speech by Japanese, the accuracy was 77 percent. To address the mismatch, the researchers introduced multilingual training, which combined a Japanese speech dataset, and improved the accuracy to 86 percent. This demonstrates the effectiveness of using L1 speech data or knowledge of L1 for pronunciation error detection in L2.

Speech Recognition Technology

Automatic speech recognition (ASR) has been investigated since the 1960s and has dramatically improved over the last decade because of the advancement of machine learning, and deep learning in particular, as well as the construction of a huge amount of speech database. It is often claimed that the state-of-the-art system outperforms most nonnative speakers and performs comparably with native speakers, given a condition of clean and fluent speech. Most notably, these high-performance ASR systems developed by big-tech companies such as Google, Apple, and Microsoft are readily available on smartphones, tablets, and PCs.

The application of speech recognition technology to L2 pronunciation learning has also been investigated since the 1990s. However, we should take into account that the standard speech recognition systems are trained with native speech datasets, and do not model nonnative speech. It is easily confirmed that even high-level nonnative speakers have difficulty in having their speech transcribed by the ASR system. This does not mean they cannot communicate with native speakers. In daily life, the context of the conversation helps. In pronunciation learning, however, we need to model nonnative speech in both acoustic feature models and symbolic phoneme sequences. This modeling will be effective when we limit the L1, for example, for Japanese learners speaking English. In any case, it will require the construction of a large-scale nonnative speech database, which involves not only the recording of speech data but also the annotation of incorrect pronunciations with a large variation in the proficiency level. This is the most critical part of the research and development of this kind of system.

The major applications of speech recognition technology to L2 pronunciation learning are pronunciation error detection and pronunciation grading, which are described in the following subsections. Pedagogical feedback is also important, but it will be generated by combining the speech analysis described in the previous section.

Pronunciation Error Detection

Pronunciation error detection is designed to identify which phoneme is not correctly articulated. The following settings are considered.

Minimal Pair of Words

We can prepare a pair of words that differs by only one or two phonemes, which are confusing to nonnative learners. For example, bat/but, sea/she, right/light, berry/very, and think/sink. Learners can then try to see if their speech is correctly recognized by an ASR system. This corresponds to phoneme or word-level pronunciation training. It can be done by simply using the existing ASR systems in smartphones, tablets, and PCs.

Prompted Text

When we extend pronunciation training to the sentence level, there are many points for possible errors. Moreover, ASR systems have not typically produced meaningful output for most nonnative speech (McCrocklin & Edalatishams, 2020). A simple and widely used solution is to use a prompted text. A sentence is presented to the learners, and it is used to guide the ASR system. Specifically, alignment of the input utterance against the prompted text is conducted. As a result, the utterance is segmented into a sequence of phonemes. Then, each phoneme is checked to see if its pronunciation is correct. This is done by comparing with the predefined confusing phonemes, which are used in minimal pairs. More generally, this process is done by computing the goodness of pronunciation (GOP) score introduced next. In the alignment process, we also need to consider the insertion and deletion of phonemes. It is well known that Japanese people tend to insert a vowel between consecutive consonants to make open syllables. This possible insertion needs to be modeled as well (Tsubota et al., 2002).

Free Input

When we allow learners to speak freely, it is very difficult not only to transcribe but also to detect pronunciation errors. In theory, we can design an ASR system to transcribe the speech and compute the GOP score for each phoneme. But it is not easy to distinguish ASR errors by the system and pronunciation errors by the learners. The distinction may not be binary by nature. We can only conclude that if the speech is correctly transcribed by the ASR system, it is intelligible.

Pronunciation Grading

Pronunciation grading measures how "good" the input utterance is. Automatic speech recognition systems based on machine learning evaluate each phoneme on how distinguishable it is from other phonemes. The most widely used GOP score for a phoneme p is defined as follows (Neumeyer et al., 2000):

$$GOP(p) \approx \frac{1}{T} \sum_t log \frac{P(p|x_t)}{\max_q P(q|x_t)}$$

Here, x_t represents a time frame in the phoneme p, and q is a competing phoneme. The probabilities are computed as the direct output of a deep learning-based phoneme recognizer (Hu et al., 2015). The probability ratio against the most competing phoneme is computed frame-by-frame and averaged over the segments of T time frames.

If this score is negative, that is, the numerator is larger than the denominator on average, the phoneme is regarded as erroneously pronounced. Note that if we predefine the competing phoneme q with a priori knowledge of confusing phonemes such as /l/ and /r/, then it is reduced to the pronunciation error detection previously described.

The GOP score can be aggregated over all phonemes in the utterance to grade the entire utterance. The standard GOP is computed with the ASR system using the phoneme set of the target L2, thus it is L1-independent. We can design L1-dependent GOP by combining the phoneme set of L1 and training a bilingual ASR system. By considering the pronunciation of L1 phonemes this will become more effective.

Nonnative Speech Modeling

It is important to model nonnative speech in the ASR system, though this is limited to a particular L1 group. This can be simply done by incorporating nonnative speech data, such as Japanese people speaking English. A problem is that it is not easy to collect such data on a large scale. Therefore, several investigations have been done using L1 speech datasets, for example, Japanese people speaking Japanese, which are readily available in major languages. Although the phoneme sets are very different between English and Japanese, we can still use a large portion of consonant models which share the same symbols. Tsubota et al. (2002) demonstrated that using this Japanese native model is as effective as using nonnative speech data (English speech by Japanese people), and that phoneme recognition accuracy was improved by 3.5 percent absolute (from 75.4 percent to 78.9 percent). Recent deep learning allows for more elegant multilingual training, in which feature extraction networks are shared between the two languages. Duan et al. (2019) demonstrated that this multilingual training using English and Japanese native speech datasets improved the word recognition accuracy from 65.6 percent to 71.1 percent.

We can model nonnative speech in the phoneme sequence by considering the typical substitution and insertion patterns. For example, the word "breath"

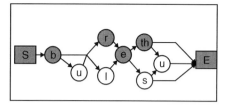

Figure 28.5 Example of a network with error prediction for the word "breath."

can be represented with b (uh) r|l eh s|th (uh), where "()" represents a possible insertion and "|" represents possible substitutions. This can be represented in a network, as shown in Figure 28.5, which ASR systems can use. It is effective for transcription, alignment, and error detection processes.

Suprasegmental Assessment

Suprasegmental factors such as accent and intonation play an important role in intelligibility. Even if every phoneme is correctly pronounced, an improper accent makes the utterance unintelligible. It happens typically in katakana words in Japanese, such as "banana" and "tomato." It is often pointed out that Japanese people tend to speak without any stress, and as a result, many Japanese people are not aware that stress is required for a proper accent because the pitch is primarily used for accent in Japanese.

Training on the suprasegmental aspects requires dedicated speech analysis because stress is not easily observed in pitch and spectrograms. Note that the GOP using the ASR system does not consider suprasegmental aspects. Therefore, stress detection based on dedicated machine learning has been explored (Imoto et al., 2002). In addition, there are many languages that depend on tones for distinction of words, such as Mandarin and Thai. In this case, pitch features can be used for analysis and feedback (Dantsuji & Tsubota, 2005; Kaur et al, 2021).

Recommendations for Research and Practice

The last several years have seen exponential improvement in the availability of free open-source speech analysis and recognition software. Originally released in the Netherlands in 1995, Praat (www.fon.hum.uva.nl/praat/) provides a visual analysis of utterances produced by users, and has been used in teaching the pronunciation of languages such as English by Thai learners (Behr, 2022), German learners (Schlechtweg, 2023), and Chinese learners with a focus on tones by learners in the United States (Chen, 2022). Other software includes WaveSurfer (https://sourceforge.net/projects/wavesurfer/) (Handley & Hamel, 2005) and Julius (https://ja.osdn.net/projects/julius/) (Shadiev & Liu, 2023), which have both appeared in the literature, but with far less frequency compared to Praat.

One of the ongoing problems with this type of software, however, is the lack of development of a clear pedagogy that takes advantage of the affordances of these tools. There is a tendency to focus on technological functions without providing clear instruction as to how they can be directly related to learners' pronunciation improvement. In addition, these tools can allow for the automatic measurement of speech fluency, which means that there is still broad scope for them to be used in speaking assessment (e.g. de Jong, Pacilly, & Heeren, 2021). These are areas where there is an obvious relationship between research and practice that can lead to making the most of technological advances in ASR and speech analysis.

There is a critical need for open educational resources that allow teachers and researchers to use these tools with nonnative speakers more accurately. To conduct research in this area, a comprehensive database of nonnative speech is essential. Two notable publicly available databases are the English Speech Database Read by Japanese Students (UME-ERJ) (https://doi.org/10.32130/src.UME-ERJ) and the Japanese Speech Database Read by Foreign Students (UME-JRF) (https://doi.org/10.32130/src.UME-JRF), but they do not have annotations on incorrect pronunciation, which are also necessary but very costly. There are spoken corpora also appearing in different languages (see Knight & Adolphs, 2015).

Future Directions

As it has been demonstrated that a large amount of data has been the key to the success of many AI applications in the past decade, it is most critical to collect datasets of nonnative speech in order to broaden the applicability of these tools. Accurate annotation of pronunciation errors has been the bottleneck, and as such, many natural language processing studies have recently adopted crowd-based data collection and annotation. We may look for this option with proper design and implementation.

Although we have emphasized L1-dependency in pronunciation errors, cross-lingual analysis and universal modeling need to be explored in the future given the enormous variety of languages. Low-resource and endangered languages need to be a particular focus in future research. This can result not only in their preservation but also in effectively passing on their correct pronunciation to future generations via these teaching materials.

References

Anderson, R. S. (1985). *Phonology in the twentieth century.* The University of Chicago Press.

Badin, P., Tarabalka, Y., Elisei, F., & Bailly, G. (2010). Can you "read" tongue movements? Evaluation of the contribution of tongue display to speech understanding. *Speech Communication, 52,* 493–503. https://doi.org/10.1016/j.specom.2010.03.002

Bashori, M., van Hout, R., Strik, H., & Cucchiarini, C. (2022). "Look, I can speak correctly": Learning vocabulary and pronunciation through websites equipped with automatic speech recognition technology. *Computer Assisted Language Learning.* Advance online publication. https://doi.org/10.1080/09588221.2022.2080230

Behr, N. S. (2022). English diphthong characteristics produced by Thai EFL learners: Individual practice using PRAAT. *CALL-EJ, 23*(1), 401–424.

Bernstein, J. (2003). Objective measurement of intelligibility. *Proceedings of the ICPhS (International Congress of Phonetic Sciences),* 1581–1584.

Best, C. T. (1991). The emergence of native-language phonological influences in infants: A perception assimilation model. *Haskins Laboratories Status Report on Speech Research, SR-107/108,* 1–30.

Chen, M. (2022). Computer-aided feedback on the pronunciation of Mandarin Chinese tones: Using Praat to promote multimedia foreign language learning. *Computer Assisted Language Learning.* Advance online publication. https://doi.org/10.1080/09588221.2022.2037652

Chomsky, N., & Halle, M. (1968). *The sound patterns of English.* Harper & Row.

Collins, B., Mees, I. M., & Carley, P. (2019). *Practical English phonetics and phonology: A resource book for students.* Routledge. https://doi.org/10.4324/9780429490392

Dantsuji, M. (1989). Onseigaku to on'inron [Phonetics and phonology]. In O. Sakiyama (Ed.), *Nihongo to Nihongokyouiku [Japanese language and Japanese language education]* (Vol. 11, 21–59). Meijishoin.

Dantsuji, M., & Tsubota, Y. (2005). Dainigengo no onsei shutoku to CALL [Speech acquisition of L2 and CALL]. *Onsei Kenkyu [Journal of the Phonetic Society of Japan], 9*(1). 5–15.

de Jong, N. H., Pacilly, J., & Heeren, W. (2021). PRAAT scripts to measure speed fluency and breakdown fluency in speech automatically. *Clinical Linguistics & Phonetics, 35*(5), 456–476. https://doi.org/10.1080/0969594X.2021.1951162

Duan, R., Kawahara, T., Dantsuji, M., & Nanjo, H. (2019). Cross-lingual transfer learning of nonnative acoustic modeling for pronunciation error detection and diagnosis. *IEEE/ACM Transactions on Audio, Speech & Language Process, 28,* 391–401. http://dx.doi.org/10.1109/TASLP.2019.2955858

Evers, K., & Chen, S. (2020). Effects of an automatic speech recognition system with peer feedback on pronunciation instruction for adults. *Computer Assisted Language Learning, 35*(8), 1869–1889. https://doi.org/10.1080/09588221.2020.1839504

Ezykin, L. (2018). English: Average vowel formants F1 and F2. https://commons.wikimedia.org/w/index.php?curid=71013415

Flege, J. E. (1995). Second language speech learning. In W. Strange (Ed.), *Speech perception and linguistic experience* (pp. 233–277). York Press.

Goss, S. (2020). Exploring variation in nonnative Japanese learners' perception of lexical pitch accent: The roles of processing resources and learning context. *Applied Psycholinguistics, 41*(1), 25–49. https://doi.org/10.1017/S0142716419000377

Handley, Z., & Hamel, M. (2005). Establishing a methodology for benchmarking speech synthesis for computer-assisted language learning (CALL). *Language Learning & Technology, 9*(3), 99-120. http://dx.doi.org/10125/44034

Hu, W., Qian, Y., Soong, F.-K., & Wang, Y. (2015). Improved mispronunciation detection with deep neural network trained acoustic models and transfer learning based logistic regression classifiers. *Speech Communication, 67*, 154–166. https://doi.org/10.1016/j.specom.2014.12.008

Imoto, K., Tsubota, Y., Raux, A., Kawahara, T., & Dantsuji, M. (2002). Modeling and automatic detection of English sentence stress for computer-assisted English prosody learning system. *Proceedings of ICSLP (International Conference of Spoken Language Processing)*, 749–752. http://doi.org/10.21437/ICSLP.2002-244

International Phonetic Association. (1999). *Handbook of the international phonetic association.* Cambridge University Press.

Jakobson, R., Fant, C. G. M., & Halle, M. (1952). *Preliminaries to speech analysis: The distinctive features and their correlates.* MIT Press.

Jo, C.-H., Kawahara, T., Doshita, S., & Dantsuji, M. (1998). Automatic pronunciation error detection and guidance for foreign language learning. *Proceedings of ICSLP (International Conference of Spoken Language Processing)*, pp. 2639–2642. http://doi.org/10.21437/ICSLP.1998-759

Kaur, J., Singh, A., & Kadyan, V. (2021). Automatic speech recognition system for tonal languages: State-of-the-art survey. *Archives of Computational Methods in Engineering, 28*, 1039–1068. https://doi.org/10.1007/s11831-020-09513-0

Knight, D., & Adolphs, S. (2015). Building a spoken corpus: What are the basics? In A. O'Keeffe & M. McCarthy (Eds.), *The Routledge handbook of corpus linguistics* (2nd ed., pp. 21–34). Routledge.

Kochem, T., Beck, J., & Goodale, E. (2022). The use of ASR-equipped software in the teaching of suprasegmental features of pronunciation: A critical review. *CALICO Journal, 39*(3), 306–325. https://doi.org/10.1558/cj.41968

Kuhl, P. K. (1993). Innate predispositions and the effects of experience in speech perception: The native language magnet theory. In B. de Boysson-Bardies, S. de Schonen, P. Jusczyk, P. MacNeilage, & J. Morton (Eds.), *Developmental neurocognition: Speech and face processing in the first year of life* (pp. 259–274). Kluewer Academic Press.

Ladefoged, P. (2001). *A course in phonetics* (4th ed.). Heinle & Heinle.

Ladefoged, P., & Maddieson, I. (1996). *Sounds of the world's languages.* Blackwells.

Lee, C.-H., & Siniscalchi, M. (2013). An information-extraction approach to speech processing: Analysis, detection, verification and recognition. *Proceedings of the IEEE, 101*(5), 1089–1115. https://doi.org/10.1109/JPROC.2013.2238591

Li, S., & Wang, L. (2012). Cross linguistic comparison of Mandarin and English EMA articulatory data. *Proceedings of INTERSPEECH*, 903–906.

McCrocklin, S., & Edalatishams, I. (2020). Revisiting popular speech recognition software for ESL speech. *TESOL Quarterly, 54*(4), 1086–1097. https://doi.org/10.1002/tesq.3006

Meng, H., Lo, W.-K., Harrison, A. M., Lee, P., Wong, K. H., Leung, W.-K., & Meng, F. (2010). Development of automatic speech recognition and synthesis technologies to support Chinese learners of English: The CUHK experience. *Proceedings of APSIPA ASC*, 811–820.

Munro, M., & Derwing, T. (2015). Intelligibility in research and practice: Teaching priorities. In M. Reed & J. Levis (Eds.), *The handbook of English pronunciation* (pp. 377–396). Wiley-Blackwell. https://doi.org/10.1002/9781118346952.ch21

Neumeyer, L., Franco, H., Digalakis, V., & Weintraub, M. (2000). Automatic scoring of pronunciation quality. *Speech Communication, 30*, 83–93. https://doi.org/10.1016/S0167-6393(99)00046-1

Newmeyer, F. J. (2022). *American linguistics in transition: From post-Bloomfieldian structuralism to generative grammar.* Oxford University Press. https://doi.org/10.1093/oso/9780192843760.001.0001

Ortega-Llebaria, M., & Wu, Z. (2021). Chinese-English speakers' perception of pitch in their non-tonal language: Reinterpreting English as a tonal-like language. *Language and Speech, 64*(2), 267–291. https://doi.org/10.1177/0023830919894

Radzikowski, K., Wang, L., Yoshie, O., & Nowak, R. (2021). Accent modification for speech recognition of nonnative speakers using neural style transfer. *EURASIP Journal on Audio, Speech, and Music Processing, 2021*(11). https://doi.org/10.1186/s13636-021-00206-4

Raux, A., & Kawahara, T. (2002). Automatic intelligibility assessment and diagnosis of critical pronunciation errors for computer-assisted pronunciation learning. *Proceedings of ICSLP (International Conference of Spoken Language Processing)*, 737–740. https://doi.org/10.21437/ICSLP.2002-241

Schlechtweg, M. (2023). Optimizing English pronunciation of German students online and with Praat. In M. Suárez & W. M. El-Henawy (Eds.), Optimizing online English language learning and teaching (pp. 233–277). Springer. https://doi.org/10.1007/978-3-031-27825-9_14

Shadiev, R., & Liu, J. (2023). Review of research on applications of speech recognition technology to assist language learning. *ReCALL, 35*(1), 74–88. https://doi.org/10.1017/S095834402200012X

Shimizu, K. (1982). *Onsei no chouon to chikaku [Articulation and perception of speech sounds].* Shinozaki Shorin.

Shimizu, K. (2008). L2 Onseigakushuu to sono rironteki haikei [L2 speech learning and its theoretical background]. *Nagoyagakuindaigaku Ronshuu Gengo Bunka hen, 19*(2), 81–87.

Shimizu, K., & Dantsuji, M. (1983). A study on the perception of /r/ and /l/ in natural and synthetic speech sounds. *Studia Phonologica, 17*, 1–14.

Tsubota, Y., Dantsuji, M., & Kawahara, T. (2000). Computer-assisted English vowel learning system for Japanese speakers using cross language formant structures. *Proceedings of ICSLP (Int'l Conf. Spoken Language Processing), 3*, 566–569. https://doi.org/10.21437/ICSLP.2000-598

Tsubota, Y., Kawahara, T., & Dantsuji, M. (2002). Recognition and verification of English by Japanese students for computer-assisted language learning system.

Proceedings of ICSLP (International Conference of Spoken Language Processing), 1205–1208. https://doi.org/10.21437/ICSLP.2002-245

Tsubota, Y., Kawahara, T., & Dantsuji, M. (2004). An English pronunciation learning system for Japanese students based on diagnosis of critical pronunciation errors. *ReCALL, 16*(1), 173–188. https://doi.org/10.1017/S0958344004001314

van Dalen, R. C., Knill, K. M., & Gales, M. J. F. (2015). Automatically grading learners' English using a Gaussian process. *Proceedings of SLaTE (Speech and Language Technology in Education)*. https://doi.org/10.21437/10.21437/SLaTE.2015-2

van Doremalen, J., Boves, L., Colpaert, J., Cucchiarini, C., & Strik, H. (2016). Evaluating automatic speech recognition-based language learning systems: A case study. *Computer Assisted Language Learning, 29*(4), 833–851. https://doi.org/10.1080/09588221.2016.1167090

Yang, R., Nanjo, H., & Dantsuji, M. (2018). Training Japanese speakers to identify nasal codas of Mandarin Chinese. *Journal of Language Teaching & Research, 9*(1), 7–15.

Zechner, K., Higgins, D., & Xi, X. (2007). Speechrater: A construct-driven approach to scoring spontaneous nonnative speech. *Proceedings of SLaTE (Speech and Language Technology in Education)*. https://doi.org/10.21437/SLaTE.2007-31

Further Reading

Eskenazi, M. (2009). An overview of spoken language technology for education. *Speech Communication, 51*, 832–844. https://doi.org/10.1016/j.specom.2009.04.005
This article reviews studies in a variety of areas of spoken language technology in education. It highlights the potential benefits and challenges of incorporating such technology into language learning and assessment.

Pennington, M. C. (2021). Teaching pronunciation: The state of the art 2021. *RELC Journal, 52*(1), 3–21. https://doi.org/10.1177/00336882211002283
While not dedicated to technology in the teaching of pronunciation, this article brings together past research to show that pronunciation has been delegated to a more minor role in communicative language teaching despite its importance. It explores how we should be teaching pronunciation and includes a discussion on how technology can contribute to improved practice in this regard.

Seileek, A. A., & Elimat, A. K. (2014). Automatic speech recognition technology as an effective means for teaching pronunciation. *The JALT CALL Journal, 10*(1), 21–47. https://doi.org/10.29140/jaltcall.v10n1.166
In this article, Selieek and Elimat investigate the effectiveness of ASR in improving the pronunciation of EFL learners. The research results indicate that ASR technology has the potential to enhance learners' performance in pronunciation by offering them accurate and timely feedback. However, the authors also recognize the necessity for additional research and development to optimize the integration of ASR into language education.

29

Vocabulary

Jang Ho Lee and Dongkwang Shin

Introduction

Vocabulary constitutes an integral part of language comprehension and use (Meara, 1996; Nation, 2013; Schmitt, 2008; Zimmerman, 1997), with research on this area having addressed the issues of the operationalization and acquisition of vocabulary knowledge and instructional approaches to vocabulary learning. In the present era of technology-enhanced language learning, researchers' interest in integrating technology into vocabulary teaching and learning has been ever increasing, evidenced by meta-analyses on technology-aided vocabulary learning since 2010 (e.g. on computer-mediated glosses, Yun, 2011; on data-driven learning through concordancing, Lee, Warschauer, & Lee, 2019; on mobile-assisted learning, Lin & Lin, 2019), as well as recent research synthesis of technology-aided vocabulary teaching and learning (Elgort, 2018; Ma, 2017).

In this chapter, we aim to introduce a range of technologies integrated into vocabulary teaching and learning in light of previous studies and academic resources. More specifically, we will discuss their pedagogical values in light of research on vocabulary teaching and learning at a broader scope. We will also propose some recommendations for future research on technology-aided vocabulary teaching and learning.

Primary Themes

In this section, we give a succinct overview of theoretical concepts needed to address the issues related to technology-aided vocabulary teaching and learning, including the operationalization and acquisition of vocabulary knowledge and instructional approaches to vocabulary learning.

Operationalization of Vocabulary Knowledge

Lexical research has operationalized vocabulary knowledge in several different ways (e.g. Henriksen, 1999; Read, 2004), but Nation's (2013) taxonomy is one of the most widely accepted frameworks. In this framework, vocabulary knowledge is suggested to comprise three aspects, namely, knowledge of form (i.e. sound, orthography, word parts), knowledge of meaning (i.e. form-meaning connection, referential and conceptual meaning, association with other words), and knowledge of use (i.e. collocation, constraints on use, syntactic patterns). Furthermore, these three aspects could be represented receptively (in listening and reading) or productively (in speaking and writing). In her recent review of research on technology-aided vocabulary developments, Elgort (2018) reported that form-meaning connection (as part of knowledge of meaning) has been the most extensively examined, followed by the knowledge of written form (i.e. orthography) and the knowledge of use.

Another widely accepted concept related to the operationalization of vocabulary knowledge is size and depth (Anderson & Freebody, 1981). Size has been "typically operationalized as knowledge of the form–meaning connection" (Schmitt, 2014, p. 915), and is related to how many words one knows, albeit superficially, in the target language. As we will discuss below, several vocabulary tests have been designed to measure this dimension of vocabulary knowledge. On the other hand, more diverse approaches have been proposed to operationalize depth, with knowledge of a word's multiple senses and derivative forms, and collocation having been suggested as part of this dimension. Among these, the importance of operationalizing and measuring collocation knowledge has been highlighted (e.g. Martinez & Schmitt, 2012; Shin & Nation, 2008), in view of its contribution to one's fluency and native-like selection of vocabulary in language use.

Discussion on the extent to which size and depth are separate constructs has not been settled (e.g. Qian, 2002; Vermeer, 2001) and is beyond the scope of this chapter. Instead, we will introduce technology-aided vocabulary tests and their pedagogical values in the Current Research and Practice section.

Acquisition of Vocabulary Knowledge

Lexical processing and vocabulary acquisition have been proposed to consist of different stages (de Bot, Paribakht, & Wesche, 1997; Jiang, 2004), and it can be assumed that each technology is associated with a particular stage of lexical processing and vocabulary acquisition; thus, it is important to discuss the theoretical frameworks of vocabulary acquisition in order to understand the role of a particular technology for vocabulary learning. Among a range of theoretical frameworks, we discuss Ma's (2014) memory-based strategic framework. In light of the literature on cognitive psychology and second language (L2) vocabulary research, Ma proposed that four psychological stages are involved in the acquisition (or "semantization" in Beheydt, 1987) of an L2 lexical item, which are: "(1) perceiving the word form; (2) accessing the word meaning; (3) building the word entry in the mind; (4) retrieving the word from the mind" (p. 42).

Ma also suggested that these internal processes are associated with, respectively, the following strategy-driven processes: "(a) discovering the new word; (b) obtaining the word meaning; (c) mapping the word meaning with form; (d) consolidating the use of words" (p. 42). Ma (2017) further noted that most technologies integrated into vocabulary learning have been geared toward the first and second processes in her framework. Based on her model, a range of technological resources for vocabulary teaching and learning will be introduced in terms of their contribution to the different stages of vocabulary acquisition.

Instructional Approaches to Vocabulary Learning

In terms of the instructional approaches to vocabulary learning, intervention research has generally adopted a distinction between incidental and deliberate (intentional) learning (Hulstijn, 2013). Incidental learning of target vocabulary is assumed to occur when the primary focus of a target activity is not related to vocabulary (having more to do with comprehending the message of the text, as in reading or listening), but a learner acquires some vocabulary included in the text through guessing, repeated exposure, or some vocabulary learning devices. For example, vocabulary learning through electronic glossing in hypertext environments (Chen & Yen, 2013; Lee & Lee, 2015) could be considered incidental. In contrast, in deliberate learning, learners' attentional resources are predominantly channeled toward target vocabulary, which may be presented in or out of sentential contexts. For example, vocabulary acquisition through a web-based learning system called Word Engine, which was introduced in McLean, Hogg, and Rush (2013), could be characterized as deliberate learning. It should be noted that, although some studies have described their technology-aided vocabulary learning as incidental, it is possible that some degree of deliberate learning may be involved, if some aspects of the target vocabulary activity (e.g. frequency of the target vocabulary, the availability of the vocabulary learning device) have effectively attracted the learner's attention. Also, the concepts of incidental and deliberate vocabulary learning should be seen as a continuum, rather than discrete categories.

Current Research and Practice

In this section, we will present a research-based introduction to technologies related to vocabulary teaching and learning, and discuss their roles and characteristics (see Appendix for the summary of the instruments and applications introduced in this section).

Online Tests of Vocabulary Size

The data on one's vocabulary size could be useful for several purposes. For example, it could serve as a valid gauge of one's performance in English classes or proficiency level (Laufer & Goldstein, 2004; Schmitt, 2010), and as a criterion against which teachers could choose a target reading text (Nation, 2006; Nation & Ming-tzu, 1999). As mentioned in the previous section, vocabulary size tests have typically been designed to measure form-meaning connections (as part of knowledge of meaning) (Nation, 2013), and some of these are accessible online. For example, Nation and Beglar's (2007) instrument called Vocabulary Size Test (www.wgtn.ac.nz/lals/resources/paul-nations-resources/vocabulary-tests), developed on the basis of the 14,000-word list extracted from the British National Corpus, is available at Compleat Lexical Tutor. In this test, ten words were sampled from each band of the fourteen 1,000-word sub-lists, which makes the entire test consist of a total of 140 testing items. This means that roughly one item would represent 100 known words. Regarding its format (i.e. a multiple choice test), some researchers (Stewart, 2014; Stewart & White, 2011) have suggested that multiple choice questions may result in an inflated estimation of about 17–25 percent compared to actual vocabulary knowledge; thus, teachers who use this test are advised to make a rather conservative interpretation of the test results.

For young language learners, the Picture Vocabulary Size Test (downloadable at www.laurenceanthony.net/software/pvst/), developed by Anthony and Nation (2017), could be used. The Picture Vocabulary Size Test, which consists of 96 items, can measure up to 6,000 words. Such a test is strong in its testing format, presenting the testing word orally and its multiple choice options as pictures, and could be conveniently employed for young learners who have not developed literacy in English.

Online Tests of Vocabulary Depth

While early studies (e.g. Goulden, Nation, & Read, 1990; Laufer, 1992; Meara & Jones, 1990; Nation, 1983) were primarily dedicated to the development of measures related to vocabulary size, later studies (e.g. Qian, 1999, 2002; Read, 1993, 1998; Schmitt, 2010; Yanagisawa & Webb, 2020) have aimed to develop measures for vocabulary depth. Some of these tests have been made available online, and we introduce three of these tests below.

The Word Associates Test (WAT) developed by Read (1993) (available at www.lextutor.ca/tests/wat/) has received a significant amount of attention as the measure of knowledge of a word's different senses and collocates. In this test, a test taker is given a series of stimulus words and asked to choose their collocates or semantically relevant words.

As another measure of depth, the Phrasal Vocabulary Size Test (PVST; www.lextutor.ca/tests/pvst/) developed by Martinez (2011) is based on the graded multi-word unit list of PHRASal Expressions List (PHRASE List), which contains the 505 most frequent non-transparent multi-word units in English. This test consists of five levels of sub-tests, with each sub-test being made from ten phrasal expressions from each band of the five 100 sub-lists, by considering its compatibility with single-word frequency lists from the British National Corpus. Thus, the first ten phrasal expressions on the first sub-test are as common as the top 1,000 words in English. It could provide a useful reference for recommending idiomatic expressions suitable for learners with a particular level of (single) word knowledge.

Finally, the Guessing from Context Test (GCT) is another test of depth (Sasao & Webb, 2018). This test has been developed based on guessing models proposed by previous studies (Bruton & Samuda, 1981; Williams, 1985), and consists of three sub-tests: (1) identifying the part of speech of an unknown word; (2) finding its discourse clue; and (3) guessing its meaning. Each sub-test contains twenty multiple choice questions. The Rasch model has been employed to validate this test, and the analysis reported in Sasao and Webb's (2018) study suggests that GCT scores can statistically differentiate four different levels associated with each sub-test.

Hypertext Glosses

Glossing has been one of the most extensively employed tools in research on reading, and has been valued for increasing the likelihood of incidental vocabulary learning and successfully enabling learners to tackle a target text including some unfamiliar vocabulary (Nation, 2013). In the pen-and-pencil contexts, the primary role of glossing has been to provide the receptive knowledge of meaning (in Nation's classification described above), which corresponds to the second stage (i.e. accessing the word meaning) in Ma's framework. In the pen-and-pencil contexts, glossing is usually placed at the side or bottom of the page.

In hypertext environments, unlike the traditional contexts in which all the glosses of the target words are printed and presented to the reader, a learner can have more control over glossing, by selecting glossed words to check their meanings. Glossing in hypertext environments (electronic glossing, henceforth) could be realized in two different formats, namely hyperlinks to the target item and tooltips by touching (Lee & Lee, 2013). In the hyperlinks format, the user clicks the glossed word in the text, which would then present glossary information on the monitor, similar to a click-on dictionary (Liu, Fan, & Paas, 2014), whereas in the tooltip format a learner could obtain the glossary information by moving the mouse cursor over the glossed word (without clicking it).

Modes of electronic glossing have been diverse: texts, audio, pictures, and videos (e.g. Akbulut, 2007; Al-Seghayer, 2001; Khezrlou, Ellis, & Sadeghi, 2017; Sakar & Erçetin, 2005). One of the advances related to electronic glossing (compared to its traditional counterpart) is that it has fewer space constraints, meaning that lexical information such as concordance lines could be presented through glossing in hypertext environments (e.g. Lee, Warschauer, & Lee, 2017). Such a characteristic of electronic glossing enables material developers and teachers to present various types of lexical information, which in turn may have the potential to contribute to vocabulary developments at later stages in Ma's framework (2017).

Several online resources equipped with electronic glossing are as follows. First, the English Listening Lesson Library Online (ELLLO; https://elllo.org/) provides an online streaming service with over 3,000 audio and video activities. This website also provides conversation scripts, and ready-made vocabulary and comprehension quizzes with audio glosses. However, it does not allow the users to directly annotate or create glosses on the text. Cobb's (2007) Hypertext (www.lextutor.ca/hyp/) is another relevant resource: When a user enters target text into a text box, the program generates new text, where words become clickable and linked to concordance samples from various corpora and the definition extracted from the online dictionary. In Text Helper (www.er-central.com/text-helper/), when the user pastes the target text into a text box and chooses one of the twenty different vocabulary levels, the program generates a list of electronic glosses for all the words beyond the selected vocabulary level. Finally, Lee and Lee (2013) provide sample HTML codes with which teachers can realize two types of glossing (i.e. hyperlinks and tooltips) with their own text materials.

Vocabulary Profiler

Vocabulary profile analysis has been employed for several purposes: to select materials suitable for target learner groups by analyzing vocabulary levels of the materials (e.g. Nation, 2006); to analyze learners' level of academic vocabulary in their writing (e.g. Morris & Cobb, 2004); and to develop graded readers (e.g. Anthony, 2014). In this section, we introduce two online programs that utilize vocabulary profile analysis.

On VocabProfiler (Morris & Cobb, 2004) at Compleat Lexical Tutor (www.lextutor.ca/vp/comp/), teachers can put target text into the text box, and choose an option among the given vocabulary lists. Then, the program presents the vocabulary profiles of the target text and highlights the words in different colors according to their vocabulary levels. By referring to this colored text, teachers could predict which words in the text may be beyond their learners' current level of English proficiency. The Online Graded Text Editor (www.er-central.com/ogte/) of Extensive Reading Central provides a similar function. It analyzes the text with the criteria of either vocabulary levels (e.g. General Service List, Academic Word List) or language proficiency levels (e.g. Common European Framework of Reference for Languages, Common European Framework of Reference Japan), and then highlights all the words beyond the target level. With this program, teachers could control the word level of the text by replacing difficult words with easier ones or may use the word list beyond the target level for deliberate vocabulary learning before introducing the text to their learners. In all, the vocabulary profile analysis would give teachers some concrete idea about the proportion of unfamiliar vocabulary in the target text for their learners as well as the likelihood of incidental vocabulary learning to occur, and whether they should equip the target text with attention-increasing devices (e.g. glossing) for such vocabulary.

Learning through a Vocabulary List

Schmitt (2008) highlights a need for deliberate vocabulary learning for L2 learners, proposing on the basis of the research evidence that "intentional vocabulary learning ... almost always leads to greater and faster gains, with a better chance of retention and of reaching productive levels of mastery" (p. 341). While incidental vocabulary learning does play an important role in vocabulary development, expanding one's vocabulary through deliberate learning in initial stages of language learning seems to be inevitable, as some amount of vocabulary knowledge would be a prerequisite for the incidental learning (e.g. guessing from context) to occur (Nation, 2013). The current and the next sections will introduce some of the technologies geared toward deliberate vocabulary learning.

One of the common approaches to deliberate vocabulary learning is to memorize a large number of words through a vocabulary list. Creating one's own word list is assumed to be effective, in view of the premises of the involvement load hypothesis (Hulstijn & Laufer, 2001), which proposes that vocabulary learning could be reinforced through learners' active engagement in the learning of target vocabulary.

List-Learn at Compleat Lexical Tutor (www.lextutor.ca/list_learn/) is an application to this end, built to enhance the efficiency of list-based vocabulary learning. In this application, when a user chooses one of the four vocabulary lists (i.e. General Service List, Academic Word List, Common European Framework of Reference for Languages, British National Corpus 20K, or the British National Corpus – Corpus of Contemporary American English 25K), the program provides various concordance samples related to the selected word. Among these examples, a user can choose an example sentence according to their proficiency level. Then, he or she can directly type in the first language (L1) meaning (equivalent) of the target word, and their own word list will be created accordingly.

Although most existing electronic dictionaries are already equipped with a function to create a user's own word list, the advantage of List-Learn lies in its feature where learners can select a sample sentence that suits their vocabulary level from a corpus.

Game-Based Vocabulary Learning Applications

The term "Gamification," which is defined as the "use of game design elements within non-game contexts" (Deterding et al., 2011, p. 1), emerged in the early 2000s, and the interest in this term has rapidly increased (Sailer et al., 2017) since then (see also Chapter 10). The elements of gamification include points, badges, leaderboards, meaningful stories, progress bars/progression charts, performance graphs, quests, levels, avatars, social elements (e.g. team-mate), and rewards (Sailer et al., 2017; Smith-Robbins, 2011). Gamification has also attracted some attention in the field of language learning (see Dehghanzadeh et al., 2021 for the systematic review of the studies on the use of gamification for ESL) as well as in the private education market, with the underlying assumption that the elements of gamification are expected to significantly boost learners' motivation to learn the target language. Thanks to the development and dissemination of mobile devices (e.g. smartphones, tablet PCs), several mobile applications using gamification have been released, with vocabulary having been targeted from the very early stages among app developers in the field of language learning (Godwin-Jones, 2010).

One example of game-based vocabulary learning applications is PHONE words developed by the Alice Education Studio, through which learners can engage in deliberate vocabulary learning (see Chen, Liu, & Huang, 2019 for an empirical study on this app). PHONE words includes three games for users, namely Tic-Tac-Toe, Tug-of-VOC, and Star VOC, in addition to the wordlist function. Tic-Tac-Toe is a game for two players, who fill in a 3-by-3 grid by answering vocabulary questions, while Tug-of-VOC is a fill-in-the-blank game, assessing the user's knowledge of word form (i.e. spelling). Star VOC is a game in which a user becomes the pilot of a spacecraft, and answers vocabulary-related questions. This application utilizes a competition ranking system, which is the element of gamification.

Duolingo (www.duolingo.com/learn) is another application that uses several elements of gamification such as points, level, leaderboard, and badges. The learning units in Duolingo are words and sentences, with various learning activities being provided in connection with four skills. The basic level is composed of vocabulary-centered learning, in which a user engages in the form-meaning matching of the basic vocabulary (e.g. man, woman, boy), topic-oriented vocabulary (e.g. food, animals), and frequently used idioms. Recent studies (e.g. Ajisoko, 2020; Loewen et al., 2019) have been conducted to verify the effectiveness of Duolingo for language learning.

Recommendations for Future Research

This section will present some recommendations for future research related to technology-aided vocabulary teaching and learning, with each relating to one of the three identified themes discussed in the Primary themes section.

Regarding the operationalization and measurement of vocabulary knowledge, development of the measure of implicit vocabulary knowledge is needed, as such a measure could enable us to delve into "learning at early stages of vocabulary development" (Elgort, 2018, p. 4). Most existing vocabulary instruments to date are explicit by nature, tapping into learners' conscious efforts to process their lexical knowledge; yet, these instruments may not be sensitive enough to measure the very initial stage of vocabulary learning. Although more implicit measures such as eye-tracking methods (Elgort et al., 2018) that could be used to this end have started to emerge, we are far from having standardized measures of implicit vocabulary knowledge, especially those that teachers could use without difficulty. It is expected that the development of a measure of implicit vocabulary knowledge would result in new revenue for vocabulary research and teaching based on technology.

Regarding the acquisition of vocabulary knowledge, the role of learners' L1 in L2 vocabulary acquisition needs to be further examined in the research on technology-aided vocabulary developments. The lack of more overt discussion on this issue appears to be partly due to a rather negative connotation attached to the term "L1" in the field (Cook, 2010). Still, learners' L1 has been proposed to play a critical role in L2 lexical processing and vocabulary acquisition, particularly in terms of establishing a new entry of the target lexical item, and connecting its form and meaning (Jiang, 2004; Lee & Lee, 2022; Lee & Levine, 2020; Ma, 2017). Thus, researchers are encouraged to examine more directly the role of learners' L1 in technology-aided vocabulary learning and its interaction with other important features of target technologies. As another recommendation regarding this theme, a vocabulary program through which learners can engage in most, if not all, stages of vocabulary acquisition should be developed, because most technologies related to vocabulary teaching and learning are designed for only a particular stage (e.g. obtaining the meaning of the target word) in vocabulary acquisition (Ma, 2014). A good example of such a technology would be "an intelligent system for vocabulary learning" introduced by Stockwell (2013), which not only presents new vocabulary through contexts along with hyperlinks to annotation, but also records each learner's clicking patterns of these hyperlinks, which can be used later to provide individualized vocabulary activities.

Finally, in view of a recent surge of interests in the employment of augmented and virtual reality (e.g. Chen & Hsu, 2020; Hsu, 2017), chatbot (e.g. Lee et al., 2020), and machine reading comprehension (e.g. Shin, Lee, & Lee, 2022) in language learning, researchers and teachers are encouraged to pay more attention to the effects of such cutting-edge technologies on vocabulary learning, with some consideration of how each fits in with different instructional approaches (i.e. incidental and deliberate). In addition, more attention is needed for the intentional vocabulary learning through technology, in view of the effectiveness of such learning as evidenced by the results of a recent meta-analysis (Webb, Yanagisawa, & Uchihara, 2020).

References

Ajisoko, P. (2020). The use of Duolingo apps to improve English vocabulary learning. *International Journal of Emerging Technologies in Learning*, 15(7), 149–155. https://doi.org/10.3991/ijet.v15i07.13229

Akbulut, Y. (2007). Effects of multimedia annotations on incidental vocabulary learning and reading comprehension of advanced learners of English as a foreign language. *Instructional Science, 35*(6), 499–517. https://doi.org/10.1007/s11251-007-9016-7

Al-Seghayer, K. (2001). The effect of multimedia annotation modes on L2 vocabulary acquisition: A comparative study. *Language Learning & Technology, 5*(1), 202–232. http://dx.doi.org/10125/25117

Anderson, R. C., & Freebody, P. (1981). Vocabulary knowledge. In J. T. Guthrie (Ed.), *Comprehension and teaching: Research reviews* (pp. 77–117). International Reading Association.

Anthony, L. (2014). *AntWordProfiler* (version 1.4.1) [Computer Software]. Waseda University. https://www.laurenceanthony.net/software/antwordprofiler/releases/AntWordProfiler140/AntWordProfiler.exe

Anthony, L., & Nation, I. S. P. (2017). *Picture vocabulary size test (Version 1.2.0)* [Computer Software]. Waseda University.

Beheydt, L. (1987). The semantization of vocabulary in foreign language learning. *System, 15*(1), 55–67. https://doi.org/10.1016/0346-251X(87)90048-0

Bruton, A., & Samuda, V. (1981). Guessing words. *Modern English Teacher, 8*(3), 18–21.

Chen, C. M., Liu, H., & Huang, H. B. (2019). Effects of a mobile game-based English vocabulary learning app on learners' perceptions and learning performance: A case study of Taiwanese EFL learners. *ReCALL, 31*(2), 170–188. https://doi.org/10.1017/S0958344018000228

Chen, I. J., & Yen, J. C. (2013). Hypertext annotation: Effects of presentation formats and learner proficiency on reading comprehension and vocabulary acquisition in foreign languages. *Computers & Education, 63*, 416–423. https://doi.org/10.1016/j.compedu.2013.01.005

Chen, Y. L., & Hsu, C. C. (2020). Self-regulated mobile game-based English learning in a virtual reality environment. *Computers & Education, 154*, 103910. https://doi.org/10.1016/j.compedu.2020.103910

Cobb, T. (2007). Computing the vocabulary demands of L2 reading. *Language Learning & Technology, 11*(3), 38–63. https://doi.org/10125/44117

Cook, G. (2010). *Translation in language teaching: An argument for reassessment.* Oxford University Press.

De Bot, K., Paribakht, T. S., & Wesche, M. B. (1997). Toward a lexical processing model for the study of second language vocabulary acquisition: Evidence from ESL reading. *Studies in Second Language Acquisition, 19*(3), 309–329. https://doi.org/10.1017/S0272263197003021

Dehghanzadeh, H., Fardanesh, H., Hatami, J., Talaee, E., & Noroozi, O. (2021). Using gamification to support learning English as a second language: A systematic review. *Computer Assisted Language Learning, 34*(7), 934–957. https://doi.org/10.1080/09588221.2019.1648298

Deterding, S., Dixon, D., Khaled, R., & Nacke, L. (2011). From game design elements to gamefulness: Defining "gamification." Paper presented at the 15th International Academic MindTrek Conference, Tampere. https://doi.org/10.1145/2181037.2181040

Elgort, I. (2018). Technology-mediated second language vocabulary development: A review of trends in research methodology. *CALICO Journal, 35*(1), 1–29. https://doi.org/10.1558/cj.34554

Elgort, I., Brysbaert, M., Stevens, M., & Van Assche, E. (2018). Contextual word learning during reading in a second language: An eye-movement study. *Studies in Second Language Acquisition, 40*(2), 341–366. https://doi.org/10.1017/S0272263117000109

Godwin-Jones, R. (2010). From memory palaces to spacing algorithms: Approaches to second-language vocabulary learning. *Language Learning & Technology, 14*(2), 4–11. http://dx.doi.org/10125/44208

Goulden, R., Nation, P., & Read, J. (1990). How large can a receptive vocabulary be? *Applied Linguistics, 11*(4), 341–363. https://doi.org/10.1093/applin/11.4.341

Henriksen, B. (1999). Three dimensions of vocabulary development. *Studies in Second Language Acquisition, 21*(2), 303–317. https://doi.org/10.1017/S0272263199002089

Hsu, T. C. (2017). Learning English with augmented reality: Do learning styles matter? *Computers & Education, 106*, 137–149. https://doi.org/10.1016/j.compedu.2016.12.007

Hulstijn, J. H. (2013). Incidental learning in second language acquisition. In C. A. Chapelle (Ed.), *The encyclopedia of applied linguistics* (Vol. 5, pp. 2632–2640). Wiley-Blackwell. https://doi.org/10.1002/9781405198431.wbeal0530

Hulstijn, J. H., & Laufer, B. (2001). Some empirical evidence for the involvement load hypothesis in vocabulary acquisition. *Language Learning, 51*(3), 539–558. https://doi.org/10.1111/0023-8333.00164

Jiang, N. (2004). Semantic transfer and its implications for vocabulary teaching in a second language. *The Modern Language Journal, 88*(3), 416–432. https://doi.org/10.1111/j.0026-7902.2004.00238.x

Khezrlou, S., Ellis, R., & Sadeghi, K. (2017). Effects of computer-assisted glosses on EFL learners' vocabulary acquisition and reading comprehension in three learning conditions. *System, 65*, 104–116. https://doi.org/10.1016/j.system.2017.01.009

Laufer, B. (1992). Reading in a foreign language: How does L2 lexical knowledge interact with the reader's general academic ability?. *Journal of Research in Reading, 15*, 95–103.

Laufer, B., & Goldstein, Z. (2004). Testing vocabulary knowledge: Size, strength, and computer adaptiveness. *Language Learning, 54*(3), 399–436. https://doi.org/10.1111/j.0023-8333.2004.00260.x

Lee, H., & Lee, J. H. (2013). Implementing glossing in mobile-assisted language learning environments: Directions and outlook. *Language Learning & Technology, 17*(3), 6–22. https://doi.org/10125/44334

Lee, H., & Lee, J. H. (2015). The effects of electronic glossing types on foreign language vocabulary learning: Different types of format and glossary information. *The Asia-Pacific Education Researcher, 24*(4), 591–601. http://doi.org/10.1007/s40299-014-0204-3

Lee, H., Warschauer, M., & Lee, J. H. (2017). The effects of concordance-based electronic glosses on L2 vocabulary learning. *Language Learning & Technology*, *21*(2), 32–51. https://doi.org/10125/44610

Lee, H., Warschauer, M., & Lee, J. H. (2019). The effects of corpus use on second language vocabulary learning: A multilevel meta-analysis. *Applied Linguistics*, *40* (5), 721–753. https://doi.org/10.1093/applin/amy012

Lee, J. H., & Lee, H. (2022). Teachers' verbal lexical explanation for second language vocabulary learning: A meta-analysis. *Language Learning*, *72*(2), 576–612. https://doi.org/10.1111/lang.12493

Lee, J. H., & Levine, G. S. (2020). The effects of instructor language choice on second language vocabulary learning and listening comprehension. *Language Teaching Research*, *24*(2), 250–272. https://doi.org/10.1177/1362168818770910

Lee, J. H., Yang, H., Shin, D. K., & Kim, H. (2020). Chatbots. *ELT Journal*, *74*(3), 338–344. https://doi.org/10.1093/elt/ccaa035

Lin, J. J., & Lin, H. (2019). Mobile-assisted ESL/EFL vocabulary learning: A systematic review and meta-analysis. *Computer Assisted Language Learning*, *32*(8), 878–919. https://doi.org/10.1080/09588221.2018.1541359

Liu, T. C., Fan, M. H. M., & Paas, F. (2014). Effects of digital dictionary format on incidental acquisition of spelling knowledge and cognitive load during second language learning: Click-on vs. key-in dictionaries. *Computers & Education*, *70*, 9–20. https://doi.org/10.1016/j.compedu.2013.08.001

Loewen, S., Crowther, D., Isbell, D. R., Kim, K. M., Maloney, J., Miller, Z. F., & Rawal, H. (2019). Mobile-assisted language learning: A Duolingo case study. *ReCALL*, *31*(3), 293–311. https://doi.org/10.1017/S0958344019000065

Ma, Q. (2014). A contextualised study of EFL learners' vocabulary learning approaches: Framework, learner type and degree of success. *The Journal of Asia TEFL*, *11*(3), 33–71.

Ma, Q. (2017). Technologies for teaching and learning L2 vocabulary. In C. A. Chapelle & S. Sauro (Eds.), *The handbook of technology and second language teaching and learning* (pp. 45–61). Wiley Blackwell.

Martinez, R. (2011). Phrasal vocabulary size test, BNC version (1-5k). https://www.lextutor.ca/tests/levels/recognition/phrasal

Martinez, R., & Schmitt, N. (2012). A phrasal expressions list. *Applied Linguistics*, *33*(3), 299–320. https://doi.org/10.1093/applin/ams010

McLean, S., Hogg, N., & Rush, T. W. (2013). Vocabulary learning through an online computerized flashcard site. *The JALT CALL Journal*, *9*(1), 79–98. https://doi.org/10.29140/jaltcall.v9n1.149

Meara, P. (1996). The dimensions of lexical competence. In G. Brown, K. Malmkjaer & J. Williams (Eds.), *Performance and competence in second language acquisition* (pp. 35–53). Cambridge University Press.

Meara, P., & Jones, G. (1990). *Eurocentres vocabulary size tests 10KA*. Eurocentres Learning Service.

Morris, L., & Cobb, T. (2004). Vocabulary profiles as predictors of the academic performance of teaching English as a second language trainees. *System*, *32*(1), 75–87. https://doi.org/10.1016/j.system.2003.05.001

Nation, P. (1983). Testing and teaching vocabulary. *Guidelines*, 5(1), 12–25.

Nation, P. (2006). How large a vocabulary is needed for reading and listening? *The Canadian Modern Language Review*, 63(1), 59–82. https://doi.org/10.3138/cmlr.63.1.59

Nation, I. S. P. (2013). *Learning vocabulary in another language* (2nd ed.). Cambridge University Press. https://doi.org/10.1017/CBO9781139524759

Nation, I. S. P., & Beglar, D. (2007). A vocabulary size test. *The Language Teacher*, 31(7), 9–13.

Nation, P., & Ming-tzu, K. (1999). Graded readers and vocabulary. *Reading in a Foreign Language*, 12(2), 355–380.

Qian, D. (1999). Assessing the roles of depth and breadth of vocabulary knowledge in reading comprehension. *The Canadian Modern Language Review*, 56(2), 282–308. https://doi.org/10.3138/cmlr.56.2.282

Qian, D. (2002). Investigating the relationship between vocabulary knowledge and academic reading performance: An assessment perspective. *Language Learning*, 52(3), 513–536. https://doi.org/10.1111/1467-9922.00193

Read, J. (1993). The development of a new measure of L2 vocabulary knowledge. *Language Testing*, 10(3), 355–371. https://doi.org/10.1177/026553229301000308

Read, J. (1998). Validating a test to measure depth of vocabulary knowledge. In A. J. Kunnan (Ed.), *Validation in language assessment* (pp. 41–60). Lawrence Erlbaum.

Read, J. (2004). Research in teaching vocabulary. *Annual Review of Applied Linguistics*, 24, 146–161. https://doi.org/10.1017/S0267190504000078

Sailer, M., Hense, J. U., Mayr, S. K., & Mandl, H. (2017). How gamification motivates: An experimental study of the effects of specific game design elements on psychological need satisfaction. *Computers in Human Behavior*, 69, 371–380. https://doi.org/10.1016/j.chb.2016.12.033

Sakar, A., & Erçetin, G. (2005). Effectiveness of hypermedia annotation for foreign language reading. *Journal of Computer Assisted Learning*, 21(1), 28–38. https://doi.org/10.1111/j.1365-2729.2005.00108.x

Sasao, Y., & Webb, S. (2018). The guessing from context test. *ITL International Journal of Applied Linguistics*, 169(1), 115–141. https://doi.org/10.1075/itl.00009.sas

Schmitt, N. (2008). Instructed second language vocabulary learning. *Language Teaching Research*, 12(3), 329–363. https://doi.org/10.1177/1362168808089921

Schmitt, N. (2010). *Researching vocabulary: A vocabulary research manual*. Palgrave Macmillan.

Schmitt, N. (2014). Size and depth of vocabulary knowledge: What the research shows. *Language Learning*, 64(4), 913–951. https://doi.org/10.1111/lang.12077

Shin, D., Lee, J. H., & Lee, Y. (2022). An exploratory study on the potential of machine reading comprehension as an instructional scaffolding device in second language reading lessons. *System*, 109, 102863. https://doi.org/10.1016/j.system.2022.102863

Shin, D., & Nation, I. S. P. (2008). Beyond single words: The most frequent collocations in spoken English. *ELT Journal*, 62(4), 339–348. https://doi.org/10.1093/elt/ccm091

Smith-Robbins, S. (2011). "This game sucks": How to improve the gamification of education. *Educause Review*, 46(1), 58–59.

Stewart, J. (2014). Do multiple-choice options inflate estimates of vocabulary size on the VST? *Language Assessment Quarterly, 11*(3), 271–282. https://doi.org/10.1080/15434303.2014.922977

Stewart, J., & White, D. A. (2011). Estimating guessing effects on the vocabulary levels test for differing degrees of word knowledge. *TESOL Quarterly, 45*(2), 370–380. https://doi.org/10.5054/tq.2011.254523

Stockwell, G. (2013). Investigating an intelligent system for vocabulary learning through reading. *The JALT CALL Journal, 9*(3), 259–274.

Vermeer, A. (2001). Breadth and depth of vocabulary in relation to L1/L2 acquisition and frequency of input. *Applied Psycholinguistics, 22*(2), 217–234. https://doi.org/10.1017/S0142716401002041

Webb, S., Yanagisawa, A., & Uchihara, T. (2020). How effective are intentional vocabulary-learning activities? A meta-analysis. *The Modern Language Journal, 104*(4), 715–738. https://doi.org/10.1111/modl.12671

Williams, R. (1985). Teaching vocabulary recognition strategies in ESP reading. *The ESP Journal, 4*(2), 121–131. https://doi.org/10.1016/0272-2380(85)90015-0

Yanagisawa, A., & Webb, S. (2020). Measuring depth of vocabulary knowledge. In S. Webb (Ed.) *The Routledge handbook of vocabulary studies* (pp. 371–386). Routledge.

Yun, J. (2011). The effects of hypertext glosses on L2 vocabulary acquisition: A meta-analysis. *Computer Assisted Language Learning, 24*(1), 39–58. https://doi.org/10.1080/09588221.2010.523285

Zimmerman, C. B. (1997). Historical trends in second language vocabulary instruction. In J. Coady & T. Huckin (Eds.), *Second language vocabulary acquisition* (pp. 5–19). Cambridge University Press.

Further Reading

Elgort, I. (2018). Technology-mediated second language vocabulary development: A review of trends in research methodology. *CALICO Journal, 35*(1), 1–29. https://doi.org/10.1558/cj.34554

This article provides a comprehensive summary of eighty-two primary studies on technology-aided L2 vocabulary learning since 2010. It offers systematic analyses of these studies in terms of instructional approaches, aspects of word knowledge, and measures of vocabulary development.

Schmitt, N. (2010). *Researching vocabulary: A vocabulary research manual.* Palgrave Macmillan.

This book provides an in-depth examination of the concepts and issues related to research on vocabulary. Part 4 covers a range of resources (e.g. vocabulary tests, corpora, concordances) that teachers can use in their vocabulary teaching.

Tom Cobb's Compleat Lexical Tutor (www.lextutor.ca).

This is one of the most useful websites, equipped with a wide range of programs built for vocabulary teaching and learning.

Appendix

Summary of the (Selected) Instruments and Applications on Vocabulary Teaching and Learning

Name	Use/purpose	Relevant work	URL
Duolingo	Game-based application for effective vocabulary learning	Ajisoko (2020); Loewen et al. (2019)	www.duolingo.com/learn
Hyperlink and tooltip glossing	To add two types of glossing to one's own text	Lee & Lee (2013)	http://dx.doi.org/10125/44334
Hypertext	To generate new text, where words become clickable and include glossary information	Cobb (2007)	www.lextutor.ca/hyp/
List-Learn	To create customized dictionaries, which are equipped with concordance samples related to the selected words	Cobb's Compleat Lexical Tutor	www.lextutor.ca/list_learn/
Phrasal Vocabulary Size Test	To measure one's knowledge of phrasal vocabulary	Martinez (2011)	www.lextutor.ca/tests/pvst/
Picture Vocabulary Size Test	To measure young learners' English vocabulary size	Anthony & Nation (2017)	www.laurenceanthony.net/software/pvst/
VocabProfiler	To calculate the percentages of different levels of vocabulary in the target text	Morris & Cobb (2004)	www.lextutor.ca/vp/comp/
Vocabulary Size Test	To measure vocabulary size	Nation & Beglar (2007)	www.wgtn.ac.nz/lals/resources/paul-nations-resources/vocabulary-tests
Word Associates Test	To measure knowledge of a word's different senses and collocates	Read (1993)	www.lextutor.ca/tests/wat

30

Grammar

S. Susan Marandi

Introduction

While few teachers today would question the importance of digital literacy, not all would welcome the challenges of teaching via technology, particularly in the case of foreign languages, where matters are further complicated by language being, at once, both the content to be taught and the means of teaching it. It doesn't help that different online venues often encourage different language styles and registers, and that even such simple choices as whether or how to use an emoji, meme, or e-breviation can change depending on the context and sometimes even the platform being used. Nevertheless, such choices are clearly decisions of discourse and, as such, fall within the realm of language teaching. More to the point, they have direct relevance to the current meaning-based discourse view of grammar as a tool to construct and express meaning and achieve communicative goals (Halliday & Matthiessen, 2004; Nassaji & Fotos, 2011). Pandemic or no pandemic, it is clear that learning how to communicate effectively online is increasingly becoming part and parcel of learning a language and its grammar; and it therefore seems logical to expect all language teachers to address this need, and to at least occasionally engage learners in online activities, if for no other reason than to enhance the authenticity and construct validity of communicative tasks.

At the same time, it is important to recognize that the role of technology should not overshadow that of pedagogy, and that any use of computer-assisted language learning (CALL) should be in line with language teaching principles and guided by them. Indeed, as the founders of the TPACK framework (Mishra, 2019; Mishra & Koehler, 2006) point out, even when a teacher has the required technological, content, and pedagogical knowledge (TK, CK, and PK, respectively), successful online teaching does not necessarily follow: The interactions among these types of knowledge (i.e. TPK, TCK, PCK, and TPACK) as well as contextual knowledge (XK) should also be part of teacher education. Obviously, this indicates that the manner of teaching grammar via technology will vary from context to context, and there are no one-size-fits-all solutions. Nevertheless, gaining a general understanding of the theoretical background of teaching grammar would appear to be a good starting point. Thus, this chapter will begin with some background knowledge about grammar teaching in general, and then will continue to discuss teaching grammar with technology.

Background

Perhaps no language skill or component has been subject to extreme views more than grammar, with language policymakers moving from the position of virtually equating language teaching to the teaching of grammar, to wholly abandoning it or even banning it from the classroom, to every possible position in between. And while people are still far from arriving at a common solution to the grammar problem, a major step toward consensus ensued from Long's (1991) prioritizing what he termed *focus on form* (FonF) over *focus on forms* (FonFs), the latter referring to the "traditional" obsession with decontextualized grammar divorced from communicative use, and the former referring to attention paid to linguistic form while the learner is attending to meaning and is engaged with an authentic communication problem. Long originally used FonF to refer to *incidental* attention to linguistic forms; however, later researchers broadened the definition to be more inclusive. Ellis, Basturkmen, and Loewen (2002), for example, clarify that FonF can be incidental or planned, reactive or pre-emptive, implicit or explicit, student-initiated or teacher-initiated.

Nassaji and Fotos (2011) elucidate how three different instructional perspectives on teaching grammar have historically existed, starting from the days when grammar was central and all classes and teaching methods gave prominence to linguistic accuracy, to the second phase when grammar almost became taboo and was largely avoided, unless implicitly and at the service of meaning, to present times when it is mostly believed that instruction should focus on both meaning *and* grammar. They further clarify that their own stance is that grammatical instruction should be one component among others in a learning environment that offers abundant opportunities for meaningful and form-focused learning, that form should be defined broadly, and that the class should offer a variety of opportunities for L2 input, output, interaction, and practice. Nassaji and Fotos (2011) go on to describe different ways of concentrating on grammar, which they believe should be complementary to each other, with due attention to the context and learner characteristics and needs. These methods of focusing on grammar might be input-based, such as through processing instruction, textual enhancement, or discourse; they could also be interaction- and output-based options, such as through interactional feedback, structured grammar-focused tasks, or collaborative output tasks. As their taxonomy forms the theoretical basis for the CALL-related grammar tasks discussed in this chapter, a brief explanation of each follows.

Input-based options give centrality to the role of input in the acquisition of language. The first, that is, *processing instruction* is based on ideas about how learners process input. It is suggested that due to limited attentional resources of the learner, they tend to prioritize forms which have more communicative value, using specific strategies to assign value to different parts of the text (VanPatten, 1996). Accordingly, it is suggested that providing processing instruction can enhance the efficacy of the input processing; this necessitates the teacher first recognizing the learners' faulty input processing strategies and then designing structured input activities aimed at changing these strategies. The usefulness of processing instruction has proven to be limited to certain linguistic forms (Nassaji & Fotos, 2011) and does not require language production.

Textual enhancement is another input-based option for focusing on grammar (Sharwood Smith, 1991). Using textual enhancement refers to making the input more noticeable in hopes of drawing the learner's attention to linguistic forms and increasing their uptake. In written input, this is usually achieved through italicizing, underlining, boldfacing, capitalizing, or color coding, whereas in oral input it is often attained through adding stress or using repetition, intonation, or even facial expressions, body movement, or gestures. Another method of input enhancement is the use of input flooding tasks that contain many instances of the target form. Textual enhancement is usually done without providing any further metalinguistic instruction and while keeping the learners focused on meaning using easily comprehensible texts requiring minimal attention. However, research suggests textual enhancement might be insufficient to bring about learning and that, to be most effective, it should also benefit from more explicit forms of enhancement, as well as corrective feedback (CF) (Nassaji & Fotos, 2011).

Yet another input-based option is to *focus on grammar through discourse.* This view doesn't merely equate grammar with syntax but sees it as the flexible use of language to achieve communicative goals within the larger discourse context. Discourse-level input, whether oral or written, is considered necessary in order to provide authenticity and to allow learners to learn about cohesion and coherence, as well as assisting them to acquire chunks of speech, formulaic utterances, and frequently occurring collocations.

Despite the usefulness of the above approaches, the shortcomings of the Input Hypothesis (Krashen, 1981, 1985) motivated some scholars to move beyond over-reliance on "comprehensible input." Long (1981, 1983), for example, pointed out the importance of *interaction* and the negotiation of meaning and form. Similarly, Swain (1985, 1993) argued that input is necessary but insufficient; she maintained that input involved semantic processing for comprehension purposes, whereas output brought about the syntactic processing required for production. These and similar views were influential in also bringing about interaction and output-based ways of dealing with grammar, as a complement to input-only methods.

One popular such method is the use of *interactional feedback*, a kind of reactive focus on form where the interlocuter negotiates meaning through the use of reformulations or elicitations, for example, recasts, clarification requests, repetition, metalinguistic feedback, direct elicitation, direct correction, and nonverbal feedback. Another is approaching grammar through *structured grammar-focused tasks*, often equated with *grammar consciousness-raising tasks*, in which the grammar point under question is presented, implicitly or explicitly, through student-initiated negotiated interaction instigated by complex activities, with the hope of developing declarative knowledge of grammar and increasing learner uptake. This is often achieved via an information gap which requires negotiation and agreeing upon a task solution, with adequate time for planning the language to be used. While the learners' attention is drawn to form, such tasks are still considered to be communicative, since the learners are engaged in meaning-focused interaction (Nassaji & Fotos, 2011). Some tasks that have such potential are: problem-solving tasks, information exchange tasks, and interpretation tasks. Learners are often required to generate the relevant language rule and to communicate directly about the language structure (Nassaji & Fotos, 2011). Finally, *collaborative output tasks* build upon Vygotskian ideas (Vygotsky, 1978, 1986) on the zone of proximal development (ZPD), scaffolding, and sociocultural theory, on the one hand, and Swain's output hypothesis (Swain, 1993) on the other. Swain believes that pushed output, that is, output which pushes learners beyond their existing proficiency level, can enhance acquisition through at least three functions: a noticing function, a hypothesis testing function, and a metalinguistic reflective function. Collaborative output tasks, such as dictogloss, collaborative jigsaws, and text reconstruction tasks are intended to bring about the collaborative production of language by the learners (Nassaji & Fotos, 2011). Obviously, many approaches to dealing with grammar include the use of more than one of the above methods, in tandem, depending on the context.

Primary Themes

Embarking on Technology-Enhanced Grammar Learning and Teaching

These days the internet and bourgeoning digital technologies are an almost inexhaustible source for language tasks and activities, and attempting to cover all of them here would be unrealistic. I will therefore limit the discussion to some of those that are more obviously in line with the theories established above, as well as being relatively easily accessible to all those who have an internet connection.

One of the more popular options for learning grammar via technology is the use of corpora. Reppen (2010) defines a corpus as "a large, principled collection of naturally occurring texts (written or spoken) stored electronically" (p. 2). These texts are analyzed using concordancing software to gain insight into how language is used (Figure 30.1).

Depending on the nature and size of the corpora, the results of corpus analyses are used as empirical evidence for a wide range of linguistic studies,

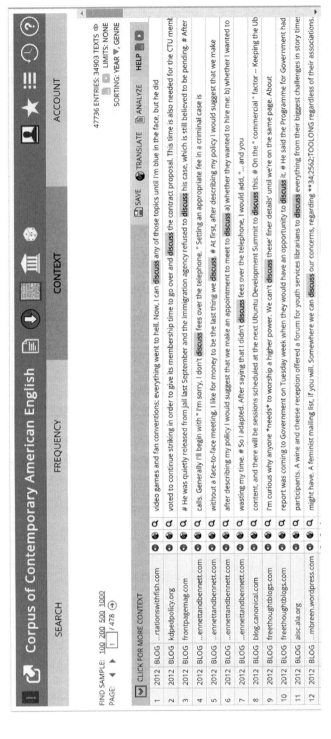

Figure 30.1 Sample corpus analysis search result (www.english-corpora.org/coca).

Activity 1: Below, you can see a list of sentences containing the words "tell" and "say." Read the examples carefully; then:

a. Explain how "tell" and "say" are used differently
b. Fill in the blanks in the text below, using either "tell" or "say." Be prepared to defend your choice.

Examples:

1 – I tried to think of something to **say** to her, but my mind went blank.

2 – He was tired of people **telling** him what to do.

3 – What would you **say** to going to the movies?

Figure 30.2 Sample activity developed on the basis of concordancing results.

such as providing descriptive grammars; comparing languages; enhancing dictionary entries; analyzing the characteristics of various genres; investigating the changes of language over time; and generally extracting vocabulary frequency lists, word families, collocations, colligations, cohesive and metalinguistic devices, connotations, register, stylistic rules, word usage subtleties, and more. All this has made corpus analysis an increasingly popular tool for language instruction, whether indirectly in the form of creating corpus-based materials and language tasks (Figures 30.2), or even through the direct involvement of learners with the actual corpora (Aijmer, 2009; Jones & Waller, 2015; Reppen, 2010; Sinclair, 2004), particularly since many open-access corpora and corpus analysis tools can now be found online. Learners are encouraged to use an inductive, discovery-based approach to learning language rules, referred to as data-driven learning (DDL) (Johns, 1991). This obviously fits in well with Nassaji and Fotos' (2011) suggestion regarding focusing on grammar through discourse and can also be considered a type of input enhancement as well as input flooding.

Despite the undeniable potential of corpora for language learning, they are largely recognized for their ability to accommodate an input-based approach. In addition, many learners or even teachers can find corpora a bit confusing and difficult to use at first. Collaborative online writing platforms, on the other hand, are usually fairly straightforward and are mastered with very little practice, and inspire an interaction- and output-based approach to teaching grammar. Platforms such as Google Docs, Zoho Writer, Etherpad, Dropbox Paper, PBworks, and MediaWiki allow learners to collaborate together on a written text via the internet, often free of charge. Some function more like online collaborative word processors, allowing for real-time collaboration on documents before they are published or shared with the wider public; these usually allow for WYSIWYG – that is, *What You See Is What You Get* – editing, as well as autosaving and exporting. Others are wiki platforms allowing for the creation of collaborative websites to which all community members can make changes, the most familiar example being Wikipedia. These venues usually include the possibility of tracking changes and displaying the page history for members, thus allowing teachers to identify the individual contributions of each student. This also enables reverting to a previous version if necessary, lessening the burden on a student if they make a mistake. Wikis are perfect for encouraging online written group projects, such as creating an online book review club; sharing experiences and exchanges with other cultures; multi-authoring stories, wikibooks, class glossaries or encyclopedias; or documenting field trips. Such activities are fully in line with Nassaji and Fotos's (2011) focus on grammar through collaborative output tasks and have the additional bonus of increasing learners' digital literacy, motivation and, if well designed, their critical thinking. The fact that such platforms allow for commenting and peer feedback also enables the teaching of grammar through interactional feedback, and since most offer a variety of text formatting and input enhancement possibilities, they are also suitable for learning grammar through textual enhancement. And, of course, they undeniably focus on grammar through discourse, as well.

While some scholars advocate the idea that there is one grammar underlying both *spoken* and *written* language and that it is the context rather than the mode that differs (e.g. Leech, 2000), others have contended that the two are very different (e.g. Carter & McCarthy, 1995) and thus need to be addressed separately in a balanced manner. While many current popular online tools appear to favor written grammar, podcasts usually favor spoken grammar, especially those that contain spontaneous speech instead of merely verbalizing written texts. Depending on how they are used, podcasts can cater to an input-based focus on spoken grammar, or lead to an interaction- and output-based approach; for example, the class can benefit from existing podcasts as a source of input of spoken language and can create their own podcast as a source of pushed output and interaction. The former can also be used as a source for flipped learning, with the learners receiving education about grammar rules before class; on the other hand, the latter can also enable the learners to create their own grammar guides or articulate their reflections on grammatical points or, in fact, any other aspect of their learning.

It bears noting, at this point, that despite all that has been said about the differences between written and spoken grammars, it could be argued that the emergence of Web 2.0 and social media has often blurred the lines between the two, since there is indubitably more fluidity and flexibility in this regard than before (Tagg, 2015). In fact, the emergence of more "conversational" forms of writing due to the influence of internet communications has long been noted by researchers (Gains, 1999; Gimenez, 2000). This does not always mean, however, that things have become less complicated for the learner; if anything, there often appear to be even more language choices for the learner to make. This is further complicated by the fact that on the internet one may often be exposed to a very multicultural community, with different ideas about acceptable norms and forms. Helping learners recognize and successfully navigate among the different norms, affordances, and limitations of the various venues should be considered an indispensable element of both language and digital literacy education. For this reason, a principled engaging in the use of social media in accordance with language pedagogy can often be invaluable for demonstrating how language norms shift from one context to another, and can better elucidate the dynamics of language. For example, microblogging platforms such as X (formerly Twitter) demand brevity; and blogs often encourage more personal, journal writing styles in comparison with many other forms of writing. Educating learners to recognize such (occasionally subtle) distinctions between the ways language is used within different forms of computer-mediated communication (CMC) by engaging with these platforms is the embodiment of focus on form in its current broad sense and is in line with a discourse-based grammar teaching method. Another merit of social media is that they are popular and relatively easy to use and can usually be managed even by people who aren't very tech savvy. However, it is important that the tasks have clearly predefined pedagogical goals, and that the learners' performance is benchmarked against the achievement of these goals.

Last but not least, although applying generative artificial intelligence (AI) in language classes has not yet become routine, as of this writing, it is swiftly gaining wider currency, particularly with the advent of the wildly popular chatbot, ChatGPT, and an exponentially increasing number of free and premium alternatives. Again, the approach to grammar can vary depending on how the tool is used: One can quite easily use it with an input-based focus, for example, employing prompts that will produce examples and exercises, or those that will facilitate input flooding tasks through generating texts that make extensive use of a particular grammar form, or one can use it merely to provide comprehensible explanations or translations for grammar rules (Peachey, 2023; Shemesh, 2023). It is also possible to employ it to support interaction- and output-based approaches to grammar; for example, through providing corrective feedback, or pushing output. It is important to bear in mind, however, that AI tools are still surrounded by a multitude of ethical and pedagogical concerns (Peters et al., 2023), and we should thus exercise careful judgement in using them.

Current Research and Practice

Although CALL studies are extremely varied, certain types of technology-enhanced grammar teaching methods are undeniably more popular than others, and the approaches mentioned by Nassaji and Fotos (2011) do not all make an equal appearance in the literature. Below are a handful of examples, and while they are by no means exhaustive, they are probably largely representative of the field in recent years.

A substantial part of recent research on technology-enhanced grammar teaching focuses on the provision of CF, often automated. For example, Bodnar et al. (2017) employed automatic speech recognition (ASR) to investigate learners' oral grammar and provide immediate CF. They were unable to find a significant difference between either the performance or the affective experiences of the no-feedback group and the group benefiting from immediate feedback via ASR. In another study, Gao and Ma (2019) investigated the use of computer-automated metalinguistic corrective feedback for writing tasks, in order to see whether the learning transferred from drills to subsequent writing tasks. While the two feedback groups (i.e. metalinguistic feedback vs. metalinguistic feedback with corrections) did improve more on the error correction post-test than the no-feedback and control groups, there was no statistical difference among the performances of the four groups on subsequent writing tasks. In a third study, Ranalli (2018) also explored automated written CF and reported that specific feedback leads to more successful corrections, a lower perception of mental-effort expenditure, and higher ratings of clarity and helpfulness in comparison with generic feedback. And in a study focused on dynamic assessment, Ai (2017) provided learners of Chinese with *graduated* CF via an intelligent computer-assisted language learning (ICALL) system, with the intention of scaffolding the learners and enhancing their potential. While the intelligent system occasionally misidentified errors, it was overall found to be effective and useful in mediating participants' learning, encouraging them to self-identify and self-correct their grammatical mistakes, particularly when the CF became more specific.

Using a different approach, Reynolds and Kao (2019) compared three groups on their use of definite and indefinite English articles when writing letters of application. All three groups received just-in-time focused CF on their misuse of articles; however, the two comparison groups received additional instruction (teacher instruction vs. digital game-based instruction) before being given the opportunity to correct their writing. Perhaps unsurprisingly, the control group obtained the least impressive results. Somewhat oddly, though, whereas only the first comparison group (i.e. the group that also received teacher instruction) significantly outperformed the control group on the *immediate* post-test, *both* comparison groups significantly outperformed the control group on the *delayed* post-test.

Kılıçkaya (2019) also explored online written CF, noting the importance of feedback timing, and observing that immediate feedback was found to be more efficient than delayed feedback. He also compared the different types of CF and found that metalinguistic and concordance feedback were preferred over recasts and direct and indirect feedback. And in yet another study on CF, Wach, Zhang, and Nichols-Besel (2021) examined the instruction techniques applied by native pre-service teachers of English when engaging in grammar instruction of nonnative pre-service teachers via multinational telecollaboration through email exchanges. The results indicate that implicit, cooperative instructions were preferred to explicit CF, leading to a high volume of uptake, as well as positive perceptions among the stakeholders.

Another popular way of addressing grammar has been by incorporating a mixture of interactive feedback and collaborative output tasks via the use of online collaborative writing platforms. Hsu and Lo (2018), for example, wrote about the potential of wikis for L2 collaborative writing. They maintain that wikis foster social-constructive learning, collaborative scaffolding, and the co-construction of knowledge, and provide learners with more opportunity to focus on form. In their study, they compare the learning of a wiki collaborative writing group with that of an individual writing group over a nine-week period. The results for linguistic complexity and quality of organization were not significant; however, the content quality and linguistic accuracy of the group benefiting from wikis had increased significantly more than the individual writing group. In a somewhat similar study, Bikowski and Vithanage (2016) investigated whether web-based collaborative writing vs. individual writing have different impacts on individual writing development. The results of their research indicate that those in the collaborative group statistically outperformed those in the individual group; it was also observed that positive attitudes existed with regard to the collaborative writing experience. Yang (2018) investigated how web-based collaborative writing can lead to indirect feedback, which fosters negotiation of meaning and brings about the construction of new language knowledge. This collaboration was particularly effective in actuating more writing progress in less proficient learners. And Abrams (2019) explored the relationship between patterns of collaboration and the linguistic features of written texts collaboratively produced by learners using Google Docs. She notes that the more collaborative and equal the groups were, the more the amount of engagement, leading in turn to longer and richer texts and better coherence – in other words, impacting meaning-making. However, the formal features of the texts, such as grammatical/lexical accuracy, syntactic complexity, and lexical richness were, perhaps surprisingly, not impacted in her study.

In Crosthwaite (2017), CF is interestingly combined with discourse-based grammar teaching. English learners were instructed in the use of corpora and DDL, then required to submit their original writing texts to the instructor, who would highlight their mistakes and return their writing. The learners would then make corrections, either using corpus analysis or not, and would highlight the corrections accordingly. This was done as part of an effort to identify which error types the learners would correct using or not using concordancing, whether or not the corrections were appropriate, and whether teacher feedback had any impact. Crosthwaite suggests that DDL might be more useful for vocabulary than grammar learning.

Studies engaging in DDL via concordancing often lead effortlessly to a combination of discourse-based grammar and grammar consciousness-raising tasks. Li (2017), for example, compared the use of verb–preposition collocations in the academic writing of two groups of advanced Chinese EFL learners, one engaged in a deductive method of learning lexico-grammatical constructions, and the other exposed to inductive DDL in the form of directly searching corpora (i.e. BNC and COCA). While both groups improved on their post-test and delayed post-test, the experimental group learning via DDL outperformed the control group on both post-tests, with a very large effect size. In another study concerned with DDL, Han and Shin (2017) looked at the impact of using the World Wide Web as a corpus and Google as the concordance for Korean learners of English who were trained in DDL regarding the use of articles, collocations, and paraphrasing. The results showed a striking improvement in relation to article use, but not collocations or paraphrasing, a result attributed partly to insufficient grammar and vocabulary knowledge. It was also noted that the learners were generally satisfied with the Google training, and in fact preferred consulting Google to consulting their bilingual dictionary when working on productive tasks. However, it was recommended that teachers provide detailed guidance and individualized feedback to maximize learning outcomes. Moon and Oh (2018) also used DDL with Korean learners of English; interestingly, however, they were concerned not with learning but *un*learning; more specifically, they attempted to help Korean learners to lower their ratio of overgeneralized use of *be*. In order to do so, they had the experimental group compare *learner* corpora with native English, utilizing the negative evidence from learner corpora to increase their grammar consciousness, as well as their motivation (as indicated by an open-ended survey). The DDL group statistically outperformed the control group on both the post-test and delayed post-test, indicating better (un)learning as well as better retention. Also, the vast majority of the members of the DDL group were satisfied with the new method, particularly students at lower proficiency levels.

In recent years, machine translation (MT) has also been increasingly used for grammar consciousness-raising. For example, Lee (2020) reports on the use of MT to improve EFL learners' writing. She had students first translate their own writing into the target language, then translate it with the help of MT, and then use the MT translation to compare the two and correct their L2 writing. Her study indicated that MT, if used correctly, can lead to a decrease in lexico-grammatical errors and to more positive attitudes, while, in addition, positively impacting students' writing strategies. In a somewhat similar study, Tsai (2020) explored the use of Google Translate for improving the writing of Chinese learners of English. Once again, the learners wrote their essays in both languages, then used Google Translate to translate their original Chinese text into English, then compared the two and corrected their L2 writing. Somewhat similarly to Lee (2020), Tsai (2020) found that using Google Translate led to better writing, that is, enriched content, more advanced vocabulary, and fewer grammatical and spelling mistakes.

Grammar consciousness-raising tasks are well suited to a variety of technologies. In a mobile assisted language learning (MALL) study, Hedjazi Moghari, and Marandi (2017) investigated the impact of texting grammar exercises to learners via short message service (SMS), using the school text message panel to send grammar exercises daily (on weekdays) over a span of twelve weeks. After sending their responses, the learners would automatically receive the correct response via another text message. The results indicated that the experimental group significantly outperformed those who practiced grammar via paper and pencil, although the effect size was relatively small. The majority of stakeholders were highly satisfied with the intervention and found it both useful and motivating for the students. Finally, Lan et al. (2016) compared the effect of information-gap vs. reasoning-gap tasks in Second Life (a virtual world where users interact via avatars) on the oral communicative accuracy and motivation of beginner learners of Chinese. The results indicated that using a task-based approach in Second Life benefited the oral communicative accuracy and motivation of both groups; however, the group with reasoning-gap tasks benefited more.

Recommendations for Research and Practice

While the recent pandemic has brought about an abrupt and previously inconceivable increase in online teaching and learning experiences, these have often been more worthy of the label emergency remote teaching (ERT), a term coined to indicate a provisional shift to an online mode during crisis times, where the focus is on an immediate and temporary solution and not building up the necessary learning infrastructure or ecosystem (Hodges et al., 2020). This can gradually build false confidence in teachers becoming accustomed to teaching online and lead to inappropriate online practices becoming normalized. For this reason, it is important that we encourage a critical approach toward CALL, including grammar teaching. It is important that our research and practice are firmly grounded in credible language acquisition pedagogy. Furthermore, frameworks such as TPACK (Mishra, 2019; Mishra & Koehler, 2006) can help ensure that sufficient attention is being paid to the different types of knowledge necessary for successful online teaching.

The SAMR framework has also been proposed as a simple yet effective way of evaluating how technology has been incorporated into teaching (Puentedura, 2006, 2013). This framework can be regarded as a spectrum and comprises four steps: The bottom step is substitution; the next is augmentation; then modification; and the top step is redefinition. Substitution means using technology to merely replace traditional tools, but without changing the function; augmentation is when the technology is used as a substitute, but the function is also enhanced. Modification and redefinition allow for task transformation: Modification refers to when the technology allows for major changes in the task, and redefinition signifies the use of technologies that permit the creation of new tasks that were previously impossible. For example, flipped learning is only possible due to the application of recent technologies allowing us to offer online grammar lessons outside the classroom, thus freeing valuable classroom time for hands-on practice and authentic interaction and negotiation.

Having a critical view toward CALL would entail recognizing the shortcomings and disadvantages of e-learning in general and CALL in particular.

> United States export control regulations prohibit U.S. businesses, such as ████████, from offering services to users in specific sanctioned regions. In order to comply with these regulations, ████████ does not allow users in certain countries or regions to access all of certain parts of our site, including certain degree program content. These countries or regions may include Iran, Sudan, Crimea, Cuba, Syria, North Korea, and are subject to change depending on U.S. export control regulations. More information about the sanctions programs administered by the Office of Foreign Assets Control (OFAC) of the US Department of the Treasury is available at https://www.treasury.gov/resource-center/sanctions/pages/default.aspx.

Figure 30.3 Example of sociopolitical hegemonies of e-learning; website name purposely withheld.

A relevant issue which is often disregarded is that of CALL hegemonies; that is, linguistic, technological, economic, educational, cultural, sociopolitical hegemonies (Marandi, 2017, 2023; Marandi, Karimi Alavijeh, & Nami, 2015). As an illustration, technological hegemonies exist when the technologies employed are not compatible with certain learner styles, strategies or intelligences, or are better equipped to deal with certain skills and subskills but not others, or are not equally equipped to serve people with special physical or educational needs. On the other hand, limitations such as that exemplified in Figure 30.3, where the user is excluded based on geographical location and political differences among countries can be classified as sociopolitical hegemonies. Such issues can be decisive in choosing which technologies to use in a given context, but unfortunately do not usually receive much attention. Research on how such hegemonies can affect the learning and teaching of grammar – or indeed, language in general – is effectively nonexistent.

Finally, it is erroneous to assume that learners have sufficient digital literacy to begin with; so regardless of which language skill or component is being addressed, it is important that the teacher ensures that all the learners have sufficient access to help whenever necessary; also, that they have sufficient awareness of matters such as online safety and privacy; copyrighted online materials and plagiarism; and identifying reliable, authentic online sources.

Future Directions

Following the amplified importance of e-learning and CALL during the pandemic, and considering the fact that newer, more advanced technologies are making an appearance almost daily, it is natural to expect that technology-enhanced grammar teaching and learning will also experience major changes in the future. Some technologies that are currently cutting-edge and exclusive will gradually become commercialized and mainstream, naturally leading to an increase in their use. Developments in current technologies such as mobile technologies, extended reality (XR) and wearable technologies, the internet of things (IoT), learning analytics, games and gamification, gesture and voice recognition technologies, and the various forms of AI (including but not limited to ChatGPT) have the potential to reconceptualize education. While it is not yet clear what implications each of these will have for the future of grammar teaching, it is conceivable that they will increase the potential for more authentic communication. However, at the end of the day, it is not the technologies themselves that will determine how well we teach grammar but, as always, the way we use them.

References

Abrams, Zs. I. (2019). Collaborative writing and text quality in Google Docs. *Language Learning & Technology*, 23(2), 22–42. https://doi.org/10125/44681

Ai, H. (2017). Providing graduated corrective feedback in an intelligent computer-assisted language learning environment. *ReCALL*, 29(3), 313–334. https://doi.org/10.1017/S095834401700012X

Aijmer, K. (Ed.). (2009). *Corpora and language teaching*. John Benjamins.

Bikowski, D., & Vithanage, R. (2016). Effects of web-based collaborative writing on individual L2 writing development. *Language Learning & Technology*, 20(1), 79–99. http://dx.doi.org/10125/44447

Bodnar, S., Cucchiarini, C., de Vries, B. P., Strik, H., & van Hout, R. (2017). Learner affect in computerised L2 oral grammar practice with corrective feedback. *Computer Assisted Language Learning*, 30(3), 223–246. https://doi.org/10.1080/09588221.2017.1302964

Carter, R., & McCarthy, M. (1995). Grammar and the spoken language. *Applied Linguistics*, 16(2), 141–158. https://doi.org/10.1093/applin/16.2.141

Crosthwaite, P. (2017). Retesting the limits of data-driven learning: Feedback and error correction. *Computer Assisted Language Learning*, 30(6), 447–473. https://doi.org/10.1080/09588221.2017.1312462

Ellis, R., Basturkmen, H., & Loewen, S. (2002). Doing focus-on-form. *System, 30*(4), 419–432. https://doi.org/10.1016/S0346-251X(02)00047-7

Gains, J. (1999). Electronic mail: A new style of communication or just a new medium? An investigation into the text features of e-mail. *English for Specific Purposes, 18*, 81–101. https://doi.org/10.1016/S0889-4906(97)00051-3

Gao, J., & Ma, S. (2019). The effect of two forms of computer-automated metalinguistic corrective feedback. *Language Learning & Technology*, 23(2), 65–83. https://doi.org/10125/44683

Gimenez, J. C. (2000). Business e-mail communication: Some emerging tendencies in register. *English for Specific Purposes, 19*, 237–251. https://doi.org/10.1016/S0889-4906(98)00030-1

Halliday, M., & Matthiessen, C. (2004). *An introduction to functional grammar* (3rd ed.). Hodder Arnold.

Han, S., & Shin, J.-A. (2017). Teaching Google search techniques in an L2 academic writing context. *Language Learning & Technology*, *21*(3), 172–194. http://llt.msu.edu/issues/october2017/hanshin.pdf

Hedjazi Moghari, M., & Marandi, S. (2017). Triumph through texting: Restoring learners' interest in grammar. *ReCALL*, *29*(3), 357–372. https://doi.org/10.1017/S0958344017000167

Hodges, C., Moore, S., Lockee, B., Trust, T., & Bond, A. (2020). The difference between emergency remote teaching and online learning. *Educause Review*, *27*, 1–15. https://er.educause.edu/articles/2020/3/the-difference-between-emergency-remote-teaching-and-online-learning

Hsu, H.-C., & Lo, Y.-F. (2018). Using wiki-mediated collaboration to foster L2 writing performance. *Language Learning & Technology*, *22*(3), 103–123. https://doi.org/10125/44659

Johns, T. (1991). Should you be persuaded: Two examples of data-driven learning materials. *English Language Research Journal*, *4*, 1–16. https://moodle.ils.uw.edu.pl/pluginfile.php/10011/mod_resource/content/2/Tim%20Johns%20and%20DDL.pdf

Jones, C., & Waller, D. (2015). *Corpus linguistics for grammar: A guide for research*. Routledge.

Kılıçkaya, F. (2019). Pre-service language teachers' online written corrective feedback preferences and timing of feedback in computer-supported L2 grammar instruction. *Computer Assisted Language Learning*, *35*(1–2), 62–87. https://doi.org/10.1080/09588221.2019.1668811

Krashen, S. (1981). *Second language acquisition and second language learning*. Oxford University Press.

Krashen, S. (1985). *The input hypothesis: Issues and implications*. Pergamon Press.

Lan, Y.-J., Kan, Y.-H., Sung, Y.-T., & Chang, K.-E. (2016). Oral-performance language tasks for CSL beginners in Second Life. *Language Learning & Technology*, *20*(3), 60–79. http://llt.msu.edu/issues/october2016/lanetal.pdf

Lee, S.-M. (2020). The impact of using machine translation on EFL students' writing. *Computer Assisted Language Learning*, *33*(3), 157–175. https://doi.org/10.1080/09588221.2018.1553186

Leech, G. (2000). Grammars of spoken English: New outcomes of corpus-oriented research. *Language Learning*, *50*(4), 675–724.

Li, S. (2017). Using corpora to develop learners' collocational competence. *Language Learning & Technology*, *21*(3), 153–171.

Long, M. H. (1981). Input, interaction, and second language acquisition. In H. Winitz (Ed.), *Native language and foreign language acquisition* (pp. 259–278). Annals of the New York Academy of Sciences 379.

Long, M. H. (1983). Native speaker/non-native speaker conversation and the negotiation of comprehensible input. *Applied Linguistics*, *4*, 126–141. https://doi.org/10.1093/applin/4.2.126

Long, M. H. (1991). Focus on form: A design feature in language teaching methodology. In K. de Bot, R. Ginsberg, & C. Kramsch (Eds.), *Foreign language research in cross-cultural perspective* (pp. 39–52). John Benjamins.

Marandi, S. S. (2017). Virtual walls and bans: E-learning/CALL hegemonies in the Iranian context. In J. Colpaert, A. Aerts, R. Kern, & M. Kaiser (Eds.), *CALL in Context: Proceedings of the XVIIIth International CALL Conference, UC Berkeley, California* (pp. 488–495). University of Antwerp.

Marandi, S. S. (2023). Virtual supremacy and electronic imperialism: the hegemonies of e-learning and Computer Assisted Language Learning (CALL). Learning, Media and Technology, 49(4), 527–543. https://doi.org/10.1080/17439884.2023.2207832

Mishra, P. (2019). Considering contextual knowledge: The TPACK diagram gets an upgrade. *Journal of Digital Learning in Teacher Education*, 35(2), 76–78. https://doi.org/10.1080/21532974.2019.1588611

Mishra, P., & Koehler, M. J. (2006). Technological pedagogical content knowledge: A framework for teacher knowledge. *Teacher College Record*, 108(6), 1017–1054. https://doi.org/10.1111/j.1467-9620.2006.00684.x

Moon, S., & Oh, S. (2018). Unlearning overgenerated be through data-driven learning in the secondary EFL classroom. *ReCALL*, 30(1), 48–67. https://doi.org/10.1017/S0958344017000246

Nassaji, H., & Fotos, S. (2011). *Teaching grammar in second language classrooms: Integrating form-focused instruction in communicative context*. Routledge.

Peachey, N. (2023). *ChatGPT in the language classroom*. Peachey Publications.

Peters, M. A., Jackson, L., Papastephanou, M., Jandrić, P., Lazaroiu, G., Evers, C. W. et al. (2023). AI and the future of humanity: ChatGPT-4, philosophy and education – Critical responses. *Educational Philosophy and Theory*, 56(9), 828–862. https://doi.org/10.1080/00131857.2023.2213437

Puentedura, R. R. (2006, November 28). Transformation, technology, and education in the state of Maine [Web log post]. www.hippasus.com/rrpweblog/archives/2006_11.html

Puentedura, R. R. (2013, May 29). SAMR: Moving from enhancement to transformation [Web log post]. www.hippasus.com/rrpweblog/archives/000095.html

Ranalli, J. (2018). Automated written corrective feedback: How well can students make use of it? *Computer Assisted Language Learning*, 31(7), 653–674. https://doi.org/10.1080/09588221.2018.1428994

Reppen, R. (2010). *Using corpora in the language classroom*. Cambridge University Press.

Reynolds, B. L., & Kao, C.-W. (2019). The effects of digital game-based instruction, teacher instruction, and direct focused written corrective feedback on the grammatical accuracy of English articles. *Computer Assisted Language Learning*, 34(4), 462–482. https://doi.org/10.1080/09588221.2019.1617747

Sharwood Smith, M. (1991). Speaking to many minds: On the relevance of different types of language information for the L2 learner. *Second Language Research*, 72, 118–132. https://doi.org/10.1177%2F026765839100700204

Shemesh, H. (2023, January 24). The ultimate guide for using ChatGPT for English learning. *The Accent's Way*, 289. https://hadarshemesh.com/magazine/chatgpt-for-learning-english

Sinclair, J. M. (2004). *How to use corpora in language teaching*. John Benjamins.

Swain, M. (1985). Communicative competence: Some rules of comprehensible input and comprehensible output in its development. In S. Gass, & C. Madden (Eds.), *Input in second language acquisition* (pp. 235–253). Newbury House.

Swain, M. (1993). The output hypothesis: Just speaking and writing aren't enough. *Canadian Modern Language Review, 50,* 158–164. https://doi.org/10.3138/cmlr .50.1.158

Tagg, C. (2015). *Exploring digital communication: Language in action.* Routledge.

Tsai, S.-C. (2020). Chinese students' perceptions of using Google Translate as a translingual CALL tool in EFL writing. *Computer Assisted Language Learning, 35*(5–6), 1250–1272. https://doi.org/10.1080/09588221.2020.1799412

VanPatten, B. (1996). *Input processing and grammar instruction in second language acquisition.* Ablex.

Vygotsky, L. S. (1978). *Mind in society: The development of higher psychological processes.* Harvard University Press.

Vygotsky, L. S. (1986). *Thought and language.* MIT Press.

Wach, A., Zhang, D., & Nichols-Besel, K. (2021). Grammar instruction through multinational telecollaboration for pre-service teachers. *ReCALL, 34*(1), 4–20. https://doi.org/10.1017/S0958344021000112

Yang, Y.-F. (2018). New language knowledge construction through indirect feedback in web-based collaborative writing. *Computer Assisted Language Learning, 31*(4), 459–480. https://doi.org/10.1080/09588221.2017.1414852

Further Reading

Heift, T., & Vyatkina, N. (2017). Technologies for teaching and learning L2 grammar. In C. A. Chapelle & S. Sauro (Eds.), *The handbook of technology and second language teaching and learning* (pp. 26–44). Wiley Blackwell. https:// doi.org/10.1002/9781118914069.ch3
In this book chapter, Heift and Vyatkina explore four technology-based pedagogies for teaching and learning grammar: tutorial CALL, ICALL, DDL, and CMC. The authors provide an overview of the historical framework and offer practical guidelines for integrating technology into L2 grammar classrooms. The chapter presents a comprehensive examination of technology's role in L2 grammar teaching and learning, providing educators with valuable insights and strategies to enhance their classroom practices.

Ko, C.-J. (2022). Online individualized corrective feedback on EFL learners' grammatical error correction. *Computer Assisted Language Learning.* Advance online publication. https://doi.org/10.1080/09588221.2022.2118783
This article explores the effectiveness of online individualized corrective feedback in improving grammatical error correction skills among EFL learners. It highlights the potential of personalized feedback in facilitating language learning and emphasizes the importance of integrating technology into language education for effective feedback delivery.

31

Conclusion

Glenn Stockwell and Yijen Wang

In this chapter, we would like to bring together several of the issues raised throughout the book by further exploring the ongoing challenges associated with using technology in language education and considering a way forward. By discussing both the causes and the realities of these challenges, we hope to provide pre-service teachers, educators, and stakeholders with valuable insights and guidance to pave the way for better integration of technology into language teaching and learning.

Fathoming the impact of recent and ongoing developments of technology on second language teaching and learning is logistically extremely difficult. In saying that, it helps to bear in mind that the way that we perform many of the tasks we do now are based solidly on the historical development of technologies that preceded those that we currently use (Haas, 1996). While awareness of these origins gradually fades over time, their presence remains apparent in various shapes and forms. A classic example of this is the use of the QWERTY keyboard, which was developed in the mid nineteenth century as a way of allowing the typebars to strike the paper in a way that key combinations caused the least amount of interference with one another. This keyboard is largely unchanged in its layout, and it has come to be used not only in physical keyboards of all shapes and sizes but also virtual onscreen keyboards and even laser projection units that allow almost any flat(ish) surface to be used as a keyboard. The replication of that mechanical keyboard from a century and a half ago remains in essence in modern tools, but these tools have also undergone massive changes in how the act of inputting text through typing takes place, in terms of the kinaesthetic sense of striking the keys, the ability to carry out shortcuts for various functions such as copying and pasting, and freeing up the locations where users can type text.

As Chapter 4 points out, however, technology makes subtle changes to the environment that we may not immediately be conscious of. Hypertext, for example, allows readers to click links in online texts, which makes it possible for them to have access to information related to what they are reading or to jump to other parts of the text. While this was heralded as a revolutionary outcome in freeing readers from material constraints of reading (see Carr, 2011, for a discussion), as Miall and Dobson (2001) observed, people found the content of literary texts to be far more confusing when read through hypertext compared to a linear manner. To this end, the evolution of technology can give rise to potentially highly useful tools or functions, but these may also bring with them unanticipated shortcomings. This is a key consideration for making decisions about how to deal with advances in technology, be they instigated by the teacher or institution or brought about by larger shifts that take place on a global scale.

It is helpful here to review the concepts of emergent and established computer-assisted language learning (CALL) (Levy & Stockwell, 2006), where emergent CALL is the use of technologies that are still relatively new to the field of language teaching and research, and established CALL is the use of technologies that have a proven pedagogical track record. These have been likened to their position on Gartner hype cycles (Gartner, 2023; see also Stockwell, 2022, for a discussion), where a new technology will typically trigger a large amount of attention when it is first released with exaggerated expectations (referred to as the "peak of inflated expectations") about what it can achieve. After this initial boom, there is typically a period of disillusionment as people come to realize that the new technology is unable to live up to these expectations, and it is not until these phases have been passed through that the technology starts to establish its place in actual practice viewed from a balanced perspective (called the "plateau of productivity" by Gartner). How these phases relate to the current volume is described in the following section.

Revisiting Emergent and Established CALL

Technology is in a constant state of flux, with new (or variants of existing) technologies that have the potential to affect the ways in which language teaching and learning take place appearing regularly. Some developments are more subtle (such as incremental increases in storage on our devices) while others make a more dramatic appearance (like ChatGPT). Similarly, the longevity of the impact that technologies have will also vary, although this rarely corresponds to the hype that surrounded their entrance. For example, there has been very little public excitement about the advances in storage, and yet we've moved from hard disk sizes of around 1GB in the mid 1990s through to 1TB (1000 times more storage and exponentially faster) at the time of writing this chapter some thirty years later, making a phenomenal impact on what we can do with a broad range of technologies. When the iPad was released in 2010, it was deemed to revolutionize education, even marking the end of books printed on paper. While it certainly has had an impact, this does not seem to be anywhere near the scale that was first predicted.

Although there is a need to explore the affordances of new technologies as they emerge, care needs to be taken to avoid an unrealistic amount of expectation (or criticism) that has the potential to mask their limitations. Artificial intelligence (AI) technologies are a typical example of this, where the reality about their development has been decades behind what was predicted (Funk & Smith, 2021), although they have existed for some time in less obvious forms such as search engines, personalized feeds on social media, and spellcheckers in word processors. At the time that this handbook was being completed, there was a phenomenal development in AI technology, in particular with the emergence of generative AI tools such as ChatGPT and advancements in machine translation, leading to both celebration and con-sternation about what these technologies mean for education in general and, of course, language education. Technologies that have the potential to trans-form or change current practices or concepts are known as *disruptive*, and AI has been described as perhaps the most disruptive technology from recent developments (Păvăloaia & Necula, 2023). The way in which disruptive technologies may affect language education is also a topic of interest, poten-tially altering how learners interact with one another and the teacher, how they access and process information, and even how they relate to the world around them (Hampel, 2019). Despite the promise of significant changes to education disruptive technologies, as illustrated with the example of the iPad above, technologies alone are not sufficient to achieve this (Reich, 2020; Säljö, 1999). The tendency to focus on the technology rather than on its use as a means of changing practice in language teaching is a point that has been made previously by Bax (2003), where he argues that many believe that if a new technology has new features, then it would be "inherently more effective" for teaching (p. 25). A brief glance at social media seems to reflect this mentality where people are posting short pieces of advice (typically anecdotal and without any research-based evidence) of how they used/could use ChatGPT, Copilot, or any of the other countless available generative AI tools to write tasks, quizzes, lesson plans, or reading passages for their students. Without any objective, empirical data to evaluate what is being created, it seems that these discussions remain very much at the "emergent" phase, describing what *might be* rather than what *is*. This is not to say that the emergent phase is not an important one – it is in fact an essential step that needs to be passed through to make sense of the complexities of new and/or disruptive technologies.

What will happen with the emergent AI technologies described above remains to be seen at the time of writing, but their possibilities are explored in Chapter 20 (digital literacies), Chapter 24 (speaking), Chapter 27 (writing), and Chapter 30 (grammar), and they are relevant to many other areas covered in this volume as well. What these chapters have done, however, is to start to move dialogue to solid pedagogies that formulate the foundation for estab-lished CALL. It should be remembered something that may be considered as "emergent" today will likely become "established" in a few years provided there is a foundation on which to base its implementation in an informed manner, and if not, it will either remain marginalized as a technology that is used by a die-hard minority or it will all but disappear from educational use altogether. There are many who feel a great deal of apprehension or resistance regarding the use of new technologies (see Chapter 21), and this has been seen with AI tools, even leading to blanket bans on their usage (Barrot, 2023). These concerns could well be attributed to fear of the unknown, and this further emphasizes the need to look at tools with a critical eye to explore the challenges that arise and to develop pedagogies that can take advantage of the affordances that tools can provide.

Some Challenges of Teaching and Learning a Second Language with Technology

While technology continuously shapes the landscape of language education, new technologies will typically bring with them new challenges that need to be addressed, as described above. The more recent developments seen in technology have raised serious concerns about academic honesty of students (and teachers), but there are other issues that have also started to come to the surface as they evolve into the realm of established CALL. Although there are several challenges that are worthy of mention in this regard, in this section we would like to focus on two issues related to technology and language learning that we believe are particularly pressing.

Cyber Cheating

Online assessment has come a long way in recent years to offer new possibilities for evaluating students' knowledge and skills in a digital environment, due to both ongoing advances in technology and of the COVID-19 pandemic, which resulted in lockdowns and made it difficult to carry out assessment face-to-face. However, alongside these advancements, academic dishonesty with technology, which has come to be known as *cyber cheating*, has emerged as a serious issue that educators and institutions must address. These include, among others, using mobile devices such as smart phones and smart watches during exams, engaging in social media to exchange exam questions and share answers, and plagiarizing by copying and pasting texts from online sources (Noorbehbahani, Mohammadi, & Aminazadeh, 2022; Parks et al., 2018). AI tools such as ChatGPT, Copilot, Jasper, and Writesonic can generate short to medium-length texts based on users' instructions. While these tools may be useful for language learners by providing valuable support to their learning process, there is a danger that they may use the tools in inappropriate ways, such as requesting "write x for me" in their stead. These academically dishonest behaviors pose serious threats for educators as they may damage the teaching and learning process as well as the credibility of assessment.

One important point to keep in mind is that academic dishonesty has always been an issue, and it is crucial to recognize that technology itself is not to blame for its existence (see also Stockwell & Wang, 2023 for a discussion on online cheating). To avoid cyber cheating, learners need to be educated about the consequences and teachers need to learn how to detect and prevent dishonesty with technology. This includes creating clear policies and guidelines on academic integrity, promoting open discussion, and providing ongoing education and training for both educators and students. The need for training has been raised in the majority of chapters throughout this volume and will be dealt with in more detail later.

Social Justice

As technologies become a regular part of our daily personal and educational activities, the focus shifts away from the technology itself to what is done with the technology, as described by Haas (1996). As this takes place, along with a general raising of awareness of the need to consider social justice in education (deMatthews & Izquierdo, 2016), there has been an increased interest in the impact that these technologies and the interactions that they facilitate have on the teachers, learners, and other stakeholders who use them (see also Chapter 3). Sometimes inequalities appear in benign places that are easy to overlook. The example of the keyboard above reminds us of a pertinent comment made by Murray (2000, p. 409) that "when speakers of languages other than English try to use their mother tongue online, they are hampered by a technology that was designed for English." In countries that do not typically use English as a language of communication, such as the Arab States, China, Japan, or Thailand, keyboards will still often be used that retain English letters (Yılmaz & Söğüt, 2022), most often in the QWERTY format.

One of the major issues is the unequal accessibility to technology. In some low-income or remote areas, the lack of access to technology and internet connections may significantly limit the opportunities for language learning (Murphy-Judy, 2023; UNICEF, n.d.; see also Chapter 8). Recently, a meme illustrating a "revised" version of Maslow's (1943) hierarchy of needs (i.e. the basic human needs presented in a hierarchical structure) with a hand-drawn addition to the base of the pyramid called "Wi-Fi" may illustrate the fundamental dependency on technology in modern society. While intended in jest, it carries a truth that in today's digital age, and internet connectivity has become an essential utility that impacts various aspects of life, including education. While equal access to education has long been a global societal problem, this challenge now includes an element that is directly related to whether people can access technology as well.

Another significant issue regarding social justice and technology in language education is exclusivity and discrimination. Technology should be designed and implemented in a manner that caters to learners from diverse linguistic and cultural backgrounds. When adopting technology into educational settings, educators must be aware of potential biases, such as gender bias, age bias, and racial bias. It is crucial to avoid assumptions, stereotypes, or even discrimination, such as assuming that the younger generation are "digital natives" – or more to the point that the older generation are less proficient users of technology (Sink & Bales, 2016) – or that male students possess superior technology skills compared to female students (Shields & Harris, 2007). In line with this, it is important to critically examine research and survey practices to ensure they align with principles of social justice. For instance, it is common to include questions about gender and age in surveys simply by following previous practices, but this can perpetuate biases and reinforce discriminatory practices and stereotypes. Instead, surveys and questionnaires should focus on collecting data that directly relate to the research objectives, ensuring that participants' identities and personal characteristics are respected and protected.

Teaching Training, Learner Training, and Administrative Responsibility

As described above, a recurring theme in this volume is the need for training for both teachers and learners. There is a clear relationship between these two, as ultimately the responsibility for training learners falls on the shoulders of teachers, many of whom have not been properly prepared themselves. The fact that teachers feel they are not receiving enough training is a problem that has been raised repeatedly in the literature on technology in language education (Son, 2018), and points to a potential breakdown in communication between teachers and the administrators of their institutions. The lack of preparedness in using technology was made glaringly obvious at the outset of the COVID-19 pandemic, where many – if not most – institutions lacked the infrastructure to deal with online classes and teachers were forced to rely on online communities to attempt to find hints on how to conduct a class mediated by technology (see Chapter 22). Should institutions have been ready for COVID-19? The pandemic was so unexpected and widespread that most educational institutions around the world were not prepared to handle fully online courses in such a short period of time. The costs of having hardware and software in place for something that may or may not occur is a burden on institutions, particularly for those that are less well funded or located where regional or national infrastructure is simply unable to deal with the massive amount of bandwidth required.

It may not be entirely fair to hold institutions solely responsible for the lack of preparedness among teachers or learners as many institutions do indeed offer courses and seminars for teachers (and learners) on technological tools, but they are often underutilized. Some teachers resist using new technologies (as discussed in Chapter 21), and even if courses are offered, these teachers may refuse to participate because they do not see how it will improve their current teaching practices. Although there is a good deal of individual variation, Farrell (2022) has pointed out that teachers' attitudes toward change may relate to the stages of their teaching career. Early-career teachers who have come into the classroom from pre-service courses to teach classes for the first time may experience a reality shock as they find that things often differ greatly from their training in terms of the available technologies and support from the institution. Thus, these teachers may not feel ready to try out new technologies or techniques until have become accustomed to their new environments (Kelchtermans, 2019). On the other hand, experienced teachers may be hesitant to change their teaching methods because they have developed their current practices over several years and believe that they are effective (Hargreaves, 2005). In other cases, the fault may not be a lack of communication between teachers and administrators when information about training courses fails to filter down to those who need it most. This may be caused by a disparity between employment conditions where part-time staff often have less access to information (Ito, 2023), and administrators may not even know this information is not being passed on.

Whatever the causes for the lack of training for teachers, ultimately it is the learners who end up disadvantaged. There tends to be a knock-on effect from this where if teachers are reluctant to change with developments in technology, they will naturally not be able to pass these technological changes on to their learners (Wang, 2021). Learners may be willing to use the new technologies, but they are unable to do this unless they are provided with adequate guidance in understanding their technological context and how to make the best use of it (see Chapter 21). As a result, teachers themselves need to be aware of this responsibility that they have to learners and be willing to expand their digital literacy skills to match their own teaching, learning, and cultural environment (as discussed in Chapters 19 and 20). An issue that is related to this is what the administrative responsibility is for institutions to ensure that teachers are properly prepared. The legal obligations for providing teachers with sufficient training to be able to perform their jobs has been raised as an issue for discussion. The responsibility for teacher education has shifted from being largely under government control in the 1970s and 1980s, institutional governance in the 1990s, through to a conflict between professionalization and deregulation policies post-2000, and the ultimate result is a lack of clarity over who is responsible for providing teacher education (Grimmett, Fleming, & Trotter, 2009). There are often assumptions that teachers have been trained prior to their employment, which is true in one sense, but at the same time does not take into consideration a teacher's ability to adapt to change. Accreditation programs in using technology in language teaching and learning have been introduced broadly, but many of these qualifications are typically neither strictly monitored nor required, meaning that their value will often depend on how well the issuing institutions compile their courses. How the government and institutions will address the issue of ensuring that teacher training is provided and how they will decide on the extent to which it should be required is still a matter for future discussion.

Concluding Remarks

As we conclude this book, we would like to reiterate the importance of understanding that the use of technology in language teaching and learning is dynamic, transforming continuously as both technology and fundamental views of language teaching and learning evolve. There is no single approach to using technology in language education, as each context is unique in terms of its individual, institutional, and societal factors (Stockwell, 2012). As has been pointed out at several points throughout this volume, technology will automatically, even if not always obviously, change the teaching and learning environment. While many of these changes will open up new possibilities, they may also create or highlight challenges that need to be addressed to make the most of the affordances that the technologies bring with them. The authors of the chapters in this volume have provided insights on how to apply a range of technologies to the teaching and learning of a second language based on their own varied experiences, pointing out these possibilities and the challenges. We would like to encourage teachers, researchers, administrators, and learners to consider their own individual roles in making the most of the possibilities and overcoming the challenges to seek out the best practices in second language teaching and learning with technology.

References

Barrot, J. S. (2023). Using ChatGPT for second language writing: Pitfalls and potentials. *Assessing Writing, 57*, 100745. https://doi.org/10.1016/j.asw.2023.100745

Bax, S. (2003). CALL: Past, present and future. *System, 31*, 13–28. https://doi.org/10.1016/S0346–251X(02)00071-4

Carr, N. (2011). *The shallows: What the internet is doing to our brains.* W.W. Norton & Company.

DeMatthews, D., & Izquierdo, E. (2016). School leadership for dual language education: A social justice approach. *The Educational Forum, 80*(3), 278–293. https://doi.org/10.1080/00131725.2016.1173152

Farrell, T. S. C. (2022). *Insights into professional development in second language teaching.* Castledown Publishers. https://doi.org/10.29140/9781914291036

Funk, J., & Smith, G. (2021). Why A.I. moonshots miss: Ambitious predictions about the future powers of computers keep turning out to be wrong. https://slate.com/technology/2021/05/artificial-intelligence-moonshots-usually-fail.html

Gartner. (2023). Gartner Hype Cycle. www.gartner.com/en/chat/gartner-hype-cycle

Grimmett, P. P., Fleming, R., & Trotter, L. (2009). Legitimacy and identity in teacher education: A micro-political struggle constrained by macro-political pressures. *Asia-Pacific Journal of Teacher Education, 37*(1), 5–26. https://doi.org/10.1080/13598660802616419

Haas, C. (1996). *Writing technology: Studies on the materiality of literacy*. Lawrence Erlbaum Associates.

Hampel, R. (2019). *Disruptive technologies and the language classroom: A complex systems approach*. Palgrave Macmillan. https://doi.org/10.1007/978-3-030-31368-5

Hargreaves, A. (2005). The emotions of teaching and educational change. In A. Hargreaves (Ed.), *Extending educational change* (pp. 278–295). Springer. https://link.springer.com/content/pdf/10.1007/1-4020-4453-4

Ito, Y. (2023). Examining a technology-focused language teacher community on Facebook during a crisis situation. *Asian-Pacific Journal of Second and Foreign Language Education, 8*, 1. https://doi.org/10.1186/s40862-022-00159-0

Kelchtermans, G. (2019). Early career teachers and their need for support: Thinking again. In A. Sullivan, B. Johnson, & M. Simons (Eds.), *Attracting and keeping the best teachers* (pp. 67–80). Springer. https://doi.org/10.1007/978-981-13-8621-3_5

Levy, M., & Stockwell, G. (2006). *CALL dimensions: Options and issues in computer-assisted language learning*. Lawrence Erlbaum Associates.

Maslow, A. H. (1943). A theory of human motivation. *Psychological Review, 50*(4), 370–396. https://doi.org/10.1037/h0054346

Miall, D. S., & Dobson, T. (2001). Reading hypertext and the experience of literature. *Journal of Digital Information, 2*(1). https://jodi-ojs-tdl.tdl.org/jodi/index.php/jodi/article/view/jodi-36

Murray, D. E. (2000). Protean communication: The language of computer-mediated communication. *TESOL Quarterly, 34*(3), 397–429. https://doi.org/10.2307/3587737

Murphy-Judy, K. A. (2023, May 31). Leadership at the crux of social justice and instructional technology in world language education [Webinar]. University of Virginia.

Noorbehbahani, F., Mohammadi, A., & Aminazadeh, M. (2022). A systematic review of research on cheating in online exams from 2010 to 2021. *Education and Information Technologies, 27*, 8413–8460 (2022). https://doi.org/10.1007/s10639-022-10927-7

Parks, R. F., Lowry, P. J., Wigand, R. T., Agarwal, N., & Williams, T. L. (2018). Why students engage in cyber-cheating through a collective movement: A case of deviance and collusion. *Computers & Education, 125*, 308–326. https://doi.org/10.1016/j.compedu.2018.04.003

Păvăloaia, V.-D., & Necula, S.-C. (2023). Artificial intelligence as a disruptive technology: A systematic literature review. *Electronics, 12*(5), 1102. https://doi.org/10.3390/electronics12051102

Reich, J. (2020). *Failure to disrupt: Why technology alone can't transform education*. Harvard University Press.

Säljö, R. (1999). Learning as the use of tools: A sociocultural perspective on the human–technology link. In K. Littleton & P. Light (Eds.), *Learning with computers: Analysing productive interaction* (pp. 144–161). Routledge.

Shields, C. J., & Harris, K. (2007). Technology education: Three reasons stereotypes persist. *Journal of Industrial Teacher Education, 44*(2), 60–72. https://scholar.lib.vt.edu/ejournals/JITE/v44n2/harris.html

Sink, J. K., & Bales, R. (2016). Born in the bandwidth: "Digital native" as pretext for age discrimination in hiring. *ABA Journal of Labor & Employment Law, 31* (3), 521–536. www.jstor.org/stable/44652937

Son, J. B. (2018). *Teacher development in technology-enhanced language learning.* Palgrave Macmillan. https://doi.org/10.1007/978-3-319-75711-7

Stockwell, G. (2012). Conclusion. In G. Stockwell (Ed.), *Computer assisted language learning: Diversity in research and practice* (pp. 164–173). Cambridge University Press.

Stockwell, G. (2022). *Mobile assisted language learning: Concepts, contexts, and challenges.* Cambridge University Press. https://doi.org/10.1017/9781108652087

Stockwell, G., & Wang, Y. (2023). Exploring the challenges of technology in language teaching in the aftermath of the pandemic. Advance online publication. *RELC Journal,* 54(2), 474–482. https://doi.org/10.1177/00336882231168438

UNICEF. (n.d.). Inclusive education. www.unicef.org/education/inclusive-education

Wang, Y. (2021). In-service teachers' perceptions of technology integration and practices in a Japanese university context. *The JALT CALL Journal, 17*(1), 45–71. https://doi.org/10.29140/jaltcall.v17n1.377

Yılmaz, A., & Söğüt, S. (2022). Language education for social justice: Reproductions or disruptions through technology. *Computers & Education, 187,* 104535. https://doi.org/10.1016/j.compedu.2022.104535

Glossary

adaptivity The ability of people or technology to change in order to fit a
specific need. For example, technology can be used to automatically provide
different content or assessment items to learners based on their responses to
earlier prompts in a learning system. Similarly, teacher and/or learners may
change their behaviors to adjust to shifts in learning environments
or technologies.

affordance What something makes possible or what it inhibits. Originally
conceived by Gibson in 1979 in his book, *The Ecological Approach to Visual
Perception*, the concept of affordances has been used broadly with
technology to show what it brings to or takes away from a teaching or
learning event.

artificial intelligence (AI) The use of technology to emulate the intelligence of
a human being. AI systems typically consist of a knowledge base, an
interface through which interactions with the AI take place, and a system of
"learning" from input received over time.

asynchronous learning A form of educational mode that allows learners to
access and complete learning materials, resources, activities, prerecorded
videos, and assignments on their own schedule, which usually takes place
through a learning management system (LMS). Instructor and learners are
able to interact through the LMS, or discussion forum or email, remotely at
different times (cf. **synchronous learning**).

augmented reality (AR) The use of technology to link between the real and
the virtual. It may be used to add multimedia information to a real world
environment, such as video to a paper-based picture book.

automatic speech recognition (ASR) – Also known as speech to text (STT),
this is a technology that converts spoken language into written text.
It enables human–computer interaction and has been applied to detect
pronunciation errors and grade pronunciation in language education.

autonomy A term used to describe the ability of a learner to be able to take
responsibility for their own learning, including the selection of content, the

manner in which this content is learned, evaluation of learning, and setting of short- and long-term goals. It is often closely associated with motivation, and like motivation it is considered difficult to accurately measure and observe.

blended learning see **hybrid learning**

CALL The acronym for computer-assisted language learning is the most enduring of the terms used to describe the field. Other terms such as technological-enhanced language learning (TELL) and technology-assisted language learning (TALL) have had some degree of usage, but CALL remains in the titles of several journals in the field (see Chapter 1 for more information).

collaboration The act of carrying out tasks and activities with others, usually with a shared goal or planned outcome. Through this process, participants are able to both share their knowledge and learn from others during the process of completing the task or activity.

communicative language teaching (CLT) An approach to language education that places emphasis on the development of communicative competence as the primary objective of learning the target language. In CLT, learning activities such as role-plays, group work, and discussions are commonly employed to facilitate meaningful communication.

corrective feedback (CF) A form of feedback on linguistic errors and mistakes provided to learners by instructors, peers, or technology, for example, automated written corrective feedback (AWCF).

critical thinking A learning objective that aims to develop learners' understanding, independent thinking, and problem-solving skills. It emphasizes the ability to consider diverse viewpoints and analyze information.

data-driven learning (DDL) A language learning approach based on language data such as corpora designed to encourage learners to make their own deductions about how the target language is used.

distance learning Although this traditionally took place through correspondence using paper-based materials, more recently it has become synonymous with "e-learning" or **online learning**. Teachers and learners may have no actual physical interaction with one another during the course of study, but there are forms of distance learning that include short-term face-to-face sessions as well.

Diversity (learner diversity) The differences between learners, such as their background language and experiences, their culture, and their motivation, agency, and aptitude for learning.

educational context A broad term which can be used to describe the various attributes of the environment in which something is taught or learned. It has been used to encompass the teaching approaches, the technologies that are available, learning support, and the overall curriculum.

extended reality (XR) An umbrella term which is used to include the various experiences of **augmented reality** and **virtual reality**, where individuals are able to experience real or virtual worlds through technology.

flipped classroom See flipped learning.

flipped learning Although some argue for a distinction with flipped classrooms, both refer to an educational approach that allows learners to access instructional materials or contents before the class, for example learning through reading online materials or watching online lectures. During class time, learners' engagement in interactive discussions and deeper learning are emphasized.

high-tech An abbreviation for high-technology, which refers to the use of sophisticated, advanced, or emerging technologies (cf. **low-tech**).

hybrid learning – Also known as "blended learning," which refers to an educational model combining traditional in-person instruction with online learning. Its flexibility provides a balanced approach between the two methods to facilitate a more interactive and collaborative learning experience.

hypertext A word, phrase, or section of text that connects to another piece of text or document. It can be used as electronic glossing for vocabulary learning (see examples in Chapter 29).

immersion The process of learning content through the target language in a manner that results in acquisition of that language. While there are different models for this, one of the most common is to start with an approach that includes a higher degree of language instruction in the early stages and gradually moves to a complete focus on the content only.

incidental learning The process of acquiring an aspect of a second language subconsciously while engaged in activities such as reading or listening. This is most commonly associated with vocabulary, but there have been cases of grammar being considered as being acquired incidentally as well.

individualized learning A plan of study tailored to an individual learner's needs and abilities. It may be designed by the teacher or by using some form of **artificial intelligence** which enables a system to adapt to a learner's changing needs (cf. **personalized learning**).

input hypothesis Based on work by Krashen, the premise is that a language can only be learned if there is sufficient input that is above the learner's current level but is still comprehensible to them. (See S. Krashen (1983), Second language acquisition theory and the preparation of teachers: Toward a rationale. In J. E. Alertis, H. H. Stern, & P. Strevens (Eds.), *GURT '83: Applied linguistics and the preparation of second language teachers: Towards a rationale* (pp. 253–263), Georgetown University Press.)

intelligent personal assistants (IPAs) Devices that allow a user to interact with them to carry out activities or tasks based on the user's commands through text, speech, or other input including GPS or online sources.

intercultural communication Communication that takes place between individuals of different cultural backgrounds. This type of communication is often the topic of research that explores how to overcome potential problems of bias and cultural stereotyping to achieve better communication.

language MOOCs (LMOOCs) and MOOCs Derived from Massive Open Online Courses, they are designed specifically for learning a language, typically with a syllabus that includes both language and content elements as well as a forum for communication among the participants in the target language.

learner training The provision of instruction in how to use a technology or technologies, ideally including an overview of not only how the use them in general but also how to apply them to specific learning strategies. This should include scope for learners to reflect on these strategies and to create their own (see K. Romeo, & P. Hubbard (2010). Pervasive CALL learner training for improving listening proficiency, in M. Levy, F. Blin, C. Siskin, & O. Takeuchi (Eds.), *WorldCALL: International perspectives on computer-assisted language learning* (pp. 215–225). Routledge).

literacy Its primary meaning has been the ability to read and write, but it has also been extended to include comprehension and communication skills. More recently the term digital literacy has been used, meaning the ability to find, evaluate, and communicate information through digital technologies.

low-tech An abbreviation for low-technology, which refers to an educational setting that lacks advanced technologies, adopting relatively fewer innovative technologies or no technology at all (e.g. relying on pencils and paper) (cf. **high-tech**).

mobile-assisted language learning (MALL) The teaching and learning of a language through the use of mobile devices. These devices may be used within a fixed environment or portably and may allow interactivity between the learner(s) and the context in which learning takes place.

motivation A highly complex concept of the feelings behind an action. In the field of language education, it is often used to refer to the degree to which learners wish to engage in language learning or the reasons behind learning a language. This is notoriously difficult to quantify and is usually measured through observing behavior associated with language learning.

multiliteracies The ability to create and interpret meaning across a wide range of modes such as visual, oral, kinaesthetic, and written modes, understanding that these may carry different meanings across different cultures.

online communities A group of people using online tools to communicate with one another on topics of mutual interest.

online learning The process of learning a language using digital tools. This learning can take place in entirely online environments where teachers and learners do not share physical learning spaces through to making up a part of a predominantly face-to-face learning environment.

open education A concept based on the belief that education is a fundamental right and that learning materials and resources should be free to use, share, and adapt by all.

Open Educational Resources (OER) Resources that arise from a movement for the creation of a public digital library of freely available digital resources.

personalized learning A plan of study where the learner is involved in the process of making decisions about what and how they learn based on their own skills, abilities, and preferences (cf. **individualized learning**).

phoneme A distinct unit of sound within a certain language that makes it distinguishable from other lexical or morphological units within that language. For example, "pat" and "bat" share the same sounds apart from the initial phoneme of /p/ and /b/, which results in a different meaning.

professional development An ongoing growth process for educators to improve their pedagogical professional expertise, such as teaching skills, curriculum design, and classroom management.

research context The factors that make up the environment in which research is conducted, such as the language(s) being learned, the experience and skills of both teachers and learning, the available technologies, and support from administration.

second language acquisition A complex process of learning the various components that make up the target language, including pronunciation, spelling, vocabulary, syntax, and pragmatics. The term is typically used to refer to the learning that occurs in both formal and informal learning situations.

self-directed learning A process of learning where an individual takes control over their own learning and which is built on the characteristics of a learner including their self-efficacy and motivation.

self-regulated learning A process of learning where an individual decides on the content of their learning and actively monitors their progress as they learn.

sociocultural theories A term used to refer to a set of theories that are associated with the ways in which society contributes to the development of an individual. At its core is the premise that language and culture are a product of the society in which they occur and that they can influence the ways in which individuals within that society perceive the world.

synchronous learning A form of real-time learning that allows instructor and learners, or a group of learners, engage in the course content simultaneously but from different places, through, for example, videoconferencing, webinars, online chat, and live streaming (cf. **asynchronous learning**).

tandem (learning) The process of two or more learners studying the language of the other engaging in activities that can enhance the learning of both languages. A typical example is when two learners exchange emails with one another in both their first and target languages and provide feedback on each other's writing.

task-based language teaching/learning A foreign or second language approach that emphasizes using meaningful and authentic tasks to encourage learners to use the target language to achieve certain outcomes.

teacher resistance The reluctance or opposition of educators to adopt or embrace new technologies or teaching methodologies into their language teaching practices.

telecollaborative learning A form of collaborative learning that using information and communications technologies such as audio- and videoconferencing. It allows leaners to engage with one another regardless of geographical boundaries.

virtual exchange An approach to language learning where learners connect with one another to communicate, interact, and collaborate, typically through the medium of technology. Through this experience, it is thought that learners have the opportunity to come in contact with other languages and cultures that help them to deepen their understanding of both.

virtual reality (VR) The use of technology to emulate reality, such as the creation of a virtual environment that represents the real world. They will typically allow participants to interact with objects and people within the environment using voice and/or text, and, if the interface allows it, kinaesthetic actions.

Index

Printed in the United States
by Baker & Taylor Publisher Services